NEW HORIZONS
World Guide

TIPS FOR YOUR
TRAVELING CONVENIENCE

1. To get a passport, you'll need baptismal certificate, expired passport or birth certificate (or a notarized affidavit of your birth which is vouched for by a relative or person who has known you a long time). You'll need two passport pictures (front view, 2½″ to 3″ square on a white background). A passport costs $9 (plus a $1 or $2 handling fee) for individuals or families traveling together. It is valid for three years and can be renewed for two more years for $5.

Apply in person at the Passport Division of the Department of State, or the Passport Agencies of the Department of State in Miami, New Orleans, Los Angeles, San Francisco, Seattle, Honolulu, Chicago, Washington, D.C., Boston, New York—or in other cities apply at the office of the Clerk of a Federal Court.

Be sure to sign your passport and keep it on your person at all times (except, of course, when your hotel concierge in some countries needs to borrow it temporarily when you register)—*not in your baggage.* Specific papers required for entry by each country from United States citizens are listed with the countries on pages that follow.

2. Before you leave the United States, it's best to have visas and tourist cards (where required) for each country you think you *might* visit, because in some foreign countries it takes a long time to get them for other countries.

3. Some travelers realize a saving by exchanging some of their money into foreign currency before leaving the United States, where one may frequently get a better rate of exchange, but be careful to note the total amount of foreign currencies that may be taken into each country. The Clipper Passenger's Currency Converter lists currency for many countries with the United States equivalents.

4. It's handy to carry a few one-dollar bills with you so that it is not necessary to cash a traveler's check or exchange a large bill into local currency in order to make small purchases in those countries where you plan only a short stop-over between planes.

5. Just as the water in one section of the United States differs from that of another, the water of many foreign countries varies; and even though it may be safe to drink, i.e., sanitary, some people may contract diarrhea due to the *change* of water. This also applies to the ice in drinks. Consult your doctor as to what medicine to take along. A good rule to follow is—when in doubt, drink bottled water.

6. Specific health documents required for individual countries are listed under CUSTOMS REGULATIONS in each chapter of this book. The general requirements are: for re-entry to the United States and for entry to most foreign countries you need a smallpox vaccination certificate. It's advisable to have this before you leave the U.S. Yellow fever and cholera certificates are required by most countries from passengers who have come from an infected area. Nearly all countries of the world have adopted the international sanitary regulations of the World Health Organization. These regulations establish the following

CONTENTS

TABLE OF

FOREWORD

No one before has ever attempted to publish a book quite like this. It is not a "travel book" in the ordinary sense at all. It does not deal with "impressions"; but rather with useful facts, carefully gathered by Pan American from its stations in all parts of the world.

As you read these facts you will come to some interesting conclusions. You will see, for example, why summer is not necessarily the best time for a vacation. You will see how the airplane has made it possible to take advantage of the fact that the seasons are reversed south of the equator. December is June (weatherwise) in Rio de Janeiro. January is July in New Zealand; in Australia; in Santiago, Chile; in Buenos Aires and in South Africa. You will see that Mexico, Guatemala and the West Indies have an even better climate in "winter" than in summer. They're only minutes away from Miami, New York, New Orleans, Houston, San Francisco and Los Angeles—or a few short hours away from any city in the United States. You will note that Europe is less than 7 hours by Jet Clipper, South America less than 5 hours.

You'll realize, too, that as in the United States, cities in Europe and elsewhere are often at their best in the winter when the theater, music and social season is in full swing; yet prices are considerably less.

You will discover that being unfamiliar with a foreign language is no longer any barrier to foreign travel. English, as you will note in country after country, has actually spread around the entire world.

As you thumb through the pages you'll probably get the urge to go somewhere. If you really need an excuse to do something about it, bear in mind that doctors all agree: vacations are a very necessary part of modern life. You owe it to your job, your health and your home life to take a vacation. There's no vacation like a trip and no trip like a trip abroad.

THIRTEENTH (REVISED) EDITION: 1966
FIRST PRINTING

ACKNOWLEDGMENT

This book was made possible through the cooperation and assistance of our employees and agents in the countries and lands served by Pan American. We also wish to acknowledge the helpful assistance given by the tourist offices and Consuls of the various countries represented. Weather chart information was supplied by the United States Weather Bureau and Ivan Ray Tannehill's *Weather Around the World,* published by the Princeton University Press. The key to pronunciation is based on W. Cabell Greet's *World Words* published by Columbia University Press.

Inquiries and comments should be addressed to Pan American Airways, P. O. Box PAA, Jamaica, New York 11430.
NOTE: *While we have made every effort to provide current and accurate information, there are frequent changes in immigration requirements, hotel rates and other facts relating to travel abroad, and we can accept no responsibility for inaccuracies and omissions.*

LIBRARY OF CONGRESS CATALOG CARD NUMBER: 54–5818
MANUFACTURED IN THE UNITED STATES OF AMERICA.

CLIPPER, PAN AM AND NEW HORIZONS, TRADE MARKS, REG. U.S. PAT. OFF.
TRADE DISTRIBUTION IN U.S. AND CANADA BY SIMON AND SCHUSTER
630 FIFTH AVENUE, NEW YORK, N. Y. 10020

TRADE DISTRIBUTION ELSEWHERE
BY FEFFER & SIMONS, INC.
31 UNION SQUARE, NEW YORK, N. Y. 10003

NEW

HORIZONS

World Guide

Pan American's
Travel Facts About 112 Countries

GERALD W. WHITTED
Publications Editor

PAN AMERICAN AIRWAYS

periods of validity for vaccination certificates: smallpox—not less than 8 days nor more than 3 years old; yellow fever—not less than 10 days nor more than 10 years old; cholera—not less than 6 days nor more than 6 months old; typhus and typhoid-paratyphoid inoculation certificates are not required under the WHO sanitary regulations as a prerequisite for admission. They are recommended, however, for visits to some countries. The record of these inoculations must be entered by the health authority in the official WHO certificate of vaccination form. Passengers should obtain a copy of the form from the Pan American Ticket Office before obtaining their inoculations.

7. Tours—or pre-arranged travel plans—are often the answer to seeing the most and doing the most. Escorted tours are scheduled frequently; independent tours start any day you wish. All reservations are assured, you know the exact cost in advance, transportation is by the most direct and advisable routes with no timetable problems, hotels are carefully selected, meeting and transfer service and advice of a local representative are always available, and well-planned sightseeing leaves plenty of free time for personal activities. Often these established travel plans can be modified or extended to suit special interests and desires. You will find a wide choice of tours available.

8. In writing abroad from the United States, it's best to use International Air Mail. Rates per half-ounce are 11 cents to the Caribbean, Central and South America; 15 cents to Europe; 25 cents elsewhere. Air mail single postcards are 12 cents each to most countries, except Canada and Mexico, where they are 6 cents.

9. If you feel you can organize a group of friends or members of an organization for a trip abroad, check on Pan Am's Tour Conductor Plan, by which you can obtain your own passage free of charge. Inquire also about special fares for groups.

10. To avoid inconvenience and Customs in each country you visit, you may send gifts to the United States duty free without declaring them or paying duty or tax, providing the value of each parcel does not exceed $10 retail and does not include alcoholic beverages, perfume containing alcohol, or tobacco. *You don't have to deduct the value of these gifts from your duty exemptions* described on the next page. You may send as many gifts as you wish but not more than one parcel a day to the same person. International Air Parcel Post is convenient and fast, Mark "Gift" on the outside of each package.

11. If you don't want to disturb your savings, you can now budget part or practically all of your expenses including air fare, hotel accommodations, meals, sightseeing, etc., on the Pan Am Pay Later Plan. You can pay as little as 10 per cent down, then pay the balance in as many as 24 monthly installments. You can make the arrangements quickly and confidentially. No collateral needed.

12. 35mm Kodachrome slides in standard 2″ x 2″ frames covering travel areas all over the world are now available, should you want to augment your collection of travel pictures with some excellent shots taken by professional photographers.

13. Many business firms and individuals who travel regularly find it very worthwhile to subscribe to the Universal Air Travel Plan. The contract requires a returnable deposit of $425, but an unlimited number of Air Travel Cards for members of a firm or family may be issued on a contract without further cost. The card entitles you to charge air travel at any of the offices of over 125 airlines and their appointed travel agents throughout the world. In addition, the Air Travel Card is now accepted as a personal credit reference by over 10,000 hotels, motels, car rental agencies, restaurants and other services.

14. Be sure to arrive at airport at least 10 minutes before the "latest check-in time" on your ticket.

HOW TO CLEAR U.S. CUSTOMS
THE EASIEST WAY

HALF THE fun of traveling is acquiring duty-free "bargains." Your purchases—within monetary limits and depending upon the circumstances—are exempt from duty if (1) they are for your personal or household use; (2) you declare them properly on your arrival in the United States; (3) your trip was not made just to buy them; (4) you didn't order them ahead of time. Bear this in mind when ordering from a representative of a foreign bootmaker or tailor soliciting orders in the United States.

INFORMATION FOR ALL TRAVELERS

Gifts valued under $10 retail can be sent to the U.S. duty free provided not more than one parcel a day is addressed to the same person. Gifts may not include liquor or tobacco. Be sure to mark the package "GIFT." These gifts need not be declared on arrival nor the value deducted from exemptions.

Plants, Foods, and Pets—many fruits, vegetables, plant seeds, flowers—including corsages—meats and pets must meet Department of Agriculture or Public Health Service requirements. Consult your nearest Pan American Office for the latest requirements.

Chinese Merchandise—no one may bring into the U.S. articles from Communist China or North Korea. Sale of such goods is not limited to the Far East; they're found in Caribbean ports too. In addition, Chinese-type articles produced in other countries may not be imported without a certificate of origin.

Trade-Marked Articles—watches, perfumes, musical instruments and similar articles whose trade mark is registered in the U.S., require written permission to import from the owner of the trade mark. If labels or other identification marks are removed, and purchase is within reasonable quantity, permission is not required. Consult a U.S. Consul about any questionable purchase.

If you have other questions—consult a Pan American office, or your purser on the aircraft, who will endeavor to supply the answers.

Questions of a legal or technical nature should be referred to a Customs officer at time of arrival.

INFORMATION FOR U.S. CITIZENS OR ALIENS IN THE U.S.

When you compute your Customs exemptions from duty and tax remember to include everything you acquire abroad. Do not overlook clothing or other personal effects, even though they have been worn or used abroad. The retail purchase price must be declared. All goods must accompany the traveler.

Exemptions—You are allowed a $100 exemption if you have been outside the U.S. at least 48 hours (except no 48-hour absence required if arriving from Mexico or the U.S. Virgin Islands), and such exemption has not been claimed within 30 days. You are allowed a $200 exemption when arriving from the U.S. Virgin Islands, Guam or American Samoa. No more than $100 can be acquired outside of these islands. For gift exemptions see travel tip No. 10 on page 9.

Art, Antiques—Bona fide original works of art (not reproductions) may enter the U.S. free of duty, and so may antiques (generally items in existence before 1830), but documents to prove authenticity should accompany them.

Liquor and Tobacco—These duty-free exemptions include 1 quart of alcoholic beverages for passengers over 21 years of age and 100 cigars. There is no limit on cigarettes for personal use. Some states have restrictions on the amount of liquor residents may bring in. In case of doubt consult any Pan Am office. You are allowed 1 gallon if arriving from the U.S. Virgin Islands, American Samoa or Guam provided no more than a quart is purchased outside of these areas.

Note—If you are not eligible for the $100 exemption, you are allowed a $10 retail value duty and tax exemption. Under the $10 ruling you are allowed a maximum of 50 cigarettes, 10 cigars or ½ lb. tobacco, 4 ounces of alcoholic beverage, or 4 ounces of alcoholic perfume.

Family Groups—All exemptions may be combined for families traveling together and applied to total value of all articles declared.

Information for Nonresidents—U.S. citizens or aliens whose residence is not in the U.S.—$100 exemption for gifts accompanying nonresident, including 1 gallon of alcoholic beverage and 100 cigars. In addition, adults allowed 1 quart alcoholic beverage and 50 cigars or 300 cigarettes or 3 lbs. of tobacco for personal use. To qualify for $100 gift exemption, nonresident must remain in U.S. not less than 72 hours and exemption may not have been claimed within 6 months. If not eligible for $100 exemption, $10 exemption allowed for accompanying articles for personal use which may include 1 quart of alcoholic beverage, 300 cigarettes or 50 cigars or 3 lbs. of tobacco, for adults.

Nonresidents in transit through the U.S. may bring with them dutiable items up to $200 in value, free from duty and tax. Consult Customs officer on arrival if you have dutiable articles over $200 in value.

MAKE FRIENDS WITH
YOUR TRAVEL AGENT

A TRAVEL agent is an expert in the complicated details of arranging travel . . . figuring out routes and itineraries, reservations and costs. Experienced travelers use a travel agent's many services because he can get confirmed hotel accommodations and other reservations in advance—so important in countries where space is limited. Furthermore, it's such a *convenience* to have all your travel details handled for you.

And remember, it often saves you *time* and *money* when you utilize the services of a travel agent. Travel agents sell on a commission basis, paid by the companies they are authorized to represent. Since they represent a wide variety of transportation, hotel and tour organizations in various price brackets, they can give you advice on filling your individual needs and wishes. A travel agent knows best how to keep your travel costs down.

PHOTOGRAPHY DATA
FOR AIR TRAVELERS

IN THE alphabetical listing of subject headings for each country in this book you will find a paragraph on PHOTOGRAPHY that describes the local availability of film, camera equipment and developing facilities. When prospects of buying supplies abroad look good, save weight and space by waiting to buy them when you get there. In countries where specific import restrictions apply, these facts are included under CUSTOMS REGULATIONS AND DOCUMENTS REQUIRED FOR UNITED STATES CITIZENS. Where there are no specific restrictions, the general rule should be to avoid bringing in quantities that would invite suspicion as to their use for other than personal reasons. Many persons carrying film in large quantities break the seals open and write their names and addresses on the packages, thus making it obvious that the film is being brought in for personal use.

As noted, in several countries the photographing of military installations and evidences of poverty is forbidden. When in doubt, inquire first and be sure to obtain permission from local people before taking their picture.

You'll probably wish to take many pictures as a record of your trip and some from your Clipper window en route, as well. Here are a few general suggestions and charts showing proper camera settings:

1. While flying, do not take movies or snapshots in either color or black and white when haze or smoke make it difficult to see the ground. A little blue haze doesn't matter much, although it's a good idea to use a haze filter.
2. To avoid possible reflection from the airplane window, hold your camera close to it without touching it. Let your body

cushion the camera from small bumps. Take your pictures from the shady side of the plane, if possible.

3. When making aerial pictures, you should use, for stills, a shutter speed of at least 1/100 of a second or faster if your camera permits. Shoot movies at 32 frames per second.

4. Be completely familiar with your camera and its results. Keep it as cool and dry as possible when traveling in humid areas. Remember to take some pictures with human interest, not just postal card monuments (have your photo subjects *doing* something). Never hand-hold your camera when shooting at less than 1/25 of a second. Follow faithfully the exposure instructions which apply, but above all don't worry about it. Everyone misses a good shot occasionally.

5. Paragraph No. 12 on page 9 tells how you can purchase professional 35mm. Kodachrome slides to augment your own collection.

6. Bear in mind that atmospheric conditions, the type of film you use and other factors may affect settings suggested.

Still Camera Settings for Kodacolor or Black-and-White Film in Sunlight
(Film with daylight speed of 50, such as Kodak Verichrome, or Ansco Plenachrome)

Landscapes	$\frac{1}{100}$ second at f/8 or $\frac{1}{200}$ second at f/5.6
Clouds (from above)	$\frac{1}{100}$ second at f/11–16 or $\frac{1}{200}$ second at f/8–11

Still Camera Settings for Kodachrome or Ansco Color Films at 1/100 Second
(For 1/200 second, use next larger lens opening)

Altitude	Bright Sun	Hazy Sun	Cloudy Bright
Below 2,000 ft.	Between 4 and 5.6	Between 2.8–4	Between 2–2.8
2,000 ft. to 4,000 ft.	f/5.6	f/4	f/2.8
4,000 ft. and up	Between 5.6–8	Between 4–5.6	Clouds from above, 8

NOTE: Always use a shutter speed of at least 1/100 second for aerial photographs.

Motion Picture Camera Settings for Kodachrome Film, Daylight Type 8 or 16 mm.
16 Frames per Second
(At 32 frames per second use next larger lens opening)

Altitude	Bright Sun	Hazy Sun	Cloudy Bright	Cloudy Dull
Below 2,000 ft.	f/8	5.6	4	2.8
2,000 ft. to 4,000 ft.	f/8–11	5.6–8	4–5.6	2.8–4
4,000 ft. and up	f/11	8	Clouds from above, f/11–16	Clouds from above, f/11–16

MAKING LIGHT WORK
OF LUGGAGE

UNDER THE agreement of the International Air Transport Association approved by all member airlines, the following amounts of baggage may be carried free of charge on scheduled International flights: First Class—66 lbs. or 30 kilograms; Economy Class—44 lbs. or 20 kilograms.

A charge must be made for all baggage in excess of this free allowance. The internationally accepted charge per kilogram or 2.2 lbs., is 1% of the normal first class adult fare for the flight concerned.

Personal articles such as purse, camera, coat, which can be carried over the arm, do not figure in your weight allowance. All other items, such as briefcases, parcels and overnight bags are weighed.

To avoid excess weight charges, weigh all your luggage on your bathroom scale before you leave home.

If you have excessive overweight, ask about Pan Am's Jet Clipper Cargo service. The rates are low. Keep this service in mind, too, when shipping items home from abroad.

You will find the 44-lb. allowance more than adequate, if like most experienced travelers, you travel "light." There is nothing more discouraging than being burdened with too much luggage. If you use simple lightweight luggage without fittings, and pack no more than 3 pairs of shoes (wearing the 4th pair), you'll be able to pack an excellent wardrobe for a 2-week to 2-month trip under the 44-lb. allowance.

Articles of clothing, except shoes, weigh surprisingly little. A man's worsted suit, for example, weighs about 2½ lbs.; a pair of flannel slacks, 1¾ lbs.; a shirt, ½ lb.; 6 pairs of wool socks, ½ lb. A woman's suit weighs about 2½ lbs.; a dress, 1½ lbs.; 6 pairs of hose, ¼ lb. Men's shoes weigh about 4 lbs., while women's average 1 to 2 lbs.

WHAT TO PACK FOR YOUR TRIP

Don't burden yourself with a lot of hard-to-care-for clothing. Undoubtedly you'll tire of wearing the same outfits often but the ease of packing and unpacking will be well worth it. Women will find that many attractive changes may be made by simply adding a scarf, a different blouse, an overskirt or a stole. Men can rely on a dark business suit, slacks and a sports jacket.

Stick to one basic color scheme. In that way you can mix and match various pieces of clothing and also keep your shoe wardrobe at a minimum.

You will not need formal clothing unless you have been invited to a formal affair. Women will find that a cocktail dress will see them through all but strictly formal occasions while a dark business suit will do nicely for men. In tropical climates, men frequently wear white dinner jackets in the evening so you may want to take one if you are visiting tropical areas.

If your trip is all sightseeing and touring with little time for socializing then leave your furs and jewelry at home. Any valuables are a liability—especially so when traveling. So don't take them unless you need them.

The temperature will ultimately decide your travel wardrobe. A handy clothes barometer can be made by jotting down the average temperatures for each place you'll visit. These will be found at the beginning of each chapter of this guide. Make a special note to pack swimsuit and robes if you'll be visiting beach areas in warm weather.

If your trip takes you to opposite extremes of climate, calculate how much time you'll spend in each. If most of your trip will be spent in a hot climate then concentrate on lightweight clothing and take a warm coat to wear in colder areas. If most of your time will be spent in cold weather, concentrate on warm clothing and take one or two lightweight summer outfits.

Ask your local Pan Am office for a complete wardrobe checklist plus copies of the "Woman's Way" booklets on Europe, Hawaii and the Far East, Bermuda and the Caribbean and on the U.S.A. These booklets give complete packing and wardrobe information. There is also a Honeymooner's Handbook and one called *Pan Am Loves Children*. Pan Am's "Baggage Handbook" supplied with each ticket also gives packing information.

HOTEL RATES

European Plan (EP)—Room; no meals included in rates.
American Plan (AP)—Room and 3 meals included in rates.
Modified American Plan (MAP)—Room, breakfast and either lunch or dinner included in rates.
Bermuda Plan (BP)—Room and breakfast. In Britain, where this plan is widely used, "B & B" is the hotels' abbreviation for bed and breakfast; both are covered by one price.

While hotels base their range of rates from lowest to highest, they often have only a very few rooms in the lowest category—often on an inside court right over the kitchen. The average traveler, who plans to spend very little time in his room, cannot always expect to get one of these bargain accommodations; there are seldom enough to go around. In budgeting expenses, plan on spending more than the lowest rates quoted.

ELECTRIC CURRENT ABROAD

Most—but not all—countries and islands in the Western Hemisphere operate on 120-volt, 60-cycle alternating current such as is used in the U.S.A. and Canada. Most—but not all—of the rest of the world runs on electricity ranging from 200 to 400 volts, 50-cycle current—nearly always alternating, but some direct current remains in a few unconverted locales. The usual American appliances will burn out on such high voltages, but many stores now sell specially made, light-weight gadgets for the convenience of travelers to foreign countries. Immersion heaters for hot liquids, coffeepot kits, electric shavers, travel irons and hair dryers are the most familiar appliances available, and most are dual-purpose for use on home current or on currents up to 230 volts abroad. All of them come with adapter plugs to fit into the kind of wall outlets (different from ours) that you'll find overseas. Adapter plugs are useful *only* for connecting an appliance to the socket. They do nothing at all toward converting high-voltage current so it will be compatible with an American appliance made to operate solely on 120-volt current. Only a transformer can do this job, and transformers are both very heavy and very expensive. One exception is the Remington transformer ($7.50), which is lightweight and can be used with any type of shaver.

MEDICAL CARE ABROAD

A new organization, Intermedic (777 Third Avenue, New York, N.Y. 10017), has been formed to enable members traveling in all parts of the world to obtain immediate help from a highly qualified, English-speaking physician.

Members are assured that professional fees will not exceed $8 for the first office visit, $10 for the first house call at the hotel, or $15 for an emergency nighttime hotel call. Intermedic provides a Directory of Participating Physicians overseas with their day and night telephone numbers. The Directory also has pages which should be filled in at home with the member's medical history, allergies and the like.

Membership in Intermedic is sold directly from its headquarters, and through travel agents. Annual dues are $5 for a Personal Membership, and $9 for a Family Membership.

WHAT WILL THE WEATHER BE LIKE?

THE CHART on pages 18–19 gives average temperatures in various cities in the United States, for each month of the year. By comparing these figures with the charts for the various countries, you can get a general impression of what kind of weather to expect abroad.

First, a few general observations. Of course, in the Southern Hemisphere, the seasons are the reverse of ours, making our winter an ideal time to visit many of the countries below the equator. Most islands of the West Indies (where you'll find only a few degrees' variation between summer and winter temperatures) are ideal for vacationing almost any month of the year. Many of the cities you will visit in various parts of the world are either seaports or near large bodies of water, which tend to moderate the weather and reduce extremes between daily highs and lows or day and night temperatures. In very warm areas, such as Bolivia or Ecuador on the equator, however, inland cities in the mountains are the most comfortable places. It is about 5 degrees cooler for every 1,500 feet of altitude than it is at sea level. The altitude of principal cities is given in the weather chart for each country. In general, cities with daily variations of not more than 12 degrees are more comfortable than localities with abrupt changes between day and night readings.

Latitude, too, is an important determining factor in climate, and in the weather chart for each country you will find the latitude of the principal city given. In the following chart, next to each United States city, the latitude and altitude are given for comparison.

With allowances for altitude and proximity to the ocean, areas of similar latitude north or south have similar climates. Compare New Zealand and the West Coast of the United States, which are about the same distance from the equator. Note that Mexico City, on about the same latitude as Honolulu, is slightly cooler, with greater variation between lows and highs because of the altitude and distance from the ocean.

Now, a look at the charts will show you, for example, that Cape Town in South Africa in June (the coolest month) is like Chicago in May, and that the summer weather there (December to February) is very near the ideal 68 degrees. The weather in western Europe is something like the weather in western United States; compare London and Seattle.

In the South Pacific, summer temperatures in Sydney, Australia (December to February), are similar to summer temperatures in Portland, Maine. Both summer and winter temperatures in the southern parts of Italy and Spain are about the same as in South Carolina.

A comparison of days of rainfall on the following chart with the rainfall figures for each country will also help give you a preview of your vacation weather. If there is as much as .01 of an inch of precipitation, the meteorologists call it a day with rain. But if the rain occurs in a month when temperatures are warm, you can usually expect mere showers in an otherwise pleasant, sunny day. If the rainy day occurs during a cold-weather month, however, the whole day is more likely to be gloomy. With temperatures below freezing, the precipitation is probably snow or sleet.

Even though weather is a logical sequence of natural causes, there's no foretelling unseasonable weather or record-setting temperatures, so don't expect the weather you experience on your vacation to conform with monthly averages every time. But wherever it's convenient, why not pack as much pleasure as possible into your trip and plan to visit a country when the weather is at its best?

AVERAGE FAHRENHEIT TEMPERATURES

+ DAYS OF RAIN

FOR CITIES IN THE UNITED STATES

TO COMPARE WITH OTHER COUNTRIES

EAST

	JAN.	FEB.	MAR.	APR.	MAY	JUNE	JULY	AUG.	SEPT.	OCT.	NOV.	DEC.
Boston Lat. N42°21'—Alt. 21'	29°	29°	37°	47°	58°	67°	72°	70°	64°	54°	43°	32°
	12*	10*	12*	11*	11	10	10	10	9	9	10*	11*
New York Lat. N40°45'—Alt. 55'	31°	31°	39°	49°	60°	69°	74°	73°	67°	56°	45°	35°
	12*	10*	11*	11	11	11	11	10	9	9	9	11*
Portland, Maine Lat. N43°39'—Alt. 160'	20°	22°	33°	43°	53°	62°	68°	67°	59°	50°	38°	25°
	12*	11*	13*	11*	12	12	11	10	10	10	11*	11*
Washington, D. C. Lat. N38°53'—Alt. 25'	35°	36°	44°	54°	65°	73°	77°	75°	69°	57°	46°	37°
	11*	10*	12*	11	12	11	11	11	8	8	9	10*

SOUTH

	JAN.	FEB.	MAR.	APR.	MAY	JUNE	JULY	AUG.	SEPT.	OCT.	NOV.	DEC.
Atlanta Lat. N33°45'—Alt. 1050'	43°	46°	53°	61°	70°	77°	79°	78°	73°	63°	52°	45°
	12	11	11	10	9	11	12	12	8	7	8	11
Asheville Lat. N35°35'—Alt. 1985'	39°	40°	47°	55°	63°	70°	73°	72°	67°	57°	46°	39°
	11	10	12	11	12	13	15	13	9	7	8	10
Charleston Lat. N32°46'—Alt. 16'	51°	52°	58°	65°	73°	79°	82°	81°	77°	68°	58°	54°
	10	9	9	8	8	11	13	13	10	6	7	9
Houston Lat. N29°45'—Alt. 40'	53°	56°	63°	69°	75°	81°	83°	83°	79°	71°	62°	55°
	10	9	8	7	7	8	10	9	9	6	8	10
Miami Lat. N25°46'—Alt. 10'	68°	68°	71°	74°	77°	80°	82°	82°	81°	78°	72°	69°
	8	6	7	7	11	13	16	15	18	15	10	8
Nashville Lat. N36°09'—Alt. 500'	39°	41°	50°	59°	68°	76°	79°	78°	69°	61°	49°	41°
	12*	11*	12*	11	10	10	11	9	8	6	9	11*
New Orleans Lat. N29°56'—Alt. 5'	55°	57°	63°	69°	76°	81°	83°	83°	80°	72°	62°	56°
	10	9	9	7	8	13	15	14	11	7	8	10

NOTE: All temperatures in this book are Fahrenheit. To reduce Fahrenheit to Centigrade subtract 32 and multiply by 5/9; to reduce Centigrade to Fahrenheit multiply by 9/5 and add 32.

* Includes days with snow.

CENTRAL

	JAN.	FEB.	MAR.	APR.	MAY	JUNE	JULY	AUG.	SEPT.	OCT.	NOV.	DEC.
Chicago	25°	27°	36°	47°	58°	68°	73°	72°	65°	54°	40°	30°
Lat. N41°52'—Alt. 595'	11*	10*	12*	11	12	11	9	9	9	9	10*	11*
Cincinnati	33°	34°	43°	54°	64°	73°	77°	75°	69°	57°	45°	35°
Lat. N39°06'—Alt. 550'	13*	12*	13*	12	12	11	10	9	8	8	10	12*
Cleveland	25°	26°	35°	46°	58°	68°	72°	70°	64°	53°	39°	29°
Lat. N41°29'—Alt. 580'	17	15	15	13	13	11	10	9	10	11	14	16
Dallas	45°	50°	57°	65°	73°	81°	84°	84°	78°	68°	56°	48°
Lat. N32°47'—Alt. 435'	8*	8*	8*	8*	9	7	5	7	5	6	6	7*
Detroit	25°	25°	34°	46°	58°	68°	73°	71°	64°	53°	40°	29°
Lat. N42°19'—Alt. 585'	13*	12*	13*	11*	13	11	9	9	10	10	12*	13*
Minneapolis	14°	17°	30°	46°	58°	68°	73°	71°	62°	50°	33°	20°
Lat. N44°58'—Alt. 815'	8*	7*	8*	9*	12	12	9	9	9	9	8*	8*
Memphis	41°	44°	53°	62°	70°	78°	81°	80°	74°	64°	52°	44°
Lat. N35°08'—Alt. 275'	11	10*	11	10	10	9	9	8	7	7	9	11
Omaha	22°	26°	38°	52°	62°	72°	78°	75°	67°	55°	39°	28°
Lat. N41°15'—Alt. 1040'	6*	6*	8*	10	12	11	9	9	8	7	5*	6*
Pittsburgh	31°	31°	40°	51°	62°	70°	74°	72°	67°	55°	43°	34°
Lat. N40°26'—Alt. 745'	16*	14*	15*	13*	13	12	12	10	9	10	12*	14*
St. Louis	32°	35°	45°	56°	66°	75°	80°	78°	71°	59°	46°	36°
Lat. N38°37'—Alt. 455'	9*	9*	11*	11	12	11	8	8	8	8	8	9*

ROCKIES

	JAN.	FEB.	MAR.	APR.	MAY	JUNE	JULY	AUG.	SEPT.	OCT.	NOV.	DEC.
Denver	31°	33°	39°	48°	57°	67°	73°	71°	63°	52°	40°	33°
Lat. N39°44'—Alt. 5280'	5*	6*	8*	9*	10	8	9	9	6	6*	5*	5*
Salt Lake City	29°	34°	42°	50°	59°	68°	77°	75°	65°	53°	41°	32°
Lat. N40°45'—Alt. 4390'	10*	10*	10*	9*	8	5	4	6	5	7	7*	13*

SOUTH WEST

	JAN.	FEB.	MAR.	APR.	MAY	JUNE	JULY	AUG.	SEPT.	OCT.	NOV.	DEC.
Albuquerque	34°	41°	46°	54°	63°	73°	77°	74°	68°	57°	43°	35°
Lat. N35°05'—Alt. 4950'	3*	3*	3*	4	4	3	8	8	5	4	2*	3*
Phoenix	52°	56°	61°	68°	76°	85°	91°	89°	86°	71°	60°	53°
Lat. N33°27'—Alt. 1090'	4	4	4	2	1	1	5	6	3	2	2	4

WEST COAST

	JAN.	FEB.	MAR.	APR.	MAY	JUNE	JULY	AUG.	SEPT.	OCT.	NOV.	DEC.
Los Angeles	56°	56°	58°	60°	63°	67°	71°	72°	70°	66°	62°	57°
Lat. N34°03'—Alt. 340'	6	6	6	4	2	1	0	0	1	2	3	6
Reno	32°	36°	42°	48°	55°	63°	71°	69°	61°	51°	41°	34°
Lat. N39°31'—Alt. 4490'	7*	6*	6*	4	4	3	2	2	2	3	4	6*
San Francisco	50°	53°	54°	56°	57°	59°	59°	60°	62°	61°	57°	52°
Lat. N37°46'—Alt. 65'	11	11	10	6	4	2	0	0	2	4	7	10
Seattle	40°	42°	46°	50°	56°	60°	64°	64°	60°	53°	46°	42°
Lat. N47°36'—Alt. 75'	18*	16	19*	16	12	9	5	5	8	13	17	16

COMPARATIVE TABLE OF CLOTHING SIZES

MEN'S

SHIRTS			HATS	
American	**European**		**American**	**European**
13	33		6½	52
13½	34		6⅝	53
14	35–36		6¾	54
14½	37		6⅞	55
15	38		7	56
15½	39		7⅛	57
16	40		7¼	58
16½	41		7⅜	59
17	42		7½	60
17½	43		7⅝	61

SHOES			SOCKS	
American	**European**		**American**	**European**
6	38		9	23
6½	39		9½	24½ (also *Cadet*)
7–7½	40		10	25½ (also *Page 2*)
8	41		10½	26¾ (also *Homme 3*)
8½	42		11	28 (also *Demi-Patron*)
9–9½	43			
10–10½	44		11½	29¼ (also *Patron*)
11–11½	45		12	30½
12–12½	46			
13	47			

WOMEN'S

DRESSES			SHOES		
American	**French**	**English**	**American**	**English**	**European**
10	38	32	4–4½	2–2½	34
12	40	34	5–5½	3–3½	35
14	42	36	6	4	36
16	44	38	6½	4½	37
18	46	40	7–7½	5–5½	38
20	48	42	8	6	38½
40	50		8½	6½	39
42	52		9	7	40
44	54		9½–10	7½–8	41
46	56		10½	8½	42
			11–11½	9–9½	43
			12	10	44

HATS			STOCKINGS	
American	**European**		**American**	**European**
21	53		8	20¼ (size 0)
21¼	54		8½	21½ (size 1)
21½	55		9	22¾ (size 2)
22	56		9½	24 (size 3)
22½	57		10	25¼ (size 4)
23	58		10½	26½ (size 5)
23¼	59		11	27¾ (size 6)
23½	60			
24	61			
24½	62			

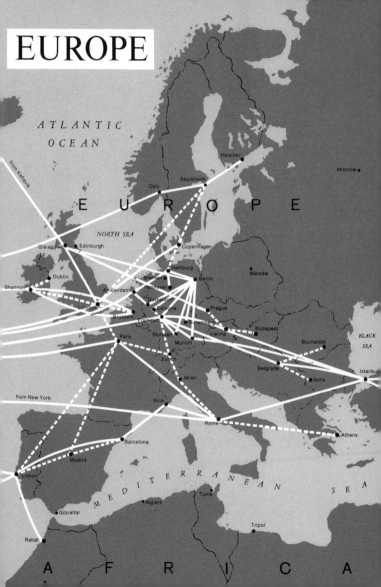

AUSTRIA

WEATHER IN VIENNA—Lat. N48°20′—Alt. 564′

Temp.	JAN.	FEB.	MAR.	APR.	MAY	JUNE	JULY	AUG.	SEPT.	OCT.	NOV.	DEC.
Low	28°	29°	35°	41°	50°	55°	58°	57°	51°	43°	35°	31°
High	36°	38°	48°	56°	65°	70°	73°	72°	65°	55°	42°	38°
Average	32°	34°	42°	49°	58°	63°	66°	65°	58°	49°	39°	35°
Days of Rain	7	5	7	8	9	10	10	8	7	8	7	7

LOCATION . . . Austria lies in central Europe, easily accessible from principal European cities.

CHARACTERISTICS . . . This beautiful country is always ready to welcome tourists. There are many new hotels and restaurants and, of course, the same beautiful scenery which has made Austria one of the famous tourist spots of the world. Here you find the Vienna, Bregenz and Salzburg Festivals, famous the world over; Vienna with its cafés; Innsbruck with its marvelous skiing in the surrounding country of Tyrol and at nearby Arlberg. The people are friendly and you can have a delightful time.

POPULATION . . . Estimated at nearly 7,074,000.

SIZE . . . 32,374 square miles; 360 miles east-west.

CAPITAL . . . Vienna (Wien), a city of 1,627,566.

GOVERNMENT . . . The State Treaty of 1955 re-established the sovereignty of democratic Austria. It is a federal republic of 9 provinces governed by a parliament which meets in Vienna.

HOW TO GET THERE . . . By Pan American Jet Clipper, 11 hours (elapsed time) to Vienna from New York via Frankfurt. By ship, 5 to 9 days to Le Havre, France, then 21 to 24 hours by train to Vienna. Western Austria is most easily reached by Pan Am to Munich and thence a 2½-hour train ride to either Innsbruck or Salzburg. Austrian Airlines provides frequent service by connecting with Pan Am in many European cities. There is also daily air service to Salzburg, Innsbruck, Graz, Linz and Klagenfurt.

ACCOMMODATIONS... The inn is a part of native Austrian life. Every village has at least one inn. Throughout Austria these accommodations are clean and comfortable. But there are first-class hotels in most places, which have private baths and excellent food. All large resorts have modern hotels and inns with modern conveniences. Except in Vienna and at festival times elsewhere, good hotels in Austria generally charge about $12 and up a day for room, bath and breakfast. Many Austrian hotels and inns have that ineffable quality termed "atmosphere." The historic *Goldener Adler* in Innsbruck has it, as does the *Goldener Hirsch* in Salzburg. Then there are the very modern hotels, like the *Europa* and the *Tyrol* in Innsbruck, the *Prinz Eugen* in Vienna, the *Parkhotel Mirabell* in Salzburg. Other famous hotels include the *Schloss* in Velden on the Wörthersee, the *Bellevue,* the *Europe* and the *Straubinger* in Bad Gastein. In Vienna the elegant new *Vienna Intercontinental* is very convenient. Other top hotels are the *Imperial,* the *Bristol,* the *Sacher* and the *Krantz Ambassador;* from about $14 single, plus about $3.60 for a meal. Among other good hotels are the *Astoria,* the *Kaiserin Elisabeth,* the *Erzherzog Rainer, Parkhotel Schönbrunn,* the *Clima,* the *Regina, Europa, Am Parkring, Capricorno* and *Kummer.* Rates at the latter are from $8 single, $10-$14 double a day with bath.

ARTS... Vienna's reputation as an art center is due to its wonderful museums filled with collections by world-famous masters. One should visit the Albertina Museum, which houses a famous collection of the etchings of Raphael, Michelangelo, Titian, Rembrandt, and Italian and German primitives. In this museum is one of the world's outstanding collections of Dürer's work. The National Museum of Fine Arts contains priceless collections. Here are represented all the great masters, such as Pieter Breughel and Dürer, the best Velasquez collection outside of Madrid, Rembrandt, Rubens, Holbein, Giorgione, Titian, Moretto, Raphael and Correggio. Don't miss the Belvedere Picture Gallery, the Vienna Museum of Natural History, the Vienna City Museum and the Imperial Palace collections.

BALLET... Famous ballet of the Vienna Opera. The ballet, like the opera and symphony, does not perform in Vienna from July 1 to September 1, when all are on tour.

BANKS... The Creditanstalt-Bankverein, the Länderbank, the National Bank and the Österreichisches Creditinstitut are Austria's principal banks. The American Express Company will cash travelers checks and so will the banks and most hotels and shops.

CALENDAR OF HOLIDAYS... New Year's Day; January 6, Epiphany; Easter Monday; May 1, Labor Day; 10 days before Whitsun Sunday, Ascension of Christ; Whitmonday; 10 days before Whitsun, Corpus Christi; August 15, Feast of the Assumption; November 1, All Saints' Day; December 8, Feast of the Immaculate Conception; Christmas and December 26, St. Stephen.

CIGARETTES AND TOBACCO... All tobacco products, including U.S. cigarettes, are available and not so expensive as in the other capitals of Europe.

CLIMATE ... Austria rarely becomes either terribly hot or bitingly cold, and the seasons slip gradually into one another without abrupt temperature changes. There are rainy days from late October to mid-December, but Vienna is always agreeable. In the mountain regions snow begins to fall in mid-November. The air is crisp, clear and cold, but sunny. Spring climate in the mountains makes Austria a skiers' paradise.

CLUBS ... Austrian Press Club, P.E.N. Club, Jockey Club, Lions, Kiwanis and Rotary.

COMMON COURTESIES AND LOCAL CUSTOMS ... The tempo of living in Austria is a bit slower than in the United States, so be patient when expecting personal service. The Austrians are very gracious. *Danke schön* is "Thank you." Many tourists take to native apparel upon arrival in Austria, but in Vienna the usual international city attire is recommended. Austrians enjoy going to their favorite sidewalk coffeehouses for coffee and the newspaper, and lately the espresso shop has become very popular.

COMMUNICATIONS ... A 3-minute phone call to the States costs ö.S. 312 ($12.15); about ö.S. 10 (39¢) per word for a cablegram. Airletters cost ö.S. 4.50 (18¢); high surcharges on other mail.

CURRENCY ... There are about 25.65 Austrian schillings to U.S. $1. One schilling is worth 4¢.

CUSTOMS REGULATIONS AND DOCUMENTS REQUIRED FOR UNITED STATES CITIZENS ... Except for duty-free limit of 400 cigarettes or 80 cigars or 2 lbs. tobacco; 2 quarts of wine, 1 quart of hard liquor, you may take into Austria anything which is for your personal use. An unlimited amount of dollars may be brought into or taken out of Austria. You need a passport but no visa.

DRUGSTORES ... In some of the drugstores within the first district of Vienna, foreign products, including American, are available.

ELECTRIC CURRENT ... Almost entirely 220 volts, A.C., although there is still some D.C. current in a few unconverted sections of Vienna. Adapters for round-prong plugs are also needed.

FAUNA ... The vast forest and rock districts of the provinces overflow with prize game. Chamois shooting is a special feature.

St. Wolfgang near Salzburg in Upper Austria, is typical of the charming villages that dot the countryside.

Stag, marmot, roebuck, and mountain cock all abound. Hunting is good throughout the country, but the shoots of Styria, Tyrol, Vorarlberg, and the Danube are particularly renowned. All hunting equipment may be rented, or brought into the country duty free. As for fishing, the mountain lakes and streams teem with brook, lake and rainbow trout, char, brook-char, pike, pike-perch, and other fish.

FLORA... The lower meadows of Oberinntal, near the Italian border, are rich in the multicolored carpets of flowers for which the Alps are famous. Throughout the Alps the forests and flowers are strikingly beautiful, especially in the spring.

FOOD... Most of the more popular Austrian dishes are part of international cuisine everywhere—*Wiener Schnitzel, goulash,* and the various *strudels,* to name a few. There are numerous other less well-known specialties worth trying, especially dishes garnished with small dumplings. And do not miss Viennese pastry such as the famous *Sacher Torte* (chocolate cake) and *Linzer Torte* (with jam). Even in the small inns food is served in substantial quantities. A Continental breakfast of coffee and rolls is taken upon arising, with a heartier second breakfast at 10 A.M. In Vienna, large towns, and resorts, dinner is from 6:30 P.M., with a light supper after the theater. Afternoon tea, called *jause,* is served after 4 P.M. and consists of sandwiches, pastry, coffee (with mountains of whipped cream) and tea.

GAMBLING... There are two large racetracks in the vicinity of Vienna. Casinos are also located in Salzburg, Bad Gastein, Seeboden, Velden, Kitzbühel, Vienna and Baden (15 miles from Vienna).

LANGUAGE... German is the official language, but English is taught in the high schools and is widely understood.

LAUNDRY AND DRY CLEANING... You can have your laundry done quickly and thoroughly and inexpensively, by the chambermaid at your hotel. Dry cleaning is fast and good in Vienna, but not so good in the provinces.

LIQUOR... Austria is both a beer- and wine-drinking country. The beer is excellent and the wines are wonderful. *Vin ordinaire* is both good and cheap. The best red wine is Vöslauer, with Ruster Burgunder a close second. But Austria is best known for its white wines, such as Dürnsteiner, Gumpoldskirchner, Grinzinger, Nussberger, Riesling, and Veltliner. Austrian champagne is good. Schnaps, distilled liquors, obtainable in great and potent variety, are also good. Whiskey is imported and expensive. Slivovitz, a South Slav drink distilled from plum juice, is popular and strong. The famous Heurigen wine of new vintage is served by the wine growers in the backyards of their premises in all the wine growing areas. Cocktails vary in price and quality, but are good at the large international bars.

MEDICAL FACILITIES... Austrian doctors and hospital facilities are generally excellent. Ski resorts have first-aid centers with resident doctors. Inquire at your hotel.

MOTION PICTURES... Motion-picture theaters are to be found in most cities. Many of the films shown are American or English, but with German sound track.

MUSIC ... There is music everywhere in Austria; for centuries Vienna has been considered the music capital of the world. From there emanated the works of Mozart, Beethoven, Schubert, Brahms, Gluck, Haydn, Bruckner, Wolf, Mahler, Lanner, the Strausses and other great artists. The Vienna Philharmonic is world renowned. Among the many famous conductors are Herbert von Karajan, Dr. Karl Boehm and Rafael Kubelik. The Vienna State Opera is superb, and the gay Volksopera is unsurpassed. These, however, like the ballet, do not play in Vienna from July 1 to September 1, although there is a great summer program of chamber music and concerts in lovely old Viennese palaces; opera and operetta in historic Theater an der Wien. In late July and August there are the important Salzburg and Bregenz festivals. In recent years, Vienna has produced its own Spring Music Festival, called *Wiener Festwochen,* during the first three weeks of June. Summer and fall festivals are also numerous, and most sizable villages have lively and colorful dances on Saturdays. The world-famous Vienna Boys Choir can be heard almost every Sunday, except in summer, at the Hofburg Chapel.

NIGHT CLUBS ... Vienna has everything from swank night clubs with floor shows to fashionable little *tanz* bars where there is always wonderful music and good wine. However, don't expect the big shows of Paris—they just don't exist. The *Cobenzl Bar* in the Vienna hills is smartest of all. You can dine and dance here with the city of Vienna and the Danube spread below you (open only in summer). The *Splendid, Eden, Moulin Rouge, Maxim* and *Eve* are all good. Vienna specializes in *intime* small bars with piano players or orchestra. You'll find them everywhere within the Ring. Among the wine gardens, try *Hengl, Rode, Setzger, Kurtz-Manhart, Maly, Toni Karas.* The native inns in the smaller towns all have *bauernstube* rooms, handsomely decorated with folk art, where in the evenings there are dancing, singing and congenial company.

PHOTOGRAPHY ... All equipment is available but expensive. Good developing everywhere, including color developing.

RELIGION ... Austria is predominantly Roman Catholic. Cathedrals, abbeys and churches are numerous and beautiful throughout the country. There are Protestant services in the larger cities.

RESTAURANTS AND BARS ... Vienna abounds in wonderful restaurants, dance-bars and small, smart eating places. Coffeehouses are a way of life here. Try *Landtmann, Rebhuhn, Opern, Demel* ("Konditorei"). You should dine once in the deep old cellars in the inner city. The *Rathauskeller* is famous, also the *Lindenkeller* and the *Griechenbeisl.* Another famous keller is the *Hofkeller,* where you can listen to zither music while you eat. The *Palais Auersperg,* a masterpiece of baroque building with restaurant, beautiful winter garden, coffee shop and bar, is interesting to see. Best international restaurants are the *Drei Husaren, Stadtkrug, Franziskaner* and the restaurants of the *Sacher* and *Imperial* hotels. For Balkan food, with the zip of music, try the *Bosna* or the *Balkan Grill;* good Hungarian food at the *Pataky.* Other excellent restaurants include *Kerzenstüberl, Deutsches*

Haus, Bierklinik, the *Weisser Rauchfangkehrer* and *Liesingerkeller.*
If, after dinner, you would like to drink wine (no food) in one of the oldest kellers in Vienna, visit the *Urbani Keller.* It's well worth it.

SHOPS AND STORES . . . Stores famous for their leather goods are Popp and Kretschmer, Nigst, Scheffel and Förster, as is the Lanz shop for native costumes. Antiques around Vienna's famous state-owned pawnshop Dorotheum. Shooting, fishing and ski equipment may be purchased locally. For smart ready-made dresses try Elegance, Farnhammer, Adlmüller and Hoechsmann.

SPECTATOR SPORTS . . . From January to June there are international ski events at all the major alpine resorts. *See* SPORTS.

SPORTS . . . Skiing tops the list. It is the national sport of Austria, and her mountains and climate are perfect for it. Skiing huts and lodges dot the countryside, and there are many fine ski resorts. One-day ski excursions on Semmering, only an hour out of Vienna, may be booked at the Intercontinental Hotel. Near Salzburg are the Bad Gastein and Hofgastein resorts with cable cars, ski lifts, jumps, and skating rinks. The Arlberg resorts, west, and Kitzbühel, east of Innsbruck, are international favorites. Obergurgl resort offers spring skiing. The St. Anton-am-Arlberg resort is known as "The Ski Capital of the World." Zürs and Lech have international competitions. Austrian ski schools, trails, runs, and incidental facilities cannot be surpassed. Austria contains over a thousand miles of perfect ski slopes. Hunting and fishing, mountaineering, bicycling and boating are also popular sports in Austria.

For golf the course at Dellach on the Wörthersee in Carinthia (Southern Austria), at Pertisau on the Achen Lake, and the course at Kitzbühel are well known. Tennis is popular; every sizable resort and all Austrian cities have good courts. There are sailing and rowing on all the larger lakes, and the Austrian rivers lend themselves exceptionally well to flat-boating. All the lake resorts offer swimming facilities. Opportunities for hiking and climbing are limitless. Trails are carefully marked, and the existence of the hut system and at least one clean, comfortable inn in every village makes it possible to range freely. All mountaineering equipment may be purchased on the spot, and professional guides are available everywhere. Many towns also provide horseback riding.

THEATERS . . . State Opera, Theater an der Wien, Volksopera, Burgtheater, Volkstheater, Theater in der Josefstadt. Plays in German only.

TIME . . . Noon in Vienna is 6 A.M. in New York.

TIPPING . . . Bellboys and porters get 2 schillings per bag and for any little special service. One schilling is also customary for the doorman who calls a cab, hat-check girl, washroom attendant, barbers and, in special cases, movie and theater ushers—which shows that Austria really is one of the least costly European countries to visit. Beauty-shop attendants get from 2 to 5 shillings; cab drivers get 10% of the meter reading; railway porters expect 2 or 3 schillings per bag, and 5 for a trunk. Museum guides get 2 or 3 schillings per sightseer.

TOURIST TAXES ... All resorts in the provinces charge a small *kurtaxe*. Air departure tax is $1.20.

TRANSPORTATION ... There are taxis, streetcars, and buses in the larger cities, but taxis are not inexpensive, except in Vienna. Chauffeur-driven and self-drive cars are available. Good train service is maintained within the country. The cable railways up and down and across mountains are remarkable and entirely safe. Riding in "fiacres" (2-horse open carriages) is a popular and charming feature of Viennese and Salzburg life.

WATER ... Water in Vienna is famous—it comes from mountain springs on aqueducts. You can drink the water anywhere in Austria.

WHAT TO BUY ... Vienna has rapidly re-established itself as a shopping center. Knitwear, petit point, fine needlework, along with the famous leather goods, antiques, crystal, porcelain and jewelry are worth mentioning. Peasant costumes may be bought almost everywhere. Also hunting, fishing, and skiing equipment.

WHAT TO WEAR ... Take with you about the same clothes required for corresponding seasons in New York, but warm clothes are needed for the Alpine evenings, and good, strong shoes always. Even if you do not plan to ski, heavy slacks or ski trousers are suggested for the provinces in winter. You will also need galoshes or fur-lined boots for walking in the provinces in winter. Formal dress may be worn at the opera in Vienna and at the Salzburg Festival. Formal dress is also worn at the more fashionable resort hotels in the evening, but by no means is this a "must," particularly for men.

WHERE TO GO—SIGHTSEEING ...

Vienna ... Perhaps for the first sightseeing trip you make in Vienna it would be best to take a standard tour around the city. The buses are excellent and modern. Just ask your hotel porter for tickets. This would make it possible for you to plan from there on what you want to see most. Because there is so much of interest to see in Vienna, it is impossible to cover it all unless you plan to stay for some time. Vienna is divided into 23 districts. The inner town, the first district, is the most important. It is surrounded by the Ringstrasse. Each section of the Ringstrasse has a different name. The one in the very center of the city is the Opern Ring, the others are the Schotten, the Dr. Karl Lueger, the Dr. Karl Renner, the Burg, the Kärntner, the Schubert, the Park, and the Stuben Ring. These take in two thirds of the Old Vienna. The other third is bounded by the Franz Joseph Kai along the Danube Canal. The Opera House, a magnificent structure, is located where the Kärntnerstrasse, the main shopping district, meets the Opern Ring. It was rebuilt after extensive war damages and reopened in November 1955. The building was designed by the famous Austrian architect van der Null, who, after realizing that he had designed the Opera House at street level (the only one in the world at that time not raised above street level), committed suicide. Tickets for the symphonies and operas can be ordered through your hotel porter, or through your travel agent at home.

From the Opera House take a walk to St. Stephen's Cathedral,

Austria offers skiing at its best and facilities are excellent. The group above is at Arlberg resort, Zürs, an international favorite.

St. Stephen's Cathedral, affectionately called "der alte Steffl," is an impressive landmark dating from the 12th century.

Heldenplatz is in the heart of Vienna and the location of the New Hofburg (Imperial Palace).

which was built in 1147 A.D. and partially remodeled from then to 1433. It suffered many war scars, but the Gothic spire (448 feet) escaped damage. The Cathedral contains many beautiful pulpits, choirs, choir galleries, and a great organ. The catacombs connect with subterranean passageways which extend under the entire area around Stefansplatz. Next on your list should be a visit to the Palace. The Hofburg Palace, whose oldest part was built in 1275 A.D. by Ottocar II, was the winter palace of the Habsburg emperors. It is now open to visitors who want to see the wonderful Habsburg collection. The renowned wrought-iron Michaeler Tor opens into the Michaeler rotunda. Off this are the imperial apartments and state suites, the private apartments of Franz Joseph, containing the personal furnishings of the Emperor, the suites of Empress Elizabeth, the gorgeous state apartments now used by the President of Austria and the rooms containing the imperial porcelain collection. Adjacent is the world-famous Spanish Riding Academy which was founded in the 16th century. In the beautiful hall the famous Lipizzaner horses are put through the Spanish paces at regular performances. A main entrance leads from the rotunda to the central courtyard of In der Burg. Here too you should visit the Schweizerhof, from which you enter to see the unique collection of the crown jewels. You should also see the Imperial Chapel, where the Vienna Boys Choir sings at Sunday Mass.

Another must is a visit to the National Library, one of the largest in the world. This contains a collection of papyri comprising 81,000 items, 1,200,000 printed books and a fabulous collection of manuscripts. The oldest known part of an illustrated Christian Bible is here, too, as well as many other interesting early books and manuscripts. There is a music collection containing 19,000 volumes of printed music and 12,000 music manuscripts, a huge library and a collection of autographs.

Other places of interest to the tourist in Vienna are the Kapuziner church, in whose crypt lie 144 Habsburgs (12 were emperors and 15 empresses); the House of Parliament; and the University of Vienna. Nearby are the Minoriten Church, the Chancellery and the Votive Church.

In the 2nd district is the Viennese Coney Island "Der Prater," with its well-known giant Ferris wheel.

The immense imperial summer palace and beautiful gardens of Schönbrunn in the western outskirts of the city are an absolute must. Don't fail to walk through the interior of this palace.

If you want to look down on Vienna from the crests of the Vienna Woods, include the Kahlenberg and Cobenzl in your sightseeing.

From Vienna there is good train service to the other fascinating tourist spots described below. Innsbruck can be reached in about 9 hours on a route that takes you to Linz, Salzburg, Kitzbühel. Styria in the south is reached in about 4 hours. There are frequent flights via Austriar Airlines from Vienna to most provincial capitals.

Innsbruck. . . The ancient and impressive city of Innsbruck in Tyrol is known as the capital of "The Land of the Mountains." The best way to see Innsbruck is to walk around the city either in the early morning or early evening. In the blocks between the station and the Maria Theresienstrasse is the so-called new town, a section rich in sights, cafés and hotels. If you would like to know Innsbruck, take a tram to the point where the Maria Theresienstrasse becomes the Herzog Friedrichstrasse, a thoroughfare which bisects the old city, the part which was within the walls. There you will find the city moat used long ago, narrow Gothic houses, pointed arcades and wrought-iron signs. The Herzog Friedrichstrasse leads directly to a little cobbled square, the Stadtplatz, which contains the world-famous Goldenes Dachl. The Dachl, a small Gothic balcony three stories high with a steeply pitched gilded roof, is a gleaming wonder. The entire neighborhood of the Dachl, containing several of those fountains for which Innsbruck is famous, is a must for sightseers. Try to visit the rococo parish church of Wilten, and be sure to make a journey on one of the two cable ascents from Innsbruck. One cable railway takes you to the Patscherkofel, the other to the Hafelekar. The entire Tyrol can be seen from there, outspread like a great relief map. Good hotels include the *Maria Theresia,* and the *Grauer Bär,* the new modern *Europa* and the *Tyrol,* and ancient inns such as the *Goldener Adler,* the *Goldene Rose* and the *Stiftskeller.* You should visit some of the night places where you will enjoy native singing and see native dancing. Tyroleans love life, celebrations and music.

Lienz in East Tyrol . . . sometimes called "the prettiest little city in Europe," set between the High Tauern peaks and the dramatic Dolomites, is a perfect spot to break the trip from the north into Italy. Around its quaint, lively square, which is dominated by an old rose castle, now the City Hall, stand attractive little hotels, some with balconies that permit a good view of events in the square. Tempting shops are tucked under the white arched arcades. They are laden with peasant linens, trimming, knit goods, wood carvings, antiques. The wrought-iron work, wood carvings and brasswork are world famous. Castle Bruck on the edge of town has a gay wine *stube,* and houses a museum with two notable collections—one archaeological, the other paintings (the ranking collection of Egger-Lienz). A new cable car up the Zettersfeld has opened a new terrain to skiers and provides sightseers with a breathtaking panorama of the Dolomites. One-day excursions from Lienz go into the Tauern (Grossglockner) to Matrei and Hinterbichl, to Meran, the Dolomites, to Venice. Lienz hotels are the *Traube* and the *Post.*

Vorarlberg—Bregenz-Feldkirch-Montafon . . . *Bregenz* on *Lake Constance,* with the nearby Bregenz Forest, is a highlight of Austria's westernmost province, Vorarlberg. An ancient Celto-Roman town and a provincial capital, it has both a quaint old quarter and a beautiful lakeside esplanade providing modern diversions. The Bregenz Festival is held from late July to late August. This city is a fine base for exploration of the Lake Constance area and starting point for the Bregenz Forest trip. The latter offers beautiful scenery, good, inexpensive inns in lovely villages, costumed folk and the work of Angelika Kaufmann, who was born there. The Rhine valley route from Bregenz leads to Feldkirch, a medieval town with a celebrated castle winecellar. The Montafon Valley, which slants southeastward from Feldkirch, is even more dramatic than the Bregenz Forest. Exotic costumes, mountain grandeur, the gourmet fare at the *Madrisa* in Gargellen are top-ranking attractions. A mountain road leads via the Montafon into Tyrol's Oberinntal.

Salzburg ... The great festival city. Here the world-famous musical event takes place from the last week in July through the month of August. It's the world's leading summer musical festival. The city is jammed with musicians and music lovers. The works of the great musical masters, particularly Mozart, are to be heard day and night, played by several orchestras and chamber groups. For many of these events there's a brand new Festival House, a dramatically designed modern building built in the side of a mountain. Salzburg has preserved its medieval character and is one of Austria's most beautiful cities. Small, but impressive mountains surround the town.

There are several organized sightseeing tours you can take, such as the city-sightseeing and Salzkammergut tour, the tour to Gaisbergspitze via Gaisbergstrasse (4,218 feet), and Grossglockner.

Of special interest are the famous Salzburg Cathedral, finest Italianate edifice in Austria, and the Hohensalzburg Fortress, which dominates the skyline. Attending the *Everyman* performance in front of the cathedral in the late afternoon, Sundays and August 15 during Festival time, is one of the most stirring experiences Europe can offer. This is theater at its very best. You must see a performance of the Aicher marionettes, which have toured many countries and have won great acclaim. One of their best performances is *The Magic Flute*, but their *Don Giovanni, Nutcracker Suite* and *Fledermaus* are a delight, too. Also, attend a chamber-music concert in the exquisite Marble Hall of Mirabell Palace. Interesting places are Mozart's birthplace in Getreidegasse—now a museum—and the house of the Mozart family, which is near the Mozarteum, Europe's most distinguished summer music school, attended by many Americans. For a stay during the Salzburg Festival be sure to arrange your reservations well in advance. You can stop at the famous, charming *Goldener Hirsch,* the Hotels *Stein, Gastschloss Mönchstein, Europa* or *Parkhotel Mirabell, Oesterreichischer Hof, Bristol;* or nearby at the *Salzburg Cobenzl, the Kaiserhof,* or the *Schloss Hotel* on the Fuschl lake. While in Salzburg, visit the charming *Till Eulenspiegel* restaurant, and the *Café Bazar,* where celebrities, tourists and natives mingle. Don't miss *Schloss Hellbrunn* with its water shows.

Zell-am-See ... The best route at present from Salzburg is via Saalfelden. Just south of this town is the famous lake resort of Zell-am-See, an Alpine lake about 2¼ miles long, a mile wide and about 225 feet deep. The town has comfortable, fairly inexpensive hotels, and is a good place to make your headquarters for trips to places in the High Tauern. Castle Rosenberg in Zell-am-See on the main square is worth seeing, as is the thousand-year-old church tower.

There are an excellent bathing beach, tennis courts and good shops. Take a trip by cable railway up the Schmittenhöhe. It takes only fifteen minutes to reach the top of this mountain, where you'll find a small chapel and a meteorological station. Zell-am-See is a winter resort, too. There are excellent accommodations and a good sparkling climate.

Bad Gastein ... High in the Alps, 47 miles south of Salzburg, is this famous old cure resort. In addition to being a summer place, it is also developing into one of Austria's leading winter resorts. There are good shops, theaters, cinemas and, of course, the casino. Beautiful mountain walks abound. Go via cable car up to the top of the Stubnerkogel for a breath-taking view of the Tauern. The radioactive springs of Bad Gastein are famous for their rejuvenating powers. The *Bellevue Hotel* and the *Hotel de l'Europe* are excellent; the bar and orchestra of the Bellevue make the wintertime particularly gay. Above Bad Gastein, reached by chairlift, is the *Bellevue Alm*— and if you have a longing to stay in a small Tyrolean lodge high up in the mountains with the world outside your balcony, make your reservations for the Alm early. It has a small swimming pool for summer—and in winter a roaring open fireplace in the bar.

Kitzbühel ... Situated between Zurich and Vienna on the main railway line is Kitzbühel, one of the best-known Austrian towns among tourists. In winter it is an outstanding skiing resort, considered second only to the Arlberg resorts by expert skiers. The town has every kind of ski slope, cable railways up the Hahnenkamm and Kitzbüheler Horn, ski lifts, any number of ski runs, including, of course, the famous Hahnenkamm run. There are excellent ski schools with expert instructors and guides. For skaters there is an ice rink. First-class hockey matches are staged there frequently. Kitzbühel is the scene of many important international winter sport competitions. There are a great many good hotels. The *Grand* and *Goldener Greif* are luxurious. Inns and pensions abound. One of the best pensions is *Schloss Münichau*, a castle where the paying guest may have every comfort. *Die Postkutsche* is a *Holiday* award-winning restaurant with Tyrolean atmosphere. Some of the places of interest to see are the Church of St. Andreas and the Frauenkirche. You should take a side trip to the Kitzbüheler Horn and to Fieberbrunn, where there are a health spring and peasant festivals. The shops of Kitzbühel are extremely interesting. It has been said of Kitzbühel that despite its yearly influx of nobility and celebrities, the local people maintain their native charm.

Styria ... This southeastern province, of which Graz is the capital, is surnamed "the green state" for its beautiful wooded countryside. Here the peasants and the visitors wear the Styrian gray and green hunting suits and the Styrian version of the dirndl, most popular in Austria. Alt Aussee is the perfect place to stay. Bad Aussee, the larger center, is lovely with its white-faced, dark-timbered houses with balconies covered with beautiful flowers. Life here is lived and also ended with a great deal of ceremony. An Aussee wedding is a sight to see, as is a funeral with the glass and ebony, plumes, and horses with their gleaming silver harnesses. There are well-known hotels here such as the *Post*. Go to Alt Aussee and take a room at the Hotel *Am See* with a balcony overlooking the lake. While having breakfast, look at the Dachstein glacier with the strange glints of morning light. Watch it, too, from a canoe on the lake (you can almost taste the ice). You should take a brine bath scented with a few thimblefuls of strong pine oil for an exhilarating feeling. Near Aussee is Bad Ischl and the famous Salzkammergut lakes, easily reached from Salzburg. The villages around the Wolfgangsee, Mondsee, Ebensee and Traunsee look like settings for the most romantic operettas.

Carinthia . . . The Province of Carinthia is in the southernmost part of Austria, bordering Italy. Carinthia's Wörthersee is Austria's best-known summer resort. This is a region of beautiful lakes and mountains, and because of its location south of the main Alpine chain, spring comes earlier and fall lasts much longer. Lake bathing is possible from mid-May until mid-October. Carinthia has excellent wintersport resorts also, such as Kanzelhöhe, famous for its perfect snow and many hours of sunshine. The highlight of Carinthia is Velden on Wörthersee, known all over Europe. It is a picturesque lake resort with first-class hotels (the *Schloss* is one of the best in Austria), an interesting program of social entertainment, including champion water skiing. There are flower festivals, *corsos,* international dancing competitions, boat races, etc. At Velden, Pörtschach or Klagenfurt you can swim, sail, water ski, play tennis or golf to your heart's content. One of the few golf courses in Austria is located in Dellach, a 15-minute drive from Velden. Millstatt and Seeboden on Millstättersee are also pleasant lake resorts with good hotels. The many castles are another interesting aspect of Carinthia. Villach is a perfect stopover for tourists traveling between Vienna or Salzburg and Venice. The ideal castle tour is from Klagenfurt via Hochosterwitz to the old walled town of Friesach and the ancient town of Gurk.

Sightseeing Along the Danube . . . During the summer months the First Vienna Danube Steamship Company provides regular steamship service along the beautiful river Danube. The loveliest stretch winds through the romantic "Wachau" valley, which is a famous attraction especially at blossom time. However, due to the strong current, it is recommended to take this trip only downstream and on less crowded weekdays.

SOURCES OF FURTHER INFORMATION . . . Austrian State Tourist Department at 444 Madison Avenue, New York, N.Y. 10022; at 2433 N.W. Lovejoy St., Portland, Oregon; at 195 South Beverly Drive, Beverly Hills, Cal.; and at 332 S. Michigan Avenue, Chicago, Ill. 60604. Every city and resort in Austria has its *Fremdenverkehrsverein* (local tourist office). The hotels and travel agencies will also be helpful to tourists. Just ask your hotel porter for any tickets including ski-lift tickets you may want for special events. Pan American's offices are at Kärntnerring 5, Vienna 1 (Tel. 526646).

BELGIUM

WEATHER IN BRUSSELS—Lat. N50°50′—Alt. 190′

Temp.	JAN.	FEB.	MAR.	APR.	MAY	JUNE	JULY	AUG.	SEPT.	OCT.	NOV.	DEC.
Low	30°	33°	35°	40°	46°	52°	55°	55°	52°	44°	38°	33°
High	39°	43°	49°	57°	64°	70°	73°	72°	67°	56°	48°	42°
Average	35°	38°	42°	49°	55°	61°	64°	64°	60°	50°	43°	38°
Days of Rain	15	15	15	16	16	17	16	16	16	17	18	16

LOCATION ... Belgium is nestled among France, Germany, Luxembourg, and The Netherlands, with 43 miles of coast line. Its oldest and most important coastal city, Ostend, is only 55 miles from Dover. Brussels is less than 1 hour's flying time from London, and is within easy reach of all European countries.

CHARACTERISTICS ... This charming country with its wonderful museums, long stretches of beaches and gay cafés is a marvelous place to take a holiday. It is clean, modern, and rich in delightful architecture. You'll eat some of the finest food on the Continent.

POPULATION ... Estimated 9,300,000; Belgium is the most densely populated country in Europe. The population of Brussels and suburbs, the largest center, is 1,439,536.

SIZE ... A small compact country of 11,755 square miles, Belgium is approximately the size of Maryland. The distance between its farthest points is less than 200 miles.

CAPITAL ... Brussels. Not only the capital of Belgium, but the heart and center of the country, it's one of the most interesting and most beautiful cities in Europe. Brussels is also the center of the country's banking and commercial activity and is the provisional center of European Common Market activities.

GOVERNMENT ... A constitutional monarchy with a parliament elected by universal suffrage.

HOW TO GET THERE ... By Pan American Jet Clipper, from

New York to Brussels, 8¼ hours (elapsed time). By ship, 8 to 10 days to Antwerp, depending on the steamer.

ACCOMMODATIONS ... Among the principal hotels in Brussels in the first-class category are the *Westbury, Metropole, Palace, Amigo* and *Brussels Residence,* with rates ranging from $8 to $14 single and $18 to $60 double. Medium-class hotels are the *Central, Grand, Splendide* and *Queen Anne,* with rates ranging from $6 to $8 single, $10 to $12 double for rooms with bath. Tourist-class hotels are the *Bearn, Boulevards, Van Belle* and *Richmond House;* $4-$5 single, $6.50-$9 double.

ARTS ... Among the many Brussels museums and art galleries the tourist should see the Royal Fine Arts Museum of Belgium, consisting of the Museum of Ancient Art containing works of the 15th to 18th centuries and the Museum of Modern Art with works of the 19th and 20th centuries.

BANKS ... Brussels banks include the Morgan Guaranty Trust Co. of New York; First National City Bank of New York; the American Express Co.; Banque de la Société Générale de Belgique (agents for various banks); Banque de Bruxelles (agents for various banks); Banque Lambert; Société Belge de Banque; Kredietbank.

CALENDAR OF HOLIDAYS ... January 1, Easter Monday, May 1 (Labor Day), Ascension Day, Whit Monday, July 21 (National Holiday), August 15 (Assumption Day), November 1 (All Saints' Day), November 11 (Armistice Day), and Christmas Day are official holidays in Belgium. Processions and pageants take place all over the country. Ask at your hotel about these colorful events. Some of the interesting festivities include the Carnival at Binche on Shrove Tuesday with the procession of the Gilles; the procession of the Holy Blood at Bruges on Monday after May 2; the Combat of the Lumeçon, a local version of St. George and the Dragon, as well as the procession of the Golden Cart of Ste. Waudru, both taking place at Mons on Trinity Sunday; Procession of the Penitents at Furnes on last Sunday in July; historic cortege and St. Guidon procession at Anderlecht. Most beautiful and spectacular is the mystery called "Jeu du Saint Sang," played every 5 years in July-August on the open square at the foot of the belfry in Bruges, relating the story of the relic of the Holy Blood belonging to the city of Bruges. Also the "Ommegang," a medieval pageant and joust held in the Grand'Place of Brussels in July.

CIGARETTES AND TOBACCO ... American cigarettes cost from 30¢ to 60¢ a pack, but local brands are good and reasonably priced. Pipes of Belgian briar are excellent and inexpensive.

CLIMATE ... No extreme temperatures at any season. May through September is the best time to visit Belgium. (Brussels is also very worthwhile visiting from December 6 through the New Year, when the city is gaily decorated.)

CLUBS ... The American Chamber of Commerce, Brussels, can advise you about the meeting days of the American Club. Rotary, Lions, Kiwanis and commercial clubs in every city.

COMMON COURTESIES AND LOCAL CUSTOMS . . . Hand-shaking when you meet or leave anyone. Bring or send flowers when invited to dinner at a private home.

COMMUNICATIONS . . . A 3-minute call to the U.S. costs 450 francs. Airmail postage to the U.S.: postcards 6.50 frs.; letter 8.50 frs. (for 5 grams).

CURRENCY . . . The monetary unit is the Belgian franc. ($1 equals 50 Belg. frs.). One franc is divided into 100 centimes.

CUSTOMS REGULATIONS AND DOCUMENTS REQUIRED FOR UNITED STATES CITIZENS . . . Passport required. No visa needed. Vaccination certificate for re-entry into the United States. You can bring in 400 cigarettes, 1 lb. of tobacco or 100 cigars, 1 opened bottle of wine or liquor.

DRUGSTORES . . . Only pharmacies are found here. They usually carry only pharmaceuticals and a limited choice of cosmetics. Other items found in American drugstores are available in general stores here.

ELECTRIC CURRENT . . . Both 220 volt and 110 volt A.C., so check first at your hotel. European plugs needed.

FAUNA . . . Deer, wild boar, hare, wild fowl and game birds, wild ducks; hunting and shooting authorized only on private property; invitations to hunting and shooting parties can be obtained through hunting clubs or associations. Fishing is highly specialized, at sea, in rivers and streams; mostly private, however. Licenses for hunting and fishing are needed.

FLORA . . . The Ardennes is beautifully wooded. Flanders abounds in pastures. The district of Ghent is renowned for its orchids and be-gonias and its azaleas are world famous. There are many beautiful public parks in most cities.

FOOD . . . Most people think that Brussels ranks close to Paris when it comes to food. Local specialties are *choesels au Madère* (elaborate kidney stew), *waterzooi* (chicken in broth), *carbonnade fla-mandes* (beef stew with beer), lobster in whiskey sauce, snipe cooked in brandy, chicken in sherry. The pastries are glorious.

GAMBLING . . . Casinos at Knokke-Le Zoute, Blankenberge, Ostend, Namur, Chaudfontaine, Middelkerke, Spa and Dinant.

LANGUAGE . . . French and Flemish are the official languages, but most people you contact will have a working knowledge of English.

LAUNDRY AND DRY CLEANING . . . All the hotels have speedy laundry and dry-cleaning service.

LIQUOR . . . Good French wines and unlimited choice of other liquors. Whiskey and cocktails about 80¢ each. Belgian beer is very good. Try Faro, Lambic, Kriek, Gueuze and Orval.

MEDICAL FACILITIES . . . There are English-speaking doctors; ask at your hotel.

MOTION PICTURES . . . All foreign pictures with subtitles in French, Flemish. Shows, except Cinerama, run continuously.

MUSIC . . . There are excellent symphony concerts and occasional ballet in Brussels at the *Palais des Beaux-Arts*. Also opera at *La Monnaie*. Ask your hotel concierge for details.

NIGHT CLUBS ... Night spots in Brussels are big and brassy and on the expensive side. You may have to pay around $4 for a highball and $20 for the bottle of champagne you're expected to buy (unless you're at the bar) but there's no cover or minimum. Some require membership fees. Negro entertainers are popular here. Among the better-known and popular places are *Cabaret Chez Paul; "Au Gaity"; The Key Club;* and the *Scotch Club. Memling* is less expensive, more intimate. *Ancienne Belgique* is an amusing music hall.

PHOTOGRAPHY ... Black-and-white still and movie films are available in Belgium at about the same prices as in the U.S. Developing of color film takes at least one week, of black and white 24 hours. La Camera, 47 rue de l'Ecuyer, Brussels, is recommended for photo purchases.

RELIGION ... While Belgium is a Roman Catholic country, there are churches of almost every denomination.

RESTAURANTS ... Some of the most famous restaurants in the world are in Brussels. Among them are: *La Couronne* and *Le Cygne* on the Town Hall Square (Grand'Place); *Au Filet de Boeuf,* Rue des Harengs; *Brussels Grill Bar,* 319 Ave. Louise; The *Carlton* and *Savoy,* Blvd. de Waterloo; *Restaurant de Londres,* 21 rue de l'Ecuyer; *Fondroy* and the *Villa Lorraine,* especially pleasant on summer evenings. There are many, many others. These are in addition to the hundreds of restaurants offering foods of many nations. On the grounds of the 1958 World's Fair, a short distance from the center of the city, the restaurant atop the Atomium is still open. Good food with a view.

SHOPS AND STORES ... Large department stores are open daily (except Sundays) from 9 A.M. to 6 P.M. Principal ones in Brussels include Au Bon Marché, A L'Innovation, Magasins de la Bourse, Galeries Anspach, and many excellent small luxury shops.

SPECTATOR SPORTS ... Soccer, tennis, bicycle races, horse races.

SPORTS ... Yachting, fishing, horseback riding, golf, tennis. You can go hiking, cycling or boating. There are Youth Hostels everywhere. The swimming is magnificent all along the coast.

THEATERS ... In Brussels plays in French at *Théâtre Royal du Parc, Théâtre du Palais des Beaux Arts, Théâtre des Galeries, Théâtre National, Théâtre de Poche.*

TIME ... Noon in Brussels is 6 A.M. in New York.

TIPPING ... 15% is added to your bill at hotels and restaurants; if not, 15% is the usual tip, except for taxi drivers, who get 20%; or a minimum of 7 frs. Bellboys get 10 frs. per bag; chambermaids 10 frs. per day. Checkroom and washroom attendants and museum guides, 10 frs.; theater ushers, 5 frs.

TOURIST TAXES ... 5 francs in Brussels, less elsewhere. Airport departure tax $1.

TRANSPORTATION ... Good tram and bus service. Taxis, chauf-

The 15th-century Town Hall dominates the Grand'Place and is surrounded by guild halls representing characteristic trades.

feur-driven cars and drive-yourself cars are plentiful but expensive. Train service is widespread and good.

WATER ... May be drunk without danger in any city.

WHAT TO BUY ... Belgian lace from Flanders, linenware, Belgian porcelain, copperware, tapestry, diamonds cut in Antwerp, exquisite jewelry, Belgian crystal, rifles, shotguns and fine cutlery.

WHAT TO WEAR ... You do not need evening clothes in this part of Europe. Both men and women should take along medium-weight clothes, with an overcoat for winter. Be sure to take a raincoat, umbrella and walking shoes and in summer a swimming suit.

WHERE TO GO SIGHTSEEING ...

Brussels ... Brussels' architectural jewel is the Grand'Place with its lovely 17th-century buildings and the 15th-century Town Hall. Nearby is the well-known little statue of Manneken Pis, the most popular citizen of Brussels. The church of St. Michel (Gothic) with its 16th-century stained-glass windows and the church of Our Lady of the Sablon (late Gothic) are magnificent monuments to be visited. Other points of interest are the House of Erasmus in Anderlecht, the 17th-century Cambre Abbey, the Royal Palace and Park, Parliament Buildings, the Archway of the Cinquantenaire and the 19th-century Palais de Justice (one of the largest buildings in the world). The battlefield of Waterloo, with its painted panorama of the famous battle and Napoleonic relics, is a short distance from the capital, as is the Castle of Gaasbeek, which belonged to Count d'Egmont.

Side Trips ... Belgium is divided into two main sectors: Flanders, the Flemish-speaking flatland of the northwest, reaching to the coast, and Wallony, the French-speaking southeastern part.

Antwerp ... a wealthy metropolis in the rich country of Flanders, is a cosmopolitan city and international business center, a mecca for art lovers and a great port, second largest in Europe and third largest in the world. Here are some of the most famous Gothic and Renaissance buildings in all Europe. The Gothic Cathedral has an exceptional carillon and many magnificent masterpieces by Rubens, which are kept covered until noon every day. The Town Hall in Market Place has a fine Renaissance façade. In one corner of the square are several old guild houses. The Museum of Fine Arts contains 16th- and 17th-century paintings by such great artists as Rubens, Memling, Breughel, Van Dyck and Jordaens. In the Museum Mayer-Van den Bergh, you'll find more Flemish masters. Other places of interest are the Steen, 10th-century castle, Butcher's Hall, and Folklore Museum. The best hotel is the *Century.* Excellent restaurants are the *Criterium, St. Jacob in Galicie* and *La Rade.*

Ardennes . . . Wooded hills and valleys, steep rocks and winding streams abundant with fish, forests teeming with deer, ruins of ancient castles, watermills and hunting lodges—such is the scenery in Ardennes and Fagne. La Roche, Ciney, Bouillon, Arlon are worth a trip. The Grottos of Han on the Lesse river are worth seeing as is the Mardasson Memorial to American troops at Bastogne. There are many wonderful country inns in this area.

Beloeil Castle . . . Residence of the Princes de Ligne. Rich museum, splendid French-style park with ornamental lakes.

Bruges . . . One of the most beautiful medieval towns of Europe. A one-time harbor, it is now visited for its picturesque old buildings and dreamy canals. The 13th- and 14th-century *Halles* (market), with 310-foot belfry; 13th-century St. Sauveur cathedral; Gothic Notre Dame church; the Holy Blood Basilica; the 13th-century Béguinage and poetic *lac d'amour;* St. John's Hospital, where Memling lived and worked and where his paintings are shown; all are a delight. The *Duc de Bourgogne* and the *Portinari* are good hotels with restaurants. The *Panier d'Or* is a *Holiday* magazine award-winning restaurant.

Ghent . . . Another place you won't want to miss. There is a beautiful view from St. Michael's Bridge. In one direction is the Enfilade des Monuments, consisting of St. Nicholas Church, Cloth Hall and adjoining Belfry, and the famous St. Bavon's Cathedral. In the other direction are several Romanesque houses and the Castle of the Counts. Other places to see are the Hotel de Ville, the Abbey de la Byloke, the Chateau of Gerard the Devil, ruins of St. Bavon Abbey.

Liege . . . Wallony's intellectual and industrial center. Its architectural pride is the 16th-century Palace of the Bishop Princes. *Le Clou Doré* offers magnificent food and accommodations.

Ostend . . . The famed coast resort has long been popular with tourists. There is the Casino, racing, tennis and golf and, of course, the thermal baths. *Knokke-Le Zoute,* farther up the coast, is the newest and finest Belgian shore resort. Here they have the annual summer film festival. There is a casino, too, and a good hotel, *La Réserve.*

SOURCES OF FURTHER INFORMATION . . . Tourist offices in Town Hall, Place de Brouckere and Central Station, Brussels; Pan American office is in the Shell Building, 55 Cantersteen (Tel. 11-64-05), Brussels. Belgian Tourist Bureau Information Desk, 589 Fifth Ave., New York, N.Y. 10017.

BULGARIA

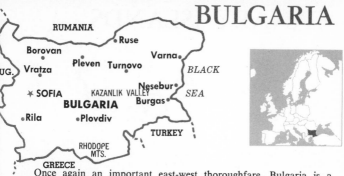

Once again an important east-west thoroughfare, Bulgaria is a warmly hospitable country that proves its welcome with countless brand-new hotels in cities and mountain and beach resorts. May through November is the best time for a visit, and the country is especially lovely in its long, golden autumn. Sofia (population 819,000) is 15½ hours from New York, elapsed time, by connections from Pan Am Jet Clippers to Belgrade.

The necessary visa ($1) is obtainable from the Bulgarian Legation, 2100 16th St., N.W., Washington, D.C. 20009, or ($4) on arrival. Rate of exchange is 2 leva to U.S. $1. Two bottles of liquor and 400 cigarettes, enter duty free. The electric current is 220 volts, 50 cycles, A.C. Tempting souvenirs of wood carvings, embroidery, pottery and blankets are found in all large cities.

De luxe hotels in Sofia are the *Balkan, Rila* and *Bulgaria*. Also recommended are the *Slavinska Besseda, Slavia, Moskva* and *Sevastopol*. Country-wide (even at Black Sea resorts) daily rates per person, including all meals, are $12 "special" class; $10 de luxe; $9 first class; $8 second class, single rooms; rates are $1 less in all classes for double rooms, and there is another $1 off if you stay more than 7 days. Sofia combines starkly modern architecture with elaborate mosques and rich Byzantine churches. Hear the choir in the great Alexander Nevsky Cathedral, and be sure to see the 13th-century Boyana church and the archaeological museum in the huge Bouyouk mosque.

Places to go in your own car or with a Balkantourist tour include Rila Monastery, a 3-hour drive from Sofia. Here, in beautiful mountain scenery, is a treasury of ancient Bulgarian art and architecture. Visit Plovdiv, where lovely old buildings and monuments are carefully preserved; the fabulous Thracian gold relics are displayed in the archaeological museum. Along the Black Sea, major sun-drenched resorts in this Riviera of the East are around Varna and Nessebur. Cabarets and gambling casinos thrive, and Varna and Burgas have open-air theater performances.

SOURCES OF FURTHER INFORMATION . . . Balkantourist, Bulgarian Tourist Office, 50 East 42 St., New York, N.Y. 10017.

CANARY ISLANDS

Long known as the "Fortunate Isles," the Canary Islands enjoy a perfect climate, magnificent scenic beauty and low, low prices. Only about 6 hours flying time from New York or San Juan, Puerto Rico, and 2¾ hours from Lisbon, the Canaries lie 72 miles off the northwest coast of Africa, but they have been Spanish provinces since 1496. (See SPAIN, page 165, for customs regulations, currency, electric current.)

Tenerife (30 by 60 miles; 491,000 population) and Grand Canary (30 by 40 miles; 454,000 population) are the two islands, of the seven that are inhabited, most popular with tourists. The major new hotel in Puerto de la Cruz on Tenerife is the *Las Vegas*, with swimming pool, rooftop night club, mini-golf; single from $7.60, double from $14.60, including all meals. Also new are the *Valle Mar, Tenerife-Playa, Belgica* and *Tigaiga*. Newest in Las Palmas on Grand Canary is the de luxe *Las Palmas Palace*, with swimming pool, gym, 18-hole golf course nearby; summer rates are $6.75 single, $9.25 double, without meals. Other good hotels are the *Gran Canaria, Gran Hotel Parque, Metropol* and *Santa Catalina*. About $15 a day covers a luxury-class room with private bath, full board, service charges and taxes. The islands also offer free-port prices on imported luxury goods and liquor.

Warmed by the Gulf Stream in winter, cooled by trade winds in summer and often months without a rainy day, these paradisical islands have daytime temperatures of 60° to 75° in winter, 70° to 85° in summer. Nights are cool enough for blankets the year round. The climate is ideal for growing luscious vegetables and fruits—Tenerife bananas are said to be the world's best—and gorgeous flowers; the Botanical Gardens of La Orotava on Tenerife are vivid with unusual tropical plants. There are two excellent golf courses (visitors' fees about $1 a day), tennis courts and year-round swimming at beaches and pools. Mountain climbers can tackle Mt. Teide (12,192 feet) on Tenerife, and there is deep-sea fishing. Buses all over the islands are very inexpensive, and taxis charge only about $3 for a full day's outing. Daily interisland flights between Grand Canary and Tenerife are only $8.50, round trip.

SOURCES OF FURTHER INFORMATION . . . Spanish National Tourist Office, 589 Fifth Avenue, New York, N.Y. 10017.

CZECHOSLOVAKIA

Most western—and Westernized—of the East European countries, Czechoslovakia offers a full program of winter and summer sports, luxurious spas, beautiful architecture, fine food, the original *Pilsner Urquell* beer and incomparable Czech glass and crystal. Prague (population over 1,000,000) is only ¾ hour from Vienna by connection from Pan Am's Jet Clipper flights, 9¼ hours direct from New York.

The necessary visa ($4) is obtainable within 2 days from any travel agent, any Czechoslovak Embassy, or at Czech frontiers and airports. Although it is not necessary to buy prepaid hotel and meal vouchers to get the visa, it is much better to make advance reservations for all such services through Cedok in Prague. Official exchange rate is 7.17 crowns per U.S. $1, but travelers with tourist visas may exchange currency at a bonus rate of 16.08 crowns per $1. Tourists who don't prepay for reservations by vouchers or checks must exchange $3 per person per day at the bonus rate. Personal belongings, including 400 cigarettes and gifts for residents up to a value of $27, enter duty free. The electric current is 220 volts, 50 cycles, A.C.

De luxe hotels in Prague are the *Alcron, Esplanade, International* and *Jalta*. Also recommended are the *Palace* and *Ambassador*. For rooms with bath, daily rates per person, including all meals, are: $14 de luxe; $9.50 first class; $7.50 second class. Prague (*Praha*) is the "Golden City of a Hundred Spires." Gothic and baroque towers soar above quaint arcaded streets surrounding the beautifully bridged Vltava (Moldau) River. Hradcany Castle is a legendary complex of palaces now converted into concert halls and museums. See the fabulous baroque Church of St. Nicholas, and St. Vitus Cathedral. Best shopping buys are glass and crystal, semiprecious stones, embroideries, wood carvings. Evenings resound with concerts, opera, ballet, clever pantomimes and hilarious marionette shows.

Visit Carlsbad (*Karlovy Vary*) and Marienbad (*Marianske Lazne*), celebrated spas that look just like movie sets. The lush Czech countryside of forests and mountains is jeweled with castles, and Cedok conducts inexpensive tours.

SOURCES OF FURTHER INFORMATION . . . Cedok, 10 E. 40th St., New York, N.Y. 10016; and Cedok, Na Prikope 18, Prague 1, and their travel agent representatives in the U.S.

DENMARK

WEATHER IN COPENHAGEN—Lat. N55°40′–Alt. 25′

Temp.	JAN.	FEB.	MAR.	APR.	MAY	JUNE	JULY	AUG.	SEPT.	OCT.	NOV.	DEC.
Low	29°	29°	31°	37°	45°	53°	56°	56°	51°	44°	37°	34°
High	35°	35°	39°	47°	57°	65°	68°	66°	60°	51°	43°	38°
Average	32°	32°	35°	42°	51°	59°	62°	61°	56°	48°	40°	36°
Days of Rain	15	14	15	12	13	12	15	16	14	17	16	17

LOCATION . . . Denmark occupies the Jutland peninsula, protruding north from Germany between Norway and Sweden, and includes a group of nearby islands, of which Funen and Zealand, where Copenhagen is located, are the largest.

CHARACTERISTICS . . . Denmark is one of the tidiest countries in Europe. Everything is bright and shining. The people are genial and gay, the food is wonderful and all too plentiful and the bars never close. Good hotels, night clubs, restaurants, shops and a palace at which the guard is changed at high noon when the King is in residence. Yachting and fishing are superb.

POPULATION . . . 4,681,469.

SIZE . . . 16,615 square miles, about half the size of Maine. No part of the country is more than 40 miles from the open sea.

CAPITAL . . . Copenhagen with suburbs, 1,500,000.

GOVERNMENT . . . A constitutional monarchy, the crown holding power with the Folketinget (Parliament).

HOW TO GET THERE . . . By Pan American Jet Clipper about 9 hours (elapsed time) from New York via London. By ship about 10 days.

ACCOMMODATIONS . . . Outstanding hotels in the heart of Copenhagen are the *Hotel d'Angleterre, Kong Frederik, Palace, Richmond, Royal* and *Imperial*. Rates average about $10 single, $18 double. Other highly recommended, conveniently located hotels are the *Alexandra, Astoria, Codan, Europa, Hafnia, Mercur* and *Termi-*

nus. Rates average $8 single, $13 double. The large *Hotel 3 Falke* (3 Falcons) is 5 minutes away by taxi. Rates from $9 single, $12 double. The new *Danhotel* near the airport offers single rooms with bath and TV from $4.35. Rates quoted do not include the 15% service charge, or the 18¢ per day for shoeshine service. Many hotels reduce their rates between October and April. Camping and youth hosteling are very popular in Denmark, and Denmark's special "park your children" facilities keep tourists' youngsters safe, happy and entertained while parents sightsee locally or tour the rest of Europe.

ARTS . . . You could spend all your sightseeing time in the wonderful museums of Copenhagen alone. Here are a few of the most outstanding: The National Museum has excellent collections from the Stone Age, Viking days and other periods in Danish history. The Arsenal has a famous display of arms, armor and uniforms. In Rosenborg Palace you will enjoy seeing the regalia of the Danish kings. The Kunstindustrimuseet houses a fascinating collection of arts and crafts of Denmark and foreign countries from the Middle Ages to the present time. The world-famous Museum of Musical Instruments is in the same building. The Hirschsprung Collection of Danish art is an interesting and representative exhibit. The Thorvaldsen Museum contains the works, tomb and the personal effects of Thorvaldsen, one of Denmark's greatest sculptors. The State Museum of Art has fine paintings from the Danish Renaissance. The Ny Carlsberg Glyptotek contains an antique collection and the largest display of French Impressionists outside of France.

BALLET . . . The Danish Royal Ballet Company is one of the finest in the world. Season at the Royal Theater in Copenhagen is September through May. Ballet and Music Festival, last 2 weeks in May.

BANKS . . . Leading banks in Copenhagen are: Landmandsbanken, Handelsbanken and Privatbanken, all with U.S. affiliations. Banking hours are: 9:30 or 10 to 3; Fridays also 4:30 to 6 P.M. American Express Office is located at Dagmarhus, H. C. Andersen's Boulevard 12.

CALENDAR OF HOLIDAYS . . . Stores are closed but museums are open on: New Year's Day; 5-day holiday from Maundy Thursday to Easter Monday; Store Bededag (public holiday fourth Friday after Easter); Ascension Day; Whit Monday; June 5, Constitution Day (afternoon); Christmas; December 26, Boxing Day. Other celebrations are June 23, Midsummer Night and July 4, celebration in the Danish-American National Park in Rebild.

CLIMATE . . . All of Denmark is warmer in the winter and cooler in the summer than the northeastern section of the United States. Winter temperatures seldom go below 30 degrees and summer averages around 68 degrees. The Gulf Stream keeps the climate equable. Best time to visit Denmark is from the middle of April to November.

CLUBS . . . There are many clubs of all kinds in Denmark. Ask the Personal Information Department of the National Travel Association of Denmark for information about clubs which may interest you. Address in Copenhagen: 7 Banegaardspladsen (in the Central Station but with its own street entrance).

COMMON COURTESIES AND LOCAL CUSTOMS ... "Thank You" (*Tak*) is the most often heard phrase in Denmark. You shake hands when you meet people and when you leave. Bring flowers when invited to dinner at a private home or send them ahead.

Time is referred to as half of the next hour rather than half past an hour; for example, 6:30 is called "half-seven."

COMMUNICATIONS ... A 3-minute phone call to the States costs 72 kroner ($11.44); 25.50 ($3.70) for a 10-word cablegram. Airmail postage to the U.S. is 60 øre for a 5-gram letter; 35 øre for a postcard. Local phone calls are 25 øre.

CURRENCY ... There are 100 øre in a krone, which is worth 6.92 kroner to the dollar. (Buying rate 6.82).

CUSTOMS REGULATIONS AND DOCUMENTS REQUIRED FOR UNITED STATES CITIZENS ... Your American passport is all you need to enter Denmark. No visa. Bring your driver's license if you plan to hire a car. If you are not living at a hotel, you must register with the local police. You can bring in and out unlimited amounts of Danish and foreign currency. Other duty-free imports are: 400 cigarettes or 500 grams of cigars or tobacco, up to 2 liters of wine or liquor for persons over 17 years of age. Air departure tax $2.25.

DRUGSTORES ... Known as *Apotek,* Danish drugstores carry American or equivalent European products.

ELECTRIC CURRENT ... 220 volts, A.C., 50 cycle. The European standard type plug is necessary in nearly all hotels.

FAUNA ... Danish forests abound in deer, hare and wild fowl and game birds. Fishing in Danish lakes, streams and along the seacoast is excellent for both sportsmen and for the great fisheries that are one of the principal industries. Graceful swans are found in the parks and sea gulls are as common as pigeons in Copenhagen. Ducks waddle around among the people in Danish parks. Denmark is principally agricultural. There is a marvelous agricultural show the last week of June in Copenhagen.

FLORA ... Denmark is a land of beautiful flowers. The parks of Copenhagen are among the most beautifully landscaped in the world. Lilacs and roses are everywhere. The beech is the national tree of Denmark. There are impressive pine forests and lovely meadows and farmlands.

FOOD ... The Danes love to eat and eat well. They have done the ultimate-most with the sandwich. There are over 200 varieties of delicious open-faced sandwiches available, the so-called *Smørrebrød,* which are the uniquely Danish variety of *smörgåsbord.* Danish dairy products, especially cheeses, are among the most outstanding in the world. The milk is marvelous. Seafood is a national specialty. Here, Danish pastries are deliciously different from the American version. The variety is infinite. Boiled cod, fried eel (*stegt ål*), and a delicious soup made of rye bread and beer are Danish national dishes, too. The

Danes are great consumers of coffee and enjoy tea.

GAMBLING ... Gambling is prohibited except at Government-controlled racetracks and other sports events.

LANGUAGE ... The official language is Danish of course, but English is understood even by the man on the street in Copenhagen.

LAUNDRY AND DRY CLEANING ... Though service is not as fast as in American establishments, Danish laundries and dry-cleaning plants are excellent. Most hotels in Copenhagen have their own facilities, and there are self-service automats, too.

LIQUOR ... Good, strong Danish beer and Danish *akvavit* (snaps) are well known, as well as Cherry Heering. Most kinds of imported liquor and wines are also available. Minimum legal age for drinkers is 18.

MEDICAL FACILITIES ... Medical care is available to tourists at a very low cost at the Government health clinics. There are excellent doctors and dentists throughout the country.

MOTION PICTURES ... English and American pictures and other foreign films are shown in Copenhagen. Better motion picture theaters include the *Alexandra,* the *Palads,* the *Palladium, Dagmar, Kino Palaeet, Tre Falke* and *Imperial.* See the local papers for time and program, which are at set hours.

MUSIC ... Opera, alternating with plays and the Royal Ballet at the Royal Theater, is one of the outstanding features of the winter in Copenhagen. There is an excellent symphony that performs at the Copenhagen Concert Hall and a visiting artist or musical group once a week during the winter. Also, in the attractive Concert Hall of the Broadcasting House, the symphony orchestra of 90 musicians gives concerts weekly. During the summer, daily concerts are held in Tivoli Gardens.

NIGHT CLUBS AND CABARETS ... Night life in Copenhagen is gay and fairly inexpensive. The clubs, now called "night restaurants," no longer require memberships, are open from about 10 P.M. on. These and other restaurants with dancing and floor shows may stay open till 5 A.M. The *Adlon* is the leading night restaurant with these hours. Others include *Lorry,* the *New Look,* the *Valencia.* There is dancing at the *Nimb,* and in the summer at the *Bellevue.* Most hotels have good orchestras and other entertainment. There are numerous sidewalk cafés and little bars.

PHOTOGRAPHY ... Copenhagen is fully supplied with all kinds of photographic equipment and supplies at prices even lower than those in Germany. Black-and-white and color films are developed quickly and well in Denmark. Most photogenic parts of the city: old canals around fish market, flower market near the main street, stock-exchange and Nyhavn, also modern residential quarters around Grundtvig's Church and street scenes in the rush hours.

RELIGION ... The state religion is Lutheran. Other churches include Catholic, Episcopal, Methodist, Presbyterian and Jewish.

RESTAURANTS ... Eating being one of the Danish national pastimes, it's hard to find a poor restaurant in Copenhagen. You'll seldom go wrong just walking into the first place that appeals to you. Have lunch on the attractive terraces of *Hotel d'Angleterre,* or *Stephan à Porta.* Sample the seafood at *Fiskehusets Restaurant* or *Krog's Fiskerestaurant.* Delightful dining in the *Langelinie Pavillonen* in the Royal Yacht Club overlooking the harbor. There is excellent French food and a Parisian atmosphere at *Au Coq d'Or.* There are also excellent restaurants in the Tivoli Park area: the *Belle Terrace, Divan I* and *Divan II* and the *Nimb,* which have lovely dining terraces. The *De 7 smaa Hjem* (7 small homes), the *7°Nations,* the *Hotel Imperial Restaurant,* the *Viking* in the Palace Hotel and the *Roof Restaurants* at Hotel Codan, Royal Hotel and Hotel Europa are also very good. *Oscar Davidsen's* is the famous sandwich emporium. They list 175 different varieties, all delicious and reasonably priced. Davidsen's is also good for seafood. *Frascati* serves both Danish and Italian cuisine on their charming sidewalk terrace. The cafeteria at the Hotel Imperial, the *Royal* and the *Lido* restaurants are inexpensive and convenient, especially when you're in a hurry. The *KAR* restaurants (no liquor) are also good and moderate.

Dinner is served from 6 P.M. until late in the evening, lunch at noon and breakfast from 8 A.M. in most restaurants. Three very good meals a day in Copenhagen cost about $6 in moderately priced places.

SHOPS AND STORES . . . Copenhagen is one of the great shopping centers of the world. Department stores in Copenhagen which sell distinctive Danish souvenirs are: Magasin du Nord, Illum, Crome and Goldschmidt. The headquarters of Georg Jensen is here. Also good are A. Michelsen and Hans Hansen. Illums Bolighus for furniture, interior decorations. The Permanent Exhibition of Danish Industrial Arts and Crafts is a good place to pick up marvelous textiles, pewter, ceramics, china and toys. Silver and furs cost much less than at home. Shops close at 5:30 P.M. weekdays (7 P.M. Fridays) and at 2 P.M. on Saturdays. There's a tax-free store at the airport.

SPECTATOR SPORTS . . . Soccer is the national sport in Denmark. Racing and trotting meets are also very popular. Bicycle racing and tennis matches are great seasonal favorites, too. See the local papers for more information on these events.

SPORTS . . . There are golf courses at Aalborg, Aarhus, Asserbo, Ebeltoft, Esbjerg, Vesterhavsbad on the island of Fanø, Elsinore, Holbaek, Kolding, Copenhagen, Nyborg, Odense, Randers, Rungsted and Silkeborg. Tennis courts are plentiful. The local club will gladly arrange for you to use their courts. Riding clubs throughout the country will give you information about hiring horses. Kajak and canoeing are favorite holiday sports. There are lovely rivers, like Gudenaa and Susaa, and the fjords. Freshwater fishing in some of the rivers may interest you, but if you prefer sea fishing, fishermen will be glad to take you out. There is great sport each year in tuna fishing in the Oresund off Elsinore. The season is from about August 15 to October 1. Sailing is ideal in Danish waters. Get information from the Danish Yachting Association, Langelinie-pavillonen, Copenhagen.

THEATERS . . . The presentations in Copenhagen's *Royal Theater,* including ballet and opera, will interest those unfamiliar with the Danish language. During the summer there are open-air performances all over Denmark, including the Viking Festival at Frederikssund June 19 to July 4 with colorful pageantry. Consult the National Travel Association for information on current programs.

Tivoli and *Dyrehavsbakken* are great big amusement parks open daily in summer. There are outdoor comedy theaters, side shows, animal circuses, band concerts and pantomime, to name but a few of the attractions at these mammoth fun fairs. Famed *Schumann Circus* performs daily in summer in the World Cinema.

TIME ... Six hours later than United States Eastern Standard Time. Denmark uses the 24-hour clock (12:01 to 24 is P.M.).

TIPPING ... All hotels and restaurants add a 15% service charge to your bill, plus, in hotels, 1.25 kr. per person a day to cover shoeshines and everything but special services. 1 krone (14¢) is the usual tip for small services. Luggage porters get 1.50 kr. for the first bag, 75 øre for each additional bag. Barbers, beauticians and taxi drivers get 10–15% of the bill.

TRANSPORTATION ... The fare on the airport bus into Copenhagen is 3.50 kroner. Taxis are inexpensive with a basic starting fare of 2 kroner. There are good trains and cross-country buses for traveling in Denmark. Little steamers take you from island to island at reasonable rates. Cars for hire are readily available through all hotel porters and most travel agencies. Rates are reasonable. A bicycle, with or without auxiliary motor, can be rented for a few kroner a day.

WATER ... The water is safe to drink all over Denmark.

WHAT TO BUY ... Danish and Greenland furs and silver, which cost much less than at home; Royal Copenhagen and Bing and Grondahl porcelain; lovely table and other linen; pewter and bronze ware; beautiful Danish furniture; Danish toys; jewelry. *See also* SHOPS AND STORES.

WHAT TO WEAR ... As there are no extremes of heat or cold in Denmark, you'll need neither very heavy clothes nor your lightest cottons. Wool suits and dresses and a warm topcoat will be fine although it is recommended that women bring their furs for the winter months. Suits and a dressy black outfit will fill a woman's needs in Copenhagen. Formal attire is seldom worn. Business suits, a topcoat and tweeds in the country for men. Bring a raincoat, too. Conservative sports clothes are favored by the Danes anywhere outside of Copenhagen. Wear conventional sport clothes for active sports.

WHERE TO GO—SIGHTSEEING ...

Copenhagen ... A wonderful way to get your first view of Copenhagen and environs is by the little motorboats that chug through the canals of the city and the surrounding coastline. Well-planned guided tours to various points of interest are available. Usually operating throughout the year, they range in price from $1.50 for the nonstop City Tour to $10.75 for the Copenhagen Night Tour. Others include all-day tours of South Zealand, all- or half-day tours of North Zealand, or historical areas. The "Lifeseeing" tours, such as the World of Tomorrow Social Tour, offer opportunities for becoming acquainted with Danish life aside from their unique Meet the Danes service mentioned under SOURCES OF FURTHER INFORMATION.

Of course, it's fun to sightsee on your own, too. The King lives in the beautiful Amalienborg Palace. The Changing of the Guard takes place at noon when the King is in residence. The royal reception rooms in Christiansborg Palace are open to visitors Thursday through Sunday. Other sights are Grundtvig's Church, which is situated in the middle of the new residential quarter of Bispebjerg, and the Church of our Saviour, with a spiral staircase outside the spire. The Copenhagen Zoo is one of the most important zoos in Europe. Orstedsparken is one of the loveliest parks in Europe surrounding a charming little lake full of graceful swans.

Other sights of interest include the Arsenal Museum, Rosenborg Castle, the University of Copenhagen, the House of Parliament in Christiansborg Palace, and the Gefion Fountain at the entrance to Copenhagen's favorite promenade, Langelinie, where you'll see the statue of the Little Mermaid. Tivoli is the famous amusement park in the center of town, where you can dance, hear a symphony, dine superbly or ride a Ferris wheel. Side trips from Copenhagen can be made through the lovely surrounding countryside. You can go to Kronborg (Hamlet's) Castle at Elsinore, 28 miles north. Bellevue Bathing Resort is only 8 miles from Copenhagen. The Deer Park is a beautiful wooded area where horses and carriages can be hired. At Lyngby there is an interesting Open-Air Museum, featuring old Danish farms (folk dances on Sundays in the summer). See the exciting Louisiana Museum in Humlebaek, 20 miles from Copenhagen. Continually changing exhibits of all kinds of modern arts. Fredensborg Castle is the lovely autumn residence of the Royal Family, set in a beautiful park. Hornbaek Beach, 40 miles from Copenhagen, is worth visiting.

Now for sightseeing farther afield. There is a good 4-day tour called "The Fairy Tale Tour," for approximately $90, which covers most of the places described below. You can have it adapted to suit your time and travel plans beyond Denmark. Or you can go on your own. The Danish Tourist Office or travel agencies will be glad to help you plan it. You can also visit southern Sweden on a 1-day tour from Copenhagen.

Aarhus . . . Denmark's second largest city is Aarhus. Located on the Jutland peninsula, overnight by boat from Copenhagen or 6 hours by train. The Town Hall is striking, ultra-modern; the cathedral, part Romanesque, part Gothic. The University is beautifully situated in an extensive park. The open-air museum is very interesting. The deer parks and wood of Riiskov preserves are wonderful. The leading hotel in Aarhus is the *Royal,* but the *Ritz* and *Regina* are both good. Singles $4–$7, doubles $7–$12. Thirty-one miles from Aarhus is Silkeborg, resort center of the Jutland region. In the heart of the lake district, Silkeborg is a charming little town. The sailing is great, the beaches are lovely, and fishing is also very popular. Travel through ιne crystal lakes in shiny little lake steamers. The best hotel in Silke-borg is the *Dania*.

Odense . . . is an enchanting city, the capital of the fairy-tale Island of Funen, second largest in Denmark. Hans Christian Andersen was born in Odense, and his house has become a museum, open to the public daily. The 13th-century Gothic church is one of the most de-lightful in Denmark. See the Funen Village, an open-air museum of Danish peasant life. It looks like something out of Andersen. The zoo is also very interesting. Excursions can be made among the lovely rolling hills. Quaint thatched farmhouses and picturebook scenery abound. The *Grand Hotel* in Odense is very good; so is the new *Motel Brasilia* on Highway A-1.

Traveling to the south of Funen you'll come to the lovely old town of Svenborg. Twisting streets and old houses; many beautiful private castles in this region. Good swimming, boating, and fishing. The Travel Association here arranges tours to the small, beautiful islands of Aerø (enchanting with 17th- and 18th-century houses), Strynø, and Langeland, well worth the reasonable cost.

Aalborg . . . is a very active city in the north of Jutland. Don't miss Jens Bang's House, a beautifully preserved Renaissance building. Night life here is very gay. The *Ambassador* and *Kilden* restaurants are known all over Denmark. There are a good golf course, fine fishing and other excellent sports facilities. Stay at the *Phønix*. Rebild Na-tional Park near Aalborg is the beautiful setting for the unique July 4 celebration. The de luxe *Rold Stor-Kro* here is excellent. For good fishing and the invigorating tang of the North Sea, stay at new *Hotel Hanstholm,* northwest of Thisted on Jutland.

SOURCES OF FURTHER INFORMATION . . . To get the most out of your stay in Copenhagen and Denmark contact the Informa-tion Department of the Danish National Travel Association. The office is in the Central Station (Tel. 11.1415). To arrange to "Meet the Danes," call Central 1946. This meeting service is international friend-ship and hospitality at its best. They will also make arrangements for you to visit Danish institutions, concerts, circuses or even Danish homes. They will provide information about restaurants, shopping, general sightseeing and special tours. The American Embassy is at Dag Hammarskjöldsallé 24 (Tel. Tria 4505); Pan Am's office is in the Imperial Building, Ved Vesterport, 4 (Tel. By 10.000). In New York the Danish National Travel office is at 505 Fifth Avenue.

FINLAND

NORWAY
LAPLAND
SWEDEN ARCTIC CIRCLE
Rovaniemi
GULF OF BOTHNIA
U. S. S. R.
FINLAND
Tampere Hameelinna
Vehoniemi
Aulanko
HELSINKI
GULF OF FINLAND

WEATHER IN HELSINKI—Lat. N60°12′—Alt. 25′

Temp.	JAN.	FEB.	MAR.	APR.	MAY	JUNE	JULY	AUG.	SEPT.	OCT.	NOV.	DEC.
Average	23°	22°	28°	39°	48°	58°	63°	59°	53°	45°	37°	28°
Days of Rain	18	16	14	12	12	13	12	16	16	17	19	19

LOCATION ... Finland lies northwest of Russia and east of Norway and Sweden. Helsinki in the south is about 250 air miles from Stockholm, 1,144 air miles from London.

CHARACTERISTICS ... Finland is a delightful and vigorous country which is unspoiled by tourists despite the fact that it offers the traveler a great deal. This land, where the Midnight Sun shines through the summer, is a paradise of virgin forests, crystal lakes (about 60,000), mountains and cascading rivers. As in all Scandinavian countries, its people are blond and blue-eyed, its cities clean, its food marvelous. This is a land of distinctive architecture, where the people are hospitable; and the rugged, rather mystic quality of the country is reflected in the Finns themselves. For an unusual vacation, Finland is the answer.

POPULATION ... 4,523,065.

SIZE ... 130,165 square miles; 724 miles and 337 miles at its longest and widest points.

CAPITAL ... Helsinki, with 496,193 inhabitants.

GOVERNMENT ... A republican form of government similar to the British parliamentary system.

HOW TO GET THERE ... By Pan American Jet Clipper from New York to Helsinki, about 10 hours (elapsed time) via Oslo and Stockholm. Or fly by Pan Am Jet to Copenhagen in 9¼ hours and make connections there for Helsinki. Helsinki is only 1 hour's flying time from Stockholm. By ship about 10 days from New York to Helsinki.

ACCOMMODATIONS ... Among the first-class hotels in Helsinki are the *Marski, Palace, Vaakuna, Helsinki, Seurahuone, Klaus Kurki* and *Torni*. There are also many less expensive but very good hotels, such as the *Hospiz, Martta, Ursula, Olympia*. Rates in Helsinki's top hotels run from $10 single and about $6.50 elsewhere.

ARTS ... There are many galleries and museums in Helsinki, and magnificent sculptures to be seen in the public squares. In the Atheneum, you will see collections of paintings by Akseli Gallen-Kallela, Albert Edelfelt, Eero Järnefelt, Juho Rissanen and other famous Finnish artists. The National Museum houses a large collection, as does the Museum of the City of Helsinki, and the Taidehalli. The museums also contain sculpture by Finland's outstanding sculptor, Wäino Aaltonen, by Jussi Mäntynen and others. There's a Permanent Design Center at Kaartinhalli House.

BALLET ... The Finnish Ballet Company of the Finnish National Opera gives performances in the Opera House, except in summer.

BANKS ... The important banks with U.S. affiliations are: Pohjoismaiden Yhdyspankki, Helsingin Osakepankki, Kansallis-Osake-Pankki. The banks and most hotels will cash travelers checks.

CALENDAR OF HOLIDAYS ... January 1 (New Year's Day); January 6 (Epiphany); May 1 (Spring Feast and Labor Day—Student Festivals); the Saturday closest to June 24 (Midsummer's Day and Finnish Flag Day); Saturday nearest the end of October, or beginning of November (All Saints' Day); December 6 (Independence Day); December 25 and 26 (Christmas and Boxing Day). Added to these are Easter, Ascension Day and Whitsunday.

CIGARETTES ... American-style local brands are *North State, Kent, Boston, Marlboro, Newport, Life* and *Milton*.

CLIMATE ... Similar to that of New England. July and August are the best times to visit Finland.

CLUBS ... Rotary Club, Lions, Jaycees, Zonta.

COMMON COURTESIES AND CUSTOMS ... The *sauna*, the famous Finnish bath, is a must when you visit Finland. Almost all homes and hotels have one. In Finland, both men and women always shake hands on meeting each other. Children should not be excluded from this ceremony. When introduced, you are also expected to mention your last name. When invited anywhere, you are expected to be prompt. This means you arrive between 7:30 and 7:35 for a dinner party scheduled for 7:30. Guests shouldn't take a drink until the host has proposed a toast to their health. Another Finnish social custom is that of observing the name day, as well as the birthday, of friends and relatives. *"Kiitos"* is "Thank you."

COMMUNICATIONS ... A 3-minute phone call to the States costs about Nmk. 40 ($12.60). Airmail postage to the U.S. is 40 penniä for an airletter or postcard; 60 penniä for a 5-gram letter. Local phone calls are 20 penniä. Dial 018 in Helsinki for newscasts in English.

CURRENCY ... The new *markka,* composed of 100 penniä, is valued at 3.20 *markkaa* (plural form) to U.S. $1.

CUSTOMS REGULATIONS AND DOCUMENTS REQUIRED FOR UNITED STATES CITIZENS ... Passport; no visa required up to 3 months' visit. You may bring in duty free: 2 liters of wine or spirits and 2 liters of beer; 400 cigarettes, 100 cigars, or ½ lb. of tobacco.

DRUGSTORES ... Chemists' shops and lots of them.

ELECTRIC CURRENT ... 110 to 220 volts, 50 cycles; A.C. The outlets are the round, two-hole European type.

FAUNA ... Most numerous among Finland's mammalian fauna are the fox, squirrel, hare, moose. In the eastern and northern parts the bear, wolverine and lynx wolf are also found. For the game-bird hunter, Finland offers good opportunities. The capercailzie, the black grouse and the hazel hen are rather common birds.

FLORA ... The flora and vegetation of Finland resemble that of northern Minnesota. More than 70% of Finland's land area is covered by forests. Predominant trees are pine, spruce and birch.

FOOD ... Some of the native foods are wonderful. Be sure to try the *voileipäpöytä* (like smörgasbord), *piirakka* (Karelian rice pastry), Finnish pancakes served with lingonberry sauce. "Fish Cock" (kala-kukko)—a strange but delicious blend of pork and fresh-water herring in a pastry loaf—reindeer steak or smoked reindeer, and in August, crayfish. Attend a crayfish party, if you can.

GAMBLING ... The National Lottery and betting on horse races.

LANGUAGE ... Finland is a bilingual country where approximately 92% of the population speaks Finnish, the rest Swedish. The tourist can easily get by in Helsinki and other big towns, as people commonly speak English, too.

LAUNDRY AND DRY CLEANING ... Laundries are plentiful. Dry-cleaning facilities are excellent.

LIQUOR ... The Finns have two rare liqueurs. Mesimarja (Arctic brambleberry) and Lakka (cloudberry or chamaemorus). Scotch and American whiskies and cocktails are also available.

MEDICAL FACILITIES ... If you need a doctor in Helsinki, dial 008 at any hour of day or night.

MOTION PICTURES ... Movies are mostly in English.

MUSIC ... The Helsinki Symphony Orchestra gives concerts during the season at the University Hall. Opera at the Opera House. A great musical event is the annual Sibelius Festival, which takes place in Helsinki during the first 2 weeks of June.

NIGHT CLUBS ... The *Teatterigrilli* restaurant has an occasional floor show and stays open until 4 A.M. Restaurants with floor shows (open to 2 A.M.) are the *Kaivohuone, Kalastajatorppa* and *Fennia.*

PHOTOGRAPHY ... Films and developing charges are reasonable. Color film is available, as are black-and-white still and movie film. There is excellent service on developing as long as you make clear exactly how long you can wait. An expert recommends the orange filter for lakes, islands and summer clouds, the dark green for full effect of the forest and landscape, and yellow for Lapland scenes. Sunsets in Finland are particularly strong and beautiful, especially in July, August and September.

RELIGION ... Lutheran and Greek Orthodox are the state churches, although all sects are represented.

RESTAURANTS ... There are dozens of restaurants in Helsinki besides the hotel dining rooms. Some of the better ones are the *Monte Carlo, Savoy, Palace, Victoria, Vaakuna, Torni, Motti* and *Walhalla*. There are also many restaurants with dancing; among these are the *Marski, Adlon, Kalastajatorppa* (a *Holiday* award winner), *Casino, Klippan, Kaivohuone* and *Fennia*. There are temperance restaurants, too: the *Kestikartano, Elanto, Primula* and *Pikapala*.

SHOPS AND STORES ... Stockmann's Department Store, Sokos, Elanto, Kalevala Koru, Artek, Bitco, Finn Flare, Ecco.

SPECTATOR SPORTS ... Racing, yachting regattas, log rolling, auto and motorcycle races, track meets, Finnish baseball (which is called *pesäpallo*), international canoeing competitions, cycling championships, tennis matches, soccer, the International Winter Games, skiing and ski-jumping competitions and reindeer races.

SPORTS ... Swimming, tennis, football, golf (you can play at midnight in midsummer), sailing, skiing, fishing, hunting. The best fishing season is from the beginning of June to the end of August. The hunting season is in the autumn. The best skiing is in Lapland during March and April, when days are long. (Ski resort hotels *Pallastunturi, Utsjoki* and *Kilpisjärvi*.) Canoeing and hiking are favorites.

THEATERS ... Almost every town in Finland has its own theater where foreign as well as Finnish plays are produced. In Helsinki: the *National Theater* at Station Square, the *Swedish Theater*. In Tampere: the new *Outdoor Theater* which has become world famous.

TIME ... Noon in Helsinki is 5 A.M., in New York.

TIPPING ... There is a 15% service charge added to your hotel bill and 11% on restaurant bills. The Finns do not encourage extra tipping. Luggage porters get 50 penniä (15¢) a bag. Taxi drivers and others are seldom tipped.

TRANSPORTATION ... Taxis are easy to get (chart in taxi translates meter reading); bus and train services excellent. Also water buses to take you to some of the outlying places. You can hire private cars with English-speaking guides. Taxi fares are identical with the meter reading but are more after 11 P.M. Self-drive cars are available for about $10 a day for the first 63 miles, then 9¢ a mile.

WATER ... Excellent.

WHAT TO BUY ... Famous Arabia rice china, pottery, Karhula-Iittala glass. *"Ryijy"* rugs, ornaments of brass, wood carvings, fabrics, hand-blocked linens, and articles made of woven birch bark, reeds, wickers. Also Finnish jewelry.

WHAT TO WEAR ... Heavy clothes in winter months (fur coat, ski togs), and lightweight clothes for the summer months. Better take a coat even in summer. Fur hats in Lapland in winter season.

WHERE TO GO—SIGHTSEEING . . .

Helsinki . . . Whereas the city of Helsinki is over 400 years old, most of the present city was built after the turn of this century. This accounts for its modern architecture. There is a lot to be seen in Helsinki, which is called the White City of the North. You should take a walk through the beautiful parks and squares where some of Finland's most magnificent sculpture can be seen. In front of Stockmann's store on the Main Square is the famous statue of the *Three Smiths*. On the Market Square is the statue of *The Maid of Helsinki Rising from the Sea,* and on Observatory Hill one of their most famous symbolic statues, *Shipwrecked.* All these have been made by outstanding Finnish sculptors. Visit the Olympic Stadium where the 1952 Olympics were held. Other places to see in Helsinki are the Parliament Building; the President's Palace, on the Market Square; the beautiful City Gardens at Eläintarha Park. Take a ferry from the foot of Aleksanterinkatu to Korkeasaari Island for a visit to Finland's only zoo. Also worth visiting are the Suomenlinna Islands just off Market Square, Tapiola suburb and Seurasaari open-air museum.

Be sure to visit the Helsinki Cathedral, a magnificent white stone structure. At the Social Museum you will see an exhibition of work protection and social welfare work. From the Stadium tower you get a wonderful view of the entire city.

Turku . . . Finland's former capital, Turku (45 minutes by air from Helsinki), was founded in the 13th century. It is Finland's oldest and third biggest city, with a population of 139,000. The Cathedral and the Castle from the 13 century, the Handicraft Museum and the Resurrection Chapel, a masterpiece of modern Finnish architecture, are some of the musts in this old city with an atmosphere of its own. Modern Turku ranks very prominently in the cultural life of the country and it is also one of the biggest ports. From Turku it is easy to make trips into the beautiful surrounding country.

Side Trips . . . From Helsinki, one of the most beautiful trips to take is to the city of Tampere. Go by train, or by motor bus and water bus. Tampere, with a population of 140,000 is clean and modern and is Finland's second largest city. Fine hotels include the *Kaupunginhotelli,* the *Tammer* and the *Emmaus.* The Tammerkoski Rapids flow through the town and many important industries are located here. Take a trip to the top of Pyynikki ridge where you will get a wonderful view of the city and its surrounding lakes. Other places to see are the Cathedral with its famous fresco paintings and Näsilinna, the provincial museum, which is on the top of a hill where you get an excellent view of Lake Näsijärvi. There are also two art museums here, which house fine collections of modern Finnish art. If you are here in the summer, try the *Rosendahl* summer restaurant and attend the *Outdoor Theater*—now world famous for its revolving auditorium. Watch ice hockey in Tampere's superb new stadium.

From Tampere you go by water coach to Aulanko through the Finnish lake regions. Food and refreshments are served on board. Aulanko is on the shore of Lake Vanajavesi, facing the town of

The Helsinki Railway Station, designed by Eliel Saarinen; Hotel Vaakuna to the right.

A View of the South Harbour in Helsinki. Helsinki Cathedral is in the background.

Hämeenlinna. The *Aulanko Hotel* is one of the finest and most modern in the country and is surrounded by the Aulanko National Park, one of the most beautiful in all Finland. The restaurant in the hotel has an orchestra and floor shows. There are riding horses, a private bathing beach, tennis courts, golf course, and, of course, the traditional Finnish *sauna*. One of the historic sights to see is the Hattula Church, which was built in 1250. The town of Hämeenlinna facing Aulanko is where Jean Sibelius was born and went to school. There's also a medieval castle built in the 13th century. From a tower high up in Aulanko National Park you get a wonderful view of the entire sur-

Helsinki Olympic Stadium, with statue of world-famous runner Paavo Nurmi in the foreground.

rounding lakeland. Take a new hydrofoil boat from Lahti for the 3-hour scenic trip to Jyväskylä.

Travel agencies offer a wide choice of tours, from 3 to 11 days' duration, which combine travel by bus and boat. Rates include all transportation, first-class hotel accommodations, all meals, guide services, entrance fees and tips.

Lapland . . . No visitor to Finland should miss a trip to Lapland, which is just as beautiful in the summer as it is in the winter. There are many legends about Lapland, one being that "it casts a spell on the visitor which compels him to return again and when he goes a second time he may stay, and if he does he'll turn into a reindeer." To reach Rovaniemi, the capital of Lapland, you may go by air in 2½ hours or by train in 17 hours. Lapland was almost completely destroyed in the war, but has been entirely rebuilt. Rovaniemi is the gateway to the North. There are two good hotels here, the *Pohjanhovi* and *Polar,* and many tourists' inns and ski lodges in various parts of Lapland.

From mid-May to mid-July there is no night in the Arctic Circle, a vast and mystic region with a strange allure. There are still about 2,000 native Lapps in existence and they are a particularly proud race. One thing a visitor MUST NOT do is stare at the Lapps in their native costumes. Lapland is rapidly becoming one of the most popular resorts in Finland. Transportation is excellent; buses will take you to the most faraway villages. In the winter it is a wonderful place to enjoy winter sports. Skiing on the treeless mountain slopes (practically unequalled anywhere else) continues far into spring. Reindeer-joring is an exclusive sport in Lapland. This is getting in a one-seated *pulkka,* following the leader (they say the driving is easy), and skimming over the snow. The annual Ounasvaara International Games held in Rovaniemi are one of the biggest winter tournaments in northern Europe. During the short period of summer, Lapland is a splendid place for the fisherman, canoeist or hiker. Fish are plentiful; trout, salmon and grayling are found in the streams, perch and pike in the lakes.

SOURCES OF FURTHER INFORMATION . . . Local tourist offices in Finland are the Finnish Tourist Association, Mikonkatu 15 A, Helsinki; or The City Tourist Office, Pohj. Esphlanaadik 17; the City Tourist Bureau, Linnankatu 14, Turku; the City Tourist and Congress Service, Rautatienkatu 18, Tampere. Pan American's Helsinki office is at Aleksanterinkatu 40 (Tel. 59-055). Other useful addresses in Helsinki are the American Embassy, Itä Kaivopuisto 21; U.S. Information Center, Kaivokatu 10; Finnish Automobile Club, Fabianinkatu 14; Suomi Touring Club, P. Esplanaadikatu 25; Suomen Turistiauto Ltd., Lasipalatsi. In New York the Finnish National Travel Office is at 505 Fifth Ave., New York, N.Y. 10017. You may want to pick up a copy of the English-language magazine *Look at Finland,* available in Helsinki.

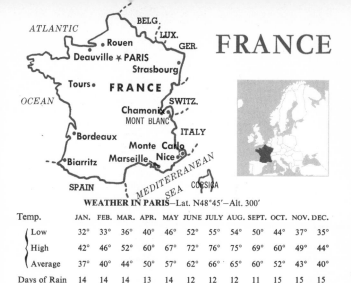

FRANCE

WEATHER IN PARIS—Lat. N48°45′—Alt. 300′

Temp.	JAN.	FEB.	MAR.	APR.	MAY	JUNE	JULY	AUG.	SEPT.	OCT.	NOV.	DEC.
Low	32°	33°	36°	40°	46°	52°	55°	54°	50°	44°	37°	35°
High	42°	46°	52°	60°	67°	72°	76°	75°	69°	60°	49°	44°
Average	37°	40°	44°	50°	57°	62°	66°	65°	60°	52°	43°	40°
Days of Rain	14	14	14	13	14	12	12	12	11	15	15	15

LOCATION ... Although France is approximately on the same latitude as Montreal, the weather is usually somewhat warmer because of the Gulf Stream. The climate is temperate. See chart above.

CHARACTERISTICS ... No one has to be told that Paris has everything for everyone. Its hotels are good, its restaurants, of course, out of this world. You can have a wonderful time in this famous, gay old city, not only during the summer season but also in winter and early spring, when there are even greater attractions in theater, music and art. Other parts of France are awaiting you, too. The Riviera, with its long stretch of fashionable and magnificent beaches, its casinos, its luxurious hotels, is ready to help you to have a wonderful time, as are the Château country, Normandy and Brittany. The people are cultivated, witty, and charming. They are also worldly-wise and sensitive to criticism. Visitors from abroad are generally appreciated and treated with special courtesy. The tourist has an advantage in being able to buy items at discount with dollars or travelers checks.

POPULATION ... About 48,000,000.

SIZE ... 212,821 square miles, about four-fifths the size of Texas.

CAPITAL ... Paris, with a population of 2,811,700 in the city itself; 7,439,000 in the metropolitan area.

GOVERNMENT ... A republic, with a Parliament which consists of a national assembly and a senate selected by all citizens.

HOW TO GET THERE ... By Pan American Jet Clipper, nonstop to Paris, about 7 hours from New York and Boston, about 15¼ hours from Los Angeles via Jet connection in New York, 10½ hours from U.S. west coast via polar route to London, then by easy connection to Paris. Through Jet Clipper service to Nice on the Riviera via Lisbon and Barcelona about 10¾ hours from New York. Connections at Lisbon for Paris (2¼ hours). By ship, 5 to 9 days.

ACCOMMODATIONS ... There are countless hotels and pensions in Paris. You can find anything you want at any price. In the de luxe group are: the *Ritz, Plaza Athénée, George V, Meurice, Crillon, Prince de Galles, Royal Monceau, Raphaël, Continental, Lotti, Lancaster* and *Bristol.* Less luxurious but very good are the *Claridge, Vendôme, Westminster, Napoléon-Bonaparte, Commodore* and others. Rates at official exchange run from about $14-$32 a day single with bath (no meals) at the top hotels. About $10 or $12 in the less swank group, and so on down from there. In the center of Paris, for businessmen, are the *Scribe* and the *Ambassador.* Singles about $11-$18 a day. Hotel space is hard to find in Paris from Easter until the end of October, and prices rise accordingly. From December 20 to March 1 some hotels in Paris and on the Riviera reduce prices as much as 20%.

ARTS ... Paris is the city for the art lover, the museum goer. Begin with the Louvre, of course. See the Venus de Milo, the Mona Lisa, the Winged Victory. Visit the Musée d'Art Moderne, the Rodin Museum, the Musée de l'Homme, the Jeu de Paume (impressionist painters), the Palais de Chaillot, Cluny, with sculptures, and exhibits of the Middle Ages, Sèvres for porcelains, Musée de l'Armée for arms and armor. Museums are closed on Tuesdays.

BALLET ... The famed Paris Opera Ballet performs each Wednesday at the Opéra all year around except in August. Many ballet and dance groups perform at local theaters.

BANKS ... In Paris, First National City Bank, 52, ave. des Champs-Elysées (8e arrt.), Tel. ELYsées 4542; American Express Co., 11, rue Scribe (9e arrt.), Tel. OPEra 4290; Barclays Bank, Ltd., 33, rue du 4 Septembre (2e arrt.), Tel. OPEra 4240; the Chase Manhattan Bank, 39, rue Cambon (1er arrt.), Tel. OPEra 4430; Morgan Guaranty Trust of New York, 14, place Vendôme, Tel. OPEra 2420; Royal Bank of Canada, 3 rue Scribe (9e arrt.), Tel. OPEra 0982; Bank of America N.T. and S.A., 28, place Vendôme, Tel. RICHelieu 55-26. Thos. Cook & Son is at 2, place de la Madeleine and 14, boulevard des Capucines.

CALENDAR OF HOLIDAYS ..: New Year's Day; Easter and Easter Monday; May 1, Labor Day; Ascension Day, 40 days after Easter; Whitsunday (Pentecost) 10 days later and following Monday; July 14, Bastille Day; August 15, Assumption; November 1, All Saints; November 11, Armistice Day; Christmas Day.

CIGARETTES AND TOBACCO ... American cigarettes cost $6.20 to $6.60 a carton, so take in as many as you are allowed. French brands, such as Gitanes and Gauloises, are much cheaper.

CLIMATE ... It seldom gets either very cold or very hot in Paris, although there are some exceptional days each season. Paris is interesting to visit in all seasons, but particularly so in autumn and spring.

CLUBS ... In Paris: Jockey Club (very aristocratic—difficult to be admitted), International Club, Racing Club de France, Touring Club, Rotary Club, Lions International. Foreign members are admitted. In Nice and Marseille: Propeller Club of the U.S.

COMMON COURTESIES AND LOCAL CUSTOMS ... You may find some customs in France new to you. Tickets are collected when you leave trains. It is customary to shake hands when you meet someone and when you say good-bye. In small buildings the elevator will take you up but you are expected to walk down. Look for the *minuterie,* those buttons you press on each floor to give you 1 minute of light in hall or stairs.

COMMUNICATIONS ... A 3-minute phone call to the States costs 59.25F. ($12); cablegrams from 1.36F. (27¢) to 2.48F. (50¢) per word, depending upon the state. Airmail postage to the U.S. is .75F. for postcards; .95F. for 5-gram letters.

CURRENCY ... There are 100 centimes in a franc (F.), valued at about 5 to U.S.$1. In many stores you can buy some French goods at up to a 20% discount by paying in U.S. or Canadian dollars or travelers checks, or by having goods delivered to your plane.

CUSTOMS REGULATIONS AND DOCUMENTS REQUIRED FOR UNITED STATES CITIZENS ... You may bring in 400 cigarettes, 125 cigars or 1 pound of tobacco in your luggage, 1 bottle of liquor with seal broken, 2 pounds of foodstuffs. You need a valid passport but no visa for stays up to 3 months.

Two still cameras of different sizes or makes with 10 rolls of film for each and 1 movie camera with 10 rolls of film may be brought in. In currency 750 francs may be taken out.

DRUGSTORES ... American products available in cities, and there is a genuine American-type drugstore on the Champs Elysées in Paris.

ELECTRIC CURRENT ... The trend is to 220 volt but some electric current is 110-115 volts A.C. In France the current is 50 cycles instead of 60 cycles as in the United States, which will affect the function of electrical equipment with moving parts. Radios, irons, shavers, etc., will operate satisfactorily; converter plugs are needed to fit sockets.

FAUNA ... In Paris, mostly poodles, dachshunds, cats and sparrows.

FLORA ... In northern and central France, a wide variety of attractive wild flowers. In the south you will see vines, mimosa, orange and olive trees and graceful cypress.

FOOD ... This is a volume in itself. French food is famous everywhere and Paris has some of the best restaurants in the world. You can find anything you want to eat in Paris at almost any price you wish to pay. Lunch can be a 2- or 3-hour affair involving several courses. The cheese is wonderful, hors d'oeuvre are usually superb, sauces are a national specialty, *pâté de foie gras* is different from anything you've had in tins. Coffee is strong but can be ordered to approximate the American taste. Try *purée de marrons,* chestnuts cooked with celery, spices and chicken consommé; wonderful snails in garlic sauce and saddle of spring lamb done in white wine with chopped tarragon. There are hundreds of other magnificent dishes and regional favorites. The wines range from ordinary to superlative, depending upon price and taste. They are served with all meals. The French rarely drink water, but you may want to order *Evian* bottled spring water. Pastries are famous, as are the *potages,* or thick soups. The French also do well by fish and salads. Milk is usually safe to drink, but make sure it's been pasteurized and purchased in a sealed bottle.

GAMBLING . . . Around Paris there is horse racing at *Auteuil, Chantilly, Longchamp, St. Cloud, Vincennes* and other nearby spots. The National Lottery has drawings every Wednesday. Nearest gambling casino in Enghien, 10 miles from Paris. Along the Riviera, and at Deauville, of course, the casinos are famous.

LANGUAGE . . . After two wars shared by the French with GIs and Tommies, many Frenchmen not only can understand English but can now even understand an American trying to speak French.

LAUNDRY AND DRY CLEANING . . . Laundry is touch and go. In some hotels it's fine, in others it's very bad. In large hotels you can get your clothes cleaned in 48 hours.

LIQUORS . . . French wines, champagnes and brandies have no peers in the world. Scotch, popular in Paris and on the Riviera, costs 80¢ and up per drink. Wine is still the national beverage, rivaled only by Pernod and brandy, and even an unknown "bar brandy" is better than you often get at home. For bar brandy ask for a *fine à l'eau.* Pernod is very popular, especially in the south. The champagne name is patented and applies only to wines from the Champagne district, just as cognac applies only to brandy of the Cognac district.

MEDICAL FACILITIES . . . The American Hospital at Neuilly is the favorite of Americans. But there are many English-speaking doctors. Ask at your hotel.

MOTION PICTURES . . . There are numerous cinema houses in Paris. Hollywood movies have French subtitles if the sign says *version original.* French is dubbed in if the sign reads *version française.* See newsstand magazine *This Week in Paris* for movies and other listings.

MUSIC . . . The Paris Opéra and Opéra-Comique are of major importance. Some of the world's greatest composers and conductors are French, so there is fine music to be heard all the time. Good music can also be heard in celebrated concert halls such as Salle Gaveau, Salle Pleyel and Palais de Chaillot.

NIGHT CLUBS AND CABARETS . . . Like food, this would take a book in itself. But in Paris take a look at the *Lido* on the Champs-Elysées, world-famous for its floor shows. Go about 9:30 for dinner and to get a good table, which must be reserved in advance. The *Crazy Horse Saloon* is a crowded striptease spot. At most night clubs there will be a bucket chilling champagne on your table, but you're usually not obliged to take it. Look in at *Au Lapin Agile* in Montmartre, a spot with atmosphere. Drop in at *Schéhérazade* or *Novy* and let yourself be carried away by old Russian atmosphere, to the strains of gypsy violins. All famous, all good. The *Nouvelle Eve* is extremely popular and has a floor show. Currently in vogue are such so-called private clubs as *Chez Castell, St. Hilaire, Blue Note, Chat qui Pêche* (for the very young), *Caméléon* (jazz), *La Grande Séverine, New Jimmy's, Bilboquet's* and *Elysée Matignon*. If you want to get real low-down, there is always the Place Pigalle in Montmartre with its many, many clubs of varying repute. Among the more reliable discotheques are *Club St-Germain* and *Le Vieux-Colombier*. There's a nightclub tour available from hotels.

PHOTOGRAPHY . . . Black-and-white and color still and movie films are available in Paris and other big cities; so are cameras. Prices are considerably higher than in the U.S. but include processing. Kodak-Pathé S.A. is located at 39, ave. Montaigne, Paris.

RELIGION . . . France is a Catholic country and there are many magnificent cathedrals which hold Mass. There are also many Protestant churches in Paris: American Cathedral, American Community Church, British Embassy Church, Presbyterian Church, Eglise l'Étoile; Église de Passy, Église du Saint-Esprit, Église de la Mission Étrangère, Methodist Church, Quakers, Russian Orthodox Church, Grande Synagogue. And in Nice, the beautiful Church of the Holy Spirit, the only American Protestant church in France outside Paris.

RESTAURANTS . . . It is always possible to find a good little out-of-the-way spot, undiscovered by tourists, which has magnificent food and cheap prices. However, here are some of the better known in Paris (most are very expensive; always best to reserve a table): *Maxim's* (also known for its meals on Pan American's first class Clipper flights) is very elegant. Dancing every evening, formal dress on Fridays; closed on Sundays. *La Tour d'Argent, Le Grand Vefour, Lasserre, Lapérouse, Chez Fabien, Le Berkeley, Joseph, Le Petit Bedon, Taillevent* and *Laurent* are outstanding. *Prunier, Le Méditerranée* and *Drouant* specialize in seafood; *Androuet* in cheese; *Pharamond* in tripe. Other restaurants with regional and foreign specialties abound. *Doucet* has three locations, good and not expensive. Consult the *Michelin Guide* for well-known restaurants in all price ranges. For the cost-conscious, there are *le snack* (lunch counters) and *le self-service* (cafeterias). For homesick Americans there are the *Champs-Elysées Drugstore,* two *Pam Pams* and the *Pub Renault,* all serving cheeseburgers, salads, milk shakes and the like. *Pavillon d'Armenonville* and *Pré Catelan* in the *Bois de Boulogne* are delightful for lunch or dinner in summer. Over on the Left Bank is *La Coupole,* beloved in the 'twenties and still doing business. *Harry's New York Bar,* famous among generations of Americans, is still at 5 rue-Daunou, and the *Café de la Paix* continues to be the crossroads of Paris. The *Ritz Bar* is a favorite meeting place of Americans (men must wear tie and coat in the Ritz). There are sidewalk cafés everywhere you turn where it is possible to sit for hours reading, writing letters, or just watching people go by while the saucers pile up. Two long-popular Left Bank cafés are the *Deux Magots* and the *Flore* in the heart of St-Germain-des-Prés.

SHOPS AND STORES . . . The two biggest and best department stores are *Printemps* and the *Galeries Lafayette. Aux Trois Quartiers* and *Samaritaine Capucines* are smaller but excellent. For linens there is *Grande Maison de Blanc*. The shops on the rue de la Paix are magnificent. The rue Royale, avenue Matignon, Faubourg St.-Honoré and cross streets near the rue Royale, the rue St.-Honoré have the smartest specialty shops. And now the big couturiers have opened what they call "boutiques" in which ready-to-wear merchandise and accessories are offered at far lower prices than in the custom salons. The *Bon Marché* is on the Left Bank. Don't miss the Swiss Village antique market near the Eiffel Tower, or *Marché aux Puces,* the famous Flea Market, reached by métro to the Porte de Clignancourt; open every Saturday through Monday, but bargains are becoming scarce.

Department stores are closed Mondays, except during the Christmas season. Beauty shops are also closed Mondays. Some shops close during August, when many Parisians take their vacation.

SPECTATOR SPORTS . . . Horse racing goes on almost all year at one track or another near Paris. Soccer is popular at the Parc des Princes and at Colombes Stadium. Tennis tournaments and championship matches take place at Stade Roland-Garros in the Bois. Boxing matches are frequent. Basketball games during the winter.

SPORTS . . . There is a new, elegant golf club at St. Nom-la-Brétèche; fine courses also at St. Cloud (card necessary), also at St-Germain, Chantilly, Mortefontaine, etc. There is skiing in the French Alps and the Pyrénées in winter. Yachting, swimming, fishing, golf, riding all along the Riviera, Deauville, Biarritz, and good fishing in Brittany.

THEATERS . . . In Paris: The *Comédie-Française,* one of the most famous theaters in the world, is open all year except in August. Grand opera may be heard all year except during August at the *Opéra.* The *Opéra-Comique* has light opera. The *Folies-Bergère* is the mecca of many Americans and there are numerous music halls, such as *Casino de Paris,* offering variety shows which you can enjoy without understanding French. Buy your seats from a broker; it saves wear and tear. Performances at 8:45 P.M. Matinees Thursday and Sunday at 3. See MUSIC for a listing of concert halls.

TIME . . . Noon in Paris is 6 A.M. in New York.

TIPPING . . . One franc is about equivalent to a 25¢ tip in the States. In addition to 12%-15% service charge at hotels, plus 10% tax, the baggage porter expects 1 to 3 francs; room service waiter, average 50 centimes per trip; chambermaid, average 25 centimes per day; doorman, 50 centimes to 1 franc for getting taxi; concierge, average at least 2 francs per day if you've made much use of his services. Most tourists leave something for restaurant waiter beyond 15% *service compris* added to check. The *sommelier* you consult for wines gets 1 or 2 francs; checkroom and washroom attendants, 40 or 50 centimes; theater and movie ushers, 50 centimes. Tour guide gets 1 franc for short tour. Beauticians and barbers 15%, usually included in bill; taxi drivers about 15% of meter reading, minimum 40 centimes.

TOURIST TAXES...Port taxes of $10 1st class, $6.50 2nd class and $3.50 tourist class collected at all seaports. Air departure tax $1.40 to European or North African cities; $5 elsewhere.

TRANSPORTATION...There are plenty of taxis but at peak hours are often difficult to find. It is advisable always to notice whether the taxi you hire has a meter. Unmetered cabs often charge exorbitant rates. Between 12 and 2 P.M. drivers won't take you anywhere except in the direction they are going. They are usually going to lunch. Taxi drivers are as volatile and excitable as ever.

After 11 P.M. taxi rates are doubled. Consult your driver before you go anywhere, because at night clubs and theaters fixed-rate cabs are waiting. There are stands for cars for hire near most of the hotels. These are more expensive than ordinary cabs. Travel—first class recommended—métro (subway) at least once. There are buses all over Paris too. You must queue up for these. Métro and bus operating hours, which vary, are posted on each station.

WATER...It's safe to drink. There are plenty of bottled waters, Perrier, Evian and Vittel, that are still or sparkling.

WHAT TO BUY...Clothes, of course, from one of the great designers, if you can afford them. If you want the very latest, don't buy dresses anywhere but at top shops or couturiers. Fashions have a 2-year patent in Paris. Shoes are not a good buy; they are apt not to be right for American feet. Paris hats are special. Lingerie, blouses, gloves, laces, china, Lalique glass, Daum crystal, cognac and champagne are all cheaper than at home. Made-to-order girdles are wonderful. Perfumes are amazingly inexpensive. Prices are standard in all stores. The handbags and umbrellas are excellent. Costume jewelry is low-priced, too. Furs are better at home. Hermès' engagement and address books are standard gifts for a man. For men there are also hand-rolled handkerchiefs, lisle socks, ties, wallets and fishing reels.

WHAT TO WEAR...Your newest, smartest clothes—what you would wear in any large city at home. You'll need a raincoat, a suit, walking shoes, evening clothes if you plan any gala night life. Men should dress as in any city. Women going to the Riviera should take their newest sports clothes, evening clothes and a fur jacket, beach clothes. Men need slacks, sport shirts, bathing trunks and robes. For skiing, what you would wear at a good resort at home, or buy your ski things abroad. Ski equipment can be rented at most resorts.

WHERE TO GO—SIGHTSEEING...

Paris...There are various ways to see Paris. You can do it on your own and discover things, or you can go on a guided tour which will probably save you time but won't give you the same feeling of working things out for yourself. You can hire a cab or walk and explore to your heart's content. Walk down the Champs-Elysées from the Arc de Triomphe; you will pass some famous restaurants and hotels. Midway is the Rond Point and from there to the place de la Concorde you may walk down a tree-lined avenue to avenue Gabriel, where you find public buildings, including the Presidential Palace and the American Embassy. At the place de la Concorde you'll find Hotel Crillon and the Marine Ministry. About two blocks away is the Church of the Madeleine. Notre Dame is on the Ile de la Cité. On the Ile, too, the Sainte Chapelle, located inside the Palais de Justice has one of the most beautiful stained-glass window arrangements in Europe. There are lectures and tours through the great cathedral that are most interesting. See also the Tuileries Gardens along the rue de Rivoli; you can't miss the Eiffel Tower, or the Opéra, which has a new ceiling painted by Marc Chagall.

Climb the hill to Montmartre, with its twisting streets and many restaurants and cafés. Sacré-Coeur stands on top of the hill and you get a magnificent view of the city below. Back in the heart of Paris you will want to see the place Vendôme, the rue de la Paix. Take a stroll down the chain of magnificent boulevards: boulevard de la Madeleine, boulevard des Capucines, boulevard des Italiens, boulevard Poissonnière, boulevard St-Denis, boulevard St-Martin, which form a wide continuous avenue of shops and theaters. Go to the Left Bank and take a look at the "Boul' Mich," or Boulevard St-Michel. The Sorbonne is nearby and the Pantheon. The Luxembourg Gardens and Palace are here, too.

Drive out through the Bois de Boulogne, with its lakes and fine restaurants and bridle paths. It's charming.

Browse at the open-air bookstalls along the Seine. Take a trip on the river, on the colorful *bateaux mouches*, and see all the familiar monuments from a different angle. Boat trips are 1 to 2 hours long, and some include lunch or dinner. Visit Les Halles, Paris' central market, at the end of a long night out, and have onion soup. Pay a visit to the Hôtel des Invalides and Napoleon's tomb. It is all fascinating.

Versailles—Fontainebleau ... There are many short trips out of Paris to the environs which are practically musts. Versailles is 12 miles away. Here are the gardens, the Palace of Louis XIV, the Grand Trianon and the Petit Trianon. You can see La Malmaison on this trip, too, the home of Napoleon and Josephine. Fontainebleau, with its Renaissance palace, its formal gardens, is fascinating. You can visit this on a standard tour or go by train. Fontainebleau, once a 12th-century fortress, was reconstructed in the 16th century and eventually became the favorite residence of Napoleon. Drive through the 42,000-acre-forest. During the summer, in the gardens of Versailles and Fontainebleau there are fountain displays, night festivals with ancient dances, fireworks, etc. These nocturnal performances are a must, and tickets can easily be purchased in most of the travel agencies.

Go to St-Germain-en-Laye, just a short trip from Paris, to see the Royal Palace with its 1½-mile-long terrace. A trip to Chantilly-Compiègne is interesting. The latter is the spot of the German surrender in 1918 and the French surrender in 1940. There is a large palace in the park with a collection of Gobelin tapestries.

At Chantilly there is a huge château set in a formal park. Chartres

Paris' famous *Arc de Triomphe de l'Etoile* is the final resting place of France's "Unknown Warrior."

The newly rebuilt harbor and the beach at Cannes is one of the most famous resorts on the French Riviera.

is about a day's trip from the city. Don't miss the Cathedral of Chartres, noted for its stained-glass windows and Gothic sculptures.

The Château Country . . . No visit to France is really complete without a trip through the Château Country, the center of which is Tours. The *Hôtel Univers* or the *Métropole* are both good here. Or stay in one of the many romantic castles in the region that have been converted into hotels, such as the *Château de Pray* outside Amboise.

Visitors to Montmartre, overlooking Paris, will enjoy the picturesque street cafés. Whitedomed *Sacré-Coeur* is seen here in the background.

Naturally, you can't miss visiting Paris' famous Notre Dame or browsing among the open-air bookstalls nearby.

Take any of the standard trips to Blois, Amboise, Chaumont, Chenonceaux, Chambord, Loches, Luynes, Langeais, Villandry, Azay-le-Rideau, Chinon. During summer months Sound and Light Spectacles are given every night in most of these châteaux similar to those in Versailles. Night trips can be arranged from Paris or from Tours. Some of the châteaux are furnished in magnificent style; some are in ruins; others are visited for their architectural interest. Azay-le-Rideau contains a kitchen which is a rarity. It has, too, a Fontainebleau tapestry ordered by Charles I for the city of Rome. Villandry is famous for its Spanish Museum, its beautiful gardens. Chenonceaux, one of the most famous châteaux, was given to Diane de Poitiers by Henry II. The gardens, ruined in 1944 by bombings have been restored. The château was unharmed.

Blois contains an ornate staircase in its inner court. Here, too, is the death chamber of Catherine de Médici, and her private chapel. Amboise is furnished with period pieces, Aubusson tapestries; there is an interesting collection of 15th- and 16th-century armors in the guardroom. Chambord is an enormous place with 365 rooms. There are innumerable turrets and spires, a wall surrounding the gardens and an estate which is the largest in France.

Visit Vouvray while in Tours. Here is where some of the finest wines in the world are made. Visit the vineyards with their acres and acres of grapes. From Tours you should go down to the cognac country if you are a brandy fancier. Here is the world-famous center for the cognac which takes its name from the city and the region.

Pyrénées—Basque Region...In southwest France the Pyrénées stretch from the Atlantic to the Mediterranean in a natural boundary line between France and Spain. Here is Bordeaux, as famous for its wines as nearby Cognac is for its brandy. On the coast of the Bay of Biscay is Biarritz, a famous beach resort made fashionable by the Empress Eugénie. There are luxurious hotels such as *Miramar* and *Le Palais,* a casino, excellent restaurants and a wonderful beach nearby. Not quite so fashionable but smart in its way is St.-Jean-de-Luz, which is less expensive. Biarritz rates are about $25 per day American Plan, if it's de luxe you want. There are also moderately priced accommodations. Pelote is a favorite local sport; or you can see a bullfight at Bayonne.

If you are heading eastward to the Mediterranean, you will go to Lourdes, site of the famous vision of Bernadette. There are many hotels and pensions here. The grotto is a national shrine and the Cathedral is composed of three churches, built one above the other with hundreds of memorial chapels donated by pilgrims to the shrine. Nearby are the baths where each year thousands of afflicted come to bathe in the holy waters. It is estimated that more than a million people make the pilgrimage to Lourdes each year. Luchon in the Pyrénées looks into Spain. It has excellent ski runs and thermal baths. There are dozens of hotels, best of which are the *Continental* and the *Sacaron.* Skiing is excellent on *Superbagnères,* a 6,000-foot peak with the wonderful *Grand Hotel* at its summit.

The tiny principality of Monaco lies near the French-Italian border on the Mediterranean Sea. Monte Carlo, the famous gambling resort here, is a short drive from Nice.

France—Chamonix with Mt. Blanc (15,781 feet), the highest mountain in Europe, in the background is a famous winter and summer resort easily accessible from Paris.

Pau is an interesting city with a fine bridge, public squares, a great castle—now a museum famed for its tapestries—in which Henry IV was born, and a renowned boulevard with a gorgeous view facing the Pyrénées. Pau is a starting point for tours of the Pyrénées.

Nîmes and Arles, old cities where Roman ruins may be seen, are on the route to Marseille and the Riviera from the Pyrénées or Carcassonne.

The French Alps ... The French Alps extend south from Lake Geneva to the Riviera. Some of the best skiing in Europe is found here and some of the most breath-taking scenery. Mt. Blanc towers over the towns of Mégève and Chamonix. From here you may visit the Mer de Glace glacier, take the cable car 9,035 feet up to the Aiguille du Midi, or go to Le Brevent with its astonishing view of the whole chain. Grenoble is both a ski and glove center. The French Alps contain nearly 30,000 guest houses and hotels from the ultra-smart to the very simple.

A fashionable watering place is Aix-les-Bains in a valley in the heart of the French Alps. The spas here are famous. And here is the famous revolving solarium. The *Splendide* is the top hotel. Annecy, a little to the north, is a quaint and charming resort.

The Riviera ... Here is France's playground, the famous Côte d'Azur. The French Riviera stretches from Toulon to the Italian border and is dotted with famous spots: Nice, Cannes, Menton, Beaulieu, Cap d'Antibes, Juan-les-Pins, St-Tropez, and, of course, Monte Carlo in the principality of Monaco.

Nice is the largest of the Riviera resorts. It has the Promenade des Anglais, a famous pre-Lenten Carnival, some fine hotels: the *Negresco, Ruhl, Plaza, Splendid, Atlantic, West End, Westminster* and *Beau-Rivage.* Out of town, but with a superb view, is the *Hostellerie de la Reine.* Single rates at the Negresco and Ruhl are $12-$23; double, $13-$29. The *Plaza* is $11-$24 single, $21-$40 double. Rates at the other hotels are mostly from $8 single, $9 double. Not so large, but smarter and more frequented by the International Set is Cannes, its yacht-dotted harbor sheltered by green hills. There are wonderful hotels, luxurious branches of Paris shops, wonderful beaches and two casinos. The beach boulevard La Croisette has the *Carlton,* the *Martinez* (the largest hotel on the Riviera), the *Majestic, Grand* and others. Between Cannes and Nice, beautifully situated at Golfe-Juan, is *Les Cocotiers* restaurant in Château de l'Aube. At Cap d'Antibes, visit *Hôtel du Cap* with the fabulous pool and restaurant of *Eden Roc.* The *Hôtel du Cap Estel* is a beautiful romantic spot with its own beach and lovely garden which is located on the low Corniche, 1 mile after *Eze-Bord-de-Mer.* At Roquebrune-Cap Martin, facing the sea, is *Hotel Le Vistaero,* all 30 of its individualistically designed rooms with private baths. The de luxe *Hôtel Provencal* and *Grand Hotel Palace* are at Juan-les-Pins.

There are, however, less swank and equally beautiful resorts along the Riviera: St-Tropez, St-Raphael, Sainte-Maxime, all with wonderful beaches, many with fine hotels and small pensions. Or try some of the smaller fishing villages such as Villefranche, Cap Ferrat and Cap d'Ail. Many hotels reduce rates as much as 20% in winter.

From Nice three roads lead to Monte Carlo and the Italian frontier. They are the Basse (low) Corniche, Moyenne (middle) Corniche, and Grande (high) Corniche. Each one runs on its different level out into the hills. From each you get that famous view of the Riviera.

At Monte Carlo there is the Casino, the most famous in the world. This is an enormous ornate building, marbled and mirrored, with crystal chandeliers everywhere you turn. There are several hotels at Monte Carlo, most famous of which is the *Hôtel de Paris.* There are the *Métropole,* the *Hermitage* and the *Monte Carlo Beach,* all of which are first rate. Along the entire Riviera there is wonderful golf, fishing, swimming and boating. It is a yachtsman's paradise, but it is fun for small boatsmen, too; there are water skiing and underwater fishing. In the winter there is skiing about 25 miles inland from the beaches. There are fine restaurants along the Riviera. *La Bonne Auberge* between Nice and Cannes, *La Réserve* at Beaulieu and *Château de Madrid* (on Middle Corniche) are the best. Also try *Le Vieux Moulin de Chez Nestou* at Cros de Cagnes, *La Colombe d'Or* in St-Paul de Vence and *Mère Terrats* in La Napoule. The *Réserve Montana* in La Napoule (see the Henry Clews sculpture museum nearby) is superb and relatively inexpensive, as is *Château de la Chèvre d'Or* in Eze Village. For a magnificent view of Nice, the Alps and the Bay of the Angels, dine high on a hill at *Hostellerie de la Reine,* just west of Nice at Place de la Lanterne.

The Riviera is both a summer and winter resort these days. The winter weather is not as warm as in Florida, but you'll find flowers and sunshine. You can take a delightful 7-day drive from Paris to Cannes by way of Avallon, St.-Seine-l'Abbaye, Vienne (home of the highly esteemed *La Pyramide* restaurant), Valence, Vaison-la-Romaine, Les Baux, Marseille and along the coast to Cannes.

Normandy and Brittany... In Normandy you will want to visit the invasion beaches of Omaha, Arromanches and Utah. Rouen is the departure point for tours of both provinces. The city was heavily damaged by bombings but has been rebuilt and is still the museum city. This is where Joan of Arc was burned at the stake. Deauville is one of the most elegant beach resorts in France, and is filled with activity during the season. The *Normandy, Royal* and *Hôtel du Golf* are the best hotels. Activities include a casino, horse racing, yachting, golf and polo. Paris shops have branches there.

Take a trip to Mont-St.-Michel, at the junction of Normandy and Brittany, which is built on a small island with a single street that climbs to the abbey founded in the 8th century. It was a prison in Napoleon's time. The cobbled street is lined with shops and restaurants, most of which feature huge fluffy omelets made on an open fire before your eyes. Very good, too. In Brittany you'll find the women still wearing white, starched coifs. You'll see cozy and ancient enclosed beds. Quimper is the tourist center. Market days, Wednesday and Saturday, are most picturesque. The square in front of the Cathedral is crowded with colored tents in which all sorts of things are sold. Dinard in northern Brittany is the largest seaside resort.

St-Malo, across the harbor from Dinard, is a walled city full of charm. It is also a battlefield site. There are many little fishing villages along the Brittany coast where traditions are preserved. The *Pardons,* religious pilgrimages, run from May to October.

There are tours of Normandy and Brittany from Paris.

SOURCES OF FURTHER INFORMATION... In Paris, contact the Direction Commissariat Général au Tourisme, 8, avenue de l'Opéra. Also the National Office for Tourist Information, 127, Champs Elysées and at 7, rue Balzac. In other French cities, see local Syndicat d'Initiative office. In New York the French Government Tourist Office is at 610 Fifth Avenue, with branches in Chicago, Los Angeles and San Francisco.

Semaine de Paris, a weekly entertainment guide and the *Paris Weekly* magazine are both in English. The *Guide Michelin* is a must if you're touring France by car or are a serious gastronome.

Pan Am's Offices in Paris are at: 138, Champs Elysées and 1, rue Scribe (Tel. BAL. 9200 for reservations—24-hour service; and BAL. 8800 for Administrative offices). In Nice, Hotel Negresco, 37, Promenade des Anglais (Tel. 88-99-11).

GERMANY

WEATHER IN FRANKFURT—Lat. N50°10′—Alt. 300′

Temp.	JAN.	FEB.	MAR.	APR.	MAY	JUNE	JULY	AUG.	SEPT.	OCT.	NOV.	DEC.
Low	26°	28°	31°	37°	46°	52°	55°	54°	49°	41°	34°	29°
High	35°	38°	45°	54°	65°	72°	74°	72°	66°	55°	44°	37°
Average	31°	33°	38°	46°	56°	62°	65°	63°	58°	48°	39°	33°
Days of Rain	15	15	15	13	13	13	15	14	13	14	14	15

LOCATION ... Germany is in the very heart of Europe. Frankfurt is about 400 air miles from London, less than 300 miles from Paris, and about 3,900 air miles from New York. The distance between Berlin, largest German city, and London is 700 air miles.

CHARACTERISTICS ... Nothing has changed the basic beauty of Germany: glorious scenery, art treasures, entertainment such as stage plays, music, gay folk festivals, and quaint ancient customs. In many ways, Germany is at present a most interesting part of Europe: the progress the country has made since 1945 in reconstruction is phenomenal. The German people have a true desire to make the tourist happy and comfortable.

POPULATION ... West Germany has a population of some 57,385,000, roughly one-third that of the United States, while in the entire country there are approximately 74,500,000 people.

SIZE ... The area of West Germany, excluding West Berlin, is 95,742 square miles, about the size of New York and Pennsylvania combined. The entire country occupies about 182,000 square miles.

CAPITAL ... Bonn, a city of 142,500 on the Rhine, is the present capital of the Federal Republic of Germany—*Bundesrepublik Deutschland,* as West Germany is officially called. The former German capital, Berlin, has a population of 3,225,600, 2,170,600 in the west sector. Hamburg has a population of nearly 2,000,000.

GOVERNMENT ... West Germany is a Federal Republic with a legislative body of two houses.

HOW TO GET THERE ... By Pan Am Jet Clipper, New York to Munich 10¼ hours; to Düsseldorf, 8¼ hours; Hamburg, 8½ hours; Frankfurt, 7½ hours; Berlin, 9 hours. Frankfurt is 10 hours from Chicago and 12¾ hours from the U.S. west coast via polar route. Also through service from Dallas, Houston, Atlanta and New Orleans. Frequent local service via Pan Am between Berlin and Hamburg, Frankfurt, Nuremberg, Stuttgart, Hanover, Cologne, Düsseldorf, Munich. By ship, about 9 days from New York to Hamburg or Bremen.

ACCOMMODATIONS ... In general, throughout the country beds in hotels or inns, including mountain hotels and converted castles, range in price from about $2 to $12 in international de luxe hotels; rooms with bath about 30% to 50% higher. Hotels add 10% to 15% service charges and, in winter, from .50 to 1 DM per night for heat. Continental breakfast, added to your bill, costs from 2.50–3.50 DM, but if you skip breakfast, hotels add 1 or 2 DM. Meals are inexpensive by United States standards. For hotel listings look under individual cities below.

BANKS ... The Deutsche Bank, Dresdner Bank and Commerzbank have U.S. affiliations. First National City Bank has a branch in Berlin's Europa-Center.

CALENDAR OF HOLIDAYS ... New Year's Day; Good Friday; Easter Sunday and Monday; Ascension Day; Whitsuntide, Sunday and Monday; May 1, Labor Day; June 17, Day of German Unity; Repentance Day, Wednesday before Sunday of the Dead, in November, a Protestant holiday; December 25 and 26, Christmas. Roman Catholic holidays of Corpus Christi, All Saints Day and All Souls Day are also observed. There are also local and regional holidays.

CIGARETTES, CIGARS AND TOBACCO ... American brands are very expensive, but German cigarettes at DM 2 per pack are very good. Try Marlboro, Stuyvesant, HB and Astor. Try thin German cigars, too.

CLIMATE ... With the exception of January, which is the coldest month, the winters are mild. There are long springs and agreeable summers; Indian summer until late October.

CLUBS ... Rotary and Lions among others; also German–American clubs.

COMMON COURTESIES AND LOCAL CUSTOMS ... Just about the same as at home, but there's little use of first names.

COMMUNICATIONS ... A 3-minute call to the States costs about DM 50; DM 10 for a 10-word cablegram to New York; DM 12 to other cities. 0.40 DM postage for an airmail postcard, 0.60 for an *Aerogramm,* 0.80 for 10-gram airmail letter. Local phone calls are 0.20 DM.

CURRENCY ... The monetary unit is the Deutsche Mark (DM), which is worth about 25¢ in United States currency.

CUSTOMS REGULATIONS AND DOCUMENTS REQUIRED FOR UNITED STATES CITIZENS ... Your American passport is all you need for entry into either West Germany or western sector of Berlin. Visa is no longer required. Adults may take in, duty free, 400 cigarettes or 75 cigars or 1 lb. of tobacco, 1 bottle of liquor, gifts to a value of $25, unlimited Deutschmarks and other currency.

DRUGSTORES ... The *Apotheke* sell only pharmaceuticals; the *Drogerie* sell standard drugs, cosmetics, etc.

ELECTRIC CURRENT ... There is 220 voltage A.C. generally prevailing all over Germany. The plugs are the round, European type. Most of the leading hotels will provide an adapter on request.

FAUNA AND FLORA ... About the same as in New York State.

FOOD ... A hamburger is *Deutsches Beefsteak,* and frankfurters are called *Frankfurter Würstchen.* Some German specialties are: dumplings and strudels in Bavaria; *Spätzle* (a special type of noodle) in Swabia and Baden. Westphalen ham; Hamburg *Schnitzel à la Holstein* and fish; New Year carp in Berlin and Northern Germany; *Berliner Pfannkuchen* (Berlin doughnuts), *Kartoffelpuffer* (potato pancakes); Helgoland lobster along the seashore; St. Martin's goose throughout Germany; Allgäu district cheese; Bodensee *Felchen* (Lake Constance trout), Rhine salmon; Alpine cheese; and countless others.

GAMBLING ... There are many licensed casinos in the resort spots such as: Baden-Baden, Bad Dürkheim near Ludwigshafen in the Palatinate, Bad Homburg and Wiesbaden near Frankfurt, Garmisch-Partenkirchen just south of Munich, Bad Neuenahr not far from Bonn, Lindau and Constance on Lake Constance, Westerland on the Island of Sylt, and Travemünde near Lübeck on the Baltic Sea. There are Ecarté Clubs in Kassel and a casino in Hanover near the famous Kröpcke Café. The German Class Lottery, the football toto and numbers lottery, all under state regulation, are very popular.

LANGUAGE ... English is understood in all the tourist centers, hotels, railroad stations and better shops.

LAUNDRY AND DRY CLEANING ... Very good everywhere.

LIQUOR ... The Germans have famous Rhine, Moselle and many other wines, Bavarian beer, Schwarzwälder (Black Forest) Kirsch (a great specialty), and Steinhäger, a form of gin. You also find all kinds of liquor, and milk bars with familiar soft drinks, juices.

MEDICAL FACILITIES ... Excellent and available everywhere.

MOTION PICTURES ... The movie theaters in all larger cities in Germany show American and English films (German sound tracks are dubbed in), as well as those of Germany and other countries.

MUSIC ... Every major German city has a philharmonic orchestra; 63 cities have permanent opera companies with ballet. Among the most important annual events are the Wagner Festival Plays in Bayreuth in July and August, the Bavarian State Opera Festivals in Munich at about the same time, the Berlin Festival Weeks with international opera companies, chamber orchestras and ballet companies in September, the International Opera Festival in Wiesbaden during the entire month of May, the Mozart Festival in Würzburg, contemporary music festivals at the Kranichstein Institute in Darmstadt and at Donaueschingen, and the popular operetta performances on the floating stage in the Rhine at Koblenz, from the end of June till the middle of September. (For others, and exact dates, consult the Calendar of Events of German Tourist Information Office.)

NIGHT CLUBS . . . See listings under cities below.

PHOTOGRAPHY . . . Black-and-white film, rolls and packs are available in all sizes; also color film. Excellent work in developing.

RELIGION . . . There are churches of all denominations.

RESTAURANTS . . . See listings under cities descriptions below.

SHOPS AND STORES . . . Store hours are 9 to 6:30; to 2 P.M. on Saturdays. In suburbs and smaller towns, 2-hour closing for lunch.

SPECTATOR SPORTS . . . Almost every sport is practiced in Germany. Soccer is as popular with Germans as baseball is with Americans. In almost every city there is a big stadium, such as the *Olympia Stadion* in Berlin and the *Frankfurt Wald-* (Woodland) *Stadion.* The famous *Sports-Palace* and *Deutschland Halle* in Berlin, where ice shows, 6-day bicycle races and hockey contests take place, have been rebuilt; so has the huge *Westfalen-Halle* in Dortmund in the Ruhr District. Tennis courts, such as those at Bad Homburg, Berlin, Hamburg, Wiesbaden, and Frankfurt, present international stars; and the *Avus,* automobile race tracks in Berlin, as well as the *Nürburg Ring* in the Eifel Mountains, attract enthusiastic fans from all over. You can watch horse races, polo games, ice hockey, and even rugby. There are also international winter sports contests in the mountains, and summer skiing events on artificial jumps near Bayreuth.

SPORTS . . . Golf, tennis, swimming, soccer, skiing, skating, rowing, fencing, sailing, boxing, volleyball, fishing, hunting, gliding, sand yachting and flying.

THEATERS . . . Performances in all larger cities. In summer open-air music and drama performances are given in ancient cathedrals, monasteries and monastery ruins and medieval castles and castle ruins throughout West Germany. In West Berlin, German Opera Berlin, Frei Volksbühne, Theater des Westens, Berliner Theater, Schiller Theater, Schlosspark-Theater, Renaissance Theater, Theater am Kurfürstendamm, Komödie, Tribüne, Hebbel-Theater and Waldbühne.

TIME . . . 6 hours later than U.S. Eastern Standard Time.

TIPPING . . . 10% to 15% service charges are included in bills, but tip chambermaid DM 1 per day; 50 pfennig per bag for luggage porters; 50 pfg. for room service, hatcheck, washroom and parking lot attendants; DM 1 for barber or beautician; 10% tip for taxi drivers; about 5% for waiters.

TOURIST TAXES . . . Moderate and only in resort places.

TRANSPORTATION . . . Excellent through trains between most important cities. Excursion trains in scenic areas have glass domes and some have dancing and movie cars. Plane service to large cities is very good, too. Car rental service, with or without driver, is available through Metro, Avis, Hertz and other Rent-a-Car systems at reasonable prices. Hired-car delivery at destination also through railroad stations. Some trains and boats will carry your car aboard.

WATER . . . Excellent to drink. Table waters are also available.

WHAT TO BUY . . . Leather goods of all kinds, photographic articles (German cameras are among the best), optical goods, china, ceramics, jewelry, wood carvings, cuckoo clocks, toys and watches.

WHAT TO WEAR . . . Dress as you would in New York City during the corresponding season. No sports clothes in the theater.

WHERE TO GO—SIGHTSEEING . . .

Frankfurt . . . Frankfurt-on-Main is the city where Goethe, author of *Faust,* was born. Coronation banquets of the emperors of the medieval German Empire were held in magnificent Römer Hall in Frankfurt for centuries. This is also a West German center of commerce and industry, and international fairs.

De luxe hotels are the new outstanding *Frankfurt Intercontinental* ($11-$20 double, European Plan), *Frankfurter Hof, Hessischer Hof* and *Parkhotel.* First-class hotels are: *Savigny, Baseler Hof, Monopol-Metropole, National* and *Excelsior.* Good tourist-class hotels are: *Inselhotel, Westfälinger Hof;* rates in these start from $3.50 and up, European Plan. The de luxe *Schlosshotel Kronberg* is 10 miles from the city.

Worth visiting in Frankfurt are the many museums, which house superb art collections. Among them are: Goethe Museum, Grosser Hirschgraben 25; Städelsches Institute of Art, Schaumainkai; Historical Museum, Saalgasse 31; Frankfurt Society of Art, Markt 44 (Steinernes Haus); Frankfurt Cabinet of Art, Börsenplatz 13-15; Zimmer Gallery Frank, Böhmerstrasse 7; Senckenberg Natural History Museum, 25 Senckenberg Anlage. There's fine ballet at the Städtische Opera; ballet groups also in the Festhalle and Kongresshalle on the Fair Grounds.

Some of the best night clubs and cabarets in Frankfurt are: *Sie-Bar, Hüttenbar, Pilotenbar, Königin-Bar, BB-Bar, Prelude* and *Three-Coins-Bar* (Hotel Frankfurt Intercontinental), *Lipizzaner-Bar* (Hotel Frankfurter Hof), *Jimmy's Bar* (Hotel Hessischer Hof). Bavarian atmosphere in the large *Maier Gustl's Oberbayern* beerhall.

Principal restaurants are: *Brasserie* and *Sylhouette Supper Club* in the Frankfurt Intercontinental Hotel; *Grillroom* in the Frankfurter Hof, *Kaiserkeller, Arnold Grill, Brückenkeller, Kupferpfanne, Salzhaus, Grillroom Parkhotel, Heyland's Weinstuben,* and *Henninger's* rotating restaurant on 400-foot tower across the Main River.

Best shopping area: Kaiserstrasse, Zeil, Hauptwache, Goethestrasse, Schillerstrasse. There's a duty-free store at the airport.

Theaters include Städtische Bühnen, Kleines Theater im Zoo, Theater am Rossmarkt, Die Schmiere.

Other cities in this area, each with its own features of interest, include Kassel, with its health resort, and Wilhelmshöhe.

Berlin . . . From Frankfurt, Berlin is 1¼ hours by Clipper. Flying is the best way for foreigners to reach the "Island City." Berlin has managed by almost superhuman effort to become an important industrial and cultural metropolis again. A variety of stage offerings, the Berlin Philharmonic Orchestra, and life along Kurfürstendamm, the Berlin equivalent of Broadway, help make the city gay and interesting. Among the night clubs are *El Panorama* atop Berlin Hilton, *Ballhaus Resi* with world-famous water shows, table phones and pneumatic mail service, and many, many others. In the Dahlem Museum are many of the paintings and sculptures of the former state museums, including 26 Rembrandts and the nearly 3,300-year-old bust of Queen Nefertiti. The National Gallery of art and antiquities is in Charlottenburg Palace. Waldbühne, a huge sylvan theater; new Philharmonic Hall; the Congress Hall, a present from the U.S.A.; the new Gedächtniskirche memorial church; the new Europa-Center; and the Hansa Quarter. The Berlin International Festival Weeks, usually in September, the Berlin International Film Festival, usually in June, a German Industries Exposition in the fall, the "Green Week," an agricultural show with equestrian, social and art events, and international sports events attract huge crowds from other countries. There are a number of luxury and good first- and second-class hotels, the best being: *Berlin Hilton, Bristol Kempinski, Hotel am Zoo, Parkhotel Zellermayer, Plaza, Tusculum, Savoy-Hotel, Ambassador* and *Hotel Berlin.* European Plan rates, from $6 single. Restaurants with excellent cuisine are *Ritz, Aben, Schlichter, Rollenhagen, Mampe, Funkturm* (radio tower), *Brüningslinden, Bonne Auberge, Kempinski Grill* and *House of Nations* in Europa-Center.

Mainz (Mayence) and **Wiesbaden** . . . are only a few miles west of Frankfurt. 2,000-year-old "Golden Mainz," where Johann Gutenberg invented movable type (see World Printing Museum), is a university town, also the center of German wine trade. This is where most Rhine River boat trips start and end. Wiesbaden, capital of Hesse, and a famous health resort, contains many art treasures. The *Hotel Nassauer Hof* and *Schwarzer Bock* in Wiesbaden, and *Europa* in Mainz, are excellent. Fifty miles south of Frankfurt is Heidelberg, alma mater of many Americans, city of the *Student Prince,* with the famous Heidelberg Castle (*Hotel Europäischer Hof, Schrieder* and *Haarlass*). Nearby is Mannheim, Europe's second largest inland harbor. Not quite 40 miles farther south is Karlsruhe, on the Rhine. Its museum and collections are worth seeing. Karlsruhe is frequently the starting point for excursions into the Black Forest. Bruchsal Palace is nearby. Southeast less than 120 miles is Ulm-on-Danube, with its famous church spire rising 528 feet. The church took 500 years to build and contains art treasures accumulated during those 5 centuries. Augsburg is slightly over 50 miles in the same direction—city of the Fuggers and Welsers, merchant princes whose origins date from the Middle Ages.

Munich (München) . . . capital of Bavaria, is a city of theaters, museums, art galleries and parks. Among many theaters are the famous Cuvilliés Theater, the National Theater, the Kammerspiele, the Residenztheater, the Prinzregententheater, the Kleine Komödie, and for operettas, the Gärtnerplatz Theater. The Deutsche Museum is the largest technology museum in Europe. Fine art collections are shown in the famous Alte Pinakothek and Haus der Kunst. Visit Munich's famous landmark, the cathedral Frauenkirche, enjoy a magnificent view from the steeple top. Other worthwhile churches are Theatiner-kirche, St. Peter and St. Michael. Also worth seeing is the Nymphen-burg Palace with its vast parks and chinaware factory, the huge Eng-lische Garten and the Tierpark Hellabrunn, Europe's largest zoo. Outstanding events are the Bavarian State Opera Festival in July and August and the Oktoberfest (last week of September and first week of October). Munich is famous for its beer, and festivals draw many visitors.

Hotels: *Vier Jahreszeiten, Grand Hotel Continental, Ambassador, Europäischer Hof, Der Königshof, Deutscher Kaiser, Regina Palast* and *Bayerischer Hof* offer first-class accommodations. Other good hotels are *Eden-Hotel Wolff* and *Excelsior.* Fine cuisine including typical Bavarian food at the top restaurants such as *Humplmayr, Weinhaus Schwarzwälder, Walterspiel* of Hotel Vier Jahreszeiten, *Kanne, Holzmüller* and *Ewige Lampe.* Schwabing is the Montmartre of Munich, with dozens of small restaurants and bars where students meet. Night spots: *Studio 15, Gisela, Der Käfig, P-1, Bei Heinz, In-termezzo, Lola Montez, Eve, Piroschka, Regina Bar* and many others. Go to the *Platzl* for a typical Bavarian stage show and to the famous *Hofbräuhaus.* Munich is the gateway to the Bavarian and Austrian Alps, with many scenic tours via the Lake District (Lake Starnberg, Tegernsee, Achensee and Walchensee).

Nuremberg . . . is one of Germany's finest medieval cities, 125 miles north of Munich, in Northern Bavaria, full of works of famous sculp-tors Adam Kraft and Peter Vischer and the woodcarver Veit Stoss. It is the city of Peter Henlein, inventor of the pocket watch (Nurem-berg Egg), of Hans Sachs and his "Meistersinger" companions and of the great painter Albrecht Dürer. It is also a toy center (Annual In-ternational Toy Fair). First-class hotels: *Grand* and *Carlton.* Typical restaurants: *Bratwurstherzle, Bratwursthaeusle, Sebaldusstuben, Schlenkerla, Heiliggeistspital, Boehm's Herrenkeller.* Places to visit: Imperial Castle, St. Sebald's Church, St. Lawrence's Church, Market Place with beautiful fountain, Church of Our Lady (see the animated clock strike at noon), Germanic National Museum, Dürer House, Fembo Museum, and the Traffic Museum.

All of Franconia and Upper Palatinate around Nuremberg is a jewel of German culture, famous for such cities as Würzburg, where the annual Mozart Festival is held in the Residence Palace (fabulous staircase and Tiepolo frescoes), Rothenburg ob-der-Tauber, Dinkels-bühl, Bamberg with its beautiful cathedral, Coburg, Bayreuth with its annual Richard Wagner Festival, the forest regions of the Fichtel Mountains with open-air plays at the Luisenburg, the city of Amberg, and Regensburg on the Danube with its famous cathedral and its boys' choir *Regensburger Domspatzen.* The entire region is dotted with ro-mantic medieval castles, monasteries, and beautiful churches.

Another tourist attraction is the Bavarian Forest along the eastern border, with vast magnificent woods and all sports facilities. Cities: Passau and Straubing. Beautiful Bavarian baroque and rococo abbeys and monasteries are found on either side of the Danube.

The German Alps . . . Another stretch of great scenery in Germany is this high mountain chain extending from Lake Constance in the west to the southeasternmost border of the country, some 150 miles. The quaint peasant architecture of the local people, their picturesque garb and simple hospitality are enchanting. Throughout the area are many mountain huts, hotels and shelters. While most are of the plain type the alpinist would expect, there are also hotels which cater to more exacting tastes. The climb has been taken out of mountain climbing in Germany for those who do not wish to exert themselves. The almost 10,000-foot Zugspitze near Garmisch-Partenkirchen (*Golf-Hotel Sonnenbichl, Wittelsbach, Partenkirchener Hof, Riessersee, Marktplatz, Posthotel,* and *Hotel Alpenhof*) and Mittenwald, the Nebelhorn near Oberstdorf, and dozens of other mountains are comfortably reached by mountain railroads, cogwheel railway and cableway. In the German Alpine country there are many health and recreation resorts, including thermal spas. Of the gems in mountain settings, Lake Königssee is considered the most beautiful. It is surrounded by natural rock walls 6,500 feet high. Of the many castles and palaces in Bavaria, best known abroad are the palaces built by King Ludwig II: Herrenchiemsee, Linderhof and Neuschwanstein. The wealth of art treasures contained in churches and monasteries such as Steingaden, Wieskirche, Rottenbuch and Ettal is astounding.

Hamburg . . . Besides its attraction as a great industrial and shipping center of tremendous reconstruction and development, Hamburg offers numerous theaters; Hamburg City Opera, Deutsches Schauspielhaus, Thalia Theater, Junges Theater; Konzert-Halle for concerts; variety shows at Hansa-Theater. Hamburg also has a planetarium and observatory and sports such as golf, tennis and sailing. All kinds of entertainment can be found in places along the Reeperbahn, St. Pauli district. Among points of sightseeing interest are the Hagenbeck Zoo, City Hall, Chile House and other characteristic business houses, the "fleete" (canals lined with quaint old buildings), fine churches and parks, and beautiful Alster Lakes in the center of the city.

Hamburg's top art gallery is the Kunsthalle, Glockengiesserwall 1. A magnificent collection of North German folklore is housed in the Altona Museum, Museumstr. 23. Among the leading hotels in Hamburg: *Atlantic Hotel, Vier Jahreszeiten* (deluxe). First-class hotels: *Hotel Prem, Alsterhof, Hotel Berlin.* Good tourist-class hotels: *Europäischer Hof, Reichshof, Baseler Hospiz.* Among Hamburg night clubs, apart from those along the Reeperbahn, are *Riverside, Society, Ambassador* and *Die Insel.* Leading restaurants: *Vierjahreszeiten-Grill, Wein-Restaurant Ehmke,* the *Ratsweinkeller* in the Town Hall, *Schümann's Austernkeller, Kleines Fährhaus, Mühlenkamper Fährhaus, Bavaria-Blick,* and *Fischereihafen-Restaurant* for seafood.

The road north leads to Lübeck, birthplace of Thomas Mann, and famous for its many medieval monuments.

Northern Germany boasts of many spas and shore resorts ideal for pleasure as well as health and recreation. Among the spas on the Baltic shore is elegant Travemünde. In the North Sea are the Isle of Sylt, linked to the mainland by a causeway, and the unique rock island of Helgoland, reachable by de luxe boats from Hamburg, Bremerhaven, or Cuxhaven.

Popular health resorts in the Harz mountains about 150 miles south of Hamburg are Bad Harzburg, Braunlage and Hahnenklee. Nearby cities include Braunschweig (Brunswick), town of Henry the Lion, and Hanover, one of the important fair and exposition centers. From late May to early September, Hanover features its Herrenhausen Park Festival of concerts, plays, ballet and illuminations.

Hanover hotels: *Grand Hotel Mussmann, Georgenhof, Kastens Hotel Luisenhof* and the new *Hanover Intercontinental.* Night clubs: *Pigalle, Eve.* Restaurants: *Georgsstuben, Bonne Auberge, Café Kröpcke, Brauerei-Gaststätten, Mandarin Pavillon, Maschsee Gaststätten.*

The third Hanseatic city, in addition to Hamburg and Lübeck, is Bremen, which combines medieval charm with outstanding examples of German reconstruction. Stay at the de luxe *Park Hotel* in a lovely park ($9 single, $12 double) or the less expensive centrally located first-class *Columbus* Hotel. Top restaurants are *Essighaus, Deutsches Haus, Flett, Die Glocke* and *Ratskeller.* Night clubs: *Astoria, Eve.*

Düsseldorf ... You won't want to miss this gay metropolis of art and fashion on the Rhine, a great business center known as the "Desk of the Ruhr." A walk through town will show the interesting contrast between old and new architecture. The *Altstadt* (Old City) harbors buildings and churches dating back to the 13th century, when West German princes made Düsseldorf their residence. The city's main boulevard, Königsallee, is known continent-wide as a fashionable shopping center. Sidewalk cafés dot the pavement—their patisseries are magnificent. Fairs, exhibitions, museums, libraries, art collections, theater, opera and concerts attract visitors the year round. During Carnival, masquerades and the Róse Monday Pageant make the city one big playground. On St. Martin's Eve, tradition calls for thousands of children to parade through the streets carrying torches and lanterns. Düsseldorf has a number of luxury and first-class hotels, best of which are the *Breidenbacher Hof* and *Parkhotel* (de luxe), and the *Gaylord, Savoy, Haus Münch, Atlantik, Esplanade* (first-class). Night spots include: *Palette, Etoile, Datscha, Töff-Töff, Eve, Kokett, Night Train, Martinique, Pferdestall, Bei Toni,* the bohemian *Fatty's Atelier,* and *Csikos* with gypsy music.

Cologne (Köln) ... dates back to the Roman era. You will see here remains of Roman fortifications, temples, invaluable mosaics and sculptures, also an important collection of beautiful Roman glass. Aside from the cathedral, one of the finest examples of Gothic architecture, Cologne is famous for her great Romanesque churches, dating from the 10th to 12th centuries, such as St. Gereon, St. Maria im

Kapitol, St. Pantaleon, St. Severin, St. Ursula with the "Golden Chamber," St. Aposteln.

Important art museums include the Wallraf-Richartz-Gallery with medieval art, Dutch paintings and an outstanding modern collection. The Schnütgen-Museum with Christian art from early Middle Ages to the baroque, the Historic Museum, the Arts and Crafts Museum, an important Ethnological Museum and the Diocesan Museum. Concerts are held at the Gürzenich and broadcasting studio. Opera and ballet in the Operahouse, Offenbachplatz, September to mid-July. There are many trade fairs and exhibitions here, too. Leading hotels are *Baseler Hof, Excelsior, Domhotel, Europa, Atlantic, Mondial* (de luxe) and *Bristol, Esplanade, Senats-Hotel, Regent, Lasthaus* and the new *Kaiser*. Night clubs: *Romantica, Eve, Goldener Spiegel, Hamo-Bar, Pigalle, Orchidee, Jazz-cellar Tabu* and *Storyville*. Luxurious restaurants: *Bastei*, on the Rhine, *Wiesel, Treppchen, Wolff, Kuckuck*. Don't miss beautiful Rhine-Park with its open-air dancing in summer.

Another city more than 2,000 years old is Aachen (Aix-la-Chapelle), less than 30 miles west of Cologne. The city's hot springs have been used for curative purposes since pre-Roman days. Charlemagne's throne of marble stands in the chapel he built here. South of Aachen is Trier (Trèves), once the capital of the Roman empire in the west, with magnificent remnants of Roman architecture.

The Rhine . . . For 150 years, a trip along the Rhine has been an essential part of the Continental "Grand Tour." The ancient cathedrals of Xanten (the Siegfried City), Cologne, Bonn (the capital) Mainz, Worms (city of the Nibelungs), Speyer and many others glide majestically by, their spires mirrored in the water. You see picturesque little wine towns nestled at the feet of vine-clad hills, and romantic medieval castles set off by terraced vineyards or steep crags.

Stuttgart . . . Is important for industry and exports. Among many sights are the Schiller Museum at nearby Marbach, the Automotive Museum of Daimler-Benz and the new Liederhalle. *Graf Zeppelin Hotel, Reichsbahn Hotel,* the de luxe *Schlossgarten-Hotel,* the moderately priced new *Rieker* and the *Park Hotel* are all good. Eat with a view atop the Fernsehturm (TV tower). Gourmet cuisine at the *Alte Post* and *Scheffelstuben* restaurants.

The Black Forest . . . only 40 miles west of Stuttgart, is a charming, sunny cluster of secondary and high mountain ranges, named "black" because of the dark firs in the dense woods. Excellent roads traverse the entire region. Thatched-roof peasant architecture is found here, as are colorful native costumes, particularly the women's headgear, differing in each valley. Baden-Baden is the doorway to the Black Forest and Lake Constance. The Black Forest is rich in curative thermal and mineral springs. In addition to cure facilities, there is plenty of activity in Baden-Baden. You may gamble at the casino, play tennis and go trout fishing and horseback riding, and play golf on a lovely 18-hole course. During "Baden-Baden Week" at the end of August, international society assembles at Iffezheim Race Course to watch the most famous stables compete for the Grand Prize.

Among the well-known hotels are *Brenners Parkhotel, Hotel Bellevue, Badhotel Badischer Hof, Europäischer Hof, Waldhotel der Selighof, Hotel Runkewitz,* and *Badhotel Zum Hirsch.* The doorway to the southern Black Forest (Hochschwarzwald) is Freiburg im Breisgau, where the magnificent "Münster" stands. Stay at the *Colombi Hotel.* Before leaving the Black Forest, a stop might be made at Badenweiler, a charming spot where spring comes early, whose healing waters were used by the ancient Romans. The de luxe *Römerbad,* the *Eckerlin* and *Parkhotel* are all very attractive places to stay. Many Black Forest resorts are also fine for winter sports.

Hohenlohe and Schwäbisch-Hall, just an hour's drive from Stuttgart, are unchanged since the early Middle Ages. Castles and palaces in the Hohenlohe area are plentiful, and the ancient Free Imperial City of Schwäbisch-Hall was already famous in the 12th and 13th centuries. On the wide stairs of the city's cathedral a series of open-air festival plays is given every summer.

Weser Hills Country ... This is a charming region in northern West Germany where all the characters in the Grimm Brothers' fairy tales and the Baron Münchhausen tales are at home. Sleeping Beauty's castle, Sababurg, still stands in the woods. Baron Münchhausen's hunting lodge is now a pilgrimage place for romantic souls. The tombstone of the much maligned Doctor Eisenbart is in Hannoversch Münden and is honored every year at a colorful folk festival. Many picturesque little towns line the Weser River banks, among them famous Corvey Abbey, founded A.D. 822; Fuerstenberg, known for its porcelain; and the Pied Piper's Hameln. There are several health resorts, such as Pyrmont Springs, Oeynhausen and Wildungen.

Westphalia ... Close to the Ruhr District lies the Westphalian Land, with brooks for trout fishing, health resorts, winter sports centers, stalactite caves, castle ruins, and picturesque mountain towns. In the south are the scenic Sauer, Sieg and Wittgenstein districts.

The Harz Mountains rank among the best winter-sports areas.

Many other places in various parts of West Germany worth visiting include: Kleve, Lohengrin's town; Nürburgring, the famous auto race course; the Hunsrück hills south of Trier; the various ranges of hills close to the right bank of the Rhine; Bergisches Land and Sauerland. Westerwald, Taunus and Vogelsberg, Rhön (birthplace of glider flying), Swabian Forest and south German mountains.

SOURCES OF FURTHER INFORMATION ... German Central Tourist Association (Frankfurt) offices; the German Tourist Information Offices in New York (500 Fifth Avenue), Chicago and San Francisco. Try the local tourist office, *Verkehrsverein.* For health resorts, see the *Kurverwaltung.* Pan Am's office in Frankfurt is at Am Hauptbahnhof 12 (Tel. 330591); in Berlin, Europa-Center and Berlin Hilton (Tel. 910611); in Bonn, Wesselstrasse 16 (Tel. 52655); in Hamburg, Colonnaden 1 (Tel. 351101); in Düsseldorf, Königsallee 82 (Tel. 2020); in Munich, 3 Lenbachplatz (Tel. 558171); in Stuttgart, Hotel Graf Zeppelin (Tel. 293944); in Hanover, Thielenplatz 3 (Tel. 27696); in Nuremberg, Karolinenstrasse 6 (Tel. 203344).

GREAT BRITAIN AND NORTHERN IRELAND

WEATHER IN LONDON—Lat. N51°30′–Alt. 245′

Temp.	JAN.	FEB.	MAR.	APR.	MAY	JUNE	JULY	AUG.	SEPT.	OCT.	NOV.	DEC.
Low	35°	35°	36°	40°	45°	51°	54°	54°	49°	44°	39°	36°
High	43°	45°	49°	55°	62°	68°	71°	70°	65°	56°	49°	45°
Average	39°	40°	43°	48°	54°	60°	63°	62°	57°	50°	44°	41°

LOCATION ... England, Scotland and Wales make up Great Britain, the largest island in Europe. Northern Ireland comprises the six northeastern counties of the island to the west.

CHARACTERISTICS ... England, despite its differences, is the closest thing to home you'll find abroad. One chief reason is the language. The English, though reserved, are friendly and unfailingly courteous. England is one of the few remaining countries in which royalty is respected, and that in itself breeds tradition and dignity. London has magnificence and the English countryside is utterly charming. There are places of historic and cultural interest from one end of the "tight little isle" to the other.

Scotland's charms are equally well worth visiting and very similar to those of England. Edinburgh, although conservative, is a lovely city, and of course the Scottish lochs and highlands are famous.

POPULATION ... The population of England and Wales is 47,023,000, which approximates that of France. Northern Ireland has a population of 1,446,000, Scotland, 5,205,000.

SIZE ... The area of England is 50,327 square miles, about the size of Alabama. Wales, with 8,017 square miles, is the size of New Jersey. Northern Ireland, with 5,459 square miles, is a little larger than Connecticut. Scotland, with 30,411 square miles (including its 186 inhabited islands), is about the size of South Carolina.

CAPITAL ... Whereas London, with a population of 8,173,000, is the capital of Great Britain, Edinburgh (population 475,338) is the recognized and administrative capital of Scotland.

GOVERNMENT ... The United Kingdom of Great Britain and Northern Ireland form a constitutional monarchy with executive power held by the cabinet and headed by the Prime Minister. Parliament consists of the House of Commons and the House of Lords.

HOW TO GET THERE ... By Pan Am's Jet Clipper services, 6½ hours to London from New York. Also from Boston, Philadelphia, Baltimore/Washington, Atlanta, Detroit, New Orleans, Dallas and Houston; direct from Chicago (7¾ hours) and Detroit. Jet Clippers fly from U.S. West Coast via the polar route in 9½ hours. Clippers serve Glasgow through Prestwick Airport. By ship, about 5 days.

ACCOMMODATIONS ... London hotels are world famous for their friendly service and atmosphere. Here are some of the best hotels in central London (average single rates $19.50): *Claridge's* is still the swankiest hostelry in town. The rooms are large and gracious. You'll be treated royally. The *Savoy*, of course, is known the world over, as is the *Ritz*. The fashionable *Berkeley* is equally fine. The *Dorchester* is very good. The *Grosvenor House* is very popular. *Brown's* Hotel is traditionally fine. The *Carlton Tower* is new, and so are the luxurious *London Hilton* and *St. George's*. The *Westbury* in Mayfair is also popular. Other good hotels include the *Hyde Park*, the *May Fair*, the *Park Lane*, *Connaught*, *President* and the *Mount Royal*. The *Strand Palace*, *Leinster Towers*, *Tavistock* and the *Cumberland* are among the pleasant and less expensive hotels. London hotel rates vary considerably depending on location of room and time of year. In a medium-price hotel they average about $9 per person, but there are many lesser-known, completely comfortable hotels where you can find more economical accommodations.

Among numerous hotels, private hotels and boardinghouses in Scotland, Americans will probably prefer the *Caledonian, George, Roxburghe, Carlton* and *North British* in Edinburgh; the *Central, St. Enoch, Royal Stuart, Tinto Firs, North British* and *More's* in Glasgow. Top rates about $14 single, $18.50 double, European Plan.

ARTS ... Foremost is the British Museum with its vast collection of the art of all ages, including some famous must-be-seens: Elgin Marbles from Greece, manuscripts of the Magna Carta, some of Shakespeare's First Folio, and important anthropological exhibits. The National Gallery in Trafalgar Square is a must for all picture lovers. It has one of the world's most brilliant collections of French, Italian, Spanish, Flemish and English painting. The Tate Gallery, Millbank, offers an excellent collection of modern art from Turner on. The National Portrait Gallery in St. Martin's Place has portraits of Britain's great by artists of their times. The Victoria and Albert Museum and the new Commonwealth Institute in Kensington should also be visited.

Besides the large galleries and museums, London also has a number of charming, intimate museums that were once the houses of great men of letters and in public life. Visiting Carlyle House in Chelsea, Keats' House in Keats Grove, or Dickens' home in Doughty Street is like going back in time. Galleries and museums in London are open usually from 10 A.M. to 6 P.M. daily and from 2 to 6 P.M. on Sundays. Admission is free in most places.

Everyone interested in Scottish history will be charmed by Edinburgh. Visit the National Museum of Antiquities on Queen Street, the Scottish Naval and Military Museum at legend-laden Edinburgh Castle, the old barracks which were turned into a National Repository in 1933. Here you will find flags, relics, historic uniforms and other objects devoted to each Scottish Regiment. Visit the Scottish National Gallery and the Royal Scottish Academy, both of which contain fine examples of past and contemporary Scottish art. These galleries are on the "Mound," a man-made hill in the center of the city. The Royal Scottish Museum is on Chambers Street.

In Glasgow, see Glasgow University and Art Gallery in Kelvingrove Park. This gallery, a work of art in itself, houses many treasures including Dali's famous painting of Christ on the Cross.

BALLET ... London's Royal Ballet Company has gained sensational success and reputation both at home and abroad. It may be seen at the Royal Opera House, Covent Garden. Many foreign ballet and dance groups may also be seen in the British Isles.

BANKS ... Morgan Guaranty Trust Company, Chase Manhattan Bank, Banker's Trust and First National City Bank, all of New York; Bank of America; Royal Bank of Canada. English banks include Westminster Bank, Lloyd's Bank, Midland Bank, Barclay's Bank, and National Provincial Bank. American Express, 6 Haymarket; Thos. Cook & Son, Berkeley Street. In Edinburgh and Glasgow: Clydesdale and North of Scotland Bank Ltd., National Commercial Bank of Scotland, and Royal Bank of Scotland. *See* CURRENCY.

CALENDAR OF HOLIDAYS ... British national holidays include the Bank Holidays on Good Friday, Easter Monday, Whit Monday and the last Monday in August; Christmas Day; Boxing Day (first weekday after Christmas). New Year's Day in Scotland only; also March 17 and July 12 in Northern Ireland only. The Queen's official birthday, celebrated in midsummer, is an occasion for pageantry but is not a public holiday.

CIGARETTES AND TOBACCO ... English cigarettes, cigars and tobacco are expensive. Cigarettes cost 49¢ to 77¢ for 20, cigars from 14¢ to $2.80 each, and pipe tobacco is $1.68 to $3.92 for 2 ounces. American cigarettes are also expensive. If you are going to other parts of Europe, you may leave cigarettes in excess of duty-free limits with the customs office to be picked up when you depart.

CLIMATE ... The British Isles enjoy a temperate climate. High summer temperatures are around 70 degrees; in winter the average low is about 35 degrees. The rainy months are November, January and February. Spring and fall are particularly delightful seasons; the winter months are apt to have fogs and mists. Northern Scotland is apt to be cool, like Maine.

CLUBS... Britain was the birthplace of the social club and many men belong to private clubs in London and Edinburgh. Some of these were founded long ago and have historic backgrounds; entry to them is invariably confined to members and their guests. Rotary, Jaycees and Lions are represented here.

COMMON COURTESIES AND LOCAL CUSTOMS... Though Britishers and Americans both speak a language called English, there are many differences that can confuse you. Remember, cricket is as serious a matter as our baseball. In Scotland, asking what's worn under kilts is not funny any more. Scotch jokes are out, too.

COMMUNICATIONS... A 3-minute phone call to the States costs £2 5s ($6.30) on Sundays and from 10 P.M. to 10 A.M.; otherwise, £3 ($8.40). Cablegrams are 1/5 (1 shilling, 5 pence) per word. Airmail postage to the U.S. is 1/3, or 18¢ per ½ oz. Airletters only sixpence (6d). Airmal postcards 8d (9¢) to the U.S.

CURRENCY... There are 12 pence in a shilling; 20 shillings in a pound, which is valued at U.S. $2.80. You may bring in unlimited amounts of all currencies. No more than declared on entry is allowed out.

CUSTOMS REGULATIONS AND DOCUMENTS REQUIRED FOR UNITED STATES CITIZENS... You can usually take in with you, without duty, 400 cigarettes (600 if in transit), 100 cigars, or 1 lb. of tobacco; 1 bottle spirits and 1 of wine or 2 of either if in use; ½ pint perfume.

Your American passport is all you'll need for identification purposes. If you plan to hire a car to drive yourself, bring your driver's license, which is also valid in Great Britain.

DRUGSTORES... Drugstores, called chemists' shops, can supply you with everything you need in the way of medicine and toilet goods. They don't usually have soda fountains, although most department stores do.

ELECTRIC CURRENT... Voltage is generally 200–250 A.C., so you'll need a transformer for an electric razor. Converter plugs of the round-prong type are also needed. Many hotels will supply electric razor adaptors.

FAUNA... A great variety of animal and bird life abounds in the British Isles, mostly of the more domestic kind. Notable among the birds is the nightingale. The forests contain deer and many species of small game and fowl.

FLORA... Mild climate and lots of rain make British gardens and countryside look like something out of a seed catalogue. The ardent English gardeners are well rewarded by beautiful colors and lush greenery. The various botanical gardens in England offer much to those interested in plants of other countries.

In Edinburgh, the Princes Street Gardens are famous for their floral clock. Glasgow also has a most beautiful botanical garden, situated in the West End, in Great Western Road.

FOOD ... Despite the generally unspectacular reputation of British cooking, there are some world-famous restaurants in Britain that have superb food. Roast beef and Yorkshire pudding are traditional British dishes. Tea is a universal meal. It can mean anything from bread and butter to a spread of cooked dishes, followed by cakes. Don't miss having hot scones. *Haggis,* a traditional Scottish dish is a pudding of liver, onion, spices and oatmeal boiled in the lining of a sheep's stomach. Then too, there is Scotch broth. Other good simple dishes are shortbread and the inevitable porridge.

GAMBLING ... Bingo and gambling casinos are enthralling Londoners nowadays, but the British will never give up betting on football, horses or dogs. There is some form of racing almost every day and night except Sundays. Bets are handled by legalized bookmakers.

LAUNDRY AND DRY CLEANING ... Good cleaning and laundry services are available at most hotels.

LIQUOR ... Beer and whisky are the Britishers' favorite drinks. Gin is popular, too, as gin and tonic, gin and bitters, gin and It (short for Italian vermouth) or gin and lime. If you order whisky you'll get Scotch. You can also get Irish whisky. Rye can be obtained, but bourbon is less readily available. Scotch whisky in Scotland is expensive. Some of the lesser-known pot still whiskies may be a mixture of Scotch and Irish whisky. There is an unlimited number of malt beverages to be had, including lager, bitter beer, mild ale, old ale and stout, to name a few. They are served at room temperature except for lager, which is closest to American beer. Minimum legal age for drinkers is 18. You can buy duty-free liquor at Prestwick, Renfrew and London airports.

MEDICAL FACILITIES ... Your hotel will direct you to the nearest private physician. If you become ill or meet with an accident in Britain, you may obtain medical care, free of charge if necessary, under the National Health Scheme.

The medical facilities in Scotland are among the best in the world. The University of Edinburgh Medical College has few equals. Hospitals are numerous and their facilities are available to all visitors.

MOTION PICTURES ... Known here as "the pictures" or the cinema, motion-picture theaters usually open at noon. Many show the best American and other foreign films as well as all kinds of British movies.

MUSIC ... In London, opera at the Royal Opera House, Covent Garden and Sadler's Wells Theater. The English were the first to perform operas sung in English on a large scale. The reception has been most enthusiastic. Modern opera, especially that of Benjamin Britten, is an integral part of the Sadler's Wells repertoire. The performances of the Royal Philharmonic and London Symphony orchestras are among the highlights of the symphony season. There are also many chamber-music groups and visiting artists from the Continent. There are concerts at the Royal Festival Hall and Royal Albert Hall.

In Scotland, the Edinburgh Festival of Music and Drama, held in late August and early September, is known the world over. World-famous conductors, orchestras, singers and opera companies appear. The Scottish National Orchestra has a concert season in Edinburgh and Glasgow, November to April. Promenade concerts are in late June and early July in Glasgow and Edinburgh. Edinburgh Castle is the headquarters for the Army School of Bagpipe Playing, so it is possible to hear that hauntingly sad music in the city. The Highlands, of course, are the best setting to hear this unforgettable music.

NIGHT CLUBS ... The British phenomenon, the pub, can mean a wide variety of establishments from London's ultra-swank West End bars, whose snack bars serve some of the best food in town, to the smoky little neighborhood pubs, with their inevitable game of darts, that are the working-class Englishman's club.

The gay night life of London centers in such places as *Murray's* on Beak Street, *Churchill's Club* in Bond Street, or *Danny La Rue's* in Hanover Square. The younger set likes to relax here. Admission fee is £1 ($2.80) per person, which includes breakfast. Dinner and wine cost approximately $13 per person and whisky is approximately $13 a bottle. The *"400 Club"* is one of the most elegant night spots in town. Also very smart and less expensive is the *Embassy*. There are floor shows and dancing at all these places. Other clubs include the *River Club* on the Embankment, *Siegi's* in Charles Street, Berkeley Square and *Les Ambassadeurs*. Membership, where necessary, can be arranged by a telephone call to the manager. Membership fees are nominal. The following London restaurants also have dance orchestras and entertainment: quite moderate in price are the *Astor, Pigalle* Restaurant, *Edmundo Ros' Club* and the theater restaurant, *Talk of the Town*. More expensive but very good is *Quaglino's* in Bury Street. London clubs change name quite frequently, so check at your hotel before you set out for an evening.

PHOTOGRAPHY ... Good supplies of cameras and equipment, black-and-white still and movie film and color film are now available. Prices are higher than in the United States. Film-developing services are good, with a 48-hour service at most shops.

RELIGION ... The official religion in Scotland is Protestant Presbyterian. In England it is Protestant Episcopal; observers are known as Anglicans. There are many other churches in Britain, including Methodist, Catholic and Lutheran, and Jewish synagogues.

RESTAURANTS ... Some of the best eating in London can be done in the dining rooms of the *Dorchester, Berkeley, Connaught, Grosvenor House, Savoy* and other fine hotels. There is usually music for dancing and the service is distinguished. *Prunier's, Mirabelle, Rules, Coq d'Or, Hunting Lodge, Stone's Chop House, Quaglino's, Caprice, Ivy* and Cunningham's *Oyster Bar* are among London's many good restaurants, and *Simpson's* in the Strand is famous for roast beef. Foreign food is found in the Soho section of town, London's Greenwich Village. Here, excellent French, Italian, Chinese, Greek, Hungarian and Jewish cookery can be found. Try *Au Jardin des Gourmets* and the *White Tower*. "Hotels and Restaurants in London," published by British Travel, and Raymond Postgate's "Good Food Guide," available locally, are good reference sources.

In Edinburgh, *Café Royal, Albyn Rooms, Handsel, l'Aperitif,* the *Epicure,* and leading hotels are all good. In Glasgow try the *Whitehall,* the *101 Club,* the *Grosvenor,* the *Royal, Rogano, Sorrento, Guy's* and the *Gay Gordon,* to name only a few.

SHOPS AND STORES . . . Harrods, Dickins and Jones, John Lewis, Harvey Nichols, Woollands, Robinson and Cleaver's, Fortnum and Mason's, Selfridge's and Simpson's are among London's top department stores. Marvelous tailors along Savile Row. Wonderful shops along Regent and Bond Streets. British designers include Digby Morton, Hartnell, Hardy Amies, Worth, and Charles Creed. Liberty's for silk prints, Foyle's for books. Shops are closed Saturday afternoons.

In Edinburgh, Anderson's, George Street, for tweeds, tartans and Highland outfits. Hamilton and Inches for Scottish silver craft. Tensfeldt, Princes Street, for souvenirs. George Cockburn, Shandwick Place, for antique jewelry and silver. McCalls, Lothian Road, for Celtic silverware and tartan souvenirs. City Glass Co., for old glass. Romanes and Paterson for tweeds, tartans, cashmeres and ladies' knitwear. Jenners is the largest department store.

SPECTATOR SPORTS . . . Horse racing goes on all year in England. The flat racing season lasts from March to December, steeplechasing is best from December to March. The first week in June is Derby Week. People come from miles around to see this world-famous race, and gypsies camp on Epsom Downs, giving the whole event a carnival air. It is one of the gayest and most interesting of events.

A visit to Lord's Cricket Ground in London is interesting. Rugby is mainly a university sport, not so popular as soccer. The biggest soccer event in England is the Cup Final, played at Wembley in April or early May. Other major sports events in England are the world-championship tennis matches at Wimbledon in London during June and July, the British Amateur and British Open Golf tournaments in May and July, respectively, and the Oxford-Cambridge boat race on the Thames in March or early April.

In Scotland, at the Highland games, which bring the clans together and are well worth seeing, you see hurling contests, wrestling, Scottish dances. Other spectator sports include golf tournaments, national and international; squash matches, association football, rugby, fencing, yachting regattas, bowling matches, horse racing.

SPORTS . . . There is a wide variety of interests for the sportsman in Great Britain. Here are some of the world's best golf courses. Near London is the famous Sunningdale course. Westward Ho! in Devon, Hoylake near Liverpool and the courses at Sandwich in Kent, to mention a few, are all excellent. In Scotland are St. Andrew's Old Course, Troon, Turnberry, Gleneagles, near Stirling, Carnoustie, North Berwick and the Old Prestwick course where you can reserve clubs in advance for £1. Some other very fine courses in Scotland within

40 miles of Edinburgh include: Gullane, Mortonhall in Midlothian, and Muirfield, one of the oldest and most illustrious courses. An open letter from your club at home will get you temporary membership.

You'll find tennis all over Great Britain. The grass courts are all good. A week-end visit is almost sure to include some tennis; the sport is nationally popular. Britain is also fine for fishing. Streams such as the Itchen, Frome and Axe have made English trout fishing famous. The dry-fly fishing here ranks with the best in the world. The moor country in western England offers the wet-fly fisherman excellent casting for salmon and trout. Fishing is also marvelous all over Scotland. The salmon fishing is world famous, but most of the salmon rivers are privately owned. It is possible to rent a boat for a month or a season. Salmon fishing is excellent in the Highlands and on the east coast. For brown-trout fishing there are innumerable hotels which own fishing streams for their guests. There are boats and guides available. For full information: "Scotland for Fishing," published by the Scottish Tourist Board.

There's good hunting in Britain for deer, hare and many kinds of game, including pheasant, partridge, wild geese and duck. Game licenses are $8.40 yearly to July 31 for as many guns as you wish and a hunting permit, or $5.60 and $2.80 for shorter periods. Most of the shooting in Scotland is done on private preserves. However, it is possible for the visitor to hire a moor for his very own, or, more modestly, to make arrangements for shooting through C. W. Ingram, 90 Princes Street; or Walker, Fraser and Steel, 58 Castle Street, Edinburgh. Pheasant, October-January; wild duck, September-February; grouse, August-December; partridge, September-January.

Britain is wonderful for the hiker and bicycling enthusiast. There is a wide variety of landscape and terrain that can be covered in a short time. The Youth Hostel movement is very popular in the British Isles. There are nearly 500 Youth Hostels offering low-cost accommodations for hikers and cyclists.

THEATERS...The National Theatre Company and the Royal Shakespeare Company offer some of the best theatrical entertainment found anywhere. You'll want to check what's playing in the famous West End theaters. London offers a great variety of plays and musical comedies throughout the year. Besides new plays, there are always revivals of Shakespeare and the classics. You buy your program, but tickets are cheap, ranging from 70¢ to $4.20 for the best seats in the house. It is best to decide when you first arrive what you are going to see and get seats in advance. You'll want to spend a few evenings at the music halls, too. The *Palladium* is the home of vaudeville. See also paragraph on MUSIC. Theater time is 7:30 or 8 P.M.

In Edinburgh there are three theaters for excellent touring companies and occasional premières. The most interesting plays are given at the International Music and Drama Festival. It was here that *Beyond the Fringe* originated. Glasgow is also well equipped to cater to the theatergoer.

TIME...Noon in London is 7 A.M. in New York.

TIPPING ... The 10 to 15% rule applies at restaurants. At hotels divide 10 to 12% among those giving personal service. In all cases bellboys, doormen and taximen are tipped extra (a shilling per bag for one or two pieces, 6d each if several small pieces). Tip 1/– (14¢) for a fare of 4/– (56¢), plus 6d for each 2/– of fare above 4/–. Don't overtip.

TRANSPORTATION ... London is a spread-out city. It will be worth your while to study the train and subway systems to various parts of it. They are good and not expensive. In both England and Scotland there are plenty of buses. Taxis are available at all times and they are reasonable. There is excellent train and plane service all over Britain. Self-drive cars are also available at an average charge of $63 a week, including insurance and unlimited mileage. Gas for 800 miles is only $15. Chauffeur-driven services are available in most towns for 21 cents per mile upwards, according to the type of car.

WATER ... The water is safe to drink throughout the British Isles.

WHAT TO BUY ... There's no purchase tax for visitors on purchases worth £5 ($14) or more if they're delivered to the ship or plane or shipped home direct.

London is the Paris of men's clothing. British tailors are the best in the world. Custom-made clothes are much cheaper than in American shops. A beautiful Scotch tweed suit costs $84 to $196, compared with $250 in New York. Wonderfully soft camel's hair coats can be bought for about the same price. Though some British tailors don't do as good a job on women's suits, you may wish to buy a length of tweed or woolen material to have made up at home. Handmade shoes cost from $33 up a pair. They wear forever, too. The British make wonderful raincoats, including the famous Burberrys that are popular with both men and women. Sweaters, socks and scarfs in lovely soft wool and cashmere are also relatively inexpensive. Fine umbrellas, long a British speciality, are for sale at very reasonable prices. Lovely old English silver sells at a fraction of its price in America. Buy Belfast linen and lace-like porcelain from Northern Ireland. Fine china and glass are a good buy, but fragile to ship.

In Scotland, buy tweeds, of course, tartans, woolens and cotton goods, silver jewelry, the kilt, if you insist, and especially Harris and Shetland tweeds. Cashmeres, too, are wonderful.

WHAT TO WEAR ... Even in the midsummer the nights in England and Scotland can get as cold as October weather. Eighty degrees is considered an unusually warm day in London. Don't crowd your luggage with light cotton or tropical worsted clothes, unless you are going to warmer climates. A simple wool suit and lightweight wool dresses and some cottons will fill a woman's daytime needs in the cities. Black cocktail dresses or dressy suits are best after 5 P.M. The British wear evening clothes much more than we do, so if you plan to go at all gala along your formal clothes. A lightweight topcoat and a warm evening wrap are musts. So are comfortable shoes for sightseeing and hiking. Casual sportswear is correct in the country. Women do not usually wear slacks.

London's famous Piccadilly Circus is a center of business activity. Eros fountain is shown in the center.

Lightweight flannel and worsted suits are fine for men in London and Edinburgh. Tweed jackets worn with gray flannel slacks are good in the country. A raincoat is definitely a must all year round for both men and women. These suggestions are primarily for a summer wardrobe. If you are going in the winter, plan to wear heavier indoor and lighter outdoor clothes than you would in the United States.

WHERE TO GO—SIGHTSEEING . . .

London . . . What you see in London is largely up to you. You can do the museums and art galleries, you can wander around the various neighborhoods which make up the second-largest city in the

The pleasant rolling countryside of Southwest England is the setting for this Inn at Yarcombe, a village in Devon near Exeter.

world, you can go down to the "City," you can poke around Soho and Chelsea. But here are a few musts on anyone's list. Westminster Abbey comes first. This old English building is England itself. Here is where the sovereigns of Great Britain have been crowned for centuries. Here is where royalty is wed, and many of the great of England are buried in the Abbey. The history of the English people can be read in these memorials.

You can't miss Big Ben at Westminster, or Eros on his Piccadilly fountain. The British Museum is a must even if you aren't a museumgoer. The Houses of Parliament are near the Abbey. Built in 1840, they are pseudo-Gothic with Victorian overtones. History is made here and you may be in on its making by obtaining passes to the debates in the House of Commons (by application to the Admission order office). There are guided tours available on Saturdays and certain other days in summer, 10 A.M.-4:30 P.M., for which it is not necessary to make advance booking arrangements.

Go to the Tower of London, scene of some of the darkest chapters in English history. It is now a museum and holds the Crown Jewels and other treasures. Within its walls is the beautiful little chapel of St. John, a perfect example of Norman architecture. Take a day to see this vast building which has stood since the time of William the Conqueror. And don't miss St. Paul's Cathedral, which was built by Christopher Wren. The graceful Renaissance dome has been a landmark for more than two centuries.

Take a bus to the "City," the financial heart of England. Here you will find "The Old Lady of Threadneedle Street" (Bank of England), Lloyd's, the Temple, Lincoln's Inn and Gray's Inn. This is where you'll find the ancient *Cheshire Cheese* pub in Fleet Street.

Go to Marble Arch on Sundays and hear soapbox orators. Watch the riders along Rotten Row, go to the world-famous London Zoo in Regent's Park. Take a look at Mme. Tussaud's Waxworks. Make a point of seeing the changing of the guard at Buckingham or St. James's Palaces. Take a look at one of the most charming churches to be seen anywhere, St. Martin-in-the-Fields in Trafalgar Square; go to St. James's Park off the Mall and watch the ducks. You can do all this by sightseeing bus or just by meandering. A wonderful way to see London is to take the No. 11 bus, which wanders over a huge territory. Travel by underground (subway). It is an interesting experience.

A half hour by train or bus from the center of London is beautiful Hampton Court on the Thames, a great palace built by Cardinal Wolsey as a private residence. The palace contains a wonderful art gallery and an interesting collection of historic English furniture. Its hundreds of square feet of windows look out on the most glorious gardens in England. There are geometric boxwood mazes for you to wander through, quaint walled Elizabethan flower beds and graceful groupings of beautiful trees and shrubs. Hampton Court is another all-day sight. From April to September you may take a daily riverboat up the Thames between Westminster and Hampton Court.

Windsor Castle definitely deserves a day of your time. It is an hour from Paddington or Waterloo Stations by train and a little longer by bus. (Daily conducted tours in summer.) Its construction started under William the Conqueror, and Henry III and Edward III both made additions to the huge building. Windsor is a royal residence. Each monarch has left the mark of his era on the interiors. There are some fine paintings by Rubens, Rembrandt and others and a wealth of British portraits. State apartments are interesting and also the Queen's Doll House. (Open subject to the requirements of the Court. Admission proceeds go to charity.) Climb the 220 steps of the Round Tower and you will be rewarded by a marvelous view of the surrounding countryside that has changed very little since Chaucer stood on the same ramparts. The best way to see the lovely Great Park that surrounds this fairyland castle is in an open carriage. The things to do and see outside of London are numerous and fascinating. In the following short description of some of the major highlights, England has been roughly divided into seven sections. The English countryside is dotted with enchanting little inns and the food is comparable with that in the large cities.

The South of England . . . English history began here in the south. Probably the most important place to visit in England, outside of London, is the ancient town of Canterbury, 65 miles to the southeast. The magnificent Canterbury Cathedral is the seat of the Church of England. This imposing Gothic church was built during four centuries. The first church was consecrated on its site in 597 A.D. The grounds around the cathedral are lovely. If you plan to go to Canterbury, make your reservations before you leave the United States. It is one of England's most popular tourist spots and the inns are booked months in advance.

Knole, outside of Sevenoaks in Kent, 25 miles south of London, is one of the showplaces of England. The house has endless corridors of gracious rooms and the park and gardens are superb. Check locally for visiting days. The whole countryside in Kent, Surrey and Sussex is dotted with quaint villages and the scenery is very beautiful. (There is a motel, *Royal Oak,* near Hythe, Kent.) For contrast, hire a car and drive along the rolling Downs by the sea.

Winchester, Salisbury, and the New Forest . . . The New Forest is so called because it was man-made. William I created this royal hunting ground and herds of cattle and very tame "wild ponies" still roam through it. Right in the center of this giant woodland is the *Parkhill* Hotel. There's also a *New Forest Motel.* Staying here, you have a wonderful base of operations for seeing Winchester and Salisbury. Winchester was the capital of pre-Norman England. Things to see include the ruins of Winchester Castle and the cathedral, a lovely church containing an amazing mixture of architectural styles that blend together very happily. Salisbury is a charming town full of quaint, lovely old houses. Salisbury Cathedral has one of the most graceful spires in the world. Nearby is Old Sarum, a fascinating hodgepodge of Roman,

Saxon and Norman ruins—a wonderful place for a picnic. The weird prehistoric ruins of Stonehenge stand on the Salisbury Plain a few miles away. Scholars date them from 1800 to 1400 B.C.

The West Country ... The town of Bath, first built by the Romans as a resort spot, is the outstanding place to visit in the west of England. Today the architecture is late Georgian, of the 18th century when Bath was the most fashionable town in England. Stroll through the Pump and Assembly Rooms. The ruins of the Roman baths are interesting, too. There are quite a few good hotels in Bath. The enchanting little town of Wells is nearby and very well worth visiting. Go to Gloucester to see the magnificent Perpendicular-Norman cathedral and a charming rural English city. The Cloisters have an interesting collection of old manuscripts.

England's southwest—Somerset, Devon, and Cornwall—has a Gulf Stream-warmed climate making it mild even in winter, with beaches, lively villages, and a cove-dotted coast, where spring comes early. You might stop at Exeter, in Devon, for a look at its Cathedral (there's a *Devon Motel* at Matford), or at fashionable Torquay. Here you will be surprised by subtropical plants, even some palms. See lush green Plymouth, from whose harbor both Drake and the Pilgrims sailed to make history. The last, most western and southern end of the island is Cornwall, with Land's End. Along its north coast with its quaint little hamlets lies Tintagel with its memories of King Arthur. Don't miss the Cornish pasties.

Oxford and Stratford-on-Avon ... There is a tremendous amount of territory to cover at Oxford. The famous university is surrounded by ancient traditions and scholarly atmosphere. See Magdalen, New and Christ Church colleges. The Sheldonian Theater is another must. From the Tower of St. Mary's Church you have a fine view of the town. The gardens are particularly lovely. Plan to stay at least two days in Oxford. There are some quite good inns. Confirm reservations in advance.

Stratford-on-Avon has been wonderfully preserved as a shrine to England's greatest poet. You will see the house where Shakespeare was born and Anne Hathaway's quaint little cottage. The town is typically Tudor England. The Shakespeare Memorial Theater has performances of the Bard's great works from April through November. Stay at the historic *Shakespeare Hotel, Alveston Manor, Welcombe Hotel* or the *Falcon Inn*. Make reservations in advance, especially during the theater season. Drive over to the sweet, cozy villages in the nearby Cotswold hills.

Visit nearby Warwick with its great Norman Castle. Sulgrave Manor near Banbury was George Washington's ancestral home.

Tewkesbury Abbey is the great church of the region. Tewkesbury is the scene of a major battle of the Wars of the Roses and the Abbey is a fine example of Norman architecture.

The Midlands and the Lake District ... Nottingham is the most historic town in this region. See Nottingham Castle. Visit the quaint old "Trip to Jerusalem" Inn, near the dungeons of the Castle. This was

The Houses of Parliament on the River Thames, with the clock tower which houses Big Ben, are one of London's famous landmarks.

Stratford-on-Avon—The Great Bard himself must have strolled the banks of the gentle Avon composing sonnets on a summer afternoon. Shakespeare Memorial Theater.

a meeting place for Richard Coeur de Lion's crusaders. Nine miles from Nottingham is Newstead Abbey, the home of Lord Byron. It has been beautifully preserved by the town of Nottingham. The gardens and ground are gorgeous.

Haddon Hall is a medieval house of great beauty. It is the property of the Duke of Rutland and is associated with the romantic Dorothy Vernon, who eloped with Sir John Manners in the sixteenth century. Chatsworth, the stately home of the Duke of Devonshire, is of interest not only for its fine collections of pictures but also as having been for short periods the house of detention of the unhappy Mary Queen of Scots. Both houses are well worth seeing.

The Lake District is a hiker's paradise. Often called "Little Switzerland," it is beautiful, full of charming little lakes, rolling hills and rugged open country. It was also the haven of great English poets, notably Wordsworth. Ambleside, Windermere (the largest lake is here), Grasmere and Keswick are all quaint little towns with good inns and restaurants. Any one of them would make a good base for seeing the Lake District.

Cambridge and East Anglia ... Cambridge is the other great university town in England. Cromwell, Wordsworth and Darwin all studied here. See King's, Trinity and St. John's College. Don't overlook the lovely chapel of St. John and King's College chapel. The gardens are beautiful. Punting on the Cam is an experience you won't want to miss. The Round Church in the town of Cambridge is an interesting relic of Norman architecture.

East Anglia is the territory of English painters. In this strangely beautiful, flat moorlike country Constable and Turner produced their lovely canvases. There are many charming towns and villages. Ely is probably the most interesting from the point of view of sights to see, principally for its ancient and beautiful cathedral.

Other Cities ... Two of the most interesting towns in all England for any tourist are York in the north, and Chester about 3 hours by train from London. Chester is a live, busy town, York a quiet cathedral town; but for an American sightseer, both have the charm that only great age brings. Both have Roman ruins, both have their ancient walls. Those in Chester are still standing so that the visitor may walk completely around them. York Minster is to many the most glorious church in all England, surely the most interesting cathedral with the most beautiful stained glass. Whoever sees the famed "Five Sisters" window or some of the simpler war memorials can never forget them. Like York, Chester is an old Roman town, but busier and gayer. You can shop in the medieval Rows, the delightful two-storied arcades with shops full of antique silver, jewelry and furniture, and almost touch and feel the fourteenth century. Either of these cities can be used as a base for a two- or three-day tour of the surrounding countryside. (In Chester, stop at the *Blossoms Hotel* and, in York, at the *Royal Station.*)

Wales ... You should try to get to Wales, which has at least a hundred old castles and a wild, unspoiled beauty even in South Wales

The Tower Bridge, spanning the Thames. Not far from here, the Romans erected the first bridge in the first century A.D.

Quaint Lower Slaughter in the Cotswolds adds charm to the English countryside.

with its coal mines. See Tintern Abbey south of Monmouth. Go to Llangollen for the annual Eisteddfod, which is a festival for musicians and dancers from all over the world. But it is the magnificent Welsh singing such as you heard in "How Green Was My Valley" which rules the occasion. Llangollen is in Denbighshire, where flows the River Dee. Go to Betws-y-Coed in Caernarvonshire. Visit Colwyn Bay, and Llandudno, modern resorts with good hotels and fine beaches. Try the *Imperial, St. George's* or *Craigside Hydro.*

Caernarvon Castle is where the first Prince of Wales was presented by his father, Edward I. The castle is forbidding and majestic. North of Caernarvon are the resort towns of Llanfairfechan, Penmaenmawr and Bangor. The highest mountain in England or Wales, Snowdon, is in this county which is famous for its steep mountain ranges and its mountain climbing. South of Caernarvon is ghostly Harlech Castle, and then Montgomeryshire, which is in Central Wales where the Wye and the Severn Rivers start their course. There are some charming towns here, and excellent fishing in the streams of Vyrnwy and Wye.

Westward on the coast is Cardiganshire, with some delightful resort towns. At Aberystwyth is a college of the University of Wales. Still going south you come to Pembrokeshire with its many Norman castles. This is the oldest county in South Wales and full of historical interest. The stones at Stonehenge are believed to have come from here. And who could resist a lighthouse named Strumble Head? Cardiff is the capital and chief city in Wales.

Northern Ireland ... Belfast, the pleasant and prosperous capital of Northern Ireland, may be reached by either air or steamer from England or Scotland. The city is surrounded by beautiful country with that soft and green quality which characterizes so much of Northern Ireland. Stay at the *Grand Central* or the *Midland*. Make trips along the Coast Road and through the famous Glens of Antrim with their steep, wooded valleys, or take a bus or train to County Down, "where the Mountains of Mourne sweep down to the sea."

Spend a few days in Portrush, County Antrim, a famous seaside resort with long stretches of sandy beach and a championship golf course. Hotels: *Northern Counties* and *Skerry-Bhan*. Visit the Giant's Causeway nearby, myriad columns of bright red and yellow volcanic stone. County Fermanagh is one of the great beauty spots of Europe. Upper and Lower Lough Erne, two lakes which divide the county, are studded with islands on which are the ruins of castles, shrines and monasteries. Stay at the *Hotel Imperial* in the island city of Enniskillen. Visit some of the lovely rose gardens of County Armagh. The city of Armagh has been the ecclesiastical centre of all Ireland for more than fifteen centuries. St. Patrick founded his church there.

Edinburgh ... Edinburgh, located on the Firth of Forth, is the Scottish capital. It is a beautiful city dominated by historic Edinburgh Castle, which sits on a rock some 270 feet high. The rock falls sharply on three sides to the gardens below it. The Castle has a long and bloody history. Here are the apartments occupied by Mary Queen of Scots when she gave birth to the child who became James I of England. See the National War Shrine here, too. The view from the Castle rock is spectacular—you look down on Princes Street, that famous and beautiful thoroughfare, which is lined with shops on one side and beautiful gardens on the other. This is the "New Town." You also see the Royal Mile (Old Town), which leads from the Castle to Holyrood Palace, the Royal residence that Her Majesty uses when in Edinburgh. Here Prince Charlie held the historic ball while at the Castle they were still fighting him. Here, too, are other apartments of Mary Queen of Scots and those of Lord Darnley, connected by an inner stairway. Next to the Palace are the ruins of Holyrood Abbey. Darnley is buried here. Parliament House, the famous St. Giles Cathedral, the Law Courts, all have marked and made Scottish history. Be sure to visit the National Gallery of Scotland.

Old Town straggles down the side of the rock. Until the middle of the eighteenth century, Edinburgh consisted of this narrow, crowded ridge. Here were built the first tall flats; the first tenements. In the latter part of that century began the expansion which is now New Town. Princes Street is the dividing line. In the center of the Gardens is the "Mound," an artificial hill constructed in the middle of the city. Visit the Zoological Park on the slope of Corstophine Hill; it is one of the largest in Europe. Visit also Craigmillar Castle, about 3 miles from the city. Greyfriars Churchyard you must see, also the Sir Walter Scott Monument, the Royal Scottish Academy and Arthur's Seat, in King's Park. This is a hill some 800 feet high. There are daily tours around the city and car hires with or without driver.

Prestwick . . . Prestwick Airport, at which you land, is situated in one of the most historic parts of Scotland. It abounds with tradition, and is near the home of Robert Burns. Visit his birthplace in Alloway and the memorial where many treasures dear to the heart of Burns lovers are on display, set in a most picturesque spot on the banks of the river Doon, with that most famous of bridges, the "Brig O'Doon" taking a prominent place in the picture.

The Auld Kirk of Alloway is the scene of Tam O'Shanter's run-in with the witches, as described in the famous poem. The scenery leaves little to be desired, and numerous hotels are situated near the airport, which, while not offering the newest in everything, retain a charm of their own. Around the airport there are 16 golf courses capable of testing the skill of the best. All are open to visitors.

Near Alloway lies Ayr, the center of the Robert Burns country. Ayr is a modern seaside resort and is filled with things to interest the devotees of Burns. Hotels are the *Station* and the *County*. From Ayr it is possible to make a "Burns" tour of Dumfries (in the south, near England), Thornhill, Cumnock and other points of interest.

Border Country . . . South of Edinburgh is the Border country, the country of Sir Walter Scott. His home at Abbotsford is worth seeing. The ruins of Melrose and Dryburgh Abbeys are nearby. Peebles on the River Tweed is the center of the Border country, a famed holiday area. There is good fishing here. North Berwick, 22 miles east of Edinburgh in East Lothian, has two golf courses and top hotels for the golfer. The *Marine* Hotel is excellent.

The Island of Arran, picturesque and colorful, lies off the coast of Ayrshire in the Firth of Clyde, southwest of Glasgow. It is about 20 miles long and is the quintessence of all Scotland.

Glasgow . . . Coming north from Ayr or Arran, you reach Glasgow, Scotland's most important seaport, largest industrial city. It is aptly called the Gateway to the Highlands. There is an excellent network of transportation, air, rail, road and sea, to take you to your desired destination. It is a city with much to see of interest. Excellent car hire facilities are available, both self-drive and chauffeur-driven. The Glasgow Art Galleries are famous; *see* ARTS. There's a good zoo at Calderpark. *See* ACCOMMODATIONS for hotels. Glasgow is an excellent shopping center, with stores offering high quality goods. Recommended are: Copland & Lye, R. W. Forsyth, MacDonalds, Wylie Lochhead, and Pettigrew & Stephen, to name only a few.

The Trossachs . . . On the way to the Highlands you come to the Trossachs, a strip of land in Western Perthshire. Tours through this region are by bus or a combination of train, bus and steamer. Gateway to this lake region is Stirling (36 miles northwest of Edinburgh), a historic town with a castle on a high rock which overlooks the spot where Robert the Bruce defeated the English at Bannockburn. Stay at the *Golden Lion Hotel*.

From Stirling you go to Callander. Here you take a bus to Trossachs Pier and stay at the *Trossachs Hotel*. Then on to Loch Katrine,

Members of the police band in Edinburgh, Scotland, take time off for a skirl on the pipes outside the city's historical castle.

Dunvegan Castle on the Isle of Skye is the oldest inhabited castle in Great Britain, the ancestral home of the chiefs of the Clan MacLeod for 800 years.

Stronachlachar, and Loch Lomond, famed in song and verse. Loch Katrine is the scene of Scott's "Lady of the Lake." There is an interesting trip, too, from Callander to Loch Tay to the northeast. Here you see thatched cottages, picturesque villages, mountains sloping to the loch shores. It is very old, very beautiful.

The Highlands ... The imaginary line of demarcation between the Lowlands and the Highlands of Scotland is drawn between the Firth of Clyde on the west and the Firth of Tay on the east. Above this line lies the rugged, beautiful but often dour country of the Scottish Highlands. Here is where you will find Balmoral Castle. Here also is the Isle of Skye with Dunvegan Castle, the oldest inhabited castle in Britain, and the ancestral home of the Clan MacLeod.

From the west coast start your tour of the Highlands at Oban (*Great Western* and *Park* hotels). This is a fine Scottish resort town, chief yachting center of the North, and base for visiting the Hebrides and taking the steamer around the Island of Mull.

From Oban go northward on the road running beside Loch Linnhe to Ballachulish, at the foot of Glencoe, scene of the sinister murder of Clan MacDonald in 1692. Nearby is Fort William and Ben Nevis, highest spot in the British Isles. The road runs beside the canal and series of lochs (including Loch Ness of sea serpent fame) that runs right across the country, from Fort William to Inverness. This modern looking little city on the banks of the River Ness is considered the capital of the romantic Highlands and, like so many other Scottish cities, was the scene of much fighting. (Hotel *Caledonian*.)

Macbeth's castle once stood in the midst of Inverness, the scene of a stormy past. Nearby is the battlefield of Culloden, where the Highlanders made their last stand against the English in 1746. You can see the names of the clans on some of the gravestones of these gallant dead. To the west from Inverness, the country is wild, the scenery more rugged and the Highlands more sparsely inhabited.

From Inverness eastward, some 15 miles, lies the town of Nairn and Cawdor Castle, still approached by a drawbridge over its moat. Farther to the east along the coast is Elgin, with its ruined cathedral, and farther yet we come to the mouth of the River Spey. This is the center of the finest salmon fishing in all Scotland. The counties of Ross and Cromarty are the heart of the best deer forests in Scotland.

There are two roads to Aberdeen—one through the resorts and seaside villages of Lossiemouth and Banff, and the other through the inland route of Keith, Huntly and Inverurie. All these places have their own particular items of interest.

Aberdeen is the most Scottish of the cities of Scotland. It is a fine holiday resort, with a pleasant climate. There are numerous good hotels, including the *Caledonian* and the *Station*. Aberdeen abounds in tradition and beautiful buildings.

Leaving Aberdeen for the south, one should travel along the road through what is known as Royal Deeside, through Ballater and Balmoral, where the Scottish home of the Queen at Balmoral Castle can be seen. Nearby is little Braemar, where the famous Royal Highland Gathering of the Clans and Highland Games are held each September. This is the chief social event of the Royal Highland Season. Following the road over the watershed at Devil's Elbow down Glen Shee, you reach Perth (32 miles northwest of Edinburgh) on the River Tay. Perth is a beautiful country town immortalized by Sir Walter Scott.

This almost completes the circle to Stirling and is near the Gleneagles golf course, with its excellent hotel. A tour of the Highlands can be made by motor coach or by car. If you want to see more rugged country and the red deer and the lonely Scottish moors, go up over the Grampians way north to John O'Groats and on to the Shetland and Orkney Islands off the north coast.

SOURCES OF FURTHER INFORMATION ... British Travel, 64 St. James's Street in London. Pan American's London office is at 193/4 Piccadilly, W 1 (Tel. Regent 7292).

The Scottish Tourist Information Center, 2 Rutland Place, West End, Edinburgh 1. Pan American is at Prestwick Airport, and at 130 St. Vincent Street, Glasgow, C.1. (Tel. City 5744). Wales Tourist and Holidays Association, 7 Park Place, Cardiff. Northern Ireland Tourist Board, 6 Royal Avenue, Belfast 1.

In New York, information and literature on Great Britain and Northern Ireland are available through British Travel, 680 Fifth Avenue. Other offices are in Chicago, Los Angeles, Toronto and Vancouver.

GREECE

WEATHER IN ATHENS—Lat. N37°59′

Temp.	JAN.	FEB.	MAR.	APR.	MAY	JUNE	JULY	AUG.	SEPT.	OCT.	NOV.	DEC.
Low	42°	42°	46°	51°	60°	67°	72°	72°	66°	60°	52°	46°
High	53°	56°	60°	68°	77°	85°	95°	95°	83°	74°	64°.	57°
Average	48°	49°	53°	60°	69°	76°	83°	83°	75°	67°	58°	52°
Days of Rain	12	11	11	9	7	4	3	3	4	9	12	13

LOCATION ... Greece occupies the southern tip of the Balkan peninsula in the eastern Mediterranean Sea. The Athens airport is on the crossroads from Europe to Egypt, Africa, Asia and the Near East.

CHARACTERISTICS ... "Cradle of civilization and birthplace of the gods, land of legend and beauty which has inspired centuries of art and the essence of philosophy, Greece welcomes the world." These long-suffering, courageous people have an economic need for foreign tourists. Since Greeks are naturally unselfish and friendly, they give visitors a warm welcome. They offer a sunny country of great natural beauty and magnificent monuments straight out of your old school-books.

Apart from its world-famed historical and archaeological relics, modern Greece provides many attractions to the traveler. The many islands and indented coastline, so characteristic of Greece, provide ideal beaches, yachting harbors and fishing places. For those who prefer the mountains and the inlands to the sea, for the huntsman, the mountain-climber, the hiker, the camper and the motorist, there is a vast wealth and variety of beautiful scenery richly scattered with relics of the Golden Age.

In organized resorts, such as the beautiful islands of Rhodes and Corfu, the gay social summer life provides a different type of holiday. For those who wish to combine a cure with their vacation, there is a large choice of famous spas rich in curative waters of every kind.

POPULATION . . . Over 8,930,000.

SIZE . . . 50,547 square miles, a slightly smaller area than Florida.

CAPITAL . . . Athens, with a total population of 2,000,000.

GOVERNMENT . . . Greece is a constitutional monarchy; also called a "crowned democracy."

HOW TO GET THERE . . . By Pan Am Jet Clipper to Rome then by Olympic Airways only 1¾ hours to Athens; or 3 hours from Beirut via Middle East Airlines. By ship from New York, 15 to 18 days.

ACCOMMODATIONS . . . There are many good hotels in Athens. In the de luxe group are: The *Grande-Bretagne, Athens Hilton, Amalia, Athénée Palace, King's Palace, Acropole Palace* and the *King George*. First class: *National, Alfa, Ambassadeurs, Olympic Palace, Alexiou, Attica Palace, King Minos, Voula Beach*. Rates at official exchange, from $7 single with bath, $9-$21 double, European Plan, at de luxe hotels; about $4 single, $6 double, at first class hotels. Reservations should be made well in advance for the period of April 1 to November 15.

ARTS . . . Athens is renowned for its classical remains dating back to the 5th century B.C. and earlier. In addition to listings under WHERE TO GO—SIGHTSEEING, sights include Acropolis with the Parthenon, Propylaea, Theater of Dionysus, Odeon of Herodes Atticus. Byzantine Churches: Saints Theodores, Kapnikarea and Saint Eleftherios. Museums: Archaeological, Byzantine, Benaki (collection of national costumes); also Zappeion Building (modern Greek art) and Zappeion Gardens.

BANKS . . . Bank of Greece, National Bank of Greece, Atlantic Bank of New York, Commercial Bank, Ionian Bank. The American Express Company is on Constitution Square. Travelers checks and letters of credit may be cashed at any bank. Banknotes may be exchanged only at the Bank of Greece or the American Express Company. Top hotels, restaurants and night clubs are authorized to exchange small amounts of foreign currency.

CALENDAR OF HOLIDAYS . . . January 1 and 6; March 25, Independence Day; Good Friday; Easter Monday; Shrove Monday; May 1; May 29, St. Constantine's Day; Whitmonday; August 15, Feast of Virgin Mary; October 28, National Day; December 25 and 26. Good Friday and Easter Sunday religious processions are splendid Greek Orthodox occasions.

CIGARETTES AND TOBACCO . . . Good, mild Greek cigarettes cost 11 drs. a pack; *Papastratos* are popular with tourists. American brands cost 30 drs. a pack.

CLIMATE . . . Mild Mediterranean climate. Spring and autumn are by far the best seasons to visit Greece. However, there are many pleasant sunny days in the winter, and even in the middle of summer the heat is often tempered by fresh breezes from the sea and mountains. The nights are invariably cool and pleasant.

CLUBS . . . Rotary, Lions, Propeller; riding, tennis, yachting, touring, golf and automobile clubs.

COMMON COURTESIES, LOCAL CUSTOMS ... Handshaking is almost *de rigueur* in Greece when you meet or leave someone. Say *ef-cha-ris-to* for "Thank you." Greeks are not too punctual, especially during the hot summer months. The summer siesta is an institution (2 P.M.–5 P.M.).

COMMUNICATIONS ... A 3-minute phone call to the States costs 360 drs. plus 6% tax; a 10-word cablegram is 92 drs. Airmail postage for letters is 6 drs.; 4.5 for postcards.

CURRENCY ... There are 100 leptae in a drachma. 30 drachmae equal U.S. $1.

CUSTOMS REGULATIONS AND DOCUMENTS REQUIRED FOR UNITED STATES CITIZENS ... Passport and vaccination certificate are required, but no visa. You can bring in 200 cigarettes, ¼ lb. of tobacco, or 30 cigars. Articles for personal use and small gifts, as well as a reasonable supply of food are duty free. Customs people, especially at airports, are courteous and efficient. Up to 2,000 drachmae may be brought in.

DRUGSTORES ... Local drugstores can supply most of your needs for American or equivalent foreign products.

ELECTRIC CURRENT ... 220 volts, 50 cycles, A.C., in cities.

FAUNA ... Aquatic birds, partridges and rabbits are found here and may be hunted. Fish are also plentiful. *See* SPORTS.

FLORA ... Pine trees on Mount Parnes near Athens. A great variety of wild flowers are found in the surrounding area.

FOOD ... The majority of tourist restaurants serve Continental food of good quality. There are also a number of typically Greek dishes like *mousaka* (alternate layers of eggplant, ground meat and white sauce agreeably spiced), *souvlakia* and *kokoretsi* (meat on small spits) and *dolmadakia* (rolled vine leaves containing rice, ground meat and spices). A great variety of excellent fish and excellent honey from nearby Mount Hymettus are available.

GAMBLING ... The Achilleion Palace on Corfu and the casino in the Grand Hotel Summer Palace on Rhodes are luxurious places to win or lose money. There is betting on horse races at the Phaleron Delta, 3 miles from Athens near the sea.

LANGUAGE ... Greek is the local language. English and French are largely understood and spoken.

LAUNDRY AND DRY CLEANING ... Modern laundries are available but a little slow even in good hotels.

LIQUOR ... Excellent bottled wines: *Achaia, Boutari, Santa-Helena, Cambas, Dekelia, Demestika, Marco, Tour-la-Reine*. Sweet wines: *Robola, Mayrodaphni, Samos, Santorini*. The Greeks like resin-flavored wine. If you don't, ask for the *aresinato* version. Local liquors: *Ouzo, Metaxa* (brandy), *Coriandolino of Rhodes*. All Continental wines and liquors are also available.

MEDICAL FACILITIES ... There are English-speaking doctors. Ask at your hotel for information. Medical Association: Roosevelt 61 (Tel. 617141); first aid service (Tel. 525555).

MOTION PICTURES ... Italian, Greek, French, British and

American films are usually shown with original sound tracks.

MUSIC ... The Athens State Symphony Orchestra plays on Sunday mornings at the Orpheus Hall in winter; Monday evenings in summer. During August and September, the Athens Festival is in full swing at the ancient open-air Odeon of Herodes Atticus. Performances include classical Greek drama, operas, concerts, dance recitals ... all with Greek artists and other nationals.

NIGHT CLUBS ... Athens is one of the most cosmopolitan and socially alive centers of the Mediterranean. Night clubs: *Acropole, Athinea, Coronet.* Near town: *Acrotizi, Asteria, Queen Anne.* Popular bars, in addition to the hotel bars: *Floca, Zonar's, Seventeen.* For local color, the tavernas are heartily recommended for dinner, dancing and floor shows. Ask at your hotel for guidance.

RELIGION ... Greek Orthodox. Churches of other denominations; Catholic, Protestant and Jewish in the center of Athens.

RESTAURANTS ... Aside from the large hotels, the best restaurants in Athens are: *Zonars, Floca, Pantheon, Dionyssos, Lucullus* and *Costis.* Outside the city: *Asteria, Psarapoulos, Leonida's, Tourkolimano.*

SHOPS AND STORES ... Open daily, except Sundays. In winter: from 8:30 A.M. to 1 P.M., and 3:30 to 7 P.M. In summer 8 A.M. to 1 P.M. and 5 to 8 P.M., except Wednesdays.

SPORTS ... *Hunting:* Visitors may hunt almost everywhere in Greece from Sept. 1 to May 15. Aquatic birds are numerous at Marathon and Souli, near Athens. Passage birds are to be found at Lake Carla, near Volos, Halkis and Limni in central Greece. The hunting season on aquatic birds and on spring turtledoves begins March 15 and ends May 15. Partridges and rabbits may be hunted from the end of August to the middle of January. For information and hunting permits, apply to the Hellenic Hunting Association, 30 Kolokotroni Street, Athens. *Fishing:* Fish are plentiful in Greek waters. Amateur fishermen will find a warm welcome at the Association of Amateur Fishermen. For information apply to Mr. Petrovikis, Commercial Bank, 15a, Aristotelous Street, Athens.

Sailing and canoeing: Enthusiasts should get in touch with the Greek Yacht Brokers Association, 39 Venizelou Street, for boat rentals. Yacht owners will want to take advantage of the facilities offered to members of the club, where they may be admitted through a member. Regattas are organized during the summer in many ports and islands. *Swimming* is particularly pleasant in the limpid, blue sea during spring and fall. There are good beaches along the coast near Athens. Facilities, however, are rather primitive, except for the new beach development of Asteria at Glyfada, a 30-minute drive and Vouliagmeni, a 40-minute drive from Athens. The waters of the Cyclades Islands and Sporades, also those of Corfu and Rhodes, are ideal for spear fishing.

Climbing and hiking: There are several mountains in Greece for hiking and camping. Mount Parnes, near Athens, is particularly popular for week-end and holiday excursions. Excellent climbing can be enjoyed on Mount Taygetos in the Peloponnese, Kithairon, Parnassus in central Greece and Mount Olympus in northern Greece. Contact the Hellenic Alpine Club, 7 Karageorge Servias St., Athens.

TIME ... Noon in Athens is 5 A.M. in New York.

TIPPING ... A 15% service charge is included in hotel and restaurant bills. You usually leave waiters an extra 10% (on plate); and be sure to leave a separate small amount for bus boy *on table.* Tip 10 drs. to concierge, chambermaid. Tip 2 drs. to movie and theater ushers, parking lot and gas-station attendants. In general, tip 5 drs. for most small services.

TOURIST TAXES ... Air departure tax $1.34 (40 drs.). From $1.50 to $4 from Piraeus by sea.

TRANSPORTATION ... While plenty of buses and trolley buses are available in Athens, visitors usually take taxis or hire cars (5 to 7 seats) for trips both in and around Athens. The rates for a car range from 3 drs. per kilometer (about 10¢ per $\frac{2}{3}$ mile), provided the car is used for return. One-way fares cost about 5 drs. per kilometer out of town. Self-drive cars are also available, and country-wide tours in modern buses with English-speaking guides.

WATER ... Safe in cities and better resorts.

WHAT TO BUY ... Dolls, in miniature national costumes; embroideries, in modern Greek and Byzantine designs; handwoven silk, linen and cotton fabrics, rugs from Soufli, Crete, Kastoria, Arachova and the islands of Mykonos and Spetsai; handwoven striped skirts, bags and sandals; laces from Aegina, Hydra and Spetsai, small islands near Athens; earthenware with classic or modern designs from Rhodes. Also Cretan pottery with Minoan designs; peasant jewelry, silver and gilded; a variety of silver and copper items from Ioannina; silver and gold ornaments from Rhodes. All these articles are to be found in shops around Athens' Constitution Square. Antiques in Pandrossu, Argentine Republic, Kriezotou and Philhellinon Streets.

WHAT TO WEAR ... Greek women are very chic and beautifully dressed, so bring something smart for dinner and evening wear, but also plenty of lightweight cottons, because in summer it gets quite hot. Sports clothing and swim suit for the island resorts.

WHERE TO GO—SIGHTSEEING ...

Athens ... Whether you want to take motorcoach tours available through travel agencies or go sightseeing on your own, here is a brief checklist of principal places in Athens and the logical sequence of side trips according to the length of your visit. Most important, of course, is the fabulous Parthenon (448–437 B.C.), which stands like a crown on the rocky hill of the Acropolis, dominating the city. Also here is the famous Erechtheum with the Caryatids supporting the porch, the Temple of Nike (Wingless Victory), and the Acropolis Museum. North of the Acropolis is the Temple of Theseus (believed to be 437–432 B.C.), best-preserved temple of Athens' classic period. Other places of interest include the Temple of Zeus, the Chapel of St. George on Lycabettus Hill (which now has a cable car to the top), the National Museum, the Benaki Museum (noted for its fine

The beautiful white island of Mykonos is a gathering spot of artists in summer. A view of the Old Church is in the foreground.

collection of Greek costumes), the Byzantine Museum and the Stadium. Also the Stoa of Attalos.

Aegina and Hydra... These two picturesque islands can be visited on a beautiful and relaxing 1-day cruise from Athens.

Delphi... about 100 miles northwest of Athens, is reached by motorcoach or train and car. Beautifully situated on the slopes of Mount Parnassus at an altitude of 2,000 feet, Delphi is world famous as the site of the Oracle of Pythia and contains excavated ruins of many ancient monuments, including the Temple of Apollo, the open-air theater, the Stadium, the Temple of Athena, and masterpieces of sculpture. *Apollo, Vouzas, Delphi* and *Amalia* hotels.

Epidaurus... about 92 miles southwest of Athens; is noted for its Sanctuary of Asclepios, ancient health resort. During July, the "Epidaurus Festival" takes place with excellent productions of classical Greek drama in this ancient theater. Also of interest are the Tholos, the Stadium and a well-preserved, open-air theater with remarkable acoustics. Hotels include the *Xenia, Amphitryon* and the *Bourtzi*.

Sounion... is 1½ hours from Athens through beautiful countryside. This is the site of the Temple of Poseidon set on a hill overlooking the Aegean Sea. There is a tourist pavilion and restaurant here, and the *Hotel Aegaeon* and *Belvedere Motel*.

Olympia... is reached by diesel train or car about 200 miles west of Athens. Located in a beautiful serene area, it is an ancient religious center, and has the Stadium where the Olympic Games were held. The Hermes of Praxiteles is among the beautiful pieces of sculpture found in the local museum. *Spap* and *Xenia* hotels.

Rhodes... Praised by poets as the "Island of Roses" and "Bride of the Sun," Rhodes is the largest and most beautiful of the Dodecanese islands, about 1½ hours by air southeast of Athens. Immaculately clean with its blue-trimmed, white-plaster houses, imposing public buildings and pleasant parks, Rhodes offers, for contrast in the old city, ruins and buildings covering the Hellenic, Roman and Byzantine periods. Most notable is the remarkably well-preserved medieval walled city of the Knights Hospitalers of St. John of Jerusalem, with fascinating castles and palaces, buildings of Byzantine and Turkish architecture. Of interest, too, are the glowing municipal flower gardens and the Museum of Rhodes, which contains, among other interesting items, the famous Venus of Rhodes. Short excursions from the city take you to the ancient cities of Lindos, with its temple of Athena on its acropolis overlooking the sea; the Kamiros whose excavations reveal life in ancient times in the same detail as Pompeii does a later period; the valley of butterflies; and the Monastery of Philerimos, among other points of interest. Vacation facilities are excellent in Rhodes. The de luxe *Hotel des Roses* and the *Ibiscos* on the beach, the *Cairo Palace, Miramare,* the luxurious new *Grand Hotel Summer Palace* and the *Hotel Thermae,* in an attractive setting, are the best and most convenient. Also very good is the *Belvedere* on the airport road; swimming pool. Prices are moderate.

Corfu ... in beauty is second only to Rhodes among the many islands of Greece. Located in the Ionian Sea, Corfu is northwest of Athens less than 2 hours by air. This internationally smart resort has lots of charm and facilities for sports; ideal for sightseeing. Hotels are the *Astir, Miramare Beach, Corcyra Beach, Xenia* and *Corfu Palace.*

Corinth ... locale of St. Paul's sermons and epistles to the Corinthians, is situated on the isthmus about 2 hours by road or train west of Athens. Chief points of interest are the temple of Apollo, fountain of Pirene, the Agora, Odeum, Theater and Museum.

Mykonos ... is reached by boat from Piraeus, the port of Athens, in about 8 hours. It is a beautiful island noted for its picturesque windmills, gleaming white, modest houses, and good bathing. One of the most fashionable Aegean Sea islands, it is a meeting place for artists in summer. Stay at the *Leto Hotel* or the *Xenia Hotel.*

Crete ... is an hour by air south of Athens, the mythical birthplace of Zeus and site of extensive remains of early Minoan civilization, including the beautiful Palace of Knossos (2nd millennium B.C.). Herakleion makes a good base for sightseeing and has a *Xenia* hotel.

Delos ... an hour by caïque (or small native motorboat) from Mykonos, is believed to be Apollo's birthplace. The excavated former religious and commercial center reveals interesting temples, clubs, markets, a theater, and private homes with beautiful mosaics.

Mount Athos ... a peninsula in northern Greece, not easily accessible, is religious territory dotted with beautiful 14th century monasteries. No women visitors are allowed on Athos.

SOURCES OF FURTHER INFORMATION ... The National Tourist Office, 4 Stadiou Street, Athens. The Pan American office is at 6, Venizelos Avenue (Tel. 612-695). The Greek National Tourist Office is at 601 Fifth Avenue, N.Y. 10017. The Greek Tourist Agency is at 565 Fifth Avenue, New York, N.Y. 10017.

HUNGARY

Always one of Europe's prettiest countries, Hungary abounds in beautiful churches, romantic castles, rugged fortresses and music everywhere. Budapest (population 1,807,299) is 13 hours from New York by Pan Am Jet Clipper and connecting airline in Vienna. May through October is the best time for a visit.

The necessary visa ($3.50) may be obtained from any travel agent accredited by Ibusz, the Hungarian Government travel bureau. Hotel and meal vouchers are purchased at the same time at a special rate of 23 florints to U.S. $1; otherwise, there are 11.74 florints to the dollar. Any amount of foreign currency may enter Hungary and be exchanged, but it is nearly impossible to reconvert leftover florints when you leave. Personal belongings, including 1 quart of liquor and 200 cigarettes for personal use may be brought in duty free. Carry with you whatever medicines, razor blades and cosmetics you are likely to need. Electric current is 220 volts, 50 cycles, A.C.

De luxe hotels in Budapest are the *Gellért* ($14.40 per person) and the *Royal* ($13). First class: the *Duna, Margitsziget* and *Szabadsag* ($12.30), and the *Astoria, Red Star, Béke* and *Palace* ($12). Rates include all meals and are for rooms with private bath; without bath, $8.80 per person. Nearly anywhere you dine or stop for a glass of wine there will be gypsy violinists to add atmosphere to *gulyás* (goulash), *fogas* (that best of all fish), rich pastries and *Tokai*. Budapest has two opera houses and three major concert halls, and in summer performances are transferred to the open-air theater on idyllic Margaret Island, in the Danube, which separates Buda from Pest. Hilly, historic Buda still has Roman, Turkish and medieval ruins that look out over the river onto flat, modern Pest. Take a Danube steamer to the castle town of Visegrad, and to beautiful Esztergom, with its great ecclesiastical buildings. Lake Balaton, a 2-hour drive from the capital, is one of Hungary's finest summer resorts.

SOURCES OF FURTHER INORMATION ... Ibusz, Felszabadulas ter 5, Budapest, Hungary, and their travel agent representatives in the U.S.

ATLANTIC

Akureyri

ICELAND

REYKJAVIK

Keflavik ▲MT. HEKLA

OCEAN

ICELAND

This green island (5 hours by Pan Am from New York) offers an unusual and interesting experience for the traveler who will stop for even a few days. Nearly half the size (39,702 square miles) of the British Isles, Iceland is a land of frost and fire with numerous volcanoes, hot springs and glaciers, beautiful mountains and fjords. Most of the population of 188,000 is concentrated in a small area near Reykjavik, the capital city of 78,000 population. These highly literate people, direct descendants of the Vikings, are friendly and hospitable. English is taught in the schools, and readily understood.

The climate is warmer than you'd expect because of the Gulf Stream. Mean temperature is 52° in summer, 32° in winter, similar to Quebec. Best time to visit Iceland is June to September when you can enjoy the Midnight Sun and, in late August, the Aurora Borealis.

To visit Iceland you need only a passport. Duty-free customs allowances include 1 bottle of liquor and 200 cigarettes. The krona is the monetary unit, 42.95 kronur equal $1, each krona being worth about 2.3¢. Good buys are sheepskins, Icelandic handmade silver, ceramics and other handicrafts. Duty-free shop at Keflavik Airport.

Top hotels in Reykjavik are the new *Saga* and the *Hotel Borg*. Rates are about $11 double. Hotels add a 15% service charge and 7½% tax, but there is no tipping. Local food specialties include *hangikjot* (smoked lamb), and various forms of dried fish. *Brennivin,* something like aquavit, is the local drink. *Naust, Glaumbaer, The Club* and *Saga* restaurants have fine seafood and smörgåsbord. Magnificent view from the top-floor Saga Hotel *Grillroom.*

Sightseeing in Reykjavik should include a visit to the University, the hot springs reservoirs from which the city is heated, and the museums. Thirty-five miles away is Thingvellir, where the Parliament (Althing), the oldest in the world, was founded in 930.

Main attractions for visitors are the Gullfoss or "Golden Fall," the beautiful waterfall about 70 miles from Reykjavik, and the Great Geysir, the famous hot springs which spouts a jet of boiling water nearly 200 feet in the air (one of the largest in the world).

The Iceland Tourist Bureau in Reykjavik arranges tours by plane and taxi. For the mountain climber there are several 6,000-foot ranges in addition to Mt. Hekla, still an active volcano with impressive views. Icelandic streams offer excellent fishing for trout and salmon.

Pan Am's office is at the Keflavik Airport (Tel. 92-2165; or -24324, ext. 5170). (Souvenir shop and duty-free store here too.) Pan Am's Reykjavik telephone is 10275. The Icelandic Consulate General is at 551 Fifth Avenue, New York, N.Y. 10017.

IRELAND

WEATHER IN DUBLIN—Lat. N53°20′—Alt. 30′

Temp.	JAN.	FEB.	MAR.	APR.	MAY	JUNE	JULY	AUG.	SEPT.	OCT.	NOV.	DEC.
Low	35°	34°	35°	37°	42°	47°	51°	50°	46°	41°	38°	35°
High	46°	47°	49°	53°	58°	64°	66°	65°	62°	55°	50°	47°
Average	41°	41°	42°	45°	50°	56°	59°	58°	54°	48°	44°	41°
Days of Rain	21	18	19	17	16	15	18	19	16	19	19	21

LOCATION . . . The Republic of Ireland is situated to the west of Great Britain. The six northeastern counties of the island which form Northern Ireland are covered under GREAT BRITAIN.

CHARACTERISTICS . . . Ireland, with its castles, lakes, greenness, and soft-voiced people will delight you. Dublin is a charming city, full of interesting things to see. And who can resist the thought of seeing Donegal, the Yeats country, Connemara, Killarney and the River Shannon? The people are hospitable, the food good. It's a perfect place for a quiet vacation with some good fishing, inexpensive hunting, wonderful golf, and fine motoring.

POPULATION . . . The total population of the island is 4,266,462, of which 2,841,000 live in the Republic of Ireland.

SIZE . . . 32,595 square miles including 5,459 square miles in Northern Ireland. Only 302 miles long and 182 miles wide, it is said that no part of Ireland is more than 70 miles from the sea.

CAPITAL . . . Dublin is the capital with a population of 593,251.

GOVERNMENT . . . The 26 southern counties of the island have an independent, republican type of government.

HOW TO GET THERE . . . By Pan Am Jet Clipper to Shannon, about 6 hours from New York. Shuttle service from Shannon airport to Dublin. By ship, about 5 days.

ACCOMMODATIONS . . . Advance hotel reservations are advised in summer. Ireland has several luxurious new hotels: the *Limerick Intercontinental* on the River Shannon overlooking the city of Limerick; the *Cork Intercontinental*, 5 minutes from downtown Cork; and the *Dublin Intercontinental* (near the American Embassy), the capital's largest and most elegant place to stay. Rates, including breakfast, in the *Cork* and *Limerick Intercontinental* are $6.23-$9.03 single, $10.01-$14.21 double; in the *Dublin Intercontinental*, single $7.81-$12.11, double $12.67-$18.97; reduced rates September through May. Among other fine hotels in Dublin are the *Royal Hibernian;* the smart *Gresham;* the *Shelbourne,* a favorite for over a century; and the *Russell*—single rooms with bath about $12 during the peak seasons of June to September, and December. Good, but less expensive, are the *Central, Clarence, Jury's* and *Wicklow*. Room rates in this type of hotel usually include a hearty Irish breakfast. Irish tourist offices can furnish complete lists of hotels and comfortable guest houses.

ARTS ... The National Museum, on Kildare Street, with its collections of Irish antiquities from Stone Age onward, is world famous. See the museum's unique hoard of Bronze Age gold ornaments and priceless treasures of Early Christian metalwork. Nearby, the National Gallery in Leinster Lawn, facing Merrion Square, within easy reach of all parts of town, has as fine a collection of old masters as can be found anywhere outside of London. Also fine works by Rembrandt, Rubens, good examples of Italian school, a wonderful Goya, "Spanish Woman"; also Hogarth works and many famous Irish painters: Barry, O'Connor, Orpen, and two Hones, among others. National Portrait Gallery is under same roof. Open every day, free. The Municipal Gallery of Modern Art, in a fine old Georgian mansion on Parnell Square, is a must. Fine works of Continental, English and especially Irish painters, such as Hone, Orpen, G. F. Kelly, Shannon, Fisher, Yeats and George Russell. Important works by the great Irish sculptor Andrew O'Connor. The Heraldic Museum in Dublin Castle where family trees are traced is the only one of its kind.

BANKS ... American Express Company, 116 Grafton Street, Thomas Cook & Son, 118 Grafton Street; Bank of Ireland; the Hibernian Bank; the National Bank; Munster and Leinster Bank and the Royal Bank are among the principal banks in Dublin. All have U.S. affiliations, and all have their head offices in College Green or Dame Street, with branches in every town.

CALENDAR OF HOLIDAYS ... St. Patrick's Day, Whitsuntide, August Monday, Christmas Day and December 26. An Tostal is an extended period of activity in Ireland. Emphasis is on outdoor events in April, May, June, with indoor attractions in the fall. Early season events are the Royal Dublin Society Spring Show, Festival of Traditional Music held in a different town each year. The Dublin Horse Show in August is a major social and sporting event. Dublin Theater Festival is in September.

CIGARETTES AND TOBACCO ... Irish and American tobacco and cigarettes are available. Of course, Irish pipes (especially good, Peterson's Dublin). Good cigars are expensive.

CLIMATE . . . Green Ireland has no extremes of temperature. The Gulf Stream makes for mild weather, but with some rain. Best months to visit Ireland are April to October.

CLUBS . . . P.E.N. Club, Rotary Club, Lions Club, Variety Club, Skal Club, Publicity Club, Royal Dublin Society, and sundry commercial clubs.

COMMON COURTESIES AND LOCAL CUSTOMS . . . Same courtesies prevail as in America with regard to sending and acknowledgment of gifts, invitations, etc. Christmas is the biggest religious and civic festival of the year; on March 17 the Shamrock is worn and sent to friends in other countries to commemorate the feast of Ireland's patron, Saint Patrick.

COMMUNICATIONS . . . Daytime phone calls to the States cost about £1 per minute. Cablegrams are 1 shilling 5 pence (1/5) a word; urgent rates 2/10. Airmail postage to the U.S. is 1/5 for a 5-gram letter; 8d (pence) for a postcard; 10d for an airletter form. Local phone calls are 4d; 6d in some hotels.

CURRENCY . . . There are 12 pence in a shilling, 20 shillings in a pound (£), worth $2.80. Dollars are usually acceptable, too.

CUSTOMS REGULATIONS AND DOCUMENTS REQUIRED FOR UNITED STATES CITIZENS . . . An American needs his passport, but no visa. You may bring in, duty free, 1,000 cigarettes, 200 cigars or 2½ lbs. of tobacco, 1 pint of perfume, 1 quart of liquor, $56 worth of gifts. The only currency restriction is an export limit of £250 ($700) in sterling or Irish notes.

DRUGSTORES . . . Same as at home, except no meals.

ELECTRIC CURRENTS . . . 220 volts, 50 cycles, A.C. Voltage of 110 is also available at first-class hotels.

FAUNA . . . Thoroughbred race horses and stud horses and dogs are famous; also all types of sporting and domestic animals indigenous to Western European countries.

FLORA . . . Plant life, vegetation, trees, shrubs and flowers indigenous to the British Isles. Hedges of fuchsia, gorse and rhododendron border many roads. Subtropical plants in the southwest.

FOOD . . . Irish food is probably closest to American food to be found anywhere outside the United States. The milk is fine, but not pasteurized everywhere. As in Argentina, roast beef and steaks are superb and inexpensive. Hams and bacon, traditionally famous, and rich cream, eggs and all kinds of vegetables are readily available. Specialties include Dublin Bay prawns, pheasant and grouse. Game and local cheese are a feature in rural towns.

GAMBLING . . . More than 100 race meets, many of 2- or 3-day duration, greyhound night racing plentiful. Famous Irish sweepstakes, several times each year, based on the Irish Derby and big English classic races, prizes running to thousands of dollars.

LANGUAGE . . . English is spoken all over Ireland and accepted as the language of the country. In some outlying rural and coastal areas, however, there are districts where the Irish language (Gaelic)

LAUNDRY AND DRY CLEANING...Laundry service is fast, reliable. Two-day service. One day on dry cleaning.

LIQUOR...There is excellent Irish whisky. Old-fashioned, pot distilled with a barley base, it is not so smoky as Scotch. After dinner have an Irish Mist—Ireland's legendary liqueur—or an Irish Coffee. Dublin's famous Guinness stout, is darker, stronger than Continental beers. For residents, the liquor restrictions are slightly complicated, but foreign visitors registered at hotels may buy a drink at any reasonable time. Prices are lower than at home, about 40¢ a drink, including Scotch. Minimum legal age for drinkers is 17.

MEDICAL FACILITIES...Excellent.

MOTION PICTURES...The Irish are among the greatest Hollywood fans in all Europe; cinemas with good pictures abound. In Dublin the leading cinemas include the *Savoy, Carlton, Capitol, Ambassador, Astor, Corinthian, Metropole* and *Adelphi*.

MUSIC...Since the day in 1742 when Dubliners saw the first performance anywhere of Handel's *Messiah*, the town has had a high standard of musical taste. There is the Trinity College Choral Society, the Royal Irish Academy of Music, and the *Feis Ceoil* (Music Festival which first introduced John McCormack), along with the Palestrina Choir in the Pro-Cathedral; and the Hibernian Catch Club, oldest male-voice choral society anywhere, founded in 1680. Concerts with famous conductors, opera and Radio Fireann Symphony Orchestra concerts during the winter in Dublin.

NIGHT CLUBS AND CABARETS...Night clubs and cabarets are missing here. Ballrooms are found in the better hotels, but the Irish wit, gaiety and conversation are at their best in such world-famous pubs as *Davy Byrnes, The Pearl* and *The Palace*. Irish coffee (a wineglass of black coffee with Irish liqueur whisky, plus fresh thick cream), makes listening at such places as *Neary's* (off Grafton Street) a treat not easily forgotten. For cocktail lounge atmosphere: *The Shelbourne, The Buttery, Gresham, Dolphin, Russell, Red Bank, Wicklow, Jury's, Searsons* and *The Bailey*.

PHOTOGRAPHY...Tourists can buy black-and-white still and movie film in Dublin, Cork, Galway, etc.; also color film, cameras and all photo equipment. Prices, particularly of cameras, are among the lowest in Europe.

RELIGION...Catholic: the Pro-Cathedral, Marlborough Street; Catholic University, St. Stephen's Green; Augustinian Church, Thomas Street; Carmelite Church, Whitefriars Street; Dominican Church, Lower Dominick Street; Franciscan Church, Church Street; Jesuit Church, Upper Gardiner Street; Passionist Church, Mount Argus. Church of Ireland: St. Patrick's Cathedral; Christ Church Cathedral; Dublin University Chapel; St. Andrews, St. Andrew Street; St. Georges, Temple Street. There are several Presbyterian churches, one being Abbey Church in Parnell Square, and several churches of Methodist and other Protestant denominations. Synagogue, Dolphin's Barn, South Circular Road.

RESTAURANTS...Among the best Dublin restaurants are the

Martello Room atop the Dublin Intercontinental, with a panoramic view of the city; *Moira,* the *Wicklow,* the celebrated *Jammet's;* try the *Dolphin,* Essex Street, for fine steaks and chops. Leading hotel restaurants, such as in the *Dublin Intercontinental, Russell, Royal Hibernian, Gresham,* and *Shelbourne Grill,* all have excellent service and food. So have the *Red Bank, Barnardos* and *Alfredo's* (dancing).

SHOPS AND STORES ... Most of the city's smart shops are in the Grafton Street area. For the ladies Sybil Connolly's, Brown Thomas and Company, Clodagh's, Irene Gilbert's, Switzer's, Neillie Mulcahy, Walpole's. For the men, Kevin and Howlin for tweeds, Hortons and Kelly's for tailoring. At Shannon, the customs-free airport, there is an international trading market with extremely low prices.

SPECTATOR SPORTS ... More than 60 racecourses in the country. Phoenix Park, Curragh, national stud headquarters, Punchestown and Leopardstown are a few that are near Dublin. Greyhound racing 6 nights a week from March to October. Hockey, cricket, soccer, Gaelic football, hurling, bicycle racing, tennis matches, automobile racing, polo, all can be seen in and around Dublin. The Horse Show held in August draws visitors from all over the world. The All-Ireland Hurling and Football finals at Croke Park draw huge local crowds every September. Hurdle racing and steeplechases all winter. Big Irish Grand National in spring, usually Easter Monday, at nearby Fairyhouse course. Go out and see one of the famous Hunt Meets, such as the Meath or the South County Dublin Harriers, even if you don't ride. There are boxing matches which have a big local following, stadium matches, basketball, billiard matches. The annual yacht regatta, at Dun Laoghaire, is a great event. Girls hurling (Camogie, twelve to a side) play in Phoenix Park. Watch or join the players at old-fashioned bowls, at one of the many park greens.

SPORTS ... There are more than twenty golf courses in the neighborhood of Dublin, some with world-wide reputations, other courses all over Ireland. Golf is almost as popular here as in Scotland. Among the best, adjacent to Dublin: Royal Dublin (Dollymount and Portmarnock, both 18-hole championship courses), seaside, very scenic; Woodbrook, another 18-hole course (seaside), licensed clubhouse, professional instructors available. Special Dublin trains stop right at the course. Some of the better-known inland courses are Castle, Clontarf, the Hermitage and Milltown.

As for fishing, a license for salmon or sea trout for single line and rod costs $2.80 for 7 days. No license for brown trout. The River Liffey has fair game fishing right near Dublin, open season from January 1 to September 30. All over Ireland there is good sport; pike, brown and sea trout and off-coast sea fishing—very good in August and September, when mackerel fishing is also at its best. Best sea-trout fisheries are along the west coast, Connemara, Donegal, and Kerry. Fishing is free on the three lakes of Killarney, excellent for both salmon and trout. There are 17 fishery districts in Eire. Licenses can be obtained from the clerk in the respective district, also from local hotel proprietors and tackle agents. Consult Irish Tourist Offices on fishing.

Dun Laoghaire, near Dublin, is headquarters for Irish yachtsmen; the Wicklow Regatta in August is the big annual event for Irish boating enthusiasts.

THEATERS ... Dublin is the home of the famous Abbey Players. There are the *Gate, Gaiety* and several smaller theaters.

TIME ... When it is noon in New York, it's 5 P.M. in Ireland.

TIPPING ... Hotels and restaurants add a 10-15% service charge onto your bill. Tip luggage porters 2/–; 6d for washroom attendant or hat check; 1/– to 2/– for parking lot or gas station attendant. Tip taxi drivers and barbers 10% of the bill; 15% for beauticians; 1/– for bell-boy or doorman.

TRANSPORTATION ... Train service good. Taxis cheap. Bus service everywhere is clean and cheap. Drive-yourself cars from $3.50 a day, plus 5¢ a mile. Drive on the left.

WATER ... Water is good to drink.

WHAT TO BUY ... Hand-woven tweeds for both men and women, suits, topcoats, skirts, lace, linen, fine whisky, Peterson pipes, walking sticks. For antiques, fine old Irish Waterford glass, old silver, a great deal of which is superior to English of the same period. You may do better to bring your tweed goods home with you to be tailored. Good handmade shoes for men in Dublin. Wonderful fisherman sweaters from County Donegal and the Aran Islands.

WHAT TO WEAR ... Medium-weight clothes and sports clothes are fine for daytime wear. Good walking shoes are essential. You really don't need evening clothes. You'll need a warm topcoat for winter touring, or buy one there. Sportsmen will need golf and fishing togs. You'll want a raincoat, but you can buy fine ones there.

WHERE TO GO—SIGHTSEEING ...

Dublin ... Dublin, the natural headquarters for all visitors to Ireland, is a city of wide streets, lovely squares and parks, and wonderful examples of 18th century Georgian architecture. There are houses and buildings by Gandon, Cassels and Johnston, who were among the greatest of 18th century architects. Ceilings by Angelica Kauffman and mantelpieces by Bossi are famous features of some of these magnificent old buildings. See Mansion House (Dawson Street), the Merrion Square home of Daniel O'Connell. Visit Ely Place, Fitzwilliam Place and St. Stephen's Green. Robert Emmet's house is on the western side and the church of the Catholic University erected by Cardinal Newman faces the square too. Visit Grafton Street; Percy Bysshe Shelley lived at No. 1, Richard Brinsley Sheridan stayed at No. 79, and Tom Moore and the Duke of Wellington attended Samuel Whyte's famous school. The provost's house on the ground of Trinity College is impressive. O'Connell Street, the finest thoroughfare in Dublin, runs north from the river. See the Nelson Pillar, the O'Connell Monument. The General Post Office near the Pillar was headquarters of the Irish Volunteers during their Easter Rising. Parnell Square has the Municipal Gallery of Modern Art, the Gaelic League and the Rotunda. Here, too, are the Gate Theater, the Rotunda Hospital. See the birthplace of George Bernard Shaw at 33 Synge Street, and that of

James Joyce at No. 41 Brighton Square. The Joyce Museum is in the ancient Martello Tower at Sandycove. Visit St. Patrick's, St. Audoens and Christ Church Cathedral. The latter dates back to Norman times; the former to 1213. The Guinness brewery, one of the world's largest, is worth a visit. Take a look at Trinity College, the Custom House, the National Library. Spend some time in Phoenix Park, one of the finest in the world, containing a race course, zoo, sports grounds, the official residence of the President, the American ambassador's residence, flower gardens, a lake and the tallest obelisk in the world—the Wellington Monument.

Seven miles south of the city is Dun Laoghaire, with a fine harbor and steamer service to Holyhead. It is a marine playground for all of Dublin, with good swimming. The old village of Dalkey, a mile or so beyond, affords a magnificent view of the bay. Bray, 4 miles farther south, is a seaside resort with a promenade and all other resort features. To the north there are picturesque seaside villages of Howth, Skerries, Rush, Lusk, and others.

Basic Side Tours ... There are daily coach tours to other interesting and picturesque spots within a 30-mile radius of Dublin. From Shannon Airport there are luxury coach tours of 2 to 6 days to Killarney and/or Connemara. Transatlantic passengers can now take a 24-hour "Medieval Tour" from Shannon Airport for the all-inclusive cost of only $20. The tour gives you a 60-mile ride through cozy villages and emerald-green countryside, tea before a turf fire in a thatched cottage, a medieval banquet (complete with songs by Irish minstrels) in Bunratty Castle, overnight accommodations at the Airport Hotel, and breakfast. And you still have time for a glorious shopping binge in the Airport Duty Free Shop before flying out of the country. *Dromoland Castle,* 8 miles from Shannon, is now a luxurious resort hotel featuring golf, shooting, fishing and other sports. You can arrange 6- and 9- and 12-day tours out of Dublin before you leave home. Or make your arrangements in Dublin. Bicycling is a fascinating way to cover Ireland. There are Youth Hostels and inns everywhere. A clockwise tour of the island is one of the best ways to see everything there is. On the way from Dublin to Cork you see the famous round towers, the Vale of Avoca, made famous by Thomas Moore. The next county is Wexford, where you will see Johnstown Castle. The Saltee Islands, famous bird sanctuary, are off the coast. Waterford comes next, then the resort of Tramore, where there is a race meet every August. In Tipperary County, known to everyone, is the great rock of Cashel. In Cashel, once the home of the Kings of Munster, stand the remains of King Cormac's Chapel, a must for all visitors.

Cork ... the third city in Ireland, on the river Lee, has the new *Cork Intercontinental* and other modern hotels. Five miles away is Blarney Castle with the famous stone. Down the river about 16 miles is Cobh (formerly Queenstown), the country's main port. Visit St. Colman's Cathedral. When you get to Killarney, the lakes, the mountains and the pervasive charm will make you want to stay a few days. The *Great Southern Hotel, Hotel Europe* and *Castlerosse* are good.

Ross Castle is one of the famous landmarks in Killarney, 100 miles from Cork in southwest Ireland.

Take some jaunting-car trips and boat trips up the lakes.

Galway... is the springboard for sightseeing in western Ireland. Here you'll find rugged coast, mountains and fine salmon fishing. Centered about Galway City are dozens of old castles, shooting lodges and country houses which have been converted into hotels and inns. One of the finest is *Ashford Castle,* Cong.

A 30-mile steamer trip to the Aran Islands, where only Gaelic is spoken, is most rewarding. Allow a full day for this.

Westport... is to the north, where you'll see Croagh Patrick, the Holy Mountain of St. Patrick, which is climbed by thousands on the last Sunday of July. The entire west of Ireland is the fisherman's delight. Lough Corrib in Connemara, Leenane, Ballynahinch, Kylemore and Recess are known to fishermen the world over. In County Mayo are many lakes in which fish abound. At certain hotels fishing privileges are available to guests.

NOTE: Northern Ireland is a part of the United Kingdom and is completely separate from the Republic of Ireland described here. Such facts as Customs Regulations and Calendar of Holidays for Northern Ireland coincide closely with those of Great Britain. (*See* page 83.) For sightseeing in Northern Ireland, *see* page 99.

SOURCES OF FURTHER INFORMATION... The Irish Tourist Board has offices at 33 E. 50 St. in New York, and in Chicago, San Francisco and Montreal. In Dublin there is a Tourist Information Bureau at 14 Upper O'Connell Street. Information also at Pan American's office, 35 Westmoreland Street (Tel. 79091).

ITALY

WEATHER IN ROME—Lat. N41°54′—Alt. 95′

Temp.	JAN.	FEB.	MAR.	APR.	MAY	JUNE	JULY	AUG.	SEPT.	OCT.	NOV.	DEC.
Low	38°	40°	44°	49°	54°	61°	66°	65°	61°	54°	46°	40°
High	52°	55°	59°	66°	73°	81°	87°	86°	80°	70°	60°	53°
Average	44°	48°	52°	58°	64°	71°	77°	76°	71°	62°	53°	47°
Days of Rain	10	10	9	9	8	5	2	3	6	11	12	12

LOCATION . . . Italy occupies the familiar boot-shaped peninsula extending from the Alps into the Mediterranean Sea.

CHARACTERISTICS . . . Italy is always gay and full of visitors. You can relax in Rome, Florence and Capri or enjoy yourself in Sicily and in the charming little towns along the Italian Riviera. The history of the modern world has its roots in Rome. You will have missed something if you don't wander around the Colosseum or see the Sistine Chapel. Rome is noisy, Latin, and very smart these days. The tourist receives wonderful treatment from everybody: in the hotels, in the shops, in the streets; even policemen are English-speaking.

POPULATION . . . Nearly 52,000,000.

SIZE . . . 760 miles long and 100 to 150 miles wide, Italy's area is 116,372 square miles, roughly the size of New Mexico.

CAPITAL . . . Rome, estimated population 2,460,994.

GOVERNMENT . . . Italy is a Republic in which all major political parties participate.

HOW TO GET THERE . . . By Pan American Jet Clipper only 8 hours direct from New York; service also via Paris, or via Lisbon, Barcelona and Nice. By ship to Venice, Naples or Genoa, 8 to 14 days.

ACCOMMODATIONS . . . The large Italian cities offer hotels for every taste and purse. During most of the year advance reservations are necessary. In Rome de luxe hotels are the *Ambassador, Bernini Bristol, Excelsior, Flora, Grand, Eden, Mediterraneo, Parco dei Principi, Cavalieri Hilton* and *Hassler.* Rates about $15 single, $20 double without meals, plus service charges and taxes. Add about $5 a day for demi-pension (two meals). First-class hotels include the *Caesar Augustus, Dei Congressi, Michelangelo, Claridge, Hermitage,* the *Raphaël, Napoleon, Metropole, Continentale, De la Ville, Eliseo, Majestic, Massimo D'Azeglio, Quirinale, Residence Palace, Forum, Ritz, Victoria, Savoy* and others. A single room runs about $14 with meals; $9 without. Second-class hotels charge about $9 and $5 respectively. Rooms without private bath are much more reasonable, usually have hot and cold running water. An extra daily charge is made for heating from about Nov. 15 through Mar. 15. Categories for hotels are fixed each year by law and approved rates are posted or available on request. During the thrift season (Nov. 1-March. 1) some resort hotels offer a 25% discount. Not to be overlooked, especially for a stay of 3 days or longer, are the many pleasant and inexpensive *pensioni,* or private lodging houses. There is no exact U.S. counterpart for the *pensioni,* some of which offer service and facilities equal to hotels, plus a congenial and less impersonal atmosphere. The *Bellavista Milton, Roxy, Washington, Tea, Texas, Villa Borghese* and *Waldorf* are among those centrally located. In addition are *La Residenza, Villa Gaia, Home in Rome, Paisiello Parioli, Villa del Parco.* Rates for full *pensione,* taxes, service and all meals included, range between $7 and $9; it is usually possible to arrange for half *pensione:* breakfast and one other meal if preferred. Outside the main cities, new hotels are gradually beginning to appear in places of tourist interest. Foremost is the *Jolly Hotel* chain, with about 40 well-equipped, reasonable new hotels scattered through Italy, Sicily and Sardinia. Italian automobile clubs have built comfortable new motels where hotels are scarce.

ARTS . . . Italy is the art lover's paradise. Museum after museum is filled with famous paintings and sculpture, tapestries, gold and jewels, ceramics. In the churches and palaces where Raphael, Michelangelo, Titian and the other great artists actually worked, you'll see their masterpieces in the original settings. Statues, mosaics and other treasures of the ancient Greeks and Romans are superbly displayed in the Lateran Museums, the National Museum (Baths of Diocletian), and the Capitoline Museum where "The Dying Gaul" and the famous Capitoline Venus are to be found. The Vatican Museums house a vast collection of the art of many ages and many peoples; the Sistine Chapel with Michelangelo's magnificent painting of the Creation, the Borgia Apartments and the frescoed Rooms of Raphael. The fascinating art of the Etruscans fills Rome's stately Villa Giulia and the Etruscan Museum in Florence. From the Pompeiian Rooms in the Naples Museum to the world-renowned painting of the Last Supper by Leonardo da Vinci in Milan, there is hardly a town in all Italy that cannot boast at least one priceless work of art.

The Uffizi Gallery in Florence, one of the world's greatest, the

Pitti Palace, the town hall museums of Siena and Perugia, the Doge's Palace and Academy Gallery in Venice are not to be missed.

BALLET ... The Rome Opera House has its own ballet company, as does La Scala in Milan, and others listed under MUSIC on page 124. Foreign companies appear frequently. The International Ballet Festival, held in July, at Nervi on the Riviera very near Genoa, features outdoor performances by leading companies in a superb setting.

BANKS ... In Rome, the Banca del Lavoro, near PAA's office, represents the major U.S. banks. Others include Banca Commerciale Italiana; Bank of America and Italy, Largo Tritone; American Express, Piazza di Spagna 38; Thos. Cook, Via Veneto 9–11. Banks and most hotels cash travelers checks at the official rate minus bank charges.

CALENDAR OF HOLIDAYS ... National holidays are January 1, April 25, May 1, June 2, November 4; religious holidays January 6, March 19, Easter Monday, Ascension Day and Corpus Domini, June 29, August 15, November 1, December 8, 25 and 26. Detailed lists of events are available. See SOURCES OF FURTHER INFORMATION.

CIGARETTES AND TOBACCO ... American cigarettes cost about 72¢ (420-450 lire) per pack. (*See* CUSTOMS REGULATIONS.)

CLIMATE ... Rome is pleasant the year round, but there is a rainy season during the winter months. April to November are months usually filled with sunny, warm days, which by midsummer turn quite hot. Climate in the rest of Italy varies from very warm to freezing. It depends on where you go and at which time of the year.

CLUBS ... In Rome: Lions, Rotary, American Chamber of Commerce, American Women's Association and American Club.

COMMON COURTESIES AND LOCAL CUSTOMS ... Dinner hour is late and so are opera and theater performances. The chaperone is still in good standing. *"Grazie"* is "Thank you" in Italian. When visiting churches, men wear coats. Women should have a head covering, wear stockings and dresses with sleeves; never slacks. For an audience with the Pope, women must wear dark, long-sleeved, high-necked dresses or a suit, a hat or veil. Men should wear dark suits. If you are not a Catholic, you need not genuflect or kiss the Pope's ring, behavior which is mandatory for Catholics.

COMMUNICATIONS ... Telephone service is not as good as in America; for a long-distance call, one must make a reservation in advance. Calls to the U.S. cost 2,825 lire per minute. Airmail rates for letters to the United States are lire 130, for postal cards lire 100. It saves time to let the porter or concierge send your cables. Regular cables cost 225 lire per word; 113 lire per word for night letters.

CURRENCY ... The monetary unit of Italy is the lira, worth about 620 to the dollar. For exchange, consult banks or your concierge and avoid sidewalk money changers. Italy has legalized operation of the *cambio* or authorized private exchange office.

CUSTOMS REGULATIONS AND DOCUMENTS NEEDED FOR UNITED STATES CITIZENS ... You'll need a passport, no visa. You may bring in unlimited dollars and lire. About 400 cigarettes, or 1 lb. of tobacco in any form, 1 bottle of liquor or 2 of wine. No restrictions on food or liquor when leaving. One still camera with 5 rolls of film, and 1 movie camera with 2 reels duty free.

DRUGSTORES... Most American products are available in the bigger *farmacie,* which are roughly similar to the American drugstores. The *profumerie,* or perfume shops, carry familiar cosmetics and toiletries as well as perfume and souvenirs.

ELECTRIC CURRENT... Italy is in the process of standardizing its current. Large areas usually have 110–127 volts, A.C., others have 150–160 volts, and all are 50-cycle. However, American-made electric appliances are very popular in Italy, and everywhere one is able to purchase plug converters and small transformers or rectifiers for local outlets and type of current.

FOOD... *Pasta* means not only spaghetti and ravioli but *pasta* of all sorts in an amazing variety of sizes and shapes. Despite everything you've heard, you won't find much garlic in typical Italian food. There are innumerable *risotto,* or rice, dishes mixed with peppers, chicken, meat, fish, onions and spices. *Pizza,* of course, is the famous baked cheese and tomato open-faced pie. *Antipasto,* the Italian hors d'oeuvre, is much the same in Rome as at home. Veal is a favorite meat and *scaloppine* is familiar to everyone. The fruits, vegetables and salads are excellent. Beef is generally good. *Polenta,* a favorite in northern Italy, is a porridgey dish of corn meal served mostly in native restaurants in the country. The northern Italians cook in butter. In the south they prefer oil. Italian cooking is rich, saucy and spicy and infinitely varied, so take it easy the first few days. Romans eat far more than Americans, especially at lunch.

Caffè espresso is the bitter, strong coffee especially brewed in *espresso* machines, Rube Goldberg contraptions which use forced, compressed steam to make the coffee. Milk is available in any milk shop, hotel, restaurant.

GAMBLING... There are Casinos at Venice, San Remo, St. Vincent (Aosta Valley), Taormina and at Campione near Como. Parimutuel betting at horse racing, trotting and dog tracks. Weekly Government-run lotteries, too.

LANGUAGE... You won't need to know Italian to get around easily in Rome or in the other principal tourist centers.

LAUNDRY AND DRY CLEANING... Laundry is wonderful and fast; Italian laundresses do careful pressing on lingerie and shirts. It is advisable to select your dry cleaner carefully. Dry-cleaning facilities are available in all hotels or in dry-cleaning shops. The prices are somewhat higher than in the States. Be sure to inquire about the available delivery time before leaving your things.

LIQUOR... Italian wines are excellent. Best known are Chianti, Frascati, Soave and Verdicchio. Valpolicella, Barolo and Merlot wines are also good. There are many brands of each kind. Gin and brandy are favorite hard liquors, but one must acquire a taste for Italian brandy. Best is Buton Vecchia Romagna. Strega is a native cordial which has quite a bite. The average price for a bottle of good wine is just under $1 in a shop. In a restaurant or hotel, of course, one must add the service. Popular American drinks are available in all bars, restaurants and first-class hotels. You can get excellent martinis in Rome. American whiskey and Scotch cost less than in New York.

MEDICAL FACILITIES ... There are many English-speaking doctors and good hospitals. Rome has the Salvator Mundi International Hospital with American-trained staff.

MOTION PICTURES ... Most are in Italian but the *Fiammetta* and the *Archimede* in Rome show exclusively English or French films in their original versions, as does the *Metro Drive-In*. Shows are at set hours, not continuous.

Rome has become a second Hollywood, and you'll run across many American actors and actresses.

MUSIC ... In this land of Verdi, Puccini, Rossini and Mascagni, opera is a gala occasion: you'll hear wonderful music and see elegant audiences at their gayest during the winter season at Naples' San Carlo, in Rome, or at famed La Scala in Milan. In Rome there is open-air opera during July and August in the matchless setting of the Baths of Caracalla, and frequent concerts in the Basilica of Massenzio, right in the heart of the Roman Forum. Also of interest are Musical May in Florence, the International Music Festival in Venice in September, outdoor opera seasons at the Campi Flegrei near Naples and in the Amphitheater at Verona; there are also excellent orchestral and chamber concerts and recitals by world-famous soloists in principal cities during the fall and winter season.

NIGHT CLUBS AND CABARETS ... From October until the beginning of June, Rome's smartest clubs are the *Cabala* (*Hostaria dell'Orso*), the *Open Gate, Pipistrello, Club 84, Cappriccio, Dave's* and the *Cabala* and *Zanzara* discothèques. In summer, night life goes outdoors, to the *Belvedere delle Rose* on the Via Cassia, the *Villa dei Cesari*, the *Casina dell Rose* in the Borghese Gardens, or to dine and dance on the rooftops of the Eliseo and Cavalieri Hilton hotels.

PHOTOGRAPHY ... Any photographic material is available in every big town, but prices are high. Film-developing facilities are available everywhere. Time for developing is reasonable, quality good. Don't mail your films from Italy. Take them out with you or have developing done in Rome at Vasari, 6 Via Ludovisi near Excelsior Hotel or Fotoptica Vicari, Via 4 Fontane near Piazza Barberini; in Milan, Via Vittor Pisani 16; or in Naples, 6-7 Via Marittima.

RELIGION ... Rome, needless to say, is Catholic and is filled with magnificent churches. The church set aside for American Catholics is Santa Susanna, near the Grand Hotel. Other churches are the American Church (Episcopal) on Via Nazionale, the English Church on Via Babuino, other Protestant churches, and synagogues.

RESTAURANTS ... No two Romans, much less visitors, will agree on restaurants. However, one should try *Passetto's*, the *Biblioteca del Valle, Capriccio's, George's, Escargots, Ernesto, Tor Fiorenza, Il Grifone, Meo Pattacca* (a 19th-century tavern), *Chianti*,

Giggi Fazi, Horti Di Galatea, Fascination, Fontanella (famous for game), *Casale Romanesco, Jerry's Luau, Scoglio Di Frisio* (Neapolitan fish restaurant), *Corsaro, Cesarina, Al Vicario;* and for the unique experience of dining in an authentic ancient Roman setting— *Da Pancrazio, Taverna Ulpia* or Pompeiian-decorated *Apuleius* on the Aventine Hill. Don't miss the *Hostaria dell'Orso.* It's reputed to have been the hotel where Dante stayed in the 13th century; the food is epicurean. Try all three *Alfredo's.* There are countless worthwhile little restaurants and *trattorias,* especially in the old parts of Rome. *Necci, Angelinos, Il Buco, Piccolo Mondo* and *Galeassi* are also very good.

Hamburgers, ham and eggs and other American fare can be found in American-style luncheonettes and restaurants such as the *California,* the *Colony* and the *New Madison House.*

Outdoor cafés are all over, since the Roman drinks innumerable small cups of *espresso* coffee. Try *Doney's, Cafe de Paris* and *Rosati's* on Via Veneto for a coffee, ice cream or cocktails.

In summer you'll dine outdoors on the Hassler Terrace, at *La Cisterna, Romolo* or *Villa Massimo* in Trastevere, at *Tre Scalini* on Piazza Navona, the most beautiful square in Rome.

In Rome and in all of Italy eating is a fine art and not to be hurried, so plan to take it leisurely and enjoy yourself. The price for a meal in a restaurant goes from a minimum of $1.50 to a maximum of about $9. Service is usually included in the check.

SHOPS AND STORES ... The main shopping center is formed by Via Condotti, Rome's Bond Street, Via Frattina, Piazza di Spagna and Via Sistina. Specialty shops in this area display a mouth-watering array of beautifully made gifts, clothing and accessories (*See* WHAT TO BUY). English is spoken everywhere. Stores close at 1 P.M., reopen from 4-7:30 P.M. in winter; in summer 4:30-8 P.M. Some shops will let you exchange things, but there are no refunds.

The closest thing to American department stores in Rome are the Rinascente, Piazza Colonna and Piazza Fiume, and CIM, Via XX Settembre; but they are far smaller than those in America. Prices are reasonable. Rome is otherwise a fairly expensive European city.

SPECTATOR SPORTS ... Horse shows, football, yacht races, speedboat tests, motorcycle races, golf, tennis tourneys, water polo. There are several tracks near Rome for flat racing and trotting races.

SPORTS ... There are fine beaches for swimming throughout Italy. Best beach resort near Rome is Fregene. There is skiing at Terminillo, 1½ hour drive from Rome. (Also in Taormina, Sicily, and of course in the Dolomites.) You can fish in lakes and rivers throughout the Apennines and Dolomites, and all along the seacoasts. Marvelous swimming and skin diving there, too. Italy has many good golf courses and tennis courts. The Rome Golf Courses at Acquasanta and at Olgiata are open the year round and Acquasanta may be reached by streetcar. There is a bar and restaurant on the grounds of both.

THEATERS ... Many theaters in Rome and Milan. Performances, except for visiting companies, in Italian at 9 P.M. Tickets $2–$5.

TIME ... When it's noon in New York, it's 6 P.M. in Italy.

TIPPING ... Station porter gets 100 lire per bag, taxi driver 15% of meter reading and the 150 lire surcharge after 10 P.M. (minimum 100 lire). Hotels add 18% to 21% service charge. Extra is expected: chambermaid 100 lire a day or 500 a week, doorman 100 for taxi, luggage porter 100 minimum, breakfast waiter 100, head porter 10% of his separate bill, barbers and beauticians 15%–20%, restaurant and night-club waiters 100 per person above 15% service, night-club head waiters 2,000-5,000 per party, hatcheck 50-100, washroom attendant 50, shoeshine boy 50, movie ushers 50, theater ushers 100, car-park attendants 50-150 (same to the helpful souls who insist on guarding your car parked on street), museum guides 300, coffee or wine café waiter 50 lire minimum, 10 lire at a stand-up bar.

TOURIST TAXES ... Air departure tax $1.12 at Rome's Fiumicino Airport; 80¢ at all others. Sea arrival and departure taxes $4.50 to $13.

TRANSPORTATION ... Airport bus fare into Rome is 800 lire ($1.30). City taxis have a surcharge after 10 P.M. and also for extra luggage and for taxis ordered by phone. Motor buses are excellent. Auto rentals are available at about $12 a day. Trains are good, first and second class, especially first- and second-class sleepers.

WATER ... Safe in tourist centers; bottled waters are available.

WHAT TO BUY ... Tortoise shell, amber, cameos, silver, handbags, men's ties, Florentine leather, straw and embroidery, olivewood boxes, gloves. Borsalino hats, Italian silks, custom-made shirts for men and blouses for women. Italian tailors are wonderful, too. Rosaries, crosses and religious statuary abound in Rome. Perfumes are not good buys in Italy. Don't buy fountain pens from street vendors. Avoid the antique and old painting racket.

High fashion for women has become very important in Italy. There are lots of fashion houses which are comparable to those in France, also boutiques featuring original accessories and sportswear.

WHAT TO WEAR ... In spring, summer or fall in Rome wear lightweight clothes such as you would at home. Prints, dark sheers are acceptable. Rome is a dressy city, so don't appear in slacks. You'll need a couple of pairs of good walking shoes. You are bound to walk a lot in Italy. Men need sports jackets and slacks, lightweight suits. The winter season is cold, but very smart. Warm clothing necessary; evening dress is worn infrequently.

WHERE TO GO—SIGHTSEEING ...

Rome ... Volumes have been written about what to see in Rome so consider this merely as a check list. There are several guided tours to the museums and art galleries and other points of historical interest. Sightseeing tours are available at any tourist office and can be booked through the concierge of your hotel. The average price for a half-day tour in town is lire 2,000 ($3.20). If you prefer to do it on your own, see: the Borghese Gallery, the Capitoline Museum, the Gallery of Modern Art, of course the Vatican Museum (*See* VATICAN CITY). Hadrian's Tomb is a short walk along the River Tiber; you don't need to be reminded of St. Peter's, the Colosseum, the Forums; take a ride out the Old Appian Way, see the Catacombs; note the Palazzo Venezia, where Mussolini held forth on the balcony; the three Basilicas: S. Maria Maggiore, St. John Lateran and St. Paul's-Outside-the-Walls.

See the Holy Child in the Church of Ara Coeli. Look at the Quirinal Palace, former home of the popes and kings; the Holy Steps (*Scala Santa*), the grave of the poet Keats, the Pantheon, built in 27 B.C., the Circus Maximus, where the first chariot races were run; the Roman Capitol; the statue of Moses by Michelangelo in the Church of St. Peter in Chains on the Via Cavour.

See the famous Baths of Caracalla; the Spanish Steps at the old church of the Holy Trinity of the Hills which lead to the Piazza di Spagna; the Capuchin Chapel on Via Veneto; the old bridges over the Tiber; and you can't miss seeing the enormous white-and-gold monument to Victor Emmanuel II. You can spend days and weeks and still not see it all.

Vatican City ... is a state within a state ruled by the Pope. Each year thousands of pilgrims from all over the world throng to Italy for religious events here. The Vatican has its own railway station, power lines, radio station and printing plant. Here stands St. Peter's, largest church in Christendom. The treasures, the works of art are innumerable and breathtaking. Over the entrance is the famed Giotto *Navicella*. Inside, the size will awe you; the nave is 151 feet high. The Treasury of St. Peter's contains the Cross of the Emperor Justinius, Charlemagne's robes, jewels and other treasures. The vaulted dome is by Michelangelo, and there are tombs of the Popes by Bernini and Canova. Take the elevator and climb 700 steps to the peak of the dome and survey all of Rome.

The Vatican itself is next, the residence of the Pope. The famous bronze doors are guarded by the equally famous, brilliantly uniformed Swiss guards. The Vatican museum may be visited from 9 A.M. to 2 P.M. Monday through Saturday. Most beautiful of all its treasures is the Sistine Chapel with Michelangelo's great masterpieces. Visit the rooms filled with magnificent painting, statuary, robes and tapestries. You need more than one visit to savor it all. Properly accredited visitors may attend group audiences with the Pope by calling the North American College (Tel. 670-658).

Side Trips ... Half an hour's drive from Rome are the vast picturesque ruins of the Emperor Hadrian's Villa. A little farther on is the Villa D'Este with its world-famous fountains. Half-day tours to both run daily, cost $4.50. Sixty miles north along the seacoast road are the painted Etruscan tombs of Tarquinia, unique, dating back to the 5th and 6th centuries B.C. 155 miles south of Rome is Cassino, the American battlefield, and 37 miles south is the beach of Anzio. North of Rome you come to Assisi, the birthplace of St. Francis, and the Basilica with frescoes by Giotto honoring him. There are excellent guided tours in tourist buses which swing on circle itineraries. These buses have sliding roofs, radios and public address systems, hostesses who speak English, bars, desks, reading lights. The circle takes in Milan, Genoa, Florence, Rome, Naples, Cassino, Perugia, Bologna, Verona and Venice. You can start anywhere and go as far as you like. See the Etruscan Gate in Perugia, the National Picture Gallery in Siena.

Florence . . . This city—"the cradle of the Renaissance"—(180 miles north of Rome) is one of the most visited in Italy. Stay at the *Excelsior, Carlton, Villa la Massa, Grand, Villa Medici, Baglioni Palace, Kraft, Anglo-Americano, Astoria, Majestic, Roma, Savoy* or at one of the city's many comfortable *pensioni*. Dine at the *Baglioni Roof, Oliviero, Buca Lapi, Buca di San Ruffillo, Da Zi'rosa, Giovacchino, Paoli* and *Sabatini* restaurants. Visit the Palazzo Vecchio, the Loggia dei Lanzi, under which is Cellini's "Perseus." See the Cathedral, or *Duomo*, of colored marble, housing Michelangelo's last statue. You'll see the Campanile (bell tower) and the great art galleries containing astonishing examples of Renaissance painting and

The renowned 100-Fountains of the Villa D'Este are illuminated on summer nights.

The Emperor Hadrian's Tomb is now part of the Castel Sant' Angelo in Rome.

The relaxed atmosphere makes the island of Capri near Naples a favorite vacation spot.

St. Mark's Basilica and the Ducal Palace, seen via gondola from the Grand Canal.

sculpture, the Uffizi and the Palazzo Pitti. Here you will see Flemish, Spanish and German masterpieces, as well as Italian.

Visit the Church of Santa Croce, with the tombs of Machiavelli and Michelangelo; the Church of Orsanmichele with its Donatello statues; the Palazzo Riccardi, residence of the Medici, with the Medici chapel containing fabulous frescoes of the Nativity by Benozzo Gozzoli; the Ponte Vecchio, the bridge across the Arno lined with shops; Ghiberti's "Door of Paradise" at the Baptistery. Visit the Boboli Gardens, which have inspired murals in Italian restaurants the world over. Save energy by hiring an English-speaking guide if your time is short. You'll need 2 or 3 days or more to do justice to the city. There is a service called "Information Please" at Via Tornabuoni 10, which provides baby sitters, nurses and guides and also gives shopping advice.

Naples ... The Bay of Naples, dominated by Vesuvius, is famous on postal cards all over the world. The best hotels are the *Excelsior, Ambassador Palace, Vesuvio, Mediterraneo* and *Royal.*

The main reason for going to Naples these days is to go on its side trips. Pompeii, with its fabulous ruins, is only a half-hour away. Two hours away from Pompeii are Sorrento and Positano and the famous Amalfi Drive, which is cut into the side of the hills. From the drive you see spread out the tiny fishing villages and the bay. You can visit the summit of Vesuvius with a guide.

Capri ... Most famous resort near Naples is the Island of Capri, celebrated in song and verse. Here are the well-known Blue Grotto, the flower-laden villas, the small beaches, the walks along the cliffs. Drive to Anacapri, a charming village with a picturesque square. Stay at the *Europa Palace* or the *Caesar Augustus*. In Capri try the *Quisisana* or *Morgano Tiberio*. Buy rope-soled shoes, scarves, cotton skirts and fishing shirts. Take the funicular to Marina Grande, the fishing village where you get a boat for a sail into the Blue Grotto. Lie in the sun on the beach at Marina Piccola. Relax and enjoy the beauty. You'll see lots of famous people here. Capri is a gathering spot for the international set.

Venice ... slightly over one hour from Rome by air, is the stuff of dreams. It is romance, beauty, an idyl. The Mecca of tourists for more than a hundred years, Venice is built on a series of small islands at the head of·the Adriatic Sea. Its main "streets" are lagoons and canals on which float the romantic gondolas, the motor launches, the canal barges, the ferryboats. There are, however, streets and bridges on which pedestrians may stroll.

Venice was in its glory during the Middle Ages when her ships controlled the richest trade routes in the world. Her decline began in the 16th century, but her renown as a romantic, beautiful spot continues. You'll want to see the Basilica of St. Mark in famous St. Mark's Square, where everyone feeds the pigeons. St. Mark's was finished in 1500 and is a magnificent example of Byzantine architecture. The interior is lined with fine mosaics. St. Mark's Square also has the famous Clock Tower, which tells not only the hours but the daily position of the sun and moon. See the Palace of the Doges with its wonderful rooms decorated by 16th-century artists. Pay special attention to the Tintorettos. See the dungeons. The Campanile, or bell tower, dominates the Square. You can't miss it.

Other important churches in Venice include Frari and Sts. Giovanni and Paolo. Visit Palazzo Rezzonico, with its magnificent 18th-century rooms; Ca d'Oro, one of Venice's oldest houses. You will want to take a gondola through the Grand Canal, lined with historical palaces. You will pass under the Rialto. See also the Bridge of Sighs.

Stay at the *Gritti,* the *Danieli,* the *Grand,* the *Europa,* the *Bauer Grünwald,* the *Park,* the *Luna* or *Cipriani* on the Island of Giudecca. Dine at *La Taverna Fenice,* which is tops; world-famous *Harry's Bar; Florian's* on St. Mark's Square, which is very popular; *La Colomba,* or *Al Graspo de UA,* famous for seafood; the *Locanda* on the island of Torcello. Also don't miss *Quadri,* the Danieli's Roof and the Gritti terrace dining room. If you have time, visit Murano and the Venetian glass factories. Cross the Lagoon by motor launch to the Lido, the famed beach resort, with its excellent hotels: the *Excelsior,* the *Grand Hotel des Bains.* Everyone rents a *capanna* and lazes in the sun. There is a casino, too. The Feast of the Redeemer, held on the third Sunday in July, is a great festival here.

In the area there are several cities, Padua and Verona, for example, which will interest particularly lovers of Shakespeare. Nearby is Vicenza, with magnificent Palladian villas and theater.

Milan . . . This economic heart of Italy has the famous Industrial Fair each April. See the famous Milan Cathedral with its pinnacles and statues. "The Last Supper," by Leonardo da Vinci, may be seen in the convent of the Church of Santa Maria delle Grazie. Milan's famous La Scala Opera holds forth from December to June. Its museum is devoted to relics of the opera. The Brera Gallery and Castle Sforzesco house works of many great masters. Stay at the *Palace, Principe Savoia, Excelsior Gallia, Duomo Grand,* the *Continental* or the *Cavalieri.* Dine at *Giannino's, Savini, Barca d'Oro, Ciro's,* the *Gourmet.*

Italian Riviera . . . The stretch of Ligurian coast from Savona to Ventimiglia is now officially called the Riviera dei Fiori (Coast of Flowers). Most important resort in this region is San Remo, which has luxurious hotels, a casino and all the attributes of a fashionable playground. Here, as on the French Riviera, you may ski just a few miles from the Mediterranean, at Mt. Bignone, which is reached by cableway. There is a golf course, too, halfway up the mountain. Genoa, about 4 hours away, is the birthplace of Columbus. Visit Staglieno, the monumental cemetery. Beyond are famous Rapallo, Santa Margherita Ligure and Portofino, an international-set favorite, famous for its seafood. There are hotels and pensions. Excellent fishing, swimming. Continuing south (3½ hours by car) you come to Pisa with the Leaning Tower, lovely cathedral and Baptistery; Campo Santo; bridges over the Arno and a citadel.

The Italian Lakes . . . Most famous of the Italian lakes which have the Alps as their background is Lake Como, about an hour away from Milan. Bellagio is the best-known resort among the many villages which line its shores. Launches may be rented to visit spots of interest. At Cernobbio you'll find *Villa d'Este,* a luxurious hotel.

Lake Lugano is partly in Italy, partly in Switzerland. The town of Lugano, which is in Ticino across the Swiss border, has a casinò. Lake Maggiore is another resort area partially Swiss. Here is the town of Stresa, the center of the district, which has good hotels: the *Grand-Hotel et des Iles Borromees, Regina Palace, Bristol* and *Milan.*

You'll find Lake Garda, a few hours from Lake Como, worth seeing. This is the largest of the Lakes. It is here that d'Annunzio lived. Pay special attention to the steep road bordering the lake.

Mountain Resorts . . . Cortina d'Ampezzo, the key resort of the Dolomites, was the site of the Winter Olympic games in 1956. There are excellent ski slopes, a bobsled track, toboggan runs, ski jumps, cableways, ski tows and skating rinks. Instructors are multilingual. There are numerous hotels and pensions. Try the *Palace Cristallo* or the *Miramonti Majestic.* Best ski season is December to March. There's summer skiing too. Other villages nearby are San Martino di Castrozza, Misurina, Ortisei. Cortina is famous also for summer skiing. Cervinia (Matterhorn-Cervin Massive) and Sestriere in the Western Alps offer excellent skiing. Sestriere is also nice during the summer and has a new golf course.

Sicily . . . Way to the south, off the toe of the boot, is Sicily, which Americans have come to know since World War II. Taormina is the beauty spot, a delightful resort with unspoiled charm. You can ski on Mt. Etna and swim in the Mediterranean. There is a de luxe hotel, *San Domenico Palace,* with a casinò. The best season is early spring. Summer is hot, but pleasantly so.

Some of the most magnificent and best preserved Greek temples and ruins are in Sicily, at Agrigento and Syracuse. Other towns of interest are Enna, Palermo, Segesta and Selinunte. Sicily is less than 3 hours by air from Rome.

Sardinia . . . Still unspoiled, Sardinia is a completely new experience. A 2-hour flight from Rome, the island is dramatically beautiful with savage mountains, extinct volcanoes, desert uplands and villages clinging to fearful cliffs overlooking the most glorious blue sea. There are charming resorts around the Gulf of Cagliari and on the gulfs of Alghero and Asinara in the north, all with wonderful underwater fishing. Brand new beachside hotels on the "Emerald Coast" between Olbia and Santa Teresa have rates of $15 to $30, including all meals.

SOURCES OF FURTHER INFORMATION . . . The official Italian tourist office is ENIT (Ente Nazionale Industrie Turistiche) with offices in New York (626 5th Ave.), Chicago, New Orleans, San Francisco, and in Italy at major points of entry. In addition, each province and many of the larger towns have their own tourist office (EPT—Ente Provinciale Turismo). Pan American has offices in Rome, Via Bissolati, 46 (Tel. 476951); and in Milan, Torre Velasca (Tel. 898-815).

LUXEMBOURG

BELG.
Clervaux
GERMANY
Wiltz
Vianden
Diekirch •
Echternach •
LUXEMBOURG
Grevenmacher •
LUXEMBOURG
✳
Mondorf les Bains
FRANCE

WEATHER IN LUXEMBOURG CITY—Lat. 49°37′—Alt. 1,025′

	JAN.	FEB.	MAR.	APR.	MAY	JUNE	JULY	AUG.	SEPT.	OCT.	NOV.	DEC.
Average Temp.	35°	38°	42°	49°	55°	61°	64°	64°	60°	50°	43°	38°
Days of Rain	15	15	15	16	16	17	16	16	16	17	18	16

LOCATION ... Crowded between Belgium and Germany, Luxemburg on the south borders France. The city of Luxembourg is about 175 air miles northeast of Paris, 110 air miles southeast of Brussels.

CHARACTERISTICS ... This tiny duchy is a mixture of Graustark and all the Lehar operettas you ever saw, and offers some of the loveliest scenery in western Europe. This is one of the wealthiest countries, per capita, in the world and is well worth a visit.

POPULATION ... Estimated 322,000, most of whom speak French and German, although there is a local language.

SIZE ... 999 square miles: 62 miles long, 37 miles wide.

CAPITAL ... Luxembourg City, with a population of approximately 72,000, is the seat of the Government and the country's largest city.

GOVERNMENT ... An independent Grand Duchy.

HOW TO GET THERE ... By Pan Am Jet from New York to Brussels, 8¼ hours. Then only a short ride by train or car or connecting air services; from Brussels, electric train service every 2 hours; from Paris, 4 fast trains on the Paris-Germany line.

ACCOMMODATIONS ... In the city of Luxembourg there are some good hotels, including the *Grand Brasseur,* the *Cravat,* the *Alfa* and the *Kons.* Rates about $7 to $9 double with bath.

There aren't many night clubs in the Duchy, but in the city of Luxembourg try the *Plaza, Charlie's* or *Chez Nous.* There are good bars at the *Cravat* and *Brasseur* hotels.

Taxis are plentiful. Laundry is good and quick service is available.

CURRENCY ... Has the same value as the Belgian franc (2¢).

Belgian francs are accepted in the Duchy, but Luxembourg francs are not accepted in Belgium.

CUSTOMS REGULATIONS AND DOCUMENTS NEEDED FOR UNITED STATES CITIZENS ... Same as for Belgium.

FOOD ... is excellent in Luxembourg. Try the *Pavillon Royal, Au Gourmet* or the *Cordial* in the capital. In Gaichel near the Belgian border two outstanding restaurants are *La Gaichel* and *La Bonne Auberge*. The *Hotel Heintz* at Vianden also has an excellent restaurant in an attractive setting. Along the Moselle River the best food is at the *Hotel Simmer* at Ehnen. Special delicacies include Ardennes ham, crawfish, trout and magnificent pastries. The wines are good, too, particularly a native sparkling Moselle. Beer is very good.

WHERE TO GO—SIGHTSEEING ... For centuries Luxembourg City was one of the most indomitable fortresses in Europe. You can still walk through the casemates, blasted out of solid rock, whose 14 miles of corridors once connected 60 outer forts with the citadel, now replaced by a park. Follow the Promenade de la Corniche for an enchanting view of gabled houses in the medieval streets far below. Pont Adolphe, stretching from hill to hill 150 feet above its gorge, is one of the handsomest bridges in Europe. The Cathedral, built in 1618, is lavishly decorated with Renaissance sculptures and heroic tombs. On Saturday mornings there is a Changing of the Guard ceremony in front of the 16th-century Ducal Palace. In the suburb of Hamm, General George Patton and 5,100 American soldiers are buried in a cemetery which Luxembourgers keep lovely with flowers.

The northern section of Luxembourg is wild and rugged. Ruins of fortresses and castles brood among the crags. There are wide rivers in which fish abound, and deep misty ravines. The middle section is pleasant, rolling farmland. To the east is the vineyard country. There are mines and steel mills in the southwest. Wild-boar hunting and deer stalking are very popular in autumn and winter. Hiking is a delight. The rivers are a paradise for canoers, and campsites and cozy hotels line the waterways. There is an 18-hole golf course near the capital.

Trips outside the capital should include: the Moselle Valley where the wine cellars of Ehnen and Remich may be visited, and where, at Grevenmacher, there are lively grape festivals in April and September; Clerveaux in the Ardennes, whose ancient buildings are beautifully illuminated on summer nights; Vianden, a fairytale Ardennes village, still dominated by its mighty castle where ghostly coats of mail still seem to clank softly; Mondorf-les-Bains, the Duchy's smart thermal-springs resort town. Don't miss quaint little Echternach, clustered around the monastery and basilica founded by St. Willibrord in the 8th century. Here, every Whit Tuesday for over 1,000 years, is held one of the world's oddest religious dancing processions. For some of the loveliest scenery in Europe, drive through the Sûre Valley and spend some time in pretty little Ettelbruck and Esch-sur-Sûre.

SOURCES OF FURTHER INFORMATION ... The Luxembourg Consulate General is at 200 East 42 St., New York, N.Y. 10017.

MALLORCA
(BALEARIC IS.)

TO BARCELONA

Soller
Valldemosa
Alcudia
Formentor
Campanet

MINORCA I.

MALLORCA
PALMA
Manacor
Porto-Cristo
Santany

IBIZA I.

(Balearic Islands)
MEDITERRANEAN SEA

FORMENTERA I.

WEATHER IN MALLORCA—Lat. 39°35′—Alt. max.: 4740′, min.: sea level

Temp.	JAN.	FEB.	MAR.	APR.	MAY	JUNE	JULY	AUG.	SEPT.	OCT.	NOV.	DEC.
Low	36°	36°	42°	46°	54°	59°	61°	65°	62°	54°	48°	47°
High	56°	66°	62°	68°	78°	81°	85°	89°	84°	75°	68°	64°
Average	46°	51°	52°	57°	66°	70°	73°	77°	73°	65°	58°	55°
Days of Rain	11	7	10	7	2	9	6	3	8	13	8	10

LOCATION ... Largest of the Balearic group of islands, Mallorca lies 135 miles south of Barcelona in the Mediterranean.

CHARACTERISTICS ... Set in the blue waters of the Mediterranean, Mallorca is a land of eternal spring where medieval architectural splendor rubs shoulders with the modern. Because of its temperate climate, its picturesque scenery and its separation from the mainland, the island has been for many years the haunt of artists, poets and writers. People from many lands make it their permanent home, and tourists visit there in increasing numbers. Its recorded history began with the Romans, who were followed by the Vandals, the Arabs, the Moors and, lastly, by European Christians, who contributed much to its artistic charm.

POPULATION ... Estimated at 350,000.

SIZE ... 1,405 square miles; about 60 miles wide, 50 miles from northern to southern tip.

CAPITAL ... Palma, a city of about 160,000.

GOVERNMENT ... Spanish provincial.

HOW TO GET THERE ... By Pan American Clipper, elapsed time from New York, about 9 hours to Barcelona. Then by connecting plane, 50 minutes from Barcelona to Palma. By boat from Barcelona, overnight. By ship from New York, 8 to 10 days.

ACCOMMODATIONS ... Hotels in Palma are excellent, and many fine, comfortable pensions and inns are found in the interior and all around the lovely coast. American Plan double rates are given here, although European Plan accommodations (without meals) are also available. De luxe hotels in Palma include the *Son Vida* (renovated 13th-century castle) and *Fénix* where rates are from $16; *Bahia Palace* and *Gran Hotel Mediterraneo,* which are from $12.50 and $14 respectively. Class A hostelries include the *Alcina, Almudaina, Araxa, Augusta, Dux, San Carlos* and *Rigel,* where doubles average $10. Excellent guest houses such as the *Casa Martin* charge about $2 with breakfast. Lower rates prevail from about November 1 to March 1.

CIGARETTES ... About the same as in the United States.

CURRENCY ... The standard of currency is the Spanish peseta, 60 to the United States dollar.

CUSTOMS REGULATIONS AND DOCUMENTS REQUIRED FOR UNITED STATES CITIZENS ... See under SPAIN.

RESTAURANTS AND NIGHT CLUBS ... There are lots of good restaurants, and prices are very reasonable—$1.50 and up. Among the best in Palma are *El Patio, Antonio's, Puerto, Triton, L'Hermitage, Club Nautico, Ritz* and *Sa Cova.* There are also numerous sandwich shops and snack bars. Night clubs, many of which have floor shows, include the *Trocadero, Tito's, Jack El Negro, Saint-Tropez.* All the top hotels have orchestras for dancing. Mallorcan folk dancing may often be seen where there is entertainment.

SPORTS ... The Mallorcans enjoy a variety of sports: bullfights, boxing, wrestling, football (soccer) from September to June, the Basque sport of *pelota,* tennis, cycle racing, yachting and trotting. Racing meetings are held in the spring and fall. Swimming may be enjoyed at many of the adjacent beaches or in the municipal or hotel swimming pools.

TRANSPORTATION ... You can ship your car or trailer from Barcelona to Mallorca for from $25 to $65, depending upon weight and the season. Many agencies in Palma rent self-drive cars, and you can also rent motorbikes and bicycles. A railway line on the island connects Palma to a number of resorts, and there is daily bus service to all principal villages. Local taxis are plentiful and cheap.

WHERE TO GO—SIGHTSEEING ...

Palma ... Although much of its attractiveness lies in its ancient architecture and art treasures, Palma has kept up with the times. Smart shops, excellent hotels, good restaurants, and a fine system of roads and transportation enable the tourist to enjoy the comforts of modern living. Palma combines the old and the modern. Its magnificent 13th-century cathedral, erected on the site of a Moslem mosque, rises in golden splendor above the bay. Nearby, in the narrow streets and winding lanes of the older city, palaces of medieval noblemen stand beside the simple homes of modern workers. Convents, quaint patios and ivy-covered churches combine to transport the visitor back in time to the Middle Ages. A visit to Bellver Castle is also recommended; the Municipal Museum is in this 14th-century stronghold overlooking the town and bay. Gordiola's Furnages, a glass factory operating since the 17th century, welcomes visitors to

The road to Formentor and Colo Mer rock formations offers spectacular views in Mallorca.

This view is of some of the hotels which line the waterfront in Palma, Mallorca.

see its ancient installations and glass-making from 10:30 A.M. to 2:30 P.M. on workdays. Northwest of Palma are the Caves of Génova, which are fun to explore. In the village of Génova, is Casa Típica Mulet, which displays a collection of Mallorcan national costumes, intricate embroideries and ceramics.

From July 1 to September 30 there are all-day excursions out of Palma on luxurious sightseeing buses. Tours, including lunch, cost around $4, but you'll want to settle down and stay for weeks in some of these enchanting spots: Formentor, dominated by the elegant *Hotel Formentor,* with superb beaches, golf, tennis, and breathtaking views of mountains and sea (doubles $10-$17, EP); the Royal Carthusian Monastery at Valldemosa, where George Sand nursed Chopin back to health and created a romantic scandal (*Pensión Hospedaje del Artista*); the charming little harbor town of Puerto de Sóller in a valley of orange trees (hotels *Edén* and *Espléndido,* among many on or near the beach); Manacor, with its archaeological museum; Porto Cristo, on the east coast near the gorgeously colored Drach and Hams Caves (pensions *Neptuno* and *Porto Cristo* are on the beach). Other lovely spots on the island are Puerto de Alcudia, with remnants of ancient walls and a Roman theater (*Hotel Club Carabela, Hotel Golf*); delightfully terraced Bañalbufar, where garden plots rise in steps above the sea (hotels *Costa Mar* and *Mar-I-Vent*). Rates in Mallorca's idyllic resorts, other than de luxe hotels, run from $3 to $8 a day, including all meals.

SOURCES OF FURTHER INFORMATION ... Information Office of Subsecretaria de Turismo, Paseo Generalísimo Franco 38-40, Palma de Mallorca. In New York, the Spanish Tourist Office, 589 Madison Avenue.

NETHERLANDS
(HOLLAND)

NORTH SEA

Alkmaar
Volendam
★ AMSTERDAM
The Hague
• Rotterdam
NETHERLANDS
(Holland)

GERMANY

WEATHER IN AMSTERDAM—Lat. N52°20′–Alt. 16′

Temp.	JAN.	FEB.	MAR.	APR.	MAY	JUNE	JULY	AUG.	SEPT.	OCT.	NOV.	DEC.
Low	31°	31°	35°	39°	45°	51°	54°	54°	49°	43°	37°	33°
High	41°	42°	47°	54°	62°	68°	70°	70°	65°	57°	47°	42°
Average	36°	37°	41°	47°	54°	60°	62°	62°	57°	50°	42°	38°
Days of Rain	10	8	11	8	9	9	11	11	10	13	11	13

LOCATION ... Across the North Sea from England, The Netherlands (Holland) is located between Belgium and Germany. Amsterdam is only 100 air miles north of Brussels and 230 air miles northeast of London.

CHARACTERISTICS ... Crisp and clean and hospitable sums up the land of tulips and canals. You'll enjoy seeing all the things you've read about; the windmills, the wooden shoes, the colorful native costumes. And you will enjoy, too, the modern hotels and good restaurants where food is prodigious and inexpensive. The Netherlands is a flat country with plenty of lakes, rivers and canals and a charm and beauty rewarding to the person who spends more than a couple of days seeing the "musts." You'll feel at home with the Dutch, who speak English with determination. The southeastern part of the country is made up of beautiful rolling hills dotted with castles, some of which are now hotels.

POPULATION ... Over 12,000,000.

SIZE ... 13,960 square miles; no town is more than 170 miles from Amsterdam.

CAPITAL ... Amsterdam, with a population of 865,703. The seat of the Government, however, is The Hague; the royal family lives at Soestdijk Palace near Baarn, 28 miles southeast of Amsterdam.

GOVERNMENT ... A constitutional monarchy ruled by a Queen and Parliament of two chambers.

HOW TO GET THERE . . . By Pan Am Jet Clipper, nonstop flights to Amsterdam from New York, 7 hours; 1 hour from London. By boat from New York 7 to 11 days.

ACCOMMODATIONS . . . From June through October you may, if you like, take the special canal boat service from Schiphol Airport to any of half a dozen Amsterdam hotels. Fine hotels here include the new *Amsterdam Hilton, Amstel,* overlooking the river of the same name, *Hotel de l'Europe* with its excellent "Excelsior" restaurant, the *Doelen,* *Grand Hotel Krasnapolsky, Carlton* and *Victoria,* all with good food and excellent bars. Average rates are $9 single, $13 double. The *American,* the *Polen,* the *Schiller* and the *Park* are all very reasonable. Rates average $5.75 single, $15 double per day, excluding a 15% service charge, and, in most hotels, breakfast is included.

ARTS . . . See the Rijksmuseum (State Museum) in Amsterdam with its collection of Rembrandt's paintings, including his famous "Night Watch;" Willet Holthuysen Museum, a 17th-century residence with a collection of porcelain, furniture, and library on the history of art; the Stedelijk Museum (Municipal Museum); Rembrandt House; Royal Palace on the Dam Square, built in 1648 by Jacob van Campen; Allard Pierson Museum, which houses a collection of Egyptian, Greek and Roman antiquities.

BALLET . . . There are two permanent Amsterdam ballet groups considered good. Outstanding foreign troupes visit during the famous midsummer Holland Festival.

BANKS . . . The principal banks in Amsterdam are: the Nederlandsche Bank, which is the National Bank; Algemenebank Nederland and Amsterdam-Rotterdam Bank. Most banks have affiliations with New York banks. Travelers checks cashed in American Express, Thos. Cook & Son, stores and restaurants and some hotels.

CALENDAR OF HOLIDAYS . . . New Year's Day; April 30, Queen's birthday; Good Friday; Easter Monday; Ascension Day; Whitmonday; Christmas; December 26.

CIGARETTES AND TOBACCO . . . Dutch tobacco is reasonably good. American cigarettes are expensive. Bring your own and pay the duty. Dutch cigars are excellent and inexpensive.

CLIMATE . . . Very moderate, mild winters, cool summers, same as in England. April to October is the ideal time to visit.

CLUBS . . . The American Businessman's Club in Amsterdam, Rotary, Jaycees and Lions Club. For women tourists there are private organizations, somewhat like hostess clubs, which help with shopping, meeting Dutch families, etc., all free of charge. Check with the local tourist office about "Get in Touch with the Dutch" program to bring together people with mutual interests.

COMMON COURTESIES AND LOCAL CUSTOMS . . . Not much different from home. Coffee is served in all offices at 11 A.M. The luncheon hour usually lasts from 12:30 to 2 and dinner is early, not later than 7 P.M. There's more handshaking here than in the States, but less than in the more southern countries, such as Belgium and France. Meal servings are large and it's better not to overorder than leave wasted food on your plate. You may have trouble learning even a little Dutch because the people would rather show you their English.

COMMUNICATIONS ... Telephone call to New York costs around $12, a cable about $5. Airmail letters up to 5 grams cost 50 Dutch cents, 20¢ for each additional 5 grams. Airmail postal cards and air-letter forms are 40 Dutch cents. You can buy stamps at a coin machine near street mailboxes and in Amsterdam mail your letter in the back of a streetcar for quick service.

CURRENCY ... The Netherlands florin, or guilder, is divided into 100 cents. It is worth about U.S. 28¢. Fl. 3.62 is worth U.S. $1 selling; Fl. 3.57 when buying.

CUSTOMS REGULATIONS AND DOCUMENTS REQUIRED FOR UNITED STATES CITIZENS ... Passport, but no visa required. Adults may take in duty free 400 cigarettes or 100 cigars or 500 grams (1.1 lbs.) of tobacco; 1 bottle of liquor, 2 of wine, 1 small bottle of perfume. Unlimited currency allowed except only 100 Dfl.

DRUGSTORES ... Only real pharmacies. Some are open 24 hours a day. Not in the drugstores, but everywhere else, are snack bars, lunch counters and cafeterias. American soft drinks are available everywhere and a favorite drink with visitors is *Chocomel*, a cold chocolate-milk drink. The Netherlands is noted for its fine candy. Also try a *Koekje* (cooky).

ELECTRIC CURRENT ... Voltage is 220 in Amsterdam and most other places except in some sections of The Hague, where it is 110. Plugs are the two-prong, round type. The 50 cycles (rather than 60 as in the U.S.) does not affect razors or radios.

FAUNA ... There is not much hunting in Holland—small game only, such as rabbits, foxes, pheasants, pigeons and partridges. Boars and deer live on reservations. Dutch cattle are world famous. There are fine horses, too, and plenty of pigs and sheep. There are bird sanctuaries at the Naarder Meer near Amsterdam, at the Isle of Texel and many other places throughout the country.

FLORA ... Oceans of flowers. In the bulb fields near Haarlem the season is from about April 1 to May 15. Aalsmeer is the center of the flower "industry," with roses, lilacs, etc. A visit to one of the flower auctions is recommended (the one at Aalsmeer is the world's largest) as well as the annual spring open-air exhibition at *De Keukenhof* in Lisse, in the center of the bulb district.

FOOD ... Dutch food is notable. Some typical Dutch dishes are *Rolpens* (minced beef, usually served with fried apples), herring, smoked eels, oysters, *poffertjes* (small fritters). Throughout Holland there are many Indonesian restaurants which you should try. The food is exotic but delicious. Some of the specialties are *nasi goreng, bami goreng, sambal goreng, sate* and *kroepoek*. They resemble some Chinese dishes. And, of course, Dutch cheeses are known the world over as being among the finest.

GAMBLING ... The totalisator is the only legal manner of betting. This pari-mutuel apparatus is in operation at the race courses (main ones are Duindigt, near The Hague, and the Sports Stadium at

Hilversum, near Amsterdam). There is also gambling in Zandvoort in a game called "Saturne."

LANGUAGE... English is understood and spoken everywhere. Dutch, of course, is the official language.

LAUNDRY AND DRY CLEANING... Available everywhere. Service is, on the whole, slower than in hotels in the States. Quality is good, prices are reasonable. Call room service and state your wishes.

LIQUOR... All kinds of liquor are available in the better bars and hotels. A specialty is *jenever* (Dutch gin). The Dutch drink this straight and chilled, just as we do Martinis and Manhattans. Try the famous Holland beer as well as *Advocaat,* an unusual egg drink. Minimum legal age for drinkers is 16.

MEDICAL FACILITIES... No American hospitals, but facilities are excellent and available everywhere. Ask your hotel clerk.

MOTION PICTURES... All types of pictures are shown, and many are American with Dutch subtitles.

MUSIC... Amsterdam Concertgebouw Orchestra is the third largest in the world and holds regular concerts. Most other large cities have municipal orchestras, and Rotterdam has a superb new Concert Hall. Orchestral music, as well as opera, drama and ballet, is featured at the annual Holland Festival held June 15 to July 15 in Amsterdam, The Hague and Scheveningen, the well-known seaside resort.

NIGHT CLUBS AND CABARETS... There are innumerable night clubs in Amsterdam. Some of the gayer and better ones are *Extase, Caramella* and *Blue Note.* Most of these places close promptly at 2 A.M. (3 A.M. on Sunday), but there are fashionable spots operated on a membership basis where you can go after that. There are several large clubs with floor shows, such as *Femina* and the *Casino.*

PHOTOGRAPHY... All sorts of photographic equipment can be purchased in The Netherlands. Developing and printing are good and quite fast for black-and-white; color takes about two weeks. Best store in Amsterdam is Capi, Kalverstraat (main shopping street). Tourists usually shoot all sorts of street scenes, bikes, the canals, Royal Palace at the Dam Square, the harbor, the various museums. If you have an eye for it, "typical" and interesting photos can be made all over town. There are even a couple of windmills left right inside Amsterdam.

RELIGION... Most members of the royal family belong to the Netherlands Reformed Church (Presbyterian), but there are all sects. The two English churches in Amsterdam are Church of England, 42, Groenburgwal, and the English Reformed Church, in the ancient and picturesque Begijnhof, right in the heart of the city.

RESTAURANTS... Dutch cooking is first-class. Fine restaurants serving excellent food can be found everywhere. A Dutch specialty is Indonesian food (*rijsttafel,* rice table). There are many outstanding Indonesian restaurants in the big cities, as well as French, Swiss, Italian and Chinese. In Amsterdam, the dining rooms of the Hotel de l'Europe and Amstel are very popular. Other excellent restaurants are the *Stuyvesant, Dikker & Thijs, Du Chat Qui Pelotte, De Groene Lan-*

teerne, the dining room of the Hotel Victoria, and *The Diamond* in the Hilton. The *Chalet Petite Suisse,* the *Boerderij* (farmhouse) and the *Lido* (overlooking a canal) are also very good. Best Indonesian place in Amsterdam is the *Waroeng Djawa.* The *Beukenhof* in Oegstgeest near Leiden is worth driving out of your way for, and *Saur's* in The Hague is famous for seafood. In all places mentioned, $3 (approximately 12 guilders) will buy you a fine meal.

SHOPS AND STORES ... Shops and stores are open from 9 A.M. to 6 P.M., including Saturday, but many large stores are closed on Monday mornings. Service is friendly and good; most attendants speak English well. Main shopping streets in Amsterdam are Leidsestraat and Kalverstraat. There are also several department stores, including the Bijenkorf (beehive), that have branches in The Hague and Rotterdam. The American tourist will find prices in Holland very reasonable. Typical souvenirs (Delft blue) are sold in a great many shops. For good and original handicrafts: C.O.S.A. in Delft. Many shops and stores accept foreign currency and travelers checks.

SPECTATOR SPORTS ... The most popular sport is soccer. Also tennis, hockey matches, cycling, swimming and sailing. Check locally on exact dates for important sport events such as "Head of the River" and varsity-student rowing matches in the spring; Internal Tulip Rally for automobiles in May; T.T. Motor Races in June; 4-day walking contest in July; international tennis matches in July; Grand Prix car races at Zandvoort; Amsterdam Olympic Day, sailing, horse races, cycle racing and baseball games. Some of these events are at resorts outside Amsterdam. The capital also has an 18-hole golf course.

SPORTS ... The many fine lakes, such as Loosdrecht near Amsterdam and De Kaag near The Hague, offer excellent facilities, and Dutch beaches are sandy and free from stones. Aside from sailing, fishing and swimming, there's sand yachting, horseback riding, golfing, shooting and tennis. Very little polo or squash. Ice skating, of course, in winter—Remember Hans Brinker. There are some fine golf courses in Holland, especially Wassenaar near The Hague, Hilversum, De Pan near Utrecht and Kennemer in Zandvoort.

THEATERS ... Practically everything is in Dutch, including current Broadway hits, with evening performances around 8 P.M. and matinees, including Sundays. No formal dress necessary. Cost per seat averages $1.50. Ask your hotel clerk about current performances.

TIME ... Noon in Amsterdam is 6 A.M. in New York.

TIPPING ... Hotel porters get 25 Dutch cents per bag. Railway station porters get 50 Dutch cents for the first bag, 30 cents a bag for two or more. Taxi drivers are tipped 10%. If service is not included in restaurant bill, tip 15%. Theater ushers are tipped a minimum of 0.25. Cloakroom and washroom attendants are tipped 15 Dutch cents. Hotels add 15% to your bill, which covers everything but special services.

TRANSPORTATION ... Because of the flat country, bicycles are used by everyone, from the Queen down, and often dominate the road. Trains between Amsterdam, The Hague and Rotterdam run every 30 minutes; every 10 minutes during rush hours. Taxis are plentiful. Rates increase between 1 and 6 A.M. The trolleys are fun and cheap. You can hire a car readily from any one of several good agencies. Hertz Rent-a-Car agents in the Hilton hotels in Amsterdam and Rotterdam. You buy "benzine" by the liter, and it comes to 54¢ a gallon.

WATER . . . Excellent everywhere, but bottled water is available.

WHAT TO BUY . . . Silverware, china, pewter, chocolates and a Dutch specialty, *hopjes* (a coffee candy), leatherwear, diamonds, cigars, cheese, gin or liquors. Clothes are also cheap. Tourist favorites are old etchings, maps, prints and old Delft tiles, which cost 3.50 to 10 guilders each (about $1 to $2.50). Don't buy flower bulbs to take home, without a certificate of health. The growers or retailers will send them on to you. Fresh flowers can also be airmailed to the States. Feather hats are the big buy in Volendam. For departing tourists, there is a tax-free shop at Schiphol Airport.

WHAT TO WEAR . . . Same type of clothing you would wear in the corresponding season at home. In the summer be sure to have a raincoat and lightweight topcoat for cool evenings.

WHERE TO GO—SIGHTSEEING . . .

Amsterdam . . . Naturally you'll want to take a trip to the wonderfully colorful tulip fields. Holland has a million acres planted with tulip bulbs which are famous throughout the world. They are one of the most beautiful sights you can imagine. Since canals are the main thoroughfares in Holland, whatever you do don't miss taking a trip through Amsterdam in one of the glass-topped motor launches. The boats go through all the important canals as well as the smaller ones. Amsterdam is a city combining the old with the new. Many of the housing projects and public buildings are magnificent examples of modern architecture. You'll find it especially interesting to visit some of the diamond-cutting factories such as Asscher's and the A. van Moppes and Zoon plant where there are daily tours during the summer. (Amsterdam is the world's headquarters for diamond cutting.) Other places of interest to the tourist are the Botanical Gardens, the Artis Zoological Gardens, and the almshouses, which are all pretty little houses surrounded by lovely gardens. You should see the New Church, which contains the tombs of Admirals de Ruyter, Van Galen, Van Kinsbergen and Van Speyk, and also see the Old Church, built in 1300, with sculptures by A. Quellijn. Absolute musts, of course, are the Rijksmuseum of classic art, the Stedelijk Museum of modern art, and Rembrandt's home, where many of his etchings and sketches are kept. The Royal Tropical Institute is unique for its excellent displays of all facets of life collected in Africa, South America and the Pacific islands.

Side Trips . . . While in Amsterdam you can make excursions to picturesque cities of Spakenburg and Bunschoten, popular with tourists. Here, perhaps more than any place in Holland, you will see the residents dressed in traditional Holland costumes. Also take a trip to Alkmaar on a Friday, or to Gouda on a Thursday to see the world-famous cheese markets.

Schiphol, Amsterdam's great airport, is just a few miles outside of the city. It was opened in 1920 and completely destroyed during the war; now rebuilt, it is 13 feet below sea level. The village of Aalsmeer near Schiphol consists of little green islands completely covered with flowers, which are gathered in the morning and are taken to the auction. Later, most of the flowers are dispatched by air to cities in and beyond Europe. Leiden, nearby, is the birthplace of Rembrandt and was the home of the Pilgrim Fathers for 11 years before they left for America in 1620. John Robinson, their spiritual leader, is buried in the baptistery of St. Peter's Church here. Only a few miles east of Amsterdam is an unusual stretch of sandy country with delightful woods and two old fortress towns, as well as some new and modern villages. Het Gooi, within 20 minutes of the city, is known for its architecture and natural beauty. The Town Hall of Hilversum, designed by the famous Dutch architect W. Dudok, is outstanding, and there is a wonderful 18-hole golf course. Artists will certainly want to go to Laren to see the permanent exhibition of works of modern Dutch artists. While there, see the Muiderslot, a medieval castle, in the same district. Several very fine hotels are the *Grand Hotel Gooiland* at Hilversum, the *Hamdorff* at Laren and the *Kasteel de Hooge Vuursche* at Baarn, in the vicinity of the Royal Palace. Further east, near Arnhem, in the center of the 15,000-acre national park, Hooge Veluwe, stands the Kröller Muller Museum, which contains the greatest collection of Van Gogh paintings found anywhere. See, too, Arnhem's charming Open-Air Museum of old Dutch houses, buildings and costumes of long ago.

The Hague ... Whereas Amsterdam is the capital, The Hague is the seat of the Government and has been since 1247, when Count Willem II built his castle there near the sea. Various Government departments are located there, including all foreign embassies. As in Amsterdam, there are many interesting buildings both old and new to be seen. Among the first places on your list should be the Knight's Hall, new addition to the Palace (built in 1280), where, the third Tuesday in September, the Queen opens the combined Chambers of Parliament in a colorful and solemn session; the Mauritshuis Museum houses a collection of famous Dutch paintings, among them 18 by Rembrandt. The Mauritshuis is the old palace of Prince Johan Maurits van Nassau, once Governor of the Dutch possessions in Brazil. The Palace is open daily to visitors. Modern art will be found in the Gemeente Museum (municipal museum).

There are excellent hotels and restaurants in The Hague. Among the better hotels are the *Des Indes, Wittebrug, Central* and *Terminus*. The restaurants in The Hague are superb. *Menangkabau Huis* is one of the best-known Javanese rice-table restaurants. Also try *De Drie Vensters* and *Chalet Suisse*. The *Beukenhof* in Oegstgeest, near The Hague, is one of the most famous restaurants in Holland, and *Saur* is wonderful for seafood. You can go to the *Royal* for French cuisine and go to the *Jachthuis* for game. The *Old Dutch Restaurant* in The Hague has excellent food and is inexpensive. While there you will want to attend a concert by the famous *Residentie Orchestra* with outstanding guest conductors and artists.

Within 15 minutes by trolley you can get to Scheveningen, which is a wonderful seaside resort. This is divided into two parts, one the old fishing village where the women still wear the traditional costumes and wooden shoes, and the other a fashionable resort, with many good hotels such as the *Kurhaus* (open all year) and all bathing facilities. It has a wonderful wide beach. For wonderful Indonesian food, dine at the *Bali Restaurant*. You will have plenty of activity to choose from here; there are tennis courts, riding schools and a famous racetrack at Duindigt. North of The Hague is the tree-shaded village of Wassenaar (there's a fine 18-hole golf course here), and to the south, one of the best-known horticultural regions, which extends as far back as the Hook of Holland and Rotterdam. The glass hothouses here are famous for their grapes, tomatoes, peaches and flowers.

Rotterdam . . . Zadkine's *Monument to a Destroyed City* is nearly the only visible reminder of the World War II demolition of Rotterdam, which is on its way to becoming Europe's most modern and dynamic city. It is a veritable open-air museum of modern architecture.

The harbor of Rotterdam is actually Europe's largest seaport, and a sightseeing tour by luxury launch of the Spido Co. (departure from Willemsplein) showing the dry docks, shipyards, etc., is highly recommended. Also well worth seeing is *The Maastunnel*, first Dutch river tunnel, 7/10 of a mile long, 45 feet under low water level, which connects the city of Rotterdam with the harbor district.

In addition to the modern center of Rotterdam with its Lijnbaan pedestrian mall and other excellent shopping facilities and entertainment, there are various museums and galleries containing unique art treasures and modern sculpture, among which is the *Boymans Museum* with its large collection of old and modern painting from Hieronymus Bosch to Vincent van Gogh. See the new Concert Hall.

Hotels are the *Rotterdam Hilton, Rijn Hotel, Atlanta Hotel, Park Hotel* and the unique *Delta Hotel* situated in Vlaardingen (6 miles from Rotterdam) overlooking the River Maas connecting Rotterdam with the North Sea (Hook of Holland). Good places to dine include *Coq d'Or, Erasmus, Old Dutch* and *Witte Paard*. The restaurant on top of the 383-foot Euromast presents a view of 60 miles.

SOURCES OF FURTHER INFORMATION . . . The Tourist Information Office in Amsterdam is at 5 Rokin; in The Hague at 38 Parkstraat and Buitenhof (Kiosk). These and others in the larger cities have a variety of maps, folders and information in English, but make reservations only in case of emergency. Local travel agencies arrange sightseeing tours. Pan American's office is in the Hirsch Building, Leidseplein, Amsterdam C., opposite the American Hotel (Tel. 234760); Schiphol Airport (Tel. 722989). The U.S. Consulate General office (Tel. 790321) is at Museumplein, Amsterdam. In The Hague the USIS (Tel. 112015) is at Lange Voorhout, the United States Embassy (Tel. 184140) at Lange Voorhout. In New York, the Netherlands National Tourist office is at 605 Fifth Avenue.

NORWAY

NORTH CAPE

ARCTIC CIRCLE FIN. U.S.S.R.

SW.

NORWAY

Romsdalfjord
Geirangerfjord   Trondheim
Sognefjord   Lillehammer
       Bergen
rdangerfjord OSLO ✶

WEATHER IN OSLO—Lat. N59°55'—Alt. 40'

Temp.	JAN.	FEB.	MAR.	APR.	MAY	JUNE	JULY	AUG.	SEPT.	OCT.	NOV.	DEC.
Low	21°	21°	26°	34°	43°	50°	56°	53°	46°	37°	30°	24°
High	28°	30°	38°	48°	59°	65°	71°	66°	59°	46°	36°	29°
Average	25°	26°	32°	41°	51°	58°	64°	60°	53°	42°	33°	27°
Days of Rain	12	12	13	10	11	10	12	15	11	12	12	15

LOCATION ... Norway extends along the western part of the Scandinavian peninsula from a latitude the same as that of Scotland to well above the Arctic Circle. Oslo is the same distance by air from London as Chicago is from New York.

CHARACTERISTICS ... Norway is a long, rangy country with vast distances. The people have a zest for life that will exhaust the average American. It is a land of fjords, mountains, valleys and plains. Up north it has the Midnight Sun, with almost constant daylight from April to mid-September. The scenery is magnificent, the people cordial, friendly and scrupulously honest. It is a rugged country, but the cities are cosmopolitan. Hotels are very good, and many new ones have been built since the war in cities as well as in the rural districts.

POPULATION ... Estimated 3,654,000.

SIZE ... 125,181 square miles, the size of New Mexico, but extends the distance from New York to San Juan.

CAPITAL ... Oslo, a city of 475,562.

GOVERNMENT ... A constitutional and thoroughly democratic monarchy with a King and a parliament known as the Storting.

HOW TO GET THERE ... Through-plane service by Pan Am Jet Clipper to Oslo. 7¼ hours from New York (or connect from Jet Clippers to Copenhagen). By ship, 7 days to Bergen, 8 days to Oslo.

ACCOMMODATIONS ... Luxury hotels in Oslo are the *Bristol,* the *Continental* and the *Grand.* Rates about $10 single, $18 double for room with bath. First class hotels include the *Ambassadeur, Carlton,* the *KNA* (Royal Norwegian Automobile Club), the *Norum,* the large new *Viking,* and the *Holmenkollen,* which is on the famous hill overlooking the city. Rates at these hotels average $7 single, $11 double. There is usually an extra charge of Kr. 2 if you stay only 1 night. There are also several "off-season" rate reductions during the year. Advance reservations are recommended, especially in summer. The Mission hotels (*Misjonshotell*) and student hotel (*Studentöyen Hotell*) are recommended if you're on a limited budget.

ARTS ... Oslo has a large variety of museums and galleries. The Viking Ship Museum is unique. The Ski Museum has exhibits tracing 2,500 years in the history of skiing. The Open Air Folk Museum is a restored Norwegian village. The Vigeland Museum in Frogner Park contains the work of Norway's greatest sculptor. The new Munch Museum, opened in 1963, has the world's best collection of the expressionistic artist's paintings and prints. The Historical Museum is devoted to exhibits of Norwegian culture. The Museum of the Polar Ship *Fram* has interesting exhibits concerning this ship's arctic expeditions. The *Kon-Tiki* raft is also on view. Also of interest are the National Gallery, the Arts and Crafts Museum, the Theater Museum and the beautifully decorated new City Hall. Most museums open at noon.

BANKS ... Den Norske Creditbank, Christiana Bank og Kreditkasse, Bergens Privatbank. Most hotels, large restaurants and stores and the American Express Company will also cash travelers checks.

CALENDAR OF HOLIDAYS ... Stores and museums are closed on: Jan. 1, May 1, May 17 (Constitution Day), Whitsun, Christmas Day, Boxing Day, Maundy Thursday, Good Friday, and Easter Monday.

CIGARETTES, CIGARS AND TOBACCO ... Take in all you are allowed; American cigarettes cost over $1 a pack. However, local brands are good.

CLIMATE ... From April to September the nights are very short, and around midsummer you can read a newspaper out of doors at midnight. Above the Arctic Circle, the sun shines 24 hours a day. Thanks to the Gulf Stream, the climate in Norway is temperate. For winter sports, January through April are ideal.

CLUBS ... Lions and Rotary Clubs in most large centers.

COMMON COURTESIES AND LOCAL CUSTOMS ... Eiderdowns take the place of top sheets even in the hotels, although you can get blankets and top sheet at some. Dress is informal. At the best resort hotels dinner jackets are expected only in winter season.

COMMUNICATIONS ... A phone call to the States costs, per minute, Kr. 21.40 at night and Kr. 28.60 in the daytime. A 10-word cablegram costs Kr. 21 to New York, Kr. 26 elsewhere in the U.S. Postage for a 5-gram airmail letter to the U.S. is Kr. 1.25; 90 øre for an airletter. Local phone calls are 50 øre.

CURRENCY ... There are 100 øre in a krone, which is valued at 14¢. There are Kr. 7.15 to U.S. $1.

CUSTOMS REGULATIONS AND DOCUMENTS REQUIRED FOR UNITED STATES CITIZENS ... Unlimited dollars, 2 bottles of liquor or 2 of wine, 400 cigarettes or 80 cigars or 500 grams of tobacco are allowed in duty free. Also no more than 1,000 kroner in, no larger than 100-kroner denominations. You need a passport, no visa.

DRUGSTORES . . . Norwegian drugstores carry many American products or their European equivalents.

ELECTRIC CURRENT . . . The voltage in Norway is 220 A.C., except for Stavanger, with 130/220 A.C.

FAUNA . . . Norwegian waters abound with many species of fish. Both salt-water and fresh-water fishing are excellent. Big-game animals include bear, moose and reindeer. Many small wild animals are found in Norwegian forests, including wolf, fox, lynx, otter and beaver. There are also game birds, grouse being the most abundant.

FLORA . . . The beautiful forests of Norway are mainly spruce, fir and pine trees. Birch trees are everywhere. The vegetation of the valleys of southern Norway is very beautiful. Wild berries are plentiful and flowers are profuse in the gorgeous spring season.

FOOD . . . Breakfast is a large meal with a cold buffet. Fish is served in great variety. Dinner is apt to be at 4:30, followed by tea and sandwiches at 9 P.M. Tourists don't have to eat at these hours, however. Good à la carte meals are available at all times.

LANGUAGE . . . English is spoken everywhere.

LAUNDRY AND DRY CLEANING . . . There are good cleaning and laundry services in all principal towns. Inquire at your hotel.

LIQUOR . . . Beer, gin and aquavit are very popular. The liquor stores (*Vinmonopolet*) carry all varieties of wine and liquor. City bars are open from 3-11:30 P.M.; liquor is served in country hotels from 1-11:30 P.M. Minimum legal age for drinkers is 21.

MEDICAL FACILITIES . . . Modern hospitals and excellent doctors are available. Ski resorts have well-equipped first-aid centers.

MOTION PICTURES . . . The latest American and English pictures are shown with Norwegian subtitles. Be on time for performances, because late-comers may not remain at the end of a program to catch the beginning. Seats may be reserved.

MUSIC . . . The Oslo Symphony Orchestra is outstanding. The beautiful Norwegian folk music, a source of inspiration to Edvard Grieg and other composers, is an important part of the life of the people. The International Festival of Music is in Bergen from late May to early June.

NIGHT CLUBS AND CABARETS . . . In Oslo *Telle Cabaret* has fine entertainment and serves all sorts of drinks. *Telle Grill* is small, exclusive and smart. The *Rainbow Room* is the biggest night club in Oslo. The Hotel Bristol has the formal *Moorish Hall*.

PHOTOGRAPHY . . . Camera equipment, black-and-white and color, still and movie film are available at reasonable prices, and developing services are good.

RELIGION . . . Norway is a Lutheran country but there are synagogues and churches of other sects.

RESTAURANTS . . . In Oslo you will find many fine places to dine and dance. The *Frognerseter* Restaurant up in the Holmenkollen Hills overlooking Oslo and the harbor has a fine dining room. The *Mirror Room* at the Grand Hotel is very attractive and serves good food. The *Bistro* in the Norum Hotel is also tops. *La Belle Sole* is outstanding. *Blom* is a favorite of the artistic set, and journalists and theater enthusiasts throng the *Theater Café* in the Continental Hotel. The *Hotel Bristol Grill* serves excellent food, and the *Moorish Hall* in the Bristol is very popular with the younger set. The *Queen* (Royal Norwegian Yacht Club), and the *King* (Oslo Rowing Club); both have large restaurants with dance floors (May through September). *Fregatten* is a delightful seafood restaurant. *Frascati* is famed for its "Saga Lunch." There are also two *Wimpy's*, with genuine American-style short-order counters.

SHOPS AND STORES ... Steen and Strom in Oslo is Norway's biggest department store. Maja Jensen is good for tinware, ceramics and toys; David Andersen and Tostrup for silver. Gresvig for sporting goods; Heimen for wood carvings and native craft products; Hjordis Egelund for souvenirs; Husfliden (Association of Home Arts and Crafts) for tapestries, sweaters and all sorts of woolens. A must is William Schmidt on Karl Johans Street. L. Galligani also is excellent for crystal and other gift items. See Forum's permanent exhibition of arts, crafts and industrial designs, and the huge new Norwegian Design Center of home furnishings.

SPECTATOR SPORTS ... Championship ski competitions are the greatest spectator attraction during the winter, and soccer during the summer. Skating races also draw crowds. The Holmenkollen ski competition near Oslo is the first week of March.

SPORTS ... Most Norwegians who can walk can ski, and Norway is one of the ski capitals of the world. Ski-touring is very popular. Huts and lodges dot the routes of cross-country runs. Norway is full of all kinds of slopes and jumps, lifts, instructors and cheerful ski lodges. Renting your skis is wiser than bringing them. Norwegian skis are the best in the world and rented ones insured against damage. Tobogganing and skating are also very popular.

The fishing in Norway is excellent too. You fish for trout and pike in almost any of the streams or lakes. Salmon fishing is magnificent, but rivers are restricted. However, several Oslo travel agencies offer fully inclusive salmon-fishing vacations; folders on these are available from the Norwegian National Travel Office in New York. Sailing and swimming also rank high. The Oslo Golf Club's course at Bogstad is ideal. There are also golf courses in Bergen, Stavanger and Trondheim. Tourists are welcome.

Norwegian alps are a mountain-climber's delight. Cyclists and hikers will find pleasant rolling countryside beneath the snow-capped peaks. Winter ski lodges become hostels for hikers and climbers in the summer months. The hunting is wonderful. Deer and moose abound. A license is inexpensive. Rabbit, fox, hare and game birds are abundant. All in all, Norway is a year-round sportsman's paradise.

THEATERS ... In Oslo the National Theater stages classical drama, modern literary plays and light comedy. The *New Theater* devotes itself to light plays. *Chat Noir* is the oldest music hall with revues. The new English Theatre Company of Norway, opened in 1965, features modern dramas in English the year round.

TIME... Noon in Oslo is 6 A.M. EST in New York.

TIPPING... Hotels add a 10-15% service charge to your bill, and no other tips are expected, except 50 øre per day to the head porter. Round off restaurant check (which has 12½% service charge) to the nearest krone; ditto for taxi drivers. Tip washroom attendants and hat-check girls 50 øre. Luggage porters get Kr. 1 for the first bag, 50 øre for each additional bag.

TOURIST TAXES... Air departure tax Kr. 15 ($2.10).

TRANSPORTATION... City buses are easy to use, and, of course, there are taxis. Bus fare from airport to Oslo is Kr. 3.50. Rates for drive-yourself cars are reasonable, but there are also countless well-organized tours around cities and around the country by boat, bus, train and plane.

WATER... Excellent.

WHAT TO BUY... Norwegian enamelware and silver are your best buys. Native craft products are beautiful. They include textiles, glassware, embroideries, brassware and leather goods. Furs are marvelous. Prices are much lower than at home, but our duty is high.

WHAT TO WEAR... Warm heavy clothing is a must in the winter. Black suits and dresses are formal enough for Oslo night life. Raincoats will come in handy. Bring medium-weight clothes for summer.

WHERE TO GO—SIGHTSEEING...

Oslo... The 900-year-old city of Oslo is full of fascinating things to see. The town is surrounded by wooded hills and distant snow-capped peaks. You'll want to see the Changing of the Guard at the Royal Palace, the beautiful buildings of the University of Oslo, the National Theater with its statues of Bjornson and Ibsen, and the Nobel Institute where the Nobel prizes are awarded. Stroll through beautiful Karl Johans Gate Park. There are band concerts and outdoor cafés here. The medieval castle, Akershus, built by Haakon V, is a must. A trip up the Holmenkollen behind the city offers a wonderful view. There's the Holmenkollen Recreation Center here too. Plan to see the Vigeland Sculpture Park, the *Kon-Tiki* raft, the Open Air Museum and the Viking Ships Museum and the other museums mentioned under ARTS. There are also regular sightseeing tours by boat down the Oslo Fjord. They start from the City Hall.

Bergen... is Norway's second largest city (7½ hours by train from Oslo or 1¼ hours by air). It has wonderful examples of medieval, Renaissance and strikingly modern architecture. A visit to the harbor will give you a good idea of native life. Just wandering around the medieval part of the city will be like going back over 500 years in local history. See the Maria Church, built in the 12th century. The Hanseatic Museum gives an excellent idea of the culture of old Norway. There is a fine art gallery and ethnological collection in the

Bergen University, another interesting sight. Other things to see include the harbor and market places, the home of Edvard Grieg, and the old Fantoft stave church. Leading hotels include the *Bristol*, the new *Norge* and the *Orion*. Rates from $7 single. Hydrofoil boat trips may be made to the beautiful fjords around Bergen. It's also the starting point for coastal express steamers to the Land of the Midnight Sun.

Stavanger ... Norway's fourth largest city is the new gateway to the Norwegian fjords (11 hours by train or 1 hour by air from Oslo). The hotel facilities here are excellent. The *Alstor Hotel, KNA, Atlantic Hotel*, the *Hotel Victoria* and the *Ocean Hotel* all have fine accommodations. In the vicinity of Stavanger you have the *Strand, Sola Hotel* and the *Viste Hotel*, well-known sea resorts.

Trondheim ... is the principal city in north-central Norway (8 hours by train from Oslo, 1½ hours by air). There is a fabulously lovely cathedral, begun in the 11th century and being restored today. Norway's great Technical College is here. The River Nid runs through the city and can be crossed by four graceful bridges. Sailing, fishing and skiing are all wonderful near Trondheim. Cozy and cheerful ski lodges offer simple accommodations. The *Britannia, Astoria, Prinsen* and *Bristol* are the good hotels in the town itself.

Lillehammer ... This charming town is one of the great skiing centers of Norway (4 hours by train from Oslo). The *Victoria* and *Kronen* are the best hotels in town, but excellent summer and winter resort accommodations are plentiful.

The Fjords ... Norway's fjords in the western part of the country are up to 100 miles long and as deep as 4/5 of a mile. The largest are shown on the map. The most comfortable way to see the fjords is on one of the coastal steamers, or you can go by car or bus, and take local ferries to see the magnificent fjord scenery. Deluxe all-inclusive coach tours, lasting 3 or 6 days, depart from Bergen and Oslo and include the famous Hardanger Fjord in their itineraries. In the early summer there is perpetual sunlight, so if you are touring the fjords at this time it is almost impossible to tear yourself away from the scenery to sleep.

North Norway ... About one-third of Norway lies north of the Arctic Circle, but even this part of the country is now easily accessible to visitors with little time if they plan well and book in advance. There are special cruises out of Bergen and round trips of 7 or 11 days by the regular coastal express steamers. Other prearranged tours are available from Oslo which combine air and sea transportation. The North Cape Certificate, which is given to those who have visited the North Cape area, northernmost point in Europe, is a rare and prized document. For the truly adventuresome, polar bear hunting safaris sail from Tromsø to Spitzbergen in June, July and August. Your own travel agent can make reservations.

SOURCES OF FURTHER INFORMATION ... Oslo Information Office, Rosenkrantzgt 28. Pan American's office at Kronprinsesse Marthasplass 1 (Tel. 410280). Norwegian National Travel Office, 505 Fifth Avenue, New York, N.Y. 10017.

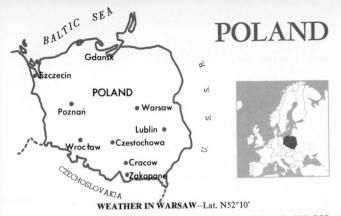

POLAND

WEATHER IN WARSAW—Lat. N52°10′

	JAN.	FEB.	MAR.	APR.	MAY	JUNE	JULY	AUG.	SEPT.	OCT.	NOV.	DEC.
Average Temp.	26°	28°	35°	46°	63°	66°	66°	64°	57°	48°	36°	29°
Days of Rain	15	15	14	14	13	13	15	13	11	12	14	15

LOCATION . . . Poland lies in central Europe.

CHARACTERISTICS . . . Poland is a country of beautiful beaches, lakes and forests, ski areas and health resorts. The climate is moderate. The Polish people are known for their hospitality, and prices are low. Best time to visit Poland is from May to September. Visitors from outside the country travel by arrangement with *Orbis,* the Polish government travel organization.

POPULATION . . . About 31,500,000.

SIZE . . . 120,359 square miles, about the size of New Mexico.

CAPITAL . . . Warsaw, a city of 1,136,000 population.

GOVERNMENT . . . Polish People's Republic.

HOW TO GET THERE . . . By Pan American Clipper to London (6½ hours), Paris, Berlin, Prague, Copenhagen or Vienna, then by Polish airlines LOT to Warsaw and all tourist centers.

ACCOMMODATIONS . . . Warsaw hotels operated by *Orbis* are the *Grand, Bristol,* and *Europejski.* Good municipal hotels are the *Warszawa, MDM* and *Polonia.* Singles $4-$7, doubles $7-$8.50, European Plan.

ARTS . . . Most outstanding are the National Museums in Warsaw, Poznań and in Cracow, where there is also the famous collection in King's Castle Wawel. Ballet and musical life in Warsaw centers around the National Philharmonic Hall. The theater is also highly regarded here. The *National Theater* and *Polish Theater,* among the many in Warsaw, and *Slowacki's* in Cracow are outstanding.

CURRENCY . . . The zloty is valued at about 24 to U.S. $1. When tourists exchange at least $20, premium coupons worth 20 zlotys (80¢)

are given for every 30 zlotys ($1.20) exchanged—a ⅔ currency bonus.

CUSTOMS REGULATIONS AND DOCUMENTS REQUIRED FOR UNITED STATES CITIZENS ... Passport and Polish visa, smallpox vaccination certificate, *Orbis* tourist vouchers to cover room and meal cost. American cigarettes are available, but 400 may be brought in; one bottle spirits, no Polish banknotes allowed in. On departure, no more currency can go out than was brought in.

ELECTRIC CURRENT ... Mostly 220 volts, A.C. 50 cycle.

LANGUAGE ... Your hotel clerk and *Orbis* guide will have a good working knowledge of English.

RESTAURANTS ... Among the best in Warsaw are the *Kameralna,* the *Jewish Restaurant, Shanghai* and those in the hotels. Vodka is the most popular drink although brandies and wines are available. Principal night clubs in Warsaw are *Kongresowa, Kameralna, Krokodyl,* and those in the Europejski, Bristol and Grand Hotels. Most clubs have music, are open until 3 A.M. The coffeehouse (*kawiarnia*) is the hub of Warsaw social life. Visit quaint old wineshops, too.

WHERE TO GO—SIGHTSEEING ...

Warsaw area ... There is a 3-hour city tour for $2.60, and *Orbis* will arrange all other tours. Car rental is available with or without chauffeur. You may bring your own car but gasoline is quite expensive. Principal sights, many rebuilt from the war's destruction are: the Old City, Nowy Swiat Street, royal residences in Lazienki and Wilanów. Near Warsaw are Zelazowa Wola (birthplace of Chopin), Nieborów Palace, Plock (oldest town), and Warka, birthplace of Pulaski, hero of the American Revolution. Newer construction includes the Muranów living quarters, modern throughways and the Culture and Science Palace. Go to "Cepelia" shops for delightful handicrafts.

Cracow area ... One of the most beautiful medieval towns in Europe, Cracow is 200 miles south of Warsaw. Here one can see the Royal Castle Wawel, St. Mary's Church (Gothic) with the famous Veit Stoss wooden altar, the old Market; and buy beautiful Polish handicrafts. Near Wieliczka are the huge salt mines and interesting Bledów Desert. Cracow's *Francuski* hotel offers good cuisine and service. Other places of interest include Czestochowa, known for its monastery in Jasna Góra, center of pilgrimages; Zakopane in the Tatry mountains, winter sports center, and summer resorts along the Dunajec River. In the north of Poland is an area of magnificent woods and lakes for hunting, fishing and relaxing, and Poznań, the city of international expositions. Just south of the Bay of Danzig is Malbork Castle, 14th century stronghold of the Order of Teutonic Knights and the best-preserved medieval structure in Central Europe.

SOURCES OF FURTHER INFORMATION ... The Polish Travel Office *Orbis,* 16 Bracka Street, Warsaw, also has correspondents in the United States. The Committee for Tourism is at Litewska Street 8, Warsaw. The consular section, Polish Embassy, is at 2224 Wyoming Ave. N.W., Washington, D.C. 20008. The Pan Am office is in the Bristol Hotel, Warsaw (Tel. 261-989 and 263-241, ext. 109).

PORTUGAL

Oporto
ATLANTIC
OCEAN
DOURO VALLEY
• Coimbra
PORTUGAL
Sintra • Fatima SPAIN
Estoril ★ LISBON
Setubal
Evara
Praia da Rocha

WEATHER IN LISBON—Lat. N38°43′—Alt. 285′

Temp.	JAN.	FEB.	MAR.	APR.	MAY	JUNE	JULY	AUG.	SEPT.	OCT.	NOV.	DEC.
Low	46°	47°	51°	54°	58°	63°	65°	67°	64°	58°	53°	47°
High	54°	56°	59°	63°	66°	77°	75°	76°	73°	68°	61°	58°
Average	50°	52°	55°	59°	62°	70°	70°	72°	69°	63°	57°	53°
Days of Rain	13	12	14	12	9	5	2	2	6	11	13	14

LOCATION ... Portugal lies between Spain and the Atlantic Ocean, a small rectangle in the southwest corner of the Iberian Peninsula. Lisbon, the capital, is 895 air miles from Paris and 319 air miles from Madrid. Among other places, the Azores, about 800 miles to the west, and Madeira Islands are an insular part of Portugal.

CHARACTERISTICS ... Lisbon is one of the pleasantest cities in Europe. Its hotels are fine and its restaurants famous. Portugal is like a picture post card. The climate is ideal, the drives and the scenery utterly beautiful. For something different, plan a trip to Portugal, where Americans are very welcome and there are not too many of them. Discover this country for yourself.

POPULATION ... Estimated 8,889,392, the population slightly exceeds that of New York City and Baltimore combined.

SIZE ... 380 miles long and 140 miles wide.

CAPITAL ... Lisbon, with an estimated population of 802,230.

GOVERNMENT ... A unitary and corporative Republic, the Portuguese constitution having been approved by plebiscite in March 1933. President of the Republic elected through college suffrage.

HOW TO GET THERE ... By Pan Am Jet Clipper only 6¼ hours (nonstop) from New York to Lisbon, 10¼ hours from Miami, 2 hours from Paris, 1 hour from Madrid. By ship, from 6 to 9 days.

ACCOMMODATIONS ... Lisbon has very good hotels to fit every taste and budget. The most luxurious hostelry in town is the magnificent new *Ritz* ($9.80 and up including breakfast). First class are the *Imperio* ($6.30), *Embaixador* ($5.75), *Avenida Palace* ($4.90), *Tivoli* ($4.90), *Florida* ($5.70), *Eduardo VII* ($4.75), *Condestavel* ($4.75), *Mundial* ($4.40), and *Fenix* ($6.30). These are minimum single rates, European Plan, plus 10% service charge and 3% tax. These are only a few of Lisbon's many hotels. Accommodations can be had for as low as $4.40 a day with all meals in the small hotels seldom frequented by tourists, but full of local atmosphere. Throughout the country are a number of Government-owned *pousadas*, or guest houses, and privately owned estalagens (inns) which are comfortable, truly-charming, and under $5 a day for room and meals.

ARTS ... There are Roman, Visigothic, Moorish, Romanesque, Gothic, Renaissance, baroque, neoclassic, and some modern buildings in Portugal. A unique Portuguese style, the *Manuelino* (15th-16th centuries), is exuberantly decorated with nautical and maritime motifs glorifying Portugal's rich Age of Discoveries. The *Mosteiro dos Jeronimos* and *Torre de Belem* in Lisbon are representative of this art.

There is an important collection of 15th- and 16th-century Portuguese paintings in Lisbon's Ancient Art Museum. See, too, the beautiful examples of Spanish, Flemish, Italian, German, and other painters, and a collection of goldsmiths' art, ceramics and tapestry. The Contemporary Art Museum in Lisbon, the Soares does Reis Museum in Oporto, the Machado de Castro Museum in Coimbra and the Grão Vasco Museum in Viseu display the most characteristic Portuguese paintings and sculptures of the 19th and 20th centuries. The Royal Coaches Museum in Lisbon, Marine Museum and the Popular Art Museum are truly remarkable. Museums are closed Mondays.

BALLET ... Portugal's national ballet group, *Verde Gaio*, features folk themes. Foreign ballets during the winter season.

BANKS ... American Express has offices in Lisbon, Estoril and Oporto. The Bank of America is represented in Lisbon, and major Portuguese banks have U.S. affiliations.

CALENDAR OF HOLIDAYS ... Stores and museums are closed on New Year's Day; June 10, Day of Camões, national poet; Corpus Christi (in June, date variable); August 15, Assumption; November 1, All Saints Day; December 1, Independence Day; December 8, Portuguese Mothers Day; Christmas Day.

CIGARETTES AND TOBACCO ... American cigarettes and tobacco are available. The most popular of the local brands of cigarettes, for 16¢ to 19¢ a pack, are *CT, SG, Sagres, Tagus, High-Life, Aviz, Português, Suave, Paris, 20–20–20* (Three Twenties), *Unic*, and *Tip-Top*. Principal tobaccos are *Francês, Superior* and *Virginia*.

CLIMATE ... Balmy but rainy weather in November, December, January at low elevations; cold and snowy in the mountains. From June to September, days are hot but humidity is low.

CLUBS ... Rotary, Lions, Turf Club, Royal British Club, Skal Club and Circulo Eca de Queiroz in Lisbon. Clube de Golfe do Estoril in Estoril; Sporting Club de Cascais and Clube Naval in Cascais. The new Clube D. Carlos I in Cascais, set in a lovely park, combines sports and sociability; its attractive restaurant is open to the public.

COMMON COURTESIES AND LOCAL CUSTOMS... A kind, warm greeting expressed by the handshake is a very important part of everyday life in Portugal. When Portuguese ladies go out in the evening, they're usually accompanied by a member of the family.

COMMUNICATIONS... Airmail postage to the States is 4$30; postcards are 3$30. A 10-word cablegram costs about U.S. 40¢ a word to New York; 48¢ a word elsewhere in the USA.

CURRENCY... The Portuguese monetary unit is the escudo, divided into 100 centavos. For example 85 escudos, 50 centavos is written Esc. 85$50. The escudo is worth about 3½ ¢ or 28$50 to the dollar. No customs restrictions on escudos or other currencies.

CUSTOMS REGULATIONS AND DOCUMENTS REQUIRED FOR UNITED STATES CITIZENS... 250 grams of tobacco, or 50 cigars, or 200 cigarettes may enter free of duty. Passport but no visa required. For stopovers in the Azores, however, you need a visa.

DRUGSTORES... No American-type drugstores, but pharmaceuticals at the pharmacies and toiletries at the perfumers. American brands are readily available.

ELECTRIC CURRENT... Power is 220/380 volts 50 cycles, A.C. in the most important cities, 110/190 volts in a few places. Standard European round-pronged converted plugs, available locally, are needed for Portuguese outlets.

FAUNA... No special birds or animals of outstanding interest for the tourist are to be found in Portugal. The Lisbon Zoo at Parque das Larangeiras, Estrada de Bemfica, however, has one of the finest collections of live animals in Europe, and beautiful gardens.

FLORA... Visit the Botanical Garden, Rua da Escola Politécnica, Lisbon, with exotic local flora, and the Greenhouse at Parque Eduardo VII, one of the best in Europe. The Forest of Monsanto is one of Lisbon's many attractions, with the belvedere of Montes Claros overlooking the Tagus River.

FOOD... Portuguese cuisine is delicious. *Bacalhau à Gomes de Sá,* a very special dish prepared with codfish, is worth trying. At the *Nicola,* one of the many cafés in Lisbon, you can try the tasty *bacalhau à Nicola,* a dish that is served on Tuesdays and Fridays. For those who like a good steak, the *bife na frigideira,* which is served in all restaurants, is a delicious dish. *Caldo verde* is a soup made with mashed potatoes and thinly sliced cabbage, unbelievably good. *Iscas com elas* is another national dish, made with thin slices of liver very specially seasoned and served with French-fried potatoes.

Almost every restaurant in Portugal has its own special dish. Cheese-making is one of the Portuguese specialties. The visitor will find delicious cheeses everywhere in the country. Cheeses from Serra, Azeitão, Serpa, Rabaçal, Ponte de Sôr and a small, fresh, white cheese made of goats' milk will be a new taste sensation for cheese lovers. Portuguese pastry is also delicious. Almost every town in Portugal has its own specialty: *Ovos Moles* in Aveiro; *Doces d'Ovos* in Viseu;

Trouxas d'Ovos and *Cavacas* in Caldas da Rainha; *Toucinho do Ceu* in Portalegre; *Queijadas* in Sintra; *Pasteis de Feijão* in Torres Vedras; *Arrufadas* and *Manjar Branco* in Coimbra; *Celestes* in Santarem; *Pão de Ló* in Alfeizerão. These last are just a few of the many kinds of pastry, almost all of them also available in Lisbon. Milk is good and safe to drink.

GAMBLING ... Casinos with roulette at resort towns, such as at Estoril (all year), Figueira da Foz, Povoa do Varzim and Espinho (during summer only).

LANGUAGE ... The official language is Portuguese. In all the big cities, it will be easy to find someone who speaks English.

LAUNDRY AND DRY CLEANING ... about the same in quality, price and speed as in the United States.

LIQUOR ... Port wine, the famous wine which comes from the Douro Valley, and Madeira wine from Madeira, are world renowned. By law, 3/5 liter of regional wine (always good) is included with fixed-price meals. The most famous wines come from Bairrada, Ribatejo and Estremadura, where the large vineyards are. You may taste the best port wines at the Solar do Velho Porto in Lisbon and in Oporto at the cellars of the old concerns which for centuries have dealt with Port. Cointreau, Benedictine, Peppermint, Aniz, and many other liqueurs are available, as well as good brandies. American and English whiskies are available in most Portuguese bars.

MEDICAL FACILITIES ... Good modern hospitals in the large towns and small first-aid stations throughout the country. Ask at your hotel if you need a doctor, or telephone Lisbon 775171.

MOTION PICTURES ... Portuguese and foreign films, including the best American pictures, are given in the original language with captions in Portuguese. Top Lisbon theaters are *St. Jorge, Tivoli, S. Luiz, Politeama, Eden, Monumental, Roma, Avalade* and *Imperio*. Show times vary; check at your hotel.

MUSIC ... You can hear fine concerts of the National Symphony Orchestra, with famous conductors, at the *Teatro Nacional de S. Carlos* in Lisbon during the winter. Every year there is an opera season featuring famous artists. Military bands in summer play concerts in the main public gardens. *Fado,* the Portuguese music of Lisbon, can be heard every night in Bairro Alto and Alfama restaurants.

NIGHT LIFE AND CAFÉS ... You'll get the best local atmosphere in the little cafés that are frequented by the Portuguese. Here, amid smoke and wine, the eerie *fado* is sung by entertainers and customers alike. Most of these haunts are in Bairro Alto, the best ones being the *Folclore, Toca, Mesquita, Tipoia, Machado, Faia, Severa* and *Parreirinha.* Gayer and more conventional are *Tagide, Negresco, Nina,* and the *Casino* in Estoril. There is dancing at all these places. Other good night spots are the *Maxime, Cave, Montes Claros, Bico Dourado,* in Lisbon; *Choupana, Ronda,* in Estoril; *Palm Beach* and *Caixote* in Cascais. Popular bars include the *Rex, York, Americano, English Bar, Lorde, Iberia.* Dining at the *Ritz* is very chic. When there is entertainment, as much as 40% in taxes may be added onto your bill, but luckily drinks are inexpensive. See also RESTAURANTS.

PHOTOGRAPHY . . . Color and black-and-white film for still and movie cameras is available in Lisbon, as well as all makes of cameras and equipment and developing facilities for black-and-white film; 8-hour service. All camera stores do reliable work.

RELIGION . . . The state religion is Roman Catholic. However, there are a few Protestant churches and two Jewish synagogues.

RESTAURANTS . . . The most elegant places to eat in Lisbon are the *Aviz;* the *Tavares, Bodegon, Gondola* (Italian cooking), *Cozinha d'el Rei, Macau* (Chinese food), *Vera Cruz* and *Negresco,* which has dancing. The food is superb, and dinner comes to about $4, including wine. The *Irmãos-Unidos Gambrinus* and *Iberia,* in the center of Lisbon's business district, are very popular and moderately priced. Typically Portuguese spots include the *Machado* and *Folclore* where you can hear *fado* and national songs, and *Mesquita* and *Faia.* Among the plushiest tea rooms in town are *Caravela, Benard, Ferrari* and the *Imperio.* Food in the *Ritz* dining room and grill is also excellent.

SHOPS AND STORES . . . Lisbon's largest department stores are Grandella, Chiado and Lanalgo. Smart specialty shops line Rua Garrett (Chiado), Rua do Ouro, Rua Augusta, Rossio and Rua da Prata. Stores are open weekdays from 9 A.M. to 1 P.M. and from 3 to 7 P.M.

SPECTATOR SPORTS . . . You must see at least one Portuguese bullfight. The bull isn't killed and the fight is not so gory as the Spanish version. The fights held in spring and summer in Lisbon (*Campo Pequeno*) are full of color.

Soccer is the most popular sport in Portugal. Roller-skating hockey is also a national sport. The most important soccer games are played in the beautiful National Stadium near Lisbon on Sundays, and throughout the country from the fall until late in spring. The roller-skating hockey matches are followed by an enthusiastic public. The Portuguese are world champions in this sport.

SPORTS . . . The deep-sea fishing enthusiast will find exciting big-game fishing in Portuguese waters. Of the many kinds of game fish, the biggest is the tuna. Boats and equipment are for hire at reasonable prices. Hunting is a great sport in Portugal, and the State Tourist Board can furnish information about shooting game in Escatelar Hunting Preserve, only 50 miles from Lisbon. From October 15 to March 31, visitors are cordially welcome to join the fox-hunting parties that go out on Sundays and Thursdays. The Tourist Board, in collaboration with Equipage Sto. Hubert, can make arrangements for you. Sailing in the Bay of Cascais is wonderful all year round, and there are international races in July and August. Golfing is mainly a tourist sport; there are good courses in resort towns. Tennis courts are also available. Horses may be hired in many large towns. Mountain climbing and skiing are both new in Portugal, but rapidly growing in popularity.

THEATERS . . . Lisbon's most important theater is the *Teatro Nacional de S. Carlos,* which houses opera, ballet, symphony music. Other good theaters which present musicals and plays in Portuguese: *Teatro Avenida, Maria Vitoria, Variedades* and the *Monumental.*

TIME . . . Five hours later than United States Eastern Standard Time. This is Greenwich Mean Time. Daylight Saving Time is observed from the first Sunday in April to the first Sunday in October.

TIPPING . . . Tip baggage porters 7$50 (around 26¢) for 2 or 3 bags; railway porters get 2$50 per bag. Tip the attendant who shows you to your room, hat-check girls, movie and theater ushers, parking-lot and gas-station attendants 2$50 each; 2 escudos to a washroom attendant, and to the doorman who calls a taxi. Taxi drivers get 10% of the meter reading. Tip 5 escudos for room service. Tips for chambermaids, waiters and shoeshine boys are included in your bill, but you'll want to give them something extra for their good service.

TOURIST TAXES . . . Sea arrival entry tax 50¢; exit tax 5% of passage plus $1. If you are traveling by air, no entry or exit tax, except for air passage purchased in Portugal.

TRANSPORTATION . . . Taxis, trolley cars and splendid buses are available in Lisbon. The subway runs under the main avenues. Good trains to principal cities, and a few excellent highways. Cars with chauffeurs are available for trips at from 1$20 per kilometer. Self-drive rentals are also available. The new airport at Faro makes the Algarve Coast easily accessible from Lisbon.

WATER . . . Water is safe to drink everywhere in Portugal. However, bottled waters are available.

WHAT TO BUY . . . Shopping in Lisbon, your best buys are cork products. Native craftsmen do amazing things with this material. You'll also find exceptionally fine gold and silver jewelry made in delicate filigree patterns, and flat silver; interesting native figurines and ceramics; rope-soled sports shoes; wines; fine embroideries and laces from Madeira and the Azores at a small fraction of their price in the States. Lovely tiles and Portuguese china are also tempting. The American Visitors Bureau, at Rua Castilho 61, will pack and mail fragile, bulky items for you. Pan Am's Lisbon office also maintains a self-service packing room where you can obtain materials and assistance for packing purchases to carry or ship back home or elsewhere.

WHAT TO WEAR . . . Lightweight street cottons are your best bet from June to September. Warm clothing is needed for the winter months, especially if you are going to mountain areas. Generally, informal sports clothes and more formal street-length wear for evening will do. Evening clothes are worn only at the most elegant resort hotels and casinos. As in Spain, the typical costume for the woman of fashion is the little black dress. If you wear sports clothes in the city, keep them conservative. Men need linen or tropical worsted suits, a light topcoat, dinner clothes, slacks and sports jackets.

WHERE TO GO—SIGHTSEEING . . .

Lisbon . . . Lisbon is a picturesque city, built, like Rome, on seven hills. The buildings are painted various pastel shades. The green hills and the blue sea make a wonderful backdrop for this colorful town. The Belem Tower, built in the early 16th century, is a wonderful specimen of the Manueline style, with some Moorish influence, as its architect (Arruda) was one of the chief builders of the Portuguese fortresses in Morocco. The view from the ramparts is breathtaking.

The churches of Lisbon represent every conceivable style of architecture. Seeing them all would be bewildering. Among the most beautiful and historically important are the Jeronimos Monastery and Church. In Manueline style, its cloisters of two pavements are regarded as among the most remarkable in the world. The cathedral blends Romanesque and Gothic styles and contains wonderful tomb sculptures of the 14th century. The city of Lisbon is crowned by a picturesque Moorish castle of the 10th century. The broad and beautiful Avenida da Liberdade runs through one of the most fashionable parts of Lisbon. Be sure to see the fabulous greenhouses of the Estufa Fria (cool garden) in Edward the Seventh Park nearby.

A visit to the harbor and the native fish market will give you an excellent chance to see the *varinas* (lady fish-vendors) in their tartan-plaid costumes, reminiscent of the Scottish dress. The botanical and zoological gardens are among Europe's finest. Black Horse Square in the lower part of the city, which was rebuilt after an earthquake in 1755, is surrounded by fine classical buildings. You will find that Lisbon's hills would be rough going if it weren't for the *ascensores,* outdoor elevators that lift you up the hills for less than half a cent. Eiffel designed the one at Rua Santa Justa. These are just a few things to see in Lisbon. The tourist could wander for days through the quaint narrow streets or along the wide modern boulevards and never cease to be interested by the unique and varied sights.

Estoril . . . Only 15 miles from Lisbon is Estoril, Portugal's fabulous seaside resort town. The beaches are magnificent and the climate is good all year round. The *Palacio Hotel* and the *Cibra* are first class. Surrounding facilities include fine golf links, swimming pool, private beaches, tennis courts, casino and splendid restaurants. Rates are from $9 single with meals, but can be much higher. The *Atlantico* with a lovely swimming pool is also a very good place to stay. Rates are from $4. There are beautiful bridle paths along the beach and up in the hills. It is one of Europe's loveliest and gayest resorts. Just beyond Estoril is Cascais, also a swank summer resort with, among other hotels, the *Baía,* the deluxe *Albatros* estalagen and the new 20-story *Estoril-Sol,* where high season rates are only $5.35 to $9; full board $4.45 additional. Top restaurants in Cascais are *Fim Do Mundo, Os Tres Porquinhos* (The three little pigs), *Boca Do Inferno, Frango Real, Muxaxo, English Bar,* among others.

A short drive from Estoril is the town of Sintra, called a little Eden by Lord Byron. Visit the Palacio da Vila, Palacio da Pena and nearby Castelo dos Mouros. There are good hotels in Sintra, including the *Central* and the *Hotel Palacio Seteais,* converted from an old castle.

Setubal . . . Is Portugal's main fishing port. See the Church of Jesus, the ruins of Cetobriga, the old fortress of St. Philip, the medieval fortress of Palmela, the marketplaces. There are very fine little restaurants. Hotels include the *Club Naval Setubalense.* Near Setubal lies one of the beautiful beaches, Portinho da Arrabida. Azeitão is an interesting little village, a center for famous wines and cheeses, with a nice rest house called *Quinta das Torres*. Nearby don't miss charming Sesimbra with the superb *Hotel do Mar*. Evora, 68 miles from Lisbon, is rich in art. Sunny and exotically Moorish, the Algarve Coast is blossoming into a year round resort paradise.

Coimbra . . . Coimbra is Portugal's university city. See the school, one of the oldest in Europe, its library and chapel, the Church of Santa Cruz, tombs of the first two kings of Portugal. *Hotel Astoria* (from $4 single plus service) and the *Bragança* (from $3) are the best. Dine at your hotel, or for lighter fare try the *Café Restaurant International, Pinto de Ouro, Café Santa Cruz* or *Nicola Café,* and for typical Portuguese food and pastry, the *Jardim da Manga.*

Oporto . . . Portugal's second largest city is the center of the wine trade and export business, 200 miles north of Lisbon. The drive up along the coast is well worth the cost of hiring a car. Things to do and see in Oporto include a visit to the Roman, Gothic and Baroque Cathedral, the little Roman Chapel of Cedofeita, the Gothic S. Francisco Church, the Soares dos Reis Museum, the Palacio de Cristal gardens, the Praça da Ribeira, a typical native market. Best hotels are *Infante Sagres* and *Grande Hotel do Porto,* where double rates begin at $5.25. Other comfortable hotels, moderately priced, are the *Grande Hotel do Imperio, Peninsular, Batalha.* The *Escondidinho, Belo Horizonte, Caravela, Le Chien qui Fume, Marisqueira, Gambrinus* are among the better restaurants.

Fatima . . . Portugal's outstanding site of devotion, 105 miles northeast of Lisbon. Aside from two big pilgrimages—May 13 and October 13—Fatima is honored on the thirteenth of each month.

Madeira is 625 miles southwest of Lisbon. The climate is perfect. The scenic beauty of the island ranks with the most famous anywhere. Funchal, the port town, has a new casino. There's sea bathing year round, and it's ideal for deep-sea fishing and other water sports. There is also good mountain climbing on the island. Madeira wine and embroideries are the chief industries. The dazzling New Year's celebrations have drawn tourists here for many years. The hotels in Funchal include the chic *Reid's Palace Hotel, Savoy, Santa Isabel, Nova Avenida, Golden Gate* and *Atlântico.*

The Azores . . . This Portuguese archipelago, 2 hours by air west of Lisbon, is interesting for its gorgeous unspoiled scenery and quaint old customs. São Miguel nearby is the biggest and most important island and provides the best tourist attractions. In the capital of Ponta Delgada, the *Hotel do Infante* is new and good; from $10.85 double with meals. The *Terra Nostra* in lovely Furnas Valley is $10 double with meals. There is also a *Terra Nostra* at the airport on Santa Maria. The climate is semitropical, around 70 degrees in summer, 50 degrees in winter. Visa required.

SOURCES OF FURTHER INFORMATION . . . In Lisbon the Secretariado Nacional da Informação, Praça dos Restauradores (or at the airport). Pan Am's office in Lisbon at Praça dos Restauradores 46 (Tel. 362181), in the Ritz Hotel and at the Portela Airport (Tel. 721101). In New York, Casa de Portugal, 447 Madison Ave.

RUMANIA

This Balkan country is eager for visitors from the West and can be reached easily by Pan Am Clipper to Paris, Vienna or Berlin, then by local airlines to Bucharest. Elapsed time from New York, 15¾ hours. The size of Oregon (91,699 square miles), Rumania's population is about 18,900,000 of which 1,450,000 live in Bucharest, the capital. Autumn is one of the pleasantest times for a visit. For entry you need a passport and visa from the Rumanian People's Republic Diplomatic Representatives at 1601 23rd Street, N.W., Washington 8, D.C. or from appointed travel agents. The monetary unit is the leu which for tourists is valued at 18 lei to the U.S. dollar. Handicraft articles are among the best buys. Electric current is 220 volts in most places.

Top hotels in Bucharest are the *Athénée Palace,* the *Lido* and the *Ambassador.* Rates, including 3 meals, are at the most only $11 per person. Reserve well in advance. Besides restaurants in these hotels, there's the *Parcul Trandafirilar, Pescarus* (summer only), and *Cina.* Best night clubs are the *Continental* and the *Melody.* Rumanian food specialties include *mititei* (spicy sausages), *sarmale* (meat and rice wrapped in cabbage leaves), pickled fish, caviar. Best wines are Murfatlar, Cotnar and Tirnave.

WHERE TO GO—SIGHTSEEING...

Sightseeing in Rumania is arranged by Carpati National Travel Office and payable in advance, through U.S. travel agent representatives. Transportation from the airport, hotel accommodations, meals, sightseeing bus or car, guides and occasionally evening entertainment are included. Motoring with your own car and without guide however can be arranged. Carpati also sells tickets for the many musical and sports events. Bucharest, the political and cultural center of the country is still a "city of gardens," although former visitors will be struck by all the new construction. Points of interest are the various museums, Opera and Ballet Theater, stadiums and park areas such as Cismigiu Gardens in the city and Baneasa and Snagov nearby. Varied tours lead through the Carpathian Mountains and Prahova Valley's health resorts to Brasov, an industrial and tourist center, and Poiana Prasov resort. Your itinerary can include the Transylvanian and Moldavian towns shown on map, Constantza, formerly Tomis, the ancient city of the poet Ovid, and modern seaside resorts. A visit to the Danube delta is fascinating for its wild life; special package tours available.

SOURCES OF FURTHER INFORMATION... Carpati National
Travel Office at 7 Blvd. Magheru, Bucharest, Rumania, and their appointed U.S. travel agents.

RUSSIA (U.S.S.R.)

WEATHER IN MOSCOW—Lat. N55°45′—Alt. 625′

Temp.	JAN.	FEB.	MAR.	APR.	MAY	JUNE	JULY	AUG.	SEPT.	OCT.	NOV.	DEC.
Low	5°	8°	15°	29°	42°	50°	54°	51°	42°	33°	21°	10°
High	14°	19°	29°	43°	60°	67°	71°	68°	56°	44°	28°	17°
Average	10°	13°	22°	36°	51°	58°	62°	54°	49°	36°	24°	13°

LOCATION ... The Union of Soviet Socialist Republics occupies one sixth of the earth's land surface, stretching across two continents from the North Pacific Ocean to the Gulf of Finland.

POPULATION ... Estimated at slightly over 224,700,000.

SIZE ... 8,000 miles wide and 5,000 miles deep, Russia occupies 8,649,489 sq. miles, 3 times that of the United States.

CAPITAL ... Moscow, with a population of about 6,800,000.

GOVERNMENT ... The U.S.S.R. is made up of 15 republics or states with representatives in the Supreme Soviet, the highest legislative authority. The administrative organ of state is the Council of Ministers (Premier, Ministers and their deputies).

HOW TO GET THERE ... Pan American Clippers connect with the Russian airline, Aeroflot, in Paris, Copenhagen, Brussels, Helsinki, Berlin, Vienna and New Delhi. Elapsed time New York to Moscow about 13 hours via Paris. Leningrad is 1 hour from Moscow.

ACCOMMODATIONS ... Best Moscow hotels are the *National, Metropole, Berlin, Sovietskaya, Ukraina, Minsk, Peking, Moskva,* and the skyscraper *Leningrad Hotel.* Accommodations should be obtained through an *Intourist* tour. See under WHERE TO GO—SIGHTSEEING.

ARTS AND BALLET ... In Moscow, two musts are the Tretyakov Art Gallery, and the Pushkin Museum of Fine Arts. World-famous Russian Ballet can be seen at the Bolshoi Theatre.

CALENDAR OF HOLIDAYS ... New Year; International Woman's Day, March 8; May 1 and 2; Victory Day, May 9; Revolution Anniversary, November 7 and 8; Constitution Day, December 5.

CIGARETTES ... Local brands at about 16-22¢ a pack. American brands at Moscow's Bereska store.

CLIMATE ... As varied as her scenery, Russian climate can mean waist-high Siberian snow and arctic blizzards with the temperature falling to 80 degrees below zero, or bathing in the Black Sea on Christmas Day. Most of the country has sharp seasonal changes. Summer is the best time to visit Moscow.

COMMON COURTESIES AND LOCAL CUSTOMS ... The average Russian has a keen sense of humor and an instinctive liking for foreigners. He can laugh at himself and has a gift for nicknames and ridiculing pomposity. He works and plays hard, and is very proud of his cultural ancestry. Your respect of these traits will increase the enjoyment of your visit. Say "Spasibo" for "Thank you."

COMMUNICATIONS ... Service to the United States: Cablegrams, 25¢ per word; telephone, $12 per 3 minutes; airmail letter, 16¢; airmail postcard, 14¢.

CURRENCY ... The monetary unit is the ruble, valued at U.S. $1.10. There are 100 kopeks in a ruble; 90 kopeks equal U.S.$1.

CUSTOMS REGULATIONS AND DOCUMENTS REQUIRED FOR UNITED STATES CITIZENS ... Passport and visa through Intourist representatives (appointed Travel Agents). Smallpox vaccination certificate is required. No limit on U.S. currency. No Russian currency allowed in or out. Keep your currency exchange slips. Reasonable quantities of liquor and cigarettes allowed duty free.

ELECTRIC CURRENT ... Both 120- and 220-volt current. Standard European type plugs are used.

FOOD ... You may find the food on the heavy side, but good. Meats, including "bifshteks," and vegetables are cooked long. *Cotleta pojarski* (chicken cutlets), *koulebiaka* (meat or fish pie) and *Zharenny carps s kashoi* (roast carp with porridge) are a few dishes to try. Soups such as *schchi* (sauerkraut soup), ice cream and of course, caviar, are excellent. Tea and some wines are good, coffee poor. If you wish, bring instant coffee and ask for *kipyatok* (hot water).

LAUNDRY AND DRY CLEANING ... Laundry is no problem, but dry cleaning is not good, and service is slow.

MEDICAL FACILITIES ... Chemist shops offer a variety of pharmaceuticals. Hospitals give free treatment even to the tourist, if he is unable to pay for it. 78% of the nation's doctors are women.

MOTION PICTURES ... Some American films are shown, but with Russian dialogue. Seats must be reserved in advance.

MUSIC ... There's a variety of concerts to choose from in Moscow. Principal concert halls are the Grand Hall of the Tchaikovsky Conservatoire, Hall of Columns, Hall of the Palace of Congresses.

PHOTOGRAPHY ... Don't take pictures in art galleries, museums, customs places, airports or railway stations without permission.

RELIGION ... Moscow has 52 churches of various denominations. Greek Orthodox is the most common.

RESTAURANTS ... For $4 to $7 you can get a meal for two in one of the national restaurants. Some restaurants have entertainment.

SHOPS AND STORES ... Most are open from 8 A.M. to 8 P.M., most are closed on Mondays. The famous department store, *Gum* (open Mondays, closed Thursdays), is an experience in itself. Interesting items to buy are: chess sets, books, records, fur hats, and some gold items.

SPORTS ... Sports are popular, especially track and gymnastics. There are many stadiums, ski centers, swimming pools and boating stations; tennis, volleyball, basketball grounds and recreation parks. International competitions are held at the Luzhniki Stadium.

THEATERS ... Repertory companies offer a wide variety of shows. Get tickets through *Intourist*. Theaters include the Bolshoi Theatre, Moscow Art Theatre and the Maly Theatre. There are some delightful puppet theaters, too.

TIME ... When it is noon in New York, it is 7 P.M. in Moscow.

TIPPING ... No tipping at all. Luggage porters carry two bags free, get 20¢ (18 kopeks) for each additional bag.

TRANSPORTATION ... In Moscow, Kiev and Leningrad the Metro, or subway, is famous for its clean, mural-covered stations. There are also buses, trams and taxis. Auto travel without guide is now permitted.

WATER ... Outside Moscow, drink *narzan,* bottled water.

WHERE TO GO—SIGHTSEEING ...

An *Intourist* itinerary, available through U.S. travel agencies, costs from $10 to $35 a day. The $35 plan includes conveyance by car to and from the airport or rail stations, de luxe accommodations in hotels, 3 meals daily, sightseeing in private car with guide-interpreter.

Moscow ... The Kremlin (built 1462-1505), the center of town, contains within its massive 65-foot walls the Grand Kremlin Palace, home of the Supreme Soviet. The Lenin Mausoleum, with the preserved body of the former premier, is just outside the Kremlin walls in Red Square, famous for military parades and exhibitions. Places to see include the Oruzheinaya Palata (Armory) with its great jewel collection, the Cathedral of Vasily Blazhenny (1554-60), Moscow University, the Minin and Pozharsky monument, the U.S.S.R. History Museum, the Museum of Lenin, the Obelisk of Revolutionary Thinkers, the U.S.S.R. Economic Achievement Exhibition with many beautiful fountains and botanical gardens and some 300 buildings, and Sokolniki Park, site of the 1959 American National Exhibition.

Other places of interest ... Intourist services cover 100 Soviet cities, including *Leningrad,* with remnants of Czarist-days atmosphere; *Kiev,* capital of the Ukraine with a gaiety about it; Caucasian mountain health resorts; cruises on the lovely Volga and Dnieper rivers; *Yalta,* site of Czar's palace and Big Three Conference; *Sochi,* on the Russian Riviera; cities of the Baltic republics, such as Riga, Tallinn and Vilnius; even into Siberia; and to the romantic, legendary cities of Tashkent, Samarkand and Bukhara.

SOURCES OF FURTHER INFORMATION ... "Intourist" is at 355 Lexington Ave., New York. (Tel. MU 2-7406).

BAY OF BISCAY

FRANCE

San Sebastian
Burgos •
Gerona •
Barcelona •
PORT.
• El Escorial
Avila •
★MADRID
Palma
Valencia •
Toledo •
S P A I N
Seville
Granda
Malaga
Cadiz
*MEDITERRANEAN
SEA*

SPAIN

WEATHER IN MADRID—Lat. N40°25′–Alt. 2,150′

Temp.	JAN.	FEB.	MAR.	APR.	MAY	JUNE	JULY	AUG.	SEPT.	OCT.	NOV.	DEC.
Low	33°	35°	38°	42°	50°	56°	61°	62°	55°	47°	40°	35°
High	48°	52°	57°	63°	72°	79°	86°	87°	76°	65°	54°	48°
Average	41°	44°	48°	53°	61°	68°	74°	75°	66°	56°	47°	42°
Days of Rain	9	10	10	10	10	6	3	3	7	9	10	10

LOCATION ... Spain, along with Portugal, occupies the Iberian Peninsula, from the Pyrenees at the French border to Gibraltar. Madrid is about halfway between Lisbon and Barcelona.

CHARACTERISTICS ... The land of the bullfight is a land of color, with skies and waters of brilliant blue. The architecture reflects the many influences that have shaped the country. Art galleries and museums filled with treasures abound. You'll enjoy the food specialties; the hotels are good, the tempo restful. There is music and gaiety in Spain, and a color that is not duplicated anywhere else in the world. Spaniards are unfailingly courteous to strangers, and while they may not always understand you, they will at least make the effort. It's a wonderful spot to rest. They won't let you hurry.

POPULATION ... About 30,000,000 on the mainland.

SIZE ... Continental Spain is 189,652 square miles, approximately 640 miles from east to west; 530 miles from north to south.

CAPITAL ... Madrid. Population 2,260,000.

GOVERNMENT ... A nominal monarchy, with Generalissimo Franco granted a life tenure as chief of state.

HOW TO GET THERE ... By Pan Am Jet Clipper, elapsed time from New York, about 9 hours to Barcelona; Madrid is 1 hour by air from Lisbon, 2 hours from Rome, and 1½ hours from Barcelona. By ship, about 7 days to Lisbon, 6 to 8 days to Gibraltar.

ACCOMMODATIONS ... De luxe hotels in Madrid are the *Castellana Hilton, Emperador, Fénix, Palace, Plaza, Ritz, Sanvy, Suecia* and *Wellington*. Single rates average about $6-$10, doubles about $8-$17. First-class hotels in Madrid include the *Gran Via, Avenida* and *Emperatriz.* Rates average $4 single, $7 double.

In Barcelona are the new *Presidente* and the *Cristal Palace;* the well-known *Hotel Arycasa; Avenida Palace,* convenient and long familiar to Americans; the *Manila* and *Ritz,* outstanding and near smart shops; the *Cólon,* facing the Cathedral, with charming local atmosphere. Rates in these de luxe hotels average about $6-$8 single, $10 to $14 double. On the road to Mt. Tibidabo is the de luxe *La Rotonda* with rooms for transients and housekeeping suites that are very popular with American families. First-class hotels in Barcelona include the *Barcelona, Condado, Roma, Majestic.* ($4 and up single, $6.50 and up double.)

During the summer, some hotels add 25% for - air-conditioned rooms, and they are legally permitted to raise their rates during fiestas and peak seasons. Rates quoted above are exclusive of the 15% service charge and numerous taxes. When official rates include these charges, they appear 30% more expensive, but there is actually little increase. Meals are about $3.50 at most de luxe hotels (plus 10% luxury tax) and $2 in first-class hotels.

There are also a number of Government-sponsored inns, some called *paradores* (converted castles) and some *albergues* (much like our motels), plain, clean, practical, in areas not served by hotels, at halfway points on main highways. Basic rates, with meals, about $4.50 a day. Regional and Continental cooking—local architectural features in all.

ARTS ... Outstanding is the Prado National Museum (not to be confused with El Pardo, residence of the chief of state) with Spain's famous art collection to which several days should be devoted; open from 10 A.M. to 6 P.M. The Royal Palace, now open to the public mornings and afternoons 10 to 1 and 3:30 to 6, contains fine examples of tapestries, paintings and furnishings. Part of the Royal Palace contains one of the world's finest collections of armor. Also worth seeing are various other museums, such as the Museum of Modern Art, the Army Museum, and the Decorative Arts Museum.

In Barcelona one has the choice of 14 museums covering all periods. Especially recommended are the Municipal Museum of Archaeology (excavations from Roman and Gothic periods) and the Archive of the Crown of Aragon (one of the most important libraries in Spain). Also see the Museum of Catalan Art, with the world's greatest collection of Romanesque murals. There are several medieval monasteries in Barcelona and in nearby Montserrat and Poblet.

BALLET ... Many prominent European and American ballet stars appear in Madrid and Barcelona during the spring. Fine European opera companies appear in both cities. There are several local ballet companies in Barcelona, most of them performing in the spring.

BANKS ... Both Barcelona and Madrid have branches of Banco Hispano-Americano (which has connections with several important U.S. banks), London and South America Bank, and others. In Barcelona, the Banco Condal has a direct telex to New York, thus permitting quick cashing of personal dollar checks.

CALENDAR OF HOLIDAYS . . . January 1 and 6; March 19, St. Joseph's Day; Holy Thursday; Good Friday; Resurrection Monday; May 1, Labor Day; Ascension; Corpus Christi and Whitmonday; June 24, St. John; June 29, SS. Peter and Paul; July 18, National Day; July 25, Santiago Day; August 15, Assumption; October 12, Columbus Day; November 1, All Saints Day; December 8, 25, 26; and in different localities many feast days, besides those big fairs, such as Barcelona's famous *verbenas* on the eves of June 24 and 29, and patroness saint's day on September 24. There is Seville's Holy Week and the popular *Feria* during the months of April and May; Pamplona's Patron Saint Day, *San Fermin,* July 7; Valencia's Patron Saint Day, *San José,* March 19, when the *Fallas* are celebrated; Madrid's festival of *San Isidro,* May 15, very typical and gay, and San Sebastian's festival of the *Assumption,* starting on August 11 and lasting the whole week. Try to visit where you can on the big days.

CIGARETTES, CIGARS, TOBACCO . . . American cigarettes cost from 16 to 22 pesetas per pack. Spanish cigarettes are black, strong, inexpensive, as are American-type and Cuban-type cigars.

CLIMATE . . . Madrid has a 2,000-foot elevation and is fairly cold in the winter and hot in the summer, but its dry climate is a help. It receives the fresh breeze from the nearby Sierra de Guadarrama which, it is said, makes it the most healthful capital of Europe. Best months are May, June, September and October.

Barcelona, situated on the Mediterranean coast, offers an ideal holiday climate. It is hot in the summer, mild in winter. Best seasons are spring, which starts as early as March, and autumn; winter does not start until November. Barcelona's hottest months are July and August, but the beautiful nearby mountains and coast are an excellent and comforting refuge.

CLUBS . . . Many exclusive, smart clubs in both cities. In Madrid, Real Club Puerta de Hierro and Club de Campo. In Barcelona there's the Polo Club, Real Club de Golf el Prat, Real Club Nautico. For visits, contact the club secretary.

COMMON COURTESIES AND LOCAL CUSTOMS . . . Spaniards are not too punctual, sometimes a little late for appointments. Luncheon is late, *aperitivo* (cocktail hour) may run as late as 9 or 9:30, with dinner served from 10 P.M. on. Ladies do *not* wear mantillas in night clubs or restaurants or for casual occasions. They are worn in church, and to bullfights.

COMMUNICATIONS . . . Day rate for a 3-minute phone call to the States is 724 pesetas; night and Sunday rate is 543 pts. Cablegrams are 23.65 pts. per word. Airmail postage to U.S. is 10 pesetas for letters, 8 for cards.

CURRENCY . . . There are 100 centimos in one peseta, worth 60 pesetas to U.S. $1. Money can be changed at the airport, in hotels, travel agencies and banks.

CUSTOMS REGULATIONS AND DOCUMENTS REQUIRED FOR UNITED STATES CITIZENS . . . United States citizens need a passport but no visa for visits up to 6 months. One bottle of liquor, one bottle of wine and about 1 carton of cigarettes for personal use may be brought in duty free. You may take 50,000 pesetas into and up to 3,000 pesetas out of Spain. Purchases up to 25,000 pesetas may be taken out of the country by visitors without permit, but show receipts for purchases to Customs. Air departure tax 85¢ (50 pesetas).

DRUGSTORES . . . A few American pharmaceuticals, but mostly Spanish or European drug items.

ELECTRIC CURRENT . . . 220 or 125 volts A.C., 50 cycles. Plug adapters can be bought locally.

FOOD . . . Spanish food is hearty, and you'll find the specialties, especially seafood, interesting. You need never fear eating any of the great variety of fruits: melons, grapes, figs, oranges, and many kinds you don't get commonly at home, all very fine. Watch for the tiny wild strawberries, the splendid seafood. Try the local specialties in the different parts of the country as you go about the countryside. There are delicate little cakes made with fruits and nuts. Spanish sweets are famous (particularly the excellent *turrones*) and suggest their Moorish ancestry. Pasteurized milk is available in Madrid and Barcelona, but not always in the smaller places where it should be boiled for safety.

GAMBLING . . . Madrid has a fine race course, as does San Sebastian, where there is good horse racing over the Lasarte course each July, August, September. Greyhound racing in Madrid and Barcelona. Lotteries. There are no casinos for gambling, but betting on football games in winter and big betting on the *jai alai* games, but you had best just watch it, unless you know something about it. It's faster than lightning, and twice as exciting.

LANGUAGE . . . The official language is Spanish, but in Barcelona they speak Catalan, and other areas have their own dialects. English is understood in large cities and tourist centers only.

LAUNDRY AND DRY CLEANING . . . Fine 1- or 2-day laundry service almost anywhere. Service is good and quick in the larger hotels. Prices are reasonable. Dry cleaning generally takes 1 or 2 days at hotels.

LIQUOR . . . You can drink sherry all through Spain, varying the type as often as you change cities. As with the food, you might well enjoy one of the dozens of wines you find featured in its native province. Spain has a great variety of wines. The reds (*vino tinto*) are truly outstanding; the whites (*vino blanco*) range from fair to fine. Prices are so low you can experiment widely until you find those you want to stick to. Those of Cataluña are delicious, always popular with Americans. There are many local liqueurs, such as anís, and several Spanish brandies, usually a little grapier than the same French grade, but very good. And they have the additional charm of being cheap, as are all Spanish distilled liquors compared with Scotch and other foreign beverages. Try local brandy and soda, or local gin and tonic. Popular American drinks are available in hotels and street bars. According to the place, prices vary from 15 to 25 pesetas, always more for Scotch. Hotel bars are open usually until 11 P.M., other bars until midnight. Minimum legal age for drinkers is 18.

MEDICAL FACILITIES ... English-speaking doctors and dentists are available in Madrid and Barcelona, with English-speaking staff in some of the better hospitals—consult your hotel clerk.

MOTION PICTURES ... British, French and American are shown at almost all theaters in both Madrid and Barcelona, usually with Spanish sound tracks. Seats must be reserved for evening shows and Sunday matinees. Check programs locally.

MUSIC ... The famous Spanish symphonic orchestras, the Sinfónica, Filarmónica and Nacional, as well as the Cuarteto de Música de Cámara and the Orquesta Sinfónica de Barcelona, give concerts all fall, winter and spring. San Sebastian has fine music each summer, especially during "Grand Week" in August as do Granada and Seville during their spring festivals. Barcelona's winter opera season ranks very high, about third in all Europe. Concerts and chamber music at the Palacio de la Música Catalana, opera at Teatro del Liceo. Best choirboy singing in Spain is at Monasterio de Montserrat.

NIGHT CLUBS AND CABARETS ... In Madrid, try the Castellana Hilton's *Rendezvous Room*. Dine and dance to good music; also *Rex, Pasapoga,* floor show, good music (closed during July and August); *Casablanca,* floor show, entertainment; *Micheleta, Lido, Flamingo, El Biombo Chino,* all with floor show, entertainment. For typical Spanish Andalusian-style dancing (flamenco) and decoration, try *La Zambra* and *El Duende.* Also good food, dancing at the *Florida* and the *Pavillon,* in the middle of Retiro Park. *Club Riscal,* summer roof garden, has good food (*paella,* the Spanish rice dish, is their specialty).

In Barcelona, some of the smartest places in summer are *La Masia* and *Tres Molinos.* For good music and floor shows without food try the *Bolero, Emporium* and *Rio.* There are many *boîtes* and *bodegas* for an evening of fun that costs very little.

PHOTOGRAPHY ... Color as well as black-and-white film is available. Also cameras. Other photo equipment is fairly expensive. There are Kodak shops in both Madrid and Barcelona, with good-quality developing taking 2 or 3 days.

RELIGION ... Roman Catholicism is the state religion. Madrid has 3 Protestant churches, Barcelona, 2. Both cities have Jewish synagogues.

RESTAURANTS ... Both Madrid and Barcelona have plenty of really good eating places. In fact, the cooking is genuinely good almost everywhere, with a variety that is bewildering. Delicacies from every part of Europe are superimposed on dozens of native dishes, game and seafood.

Probably the most famous restaurants are Madrid's *Jockey Club, Club 31, Commodore, Las Lanzas, Puerta de Moros* and *Horcher's.* Each is a de luxe, exclusive gourmet's delight, with a superlative cuisine and a fine setting. Best restaurants in Barcelona are: *Reno, Milan,*

Finisterre, Guria, Petit Soley, La Masia (closed in winter) and *Glaciar*. Near the waterfront and famous for seafood are *Casa Costa* and *Caracoles*. Both cities will serve you their own famous specialties along with dishes each province claims for its own: Valencia's *paella* —yellow rice, with chicken, seafood, lobster or snails; *zarzuela de mariscos* (a wonderful shellfish dish) and *butifarra a la Catalana*—an excellent Spanish sausage—come from Barcelona. The Bilbao and San Sebastian locale offers three famous seafood dishes: *chipirones en su tinta; anguilas,* baby eels, which you'll like; and *bacalao a la Vizcaina,* sophisticated version of codfish. A specialty of Castille is *cochinillo asado*—savory suckling roast—said to be best in Segovia, where *Mesón de Candido* is a world-famous restaurant. Another superlative place to have a real Spanish meal while in Madrid is the small, charming *El Pulpito,* above the former hideout of Luís Candelas, the Castilian Robin Hood, where you see wonderful food cooked right before you. It has been operating in the same little spot since the Declaration was signed in Philadelphia. Also typical and very good are *Mesón de San Javier* (wonderful baked chicken), *La Barraca* (with *paella* the specialty), *Hogar Gallego* (seafood), *Sobrino de Botin* (suckling pig), *Edelweiss* (German-style food), and *Casa Valentin, Luigi's* (Italian), *El Bodegón* (Spanish-European food). At the better restaurants, telephone for a reservation.

SHOPS AND STORES ... Shops open at 9 A.M. Everywhere throughout the country they close at 1:30, reopen about 4 P.M. (4:30 in summer). Closing time is usually about 7:30 P.M. Besides on local festivals and feast days, which vary, they close on major Holy Days of the Roman Catholic Church, such as Good Friday, November 1, *Todos Santos* (All Saints' Day). *See* WHAT TO BUY.

SPECTATOR SPORTS ... Seeing at least one bullfight is a tourist must. All the bigger towns have their bull rings, most have their favorite matador. The pomp and color, the pageantry, the crowds, all add up to a fabulous show. Madrid, Barcelona, Cartagena, Málaga, Seville and Toledo among others, have important rings. The season starts in spring and lasts through October. There are important bullfights at both Madrid and Barcelona every Sunday and feast day during the season, and usually on Thursdays, as well.

Madrid's fine racetrack, the *Zarzuela,* one of Europe's best, has good racing on Sundays and holidays from February until June, and in October and November. Seville's Pineda course is open both spring and September, October. Spain's best racing is perhaps at the magnificent Lasarte course at San Sebastian. There are many big races run off here during August and September, some of international importance.

Pelota (or *jai alai*), is extremely popular the year round. Brilliant professionals appear on courts in at least 8 or 10 cities, including Madrid and Barcelona, with matches nightly. San Sebastian has first-rank matches during the summer. The football (soccer) season runs from September until June, with every town of any size having its own team. The Spanish League is large, divided into 3 divisions, with the usual finals and important cup play.

SPORTS . . . Winter sports will be good in Spain from December until April and are centered in La Molina, Puigcerda, Nuria and Candanchu (Huesca) in the Catalan Pyrenees, in the Guadarrama near Madrid, and Sierra Nevada, near Granada. There are good skiing, races and contests in all these winter centers. Fishing and hunting in Spain are among the best in Europe: mountain streams with trout, splendid salmon fishing (so much so, it is said, that 5,000 natives make their living fishing salmon, all with lines—no netting allowed in Spain). Sea fishing is good all along the coasts, with tuna taken from several centers. There's good hunting in the mountains, for deer, chamois, wild boar, and splendid duck shooting along the Guadalquivir River, famous everywhere. There are pigeon shoots all over Spain, spring, summer and fall. The country has over 20 golf courses which offer temporary memberships to guests. Tennis is played everywhere. Public bathing pools in all the big cities, wonderful surf bathing at San Sebastian and all along Spain's extensive coast.

THEATERS . . . Madrid's theaters and those all over the country start very late, by our standards, about 10:30 P.M. and sometimes even a half-hour later. Everything's in Spanish, of course.

TIME . . . Noon in New York is 6 P.M. in Spain.

TIPPING . . . The standard tip of 5 pesetas is handed to the hotel attendant who opens your room, the doorman who gets a taxi, shoeshine boy, hatcheck girl, theater usher, parking-lot and gas-station attendants. Luggage porters are tipped 5 pts. per bag. Room-service waiters, taxi drivers, barbers and beauticians are tipped 10% of their bills. Tour guides are tipped 15-25 pts. Waiters and bartenders are tipped 5% of the bill, which already includes service charges.

TRANSPORTATION . . . Taxis are plentiful and very inexpensive. Everyone, visitors and residents alike, jumps into a taxi upon the slightest excuse, although city bus and streetcar services have improved. Intercity trains are also being modernized. Important changes for the better include the *"Talgo,"* smart Irun-Madrid, Madrid-Barcelona stainless-steel diesel train, and also the new "TAR" trains, which run regular schedules between Madrid and the more important cities, such as Barcelona. Spain's Iberia and Aviaco airlines are recommended for long cross-country trips. For shorter distances hired cars are easy to arrange and reasonable in price. Modern sightseeing buses cover the country on very well-organized tours. The concierge at your hotel can recommend reliable travel agents. Tour companies offer all-inclusive 2-week tours for about $15 to $20 a day.

WATER . . . Fine in Madrid and Barcelona. In small towns better stick to bottled water. Best (natural) are Solares and Fournier.

WHAT TO BUY . . . Jewelry and Toledo ware; Talavera porcelains; mantillas; linens, gloves, lace and leather goods of every kind are superior; Spanish perfume is good, cheaper than French; and plenty of good pottery, glassware. Festival and Casa Bique are good shops for Spanish products. Women's dresses made by the best Spanish couturiers are available in Madrid, Barcelona and San Sebastian at very reasonable prices, from Balenciaga (called *Eisa* in Spain), Pedro

Rodriguez, Asunción Bastida, Pertegaz, and others. Men's suits custom made at $50-$80 can be ordered in Barcelona at Rabat, and El Dique Flotante, or in Madrid at González y García, Peñalver, Montero and many others. Made-to-order shoes cost between $16 and $23. Sherries and brandies are of course good buys.

WHAT TO WEAR ... Spaniards are a well-dressed people and somewhat conservative in their attire, therefore ladies' slacks are not worn in cities. Evening clothes are not necessary for tourists. Sports and beachwear will be needed for seaside resorts; and bikinis are now accepted in internationally-minded resorts. Flat-heeled walking shoes should also be included if tourist haunts such as Toledo and the Escorial are to be visited. Lightweight suits for men for city wear, sports clothes elsewhere. It is customary to wear a jacket and tie in cities even in summer, though, strangely enough, hats are rarely seen either on men or women. When entering a church, however, women wear hats or cover their heads with mantillas.

WHERE TO GO—SIGHTSEEING ...

Madrid ... Top on your list for sightseeing in Madrid will be the famous Prado National Museum and other museums mentioned under ARTS. Also, by all means visit University City. With one of the finest campuses of its type in Europe, it embraces all the arts and sciences. It was completely destroyed during the Civil War, and completely rebuilt since 1939. A stroll through the Retiro Park, with its beautiful gardens, statues, fountains and artificial lakes is well worth while.

Toledo ... is a short drive from Madrid, the home of El Greco, and famous for its tempered steel as well as for its gold Damascene works. Visit the Cathedral, the Church of Santo Tomé, and the Jewish synagogue. A splendid view of the city may be had from the hill just beyond. *El Escorial* is famous for its monastery-palace, built by Phillip II, which houses the tombs of the kings of Spain as well as other great persons. *Hotel Filipe II* is delightful. *Avila*, the medieval walled city, is the home of the famous Spanish mystic, Santa Teresa. *Segovia* is famous for the castle known as the Alcázar and for the unsurpassed magnificence of its Roman aqueduct.

Barcelona, (2 million inhabitants), founded in the 2nd century B.C., lies within a hilly amphitheater facing the Mediterranean. Besides being the most cosmopolitan city in Spain and one of the most beautiful and historic seaports of the Mediterranean, Barcelona is rich in fine churches, lovely fountains, monuments, religious and civic buildings, and has a charming old Gothic Quarter.

Be sure to visit the Gothic Cathedral, built almost directly over the site of a Roman temple to Jupiter. Several great museums are in mountainous Montjuich Park, famous for its fountains and view of the city. Here, too, is *Pueblo Español*, in which each building represents the architecture of a different province. You can watch Spanish handicrafts in the making, and buy the results. A replica of Columbus's *Santa Maria* is in the harbor to which he returned in triumph in 1493. In the Salon del Tinell on Plaza del Rey in the Gothic Quarter, Isabel and Ferdinand formally welcomed Columbus, and here the first American Indian was baptized. See the superb fountain of Montjuich; usually illuminated from 9-11 P.M. on Saturdays, Sundays and holidays. See the unique Sagrada Familia church.

Costa Brava, known as the Spanish Riviera, stretches north from Barcelona to the French frontier. Few large de luxe hotels, but many small inns where comfort and food are supreme. Small night clubs, wonderful food, bathing, etc., and excellent personal service. Tops on the Costa Brava are *Hostal de la Gavina* in S'Agaro and *Cap Sa Sal* in Bagur. Other good hotels are the *Rigat Park, Carabela* and *Monterey* in Lloret de Mar, and the *Ancora* and *Delfin* in Tossa de Mar.

Valencia ... Ancient, beautiful Valencia, rich in historical interest, lies in the heart of the "Huerta de Valencia," the rich plain that has Spain's choicest orange and lemon groves. *Hotel Excelsior, Hotel Astoria, Hotel Reina Victoria.* The climate is dry and very mild, the lush land produces several crops each reason; there are flowers in profusion everywhere. The province was once the independent Moorish kingdom of Valencia (1021 A.D.); it was retaken by Spain's national hero, El Cid, and then lost again to the Arabs. It belonged to Aragon, then to Castile. See the many white houses, showing the Moorish influence, the many monuments.

Valencia's lures are its gay fiestas, the smell of orange blossoms, its wonderful clear sky. The whole countryside is a garden, and it is almost always spring. The fig, pomegranate, and palm trees add to the riot of color, with hundreds of streams crossing the country everywhere. The almond trees and the olive add more green to the landscape. The Cathedral, built on a former mosque, has beautiful paintings by Goya. See the palatial Dos Aguas Palace, the Museo de Bellas Artes. Although it is wonderfully beautiful at any time of the year, try to visit Valencia in March for its greatest feast day, March 19.

Málaga is farther south along the coast. This Andalusian city is the center of Spain's Costa del Sol: wonderfully even, mild winters, beautiful park, fine harbor. Its museum, left to the city by the painter Muñoz Degrain, is famed for its Murillo and other more modern masterpieces. The National Golf Tournament is played here each winter, and there are tennis matches, yachting. There are horse races in February.

Costa del Sol begins at Estepona and reaches its liveliest point at Torremolinos. Numerous new resort hotels with pools, beaches, entertainment.

Seville (460,000 population) is of enormous importance, an artistic and archaeological center, with the architecturally resplendent *Hotel Alfonso XIII*, with museums of interest, great churches, monuments, works of art. The fine arts museum has the best Murillos, the archaeological museum has Roman and Arabic art. Under Moorish rule for over 500 years, the city has Arabic architecture everywhere. See the Alcázar, and, as part of the Cathedral, the famous Giralda Tower, 12th-century minaret. The glorious Maria Luisa Park; the Palacio de las Dueñas, belonging to the Duke of Alba; the houses with their iron gates—all these and more will delight the tourist. Holy

Alcazar Castle is in the historic city of Segovia near Madrid.

The fishing village of Tossa de Mar makes an interesting stop along the Costa Brava.

Week, and the fair which follows it with a full week of bullfights, is the time to see the great city at its glorious best. Hotels include the *Alfonso XIII, Cristina, La Rabida, Madrid.*

Granada ... With its Alhambra, is where our Washington Irving lived and wrote; Córdoba with its Mosque-Cathedral, its fairs, and its romerías or tours will interest you. It's in these southern cities of Andalusia that you see authentic flamenco dancing.

Getting back to central Spain (107 miles northwest of Madrid), you will like Salamanca, old university town on the banks of the River Tormes, its Plaza Mayor, with its fine Town Hall, its magnificent arcades, and the baroque-style Pabellón Real (Royal Pavilion).

San Sebastian ... World-famous summer resort and capital of the province of Guipuzcoa, one of the three that form the Basque country, shouldn't be missed. Its beach, famed La Concha (called "the shell" because of its shape), is visited by both Spaniards and foreigners by the thousands each season. The best of sports car and yacht races, famous stake races for horses at Lasarte, the best Basque ball players anywhere, and the very best bullfighting all are seen during the summer. Stay at *María Cristina, Londres* or *Continental Palace Hotel;* get there if possible during the "Grand Week" in August, and make reservations in advance.

The Balearic Islands ... Can be reached by air in 35 minutes from Barcelona. See index for chapter on Mallorca.

SOURCES OF FURTHER INFORMATION ... The Spanish Tourist Office in New York is at 589 Fifth Avenue, and there are others in Chicago, Dallas, San Francisco and Toronto. Within Spain, folders in English, maps, lists of shops, etc., are available at Municipal Tourist Information Offices, and State Tourist Information Office. Information on sightseeing tours is available at these offices or at the larger travel agencies. Tickets for local events are available through your hotel porter. Feel free also to call upon Pan Amercan for information: in Barcelona, Calle Mallorca 250 (Tel. 215.20.58); in Madrid, Edificio España (Tel. 241.42.00) and Palace Hotel lobby.

NORWAY   FINLAND
• Riksgränsen
Kiruna
Luleå
SWEDEN
Östersund   *GULF OF*
Rättvik   *BOTHNIA*
Karlstad   • Uppsala
★
STOCKHOLM
Marstrand   • Visby
Gothenburg
Malmö   Kalmar

SWEDEN

WEATHER IN STOCKHOLM—Lat. N59°16′—Alt. 35′

Temp.	JAN.	FEB.	MAR.	APR.	MAY	JUNE	JULY	AUG.	SEPT.	OCT.	NOV.	DEC
Low	22°	21°	24°	31°	40°	49°	54°	52°	46°	38°	31°	24°
High	31°	32°	36°	46°	57°	67°	71°	67°	59°	48°	39°	33°
Average	27°	27°	30°	39°	49°	58°	63°	60°	53°	43°	35°	29°
Days of Rain	15	13	14	11	12	12	15	16	14	16	15	17

LOCATION . . . Sweden occupies the eastern portion of the Scandinavian Peninsula. Stockholm, the principal city, is 258 air miles east of Oslo, Norway, about 875 miles northeast of London.

CHARACTERISTICS . . . Cleanliness and efficiency, neither one of them obtrusive, are notable in Sweden. One of the most progressive countries in the world, it likes tourists; its hotels make them welcome, its restaurants offer wonderful food, and the scenery itself is an invitation. The Swedes are strong, happy, vigorous people whose zest for life communicates itself to you. Summer with the Midnight Sun is unforgettable. The sportsman will find fishing, skiing and sailing in abundance. It's the land of "Swedish modern" and social reforms.

POPULATION . . . 7,621,000, roughly equal to the population of Michigan, about half that of California.

SIZE . . . 173,665 square miles; it is 978 miles long, 310 miles wide.

CAPITAL . . . Stockholm, population 799,000.

GOVERNMENT . . . A constitutional monarchy with a King and a *Riksdag*, or Parliament, of two chambers.

HOW TO GET THERE . . . By Pan Am's through-plane service from New York, about 8¾ hours to Stockholm, via Oslo, or connect from transatlantic Jet Clippers to London (6½ hours) or Copenhagen (9 hours). By ship 8 to 10 days from New York to Gothenburg.

ACCOMMODATIONS . . . Stockholm has a hotel or pension to suit every budget. No matter where you stay, you will find cleanliness and friendly service. Best known is the *Grand Hotel*, beautifully situated opposite the Royal Palace. Rates here begin at about $11 single; $17 double with bath. Other first-class and very popular hotels with somewhat lower rates are *Stockholm, Gillet, Continental, Malmen, Carlton, Foresta* (has heated outdoor pool), *Apollonia, Strand, Palace, Sjöfartshotellet* (Seafarers) and the resort hotel *Grand Hotel Saltsjöbaden.* Most hotels add a 15% service charge, but prices are still lower than in the United States. You can get a very good single room for less than $5 in student hotels such as *Domus* and *Jerum,* open to tourists in summer. It is advisable to make your reservations in advance, especially during the summer months. Hotels in other areas are listed under WHERE TO GO.

ARTS . . . The *Vasa,* submerged in Stockholm harbor for 333 years, has become the city's newest museum. The National Museum and the Modern Museum have excellent collections of Swedish and foreign paintings. The Stockholm City Museum contains exhibits illustrating the history of the city from the Stone Age until the present time. The unique Skansen, an outdoor museum beautifully situated on a hilltop, has exhibits showing life and work in Sweden centuries ago, as well as houses and farms of that time. At Skansen you will find beautiful parks, excellent restaurants and a large zoo. The home of Carl Milles, the famous sculptor, beautifully situated on the Island of Lidingö near Stockholm, has been transformed into an outstanding museum, which contains antique sculptures as well as Milles' own works. Waldemarsudde, formerly the home of the late Prince Eugen, contains a fine collection of the works of the "Painter Prince" and his contemporaries. Parts of the Royal Palace, the Drottningholm Palace and the Pavilion of Gustavus III at Haga can also be seen.

Also well worth seeing are the Historical Museum, remarkable for its excellent display technique, the Nordic Museum with the Royal Armory, the National Maritime Museum, the Technological Museum and the Museum of Natural History. The annual Stockholm Festival of opera, concerts, ballet, drama and movies is held the first 19 days in September. And, although of commercial inspiration, the October Scandinavian Design Cavalcade is famed for the artistry of craftsmanship on display.

BALLET . . . The famous Royal Opera Ballet performs in the Royal Opera in Stockholm. In June, the Royal Opera Ballet gives performances as part of the Stockholm Festival.

BANKS . . . Banks connected with the larger American banks are found in Stockholm and other principal cities. Currency may be exchanged at Stockholm's Airport from 6 A.M. to 8 P.M.

CALENDAR OF HOLIDAYS . . . Legal holidays are January 1 and 6; Epiphany; Good Friday; Easter Sunday; Easter Monday; May 1, Labor Day; Ascension Day (40 days after Easter Sunday); Whitsunday (50 days after Easter Sunday), Whitmonday; Midsummer Day (Saturday following June 20); All Saints Day (Saturday nearest November 1); December 25 and 26. Easter Eve, Whitsun Eve, Midsummer Eve and Christmas Eve are bank holidays. Shops are normally open between 9 A.M. and 6 P.M. on weekdays and between

9 A.M. and 2-4 P.M. on Saturday and bank holidays, though most of them close at 2 or 3 on Saturdays during the summer. Particularly colorful are the Mid-summer and Christmas celebrations. Other interesting events—which do not have the character of legal holidays—take place on April 30, Walpurgis Night; June 6, Swedish Flag Day—Sweden's National Commemoration Day; and December 13, Day of St. Lucia.

CIGARETTES AND TOBACCO ... All brands of American cigarettes and tobacco can be obtained in Sweden, though the prices are high due to heavy taxation. American cigarettes cost about 75¢ a pack. Local cigarette brands—the best of which compare favorably with American brands—begin at 3.35 kronor a pack. Cigars—local as well as a rich selection of foreign brands—are available at about the same prices as in the United States.

CLIMATE ... Misconceptions about the climate in Sweden are common, perhaps due to the country's proximity to the Arctic Circle. However, the climate in southern and central Sweden is very much the same as in New England; the winter on Sweden's west coast is milder than the New York winter. The summer is pleasantly warm and the discomforts of high humidity are unknown. The long hours of daylight during the late spring and summer add to the pleasure. The midnight sun can be seen north of the Arctic Circle from early June to the middle of July. Although the period from June 1 to September 1 is the time most tourists visit Sweden, May and particularly September, which generally is sunny and dry, would also be excellent choices.

CLUBS ... Lions International Club (the European Host Club); Rotary International; the Royal Automobile Club and the Swedish Automobile Association; American Club of Stockholm; Junior Chamber of Commerce International; International Women's Club.

COMMON COURTESIES AND LOCAL CUSTOMS ... If you are invited to dine at the home of Swedish friends, arrive promptly and ready to eat. There is generally no cocktail hour. Much formal toasting goes on at a Swedish dinner party. Never toast your hostess if there are more than six at the party, because she is obliged to toast each gentleman, but toast the other ladies. If you are the guest of honor, make a toast of thanks at the end of the meal. In restaurants in the bigger cities you have to wear a tie, and when dancing, formal dinner jackets may be required at some first-class restaurants, except during the summer. You may have heard the Swedes described as rather formal, but there is a definite trend away from formal manners, and many families participate in the "Sweden at Home" program, which enables visitors from abroad to get to know local people in their everyday environments. Advance arrangements may be made through the Swedish National Travel Office, 630 Fifth Avenue, New York, N.Y. 10020.

COMMUNICATIONS ... From 10 A.M. to 10 P.M., a 3-minute phone call to the U.S. costs kr. 62.25; from 10 P.M. to 10 A.M., kr. 46.65. A 10-word cablegram to the States cost kr. 17.65, and you can send your cables over the hotel telephone. Letters of 5 grams (.17 ounces) are sent via airmail for 60 öre to the United States, postcards for 35 öre; international airletters cost 60 öre.

CURRENCY ... The monetary unit is the krona (plural kronor), which is divided into 100 öre. There are banknotes for 5, 10, 50, 100, 1,000 and 10,000 kronor. According to the official rate of exchange, you get approximately 5.18 kronor for your dollar.

CUSTOMS REGULATIONS AND DOCUMENTS REQUIRED FOR UNITED STATES CITIZENS ... Medicines for private use, 2 quart bottles of liquor or wine, reasonable quantities of film, 400 cigarettes or 100 cigars or 1 pound of pipe tobacco may be brought in duty free. Firearms cannot pass customs without special permission. You are allowed to bring in 6,000 kronor. Your passport is all that is necessary to enter Sweden. If you wish to stay for more than 3 months, you will have to get a special permit from the alien authorities. However, this is a mere formality and the permit is very easy to obtain. Bring your driver's license if you wish to hire a car.

DRUGSTORES ... No drugstores exist, in the American sense of the word. However, there are restaurants of the cafeteria type (often called "milk bars") everywhere, and there are pastry shops, called *Konditori,* where you can have coffee, tea, sandwiches and delicious pastry. Cigarettes are bought in tobacco shops or from automats. Drugs and medicines can be had at pharmacies, called *Apotek.*

ELECTRIC CURRENT ... The voltage in most places in Sweden, including Stockholm, is 220 A.C., although 115 and 127 voltages are also used, particularly in the provinces. It is all 50 cycles and nearly everywhere alternating current. The plugs and outlets used in Sweden are different from the ones in the United States, so bring along an inset of the type that is screwed into a standard lamp socket.

FAUNA ... Sweden stretches from the 55th parallel in the south to the 69th in the north—as does Alaska. Sweden's fauna, therefore, is very much the same as that of Alaska and Canada. The zoo at the above-mentioned Skansen outdoor museum offers an excellent exhibit of Sweden's wild life. There are reindeer (domesticated by the Lapps), moose, bear, wolf, capercailzie, black cock, hazelhen, ptarmigan, woodcock, crane, wild goose.

FLORA ... Birch, mountain birch, juniper tree, pine, "arctic" raspberry, wild strawberry and raspberry, cloudberry, bilberry, lingonberry.

FOOD ... The great smörgåsbord tables have even surpassed the level of their pre-war lavishness. There are delicious pressed meats, sausages served hot and cold, salads, fish dishes and innumerable vegetable dishes. Remember when you're eating it that this is merely a first course and the main meal is to follow. *Snaps* is drunk with this part of the meal. The Swedish are famous for their dairy products and fine fish dishes. Be sure to eat crayfish in August. Swedish pastries are rich and delicious. Morning coffee and rolls will be served in your room at the hotel—larger breakfasts can be had in the dining room.

Food in self-sufficient Sweden is plentiful. Mealtimes are about like those at home. Dinner is served beginning at 5 P.M.

GAMBLING ... Gambling casinos are not allowed in Sweden. Horse racing every Saturday and Sunday. Racetracks in Stockholm and also in Gothenburg, Malmö, Karlstad, Gävle, Örebro and Ostersund. Only pari-mutuel betting.

LANGUAGE ... Swedish is the official language. English is spoken and understood by most people, especially in the cities. How do you do and good-bye in Swedish are *goddag* and *adjö*. Thank you, which is used on every occasion, is *tack så mycket* or *tack, tack*.

LAUNDRY AND DRY CLEANING ... Cleaning and laundry facilities are good everywhere and of high quality, but they are more expensive than in the States—a suit costs about $3 to $5 and generally takes a few days. If you want it quicker there will be an additional fee. You will find dry-cleaning shops everywhere.

LIQUOR ... All American drinks and cocktails are available. Cocktails cost about $1.25, *snaps* about 75¢. Liquor is not served in restaurants before noon. Minimum legal age for drinkers is 18.

MEDICAL FACILITIES ... Stockholm and most of Sweden have excellent doctors, dentists and modern medical facilities. Most doctors speak English. Ask at your hotel, should you need a doctor.

MOTION PICTURES ... Stockholm has about 130 theaters. American pictures with their original sound track are the most popular. French, British and Swedish films are also shown. See the daily paper for times, programs and theaters.

MUSIC ... The Royal Opera in Stockholm, one of the oldest opera houses in the world, is famous for its high artistic standards. The season is from August to June. Concerts are given at the Stockholm Concert Hall from September to May. Permanent symphony orchestras outside of Stockholm are found in Gothenburg, Malmö, Hälsingborg, Norrköping and Gävle. The Stockholm Festival offers outstanding opera performances and concerts. The concert repertory in Sweden includes internationally known works as well as the works of modern and classic Swedish composers. Concert halls are closed in the summer, but there are open-air concerts given in the parks, notably the Skansen in Stockholm. Also open in summer is the Drottningholm Court Theater, its delightful 18th-century décor still intact.

NIGHT CLUBS AND CABARETS ... Many restaurants are open until 3 A.M. and feature floor shows. Among the best in Stockholm are: *Ambassadeur, Bacchi Wapen, Hamburger Börs, Club Opera, Cecil, Berns* and *Strand Hotel*. Swedish jazz is exceptionally good, and the best places to hear it are the *Nalen* dance palace on Regeringsgatan in Stockholm (open winter only), and the jazz restaurant *Gyllene Cirkeln*.

PHOTOGRAPHY ... Every kind of photo equipment is available. A color-movie film, 8 mm., costs about $3.50. Developing takes about a week for ordinary pictures, but can be rushed. The best-known shops, which do an excellent job, are: Hasselblads Fotografiska AB,

Hamngatan 16; Nerliens Foto AB, Kungsgatan 19; and Molanders, Regeringsgatan 13, all in Stockholm.

RELIGION . . . Sweden is a Protestant country. The State Church, of which almost everyone is a member by birth, is Lutheran. There are Catholic, Methodist, Episcopal, Christian Science churches and Jewish synagogues in Stockholm and elsewhere.

RESTAURANTS . . . There is a lot of superb eating to be done in Stockholm. Everyone will soon find his favorite place to dine, but here are some of the best: the *Operakällaren,* one of Europe's great restaurants; the *Riche,* serving primarily French food, is first class, and so is the *Teatergrillen. Stallmästargården* is a must. *Den Gyldene Freden* is typically Swedish and *Berns* is a big restaurant with floor shows and excellent French and Chinese cuisines. *Hamburger Börs, Djurgårdsbrunns Wärdshus, Maritim, La Ronde, Strand's Roof Terrace, Bacchi Wapen, Stortorgskällaren, Fratis, Cecil* and the *Solliden* in Skansen are all very good. The dining rooms of most hotels have very fine food, especially the swank *Grand Hotel Restaurant.* You can eat elegantly and superbly for $15 a day in Stockholm, you can eat well for half that figure, and you can eat quite adequately for only $4 a day. Expensive dinners start at around $4, but a very satisfying meal can be had for as little as $1.50. Milk bars serve good, inexpensive, lunch-counter food. Wine and beer restaurants are good, too.

SHOPS AND STORES . . . In Stockholm: K. A. Anderson for fine jewelry; Atelier Borgila for unique, modern silverware; Fritzes for books; try Svenskt Tenn for pottery and textiles; note Sörmans, Nordiska Kristallmagasinet and Svenskt Glas for glass; Williams, Leja and Valdy's are fine exclusive women's apparel shops; Bastman's for sporting equipment; Palmgren's for luggage and exquisite leather goods; Nordiska Kompaniet (NK)$_e$ is the largest department store (see their modern furniture); and Åhléns and Paul U. Bergström is the newest. Morris, Skoglunds and Ströms are excellent men's shops. There are numerous exhibitions and shops that specialize in ceramics, pottery, textiles and handicraft products; the main shopping district in Stockholm consists of the new Sergelgatan shopping mall; Kungsgatan, Drottninggatan, Hamngatan and adjacent streets. For bargains in antiques, try the Old Town.

SPECTATOR SPORTS . . . Racing is very popular in and around Stockholm. The season begins in May and lasts through November. Täby is the principal track. Trotting races are held at the Stockholm Trotting Club during most of the year. Soccer, field and track events are followed with enthusiasm. Athletic and gymnastic exhibitions are held all year around at Stockholm's many gymnasiums. Yachting races and tennis matches enjoy seasonal popularity.

SPORTS . . . Sweden is a sportsman's paradise. The Swedes are an athletic, outdoor people, and their facilities are of the finest. The lakes and mountain streams offer excellent fishing. Salmon and salmon trout, pike and perch are in abundance. There is tuna and other big-game fishing on the west coast. Golf is nationally popular. There are good courses throughout the country; Kevinge, Djursholm,

Drottningholm, Lidingö and Saltsjöbaden are the best near Stockholm. The courses and clubhouses are open to tourists. Good tennis courts are found all over Sweden. Stockholm has indoor courts for year-round play. Yachting is popular and fashionable in the Stockholm archipelago. Sailing and swimming are favorite summer sports. Boats can be rented at Saltsjöbaden's *Grand Hotel* and at N. K. Kristenson "Marina" harbor. The beaches on the archipelago are lovely. The mountains in the north are a hiker's paradise; guides are available. The end of summer is the best time of year. As in all Scandinavian countries, nearly everybody skis in Sweden. Accommodations, skis and guides are available at moderate rates. Other winter sports include skating, tobogganing and curling. There are exhibition skating matches.

THEATERS . . . The Royal Dramatic Theater season is from September to June. As part of the Stockholm Festival, special performances are offered at the beginning of September. The *China Variety Revue Theater* has a Continental revue program from April to September. The *Drottningholm Court Theater,* established in the 18th century by King Gustav III and preserved exactly in its original form, is unique, charming and definitely worth seeing. Rococo operas are performed during the Stockholm Festival, and also earlier in the summer. The *Skansens Friluftsteater* is a beautiful open-air theater in the Skansen, where Shakespearean plays are presented in summer. There is also an English-language theater open in summer. In Uppsala, the *Uppsala Castle Theater* is outstanding. Ticket prices at all these theaters are moderate, ranging from 80¢ to $5.

TIME . . . Six hours later than U.S. Eastern Standard Time.

TIPPING . . . Restaurants and hotels have a service charge of 10 to 15%. Tip porters 1 krona per bag, and give 50 öre for most small services. Hat-check girls and washroom attendants get 50 öre. Follow the 10 to 15% rule when tipping cab drivers, beauticians and barbers.

TOURIST TAXES . . . Air departure tax $3.

TRANSPORTATION . . . The transportation system in Stockholm includes buses, trams and a brand-new subway. Bus fare from the airport into Stockholm is kr. 7. Taxi fares are reasonable and cabs can be ordered by telephone. Longer trips may be made by bus, train, or air. Cars for long trips may also be hired with or without a chauffeur. The Swedish State Railways trains are regarded as the best and the most modern in Europe. They offer two classes, but most people go second class, which offers the same standard as the American railroad coaches. There are organized tours to nearly every place.

WATER . . . The water is safe to drink in every town in Sweden. Bottled water may be necessary on prolonged hiking trips and fishing expeditions. Inquire at the local village.

WHAT TO BUY . . . Glass and crystal are your best buys. Pottery, pewter and silverware are excellent. Cutlery made of famous Swedish steel and stainless tableware are quite reasonable and should be high on your list. English and Swedish textiles are of very fine quality. Modern furniture is tempting, too. Smaller pieces can be dismantled for shipping. There are many bargains to be had in various native handicrafts. Shipment of bulky articles can easily be arranged.

WHAT TO WEAR ... Stockholm winters are only a little cooler than in northeastern U.S. Bring woolens and tweeds. Summer temperatures are normally very comfortable, with averages around 60 degrees (even far north); high humidity is unknown in Sweden. Eight hours of sunshine per day is the average during the summer months. You can leave the lightest summer clothes at home, but bring your topcoat as the nights may be chilly. Raincoats are a must. Sports clothes in the country and for general sightseeing wear are correct. Simple black dresses or dressy suits will be all you need in Stockholm. Formal clothes are rarely worn except at gala openings and banquets and when dancing in first-class restaurants. Flannels and sports jackets during the day and business suits in the evening are correct for men. Rugged, simple clothes are worn in the mountains. The Swedish are conservative about clothes, so wear conventional outfits for active sports, except at the beach.

WHERE TO GO—SIGHTSEEING ...

Stockholm ... Stockholm is one of the loveliest cities in the world. The architecture is a perfect blend of centuries of good taste. Beautiful, clean modern buildings are in perfect harmony with 17th-century baroque. It's a good idea to take a boat ride through the waterways and around the islands of the city for your first bout of sightseeing. You'll get a fine over-all impression of this charming city. The Town Hall is Stockholm's trademark and one of the most beautiful buildings in Europe. The medieval section of town is called the "City between the Bridges." Here you'll find quaintly twisting little streets lined with artists' studios and curious little shops; the old church of St. Gertrud chimes the hours. Riddarholm Church is the burial place of many of Sweden's kings and queens. See the wonderful art collection at the Waldemarsudde, mentioned under ARTS. Take a night boat ride to Djurgården. Beautiful parks and magnificent buildings are found in this region. A landau ride by moonlight is wonderfully romantic here. Take a day to see Drottningholm Palace, three-quarters of an hour from the center of town by a little lake steamer. There is a fine inn here with atmosphere and good food. The palace, breath-takingly lovely, has been called the Swedish Versailles. There are many excellently planned tours of various parts of the city; private guides are available. Millesgården on the island of Lidingö (25 minutes by tramway from the center of Stockholm) is the home of the famous sculptor Carl Milles. It is surrounded by a charming terraced garden and contains a rich and unique collection of antique sculptures and works by the artist. *Vasa*, the 17th-century man-of-war salvaged from Stockholm harbor, is now a special museum on Djurgården Island.

Side Trips ... Recently a tour has been organized with special consideration for guests from America: the Sunlit Nights Land Cruise of the Swedish State Railways, 8 days aboard a special luxury train. It takes you to the fabulous region of the Midnight Sun. You travel north from Stockholm in easy stages, visiting the romantic province

Stockholm's Concert Hall with its busy flower market in the foreground is just one of the capital's many cultural centers.

of Dalarna, to beyond the Arctic Circle and back, stopping to visit the colorful, nomadic Lapps and their reindeer herds, waterfalls, open-pit iron mines. For 4 days of the trip you are under the Midnight Sun, and never see darkness. There are also Midnight Sun plane excursions from Stockholm; round-trip flights to Kiruna are $90, including meals and ground excursions.

Uppsala is about 40 miles north of Stockholm (50 minutes by train). In nearby Old Uppsala there are burial mounds of ancient chieftains. The University was founded in the 15th century. The Renaissance Castle and Cathedral are very lovely and interesting historically. Stay at the *Gillet,* the new *Rullan* or at the *Stadshotellet* for about $5-$6 a night. A 20-minute drive north of Uppsala takes you to the picturesque fishing village of Öregrund, where the *Hasselbacken* restaurant is a charming place to dine.

Inquire about the excellent Nils Holgersson trip all over Sweden.

Dalarna . . . Heading northwest you come to the charming province of Dalarna. Rättvik on Lake Siljan is the central point for excursions in this region. Many of Sweden's outstanding artists and poets have come from Dalarna. It is a great ski center, and world champions belong to its clubs. Good accommodations and instruction are available and the skiing is wonderful. Summer is equally lovely in this region. See "The Road to Heaven," an open-air allegorical play performed at the village of Leksand each July. Hiking and mountain climbing are popular. There are Youth Hostels throughout the region as well as quaint inns. Gay festivals are a feature of Dalarna.

Lapland . . . The northernmost part of Sweden is the unspoiled arctic region of Lapland. Arctic flora, mountain peaks shimmering in the sun and dazzling mountain lakes make Lapland serenely and gloriously beautiful. This is truly the Land of the Midnight Sun. The northern lights are here in all their blazing glory. The Swedish Touring Club has done much to enable the tourist to see this province. Trails have been cut through the forests, bridges and paths have been made, and much money has gone into building railroads through the rugged terrain. Boating facilities are available on the mountain lakes,

The neat little island of Riddarholmen in Stockholm shows how inlets, bays and straits form a network, setting off each section of the city.

Near the seaport city of Kalmar in the picturesque southeastern section of Sweden stands historic Kalmar Castle.

Only 45 minutes by little white steamer from Stockholm is Drottningholm, the King's old summer palace. This view is of the elegant Palace Gardens.

fishing is popular, and hikers and climbers will find endless attractions here. The culture of the primitive Lapps is much as it has been for centuries. The Swedish government has done a great deal to protect these people against exploitation. Kiruna or Abisko are the best bases of operations for seeing Lapland. Guides, accommodations and tourist information are available. A comfortable way to see this area for about $112 is to take an all-inclusive North Cape tour, 7 days by de luxe bus, starting at Kiruna.

Skåne . . . Skåne, the southernmost part of Sweden, is a fertile farm area with rolling plains and beechwood-clad ridges. It is sometimes known as the Château Country because of its hundreds of castles and fine mansions, among them Glimmingehus and Trolleholm. Malmö is the third largest town in the country. It is a busy modern port. The modern architecture in the city is of the best. The *St. Jorgen* and *Plaza* hotels are both brand new. Lund is an old university town, also the site of Scandinavia's finest Romanesque cathedral. Hälsingborg (opposite Denmark's Helsingør) is the main port of entry for motorists. Nearby Båstad is one of the best resorts. Malmö is 2 hours by air from Stockholm, 6 hours by train.

Gothenburg . . . Sweden's second city is Gothenburg (Göteborg). It is a vital port town and under 2 hours by air from Stockholm. There are theaters, a fine shopping district, modern housing developments and beautiful parks. Fishing, sailing and boating are all popular. So are golf and tennis. The regattas at nearby Marstrand are world famous. From Gothenburg to Stockholm, or vice versa, one can travel via the famous Overland Waterway (Göta Kanal), a 3-day trip. The new *Grand Haglund* and *Park Avenue Hotel* are first class. Rates begin at $8 a day. The *Palace*, the new *Opalen* and the *Eggers* are also recommended. Average single rates are $7.

Kalmar . . . This magnificent old city is a good headquarters for trips to Orrefors, Kosta and other great glass factories. Daily summer Crystal Tours of the region (4 hours, $3) are available.

Visby . . . The Isle of Gotland in the Baltic Sea should be a must on your list. Its capital, Visby, is the only walled city in northern Europe. In the Middle Ages it was a great trading center, and it contains many fine buildings of that era. There are more than 90 medieval country churches on the island, many of them exquisite. Stora Karlsö island, just off the coast of Gotland, is a bird sanctuary with interesting flora. Visby is an hour by air from Stockholm.

SOURCES OF FURTHER INFORMATION . . . Svenska Turisttrafikförbundet (Swedish Tourist Traffic Assoc.), Klara v. Kyrkogata 6, Stockholm (general information); Tourist Information Office at Gustav Adolfs torg 20; KAK (Royal Automobile Club), Södra Blasieholmshamnen 6, Stockholm (motoring); hotel accommodation service at "Hotellcentralen" in the Central Station (Tel. 24 08 80). Pan American's office at Jakobstorg 1, Stockholm (Tel. 23 19 20). In the United States write for descriptive literature to Scandinavia House, 505 Fifth Avenue, New York, N.Y. 10017; or Scandinavian Travel Commission, 612 South Flower St., Los Angeles, Cal. 90017.

SWITZERLAND

FRANCE
GERMANY
Basel
Zurich
AUSTRIA
Lucerne
BERN ★
Chur
SWITZERLAND
LAKE
GENEVA Lausanne
St. Moritz
Montreux
Locarno
Geneva Zermatt
Lugano
MONT BLANC
ITALY

WEATHER IN GENEVA—Lat. N46°12'–Alt. 1,237'

Temp.	JAN.	FEB.	MAR.	APR.	MAY	JUNE	JULY	AUG.	SEPT.	OCT.	NOV.	DEC.
Low	28°	28°	31°	41°	50°	57°	60°	59°	51°	42°	35°	29°
High	30°	37°	44°	52°	61°	66°	70°	69°	63°	53°	42°	35°
Average	29°	33°	38°	47°	56°	62°	65°	64°	57°	48°	39°	32°
Days of Rain	12	13	13	15	15	15	14	13	12	12	12	13

LOCATION ... Almost in the exact geographic center of Europe, Switzerland is next door to France, Italy, Austria and Germany. Geneva and Zurich are less than one hour by air from Paris; less than two hours from London, Brussels and Amsterdam.

CHARACTERISTICS ... A matchless variety of attractions. The Alps, the Swiss lakes, picturesque old villages, sparkling modern cities, rustic simplicity, swank resorts have attracted generations of vacationists, winter and summer, to this small but vital country. The Swiss treat the tourist with cordiality and warmth. Swiss efficiency has not been exaggerated, nor have Swiss honesty and cleanliness, all traits which give industrious Switzerland an importance far out of proportion to her size.

POPULATION ... About 5,840,000. Zurich, Switzerland's largest city, has a population of 440,000; Basel has 207,000; Geneva and Berne, the next largest cities have less than 200,000 inhabitants each.

SIZE ... Slightly under 16,000 square miles; 180 miles wide, 130 miles long.

CAPITAL ... Berne, population 163,172.

GOVERNMENT ... A Federal Republic. Each of Switzerland's 22 cantons (states) sends representatives to legislative bodies corresponding to the U.S. Senate and House of Representatives. Switzerland, founded in 1291, is the oldest existing democracy.

HOW TO GET THERE ... By Jet Clipper from New York to London, Paris or Frankfurt with connections to Zurich, 11 hours. Or from the U.S. West Coast about 10½ hours to London via Pan Am's polar route, then to Zurich. Zurich is 1½ hours from Rome by air. Geneva is a 1½ hours' flight from London. By ship 5 to 9 days to West Atlantic or Mediterranean ports and then overnight by train. Switzerland is the crossroads of the European railway network; from London and Paris the Simplon Express passes through Lausanne to Italy, and the Arlberg Express passes through Basel, with connections to Klosters, Davos, Arosa and St. Moritz, on the way to Vienna. "Europabus" from Amsterdam goes to Basel, Lucerne, Interlaken and Montreux with connections to Milan or Nice. You can even go by Rhine boat from Rotterdam to Basel in summer.

ACCOMMODATIONS ... Although some are more elegant than others, there's no such thing as a bad Swiss hotel: as far as service, basic comfort, cleanliness, courtesy and honesty are concerned, all are first class. Rates in luxury hotels are about $10 to $15 per day per person. If you can dispense with the trimmings, you can be just as comfortable in a more modest hotel for half the price. Some resort hotels offer attractive off-season rates. For names of hotels in each city, see listing under individual cities.

ARTS ... The city art museums of Zurich, Geneva and Basel have fine permanent collections. The best Holbeins on the Continent can be seen in Basel, and the Art Museum in Berne houses the great Paul Klee collection. Even the museums of the smaller cities often feature temporary exhibits of outstanding interest. Many private collections, such as the famed Reinhart collection of modern European masters in Winterthur, may be viewed with special permission.

BALLET ... Although Switzerland has no national ballet, major companies touring Europe almost invariably play the larger Swiss cities. The Paris Opera Ballet, the ANTA Ballet and the Marquis de Cuevas' Company usually visit Lausanne in June.

BANKS ... American Express and Thos. Cook & Son have branches in all major Swiss cities. The Swiss Bank Corporation, the Union Bank of Switzerland and Crédit Suisse have foreign departments that correspond with American banks. Travelers checks may be cashed at banks, railway stations, large hotels and stores.

CALENDAR OF HOLIDAYS ... August 1, Swiss Independence Day, is celebrated everywhere with fireworks displays. Other national holidays are: Christmas, New Year's Day, Good Friday, Easter and Whitmonday, Ascension Day and Corpus Christi Day in predominately Catholic regions. Stores and museums close on holidays.

CIGARETTES AND TOBACCO ... Imported U.S. brands may be found generally at about 40¢ a pack. Swiss, British and American brands made in Switzerland run from 20¢ to 30¢ a pack and are usually milder than American cigarettes, but quite good. Matches are not given free when you buy tobacco. Pipe tobacco and cigars are available in all price ranges.

CLIMATE ... Seasons and temperature ranges are similar to those of the northern U.S., without the extremities of heat and cold. Nights are cool even in the hottest part of the summer. Weather is best from May to September and from December through March. The clearness of the air and absence of wind make it possible to get a good tan in December in the high mountain regions; sunglasses are a must in winter and summer. The Ticino—southern Switzerland—has palm trees and a balmy, California-like climate.

CLUBS . . . Rotary and Lions meet regularly in larger cities. Switzerland's two major auto clubs, TCS and ACS, are affiliated with American clubs. Local U.S. Consulates give information concerning meetings of the Swiss Friends of the U.S.A. and the Swiss Society for Cultural Relations with America, as well as local American Women's Clubs and other organizations. Use of the facilities of private golf, tennis, yacht and sports clubs may usually be arranged through hotels, or upon presentation of membership cards of similar U.S. clubs.

COMMON COURTESIES AND LOCAL CUSTOMS . . . The Swiss, although friendly, are a bit more reserved than Americans. Only members of the family and intimate friends are on a "first name" basis. Men not only tip their hats to ladies but to friends of the same sex, and there's a lot of handshaking. But, in general, the forms of etiquette and good manners are the same as at home. Kady is a service in Zurich which can provide you with baby sitter, translator, shopping service, etc.

COMMUNICATIONS . . . The superefficient Swiss Post Office operates telephone and cable systems. Calls may be dialed anywhere within Switzerland. Transatlantic telephone and cable service is excellent. Basic airmail rate to the United States: letter, 75 centimes; postal card, 55 centimes.

CURRENCY . . . The monetary unit is the Swiss franc divided into 100 centimes. Current rate of exchange is approximately 4.30 Swiss francs to the dollar. Switzerland has no currency restrictions and is the most advantageous country in Europe for buying the currency of other countries you plan to visit.

CUSTOMS REGULATIONS AND DOCUMENTS REQUIRED FOR UNITED STATES CITIZENS . . . No visa required, only a valid U.S. passport. Personal effects, including 2 cartons of cigarettes, or 100 cigars, or 500 grams of tobacco, 2 bottles of wine or 1 bottle each of wine and liquor and 1 pint of perfume. Amateur camera equipment and film are admitted free. Special permission must be obtained from the Swiss Consulate for unusual or professional photographic equipment. Regulations on Swiss watches are likely to vary with the make, so check with the United States Customs before attempting to bring them back.

DRUGSTORES . . . Swiss drugstores carry all the pharmaceuticals you need, including many familiar U.S. brands, but no chocolate sodas (for ice cream and soft drinks, go to a "tearoom"), cigarettes or household appliances. American products are available at most department and grocery stores.

ELECTRIC CURRENT . . . Most of Switzerland is supplied with alternating current, 220 volts, 50 cycles; American plugs do not fit Swiss sockets. In some Alpine valleys, there is direct current or some unusual voltage like 125 or 150. Always ask hotel staff before using your own electric appliances to avoid damage.

FAUNA . . . Good hunting and fishing, but cantonal licenses are necessary. Most streams and lakes are restocked annually with game fish (mainly trout and perch). If you are interested in wild life, the Swiss National Park in the Grisons is well worth a visit.

FLORA . . . Tremendous variety of wildflowers in the Alpine regions. Edelweiss, which grows only in almost inaccessible mountain areas, is more or less the national flower. The extravagantly flowered Alpine meadow, which bursts forth spontaneously in all its glory each spring, is as much a symbol of Switzerland as the tulip field is of Holland. Especially lovely, in a spectacular setting, is the Alpine garden on the Schynige Platte (6,781 feet) near Interlaken.

FOOD . . . Cuisine in Switzerland is French, German or Italian according to the language spoken in the region. By U.S. standards, restaurant prices are extremely low. A first-class meal, without wine or coffee, in an ordinary restaurant costs around $2.50, and a gastronomic treat, with fine wines, in a de luxe restaurant can be had for about $8. Servings are much larger than we are accustomed to at home. Each region has its specialties in food and wine: melted cheese dishes (*fondue* and *raclette*) in the French-speaking regions; roasts with rich sauces, wonderful sausages, and *rosti* (something like hashed brown potatoes, only better) in the German-speaking parts; delicious air-dried meats sliced paper-thin (*Bindenfleisch*) in the canton of Grisons and in the Valais. Don't hesitate to ask the restaurant proprietor to describe the local specialty—a little interest will often pay gastronomic dividends. Bread, butter and water are usually served only upon request. Water is completely safe everywhere. Pasteurized milk is generally available and safe to drink. The continental breakfast—rolls, butter, jam, coffee, tea or chocolate—is the rule in Switzerland, but you can always order your orange juice, bacon and eggs, and cereal. *Coca-Cola* is on sale just about everywhere but you should also sample the various Swiss wines.

GAMBLING . . . Many resorts and resort cities have casinos with gaming rooms. *Boule,* a modified form of roulette, is the only game. Don't expect to make a killing—the limit per bet is 5 francs. There is occasional horse racing in larger cities with parimutuel betting, and winter racing (on snow tracks) in Davos, Arosa and St. Moritz. If you're really interested in losing money, there are also the national lotteries and football and soccer pools.

LANGUAGE . . . French, German and Italian are recognized by the Swiss Government as official languages. There's a fourth, Romansch (Rhaeto-romansch), consisting of a pre-Roman stock of words and a strong substratum of Latin elements, believed to be the language of old Helvetica. It is spoken by about 40,000 people in the canton of Grisons. English, however, is spoken and understood in most places where tourists are likely to go. It's best though, to speak slowly and clearly and to avoid slang expressions.

LAUNDRY AND DRY CLEANING . . . Available in large cities and resort hotels. Service is excellent, work beautiful, prices outrageous. Don't complain if you pay over $3 for a dry-cleaning job—your Swiss host pays the same price. Not all hotels are equipped to do your laundry overnight.

LIQUOR ... Bar prices are slightly lower than in the States. Bottled goods—Scotch, bourbon, gin—cost about the same. Swiss wines are very good, but unlike French wines they are not aged. It pays to ask the head waiter or restaurant proprietor to recommend wines. Swiss liquors, *Marc, Kirsch, Pflumli,* are renowned and potent.

MEDICAL FACILITIES ... Swiss doctors and hospital facilities have a well-deserved high reputation. All hotels have house physicians. There is a Swiss spa or sanatorium for almost every ailment. The Swiss National Tourist Office (see end of this section for addresses) publishes a descriptive listing of these.

MOTION PICTURES ... Current American and British films are shown with English sound track. German, French and Italian films carry subtitles in other languages, but not English. Movie performances are not continuous; often seats must be booked in advance (ask your hotel concierge) as in American legitimate theaters. Children under 16 are generally not admitted to evening shows.

MUSIC ... Larger cities feature regular concerts with outstanding local and visiting talent. Geneva, Zurich, Basel, Lucerne and Berne have their own opera houses. Check with the Swiss National Tourist Office for program of events and information concerning International Music Festivals in Lucerne, Montreux, Zurich, Ascona, the Engadine and other places.

NIGHT CLUBS AND CABARETS ... See listings for each city under WHERE TO GO.

PHOTOGRAPHY ... Film is available everywhere in all sizes and film speeds, color and black-and-white, still and movie. Good black-and-white and Ektachrome processing in 24 hours at local photo shops; one week for Kodachrome.

RELIGION ... Although individual regions in Switzerland are predominately either Catholic or Protestant, there are churches of the other denominations. Synagogues and Christian Science churches are found only in larger cities, Protestant services in English in larger cities. Hotels and local tourist offices give information on services.

RESTAURANTS ... Recommended ones for each city are listed under WHERE TO GO. Restaurants in the railroad stations, called *Buffet de la Gare,* are usually excellent. *Movenpick* is a popular snack-bar chain in several cities. Most trains have dining cars serving snacks, drinks and fine meals.

SHOPS AND STORES ... In Zurich, be sure to visit the Heimatwerk, not only a shop but a landmark. Native Swiss handicrafts are featured here. Prices are high, but values superb. See others listed for each city under WHERE TO GO. There are tax-free shops at the International Airports in Zurich and Geneva.

SPECTATOR SPORTS ... Soccer, football, cross-country bike racing. Swiss folklore sports: wrestling and *hornussen,* which the Swiss claim is a combination of golf and baseball.

SPORTS ... Follow the Swiss themselves if you're interested in active sports. Swimming, boating, mountain climbing, tennis, golf, horseback riding, rifle shooting, trap shooting—there are excellent facilities for practically every sport. The Swiss ski schools are government supervised and very moderate in price—the same is true of mountain-climbing schools. Before embarking on either of these sports, even if you're an expert, a short course is advisable—the Swiss themselves enroll in them every year at the beginning of the season. If you can't bring your own ski equipment, excellent skis and ski boots may be rented at a nominal cost. Ski-boating is the newest craze at St. Moritz. You can rent one of these plastic soup plates for about 50¢ a day. No special skill is required to have a lot of fun with a ski-boat, and the chance of broken bones (or dignity) is minimal.

THEATERS ... Legitimate theaters in larger cities—plays in the language of the region: French, German or Italian. Performances generally begin at 8:15 P.M. Top price for tickets is around $3.

TIME ... Noon in Switzerland is 6 A.M. in New York.

TIPPING ... 12 to 15% is the general rule. When tip is included in your hotel bill or restaurant check, it is not necessary to give more unless you feel that the service has been exceptional. Porters get 80 centimes for each bag they carry.

TOURIST TAXES ... Hotels in resort areas usually add a nominal Tourist Tax to your bill.

TRANSPORTATION ... The Swiss Federal Railways adhere almost 100% to schedule. First class is excellent; second class is comfortable and clean, but sometimes crowded. Be sure to ask your travel agent about special holiday tickets on Swiss railroads, alpine postal buses and lake steamers. You can save up to 50% on rail fares if you do enough traveling. Out-of-the-way regions may be reached on the safe, comfortable Post Office buses. Local tram and motorbus transportation is convenient, comfortable and rapid. Taxis are apt to be expensive; look for cabs marked *Klein Taxi* or *Petit Taxi*—the tariff is considerably lower. Car rental is best arranged in advance through your travel agent, or through the concierge of your hotel. Rates: Cadillac with English-speaking driver, $52.50 per day, Ford, Chevrolet or Buick, $37.50 including 150 kilometers a day. Drive-yourself rentals come to around $10 per day for light American cars, $4 to $8 a day for European cars, with a surcharge of from 4¢ to 10¢ per kilometer. Deposit required: $50-$100. These rates include public liability and property damage insurance for unlimited coverage. You must have a U.S., Canadian or West European or International driver's license.

WATER ... Completely pure and safe everywhere, unless otherwise noted in large red letters. All Swiss bottled waters (Henniez, Passugger, etc.) are carbonated, but many restaurants sell imported waters that aren't.

WHAT TO BUY ... Best bargains are watches. Popular Swiss makes sell for about 40% less here than in the States, and there are even better buys in lesser-known makes. Prices are strictly controlled and the same everywhere, but the larger shops usually have a better selection. If you buy a gold watch or jewelry worth more than 500 Swiss francs, an export certificate will save you 3.6%. Other good buys are wood carvings, handwoven and embroidered textiles, ceramics, music boxes and jewelry.

WHAT TO WEAR . . . You'll be comfortable in the same clothing you would wear in San Francisco, Chicago or New York at the same time of the year. Compulsory formal dress is unusual—men will be safe with dark suits, and women with cocktail dresses.

WHERE TO GO—SIGHTSEEING . . .

Zurich . . . Best introduction to Switzerland's largest city is through one of the conducted sightseeing tours, sponsored by the Official Tourist Bureau. These leave the Central Station at 10 A.M. and 3 P.M. every day. Zurich is one of the centers of international banking, finance and insurance; its University Medical School and Technological Institute have earned a high position in the world of education, and its hospitals and clinics are among the world's best. In fall and winter, and during the June Festival, first-rate productions, featuring internationally celebrated stars, may be seen at the Municipal Opera House, the Civic Theater (*Schauspielhaus*), and the Concert Hall (*Tonhalle*). Zurich's Art Museum is well worth a visit; its permanent collection is small but very strong in modern French and German schools. Summer sports: golf (Dolder Grand Hotel and private clubs), tennis (Dolder Grand and Baur au Lac Hotels, and private clubs), swimming (pool with artificial waves at the Dolder Grand, large indoor swimming pool, heated, for winter use, public beaches on the Lake at Zurich), sailing, rowing and pedal-boating on the lake. All Europe shops on Zurich's Bahnhofstrasse. Grieder is a de luxe department store; Jelmoli, Globus and Oscar Weber are more popularly priced. The Grossmunster Cathedral, the Fraumunster, Wasserkirche, and St. Peter's churches were centers of the Protestant Reformation and are well worth visiting. De luxe hotels: *Dolder Grand, Baur au Lac*. Very good, but less elegant: *Carlton-Elite, St. Gotthard, Ascot, Eicher, Savoy, Central, Sonnenberg* (magnificent view of city and lake), *Bellerive, Eden au Lac, Storchen*, among others. Some restaurants with local atmosphere: *Walliser Kanne, Veltliner Keller, Opfelchammer, Kronenhalle, Astoria* and, especially, the *Zunfthauses*, or ancient guildhall restaurants. *Kranzler, Kropf* and *Bahnhofbuffet* are excellent inexpensive restaurants. If you are homesick for an American-style restaurant, try one of the *Movenpicks* (Paradeplatz, Sihlportplatz, Claridenhof). The *Hermitage* and *Alexander* are excellent lakeside restaurants just outside Zurich. Most popular night clubs are the *Terrasse, Perroquet, Embassy, Börse* and the *Odeon*—but don't expect too much. Midnight closing is the rule.

Geneva . . . One of Europe's most cosmopolitan cities, Geneva is headquarters for dozens of international organizations, including the Red Cross, World Council of Churches, International YMCA, International Labor Office, World Health Organization, and the European Office of the United Nations, which now occupies the impressive "Peace Palace" that was built for the League of Nations. It is hard to imagine a city with a more romantic setting: it lies at the outflow of the flashing Rhone from Lac Leman in the shadows of mighty Mt. Blanc, the Alps' highest peak. Geneva has some interesting specialized museums: Palais Eynard (regional birds in dioramic settings); Ariana Museum (porcelain and pottery); Voltaire and Jean-Jacques Rousseau museums; Museum of Old Musical Instruments; Art and History Museum. Then, too, there are exciting lake and river promenades, vast parks and smart shopping streets. An early morning or late summer evening stroll along the Quai du Mt. Blanc, the Quai Wilson, and through the Parc Mon-Repos is fascinating, but the most exciting spectacle of the largest city in *La Suisse Romande* (French-speaking Switzerland) is the Park of Ariana with its exquisitely landscaped gardens and monumental cream-colored buildings, now the European Headquarters of the United Nations. Boats leave from Quai du Mont-Blanc, offering a choice of from ½ hour to a full day's sightseeing on Lake Geneva. Geneva's de luxe hotels are the *Genève Intercontinental,* an 18-story building with a superb view of Lake Geneva and Mt. Blanc. *Beau-Rivage, Les Bergues, De la Paix, Richemond, President* and *d'Angleterre*—all facing the lake—and the new streamlined *Du Rhône,* overlooking the river. There are many less expensive but equally comfortable hotels scattered throughout the city: the Hotel Bureau, located in the Cornavin Station, is most helpful when, as is often the case, rooms are scarce in Geneva. The *Fêtes de Genève,* held annually in August, is one of the Continent's gayest celebrations. Other annual events of interest: Exposition of Watches and Jewelry (September), Automobile Show (March). *L'Or du Rhône, Amphitryon, Le Globe, Chandelier, Bonassi* and *Le Béarn* are among Geneva's most elegant restaurants; for local atmosphere the *Auberge à la Mère Royaume* and *Le Mazot* are recommended. *Le Gentilhomme* in the Richemond Hotel is also good. Exquisite outdoor restaurants include *La Perle du Lac* and *Parc des Eaux Vives. Café Landolt* is the meeting place of students, intellectuals and Bohemians. Night clubs are a bit on the rowdy side and far too expensive for what you get: *Ba-Ta-Clan, Moulin Rouge, Monique, Piccadilly.*

Basel... Second to Zurich in size, Basel (Basle) is splendidly situated on the Rhine and is an entry point from both France and Germany. This city is the seat of the important Swiss chemical industry, the Bank of International Settlements, and is the home port of the ever-growing merchant fleet that has made the "Swiss Navy" a reality. The Cathedral, built in the 11th century on the site of a church that was then 400 years old, is well worth visiting, if only to see the charming square and medieval houses that surround it. An outstanding collection of Holbeins (he did much of his best work in this city) is on exhibit at the Art Museum, along with interesting modern works: Picasso, Braque, Klee, Chagall, and others. People who know about zoos say that Basel's is one of the world's best—it's only a 5-minute walk from the Central Station. The *Three Kings* is internationally famous and one of Switzerland's oldest hotels—its guest books date back almost a thousand years. Lunch on the terrace overlooking the Rhine is unforgettable. Somewhat less romantic, but equally comfortable are hotels *Euler* and *Schweizerhof*. The *Drachen, International* and *City* hotels are modern and conveniently located. Recommended restaurants include the *Schlüssel, Stadtcasino, Schützenhaus, Walliser Kanne* and the *Kunsthalle*. Basel goes wild each year during the *Fasnacht* (carnival) celebration in February. The Swiss Industries Fair (April) is one of Europe's most important industrial expositions.

Berne . . . Capital of the Swiss Confederation, Berne is probably the most picturesque of the larger cities, chiefly because of its arcaded streets and decorative medieval fountains. Berne's most heralded attractions are the celebrated Clock Tower, with its hourly display of mechanical figures, and the Bear Pit, which has been maintained by the municipality since the 16th century. When visiting Berne's Old City, you'll see the Town Hall, the lovely Gothic Cathedral and the Rose Gardens. A short walk beyond the Federal Capitol brings you to the Kleine Schanze, which offers a magnificent panorama of the snow-capped peaks of the Bernese Alps. Leading hotels are the *Schweizerhof* and the *Bellevue Palace*. A restaurant with typical Bernese atmosphere is the *Kornhauskeller*. For daily guided tours of varying duration to Bernese Oberland points of interest, inquire at the Official Tourist Office or your hotel.

Lucerne . . . Less than an hour from Zurich by train, this is the storybook Swiss city and one of the country's principal tourist attractions. The city's chief landmarks are the 14th-century covered bridge that crosses the River Reuss, and the familiar Lion Monument commemorating the heroic attempt of a company of Swiss Guards to save the life of Marie Antoinette. Visit the Museum of Transport with its antiquities and miniature models; also see Tribschen, the house where Wagner lived when he wrote some of his greatest operas. Lucerne is the capital of Central Switzerland's vacationland and only a short distance from the Rigi, Pilatus, Burgenstock (an ideal spot for a longer stay—three fine hotels and every imaginable facility) and Engelberg, for winter and summer sports. A trip by boat on Lake Lucerne is delightful. The Lucerne Music Festival begins in August. New hotels are the *Astoria* and the *Hotel Luzernerhof*. Leading hotels are the *Carlton-Tivoli, National, Palace* and *Schweizerhof*. Typical restaurants: *Zum Wilden Mann, Old Swiss House, the Stadthof* and the popular *Stadtkeller*. The *Aklin*, in nearby Zug, is among the finest in Switzerland. For a pleasant meal on what seems to be the top of the world, take a mountain railway to the peak of Pilatus, Rigi, or the Stanserhorn, between 6,000 and 7,000 feet high and topped with restaurants.

Lausanne . . . A half hour by train or 3 hours by boat from Geneva, Lausanne is the cultural, educational and medical center of French-speaking Switzerland. In the romantic lakeside suburb of

These picturesque buildings are storehouses for hay and grain in the area of Zermatt and the Matterhorn.

Ouchy, where Byron lived, is the palatial *Beau Rivage,* a favorite of visiting European royalty and ex-royalty. In Lausanne proper the *Palace,* the new *Continental,* the *de la Paix* and the *Royal* are the leading hotels. Fine restaurants include *La Grappe d'Or, Mistral, Les Palmiers* and *Café à la Pomme de Pin.* Visit Vevey, a charming village rich with memories of Rousseau, Victor Hugo, Thackeray, Courbet, Byron and others, fifteen minutes from Lausanne, and Montreux, to see the historical Château de Chillon and for side trips to Rochers de Naye, Les Avants, Château d'Oex and Gstaad. Tops in Vevey are *Trois Couronnes Hotel* and the *Rive Reine* in Vevey-La Tour-de-Peilz.

Interlaken . . . Chief resort town of the Bernese Oberland, Interlaken is famed for its superb view of the Jungfrau. The fine Casino features performances of native Swiss folklore: dancing, yodeling, alphorn playing, flag throwing; summertime open-air plays. Excellent connection to *Jungfraujoch* (Europe's highest railway station, almost 12,000 feet) for an incomparable Alpine and glacial panorama. Grindelwald, Murren, and Wengen are charming resort towns en route. Leading hotel in Interlaken is the *Victoria-Jungfrau.*

The Valais . . . Here is the beautiful Rhone Valley, beginning at Martigny (turn-off point for the new Grand St. Bernard road tunnel). It passes through Sierre and Sion, with picturesque vineyards and ancient ruins, Visp (the junction for *Zermatt,* celebrated summer and winter resort at the base of the Matterhorn), and ends at Brig, the beginning of the railway tunnel, through which the Simplon Express passes daily.

The Grisons . . . From Chur, Grisons' capital, there are direct connections for Switzerland's legendary resorts: St. Moritz, Arosa, Davos, Klosters, Pontresina, Flims and Sils Maria, best known for winter sports, but equally exciting in the summer. The trip by Postal Bus from St. Moritz through the Maloja Pass, along Lake Como to Lugano offers some of the most exciting scenic splendors of Switzerland, with a bit of the Italian Lake Country thrown in as a bonus. Nature lovers should see the small but lovely Swiss National Park.

Northeast Switzerland . . . Off-the-beaten-path Switzerland, largely ignored by American tourists, is rich in attractions: pleasant rolling green country, the Rhine, lazy and meandering here; friendly, unspoiled peasantry, rich in folklore; relaxation, quiet. St. Gall, Switzerland's textile and embroidery center, is the principal city of this region. Its Cathedral and Abbey are regarded as outstanding examples of rococo architecture, and the exquisite Abbey Library is one of the show places of Europe. Near Schaffhausen one may watch the spectacular Falls of the Rhine, while enjoying freshly caught trout or salmon at *Schloss Laufen,* and then proceed to the village of Stein-am-Rhine, a beautifully preserved 16th-century town. Not far away is lovely Lake Constance. Tourists can see the Landsgeminde: the citizenry meets in the town square to decide upon important municipal issues. Near Appenzell is the imposing Santis peak, with its breathtaking air-cable railway. From this 8,000-foot peak parts of Germany, Austria, and the Alpine range are visible. Throughout this region delightful country inns, very reasonably priced and serving delicious meals, may be found. Charming hotels in St. Gall are the *Hecht, Metropol* and the *Walhalla.*

The Ticino ... The Italian-speaking section of Switzerland officially begins at Airolo, the exit of the St. Gotthard Tunnel, but the region most attractive to vacationists is concentrated in the Lugano-Locarno area. These two cities share the fabulous lakes of Lugano and Maggiore with neighboring Italy. From March through November one may be reasonably sure of warm, sunny weather in the Ticino. Tennis, golf and water sports (including water skiing) predominate. In Lugano, see the art gallery at Villa Favorita and the impressive Bernardino Luini frescoes in the tiny church of Santa Maria degli Angioli. Funiculars take you to the heights of Monte Bre, Monte San Salvatore and Monte Generoso, each offering a superb panorama. Lugano's leading hotels are the *Splendide-Royal, Bristol, Europa Grand, Du Lac,* the ultramodern *Ring* and the *Palace.* Just outside Lugano is *La Romantica.* Housed in the former villa of an Italian nobleman, this restaurant is the last word in old-world elegance and its terraces offer a rare view of Lake Lugano. Locarno, on Lake Maggiore, is smaller and more resort-like than Lugano. Nearby Ascona is a favorite resort of European artists, writers and musicians—gay, informal. The delightfully primitive mountain village of Ronco is worth a day's excursion. The lake view from its churchyard is unforgettable. Also recommended is a visit to the Isle of Brissago. The Botanical Gardens are world famous. Resort hotels in this area are generally open only from mid-March through October.

SOURCES OF FURTHER INFORMATION ... The Swiss National Tourist Office, Talacker 42, Zurich, with offices in New York (10 West 49 Street), San Francisco (661 Market St.), and many European countries. Local tourist offices are to be found in every city or resort throughout Switzerland (usually marked in German *"Verkehrsbüro"* and in French *"Bureau de Renseignements"*). American Embassy at Berne, Consulate General at Zurich, Consulate at Basel. Pan American is at 46, Bahnhofstrasse, Zurich (Tel. 237704).

YUGOSLAVIA

ITALY AUST.
Opatija Ljubljana HUNGARY
Portoroz
Lovran Zagreb RUM.
Rovinj Kralievica
Rab Crikvenica
Zadar BELGRADE
Biograd Sarajevo
Dubrovnik YUGOSLAVIA
Hercegnovi Titograd BULG.
Budva Bar Skopji
ADRIATIC ALBANIA GREECE
SEA

WEATHER IN BELGRADE—Lat. N44°47'—Alt. 394'

	JAN.	FEB.	MAR.	APR.	MAY	JUNE	JULY	AUG.	SEPT.	OCT.	NOV.	DEC.
Average Temp.	33°	35°	46°	54°	63°	68°	72°	72°	66°	54°	43°	35°
Days of Rain	12	13	15	14	15	16	12	10	12	12	12	13

LOCATION . . . On the Adriatic Sea, bordering on Austria, Greece, Italy, Albania, Bulgaria, Hungary and Rumania.

CHARACTERISTICS . . . With its beautiful mountain and coastal resorts, lively festivals, low prices and hospitable people, Yugoslavia is a vacation paradise. Best times to go are April to October for the coast, December to April for winter sports.

POPULATION . . . Approximately 19,294,000.

SIZE . . . 98,766 square miles: 550 miles long, 250 miles wide.

CAPITAL . . . Belgrade, with a population of 820,000.

GOVERNMENT . . . A Socialist Federal Republic of Serbia, Croatia, Slovenia. Bosnia-Herzegovina, Macedonia, Montenegro.

HOW TO GET THERE . . . By Pan Am Jet Clipper in 11¼ hours from New York to Belgrade, with stops at London and Frankfurt.

ACCOMMODATIONS . . . Best hotels in Belgrade are the *Metropol, Majestic, Kasina, Slavija, Moskva, Palace* and *Excelsior.* No hotel in Yugoslavia charges more than $14 a day for a room with bath and 3 meals, and there are many new resorts on the Dalmatian coast where all-inclusive rates are only $4 to $6. Some of the country's most distinguished luxury hotels are the new *Intercontinental Esplanade,* the *Palace* and the *International* in Zagreb; the *Lev, Turist* and *Slon* in Ljubljana; the *Kvarner, Amalia, Atlantic, Belvedere, Ambassador* and *Slavija* in Opatija; the *Marjan, Park* and *Bellevue* in Split; the *Europa* in Sarajevo. There are also many modern rural motels where $4 is tops for a double room, and highways have recently improved.

ARTS . . . Music, drama and folklore festivals abound in summer. The best-known are at Dubrovnik in July-August; at Bled and Split in July-August; Sarajevo in July; Opatija from June 1 to September 30.

CURRENCY . . . The Yugoslav dinar is valued at 1,250 to U.S. $1.

CUSTOMS REGULATIONS AND DOCUMENTS REQUIRED FOR UNITED STATES CITIZENS . . . Passport; visa acquired upon entry. 3,000 dinars (in 100-dinar notes) and unlimited foreign currency may be brought in. Duty-free allowances: 400 cigarettes, or 20 cigars; 1 bottle of wine, ½ pint of other spirits.

The walled city of Dubrovnik is one of the most popular resorts on Yugoslavia's fabulous Adriatic coast.

FOOD... Fruits and vegetables have a picked-an-hour ago freshness, and meats are often fragrantly grilled over open fires. Yugoslavs are devoted to raw onions and highly spiced seasonings, but hotels lean mostly toward Viennese-style cookery. Yugoslavia produces superb wines and beer, and *sljivovica* (plum brandy) is potent and popular. Imported liquors cost about the same as in the States.

LANGUAGE... English is spoken in tourist centers.

WHERE TO GO—SIGHTSEEING...

Belgrade... The National Museum is known for its unusually fine medieval frescoes, icons and illuminated manuscripts. Belgrade is a city of lovely parks, the most famous being the prehistoric fortress park of Kalemegdan, high above the junction of the Sava and Danube rivers. Consult Belgrade's *Putnik Beograd* about the spectacular hydrofoil trips down the deep-gorged Danube to the Rumanian border.

Capitals of the other republics—Zagreb, Ljubljana, Sarajevo and Titograd—are also rich in medieval castles, museums, art galleries, and impressive monuments. Skoplje is being rebuilt.

Adriatic Coast... An ideal vacationland of sandy beaches, enchanting islands, colorful festivals and fine resort hotels. The "Pearl of the Adriatic" is Dubrovnik with its ancient city walls and medieval streets. Fort Lovrjenac, built in the 14th century, is often a setting for festival performances. There are water sports of all kinds and frequent open-air concerts. Best hotels: *Excelsior, Argentina, Adriatic, Neptun, Dubrovnik, Petka*. Also famed for sports, festivals, balmy climate and luxuriant vegetation is Opatija, coastal resort conveniently near Postojna Cave, historical Pula, and the Plitvica Lakes on 16 levels with waterfalls between. Other outstanding seaside resorts are Budva, Crikvenica, Hercegnovi, Portoroz, Split, and the delightful islands of Rab, Hvar and Sveti Stefan (fine accommodations). Famous resorts in the lake districts are Bled, Bohinj and Ohrid.

Major winter-sports centers are Planica, just south of the Austrian border, where international ski jumping contests are held in late March; Pokljuka, and Poherje near Maribor in the Slovene Alps.

SOURCES OF FURTHER INFORMATION... The Yugoslav State Tourist Office, 509 Madison Avenue, New York, N.Y. 10022. Pan Am's office: Marsala Tita 18, Belgrade (Tel. 20949); and in Hotel Slavija, Belgrade (Tel. 48487).

THE MIDDLE EAST

CYPRUS

A Mediterranean island of pine-clad mountains, soft sand beaches, historic antiquities and modern, comfortable hotels, Cyprus is 60 miles west of Syria, 40 miles south of Turkey. The capital city of Nicosia (population 90,000) is 1 hour by Middle East Airlines from Beirut.

Only 140 miles long by 60 miles wide (3,572 square miles), the island has a population of 581,000. With a climate comparable to that of Greece, every season is beautiful. For a stay of less than 3 months you need only a passport, a smallpox vaccination certificate and a ticket to leave. Duty-free allowances of ½ lb. tobacco in any form, 1 bottle of spirits. There are 1,000 mils in one Cyprus pound, valued at U.S. $2.80. No more than £10 may be imported. The electric current is 240 volts, A.C., 50 cycles.

Hotel rates in towns, mountain and beach resorts run from $5 to $12 per day for a room with bath and 3 meals. De luxe hotels in Nicosia are the new *Cyprus Hilton,* the *Saray, Ledra Palace* and *Regina Palace.* First class hotels include the *Acropole, Catsellis Hill, Cornaro, Louis, Crown* and the *Hilarion* near the airport. Cyprus is known for its citrus fruits, melons and wines. Another Cypriot pride is "Lefkaritika" lace, handmade in the Larnaca district for over 2,000 years. English is widely understood all over the island.

WHERE TO GO—SIGHTSEEING ...

The old quarter of Nicosia is still ringed with walls built by the Venetians in 1567. In the center is the beautiful Gothic Selimiye Mosque, converted from the St. Sophia Cathedral that was begun in 1209. Near the 17th-century Church of St. John is the Cyprus Folk Art Museum with delightful island costumes and handicrafts. The National Museum is outstanding for its historical and archaeological collections, beginning with neolithic tools and vessels made by the island's first settlers about 6000 B.C.

There are de luxe and first class hotels all around the island. Famagusta, famed for some of the world's finest beaches, was the setting for Shakespeare's *Othello.* Kyrenia harbor, popular with yachtsmen, is presided over by a Byzantine fortress. Nearby are romantic old Bellapais Abbey and St. Hilarion's Castle. Limassol is known for its spirited carnivals and festivals. At Mt. Troodos there is fine skiing from January to March. Beautiful Cyprus was, appropriately, the birthplace of Aphrodite, Goddess of Love and Beauty.

SOURCES OF FURTHER INFORMATION ...

Cyprus Government Tourist Office, Nicosia, Cyprus. Cyprus Tourist Office, 165 E. 72 Street, New York, N.Y. 10021.

IRAN

WEATHER IN TEHERAN—Lat. N35°41′—Long. E51°25′—Alt. 4,000 ft.

Temp.	JAN.	FEB.	MAR.	APR.	MAY	JUNE	JULY	AUG.	SEPT.	OCT.	NOV.	DEC.
Low	20°	24°	39°	49°	58°	66°	72°	71°	64°	53°	43°	27°
High	45°	50°	59°	71°	82°	93°	99°	97°	90°	76°	63°	51°
Average	33°	37°	49°	60°	70°	80°	85°	84°	77°	64°	53°	39°
Days of Rain	3	3	6	3	1	–	1	–	–	–	4	3

LOCATION ... Iran, one of the world's oldest empires, lies in southwestern Asia, and is an important country in the Middle East.

CHARACTERISTICS ... Iran, or Persia as it was formerly called, is the land of sunshine, roses and poetry. Although the age-old way of life is fast giving way to Westernization, Iranians cling to traditional customs of hospitality and are delighted when visitors appreciate the artistic contributions of this ancient country.

POPULATION ... Estimated at nearly 23,000,000.

SIZE ... 636,293 square miles, 3 times the size of France.

CAPITAL ... Teheran, with a population of 2,000,000.

GOVERNMENT ... Iran is a constitutional monarchy ruled by H.I.M. Mohammad Reza Shah Pahlevi and a Parliament and Senate.

HOW TO GET THERE ... Direct service by Clipper from New York, Paris, Rome, Beirut and other major world centers, 16½ hours from New York, 5¾ hours from Rome, 2 hours from Beirut.

ACCOMMODATIONS ... Just outside the city, with a superb view of the Elburz Mountains, is the luxurious new *Royal Tehran Hilton* with complete resort facilities. Singles from $9, doubles from $12. Other first-class Teheran hotels: the *Park, Sina, Caspien, Commodore, Excelsior, Tehran Palace, Semiramis* and *Carlton*. A few minutes from the business area are the *Keyhan* and *Vanak* hotels. Rates for a single room with bath in the better hotels start at about $8, plus service charges. The long-popular *Darband Hotel,* on top of Elburz Mountain, 35 minutes from the city, is at its best in summer.

ARTS ... Iran has gained world fame for fine rugs and delicate miniature paintings. Samples of these and other works of art are on display at the museums in Teheran. Also, don't miss the antiquities.

BANKS ... Bank Melli Iran, Bank Bazergani and the Central Bank have U.S. affiliations. The Bank of America has a representative in the Foreign Trade Bank of Iran.

CALENDAR OF HOLIDAYS ... As in many other Moslem countries, the day of rest is Friday, at which time most places are closed. Stores and museums are closed on 27 legal and religious holidays during the year.

CIGARETTES AND TOBACCO ... Local brands of cigarettes are about 15¢ a pack.

CLIMATE ... Teheran, Isfahan and Shiraz can be very hot in summer, cold in winter. April to mid-June and mid-September to mid-November are the best times to visit Iran.

CLUBS ... American Club, American Officers Club, Teheran Club, Iran Club, Masonic Lodge, Rotary, Lions, Iran-American Society, Gorgan Club and American Business and Professional Group of Teheran.

COMMON COURTESIES AND LOCAL CUSTOMS ... There is no limit to true Iranian hospitality, and you'll be offered tea at the most unexpected times. *Merci* is the usual way to say "Thank you."

COMMUNICATIONS ... A 3-minute phone call to the States costs 1150 rls. ($12.50). Airmail postage for postcard or airletter is 8 rls.; 24 rls. for a 5-gram letter.

CURRENCY ... The monetary unit is the rial, with a fluctuating exchange rate of about 75.75 rials to U.S. $1, but a better rate can often be legally obtained at licensed exchange companies.

CUSTOMS REGULATIONS AND DOCUMENTS REQUIRED FOR UNITED STATES CITIZENS ... Passport; tourists need no visa for visit up to 15 days. Duty-free imports are limited to 100 cigarettes, 10 cigars, or ½ lb. of tobacco and 1 opened bottle of liquor.

DRUGSTORES ... Drug products are available in better stores.

ELECTRIC CURRENT ... 220 volts—50 cycles A.C.

FOOD ... Food is interesting here. Restaurants feature European and Middle Eastern food. The top ones are the *Coq d'or, Hot Shoppe, Chez Farid, Chetnik* and *La Residence*. More modest are *Leon's Grill* and *Mehrabad Airport Restaurant*. Dining rooms at the *Royal Tehran Hilton* and *Park Hotel* are also good. For the national specialty *chelow-kebab* go to *Fards* in the Shemiran suburbs, the *Shamshri* at the covered bazaar entrance, the *Palace Hotel*, or *Reghabi's* on Avenue Amir Kabir. Fine chicken kebab at *Hatam's* on the Pahlavi Road. Local lamb is excellent, and try the famous Iranian caviar.

LANGUAGE ... The official language is Farsi but English and French are usually understood by personnel in hotels.

LAUNDRY AND DRY CLEANING ... Good, with low prices.

LIQUOR ... Vodka, beer and wine are the most popular local drinks. Foreign liquors are available but pretty expensive.

MOTION PICTURES ... Films are occasionally shown in English, but Iranian is more often dubbed in. Best theaters are *Moulin Rouge,*

Plaza, Radio City, Royal, Odeon Central, Diana, Mahtab and *Empire.*

NIGHT CLUBS ... For entertainment and dancing: *Royal Tehran Hilton, Vanak Hotel; Miami, Colbeh* and *Shoukufé Now.*

RELIGION ... The official religion is the Shia sect of Islam.

SHOPS AND STORES ... The Feroushgah Ferdowsi department store carries all kinds of (expensive) imported goods. You can bargain in street markets and in the huge covered bazaar for lovely Iranian copper and brass, silver, Persian miniature paintings. Other good buys are semiprecious stones, textiles and embroideries, *geeveh* (Persian slippers). Persian carpets cost about the same as at home. Stock up on camera film in Teheran; it's scarce in smaller towns.

TIPPING ... Hotels and restaurants add 10% to 15% service charges to your bill, but tip 10 or 20 rials for most small services. Taxi drivers are not tipped, however.

TRANSPORTATION ... Taxis are plentiful and inexpensive, costing 20 rials anywhere in town and 60 to the suburbs.

WATER ... Potable in Teheran and other cities with filter systems; elsewhere travelers are advised to drink only boiled water, tea or sterilized bottled drinks. Pure bottled water is not available.

WHAT TO BUY ... Rugs, jewelry, semiprecious stones, miniatures, silverware and brassware, "geeveh" (Persian shoes), embroidery.

WHAT TO WEAR ... Summer requires the lightest-weight clothing, but should include jackets for men and long-sleeved apparel for women. A light jacket or wrap is usually needed in the evenings when dining outdoors. Warm clothing for winter.

WHERE TO GO—SIGHTSEEING ...

Teheran ... The handsome range of bare rugged Elburz Mountains is a striking feature of the Teheran area. In the city itself, one should not fail to visit the royal palaces, interesting government buildings, the covered bazaar, Houses of Parliament, Sepah Salar Mosque, the Crown Jewels, the Golestan Palace Museum, Archaeological Museum, Ethnological Museum, Museum and School of Fine Arts, the National Library, and the University of Teheran. See the Sepahsalar Mosque, Reza Shah's Mausoleum and rug-washing in the ancient city of Rey.

Isfahan ... This city is exciting with its fabulous Blue Mosque, among many others, and its exquisite mosaic tiles. The old summer Palace of the Shahs of past dynasties contains interesting ancient paintings. Shopping is fun at the bazaar, one of the most lively, and there are good buys. The *Shah Abbas, Isfahan* and *Irantour* hotels are good.

Shiraz ... The city of roses, nightingales and heroes—Darius, Xerxes and Artaxerxes, whose tombs are only 40 miles from Shiraz among the famous ruins of Persepolis (500 B.C.). In Shiraz, the *Park* and *Park Sa'adi* (air conditioned) hotels.

Other points of interest: the resorts on the Caspian shore, the mammoth oil refinery at Abadan, the gold-domed mosque in the shrine city of Meshed, and the 18,550-foot peak of Mt. Damavand.

SOURCES OF FURTHER INFORMATION ... Pan Am office in Teheran on Ave. Shah Reza at Ave. Villa (Tel. 65991). Consulate General of Iran, 30 Rockefeller Plaza, New York, N.Y. 10020.

IRAQ

WEATHER IN BAGHDAD—Lat. N33°21′—Alt. 112′

	JAN.	FEB.	MAR.	APR.	MAY	JUNE	JULY	AUG.	SEPT.	OCT.	NOV.	DEC.
Average Temp.	49°	53°	60°	71°	82°	90°	94°	94°	88°	78°	61°	53°
Days of Rain	5	5	4	3	1	0	0	0	0	1	4	5

Baghdad, the exotic city of the Arabian Nights, is now a modern city of 630,000, 18 hours by Jet Clipper from New York. The climate is hot in summer. Spring and fall are the best times to visit.

To visit Iraq you'll need a passport, visa and vaccination certificate. You may bring in one bottle of liquor and 200 cigarettes. Air departure tax is 500 fils ($1.40). The unit of currency is the Iraqi dinar divided into 1,000 fils and equal to $2.80. The electric current is 220 volts, 50 cycles, A.C. Drugstores have American products; leading department store is *Orosdi-Back*. Mustansir and Rashid streets for souvenirs. Iraqi goods, such as brassware and rugs, are in the bazaars where you bargain.

Among the several hotels, the newest are the first class, air-conditioned *Baghdad Hotel* with single rates from $10, European Plan, and the *Ambassador* and *Khayam* with rates from about $9, including breakfast. At hotel restaurants which feature European cuisine, dinner costs about $3. One famous fish dish is *samak masgouf;* also try *kusi,* stuffed roasted whole lamb. *Araq* is the potent national drink. American drinks are available in all hotels. Best night clubs are *The Auberge, Select* and *The Embassy* (which are also restaurants). Arrive about 10 P.M. for dinner and floor show.

Outstanding points of interest are Tell Harmell and Tell Mohammed excavations, famous Kadhimain Mosque with pure gold domes, tomb of Sitt Zubaidah, ruins at Agarguf 20 miles away; Arch of Ctesiphon, one of the wonders of the ancient world, 25 miles away; the ruins of Babylon (55 miles) with Nebuchadnezzar's Procession Street, famous Hanging Gardens, throne room of the legendary "writing on the wall" and Lion of Babylon.

Pan American's office is on Saadun Street (Tel. 88300).

ISRAEL

WEATHER IN JERUSALEM—Lat. N31°46′—Alt. approx. 2,500′

Temp.	JAN.	FEB.	MAR.	APR.	MAY	JUNE	JULY	AUG.	SEPT.	OCT.	NOV.	DEC.
Low	38°	41°	45°	51°	56°	62°	65°	64°	62°	59°	50°	43°
High	51°	55°	62°	70°	78°	84°	87°	88°	85°	80°	66°	56°
Average	45°	48°	54°	61°	67°	73°	76°	76°	74°	70°	58°	50°
Days of Rain	12	12	8	4	2	0	0	0	0	2	6	9

LOCATION ... On the southeast coast of the Mediterranean.

CHARACTERISTICS ... Here you will have the thrill of seeing a nation in the making, where modern garden cities lie adjacent to ancient sites. The Holy Land, with all its wonderful scenery and Biblical sites, offers inspiration to people of all faiths. There are modern and even luxurious hotels. The climate is sunny and warm. You are assured of a pleasant welcome, for the Israelis are eager to let the world know what they are doing.

POPULATION ... Estimated 2,356,000.

SIZE ... About 7,993 square miles, smaller than Massachusetts.

CAPITAL ... Jerusalem, a growing city of more than 167,400.

GOVERNMENT ... An independent republic, established in 1948, with a President and a Parliament.

HOW TO GET THERE ... By Pan Am Jet Clipper to London, Paris, Rome, Vienna, Istanbul. Then by connection, elapsed time from New York to Tel Aviv via Rome, 14¼ hours. By ship about 15 days.

ACCOMMODATIONS ... The luxurious new *Caesarea Hotel,* adjacent to the famed golf club, is on the Mediterranean, midway between Haifa and Tel Aviv. The *Semadar Villa Hotel* has also opened in Caesarea. The *Tel Aviv Hilton, Deborah, Sheraton Tel Aviv* and the *Dan Hotel* are the best in Tel Aviv. The *Ramat Aviv Hotel,* on the edge of town, is a self-contained resort. The *Sharon Hotel* and *Accadia Grand,* at Herzlia-on-the-Sea, and the small hotel *Tadmor* are also good. All have kosher kitchens.

The best hotels in Jerusalem are the *King David,* the *Eden,* the *Judea Gardens,* the *Holyland* (3 miles out of town), the *President* (which has a fine swimming pool) and the *Kings Hotel.* Others are the *Or Gil* and the Y.M.C.A. Rates with breakfast in better hotels average $10 single, $19 double; about $6 single, $8 double in others; doubles from $7 to $28 at resorts. Rates are slightly lower in winter.

ARTS... Permanent and transient exhibitions of paintings appear in Tel Aviv, Haifa, and Jerusalem, as well as in the smaller cities. Most galleries and museums are closed on Fridays. Opened in Jerusalem in May, 1965, was the superb new Israel Museum, composed of the Bezalel Art Museum, the Billy Rose Art Gardens, the Bronfman Archaeology Museum and the Shrine of the Book. The latter is a unique cavelike structure specially designed to display Israel's collection of Dead Sea Scrolls.

BALLET... Several ballet groups present dances. Inbal, a Yemenite dance group, is famous.

BANKS... Banks are open from Sunday through Thursday from 8:30 A.M. to 12:30 P.M. and 4 to 5 P.M.; Fridays from 8:30 A.M. to 12 noon.

CALENDAR OF HOLIDAYS...

Jewish Holidays... (Rosh Hashanah) in September or October; Yom Kippur ten days later; Succoth four days later, culminating on the eighth day with Simhat Torah; the week of Hanukkah (The Feast of Lights) in late November or December; Purim, in early March, and in April, Passover. May and early June are crowded with religious and national celebrations, such as Lag B'Omer and Shavuoth. Independence Day celebration is held May 6.

Christian Holidays... (In Jerusalem) Christmas begins on the evening of December 24, the Eastern Christmas on January 6. Other celebrations of interest are: the Pilgrimage to Cana in Galilee on the Second Sunday after Epiphany, the Easter (Western) services on Good Friday, Easter Sunday and Monday; the Feast of Our Lady of Carmel, on the Sunday after Easter on Mt. Carmel; Pentecost ceremonies in May; the Feast of St. John; the Feast of Elijah on Mt. Carmel in mid-July; the Feast of Transfiguration on Mt. Tabor.

CIGARETTES AND TOBACCO... American cigarettes are available. Local Virginia brands are 30¢ to 35¢ a pack.

CLIMATE... Israel basks in a Mediterranean climate with unbroken sunshine during most of the year and fair, sunny weather with short spells of rain from November to March.

CLUBS... There are 30 Rotary Clubs in Israel. Other clubs in Tel Aviv include Automobile Club & Touring Association of Israel, Citrus House, Tel. 67612; Commercial and Industrial Club, 32, Yavne Street, Tel. 62667; in Jerusalem the Touring Club, Tel. 5783.

COMMON COURTESIES AND LOCAL CUSTOMS... Israelis are pleased if they hear you speak even one word of Hebrew. The most used word is *Shalom,* meaning "Peace," an all-purpose greeting. Everything is closed on the Sabbath (Saturday), including nearly all means of transportation except taxis.

COMMUNICATIONS ... A 3-minute call to the U.S. costs IL. 31.75 ($10.63); cablegrams are 90 agorot per word. Postage for a 5-gram airmail letter to the U.S. is 70 agorot; 35 for an airletter form. Local phone calls cost 20 agorot.

CURRENCY ... is the Israeli pound, which is divided into 100 agorot. The rate of exchange for tourists is IL. 3 to the $1.00.

CUSTOMS AND CURRENCY REGULATIONS FOR UNITED STATES CITIZENS ... You may bring into Israel duty free all your personal effects, 250 cigarettes or 50 cigars, traveling accessories and gifts whose value does not exceed $40. Import license required if value is over 200 Israeli pounds. Tourists need a passport but no visa. Undeveloped film must be passed by the censor when you leave the country, so keep a record of scenes. Black-and-white film can be developed and printed. PLEASE NOTE land entry can only be made through the Mandelbaum Gate in Jerusalem.

DRUGSTORES ... In the larger cities of Israel drugstores containing some American goods or their equivalent may be found.

ELECTRIC CURRENT ... 220 volts, A.C. single phase, 50 cycles.

FAUNA ... Wild pig and duck abound near the Jordan swamps, and in the wasteland of the Negev the gazelle is seen occasionally. Wild animals include the jackal, bear and wild boar. There is a variety of wild bird life among which the eagle, falcon, owl, stork and quail are abundant, also many colorful subtropical birds.

FLORA ... Israel's variegated climate supports a wide range of plants and flowers which splash the landscape with color. Many of the country's barren hills have been planted with trees as part of an intensive reforestation program.

LANGUAGE ... You will have no language problem.

LAUNDRY AND DRY CLEANING ... Normal service isn't fast but for a 20% surcharge you can cut the time in half.

LIQUOR ... Whisky and soda is about $1 (IL. 3). There are some good local wines such as Adom Atic, a red dry wine, and Carmel Hock, a white dry wine; Chablis, Pommereau and Carmel Port, Rishon, Cognac and cherry brandy are also popular.

MEDICAL FACILITIES ... Good, with English-speaking doctors.

MOTION PICTURES ... American and European films. Shows are at set hours; reserve seats in advance.

MUSIC ... Israel's musical life is a rich one. The Music Festival during Passover is a major event, as is the International Music and Drama Festival in summer. The Israel Philharmonic serves under famous guest conductors. Chamber music is also popular. Israel National Opera performs year around with well-known guest artists.

NIGHT CLUBS AND CABARETS ... Most first-class hotels feature dance orchestras nightly or on week-ends. The night clubs in Jaffa and Tel Aviv present nightly floor shows.

PHOTOGRAPHY ... Films and camera accessories are available in all larger cities.

RELIGION ... A synagogue tour taking in synagogues of different communities in Jerusalem takes place on Friday afternoons. There are three main Christian communities: Roman Catholic, Greek and Russian Orthódox, and Protestant.

RESTAURANTS ... Excellent eating places serving Central European and oriental dishes. Hotels and night clubs also serve fine food.

SHOPS AND STORES ... The Maskit and Wizo Shops in Jerusalem, Tel Aviv, and Haifa for oriental and modern gifts. Rivoli in Tel Aviv for practical and luxury items. Shops and stores are open from 8 A.M. to 1 P.M. and 3 P.M. to 7 P.M. Sunday through Thursday, and from 8 A.M. to 3 P.M. on Fridays. Shops and stores are closed on Saturdays and holidays.

SPECTATOR SPORTS ... Several stadia throughout the country offer football and basketball games. The Ramat Gan Sport Stadium, near Tel Aviv, is the best known.

SPORTS ... Football, basketball, swimming, skin diving and tennis are the most popular sports. Yachting and boating are also popular. There's a fine 18-hole golf course at Caesarea, as well as skin diving and horseback riding.

THEATERS ... There are four main theatrical companies in Israel: the internationally famous *Habimah;* the *Ohel,* the workers' theater; the new *Chamber* theater group; and the Israel opera.

TIME ... 7 hours later than U.S. Eastern Standard Time.

TIPPING ... Not as prevalent as at home. Taxi drivers are not tipped, but barbers and employees in the better hotels are usually given 10-15% tips. At most hotels and restaurants tipping is covered with a 10% surcharge on your bill; 25% in night clubs.

TRANSPORTATION ... Bus fare from the airport into Tel Aviv is about IL. 1. Cars can be hired with a driver or a driver-guide. Israel has two internal airlines, Avitours and Arkia. Luxury air-conditioned coaches leave Tel Aviv daily to tour various parts of the country. Typical prices are: 3-days' tour of Galilee, IL. 107 ($36); 2-days' tour of Jerusalem, IL. 68.65 ($23) (both the above prices include board and lodging); 1-day's tour of the Negev IL. 21 ($7).

WHAT TO BUY ... Yemenite and Persian filigree work, carpets, tapestry and embroidery, metal-chasing, and ceramics are recommended. Religious articles and books are also expertly produced. Ladies' and men's made-to-measure suits, furs, knitwear and fashion goods are extremely reasonable under special export scheme for visitors.

WHAT TO WEAR ... Light clothing for summer days, and fairly warm clothing for the winter months. Jackets, boleros, and sweaters are useful for summer evenings. Do not forget your sunglasses. Bring rubber overshoes or galoshes for the rainy winter months.

WHERE TO GO—SIGHTSEEING ...

Tel Aviv ... Founded in 1909, this very modern city grows larger, busier and more beautiful every day. Broad boulevards, balconied apartment buildings, numerous parks and gardens and sidewalk cafés give an effect of graciousness amid all the bustling activity. This is Israel's commercial, social and cultural center, with fine theaters, frequent concerts and art exhibits. Adjacent Jaffa, one of the world's most ancient towns, offers many picturesque corners, as well as New and Old Testament sites. 33 miles south of Tel Aviv is Ashkelon, birthplace of Herod, which now has an Antiquities Park, Israel's longest white sand beach and smart new resort hotels.

Haifa . . . This "Gateway to Israel" is a major Mediterranean port. Visit the waterfront dock area in the early morning. Be sure to see the Bahai Gardens and gold-domed Bahai Temple. Take the Panorama Road up Mt. Carmel, where beautiful homes and de luxe hotels overlook the crescent-shaped harbor. On this mountain Elijah called down heavenly fire to triumph over the priests of Baal. There is a pilgrimage to Elijah's Cave every April. The Carmelite Order was founded in the Carmelite monastery, which has a domed church in the shape of a Greek cross; a double stairway leads up to the magnificent altar with Caraventa's famous statue of Our Lady of Carmel. Excavated treasures of Caesarea, capital of Judea, are in Haifa's Municipal Museum of Ancient Art. On the coast north of Haifa is Acre, site of the Crusader Fortress of Richard the Lion Heart, and the great mosque of Jazzar Pasha. East of Haifa is Nazareth, where Christ lived as a child. Five miles north is Cana where He performed His first miracle. On to Tiberias, famed health resort on the beautiful Sea of Galilee. Then go to the Holy Places of Mt. Beatitude (scene of the Sermon on the Mount), Tabgha (where the multiplication of loaves and fishes occurred), and Capernaum, with ruins of the synagogue in which, according to tradition, Christ taught.

Jerusalem . . . At least 4,000 years old, this divided heart of the Holy Land today combines a striking modernity with relics of a rich past. On Mt. Herzl, overlooking Jerusalem, is the tomb of Theodore Herzl, founder of modern Zionism. On Mt. Zion is the tomb of King David, builder of a more ancient Jewish state. Here, too, is the Chamber of the Last Supper. A number of Christian churches are in the suburb of Ein Kerem, birthplace of John the Baptist. Modern additions to Jerusalem include the great new Israel Museum, the New Hebrew University; the Hadassah Medical Center (where the Chagall windows are installed); the Knesset (Israel's Parliament); the giant structure of the Y.M.C.A.; the Israel Touring Club in Talbia, surrounded by lovely gardens. In contrast is the Mea Shearim quarter, where ultra-Orthodox Jews cling to ancient restrictions on conduct.

The Negev . . . Go south from Jerusalem to the ancient Negev city of Beersheba. A scenic highway takes you to Sodom and the Dead Sea, 1,292 feet below sea level. Good roads and fine new hotels have greatly changed the bleakness of the Negev. In its southern point are King Solomon's copper mines, and the attractive Red Sea port of Eilat, near the spot where the Queen of Sheba's ships docked. The *Queen of Sheba, Eilat,* and *Tropicana* hotels are on the seafront.

SOURCES OF FURTHER INFORMATION . . . Israel Government Tourist Centers: 574 Fifth Avenue, New York; others in Chicago, Los Angeles, Beverly Hills, Montreal, Paris, London, Rome, Zurich. In Israel, Lydda Airport and principal cities. Pan Am's office in Tel Aviv is at 38 Achad Ha'am Street (Tel. 64422).

JORDAN

IRAQ

SYRIA

AMMAN ★

Jerusalem

MT. ZION

Bethlehem **SAUDI ARABIA**

DEAD SEA

JORDAN

Petra

● **Ma'an**

WEATHER IN JERUSALEM–Lat. N31°46′

Temp.	JAN.	FEB.	MAR.	APR.	MAY	JUNE	JULY	AUG.	SEPT.	OCT.	NOV.	DEC.
Low	38°	41°	45°	51°	56°	62°	65°	64°	62°	59°	50°	43°
High	51°	55°	62°	70°	78°	84°	87°	88°	85°	80°	66°	56°
Average	45°	48°	54°	61°	67°	73°	76°	76°	74°	70°	58°	50°
Days of Rain	12	12	8	4	2	0	0	0	0	2	6	9

LOCATION . . . The Hashemite Kingdom of Jordan is an Arab country and member of the Arab League. It is situated in the heart of the Arab world. On the north, it is bounded by Syria, on the northeast by Iraq, on the east and south by Saudi Arabia, and on the west by Israel.

CHARACTERISTICS . . . Jordan comprises Trans-Jordan proper and Central Arab Palestine and includes some of the most sacred shrines of Islam and Christianity. Within its boundaries lie Bethlehem, the birthplace of Jesus; Jericho, the oldest walled city in the world; Hebron, where Abraham was buried; the River Jordan; the Dead Sea; the Mount of Olives and the ancient walled city of Jerusalem, the holiest city in Christendom. Tourism for years has been the main industry of this country and tourists are sure to receive a hearty welcome by all. Jordanians often seek to promote direct contact between groups of tourists and inhabitants through various social gatherings and the Visit-an-Arab-Family program. There are comfortable hotels in Jordan and the climate in general is ideal.

POPULATION . . . The population, which is preponderantly Moslem Arab, is estimated at 2,000,000, of whom about 15% are Christians. Besides the Moslem and Christian Arabs, there are fair Circassians, swarthy Copts, Persian Bahais, Syriacs, Turcomans, White Russians, and 300 Samaritans who are descended from Biblical times.

SIZE . . . 37,301 square miles; 236 miles long, 87 miles wide.

CAPITAL . . . Amman, the ancient Philadelphia, is the busy and growing capital of Jordan with a population of over 300,000.

GOVERNMENT . . . A constitutional monarchy.

HOW TO GET THERE . . . By Pan American Jet Clipper to Beirut, Lebanon, 13½ hours from New York; then by connection to Jerusalem (via Middle East or Royal Jordanian Airlines) or Amman. From Beirut it is about 1 hour. There is also an overland route by car from Beirut via Damascus to Amman or Jerusalem. Or go to Beirut, Alexandria or Port Said by ship, then by air.

ACCOMMODATIONS . . . There are fine hotels in all the major cities, and many have central heating. In Jerusalem, the de luxe new *Jerusalem Intercontinental* is completely air conditioned and overlooks the Old City; from $8 single, $11.50 double, European Plan. Also good: the *Ambassador, Orient House, Ritz, American Colony, Shepherd* and the *National Palace*. Rates from $6 single with bath and all meals. In Ramallah (10 miles from Jerusalem and 4 miles from the airport) are the *Grand Hotel* and the *Carlton*. In Amman are the *Amman Club* and the *Philadelphia*, both about $8.45 single, including meals. The luxurious new *Jordan Intercontinental* has rates from about $10 single, $17 double, European Plan. Modern and very popular is the first-class *Dead Sea Hotel* on the shore of the Dead Sea, 1290 feet below sea level. It is near Jericho, midway between Amman and Jerusalem and about 25 miles from both. Reserve hotel space well in advance, especially at Christmas and Easter. There is an additional 25% charge during these peak seasons; hotels have 10% service charges the rest of the year. In the countryside handsome new rest houses are going up near historic sites; these provide meals and accommodations, and there is even an antiquities authority on hand in each.

BANKS . . . In Amman, the Arab Land Bank, Arab Bank, Jordan National Bank and Ottoman Bank have U.S. affiliations.

CALENDAR OF HOLIDAYS . . . Museums are closed but stores are usually open on legal holidays: Arbor Day, January 15; Arab League Day, March 22; Independence Day, May 25; King Hussein's ascension to the throne, August 11; King Hussein's birthday, November 14; Good Friday; Christmas.

There are several Moslem feasts based on the lunar calendar. For Christians, Christmas and Easter are most important with ceremonial pageantry. Tourists will find it specially interesting also to attend the Samaritan Passover feast on Mount Gerizim near Nablus. This feast generally falls in April and is celebrated by slaughtering sheep as sacrifice according to ancient Samaritan tradition. Jordan Army Field Day in Amman on May 9 is a special event. Tourists will love this spectacular exhibition of outstanding horsemanship, swordsmanship and sportsmanship.

CIGARETTES AND TOBACCO . . . Local cigarettes such as *Friends, Gold Star* and *Select* cost 120 fils per pack; filter brands are *Reem, Petra, Philadelphia* and *Ambassador*. American brands are 180 fils per pack.

CLIMATE . . . The country offers a vast range and contrast of climate and scenery, from the temperate heights of the rugged, purple-hued mountains of Moab to the gently rolling hills of Judea, the deep tropical depression of the Jordan Valley and the Dead Sea and finally the dry, arid desert of the eastern plateau. Jericho, 845 feet below sea level, is an excellent winter resort. *See* WEATHER CHART on page 210.

CLUBS... The Y.M.C.A., Lions Club, Rotary Club, Masonic Lodge, Orthodox Club, Sporting Club. A tourist would have to be accompanied by a member to make use of these clubs.

COMMON COURTESIES AND LOCAL CUSTOMS... Jordanians are extremely friendly and hospitable. A guest is considered a sacred trust, and you'll have many occasions to say, "Shookran" (Thank you).

COMMUNICATIONS... A 3-minute call to the States costs $10.50 (3.750 dinars); day-rate cablegram to the U.S. is 108 fils per word, with a 10-word minimum. Airmail postage to the U.S. is 40 fils for a postcard or airletter; 80 fils for a 5-gram letter. Local phone calls cost 10 fils.

CURRENCY... There are 1,000 fils in the Jordanian dinar (JD), which is equivalent to $2.80, or £1. No more than JD 10 allowed in or out of Jordan.

CUSTOMS REGULATIONS AND DOCUMENTS REQUIRED FOR UNITED STATES CITIZENS... Tourists may procure visas at Jordan consulates or at Jordan frontier ports, if they arrive via a neighboring Arab country or hold a visa to an Arab country. A gratis visa is granted to tourists staying in Jordan for a week or more. As for travel between Jordan and Israel, only a one-way crossing is permitted. American visitors in Jordan wishing to cross over into Israel must contact their consulate three days in advance for arrangements to be made, but cannot thereafter return to an Arab country. The visitor may bring duty free into the country personal effects, a pair of binoculars, one camera, one typewriter, one transformer, one projector, 200 cigarettes or 25 cigars or ½ lb. of tobacco, one liter each of wine and spirits. He may not bring in radios, phonographs or records unless willing to pay the duty on these.

DRUGSTORES... European and American pharmaceuticals and cosmetics are stocked.

ELECTRIC CURRENT... 220 volts A.C.; 50 cycles.

FAUNA... The mule, camel, Arabian horse and cattle in general, as well as poultry, migratory and local birds. Among wild animals Jordan has the jackal, hedgehog, gazelle, mole, bat, field mouse and fox.

FLORA... Jordanian flora is similar to that of southern Europe. Jordan is rich in all kinds of flowers.

FOOD... All the hotels serve continental food of good quality and variety. Tourists should try some of the delicious Arab dishes, such as barbecued lamb, rice and stuffed vine leaves.

LANGUAGE... Arabic is the common language in Jordan. The tourist, however, can get along with English or French. The majority of the people are bilingual and many speak more than two languages.

LAUNDRY... Laundry is excellent and inexpensive.

LIQUOR . . . Arak is the native drink. It is flavored with anise and may be taken straight or with water. Whisky is another favorite drink. If you order whisky you'll get Scotch. Bourbon is rare. Popular American drinks and cocktails are available in all hotels and bars. Prices are reasonable. Minimum legal age for drinkers is 18.

MEDICAL FACILITIES . . . Most doctors are graduates of American and British universities and speak English fluently.

MOTION PICTURES . . . The motion-picture houses show American, European and Arabic films. Shows are at set hours.

MUSIC . . . Familiar dance music in night clubs. Jordan's own Arabic music is hauntingly unforgettable, particularly when heard on a moonlit night in Amman's 2,000-year-old Roman Theatre.

NIGHT CLUBS . . . There are night clubs in Amman hotels, at the Dead Sea Hotel and outdoors in Jerusalem during summer. Typical of Jordan are the attractive garden cafés that have orchestras and occasional floor shows.

PHOTOGRAPHY . . . Tourists may take photographs of sites of religious, historical or scenic interest but may not take pictures of scenes of squalor or of military installations. Color and black-and-white films are available for still cameras; Kodachrome for movie cameras. Ektachrome and Kodacolor are processed in Amman and Jerusalem.

RELIGION . . . Most Jordanians are Moslem, but there are churches of nearly all denominations.

RESTAURANTS . . . Among best restaurants in Jordan are the *National* in Jerusalem and the *Ali Baba, Al Shark* and *Roy* in Amman.

SHOPS AND STORES . . . Fixed prices in the stores. Bargaining is expected in the *souks*.

SPORTS . . . Football, basketball, boxing, swimming, tennis and horse racing are the most popular sports. The Sunday races on Dead Sea shore, 1,290 feet below sea level, are the "lowest sport on earth."

TIME . . . 7 hours later than U.S. Eastern Standard Time.

TIPPING . . . Tip luggage porters 100 fils for 2 or 3 bags; 50 fils for any small services of any kind; 10-20 fils for shoeshine boy. Tip waiters 10% of the bill if no service charge is included. Taxi drivers are not tipped.

TRANSPORTATION . . . Taxi fare from the airport into Amman is about $1.50 (532 fils). All the historical and religious sites are easily accessible by car. A network of autobuses connects all the major towns and cities, but the usual means of transport is the taxi. Cabs in Jordan are very comfortable and inexpensive. One can take a taxi for 10 miles for about $2.50. Cab companies have arrangements between all the major towns and cities whereby a person can hire a seat in a car and thus travel comfortably and very cheaply indeed.

WATER . . . Water is safe to drink throughout Jordan cities and well-established villages. Bottled water can be had, too.

WHAT TO BUY . . . Tourists love the delicate bronze and silver work, the fascinating oriental jewelry, the exquisite mother-of-pearl products, the rich cross-stitch-embroidered linen work, the attractive

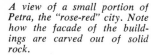

A view of a small portion of Petra, the "rose-red" city. Note how the facade of the buildings are carved out of solid rock.

In Jerusalem, from the Mount of Olives, you can see the big Dome of the Rock (Mosque of Omar).

Crusader jackets of Bethlehem, products of the famous olivewood industries, and the colorful Palestine pottery. Also religious art. These goods can be bought very cheaply.

WHAT TO WEAR . . . Light clothing for summer and warm clothing for winter. Raincoats and overshoes for the rainy months, sunglasses, wrap for cool evenings, comfortable sightseeing shoes.

WHERE TO GO—SIGHTSEEING . . .

Jerusalem . . . The city is bisected by the Armistice line resulting from the Palestine hostilities of 1948, leaving a large part of the New City in the hands of the Jews and the Old City in the hands of the Arabs. The Old City proper is enclosed by a 40-foot wall forming an irregular quadrangle about 2½ miles in circumference. The two principal streets intersect in the middle of the city and divide it into four quarters. The most impressive section is the Harem esh Sherif, or Place of the Temple, in the Moslem quarter. The vast majority of the Holy Places are in the Old City or its environs under Arab control. Many of them are sacred to all three faiths.

Church of the Holy Sepulchre . . . A collection of chapels housing the tomb in which Christ was laid to rest after the Crucifixion: the most venerated shrine in Christendom. *Via Dolorosa* . . . The way of the Cross along which Christ walked from the Court of Pilate to the hill of Golgotha, marked by 14 stations. *Garden of Gethsemane* . . . The retreat where the Savior passed his last hours of agony on the night before he was crucified, where he was betrayed by Judas. *Mount of Olives* . . . The grove of trees overlooking Jerusalem from which the Master ascended to Heaven within view of his disciples. *Tomb of the Virgin Mary* . . . The Church of the Assumption where Mary, mother of Jesus, was interred by the Apostles.

The Dome of the Rock . . . An octagonal mosque erected on the ancient site of the Temple of Solomon by Abdul Malik Ibn Mirwan in the 7th century to commemorate the ascension of Mohammed; second only to Mecca as an Islamic shrine. *Aqsa Mosque* . . . A Romanesque churchlike structure built over the Stables of Solomon, to which God conveyed Mohammed from Mecca in one night. *Wailing Wall* . . . A remnant of Herod's Temple where the Jews gathered for centuries to weep over the destruction of Jerusalem. *Citadel* . . . A 14th-century group of towers on a massive sub-structure at the bottom of a moat, forming a fine example of the ancient wall towers of Jerusalem; sometimes called the Tower of David.

Palestine Archaeological Museum . . . Constructed with the aid of the Rockefeller Foundation. Contains many Dead Sea scrolls and a priceless collection of antiquities. *Bethany* . . . One and a half miles southeast of Jerusalem; home of Mary and Martha; Lazarus' tomb; excavation of 4th- and 12th-century churches. *Bethlehem* . . . About 10 miles south of Jerusalem; Church of Nativity of Christ; Milk Grotto; Shepherd's Fields; Fields of Boaz. *Nablus* . . . About 41 miles north of Jerusalem; Jacob's well where Christ talked to the woman of Samaria; ancient Samaritan community. *Sebastia* . . . About 50 miles north of Jerusalem; the Samaria of the Bible where St. John the Baptist is supposed to be buried; nearby is the Church of St. John, a Crusaders' edifice of the 12th century.

Emmaus . . . 13 miles northwest of Jerusalem; the Church of the Franciscan Monastery stands on the site where Christ appeared to his disciples after the Resurrection. *Hebron* . . . South of Jerusalem, 27 miles; tombs of the Prophets Abraham, Isaac and Jacob; Oak of Mambre, where the angels appeared to Abraham. *Jericho* . . . 24 miles northeast of Jerusalem; ruins of the old Canaanite city brought down by Joshua; Elisha's Fountain; Mount of Temptation; the magnificent Umayyad Palace ruins. *Jordan River* . . . 27 miles northeast of Jerusalem; the world's most famous river flowing from the Lake of Tiberias to the Dead Sea for 184 miles; Christ's Place of Baptism near Jericho; Allenby Bridge. *Dead Sea* . . . 25 miles east of Jerusalem. The lowest spot on earth, the shore of the Dead Sea is 1,290 feet below normal sea level and the bottom is 2,600 feet below; site of the destruction of Sodom and Gomorrah and the rescue of Lot, but today is a delightful resort. *Jerash* . . . 36 miles from Amman; built by the soldiers of Alexander the Great. It reached great heights under the Romans and even in ruins is one of the ancient world's best-preserved cities. Restoration is interesting to watch.

Petra . . . For those who have dreamed of an adventurous trip to Tibet or the other great Shangri-las of the world, the great southern desert plain of Jordan offers a spectacle forgotten for over 500 years. The secret city of Petra, with its tombs and temples elaborately carved from the red rocks of the hidden valley, is reached by car from Amman, and then by a 20-minute horseback ride through the canyon into the city. Horses are provided at the police station in Wadi Musa.

SOURCES OF FURTHER INFORMATION . . . Jordan Tourist Bureau, 530 Fifth Avenue, New York, N.Y. 10036. Offices in Jordan at the international airport, and in Amman and Jerusalem.

LEBANON

	JAN.	FEB.	MAR.	APR.	MAY	JUNE	JULY	AUG.	SEPT.	OCT.	NOV.	DEC.
Average Temp.	56.5°	57.7°	61.2°	66°	71.8°	77.7°	82°	83.1°	80.8°	76.1°	67.3°	60.6°
In. of Rain	7.3	5.7	3.9	2.2	.8	.1	0	0	.3	2.1	5.3	7.5

LOCATION . . . Lebanon occupies a small strip of land at the east end of the Mediterranean, bordered by Syria on the north and east.

CHARACTERISTICS . . . This is a wonderful little country, which has within its boundaries some of the most magnificent ruins in the world, the famous Cedars of Lebanon, modern cities and old villages which turn the clock back hundreds of years. There are wonderful beaches; within a short distance there are high mountains on which skiing is excellent. It is the Biblical "Land of Milk and Honey," with orange and olive groves, banana plantations, wonderful wild flowers and crystal-clear rivers gushing from grottos. It is a fascinating mingling of the old and the new.

POPULATION . . . 2,200,000; the country has a slightly larger population than Philadelphia.

SIZE . . . About 120 miles long and varying from 30 to 35 miles in width, total area is 4,015 square miles.

CAPITAL . . . Beirut, with a population of about 600,000.

GOVERNMENT . . . An independent republic.

HOW TO GET THERE . . . By Pan American Jet Clipper service from New York to Beirut, only 13¾ hours. By ship about 14 to 21 days depending on the steamship line.

ACCOMMODATIONS . . . Best by far in Beirut is the new *Hotel Phoenicia Intercontinental*. Completely air-conditioned; every room with a balcony and a view; restaurants, night club; swimming pool. Rates $12-$15 single, $15-$19 double. Other good Beirut hotels are the *St. George,* which has a bathing beach, the *Riviera, Coral Beach, Bristol, Excelsior, Carlton;* from $9 single, from $12 double the year round. Also the air-conditioned *Alcázar, Commodore, Le Beryte, Normandy* and *Biarritz,* with rates about $8 per day single and $12 double. Good second-class hotels are the *Palm Beach, Pacific, Charles* and *Capitole;* about $6 single, $9 double. A few hotels include breakfast and service charges in rates.

ARTS ... The National Art Museum, Sursock Museum and the Museum of the American University in Beirut.

BALLET ... The Baalbek Art Festival (July 15-August 31) offers famous theatrical troupes, orchestras, ballet and folklore. There is Lebanese folk dancing the year round at the Phoenicia Theater.

BANKS ... Beirut is one of the world's greatest banking centers, and numerous American banks have branches in the city.

CALENDAR OF HOLIDAYS ... There are 23 legal holidays in the year. Stores close, but museums stay open. Museums close every Monday.

CIGARETTES AND TOBACCO ... American brands cost 165 piasters per pack. Local cigarettes are excellent and cost from 40 to 110 piasters.

CLIMATE ... There are 4 distinct seasons, but it is almost always cold in the mountains and usually quite warm near the sea. April through November is the best time to visit Lebanon.

CLUBS ... Lions, Masonic Lodge, Propellor, Rotary, St. George's and Skal. A tourist would have to be accompanied by a member to make use of any of these clubs in Beirut.

COMMON COURTESIES AND LOCAL CUSTOMS ... The Lebanese are extremely hospitable. A guest is a sacred trust. Say *Marhaba* for "hello"; *Shookran* for "Thank you."

COMMUNICATIONS ... A 3-minute phone call to New York is L£45.90 ($15); a 10-word cablegram is L£14.80. Airmail postage to the U.S. is 70 piasters for 5-gram letters; 50 piasters for a postcard.

CURRENCY ... There are 100 piasters in the Lebanese pound (L£). The average rate is $1 United States equals L£3.06. However, the open market for exchange fluctuates daily.

CUSTOMS REGULATIONS AND DOCUMENTS REQUIRED FOR UNITED STATES CITIZENS ... Passport and visa required. For passengers holding visas for countries beyond, a transit visa for 15 days is issued on arrival. Vaccination certificate. Duty-free allowance: 500 grams of tobacco, 500 cigarettes allowed between June 1-October 31; 1 quart of liquor.

DRUGSTORES ... All are stocked with American and European brands of toilet articles and patent drugs.

ELECTRIC CURRENT ... The current in Beirut is 50 cycles, 110 volts, A.C. No transformer is necessary for radios, electric razors or American electrical appliances that run on 50-cycle current.

FAUNA ... Principally the mule, Arab horse, and cattle in general, as well as poultry, migratory and local birds. Fish of various forms common to the Mediterranean.

FLORA . . . Lebanese flora is similar to that of Southern Europe. It is rich in flowers, and the Cedars of Lebanon are outstanding.

FOOD . . . Barbecued meats and chicken; rice dishes and wonderful dishes cooked in grape leaves are native here. A majority of tourist restaurants serve continental food of considerable sophistication. Milk is bottled and pasteurized; you can drink it with safety in the better restaurants and hotels (but ask for the bottle!).

GAMBLING . . . The *Casino du Liban,* a 10-mile scenic drive north of Beirut, has all games similar to Monte Carlo and superb floor shows.

LANGUAGE . . . Arabic, French and English. You should have no difficulty when using only English in Lebanon.

LAUNDRY AND DRY CLEANING . . . Laundry is good and inexpensive. Dry-cleaning establishments are modern.

LIQUOR . . . Arrack is the national drink; drink it cautiously. At the better restaurants and hotels you can get cocktails and most of the European liquors. A great variety of American liquors is available.

MEDICAL FACILITIES . . . There are excellent hospitals with English-speaking doctors, among them the Hospital of the American University; St. Joseph's Hospital; St. Charles Hospital.

MOTION PICTURES . . . There are many motion-picture theaters; mostly American films are shown. The theaters in Beirut include: *Radio City, Dunia, Roxy, Capitole, Rivoli, Al Hamra, Empire, Metropole, Byblos, Saroulla, Edison,* the *Strand* and *Starco.*

MUSIC . . . There is no national symphony, but there are concerts presented by the Lebanese Academy of Arts.

NIGHT CLUBS . . . Beirut has nearly 150 night clubs. Dinner and supper music at the *Black Elephant, Caves du Roy, The Casbah* at the Commodore Hotel, *Le Paon Rouge* at the Phoenicia Hotel, *Beachcomber* at the Coral Beach Hotel, *Casino du Liban.*

PHOTOGRAPHY . . . You can purchase all types of films in Beirut—color, black-and-white, both still and movie. Prices are about the same as in the United States. Kodak is at Place de l'Etoile, Beydoun Bldg., Beirut. There are many good subjects in and around Beirut. Pigeon Rock and, of course, Baalbek are favorites.

RELIGION . . . There are churches of all denominations.

RESTAURANTS . . . In Beirut *St. George Grille* and *L'Age D'or* at the Phoenicia are outstanding. There's good food also at *Costebelle* and *Temporel;* wonderful fish at *The Seven Seas;* Spanish dishes at *Restaurant Espagnol* and Italian dishes at *Quo Vadis* and *Giovanni.* Local specialties at *Barmaki, Bahri, Ajami, Pigeon Rock* and *Sinbad.*

SHOPS AND STORES . . . There are excellent shops in which you can find merchandise from both East and West. Some of the better known in Beirut are: Asfar, Sarkis, Barakat, Achkar et Cie. You may bargain in the bazaars, but feel your way in the better places.

SPECTATOR SPORTS . . . Horse racing, soccer, basketball (the latter is extremely popular), wrestling, boxing.

SPORTS...Tennis, swimming, skiing, golf, fishing, shooting, aquaplaning, water polo, water-skiing, volley ball, ping pong, ice skating at Bristol Hotel Rink. Bowling is becoming popular in Beirut.

THEATERS...Well-known European theatrical troupes appear throughout the year, often at *Casino du Liban.*

TIME...7 hours later than U.S. Eastern Standard Time.

TIPPING...Hotels and restaurants add 10 to 12% service charge to your bill. Tip shoeshine boys and washroom attendants 25 piasters; 50 to the doorman. L£5 for the concierge. Otherwise, a L£1 tip is standard for everybody from parking-lot attendants to baggage porters.

TRANSPORTATION...As Lebanon is such a small country, it doesn't cost very much to see a lot of it. You can take a taxi for 10 miles for about $2. Buses are not recommended.

WATER...In Beirut and in mountain resorts it is very good and you can drink it safely, but it's risky in the small villages.

WHAT TO BUY...The most popular things are the beautiful brocades (which can be bought for about $8 per yard and cost $25 per yard in the U.S.), embroideries, rugs, brass objects, inlaid ivory furniture, hammered Persian silver, gold filigree jewelry and leather goods.

WHAT TO WEAR...Take along your very best clothes, about the same weights as you would wear in New York City for the corresponding season. Swimming suits are essential from April through September; the beaches are beautiful and the water excellent. Raincoats are necessary from October to May. Snow is heavy in the mountains, and you'll want ski clothes.

WHERE TO GO—SIGHTSEEING...

Beirut...Beirut is a harbor with docking space for huge ships. You should see the National Museum. Visit the American University, the largest American educational unit outside the United States; the Oriental Library of the French University; the Great Mosque built in the 12th century; the Pigeon Grotto. Take a tour of the residential (Ras Beirut) section and see the modern apartment houses.

Trips to the North...From Beirut take the beautiful coastal road to Byblos and Tripoli. which is like going back through history. In Tripoli see the Crusaders' fortresses, the monastery of the dervishes, the ancient mosques and Turkish baths and towers built by the Mameluke Sultans in the 14th and 15th centuries. Going via the Sacred Valley you reach the famous Cedars of Lebanon, which certainly no one should miss seeing. Here, too, is a famous winter resort with wonderful skiing from January until April. There is "spring snow" which gives an ideal surface. Here you ski beneath and near the famed Cedars and stay at good hotels. There are high mountains, some of them 10,000 feet, and expert skiers from everywhere come here. The Cedars of Lebanon, oldest in the world, date back to 4000 B.C.; they were used in building Egyptian tombs and Roman ships.

From Tripoli you can take one of the most beautiful tours in Lebanon, through the "Sacred Valley" and the "Cedars of the Lord," which is the birthplace of the Maronite order of monks. The monas-

Of the original 54 imposing columns which surrounded the Temple of Jupiter, six still stand among the ancient Roman ruins at Baalbek, 35 miles northeast of Beirut.

Pigeon Rock, one of the landmarks near Beirut, is one of many good subjects for the camera fan in sunny Lebanon.

teries may be reached only by paths which are really steps cut into the steep rocks. Laqlouq is another important winter resort in this area. The "Sacred Valley" is ringed with precipitous hills on whose slopes are crowded dozens of tiny villages.

If you have time you should go eastward from Tripoli to Baalbek and see the magnificent Roman ruins, including the Temple of Jupiter. The villages above Beirut are clustered together in the hills. A trip from Bikfaya to Souk el Gharb is an unforgettable sight.

Resorts in the South... Most of Lebanon's famous summer resorts are situated along the Beirut-Damascus highway. Best known are Aley and Bhamdoun. Here from July to October there is a gay social season. Tennis tournaments, battles of flowers, water sports, automobile and horse racing and other special activities take place. Aley's climate is mild and there are many things to do and see. There are night clubs, and good hotels, the *Grand, Hotel Gebeily*, the *Panorama*, the *Rond Point*, the *Montania* and *Tanios*. The Grand has a night club. Bhamdoun has a lot to offer, too, including a view of the valley of Hammana. *Ambassador Palace, Esplanade,* or *Shepherd Hotel*.

SOURCES OF FURTHER INFORMATION... Pan American offices in Phoenicia Hotel and Riad-El-Solh Square, Beirut (Tel. 2-21934).

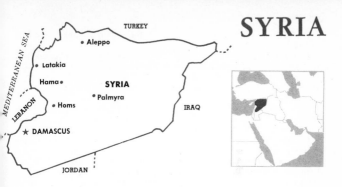

SYRIA

	JAN.	FEB.	MAR.	APR.	MAY	JUNE	JULY	AUG.	SEPT.	OCT.	NOV.	DEC.
Average Temp.	46°	49°	52°	61°	70°	75°	80°	82°	77°	68°	56°	47°
Days of Rain	4	5	3	6	0	1	0	0	0	5	5	5

LOCATION ... Syria's boundaries touch Turkey, Iraq, Jordan, Israel and Lebanon. Its Mediterranean coastline is about 200 miles long.

CHARACTERISTICS ... Syria is predominantly Arab in character and culture, though the urban Arab is adopting Western dress and habits to an increasing extent. Syria is a country of considerable interest, with its ruins of ancient civilizations and its historical monuments, reflecting the imprint of a hundred conquerors. It's a fantastically old land of Biblical fame, and traces of its exotic past may still be seen behind the modern facades of its cities.

POPULATION ... 5,180,000.

SIZE ... 71,228 square miles.

CAPITAL ... Damascus, with a population of 557,000.

GOVERNMENT ... A republic.

HOW TO GET THERE ... By Pan American Jet Clipper to Beirut-Damascus airport is 13¾ hours elapsed time from New York, 2¾ hours from Rome. By ship 18 to 21 days.

ACCOMMODATIONS ... Among the better hotels in Damascus are the *New Omayad*, the *New Semiramis, Orient Palace, Cattan Hotel*. In Aleppo, the *Baron* and *Ambassador* are best. In Lattakia, try the *Casino Hotel;* in Palmyra, the *Zenobia Hotel*. In first-class hotels rates are about $9 single, $14 double, including meals and service.

ARTS ... *See* Where To Go—Sightseeing.

BANKS . . . No American banks, but the principal banks have U.S. affiliations.

CALENDAR OF HOLIDAYS . . . The chief Moslem religious holidays are: the 3-day feast, Al Fitr, which takes place immediately after the month of fasting (Ramadan), and the Feast of Sacrifice (Qurban) which lasts 4 days. Christian shops are closed on Sunday and Moslem shops on Friday.

CIGARETTES AND TOBACCO . . . American cigarettes cost 50¢ a pack. Local brands (a mixture of Syrian and Turkish tobacco) *Star, Orient* and *Alhamra* are cheaper.

CLIMATE . . . Syria's coastal area is warm and rainy in winter, relatively hot in summer. In the interior (Damascus, Aleppo, Homs, Hama) winter is cold, summer hot. In the desert area (Palmyra) there are extreme fluctuations of temperature between night and day.

CLUBS . . . The most important clubs in Damascus are the Orient Club (Al Chark) and the Families Club. There's also an Orient Club in Aleppo. Lions in both cities as well as Rotary.

COMMON COURTESIES AND LOCAL CUSTOMS . . . It is considered only polite to accept a small cup of Arabic coffee or *gazoz* (a local carbonated drink) when visiting friends or business houses. *Shookran* is "Thank you." Arab people are particularly generous, and it can be very embarrassing to admire greatly some object in an Arab's home only to have your host present it to you. Remember that many of the strict Moslem rules are followed to the letter, particularly with regard to home life and the women of the family, although women are gradually emerging from behind veils. It is customary to take a gift when visiting someone's home.

COMMUNICATIONS . . . A 3-minute phone call to the States costs L.S. 57.50 ($15), plus L.S. 2.60 to place the call. Day-rate cablegram to the U.S. is L.S. 2.15 per word for a 7-word minimum. Airmail postage for letters to the U.S. costs L.S. 1.05; postcards 90 piasters.

CURRENCY . . . The Syrian pound, divided into 100 piasters, is worth L.S. 3.80 to L.S. 4 to U.S.$1.

CUSTOMS REGULATIONS AND DOCUMENTS REQUIRED FOR UNITED STATES CITIZENS . . . Passport and visa required. There is no fixed exemption on personal effects; duty assessment is left to the discretion of customs officers, but regulations are subject to frequent change, so check with your local Pan American office or Syrian Consul for last-minute changes.

DRUGSTORES . . . Drugstores follow the French and English rather than American system of filling prescriptions.

ELECTRIC CURRENT . . . 110 volts, A.C. 50 cycle. Adapter plugs for round prongs are needed but can be purchased locally.

FAUNA . . . Of interest to tourists are the camel and ever-present patient donkey of Damascus, Arab horses, and the gazelle, which can be found in the desert.

FLORA . . . Plants of interest are tarragon, safflower and caraway (which produces caraway seed). Trees include pistachio, apricot, nut, poplar, *platanus orientalis,* apple and cactus fruit. Several varieties of grape are also grown locally.

FOOD ... Both European and Syrian foods are offered in restaurants. Usually, a meal costs $1, and you can dine royally for $2 in the better places. A 10% service charge is normally included. Pasteurized milk is now available.

GAMBLING ... There is gambling in some night clubs.

LANGUAGE ... The official language is Arabic, but English and French are easily understood. The usual greeting is made by raising the hand while saying *marhaba* (hello).

LAUNDRIES AND DRY CLEANING ... Laundries, including those with dry-cleaning facilities, can be found throughout the country. Hotels can also take care of your laundry.

LIQUOR ... The better hotels and restaurants have bars where familiar brands of whisky, usually Scotch, are available, also wine, cognac and beer. Try *arrack,* made from grapes flavored with anise.

MEDICAL FACILITIES ... There are many Government hospitals and sanatoriums in both Damascus and Aleppo with English-speaking doctors. Inquire at your hotel or of Pan American.

MOTION PICTURES ... Damascus theaters show mostly films in English and French with Arabic subtitles. Shows at 3, 6:15 and 9:15 P.M. Reserve seats in advance.

MUSIC ... The prevailing music is Arabic. Some chamber music in the "Club of the Friends of Art" and other clubs.

NIGHT CLUBS AND CABARETS ... The *Orient Club* (*Al Chark*) on Najmeh Square, Damascus and the *Casino International* have dancing, drinks and gambling. Others which also have restaurants include the *Airport Restaurant, Caravan* and *Semiramis. Ashbilia* in Doummar near Damascus is open only during the summer.

PHOTOGRAPHY ... Photographic equipment and supplies, including color films for movie cameras and developing service for black-and-white still pictures, are available in Damascus and Aleppo, but it's wise to bring color film with you. Photographing military installations is prohibited and taking pictures in many parts of Syria is frowned on. It's best to ask about this.

RELIGION ... 85% of the people are Moslems. Other sects are: Catholic, Protestant, Syriac, Greek Orthodox.

RESTAURANTS ... The chief restaurants in Damascus are the *Candles, Laterna Caves du Roy, Alcazar, Oasis, Swiss, Assri Club, Airport Restaurant; Orient Restaurant;* the *New Omayad, New Semiramis* and *Cattan* hotels. All serve both Western and Arabic meals.

SHOPS AND STORES ... Shopping hours are normally from 9 A.M. to 7 P.M. (often closed from 1 to 4 P.M. for lunch). Prices are moderate. *Souk* vendors expect you to bargain. Shops are closed on Friday, some on Sunday.

SPECTATOR SPORTS ... From time to time, basketball or football matches are held in Damascus. Tickets are sold in most markets.

TIME ... When it's noon in New York, it's 7 P.M. in Syria.

TRANSPORTATION . . . Buses, taxis and, in Damascus and Aleppo, electric trolleys and cars for hire (with driver).

WATER . . . Potable in Damascus. No bottled water available.

WHAT TO BUY . . . Beautiful hand-worked copper and brass trays with silver inlay (from 8 inches to 4 feet in diameter); hand-loomed brocades, wood and mother-of-pearl inlay work, items from the glass-blowing "factories," mosaics and embroideries.

WHAT TO WEAR . . . Light clothing for summer, warm clothing and topcoat or raincoat for winter months.

WHERE TO GO—SIGHTSEEING . . .

Damascus . . . Damascus is the oldest continuously inhabited city in the world, dating back 6,000 years, and abounds with local color. See the Omayad Mosque, originally the church of John the Baptist, built by Theodosius in the 4th century and later converted into a Moslem basilica. The silence of its magnificent carpeted interior offers a startling contrast to the noise of the city.

Other places of interest include the Azem Palace, the home of Judas, the chapel and home of Ananias, the tomb of Saladin, the place at the city gate where Paul was lowered in a basket to escape the Roman soldiers, the Museum of Damascus, St. Paul's Church, the historical gates of the city, and the street of Biblical times called Straight, still one of Damascus's most important thoroughfares, running through the Grand Bazaar and connecting the old East and West Gates.

To wander through the crooked, narrow streets of the Grand Bazaar is to get the real atmosphere of the East, the smell of spices and garlic, exotic perfumes, the sight of beautiful brocades, Oriental rugs, brass and copper, inlaid ivory, and magnificent jewelry along with American dime-store items. More fascinating still is the swarming mass of people representing every nationality imaginable.

Side Trip . . . In Aleppo, about 225 miles from Damascus, places of interest are: the Museum of Aleppo, the Citadel of Aleppo, the historical gates of Aleppo, the Great Mosque. Stay at the *Baron Hotel* or *Ambassador Hotel*. Worthwhile, too, is a trip to the historical monuments of Palmyra, which is best made by air. (*See* PAA office.) In this town there are monuments of ancient civilizations, especially that of the reign of Queen Zenobia. See also the ancient cemeteries with their wonderful decorations, the Citadel of the Ma'anites. Stay at the *Zenobia Hotel*. Maloula, probably the only village where Aramaic, which Jesus spoke, is still used, is an interesting hour's drive from Damascus. The remarkable Crusader Castle, *Krak de Chevaliers,* oldest and best-preserved fortress of its kind in this area, lies a 4-hour drive to the northwest.

SOURCES OF FURTHER INFORMATION . . . Tourist agencies in Damascus organize trips and provide guides who speak English. Pan Am's representative is Hitti and Khoury Freres, Sharia al Nasr. (Tel. 12500). Arab Information Center, 757 Third Avenue, New York, N.Y. 10017.

TURKEY

WEATHER IN ISTANBUL—Lat. N41°10′—Alt. 30′

Temp.	JAN.	FEB.	MAR.	APR.	MAY	JUNE	JULY	AUG.	SEPT.	OCT.	NOV.	DEC.
Low	38°	36°	40°	46°	55°	62°	67°	68°	62°	57°	49°	43°
High	46°	45°	52°	60°	71°	78°	82°	82°	75°	68°	58°	51°
Average	42°	41°	46°	53°	63°	70°	75°	75°	69°	63°	54°	47°
Days of Rain	10	8	9	7	7	5	2	4	6	7	11	12

LOCATION . . . Except for the area south of Bulgaria and east of Greece on the European continent, Turkey lies in Asia, occupying the peninsula of Asia Minor, across the Black Sea from Russia and across the Mediterranean from Egypt. Istanbul, divided by the Bosporus Strait, is astride two continents. It is 843 air miles from Rome.

CHARACTERISTICS . . . Turkey is a wonderful vacation spot which is rapidly growing more popular with cosmopolites who are discovering for themselves its wonderful scenery, splendid climate, classic examples of Byzantine architecture, and atmosphere of sophistication. The Turkish people are extremely cordial and international-minded. If you are looking for something different with the exotic atmosphere of the East, you'll like Istanbul.

POPULATION . . . 31,118,000 (1,976,835 in Istanbul).

SIZE . . . 880 miles long and 390 miles wide, Turkey occupies 301,381 square miles. It's slightly larger than Texas.

CAPITAL . . . Ankara, population 874,481.

GOVERNMENT . . . A Republic with a National Assembly elected by universal suffrage. The President is elected by the Assembly.

HOW TO GET THERE . . . By Jet Clipper from New York to Istanbul, 12½ hours; 45 minutes more to Ankara which is also served by Middle East Airlines—routings via London, Paris, Frankfurt, Munich, Belgrade, Vienna and Rome. By ship, about 15 days. Airport bus fare is 3 lira.

ACCOMMODATIONS . . . The beautiful *Istanbul Hilton* has 440 rooms (some air-conditioned), each with bath and balcony, and every·thing from swimming pools to a glass-enclosed night club; single from $13.35, double from $16.70. The *Divan Hotel* is also modern and comfortable and serves fine food; single from $8, double from $10. Next best are the *Park, Kennedy, Santral* and the *Opera*. The dé luxe 150-room *Çinar Hotel*, at Yesilköy near the airport, is beautifully located on the Marmara Sea and has a supper club, pool and private beach. Nearing completion are the elegant new *Grand Hotel Tarabaya* and *Hisar* on the Bosporus near Istanbul. In Ankara the *Kent* and *Balin* are first class; about $8 single, $12 double. Others are the *Modern Palas, Bulvar Palas* and the *Barikan;* rates from about $5 single, $9 double.

New hotels for tourists include the luxurious *Grand Hotel Ephesus;* the *Tusan* in nearby Kusadasi; the *Kismet* and *Kilim* in Izmir on the Aegean Sea; and others at Troy; at Samsun on the Black Sea; and at Kilyos, an hour from Istanbul.

ARTS . . . Istanbul's fine Archaeological Museum contains the sarcophagus of Alexander the Great. Nearby is the Museum of Oriental Antiquities containing an excellent collection from ancient Hittite, Assyrian and Egyptian civilizations. The Museum of Mehmet the Conqueror, the Çinili Kösk, is a jewel. Don't miss the Kariye Camiî where restoration of the Byzantine mosaics and frescoes make it a major art museum. Other museums are the Naval Museum, Museum of Islamic and Turkish Art, Municipal Museum, and nearby the Mosque of Sultan Ahmet, a unique example of 6th-century Byzantine mosaics, thought to be on the remnants of the passage of the Great Palace and unimaginatively called the Museum of Mosaics. At Besiktas see the Museum of Paintings and Sculpture.

BANKS . . . The American-Turkish Foreign Trade Bank, Ottoman Bank, Iş Bank, Central Bank, Yapi ve Kredi Bank, Holland Bank, Bank of Rome, and Italian Commercial Bank all cash travelers checks.

CALENDAR OF HOLIDAYS . . . New Year's Day; April 23, Children's Day; May 1, Spring Day; May 19, Youth Day; May 27, Liberty Day; August 30, Victory Day; and October 29, Republic Day —all stores close. Two Turkish religious (Moslem) holidays are kept: Seker Bayram and Kurban Bayram, the dates of which vary from year to year.

CIGARETTES AND TOBACCO . . . Excellent Turkish cigarettes and tobaccos processed in the American manner. *Yeni Harman, Samsun, Camlica* and *Bafra* are popular brands. Prices are 10¢ to 33¢ a pack. American cigarettes are not available.

CLIMATE . . . Istanbul has much the same climate as New York. In summer the heat is tempered by cool breezes from the Bosporus by way of the Black Sea. Ankara, which has an elevation of 2,600 feet, has a drier climate with cool nights all summer long. Southern Turkey has a climate comparable to Florida. In general the best time of the year to visit Turkey is between June and December, and the

Indian summer, September to November, is particularly delightful.

COMMON COURTESIES AND LOCAL CUSTOMS... The fez is outlawed now in Turkey and will be seen only as a purchasable curio in the bazaars, and women are no longer veiled. The Turks are very sensitive on these questions, so tread lightly. Turks always shake hands on meeting both men and women, and they are warmly friendly and helpful. *Teshekkür ederim* is "Thank you" in Turkish.

COMMUNICATIONS... Airmail postage to the States is 2.25 liras for a 5-gram letter; 1.80 for a postcard. A cablegram costs 4 lira a word; 144 lira for a 3-minute call to the States.

CURRENCY... The monetary unit is the lira (which contains 100 kurus). United States $1 equals 9.00 Turkish lira. Money can be exchanged at any bank or hotel.

CUSTOMS REGULATIONS AND DOCUMENTS REQUIRED FOR UNITED STATES CITIZENS... Passport only; no visa for tourists. Duty-free allowances: 50 cigarettes or 20 cigars; 1 opened bottle of liquor. You can bring in 500 Turkish lira and take out no more of any currency than brought in. Air departure tax 10 lira ($1.10).

DRUGSTORES... Most American and European drug products and cosmetics are available.

ELECTRIC CURRENT... The voltage is 110 A.C. in most sections on the European side, 220 A.C. on the Asiatic. Adapter plugs must have round prongs. Hilton Hotel: 220 A.C., 50 cycles.

FAUNA... Wild boar, pheasants, hares, partridge, quail, woodcock, deer.

FLORA... Wonderful flowers—abundant roses, carnations, tulips, violets, chrysanthemums, brown orchids, gladioli, hydrangea and many other well-known varieties.

FOOD... Try *börek,* a delicious thin pastry filled with white cheese, egg and parsley; *dolmas,* grape or cabbage leaves filled with ground beef and served with sour cream; chicken or turkey stuffed with *iç pilav,* rice cooked with currants, pine nuts and spices; *kiliç,* swordfish grilled on a spit with bay leaves, and, of course, *siskebap.* Pasteurized milk is available. Better hotels serve international food. Prices run $2 and up. Turkish beer is good; avoid local gin.

GAMBLING... Racing with pari-mutuels at Istanbul and Ankara. There is a monthly national lottery. No gambling in the night clubs.

LANGUAGE... English is spoken in hotels and principal shops and restaurants. Turkish is the official language. French is also spoken in most circles in Istanbul and Ankara.

LAUNDRY AND DRY CLEANING... Hotels can handle both laundry and dry cleaning. Avoid sending unusual materials or women's clothing with ornaments, sequins, etc. Prices are much the same as in the United States and service is reasonably good.

LIQUOR... Turkey makes some good red and white wines. Their liqueurs are comparatively good and varied. Roseleaf, banana, strawberry, tangerine, sour cherry are some of the flavors. Turkish vermouth and brandy are fair; the vodka is very good. Local liquors are inexpensive. *Raki* is a native drink flavored with anise. It is drunk only with *meze* (Turkish appetizers—marvelous!) and not as a highball. Popular American drinks are available at the Hilton, Çinar, Divan and Park Hotels. The Screwdriver (orange juice and vodka) is a famous drink here as is the vodka martini.

MEDICAL FACILITIES . . . The Admiral Bristol Hospital (more familiarly known as the American Hospital) in Istanbul is modern and staffed with English-speaking doctors. There are many English-speaking private doctors available. Consult your hotel.

MOTION PICTURES . . . *Yeni Melek, Atlas, Ar, San, Konak* and *Site* are downtown Istanbul theaters which show American and British films with English sound track and Turkish titles, as well as European films in various languages. Reserve seats in advance.

MUSIC . . . Istanbul has a symphony orchestra. There are opera and ballet, too. Radio Istanbul and Radio Ankara have symphony and philharmonic orchestras.

NIGHT CLUBS AND CABARETS . . . In Istanbul you'll want to take in the entertainment and dancing at the glass-enclosed *Sadirvan Supper Club* set in the garden of the Hilton among the fountains for which it is named. They also have a *Marmara Roof* night club and *Karagöz* (puppet decor) bar adjoining their Terrace Restaurant. Others include the *Taksim Casino* (outside in the summer), *Angelo, Kervansaray, Parisienne* (Cordon Bleu)—all near Taksim Square—the *Wagon Bleu* with orchestras and floor shows of European and local entertainers, and the new *Club X* and *Club 12. Bogazici,* an elegant restaurant-night club, and the *Çinar Pavillon* are new. In Ankara the top night club is *Süreyya's* (open in winter only), also the *Ankara Palas, Club 47* (where the doors are closed after the 47th person enters), *Balin Pavyonu* and *Bulvar Palas.*

PHOTOGRAPHY . . . All kinds of film are usually available in Istanbul, Ankara and Izmir at slightly higher than U.S. prices. Ektachrome processing in Ankara and Istanbul. Foto Sabah and Burla Biraderler can give 24-hour service.

RELIGION . . . Turkey is a Moslem country, but there are many Christian churches, including Catholic, Greek Orthodox and Protestant, as well as Jewish synagogues. Most American Protestants attend the Dutch chapel, located just off the main street of Istanbul.

RESTAURANTS . . . In Istanbul, the Hilton offers the *Bosporus Terrace* coffee shop and the glamorous *Sadirvan Supper Club.* Wonderful food may be had at the *Divan* and *Park* hotels, the *Oriental,* at *Abdullah Efendi* on the main street and at *Süreyya* in Bebek. Worth the 20-minute drive is *Abdullah's Farm* at Emirgan. For lunch, try *Konyah* and *Pandelli's* in the famous *Misir Çarsisi* (Spice Bazaar) or *Liman Restaurant* near the docks; *Çinar* on the beach near the airport with American bar. While sightseeing up the Bosporus, stop at *Fidan* or *Sule,* where the seafood is marvelous and the view delightful. *Divan Hotel, Lebon, Markkiz* are all excellent for tea, ice cream and pastries. In Ankara, tops are the *Bekir* and *Washington* restaurants, the *Barikan, Kent* and *Bulvar Palas* hotels.

SHOPS AND STORES... The main shopping area is all along the main street in the European section of Istanbul. Most shops are open daily except Sunday from 9 A.M. to 7 P.M. For travelers the best and favorite shopping for all Turkish novelties is in the famous bazaars in the old section of Istanbul.

SPECTATOR SPORTS... There is horse racing, soccer, wrestling, boxing, track meets, basketball, tennis and golf.

SPORTS... Swimming, sailing and fishing are excellent in the waters of the Bosporus, Aegean Sea, Black Sea and Sea of Marmara. Hunting wild boar is a favorite national sport. Horseback riding can be arranged. Winter sports include sledding, skiing at the famous slopes of Bursa at the foot of Mount Olympus.

THEATERS... There are several theaters in Istanbul and Ankara where plays in Turkish are produced. Companies visiting Turkey perform English and French plays. Tickets for matinees or evening performances can be purchased through your hotel at between $2 and $3.

TIME... When it's noon in New York, it's 7 P.M. in Istanbul.

TIPPING... Tip porters 1 lira per bag; shoeshine boys, washroom and parking lot attendants and theater ushers get 50 kurus; 10% for barber or beautician, and for taxi driver. If no service charge is included, tip waiter 10% of the bill. Hotels have 10% service charges, but give the chambermaid 1.50 lira for each day's stay.

TRANSPORTATION... There are taxis and buses in Istanbul, and a 1-minute subway between Pera and Galata. Ferries link the European and Asiatic shores. The trip takes about 20 minutes. Taxis charge about 5.00 Turkish lira within the new section of the city and 7.50 Turkish lira from the new section to the old section (where the bazaars and mosques are). Bus tickets vary in price with the distance. Buses are marked with origin and destination. Taxis are comparatively inexpensive and the easiest mode of transport for tourists because city traffic is overwhelming.

WATER... Water is safe to drink, but there are many fine bottled table and mineral waters if you prefer.

WHAT TO BUY... Gold and silver hand-embroidered handbags and exquisitely painted filmy scarfs, bed jackets of silky mohair, attar of roses and other perfumes, wonderful candies, silver and gold filigree, rugs and carpets. Bursa silks, ceramics, hand-carved meerschaum pipes, costume jewelry—handmade brass and copper ashtrays, siskebap skewers and martini stirrers, Turkish slippers, Turkish "towels" beautifully embroidered in original designs, Kütahya tiles and wonderful old copper. In the bazaars it is best to bargain.

WHAT TO WEAR... In Istanbul you will need lightweight clothes in the summer, warm clothes in winter. Raincoats are essential in the rainy season as rain is very heavy and often quite sudden. Beach clothes are essential for both men and women. In Ankara you will need warmer clothes in winter than you do in New York or Istanbul. A light topcoat is a good idea. Men will need sports jackets and slacks, medium-weight suits for spring and winter and light suits for summer. Evening or dinner clothes are usually not necessary.

WHERE TO GO—SIGHTSEEING . . .

Istanbul . . . Türk Ekspres has a sightseeing bus service from the Hilton and Çinar. Wagon-Lits/Cook and Turist Seyahat, Inc. offer tours at $2.80 for a half day. Individual guides with cars charge around $27 per day. The Aya Sofia, a thousand years older than Saint Peter's Cathedral in Rome, is considered by architects to be one of the seven wonders of the world. Near it is Saint Irene, the oldest church in Istanbul; the fountain of Sultan Ahmet III, the Yerebatan Cisterns, built by the Emperor Justinian; Sultan Ahmet, called the Blue Mosque; the ancient Byzantine hippodrome and the Mosaic Museum, conveniently grouped for sightseeing. A short distance away are the marvelous Süleymaniye Mosque and the Mosque of Beyazit. In Istanbul there are over 400 mosques, some of which were once churches; some are decorated with beautiful old tiles, and all are interesting. Dolmabahce Palace, former home of the sultans, is now a fascinating museum. See the Edirne Gate, the Kariye Camiî, containing some of the most glorious mosaics and frescoes from the Byzantine period, and by all means drive out along the old Byzantine Walls to the Castle of the Seven Towers. A whole day can be spent in the Topkapi Palace and the newly opened mysterious and fascinating Harem section. Don't miss the fabulous horde of treasure and precious stones in the Treasury or the porcelain collection, which is one of the finest and largest in the world. Go to the famous Kapali Çarsi and be sure to take a ferry ride up the Bosporus and to the Princes Islands.

Other Trips . . . From Istanbul you may go by ferry to the health resort of Yalova and on to Bursa at the foot of Mount Olympus. Turkey is rich with the history of Christianity. Ephesus was the last home of the Virgin Mary, and the shrine there is respected by Moslems and revered by Christians. St. Paul was born in Tarsus; St. Peter's Grotto near Antakya was the first Christian church; Iznik was the site of the first Christian Council. Highways to historic sites have been greatly improved. The Tusan chain of very modern motels along the Aegean coast charge only $5 a person for room with bath, balcony and meals.

Ankara . . . You may fly from Istanbul to Ankara, seat of the Turkish Government, in 45 minutes or make overnight trip by train. Be sure to take the trip to the fortress in time to watch the sunset at Akkale. See the Ahi Elvan Mosque, the Arslanhane Mosque, the Roman Aqueduct, the Orman Çiftliği (the model farm founded by Atatürk). You will see the Government buildings, the Presidential residence at Çankaya and other buildings and monuments of interest. Visit the Turkish National Theater and the tomb of Atatürk.

SOURCES OF FURTHER INFORMATION . . . In Istanbul, Türk Ekspres, Wagons-Lits/Cook and Turist Seyahat travel agencies; Pan American's office at Istanbul Hilton Arcade (Tel. 474530) and Ankara Palas Otel (Tel. 13681/11032). In Ankara, Ministry of Press, Radio and Tourism. Turkish Information offices at 500 Fifth Avenue, New York, N.Y. 10036.

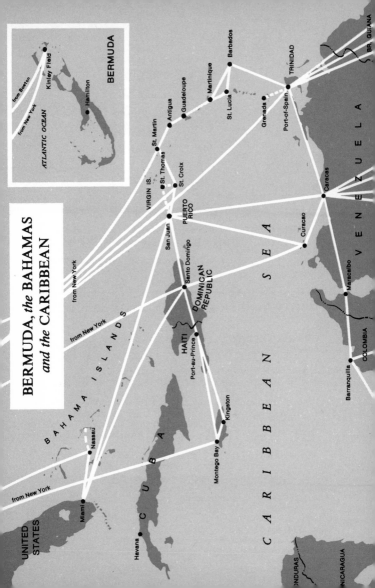

ANTIGUA

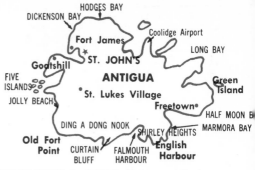

WEATHER IN ST. JOHN'S—Lat. N17°03′—Alt. approx. sea level

	JAN.	FEB.	MAR.	APR.	MAY	JUNE	JULY	AUG.	SEPT.	OCT.	NOV.	DEC.
Average Temp.	76°	76°	77°	78°	79°	80°	80°	81°	81°	80°	79°	77°
Days of Rain	20	15	14	13	15	16	19	18	18	19	19	20

LOCATION ... Antigua (pronounced An-tee′-ga) is an island in the Lesser Antilles, southeast of Puerto Rico, 1,776 miles from New York.

CHARACTERISTICS ... Antigua is one of the loveliest of the Caribbean islands, surrounded by fabulous beaches. The swimming is superb, with coral sand extending far out into the clear, colorful sea. This is an ideal spot for a holiday the year round.

POPULATION ... 64,000, of which the majority are colored.

SIZE ... Antigua is 108 square miles, about 16 miles across at any point, with headlands extending out all around the island.

CAPITAL ... St. John's, with about 21,000 population.

GOVERNMENT ... Antigua is a British Colony.

HOW TO GET THERE ... By Pan American Jet Clipper, less than 4 hours from New York nonstop.

ACCOMMODATIONS ... Most of the hotels are new. Unless otherwise mentioned, the rates quoted are the minimum, single and double, Modified American Plan (includes breakfast and dinner), December 15 through April 15. Rates are lower the rest of the year. *Anchorage Hotel,* 2 miles from St. John's on Dickenson Bay; all water sports; $28 and $42. *Caribbean Beach Club* is near St. John's; air-conditioned rooms and suites on the beach; water sports, entertainment; $24 and $38. *Curtain Bluff,* with handsomely decorated rooms, faces sea and constant breeze; snorkeling, scuba diving, other water sports; $35 and $54. *Antigua Horizons* on coral sand beach of reef-protected bay; fine French cuisine; $32 and $44. *Jolly Beach Hotel* in 350 acres of tropical splendor; central air conditioning; $28 and $48 AP. The fabulous new *Marmora Beach Hotel* with beach and fresh-water pool; air conditioned; gambling casino, nightly entertainment; $32 and $38. *Hawksbill Hotel* has 4 oceanfront beaches; all sports, including skin diving, water skiing, yachting, tennis; $36 and $46. *Admiral's Inn* at Nelson's Dockyard is small, attractive; $22 and $28. *Blue Waters Hotel* nestles in lush tropical landscaping; all sports; $34 and $40. *Half Moon Bay Hotel* offers sea or pool swimming, 9-hole golf course; $35 and $44. *The Inn,* with rooms on both hill and beach-side, has all water sports; $30 and $46. *Galley Bay Surf Club,* 4 miles from St. John's; fine beach; $27 and $42. *Antigua Beach Hotel,* with *Jabberwock Club,* is at Hodges Bay; pool and beach; $27 and $43 AP. The *Beachcomber,* on the north shore, is small and informal; $20 and $30. *White Sands,* Hodges Bay, has pool and beach; $20 and $32. The *Lord Nelson Club* has rooms smack on the beach; $16 and $24. *Sugar Mill Hotel* overlooks beautiful Parham Sound near the airport; $12 and $18 AP. Hotels add 10% service charge in lieu of tipping.

BANKS...Barclays Bank (D.C. & O.), Royal Bank of Canada and Bank of Nova Scotia.

CALENDAR OF HOLIDAYS...New Year's Day; Good Friday; Easter Monday; Whitmonday, first Monday in May; May 24, Dominion Day; Queen's Birthday (in June); first Monday in August; November 14, birthday of heir to the throne; Christmas Day; Boxing Day. Early closing days, Thursday and Saturday.

CIGARETTES AND TOBACCO...American and English cigarettes cost $4-$5 B.W.I. (U.S. $2.44-$3.05) per carton of 200.

CLIMATE...The climate is delightful in both summer and winter. September and October have a relatively high humidity, although the low year-round average is one of Antigua's attractions.

CLUBS...The American Mill Reef Club and a number of social clubs in St. John's are open only to members or by invitation. The sports clubs which offer tennis, golf, etc., welcome visitors at all times.

COMMON COURTESIES AND LOCAL CUSTOMS...Negroes are referred to as "colored people." Ladies do not wear shorts in St. John's while shopping. Men wear coats at dinner. Visitors should remember that there is no color bar in Antigua and that all hotels, bars and some clubs are interracial.

COMMUNICATIONS...In U.S. currency: a 3-minute phone call to the States costs $8-$10; a 10-word cablegram is $2.40. Airmail postage is 15¢.

CURRENCY...West Indian dollar valued at about U.S. 61¢. American currency should be converted, but is sometimes accepted.

CUSTOMS REGULATIONS AND DOCUMENTS REQUIRED FOR UNITED STATES CITIZENS...Proof of nationality for visitors from the U.S. who hold return tickets. No visa is required. Yellow fever and cholera certificates required if coming from infected areas.

DRUGSTORES...Harper's, the Corner Drug Store and O'Neal's are well stocked with drugs, patent medicines, toiletries.

ELECTRIC CURRENT... 110 volts, A.C. in most hotels, but 220 volts elsewhere on the island.

FAUNA... Dove, pigeon, some migratory duck, yellow breast, blackbirds, reef fish, tarpon and bonefish.

FLORA... Red lilies, roses, hibiscus, bougainvillaea, poinsettia, mahogany, coconuts, royal palms, cabbage palm, palmetto, fig, banana, plantain, avocado, citrus, papaya, mangoes in season.

FOOD... West Indian cookery is influenced by the ancestry of its settlers, in this case, the English. Much food is imported. Local supplies of fresh pasteurized milk are available.

GAMBLING... Roulette, blackjack, dice and slot machines at the Marmora Beach Casino.

LAUNDRY AND DRY CLEANING... Excellent services.

LIQUOR... Sold at duty-free prices.

MEDICAL FACILITIES... Hospital and English- and Canadian-trained doctors.

MOTION PICTURES... Two movie houses in St. John's, English and American films shown. Movies also at hotels.

MUSIC... Steel bands playing calypso and local dance orchestras.

NIGHT CLUBS AND CABARETS... There are several small night clubs, and most hotels feature dancing and floor shows.

PHOTOGRAPHY... Developing and printing (black-and-white only) done quickly and well. Bring color film with you.

RELIGION... Anglican (Church of England), Catholic, Methodist, Moravian and Seventh Day Adventist churches.

SHOPS AND STORES... Shops specialize in beach and sportswear, underwater gear, local handicrafts and recordings.

SPECTATOR SPORTS... Cricket and football.

SPORTS... There are tennis and golf, horseback riding and every possible kind of water sport. Fishing sloops can be chartered. At neighboring Barbuda there's exciting skin-diving.

TIME... Noon in Antigua is 11 A.M. in New York.

TRANSPORTATION... Taxi fares from the airport to hotels range from U.S. $1.25-$10. Taxi fares otherwise are charged on a round-trip basis. You can rent a self-drive car, and your state driver's license, presented at police headquarters, entitles you to a visitor's license.

WATER... Resorts serve purified rain water.

WHAT TO WEAR... Light clothes, summer suits, shorts. Evening clothes are not essential and rarely worn. Coats in evening.

WHERE TO GO—SIGHTSEEING... Dockyard at English Harbor, where Nelson, Rodney and Hood were stationed in the Royal West Indian Squadron while pursuing the French and Spanish Fleets, is of unusual interest; also near English Harbor is Clarence House, the country house of the Governor, built in 1787 by the Duke of Clarence, who later became William IV. Fig Tree Drive in the mountainous tropical part of the island can be seen by automobile.

SOURCES OF FURTHER INFORMATION... Antigua Tourist Board in St. John's. Pan Am's office is at 37 High Street (Tel. 241).

BARBADOS

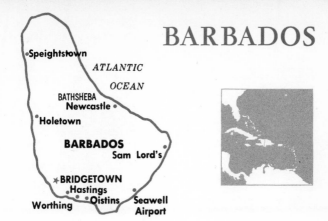

WEATHER IN BARBADOS—Lat. N13°4′—Alt. approx. sea level

	JAN.	FEB.	MAR.	APR.	MAY	JUNE	JULY	AUG.	SEPT.	OCT.	NOV.	DEC.
Average Temp.	77°	76°	77°	78°	80°	81°	80°	80°	80°	80°	79°	78°
Days of Rain	14	12	11	9	11	17	19	18	16	17	16	16

LOCATION . . . The most eastern of the West Indian islands.

CHARACTERISTICS . . . Flying fish play around this colorful West Indian island, where the natives speak with a British accent. The rum is marvelous and so is their weather the year round. Here are some of the finest bathing beaches in the world. The perfect spot for either an active or a relaxing vacation.

POPULATION . . . Estimated 243,417.

SIZE . . . Barbados is triangular in shape and is 21 miles long by 14 miles across the widest part. Total area is 166 square miles.

CAPITAL . . . Bridgetown and environs have an estimated population of 11,304.

GOVERNMENT . . . Barbados now has complete internal self-government.

HOW TO GET THERE . . . By Pan American Jet Clipper from New York in 4¼ hours. By ship, from New York or New Orleans.

ACCOMMODATIONS . . . De luxe hotels are the *Colony, Coral Reef, Eastry House, Miramar, Sam Lord's Castle* and *Sandy Lane;* winter rates about $45-$60 double, MAP. Other good beachside hotels include *Bonnie Dundee, Caribee, Paradise Beach, Royal-on-Sea, St. Lawrence* and *South Winds* (average winter rates about $30 double, MAP); and the *Accra Beach, Royal Caribbean, Crane, Ocean View, Sandy Beach, San Remo, Marine, Bagshot House, Windsor* (average winter rates about $27 double, AP). Guest houses which have rooms with private baths include the *Blue Caribbean, Contentment,*

Excursions from Bridgetown take you through the rolling countryside and sugarcane fields of Barbados.

The Harbour Police still dress like Lord Nelson's sailors. Police band concerts are colorful events.

Foster House, Pink House, Rhondda and *Torrington;* winter rates about $17 double, AP. The winter season is generally considered to be December 15 to April 15; lower rates the rest of the year.

COMMUNICATIONS ... In local currency, a 3-minute phone call to the States costs about $15.48 (U.S. $9.44). Airmail postage to the U.S. is 12¢ W.I. for a postcard; 24¢ W.I. per ½ ounce for letters.

CURRENCY ... The U.S. dollar is valued at $1.68 B.W.I. U.S. notes and travelers checks are accepted by most hotels.

CUSTOMS REGULATIONS AND DOCUMENTS REQUIRED BY UNITED STATES CITIZENS ... Proof of identity. While a birth certificate is *not* accepted as proof of identity in Barbados, it may be used as proof on returning to the United States. The official recommendation of proof of identity in Barbados is a passport, current or expired, but bona fide visitors returning within 6 months will encounter little difficulty in satisfying the immigration officials. Smallpox vaccination is required for entry to Barbados. 200 cigarettes or 50 cigars may be brought in duty free.

ELECTRIC CURRENT ... Same as in the U.S.

FOOD ... You'll get very fine continental cooking but do try some local dishes: *bonavist* (small white beans) combined with pumpkin and herbs in a traditional soup; *eddoes,* a starchy substitute for potatoes, as is breadfruit. *Jug-Jug,* a holiday dish, is a mould of green peas, chopped ham and salt beef or pork. *Coo-coo* is a savory pudding made with cornmeal. Barbadian Black Pudding is a kind of sausage stuffed with richly seasoned mashed sweet potatoes. Roast suckling pig is an island specialty. Most famous and popular dish is flying fish, prepared in innumerable ways. Try sea urchins, too, with their delicate flavor. The more exotic fruits include fig bananas, guavas, mangoes, shaddocks, avocados. The island's tap water is perfectly safe to drink.

LIQUOR . . . Imported liquors are sold at low, duty-free prices. The famous Barbados rum costs about $1 a bottle and is great served on the rocks and in Planter's Punch, Sangaree (with Madeira wine and curaçao), Cuba Libre and many other drinks.

MEDICAL FACILITIES . . . So good that people from all over the Caribbean come to Barbados for medical and dental care.

NIGHT CLUBS AND CABARETS . . . The larger hotels feature nightly dancing and floor shows with steel bands, "limbo" dancers and calypso singers. Many hotels have one "big night" a week for special balls and entertainment; among these are the *Sandy Lane, Colony Club, Bonnie Dundee, Island Inn, Blue Water Beach, Paradise Beach* and *Coral Reef*. Dancing nightly at *Cloud 9* night club.

RESTAURANTS . . . Good places to eat in Bridgetown are the *Flying Fish Club, Oasis, The Chatterbox, Hong Kong* and *Goddard's*. Light snacks may be found at the *Beau Brummel* in Hastings and at *Luigi's* Italian restaurant. The *Fiesta, Welsh Harp, Pied Piper, Bamboo* and others, all night spots, also serve meals with drinks. Crane Hotel has the *Fish Pot*, and the Caribee has *Top o' the Isle*, both famous for seafood dishes.

SPORTS . . . There are 9-hole golf courses at the Rockley Golf Club and Sandy Lane Golf Club. Tennis at the Savannah Club and The Royal Barbados Yacht Club. Your hotel can arrange horseback riding at very low rates. Spectator sports include cricket, polo, horse racing. Water sports, however, are Barbados' greatest attraction. The average temperature of the water is 75 degrees. The Paradise Beach Club, in St. Michael, close to Bridgetown, has one of the best beaches. Other especially good ones are at the Aquatic Club, Colony Club, Coral Reef, Sandy Lane, Accra Beach, Rockley Beach, Kingsley, Miramar, Crane and Sam Lord's. Barbados is the best place to learn —or to perfect—snorkeling and aqualung diving, with excellent instructors to help. Winter rates for snorkeling lessons are about $3 per 15 minutes; $12 for a lesson in aqualung diving. Basic equipment available on the island. Great catches of flying fish, barracuda, dolphin, wahoo and kingfish are the reward of the sport fisherman; charter launches with fishing gear at reasonable rates. Visitors may have temporary memberships in the Barbados Cruising Club and the Royal Barbados Yacht Club, both of which sponsor frequent regattas. Fine water skiing on the calm Caribbean side of the island.

TIPPING . . . In local currency, tip 25¢ (about 15¢ U.S.) for all small services. Tip 10% of bills presented by waiters, barbers, beauticians, taxi drivers, and others.

TRANSPORTATION . . . Fixed taxi rates from the airport to the island's southern resorts are $4 B.W.I. per car; $9 B.W.I. per car to west coast hotels; full-day sightseeing tours by taxi cost $24 B.W.I. per car, or $6 B.W.I. per seat. You may obtain a free driving permit by presenting your state driver's license at the airport's Immigration

Desk. Self-drive cars rent for about $45 B.W.I. a week and up. (Traffic moves on the left, as in Britain.) Aquatic transportation includes the glass-bottomed *Seascape,* which makes regular trips over the colorful coral reefs; the luxurious *Carlotta,* which makes three 5-day cruises a month through the Grenadine Islands; and there are many yachts that make cocktail cruises and moonlight cruises for $10.25 B.W.I. per 2½-hour cruise.

WHAT TO BUY ... Duty-free French perfumes, British textiles, Japanese cameras, Danish silver, German optical goods, Oriental silks.

WHAT TO WEAR ... You'll *shop* for duty-free cashmeres, English flannels and doeskins, Scottish woolens and tweeds, but you'll *wear* lightweight summer clothes the year round in Barbados. Evening clothes necessary in the winter season. Tailors and dressmakers can whip up clothes in a hurry, and for women there are ready-mades of Irish linen, Liberty silk, fine cottons sold in smart *boutiques.*

WHERE TO GO—SIGHTSEEING ...

Bridgetown ... In Bridgetown, the capital, you must see St. Michael's Anglican cathedral, which was rebuilt of coral rock in 1780 after the original building had been blown down during a hurricane. George Washington and his half brother, Lawrence, went to church here when they visited Barbados in 1751. Other places of interest to the visitor are Codrington College on the Atlantic, the oldest university college standing in the British colonies; St. John's Church, which contains the tomb of Fernando Palaeologus, one of the last descendants of the Christian Emperors of Greece, who died in 1678. There is a fine view of the Bathsheba coast from St. John's Church.

The Barbados Museum, an interesting place to see, is in St. Michael, 1½ miles from Bridgetown. Bathsheba, 14 miles from the town, is a beautiful seaside resort. Go to Welchman Hall in the center of the island where a tropical garden is bursting with many varieties of exotic flowers, trees and plants. In the Scotland district of northeastern Barbados, potters make attractively crude cooking pots and dishes as they have been made here since the 16th century. At Holetown there is a monument commemorating the first landing of the British in 1605. Wear thick-soled shoes to explore the animal-flower cave at North Point in St. Peter parish.

SOURCES OF FURTHER INFORMATION ... Carib Publicity Co. Ltd., Room 210, K. R. Hunte's Building, Bridgetown, publishes *The Bajan* and *South Caribbean Magazine* (1st of each month) and *The Barbados News* (15th of each month) of special interest to tourists. The Barbados Tourist Board maintains an Information Bureau at Port of Bridgetown and at Seawell Airport. Also at 355 Lexington Avenue, New York City; 150 Eglinton Ave. East, Toronto; 229 Kensington High Street, London, W8, England. The Pan Am office in Bridgetown is in the K. R. Hunte Building (Tel. 6006).

BERMUDA

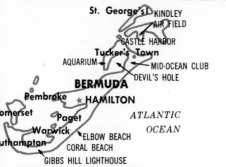

WEATHER IN BERMUDA—Lat. N32°20′—Alt. 50′

	JAN.	FEB.	MAR.	APR.	MAY	JUNE	JULY	AUG.	SEPT.	OCT.	NOV.	DEC.
Average Temp.	63°	63°	63°	65°	70°	75°	79°	80°	78°	74°	69°	65°
Av. Daily Hrs. of Sun	5	5	6	8	9	10	9	8	6	6	6	5

LOCATION . . . Approximately 753 statute miles southeast of New York.

CHARACTERISTICS . . . Bermuda is a place for tourists to enjoy bicycling, tennis, golf, swimming, sailing, skin-diving, fishing and relaxing in an atmosphere of semitropical beauty. While one can dance after dinner at some of the hotels, there is little night-club life.

POPULATION . . . Estimated at 45,000.

SIZE . . . The 300 islands of "Bermuda" cover 21 square miles. The largest island is 20 miles long, a maximum of 1 mile wide.

CAPITAL . . . Hamilton, with a population of 3,700.

GOVERNMENT . . . Since 1685, the Governor has been appointed by the British Crown to represent the Queen. Politically these islands hold a unique place among the possessions of the Crown. Bermuda has its own elected House of Assembly and a Legislative Council and is officially designated as the oldest self-governing colony in the British Commonwealth.

HOW TO GET THERE . . . By Pan American Jet Clipper, flying time from New York or Boston, about 2 hours. By ship from New York, 40 hours.

ACCOMMODATIONS . . . Rates given are for two in a double room during the high season, which is spring and summer. Fall and winter rates are less in most cases. Breakfast and dinner are included on Modified American Plan (MAP).

Among the larger hotels: *The Castle* in Tucker's Town, modern and luxurious, swimming pool, 18-hole golf course, private beach, tennis courts, fishing, dancing nightly, $36 to $48 MAP; the luxurious new *Carlton Beach* in Southampton, with every room overlooking the water, $38 to $50 MAP; the glamorous *Princess,* with an 18-hole course, swimming pool, night club, $32 to $46 MAP. The handsome *Bermudiana Hotel* overlooks the harbor on the outskirts of Hamilton, $24 and up MAP. *Elbow Beach Surf Club,* on its own beautiful beach, is a gay social spot with dancing nightly, social directors, group activities, $37 to $51 MAP. The *St. George Hotel* in historic St. George has a special Family Plan and children's playground, swimming pool, golf course, beach facilities, dancing, $24 to $36 MAP. *Inverurie* on the harbor in Paget, $26 to $30 MAP. Some cottage suites.

Smaller hotels, which accommodate about 50, are: *The Briton* on Langton Hill overlooking Hamilton, $28 to $36 MAP; *Ariel Sands,* South Shore, Devonshire, from $26 MAP; *Buena Vista,* Harbour Road, Paget, $26 to $32 MAP; *Horizons* in Paget near Coral Beach, new swimming pool, $30.50 to $44.50 MAP; *Palmetto Bay* on Harrington Sound, good food, attractive cottages, $28 to $38 MAP; *Waterloo House* on harbor close to Hamilton has gracious service, good food, pool, $29 to $43 MAP; *Pomander Gate* in Paget is an old Bermuda mansion with picturesque cottages, magnificent flower garden, swimming pool, $30 to $50 MAP. *Deepdene Manor,* recently reopened, is $26 to $30 MAP.

Bermuda abounds in cottage colonies, which offer the same service as hotels but provide a quieter, more private vacation. Rates are about the same as at hotels. Most are Modified American Plan. The following are typical: *Cambridge Beaches* in Somerset—small cottages, and rooms in main house, all rooms with bath, rates $38 to $52, American Plan; *The Ledgelets* in Somerset—small cottages, and rooms in main house, all rooms with bath, rates $32 to $40, MAP; *Lantana Cottage Colony* also in Somerset, rates $36 to $46, MAP; *Bermuda Cottages* in nearly all locales, $30 to $34 including breakfast, $40 to $44 including dinner at choice of restaurants or served by maid.

There are many others. Rates at hotels and guest houses may vary occasionally. Alternate plans, such as the Bermuda Plan (room and breakfast) are often available. Accommodations in private homes, usually on the Bermuda Plan, are $7 to $8.

ARTS ... The Bermuda Historical Museum in Hamilton, the museum attached to the Aquarium, and a continuous art exhibit in the Hamilton City Hall offer an excellent insight into Bermuda history.

BANKS ... Bank of Bermuda; Bank of N. T. Butterfield and Son.

CALENDAR OF HOLIDAYS ... New Year's Day; Good Friday; May 24, Commonwealth Day; the Queen's Birthday (celebrated in June); Cup Match Days, Thursday and Friday before first Monday in August; November 11, Remembrance Day; Christmas; December 26, Boxing Day.

CIGARETTES AND TOBACCO ... American cigarettes cost the same as in the States. There are English tobacco, pipes and cigarettes.

CLIMATE ... Bermuda has pleasant summer weather from May to mid-November. Winter months have springlike temperatures. There are occasional quick unexpected showers.

CLUBS ... American Legion, American Society, Pilot Club, Bermuda Bridge Club (visitors may join for a small fee), English-Speaking Union, Garden Club, Kennel Club, Moose, Lions and Rotary, and many others.

COMMON COURTESIES AND LOCAL CUSTOMS ... Men must wear coats and ties in better restaurants, and golf hose should be worn with shorts in restaurants. No abbreviated clothing is permitted on the streets. When driving, always keep to the left side of the road.

COMMUNICATIONS ... Cable telephone to U.S., Canada, West Indies and England 24 hours a day. A 3-minute station-to-station eastern U.S. call is £2.5 ($6.30). Airmail to U.S., Canada is 8d, or 12¢.

CURRENCY ... American and Canadian money are accepted. Bermuda has its own money valued about the same as the English pound. No Bermuda money may leave the Island; English banknotes can be used by residents of the sterling area. The pound is now at $2.80.

CUSTOMS REGULATIONS AND DOCUMENTS REQUIRED FOR UNITED STATES CITIZENS ... No passport or visa required but return ticket or onward transportation is essential and for U.S. Immigration authorities, proof of U.S. citizenship, such as an old passport, birth or baptismal certificate or voter's certificate. 200 cigarettes or 100 cigars or 1 lb. tobacco allowed duty free. There is an air departure and sea arrival tax of $2.85 each.

DRUGSTORES ... Several drugstores in Hamilton, Somerset, St. George and one in Paget carrying everything to be found in the States. Larger hotels carry moderate supplies of toilet articles.

ELECTRIC CURRENT ... 110 volts A.C., 60-cycle service.

FAUNA ... 11 species of birds call Bermuda home. But each year 50 to 100 different species seek shelter from ocean storms. Game fish abound in Bermuda's waters (*see* SPORTS).

FLORA ... Probably the most outstanding plant is the Easter lily, in bloom February through May. There are many other well-known flowering plants such as the poinciana and the frangipani. Of the woody plants, the oleander and hibiscus bloom profusely from April to September. Other notable shrubs and climbers include bougainvillaea and passion-flower vine.

FOOD ... Bermuda lobster is a famous local dish. Cassava pie, a Christmas dish in which the root of the cassava plant is grated to make a flour or meal, is filled with chicken or pork and baked. Sweet-potato pudding is native, too. Meals at the hotels, however, are similar to those served in first-class hotels in the United States. Milk is pasteurized.

LANGUAGE ... English.

LAUNDRY AND DRY CLEANING ... Same as in the U.S.

LIQUOR ... The chief local drink is West Indian rum. Popular

American drinks are available and range from 50¢ to $1. Bars in restaurants open on Sundays at noon, are closed from 2:30 to 6 P.M. Closing time on weekdays, and from 6 P.M. on Sundays, is midnight; 1 A.M. in hotels. Public bars open every day from 10 A.M. until 1 A.M. and are closed all day Sunday. Legal minimum age for drinkers is 18.

MEDICAL FACILITIES . . . Excellent.

MOTION PICTURES . . . There are two motion-picture theaters in Hamilton, one each in Somerset and St. George.

MUSIC . . . Local bands excel at calypso and popular American music. There are American and English bands, too.

NIGHT CLUBS AND CABARETS . . . There is dancing and entertainment nightly at nearly all the big hotels. Try, too, the lively *Forty Thieves* in Hamilton—open until 3 A.M.

PHOTOGRAPHY . . . Black-and-white and color in still and movie film available at approximately the same price as in the U.S. Pictures (other than movie film) can be developed in Bermuda, overnight service on black-and-white and color film. The pastel houses and brilliant flowers lend themselves particularly well to color photography.

RELIGION . . . Bermuda is Protestant Episcopal (Church of England), but many other denominations have large congregations.

RESTAURANTS . . . *Tom Moore's Tavern* in Bailey's Bay is famous. *The Plantation* at Leamington Cave is noted for its lobster. *The Penthouse Club* with its open air terraces overlooking the harbor, *The Waterfront* located right on the harbor on East Broadway, an extension of Front Street, and *Ace of Clubs* on Front Street in Hamilton are all popular spots for lunch and dinner. The *Hog Penny Restaurant* and *Horse and Buggy* are new. *Waterlot Inn* in Southampton and *The Breakers* overlooking the beach in Smith's Parish are excellent, as is *Fourways* in Paget.

SHOPS AND STORES . . . Trimingham's and H. A. and E. Smith are famous for sweaters, tweeds and Bermuda doeskin. For "Made in Bermuda" playclothes designed by Poly Hornburg, try the new Calypso Shop on Front Street. A. S. Cooper on Front Street sells Wedgwood china, and William Bluck and Company have many fine bargains in antiques. Most of the better stores are located in Hamilton and are open weekdays from 9 to 5, except Thursday afternoon.

SPECTATOR SPORTS . . . Cricket matches are played Thursdays and Sundays. Soccer and rugby are played from October to April. Water carnivals at hotel swimming pools. Sailing races all year for small boats of all classes. The Newport R.I.-Bermuda Race occurs every even-numbered year, the outstanding blue-water race in the world.

SPORTS . . . Golf, tennis, sailing (there are small boats for hire which you can sail yourself; larger craft with crew; charter sloops with boatmen). Many classes of smaller yachts are raced on Thursdays and Sundays throughout the year: International One-Designs, 5.5 meters, International 14-ft. dinghies, Luder 16's, snipes and fireflies.

The annual Bermuda Game Fishing Tournament is held from May until November. A special tournament is held in winter. World record amberjack, bonefish and wahoo have been taken from Bermuda waters, and eminently respectable catches of marlin, blue and white tuna, mackerel and dolphin are frequent. Boats, complete with tackle and bait, may be chartered for a day's deep-sea fishing for about $75 for parties of 6 or less. Water-skiing equipment may also be rented. The golf clubs in Bermuda are excellent. Mid-Ocean Club is world famous. Other golf clubs: Riddell's Bay Golf and Country Club, Belmont Golf Club, The Castle Club, Southampton Golf and Beach Club, St. George Hotel and Queen Park Golf Course. Swimming in pools or at beaches. Equipment for golf, cycling, fishing and skin diving may be rented.

TIME . . . Noon in Bermuda is 11 A.M. EST, in New York.

TIPPING . . . About the same as in the U.S.

TRANSPORTATION . . . Bicycles may be rented by the hour, day or week. Prevailing rate is $8 a week for bicycles, $23 a week for motor-assisted cycles. There are no automobiles for hire, but there are English taxis with fringed tops like old-time carriages. Taxi fare from airport into Hamilton, $3.50. Passenger ferries take you from one point to another. Buses traverse the Islands but are apt to be crowded and slow. There are no trains in Bermuda.

WATER . . . The water is excellent to drink.

WHAT TO BUY . . . Tweeds, cashmere and shetland sweaters, British and Scotch woolens, English leather goods, perfume (much lower than in the States), English pipes and tobaccos, English china (Wedgwood, Spode), silver (great savings here), doeskin gloves and men's doeskin slacks. West Indian trinkets and gadgets, cedar boxes.

WHAT TO WEAR . . . Women: for spring and summer—cottons, prints or pastel silks. Shorts and slacks (Bermuda or knee-length shorts preferable). Tweeds, sweaters and woolens in winter and late fall. Cocktail dresses of seasonal type. A lightweight raincoat is advisable in the winter months. Men: Bermuda shorts and slacks in warm weather. Ties and coats are required in all restaurants, and in all bars after 7 P.M. Lightweight jackets with shorts, slacks in summer, wool suits in winter. Black or white dinner jackets the year round. White in summer is more comfortable. Raincoat, swimming trunks, sports shirts and a beach robe are essentials. Distinctive Bermuda shorts best purchased locally.

WHERE TO GO—SIGHTSEEING . . . Not to be missed are 17th-century St. George's with Fort St. Catherine, the Aquarium, Leamington and Crystal Caves; Gibb's Hill Light, Devil's Hole, and the south-shore beaches. A trip through the Marine Gardens in glass-bottom boats is interesting. You may attend fascinating Supreme Court trials at Sessions House, but wear "city" clothes there.

SOURCES OF FURTHER INFORMATION . . . Bermuda Trade Development Board, 620 Fifth Avenue, New York; 6 N. Michigan Avenue, Chicago, Illinois; 111 Richmond Street West, Toronto, Ontario; Sackville House, 40 Piccadilly, London, W.I.

Pan Am's office is at 61 Front Street, Hamilton (Tel. 1-1051).

CAYMAN ISLANDS

CARIBBEAN SEA

CARIBBEAN SEA

Grand Cayman, West Indies, is 22 miles long and 8 miles wide, the largest of the three Cayman Islands. It is located south of Cuba, northwest of Jamaica, and is reached by LACSA airlines in about 2 hours from Miami or by connection with Pan American flights to San José, Costa Rica, or Jamaica (45 minutes). All you need for entry is some form of identification such as birth certificate; smallpox vaccination certificate for re-entry to the United States.

This delightful island is, more than many Caribbean islands, the place to get away from it all. The natural aspects of the island and the attitude of the people (population about 8,000) are still unspoiled, but new free-port prices on luxury goods are enlarging tourism.

A low island of coral limestone, Grand Cayman is heavily covered with a luxuriant growth of mangroves, sea grapes, palms, hardwoods, breadfruit, mangoes and varieties of citrus: oranges, limes and grapefruit, and numerous tropical fruit trees including almonds. A spectacular crescent beach of powder-fine white coral extends for 6 miles along the west end of the island. Wonderful for swimming. There are numerous other beaches and small coves bordering the irregular shore-line. Fishing is excellent, also wintertime hunting in the ponds and swamps. A small yacht club is available to tourists. There's also a beach club with cottages, dancing to native bands.

Among the things to see and do: A drive to the east end of the island (by rented bicycle or car) which will show the visitor how people can live happily and peacefully off the land and sea without poverty; the Turtle Kraal in North Sound; a picnic on Rum Point; "Hell," the weird coral formation on the north end of the island, now has a night club and post office with a unique postmark. Saunter along spectacular West Beach. There are many caves and "blow holes" along the ragged shore.

Hotels, in or near George Town, the capital, are: The de luxe *Beach Club Colony,* $20-$35 double, American Plan (with meals); *The Tortuga Club,* $40 double, AP; *Galleon Beach,* $18 per person, European Plan (without meals). The affiliated *Coral Caymanian* is $15 per person, EP. The *West Indian Club* has luxurious apartments with maid service; weekly rates are $196 for 1-bedroom, $280 for 2-bedroom. *Pageant Beach* is adapted for family vacations; $30-$35 double, AP. *Bay View,* a commercial hotel, has a swimming pool; $10-$13 double, EP. The homelike *Glen and Sandy Cottages* are $20-$25 double, EP. *Sunset Lodge Guest House* is $20 double, with two meals. On Cayman Brac Island, *Buccaneer's Inn* is $28-$32 double, AP. All rates appreciably lower from mid-April to mid-December.

CUBA

WEATHER IN HAVANA—Lat. N23°08′—Alt. 30′

Temp.	JAN.	FEB.	MAR.	APR.	MAY	JUNE	JULY	AUG.	SEPT.	OCT.	NOV.	DEC.
Low	65°	65°	67°	69°	72°	74°	74°	75°	74°	73°	69°	67°
High	79°	79°	81°	84°	86°	88°	89°	89°	88°	85°	81°	80°
Average	72°	72°	74°	76°	84°	81°	82°	82°	81°	79°	75°	74°
Days of Rain	8	6	5	5	10	13	12	14	15	15	10	8

LOCATION . . . Cuba lies in the West Indies 90 miles from the Florida Keys and 130 miles from the coast of Yucatan, Mexico.

POPULATION . . . Estimated 7,203,000.

SIZE . . . The largest island of the West Indies, Cuba is 760 miles long and ranges from 25 to 125 miles wide. The area of 44,218 square miles is slightly larger than the area of Tennessee.

CAPITAL . . . Havana, population nearly 1,000,000.

HOW TO GET THERE . . . Flying time from Mexico City to Havana is about 3¼ hours via Cubana Airlines. Service also from Madrid and Prague.

CUSTOMS REGULATIONS AND DOCUMENTS REQUIRED FOR UNITED STATES CITIZENS . . . Passport containing endorsement authorizing travel to Cuba, issued by the Passport Office, Washington, D.C. Visa, obtained in the U.S. from the Embassy of Czechoslovakia, Washington, D.C. Ticket to leave Cuba. Duty-free allowances: 200 cigarettes for personal use, 2 bottles of liquor. No more than 50 pesos in Cuban currency may be brought in. Jewelry and other valuables must be declared upon entry. All passengers arriving in Cuba must have sufficient funds to cover expenses during stay. Food is high; plan on U.S. $25 a day for room and meals.

SOURCES OF FURTHER INFORMATION . . . Czechoslovakia Embassy, 2349 Massachusetts Avenue, N.W., Washington, D.C.

DOMINICAN REPUBLIC

WEATHER IN SANTO DOMINGO—Lat. N18°28′—Alt. approx. sea level

Temp.	JAN.	FEB.	MAR.	APR.	MAY	JUNE	JULY	AUG.	SEPT.	OCT.	NOV.	DEC.
Low	66°	66°	67°	69°	71°	72°	72°	73°	72°	72°	70°	67°
High	84°	85°	84°	85°	86°	87°	88°	88°	88°	87°	86°	85
Average	75°	76°	76°	77°	79°	80°	80°	81°	80°	79°	78°	76'
Days of Rain	9	6	7	9	14	14	15	14	14	13	11	9

LOCATION ... The Dominican Republic and Haiti occupy the island of Hispaniola about 50 miles southeast of Cuba and about the same distance west of Puerto Rico.

CHARACTERISTICS ... This little country is the spot where Columbus landed on his first voyage to the New World, and where he is buried. It is a curious combination of centuries-old civilization and modern efficiency with contemporary buildings, spotless streets, supermarkets, luxurious hotels. The hotels are modern, elaborate and efficiently operated, the beaches are good, the fishing and hunting excellent.

POPULATION ... Estimated 3,334,000.

SIZE ... 18,816 square miles; 200 miles east-west, 150 miles north-south.

CAPITAL ... Santo Domingo, with about 367,000 population.

GOVERNMENT ... A republic.

HOW TO GET THERE ... By Pan American Jet Clipper to Santo Domingo: 3½ hours nonstop from New York and about ¾ hour from San Juan. By ship, about 6 days from New York.

ACCOMMODATIONS ... In Santo Domingo, the best hotel is the

ultramodern, 315-room *El Embajador* (the Ambassador). An Intercontinental Hotel, it is completely air-conditioned and elegant, has a
superb swimming pool, golf course, tennis courts, casino and *Embassy
Club* (night club). Rates start at $15 single, $21 double, December
16 to April 30; other times from $11 single, $15 double. Add $7 for
breakfast and dinner, $10 for all meals. Suites are also available.
Another Santo Domingo hotel is the 150-room *Hispaniola,* which also
has a swimming pool. Rates here from $10 single, $14 double, European Plan. Monthly rates also available. The *Jaragua* hotel on the sea
is 5 minutes from downtown. Many of its 250 rooms have private
terraces. Suites face sea and pool. Cottages. Casino, music, entertainment. Single rates from $11, double from $14. The 75-room *Commercial Hotel* is located in the downtown area. Rates here start at $6
single, $10 double, European Plan (without meals).

ARTS... The magnificent new National Gallery of Fine Arts on
Avenue Máximo Gomez in the capital shows painting, sculpture and
ceramics by Dominican and foreign artists. Paintings and sculptures
are available for purchase.

BALLET... There is an Academy of Ballet which occasionally
presents public shows at the local theaters.

BANKS... In Santo Domingo: the Royal Bank of Canada, Chase
Manhattan Bank, First National City Bank of New York, Dominican
Reserve Bank, Bank of Nova Scotia, Agricultural and Credit Bank of
the Dominican Republic, the Central Bank, Bank of Credit and Savings. Banking hours are from 8 to 12:30 Monday through Friday, except for one additional hour Friday afternoons.

CALENDAR OF HOLIDAYS... January 1; January 6, Three
Kings Day; January 21; La Altagracia's Day; January 26, Duarte's
Day; February 27, Independence Day; March 19, St. Joseph's Day;
April 14; Pan American Day; May 1, Labor Day; May 30, Liberty
Day; June 14, Anniversary of the invasion of Maimón, Estero Hondo
and Constanza; June 19, Anniversary of the invasion of Luperón;
August 16, Restoration Day; September 24, Our Lady of Las Mer-
cedes Day; October 12, Columbus Day; November 1, All Saints Day;
December 8, Day of Immaculate Conception; December 25.

CIGARETTES... Locally manufactured cigarettes cost from 20¢
to 60¢ a pack. Tobacco has been grown and appreciated here since
before Columbus came.

CLIMATE... The weather is warm and tropical, but seldom uncomfortable. The cool season between November and March is particularly pleasant with warm sunny days and cool evenings.

CLUBS... The Santo Domingo Country Club and La Voz de Santo
Domingo (luxuriously appointed and air-conditioned) offer facilities
for tourists; Club #16 de Mayo, Golfito Tennis Club. Also Rotary.

COMMON COURTESIES AND LOCAL CUSTOMS... It is
customary for a jacket and tie to be worn in most of the hotels after
6 P.M. The wearing of shorts and beach-type wear is not approved of
in the downtown area. When visiting local churches, women should
wear a veil or hat. It is customary to shake hands when introduced,

and introductions are made formally. *Gracias* is "Thank you."

COMMUNICATIONS... A 3-minute phone call to the States costs $8 to $9; cablegrams are 21¢ a word to New York; 26¢ to other cities. Local phone calls are 10¢. The airmail rate for letters to the United States is 10¢ per ½ ounce; 9¢ for postcards.

CURRENCY... The monetary unit is the Dominican peso on par with the U.S. dollar. U.S. bills are fully acceptable both in shops and hotels. There are no currency restrictions.

CUSTOMS REGULATIONS AND DOCUMENTS REQUIRED FOR UNITED STATES CITIZENS... Passport and visa required. Ticket to leave the country also required. Visitors not holding small-pox vaccination certificate will be vaccinated on arrival. Tobacco products to a value of $5 and liquor to a value of $5 admitted duty free.

DRUGSTORES... All very modern with United States products.

ELECTRIC CURRENT... Same as in the U.S.

FAUNA... Colorful tropical birds, flamingos, parrots, etc. Deer were imported as an experiment and are said to be breeding in the mountainous section of the Republic.

FLORA... Beautiful tropical flowers of all varieties. Banana, palm and coffee trees in abundance. Pineapples, avocados, other fruits. Sugar cane, of course, and tobacco.

FOOD... The food is naturally Spanish; *sancocho,* for instance, is a heavy, creamy soup containing 18 ingredients, such as pork, yams, Spanish sausage, onions, pumpkins and tomatoes. Very fine indeed. There is the inevitable *arroz con pollo;* cassava baked with cheese and boiled eggs; and *pastelitos*—pastries filled with chicken or other meat. The hotels and restaurants serve international food, too.

GAMBLING... Nightly at the El Embajador and Jaragua hotels and Voz de Santo Domingo. There are weekly lotteries with prizes ranging from $30 to $50,000. Pari-mutuel betting at the modern race-track Perla de las Antillas.

LANGUAGE... The official language is Spanish but English is spoken and readily understood by almost everybody. The typical greeting is *¿Cómo estamos?* or *¿Qué hay—Cómo estamos?*

LAUNDRY AND DRY CLEANING... Very good and available at several places in Santo Domingo. Hotel Embajador offers special services to guests. Prices vary depending on the type of clothing.

LIQUOR... Wonderful Dominican rum can be obtained at very reasonable prices. Popular American drinks are also served at approximately the same prices as at home.

MEDICAL FACILITIES... Most hospitals have very competent English-speaking doctors on their staffs. The hospitals in Santo Domingo are among the most modern and best equipped of the Antilles.

MOTION PICTURES... In the capital, there are several motion picture theaters showing current American, Mexican and European films. The *Lido, Santome, Elite, La Voz de Santo Domingo, Leonor* and *Rialto* are air-conditioned. English-language films carry Spanish subtitles.

MUSIC ... There is the National Symphony Orchestra, which presents a series of concerts each year. Native music is lovely. The national dance is the *merengue.* American music is also heard.

NIGHT CLUBS AND CABARETS ... El Embajador hotel has a night club with floor shows and music for dancing. Dancing, too, at La Hispaniola Hotel and in *El Patio Español* at the Jaragua Hotel. The air-conditioned *Voz de Santo Domingo* also offers good music for dancing. The beautiful *Teatro Agua Luz* is outstanding for its floor shows and dancing waters shows.

PHOTOGRAPHY ... Prices of photographic equipment are a little more expensive than at home. There are facilities for film developing. It takes around 3 days to do a good job. The Santo Domingo Gift Shop and Farmacía Esmeralda are among the places where photo equipment and films may be purchased. Good spots for taking pictures are the ruins, the Cathedral, Columbus Castle, The Altar de la Patria and the beaches. Don't photograph military subjects.

RELIGION ... The religion is Roman Catholic. There is, however, an Episcopal Church, with services in English, located on Independence Avenue in Santo Domingo. Catholic churches offer Mass each day from 5:30 through 7:30 A.M. On Sundays, Mass is said at the Convento Dominico from 6:30 A.M. through 8:30 A.M.; last Mass at 11 A.M. Cathedral services begin at 6:30 A.M. with High Mass celebrated at 9 A.M. Last Mass at 12 noon.

RESTAURANTS ... Aside from the good, new hotel restaurants, there are many restaurants where European, American, Chinese and native food is served. Among the best known in the capital are *Mario's,* an air-conditioned Chinese restaurant; *El Dragon, Europa, Lina* and *Pan American,* also Chinese-American restaurants with air-conditioning. *Terazza Hollywood* is well known and try *El Vesubio, Cesare,* or *Italia* for Italian specialties. These restaurants are within five minutes' taxi ride from the hotels.

SHOPS AND STORES ... The main shopping street in Santo Domingo is Calle el Conde. Some of the principal stores are La Opera, Cerame, El Palacio, La Puerta del Sol, Casa Lopez de Haro, Dragón de Oro (specializing in Chinese products), Artes Dominicanas handicraft shops at Arzobispo Nouel 16 and at the airport. There are two free port stores located on the grounds of Centro de los Héroes de Constanza, Maimón y Estero Hondo. Tax and duty-free prices on liquors, perfumes, cameras, watches, glass and chinaware, jewelry and miscellaneous wearing apparel. A visit to the Mercado Modelo (Model Market) should be included on shopping expeditions. This market is an excellent example of modern design and cleanliness. Shopping hours are from 8 A.M. to 12 noon, and from 2 to 6 P.M.

SPECTATOR SPORTS ... Horse racing at the Pearl of the Antilles track, baseball from April through September; cockfighting on Sunday afternoons in numerous places. A new, modern baseball stadium is located within 10 minutes' taxi ride from all the hotels. Dominicans are mad about baseball and their own league is outstanding.

SPORTS ... The Santo Domingo Country Club and El Embajador Hotel each have an interesting golf course and a pool. Privileges are extended to visitors. Beach swimming is excellent at Boca Chica. Small sailing boats may be hired. Riding horses are available, too. The *Hotel Hamaca,* on a pretty lagoon, has boats and water skis.

THEATERS ... Stage shows and TV shows are shown at *La Voz De Santo Domingo.* Radio and television theater daily including Sunday. Also TV station *Rahintel* presents daily programs.

TIME ... Same as U.S. Eastern Standard Time.

TIPPING ... The usual 10 to 15%, as in the States.

TRANSPORTATION ... Self-drive cars about $8 a day, plus 7¢ a mile. Country highways are excellent. Taxis and carriages charge $3 an hour, or $20 a day, for sightseeing. Bus fare from the airport into the capital is $1.50; $8 for a taxi.

WATER ... With the emphasis on public health in this country, it is sure to be drinkable. Hotels serve bottled water on request.

WHAT TO BUY ... Tortoise-shell boxes and accessories, embroideries, woven baskets. Handicrafts of local mahogany, green ebony, Dominican oak, etc., at Artes Dominicanas. Imported luxuries.

WHAT TO WEAR ... Santo Domingo and other coastal cities are warm. You will need summer clothes, beach things; dinner clothes at the top hotels. The mountain resorts of Constanza and Jarabacoa are much cooler, so take topcoats and a warm dress or two. Men will need linen or cotton suits, medium-weight jackets and slacks for the hills, beach clothes and summer dinner clothes.

WHERE TO GO—SIGHTSEEING ...

Santo Domingo ... The first thing you notice is the cleanliness, the spotlessness of the city. This is partly because the city has been almost completely rebuilt since the hurricane of 1930 which practically destroyed it, and partly because the people have been very determined to make civic improvements. Don't miss the cathedral: the Basilica of Santa Maria la Menor, which has some wonderful carvings, a treasure room, the Columbus tomb and the Columbus Cross. In the heart of the original city of Santo Domingo are the ruins of Alcázar de Colón, built by Don Diego, Columbus' son, which have been completely and beautifully restored. The Tower of Homage, the oldest stone fortress in the Americas, is now a prison which may be seen only from the outside. Also on the outskirts of the capital on a brand-new campus is the University of Santo Domingo, the oldest university in this hemisphere. It dates back to 1538. The new National Capitol cannot be missed. It is built of pink stone and stands in the western part of the city. Organized tours in modern limousines with English-speaking guides vary from $4.50 for the half-day city tour to $6.50 for tours to San Cristobal and Boca Chica.

San Cristobal is about 20 miles from the capital. It is reached by the Sánchez Highway, along which is the Santo Domingo Country club. The city has many attractions, especially the two lovely natural pools at La Toma. The *Hotel San Cristobal* is delightful. Rates are $11 single, $22 double, including all meals.

El Embajador, an Intercontinental hotel in Santo Domingo, offers the ultimate in comfort.

The interior of the Dominican Republic is also becoming a tourists' paradise. Roads are good. The coffee and sugar plantations, the rice paddies and the tobacco farms are interesting to see. At Jarabacoa is the *Hotel Montaña,* high in the Cordillera Central. Rooms facing the valley have superlative views. American Plan rates are about $8 single, $16 double. Offered here are a swimming pool, children's playground and horse-back riding. San Juan, the center of the ancient Carib Indian civilization, has the *Maguana Hotel* with European Plan rates of $7 double. This is off the beaten track. The hill resorts are cool.

Santiago ... Three hours by car is Santiago, the second city of the Republic and capital of the fertile valley of Cibao, in the heart of the Dominican agricultural region. The *Hotel Matum* is about $8 per person, AP; the *Mercedes* is a little less. *Nueva Suiza,* 4000 feet above sea level at Constanza is a pleasantly cool retreat; $8 per person, American Plan.

SOURCES OF FURTHER INFORMATION ... The Director General of Tourism, Santo Domingo. The Pan American office at Edificio Copello, El Conde St. (Tel. 2-2515). Other useful local telephone numbers are: U.S. Embassy, 9-4141; Immigration Department, 3-1977. Dominican Republic Tourist Office, 630 Fifth Avenue, New York, N.Y. 10020.

GRENADA

WEATHER IN ST. GEORGE'S—Lat. N12°07'—Alt. approx. sea level

	JAN.	FEB.	MAR.	APR.	MAY	JUNE	JULY	AUG.	SEPT.	OCT.	NOV.	DEC.
Average Temp.	76°	76°	77°	78°	79°	78°	78°	79°	79°	79°	78°	77°
Days of Rain	14	8	8	7	10	17	20	21	18	16	17	16

LOCATION ... The most southerly of the Windward Islands group, Grenada is only 109 air miles from Trinidad.

CHARACTERISTICS ... This little British island is called the Isle of Spice, because of the cocoa, nutmeg and clove that grow here. From end to end the island is only 21 miles long, but in this small area there is a great variety of scenery. St. George's lies on a point of land, and the streets rise rather sharply from the bay. Its red-roofed houses are pale pink and green; the effect is charming. There are mountains, valleys, and rockbound coasts where the surf thunders, a calm harbor where the water is deep blue and quiet. And 2,000 feet above sea level is Grand Etang, a volcanic lake. This is a tropical isle, quiet and peaceful, with a rainy and a dry season. The hot days are tempered by trade winds; the swimming is superb, the whole place utterly beautiful and peaceful and just made for the traveler who wants to relax in sunshine.

SIZE ... 21 miles long and 12 miles wide at the broadest point.

POPULATION ... Estimated 88,677.

CAPITAL ... St. George's (population about 10,000).

GOVERNMENT ... A British colony with a Minister, Executive and Legislative councils, and a royally appointed Administrator.

HOW TO GET THERE ... By Pan Am Jet Clipper to Trinidad or Barbados (in 4½ hours), then 45 minutes to Grenada. Grenada is 1¾ hours' flying time from St. Lucia; 2½ hours from Martinique; and 3½ hours from Antigua (all by British West Indian Airways connection with Pan Am flights). By ship about 14 days from Montreal.

ACCOMMODATIONS . . . Rates given here are double, summer (May 1 to November 30) and winter. The *Grand Anse Riviera Hotel* has kitchenette suites, $10 and $15, EP. The *Silver Sands Hotel* on beautiful Grande Anse Beach has rates of $21 and $28, Modified American Plan (two meals). The following all operate on full American Plan: *Spice Island Inn,* air-conditioned, separate cottage suites along 1,200 feet of Grande Anse Beach; $28 and $48. The *Calabash* features Indian and French cuisines; $35 double in winter. The *Grenada Beach Hotel* is air-conditioned, rooms have private balconies; $28 and $48. The *Islander Hotel* overlooks the bay and harbor of St. George's; $16.20 and $21.80. *Ross Point Inn* on the sea with private beach specializes in West Indian cuisine; $15 and $19.50. The *Crescent Inn,* with home-like atmosphere, overlooks the Yacht Basin; $13.50 and $18. At the *St. James Hotel,* in a cool and quiet section of St. George's, rates are $19.20 and $21.60. *Green Gables* and *Elite* are small, comfortable guest houses with year round rates of $10.80 and $12. 10% service charge is added onto your bill in lieu of tipping, except for special services. In addition, there are furnished seaside cottages ranging from $30 to $60 per week. Clubs offer swimming, yachting, tennis and golf.

CURRENCY . . . The West Indies dollar, worth about U.S. 60¢.

CUSTOMS REGULATIONS AND DOCUMENTS REQUIRED FOR UNITED STATES CITIZENS . . . Tourists need only proof of nationality; no passport. No duty-free allowances on liquor but 100 cigarettes or 1 lb. of tobacco and 1 roll camera film allowed.

ELECTRIC CURRENT . . . 240 volts, A.C., 50 cycles.

LIQUOR . . . West Indian rum, of course. Imported liquors, such as Scotch, are much cheaper than in the States.

RESTAURANTS . . . In St. George's *Rocky's Terrace* features Chinese food, while *Nick's* and *The Nutmeg* specialize in local dishes. Go to *Franco's* for ice cream.

WHERE TO GO—SIGHTSEEING . . .

St. George's . . . Drive along the wharf past the Botanic Gardens via Woodlands to Morne Jaloux, returning via Richmond Hill. Drive through the Sendall Tunnel which connects the quay side of St. George's with the shopping center. Explore the historic old battlements of Fort George and Fort Frederick, which offer lovely views of the quaint and picturesque little town. Take a trip to Grand Etang, a volcanic crater lake nearly 2,000 feet above sea level, and don't miss Annandale Falls, a shimmering cascade of clear, fresh water spilling down amid giant tree ferns. Enjoy the novelty of visiting nutmeg-processing stations at Grenville and Gouyave, where the pungent aroma of spices is reminiscent of the Far East. Scenic shore excursions can be arranged to all parts of the island. Swim, snorkel and water ski at some of the most beautiful beaches in the Caribbean, and cruise to the Grenadines.

SOURCES OF FURTHER INFORMATION . . . The Grenada Tourist Board, St. George's, Grenada, West Indies. Caribbean Tourist Association, 20 E. 46 St., New York, N.Y. 10017.

GUADELOUPE

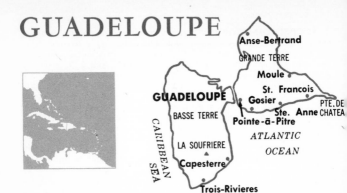

WEATHER IN POINTE-A-PITRE—Lat. N16°—Alt. approx. sea level

	JAN.	FEB.	MAR.	APR.	MAY	JUNE	JULY	AUG.	SEPT.	OCT.	NOV.	DEC.
Average Temp.	76°	76°	77°	79°	80°	80°	80°	81°	81°	80°	79°	77°
Days of Rain	19	15	15	13	18	21	22	22	20	19	20	19

LOCATION ... The French Overseas Department of Guadeloupe consists of Grand-Terre and Basse-Terre, connected by a bridge, and lying about 62 air miles south of Antigua and 120 miles northwest of Martinique. Nearby small dependency islands are Les Saintes, Marie-Galante, Petite Terre and Desirade.

CHARACTERISTICS ... In Guadeloupe, popularly called the Emerald Isle, you'll find the climate delightful, the atmosphere relaxed and informal, the scenery picturesque and the people friendly.

SIZE ... A total area of 687 square miles. Population: 277,000.

CAPITAL ... Basse-Terre, but Pointe-à-Pitre, 40 miles away, is the chief commercial town, with a population of over 45,000.

GOVERNMENT ... A department of France similar in relationship to France as Hawaii is to the United States.

HOW TO GET THERE ... By Pan American Jet Clipper, 4½ hours from New York; 4¾ hours island hopping, from Miami. By ship from New York, about 8 days.

ACCOMMODATIONS ... *La Caravelle* at Ste. Anne is new and completely air-conditioned. It has nightly entertainment and dancing, a free-port shop, swimming pool, private beach, and a cuisine by chefs imported from France. Modified American Plan (MAP) rates (2 meals) are from $46 double in winter, from $34 in summer. The air-conditioned *La Vieille Tour* at Gosier has beach, pool, night club. MAP winter rates $25 single, $35 double. The luxurious new *Fort Royal* fronts on 1,000 yards of beach and provides both hotel and cottage accommodations; choice of Creole, Parisian and American cuisines; from $56 double in winter, $36 in summer (MAP). The *Grand Hotel* in Pointe-à-Pitre is centrally located, serves good food. MAP winter rates from $17 single, $24 double. The *Grand Large* is tiny but has an excellent French restaurant and white sand beach. The *Rocroi Beach Hotel* is 3 miles from Basse-Terre on a black sand beach, $22 double American Plan (3 meals). The new *Relais de la Soufrière*, at an elevation of 2,200 feet, is a take-off point for conducted excursions to the volcano and tropical forest; $8 double, European Plan. Near here, too, is *Hotel Karukera*, same rates. *Hotel du Fort Josephine* is new, beautifully situated on an islet overlooking Les Saintes; European Plan rates $10 per person. Hotels add a 10% service charge in lieu of tips.

CUSTOMS REGULATIONS AND DOCUMENTS REQUIRED FOR UNITED STATES CITIZENS... Refer to Martinique, page 268, for regulations and general facts such as Calendar of Holidays, Cigarettes, Currency, Food, Liquor, Music, Religion, Water and What to Wear. Air departure tax $3.

SHOPS AND STORES... Perfume, French wines and local rum are true bargains. Stores are open from 8:30 A.M. to 12:30 P.M. and 2:30 P.M. to 5 P.M., except Sundays and holidays.

SPORTS... Guadeloupe is an ideal place for spear and rod fishing, water skiing at the Yacht Club, riding, hunting and hiking.

TRANSPORTATION... Buses to all areas of the island are available at very low cost. There are numerous drive-yourself car agencies. Taxi fare from airport to Pointe-à-Pitre is 5 francs ($1).

WHERE TO GO—SIGHTSEEING... The roads are good on both islands, and there are a number of interesting things to see and do all within easy reach of Pointe-à-Pitre. Principal historic sights include Sainte-Marie de Capesterre, where Columbus landed in 1493, and Fort Fleur d'Epée at Gosier, as well as rock engravings recalling early life at Trois-Rivières. The beaches are delightful. For white coral sands there's the limestone island of Gosier, Sainte-Anne, Sainte-François, Moule and Port-Louis, and for black ferruginous sand there's the beach of the Rocroi Beach Hotel, among others.

The thick tropical forests offer interesting areas for hiking, especially the Victor Hugo trail and Merwart trail. The volcanic peak of La Soufrière offers an interesting climb. Other beauty spots include the mountain lakes (the Grand-Etang, the Etang Lombi and the As de Pique) and waterfalls such as the Saut de la Lézarde, the Carbet and the Coulìsse. The island of Grande-Terre, which has a flat terrain, offers a picturesque coastline, especially between Pointe des Château and Moule (a principal harbor town during the 18th century), and in the vicinity of Anse-Bertrand.

SIDE TRIPS... The nearby French islands of Marie Galante, Désirade, St. Barthelony and St. Martin by boat or plane.

SOURCES OF FURTHER INFORMATION... L'Office du Tourisme, Pointe-à-Pitre, or in New York at the French Government Tourist Office, 610 Fifth Avenue. Pan Am's office in Pointe-à-Pitre is at 34 Rue Achille Rene (Tel. 1281).

HAITI

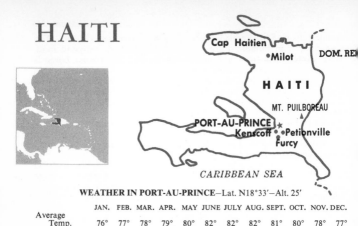

WEATHER IN PORT-AU-PRINCE—Lat. N18°33'–Alt. 25'

	JAN.	FEB.	MAR.	APR.	MAY	JUNE	JULY	AUG.	SEPT.	OCT.	NOV.	DEC.
Average Temp.	76°	77°	78°	79°	80°	82°	82°	82°	81°	80°	78°	77°
Days of Rain	5	7	10	14	16	9	9	13	16	14	9	5

LOCATION ... Haiti occupies the western third of the island of Hispaniola (next to the Dominican Republic) between Cuba and Puerto Rico.

CHARACTERISTICS ... Colorful Haiti with its voodoo drums, its fascinating capital and its twin wonders, La Citadelle and Sans Souci Palace, has a lot to offer the visitor in search of the exotic. The crowded, colorful streets of Port-au-Prince filled with Negro women carrying baskets on their heads contrast with modern automobiles, smart shops and excellent hotels to make a fascinating sight.

Haitians are a proud people because of their hard-won emancipation from slavery. Foreigners are welcomed as equals. There are no race or class prejudices. The Haitian is invariably friendly and self-reliant. Theirs is a soft-spoken and gentle hospitality.

POPULATION ... About 4,500,000, mostly Negroes or mulattoes descended from the French settlers. There are about 2,000 white foreigners.

SIZE ... 10,714 square miles, approximately the size of Maryland.

CAPITAL ... Port-au-Prince with a population of 250,000.

GOVERNMENT ... An independent republic with a President and National Assembly of two houses.

HOW TO GET THERE ... By Pan American Jet Clipper from New York to the new International Airport at Port-au-Prince in 4¾ hours; also island-hopping flights from Miami via Jamaica. By ship about 3½ days from New York.

ACCOMMODATIONS ... There are a number of fine hotels in Petionville, up the mountain above Port-au-Prince, 10 to 15 minutes by car: *El Rancho, Ibo Lele, Choucoune, Villa Creole, Montana* and, still higher, the *Dambala*. All have swimming pools; rates from $14 to $30 single, and $24 to $50 double, including meals. Less expensive hotels here include the *Marabou*. First-class hotels in Port-au-Prince include the *Castel Haiti* with European Modified and American Plan rates. Older first-class hotels are *Sans Souci, Splendid* and the *Plaza;* all have swimming pools. Fairly good second-class hotels, some with private bath, at rates from $5 to $10 a day with meals: *Oloffson, Excelsior* and *Park* in Port-au-Prince. Pensions in Petionville: the *Clerveaux, Star, Doux Sejour, Green Garden, Salvador.*

ARTS...The Centre d'Art has become an internationally important art exhibition center. Here the primitive paintings and sculptures of native Haitians are displayed, and more and more Americans are buying them. The Foyer des Arts Plastiques is another center for primitive art. The National Museum has exhibits depicting the history of Haiti. The Museum of Ethnology has an interesting voodoo section devoted to objects and displays relating to voodoo rites.

BALLET...No formal ballet, but it is possible to see voodoo dances in the hills near Port-au-Prince. You may not see the real religious ceremony but you will see enough to satisfy your curiosity.

BANKS... The National Bank of the Republic of Haiti; the Royal Bank of Canada; Banque Agricole et Industrielle; Banque Colombo-Haïtienne; Banque Commerciale d'Haiti.

CALENDAR OF HOLIDAYS...New Year's Day (Independence Day); January 2, Forefathers Day; April 14, Pan American Day; May 1, Labor Day; May 18, Flag Day; Ascension Day; Corpus Christi; August 15, Assumption; October 17, Dessalines' Death Anniversary; October 24, UN Day; November 1, All Saints Day; Christmas.

CIGARETTES AND TOBACCO...American cigarettes cost 40¢–60¢. Principal local brand, *Splendid,* costs 25¢ and 30¢.

CLIMATE...Port-au-Prince has a sunny, dry climate, not unlike Arizona. The nights are cool the year round. The new hotels in suburban Petionville (4 miles from city, elevation 1,500 feet) are making this a popular summer resort.

CLUBS...The Petionville Club with foreign resident members; the Turgeau Club, the Cercle Bellevue, and Club Port-au-Princien are the exclusive Haitian clubs. For other clubs *see* SPORTS.

COMMON COURTESIES AND LOCAL CUSTOMS...Although Haiti became independent early in the 19th century (following more than a hundred years as a French possession), the Haitians are proud of their French heritage, and French remains the official language. This is a completely foreign land where the aristocracy is mostly mulatto. It is, in fact, the oldest Negro republic in the world.

COMMUNICATIONS...A 3-minute phone call to the States costs $4.50 on Sundays; $6 on weekdays. Cablegrams to the U.S. about $3, depending upon city. Airmail postage to the U.S. is 12¢.

CURRENCY...There are 100 centimes in a gourde, which is worth U.S. 20¢. No exchange restrictions. In fact, U.S. currency is accepted without question in Port-au-Prince.

CUSTOMS REGULATIONS AND DOCUMENTS REQUIRED FOR UNITED STATES CITIZENS ... For a stay of up to 30 days, only proof of identity is required. Smallpox vaccination certificates. Transportation ticket out of the country. One carton of cigarettes or 50 cigars or 2 lbs. of tobacco and 1 bottle liquor allowed duty free.

DRUGSTORES ... At La Belle Creole Department Store there is a complete drug and cosmetic section stocked with standard American products. There is a luncheonette just like at home, and you can have ice cream, called *crème à la glace*, if you like.

ELECTRIC CURRENT ... 110 volts, 60 cycle, A.C.

FLORA ... Palms, bougainvillaea, hibiscus, frangipani, mimosa, mahogany trees and all the other tropical trees and flowers you might expect and some that you wouldn't.

FOOD ... Rice and beans are the mainstay of Haitian cooking. They are served as a separate course at the main meal of the day. Native cooking makes excellent use of spices. Local seafood is wonderful, particularly *langouste* (rock lobster). Avocados appear frequently at meals; sweet-potato pudding is a national dish. Mango pie is another national favorite. Coconut ice cream is popular. Fruits such as bananas, figs, mangoes are plentiful. Haitian coffee is famous.

LANGUAGE ... French is the official language. However, most of the people speak Creole, a patois of French, African, Spanish and English origins. The tourist can get along easily with English.

LAUNDRY AND DRY CLEANING ... Laundry is good and cheap. There are several good dry-cleaning establishments.

LIQUOR ... Haitian rum is well known the world over. It is light and good. Champagnes are plentiful and quite cheap. Brandies and whiskies are sold at low, free port prices.

MEDICAL FACILITIES ... New hospitals have been built: General Hospital; Asile Français; Canape Vert Hospital; Hospital Schweitzer. There is an American wing of St. Francis de Sales Hospital.

MOTION PICTURES ... *Rex, Paramount, Capitol,* and new drive-in *Etoile Ciné* theaters showing mostly French-language films.

MUSIC ... There is a national orchestra, but the music of Haiti is in its drums; they fill the air each weekend. At the hotels and night clubs there are small but good dance bands.

NIGHT CLUBS AND CABARETS ... On Saturday evenings, "everyone" drives to the *Cabane Choucoune* at Petionville, a few miles up in the hills. This is a circular building with a thatched roof where the elite of Haiti and the foreign colony dance the merengue. The new *La Ronde* Club at Hotel El Rancho also attracts large Saturday night crowds. *Shango Night Club* at Hotel Ibo Lele has very good floor shows on Friday nights. The *Don Pedro Club* has typical Haitian music and atmosphere, is frequented by the uninhibited merengue lovers on Saturday night. The open-air *Théâtre de Verdure,* in the waterfront exposition section, has regular performances of folklore music and dancing.

PHOTOGRAPHY ... All supplies are readily available. Black-and-white film can be developed in 3 days.

RELIGION . . . Catholicism is the dominant religion, but there are several Protestant churches.

RESTAURANTS . . . Food at the hotels is good. *Aux Cosaques* is a true Haitian restaurant; Haitian seafood and beef specialties are superb and moderate in price. *Le Picardie* in Petionville and *Shango* have excellent French cuisine. Other good restaurants are *Berliner Hof, Don Allen's Rendezvous* and *Le Rond Point*.

SHOPS AND STORES . . . Among many interesting shops: Fisher's Corner Shop, Carlos, Paquin's, Gift Fair, Store Club, Red Carpet, Haitian Craft. Meinberg's factory for mahogany items. Marie Jeanne and Lamp Post shops specialize in shoes. La Belle Creole and Little Europe have the largest selection of imported luxury items. Cameras and optical equipment at the Camera Center and Rudy's. Haiti enjoys a trade comparable to free-port areas, with luxuries at low bargain prices.

SPECTATOR SPORTS . . . There are none, really, unless you include watching a voodoo dance. There is cockfighting, of course. The national game is soccer.

SPORTS . . . Tennis, golf, swimming, horseback riding (which is particularly fine) are available. At all hotels except pensions there are good swimming pools; some have one or more tennis courts. Spear fishing is a popular native sport, and you can hire boats and an instructor if you wish. There is excellent duck shooting within a few hours of Port-au-Prince and pigeon and wild guinea hen shooting year round. Arrangements can be made with tour operators for guides and guns.

THEATERS . . . Théâtre de Verdure is the principal theater.

TIME . . . Same as United States Eastern Standard Time.

TIPPING . . . Many hotels and restaurants now add 10% to your bill, which takes care of all tips, except for 50 centimes a bag for luggage porters. Taxi drivers are not tipped.

TOURIST TAXES . . . Air and sea arrival and departure taxes $2.

TRANSPORTATION . . . You can hire a car complete with chauffeur for about $20 a day. Or you can take your choice of the "personalized" ground tours offered. You may also fly, except on Sundays and holidays, to the Citadelle, about a 45-minute flight from the capital. Incidentally, if you hire a car, the chauffeur usually pays his own expenses. Share-the-ride taxis go anywhere in town for 10¢. Limousine fare from the airport into Port-au-Prince is $1 per person, $3 in a private car; to Petionville, $1.50 in limousine, $4.50 in private car. Drive-yourself service is also available. Your U.S. driver's permit and tourist card will get you a temporary license.

WATER . . . Generally safe in hotels and restaurants of principal cities. Use caution elsewhere especially when traveling in the country.

WHAT TO BUY . . . Mahogany products, beautiful bowls, figures and furniture, sisal and straw products. Haitian rum is excellent and cheap. Pick up a voodoo trophy, if you can find an authentic one. Tortoise-shell combs and jewelry are fine here. Hand-made laces and embroideries are particularly beautiful, and so is the local artwork.

WHAT TO WEAR . . . Light summer clothing similar to that worn in Miami. For the hills you'll need a topcoat and sweaters.

WHERE TO GO—SIGHTSEEING . . .

Port-au-Prince . . . Port-au-Prince is unlike any capital city you have ever seen. It is a mixture of elegance and crudeness, of sophistication and primitiveness. The streets are jammed with automobiles and burros. Haitian women walk with huge baskets of vegetables on their heads; there are pseudo-châteaux and houses on stilts. But everywhere there is color, gaiety and charm. While in Port-au-Prince, visit the Iron Market, which is filled with an amazing variety of merchandise. Everything is for sale here: foods, clothes, leather goods, junk of all sorts and some fine things. Saturday is the biggest day, but the market is never closed.

Visit the National Museum which displays, among other things, the diamond crown of Emperor Soulouque, who ruled Haiti more than a century ago. See, too, the anchor of the Santa Maria, which allegedly was wrecked in Haiti. In the Museum of Ethnology there is a permanent exhibit of Indian and African relics. Be sure to see a typical woodwork shop where bowls and furniture are made of mahogany.

Sans Souci and La Citadelle . . . To visit King Henri Christophe's Sans Souci Palace and his incredible mountaintop Citadelle, you must go to Cap-Haitien and Milot. If you drive from Port-au-Prince, a car with chauffeur (who pays his own expenses) is $100 for 2 days and a night. On the drive up-island you will see sisal fields, thatched huts, banana trees and plantations growing that delicious Haitian coffee. The drive takes 4½ hours, or you can fly the distance in 40 minutes. In Cap-Haitien, an enchantingly picturesque Creole city, is the *Hotel Mont Joli* with a large swimming pool overlooking the town; rates start at $10 single, American Plan. Two other first-class hotels are the immaculately clean *Beck Hotel* and *Hostellerie du Roi Christophe*. Pension *André Dupuy* is less expensive, but lacks private baths.

From Cap-Haitien, it is a 15-minute drive to Milot and Sans Souci, built in the early 19th century as an exact replica of Frederick II's Sans Souci at Potsdam. Here, in marble-floored, mahogany-paneled rooms hung with Gobelin tapestries and furnished with every luxury, Christophe held his bizarre court in pompous imitation of the French court at Versailles. It is a 2-hour climb to the Citadelle, which took 13 years and the labors of 200,000 men to build. Every stone, every cannon, and enough supplies for a garrison of 15,000 soldiers to withstand a year's siege were dragged up the mountain by sheer manpower. It is a fantastic memorial to human indomitability—and conceit.

SOURCES OF FURTHER INFORMATION . . . There is a tourist information office at the site of the former exposition in Port-au-Prince, Pan American's office at Place de la Republique Argentine Cité Exposition (Tel. 3200 and 3451). In New York the Haiti Tourist Information Bureau is at 30 Rockefeller Plaza. There are others in Chicago and Miami.

JAMAICA

CARIBBEAN SEA

WEATHER IN KINGSTON—Lat. N18°—Alt. 25'

Temp.	JAN.	FEB.	MAR.	APR.	MAY	JUNE	JULY	AUG.	SEPT.	OCT.	NOV.	DEC.
Low	67°	67°	68°	70°	72°	74°	73°	73°	73°	73°	71°	69°
High	86°	86°	86°	87°	87°	89°	90°	90°	89°	88°	87°	87°
Average	77°	77°	77°	79°	80°	82°	82°	82°	81°	81°	79°	78°
Days of Rain	5	4	4	5	7	6	7	9	10	12	7	5

LOCATION ... The island of Jamaica lies in the Caribbean Sea about 550 miles south of Miami, Florida.

CHARACTERISTICS ... Long famous as a resort, Jamaica has a great deal to offer the tourist. Kingston is colorful, with fine shops, wonderful drives and good hotels. The north coast, which includes such well-known resorts as Montego Bay and Ocho Rios, is where the international set are to be found during the season. There are super-luxurious hotels, white coral beaches lapped by cerulean blue waters which are always warm, golf courses, fishing, yacht clubs and all the other things that give glamour and luxury to a vacation.

POPULATION ... Estimated at 1,750,000.

SIZE ... Largest of the West Indies islands, Jamaica is 145 miles long, 45 miles wide, and covers an area of 4,411 square miles.

CAPITAL ... Kingston, with a population of approximately 400,000.

GOVERNMENT ... An independent Dominion within the British Commonwealth, with an elected Prime Minister and a Governor-General, appointed by the Queen.

HOW TO GET THERE ... By Pan American Clipper, Montego Bay is 1¼ hours from Miami, 3¾ hours from New York, 2⅓ hours direct from Haiti. Kingston is ½ hour from Montego Bay and has direct 3½ hour Jet Clipper service from New York.

ACCOMMODATIONS ... Most Jamaican hotels are operated on both American and European Plans, with Continental and Modified American Plans available. The rates are substantially lower during the summer. The *Sheraton Kingston* is the largest hotel in the capital; the newly renovated *Myrtle Bank* is conveniently close to the downtown shopping area. In the Parish of St. Andrew, a suburb of Kingston, there is *Courtleigh Manor*, near Liguanea golf course. The *Mona, Blue Mountain Inn, Terra Nova, Liguanea Terrace, Flamingo* and *Green Gables* hotels are also in this area. Double rates average $28, Modified American Plan in winter. At *Morgan's Harbour* in Port Royal is Kingston's only beach resort; yacht marina. Other hotels throughout the island are listed under WHERE TO GO.

ARTS ... The Institute of Jamaica, which contains the Science Museum and Library, the History, Art and Exhibition Galleries. The island's leading painters operate The Gallery on Constant Spring Road.

BANKS ... In Kingston: Barclay's Bank, Royal Bank of Canada, Canadian Imperial Bank of Commerce, Bank of Nova Scotia (all with branches throughout the island), Bank of London and Montreal, and the First National City Bank of New York. Banking hours: 8:30 A.M. to 12:30 P.M. on weekdays. Saturdays they close at 11:00 A.M.

CALENDAR OF HOLIDAYS ... New Year's Day; Ash Wednesday; Good Friday; Easter Monday; Labor Day (May 23); the Queen's official birthday in June; Independence Day (first Monday in August); Christmas Day; Boxing Day (December 26).

CIGARETTES AND CIGARS ... The manufacture of cigars and cigarettes is one of the leading industries in Jamaica. American cigarettes are available at all hotels and stores at 60¢ to 70¢ a pack.

CLIMATE ... The "High Season," mid-December to mid-April, is perfect, with sunshine every day and cool nights. The summer season is now as popular as the winter, making Jamaica an all-year tropical paradise. The constant trade winds keep the island far cooler than many resorts on the United States Eastern seaboard.

CLUBS ... The Royal Jamaica Yacht Club, the Jamaica Club, St. Andrew Club, Liguanea Club, Caymanas Golf and Country Club, Rotary, Lions and Kiwanis clubs. There are also a YMCA and a YWCA. (*See* others under SPORTS.)

COMMON COURTESIES AND LOCAL CUSTOMS ... Short shorts and swim suits are *not* worn on city streets.

COMMUNICATIONS ... A 3-minute call to New York costs £3.4 (about $9). A cablegram is 1/8 per word. Airmail postage to the U.S. is 6d (7¢) for postcards and airletters; 1/– (14¢) for 5-gram letters.

CURRENCY ... The Jamaican pound is worth $2.80. There are 20 shillings in a pound (£); 12 pence (d) in a shilling (1/–).

CUSTOMS REGULATIONS AND DOCUMENTS REQUIRED FOR UNITED STATES CITIZENS ... No passports or visas are required for a stay of up to 6 months, provided the trip originates and terminates in the continental U.S. and the traveler has a return ticket and some proof of citizenship. Visitors fill in a Disembarkation Card prior to arrival, which must be returned to the Immigration authorities on departure. Vaccination certificates are required if the passenger comes from an infected area. No household pets are allowed. Allowed in duty free are: 1 carton of cigarettes; 50 cigars or ½ lb. tobacco; 1 pint of liquor or 1 quart of wine. No foreign rums are permitted. Also necessary for return entry is some sort of proof of U.S. citizenship such as a birth certificate, naturalization papers or old passport.

DRUGSTORES ... There are several very good drugstores, which carry all well-known brands of medicines and toilet articles. They don't usually have soda fountains.

ELECTRIC CURRENT ... 110 volt, 50 cycle, A.C.

FAUNA ... Commonly seen birds include the kling-kling, canary-like saffron finches, brown pelicans, green parrots, several species of hummingbird, mocking bird (called nightingale) and turkey buzzard (called John Crow); in all, there are about 52 species of birds peculiar to the island. The most unusual wild mammal is the mongoose, and there are no poisonous reptiles.

FLORA ... Wonderful fruits, obtainable at all seasons of the year, beautiful trees, shrubs, flowering plants, ferns (of which there are over 500 species), exquisite orchids (about 200 species are found, 73 of which are indigenous to Jamaica), the silk-cotton tree or ceiba, the poinciana and bougainvillaea.

FOOD ... Local foods include green banana, which is eaten boiled, yam, cocoa, breadfruit, ackee, plantain, rice and peas, and fish. Soups such as pepper pot and red pea. Fruits include mangoes, pineapples, oranges, tangerines, limes, grapefruit, ortaniques, bananas, papaya, sweetsop, soursop, star apple, naseberry, otaheite apple, melon, rose apple, guinep, avocado pear, ugli fruit and strawberry.

GAMBLING ... There is horse racing at Caymanas Park Race Course, 10 miles from Kingston. There are 42 meets a year, including 3 sweepstakes with many legal off-track betting outlets.

LAUNDRY AND DRY CLEANING ... Laundry is good. Hotels have 24-hour service. Numerous excellent dry-cleaning establishments with 24-hour service.

LIQUOR ... Jamaica rum is world famous and the coffee liqueur, Tia Maria, is gaining great popularity. All brands of imported liquor are available in free-port shops at much lower cost than at home.

MEDICAL FACILITIES ... Excellent doctors, dentists and hospitals are available. The most modern hospital is located at the University of the West Indies. Others in Kingston are the Kingston Public Hospital, Nuttall Memorial Hospital and St. Joseph's Sanitarium. There are 24 hospitals throughout the island.

MOTION PICTURES ... In Kingston and its suburbs, the *Carib, Regal* and *State* are air conditioned. Open-air theaters are the *Odeon, Tropical, Palace, Majestic, Mona, Rialto, Queens and Kings, Harbour View* and the *Boulevard* Drive-ins. The latest English and American films are shown. There are also theaters in Montego Bay, Ocho Rios, Port Antonio and Mandeville.

MUSIC . . . Concerts at the *Ward Theater, Carib, Regal* and *State* in Kingston. Calypso is heard everywhere.

NIGHT CLUBS AND CABARETS . . . Kingston area: *Cloud 9* at Half-Way-Tree; *Ferry Inn* on Spanish Town Road. Ocho Rios area: *Club Maracas* and *Brown Jug.* Montego Bay area: *Reef Club* on Coast Road and *Yellow Bird* downtown; *Cellar Club* on Union Street; *Rum Barrell Inn* and *Club 35* downtown; *Ridgely's* near Doctor's Cave.

PHOTOGRAPHY . . . Black-and-white and color still and movie film are available as well as cameras and other photographic equipment. Stanley Motta, Ltd., Caribbean Camera Center and Swiss Stores will sell German and Japanese cameras in bond for delivery on departure from the island at savings of about ⅓ over U.S. retail prices. First-class developing services on the island.

RESTAURANTS . . . In downtown Kingston: the *Caprice, Jamaica Arms* and *Paul's 104.* In the Half-Way-Tree area: the *Continental, La France* and *Terra Nova.* There are several very good Chinese restaurants, such as the *Cathay* in downtown Kingston; *Oriental, Fah Mee* and *Asia* restaurants in the Half-Way-Tree area. Seven miles away, in the foothills of the Blue Mountains, are the *Blue Mountain Inn, Casa Monte, Stony Hill,* and *Ferry Inn* on Spanish Town road, where good food and wines are served amidst beautiful surroundings.

SHOPS AND STORES . . . The largest stores in Kingston are on King Street and Harbour Street. Shops are open from 8:30 A.M. to 4 P.M. except on Wednesdays, when they close at 1 P.M., unless a large cruise ship is expected that day; then they will keep open until later in the afternoon for tourists. Thursday is early closing day outside Kingston. The "free port" shops in Kingston, Montego Bay and Ocho Rios sell all types of luxury articles at about 50% savings. The 2 airports have similar shops for liquor.

SPECTATOR SPORTS . . . Cricket and football, horse racing, polo, yachting regattas, tennis and golf tournaments, boxing, cycle racing and skeet shooting.

SPORTS . . . Golf at 9 clubs; visitors' cards can be arranged. Some of the best are: Caymanas Golf Club and Constant Spring Club, both near Kingston; Manchester Club in Mandeville; Upton at Ocho Rios; Cardiff Hall course at Runaway Bay; famed Tryall Club near Montego Bay; Rose Hall course near Half Moon hotel. Tennis clubs include posh Montego Bay's Racquet Club and Fairfield Country Club, both open to all guests in the area; Manchester Club in Mandeville. Polo, horseback riding. There are several stables where you can hire horses, particularly at Good Hope near Falmouth. The Royal Jamaica Yacht Club and Montego Bay Yacht Club hold frequent regattas in winter. Most hotels have their own fresh- or saltwater swimming pools, but most visitors cannot resist the miles of white sand beaches and crystal-clear sea. Snorkeling and scuba equipment may be rented, and the water-skiing is unsurpassed. Rafting down the Rio Grande near Port Antonio is exciting, spectacular and completely safe. There is good fishing for mullet in mountain streams, and the sea abounds in such big game fish as blue marlin, wahoo, dolphin, barracuda, tarpon, bonefish, snook and small tuna. Less energetic visitors will enjoy the magic panorama of the undersea world from glass-bottomed boats. The water is so clear that you can catch all the brilliant colors of the reefs even on film.

THEATERS ... Plays at the *Little Theater* and *Ward* in Kingston.

TIME ... Same as United States Eastern Standard Time.

TIPPING ... About the same as at home, 10-15%. Tip 1 shilling in place of a quarter; 6 pence instead of a dime.

TRANSPORTATION ... Most taxis are metered. Drive-yourself cars rent for $50 to $80 a week with unlimited mileage; your state driver's license is acceptable. Scheduled limousine transfer facilities are available with all drivers qualified tourist guides; make reservations through your travel agent. The daily diesel train run from Kingston to Montego Bay provides a unique view of the Cockpit Country, and there's also diesel train service through shadowy, tropical jungles from Kingston to Port Antonio.

WATER ... Modern pipeline supply. Safe in all hotels.

WHAT TO BUY ... Liquor, tweeds, English doeskin, jippi-jappa straw goods, English china, woolens, perfumes, cameras, watches, and golf balls are among the best buys.

WHAT TO WEAR ... Lightweight summer clothes all year. Conservative dresses for women in Kingston and Mandeville, but everyone's in shorts and slacks during the day in North Coast resorts. Men seldom wear coats during the day, but always for evening. For night life, most people wear evening clothes. Bring lots of swim suits.

WHERE TO GO—SIGHTSEEING ...

Kingston ... Don't miss a trip to the Institute of Jamaica, which is located on East Street. There is everything there representing the past and present of the island, Arawak carvings, ancient almanacs and live Jamaican animals. There are also the Art, Natural History Galleries and the Lecture Hall. This museum contains some interesting relics of the early days of the islands.

At the Hope Botanic Gardens, 5½ miles from Kingston at an elevation of nearly 650 feet, there are over 200 acres under cultivation. There is a magnificent collection of orchids, tropical trees, citrus, coffee, fruit and other tropical plants. Peacocks stroll regally through the grounds, and there is a modern zoo. Don't miss the Folk Museum in historic Spanish Town, west of Kingston.

You'll be interested in visiting "Morgan's Harbor," on the site of the old naval dockyard at Port Royal across the harbor from Kingston. The old naval dockyard was originally known as King's Yard when Port Royal was the capital of Jamaica and was the site of King's House, which was the residence of the Governor in the time of Captain Morgan. This 10-acre site has been completely fitted out with luxurious facilities for tourists, such· as salt-water swimming pool, white sand beach, a restaurant specializing in seafood, beach cabañas, dancing to calypso bands. It also includes a complete yacht marina with power and sailing boats for hire and all facilities for repairing and reprovisioning yachts. Guests at all the main hotels will be given complimentary membership to the club.

North Shore Resorts—Montego Bay ... Of all the lovely Caribbean resorts, Montego Bay on the North Coast is by far the best known to travelers. It is the seaport and chief town of the Parish of St. James, about 113 miles from Kingston. One of its features is its unsurpassed sea bathing. The deep blue water, the temperature of which ranges from 70 degrees to 80 degrees the year round, is delightful. Here the gentle, prevailing trade winds make the Bay ideal for sailing. The few remaining traces of the island's aboriginal Arawaks can be seen at kitchen middens in the areas of Tryall, California and Williamsfield, while an Arawak rock carving is to be seen at Kempshot. The town derives its name from manteca (or lard) which the Spaniards shipped from this picturesque bay. The ancient British fort still stands and the town's courthouse has been called a model of colonial architecture.

Montego Bay offers a wide variety of sports, including tennis, sea bathing, horseback riding, polo, golf, badminton, fishing and alligator shooting. It also has some of the most beautiful hotels in the island. Among internationally known hotels on the "Gold Coast" hotel strip are *Montego Beach* and *Sunset Lodge,* two beach-side hotels favored by the international set. Nearby is the luxurious beach resort community of *Round Hill. Bay Roc, Casa Blanca, Colony, Racquet Club* and *Tryall* are among Montego Bay's fine hotels. Most of them have bathing clubs and private beaches. *Gloucester House,* a modern, conservative but excellent hotel on the Bay, is within a hundred yards of *Doctor's Cave Beach Club.* Directly behind Doctor's Cave Beach facing the Caribbean is the *Casa Montego. Beach View* and *Hacton House* are very good hotels facing the sea. *Montego Inn* is near the center of town, while *Half Moon Hotel* and the *Driftwood Inn* are situated about 4 miles out along the coast, as is the excellent *Royal Caribbean* on picturesque Mahoe Bay. Smaller and attractive hotels are *Holiday House, Miranda Hill, Harmony House* and *Blairgowrie.*

Doctor's Cave Beach Club is world famous for its coral sands and crystal-clear water. There is an excellent reef, and much of the area's social life centers around its Riviera-like setting. Membership is available to guests at all Montego Bay hotels, and water skiing, skin-diving and sailing are among the many aquatic activities it offers.

Ten miles inland from Falmouth, in neighboring Trelawny, is *Good Hope* (open in the winter), an 18th-century great-house in the center of a 6,000-acre cattle ranch. It offers horses and good trails for riding, and the easy, gracious life on a plantation home set in the midst of tall, waving coconut palms. It has its own private beach.

Rates in the Montego Bay area average $34 double during the summer and $50 double during the winter, Modified American Plan (2 meals). All other plans are also available at most hotels.

Ocho Rios ... About 65 miles east of Montego Bay in the Ocho Rios area, dotted with numerous hotels and guest houses, strung out along the beautiful coastline like pearls on a string. They include the luxurious *Plantation Inn, Carib Ocho Rios, Shaw Park Beach Club* and the *Falcondip.* Near St. Ann's Bay are the 176-room *Jamaica Hilton* and the new *Runaway Bay* hotels. At the other end of the string, near Oracabessa, are the new *Golden Head* and the 200-room *Playboy Club.* In between lie *Jamaica Inn,* ever-popular *Tower Isle,* the *Windsor,* the delightful *Silver Seas,* and the cottage-type colony of *Sans Souci.* Four miles from Ocho Rios village, Dunn's River tumbles down palm-shaded falls into the sparkling Caribbean. This is one of the island's best-known beauty and bathing spots, where you can splash from the warm salt sea into the cool fresh foam of the falls. Hotel rates around Ocho Rios are approximately the same as in Montego Bay.

Port Antonio ... has the island's heaviest rainfall and is consequently more lushly tropical. It boasts the fabulous resort of *Frenchman's Cove,* the *Jamaica Reef* of Errol Flynn fame, and charming *Bonnie View,* from which—as the name implies—there is a superb view. Don't miss the Blue Hole, with its somewhat sinister, unfathomed beauty, or the famous raft trip down the Rio Grande rapids.

SOURCES OF FURTHER INFORMATION ... Offices of the Jamaica Tourist Board in North America are: Pan Am Building, New York, N.Y. 10017; Champlain Building, 37 South Wabash Avenue, Chicago; 901 Ainsley Building, N.E. First Avenue and Flagler Street, Miami; 3440 Wilshire Boulevard, Los Angeles 5; 209 Post St., San Francisco 8; 403 Jos. Vance Building, Seattle; King Edward Hotel, Toronto. Head Office in Jamaica is 80 Harbour Street, Kingston. Pan American is at 117 Harbour Street, Kingston; Casa Montego Arcade, Montego Bay; 2 Pineapple Place, Ocho Rios.

Any time is the time for a Planter's Punch on the beach at Round Hill near Montego Bay.

MARTINIQUE

Guadeloupe 80 miles

▲ MT. PELEE

● St. Pierre

MARTINIQUE

★ **FORT-DE-FRANCE**

ATLANTIC

OCEAN

CARIBBEAN

SEA

WEATHER IN FORT-DE-FRANCE—Lat. N14°38′—Alt. approx. sea level

Temp.	JAN.	FEB.	MAR.	APR.	MAY	JUNE	JULY	AUG.	SEPT.	OCT.	NOV.	DEC.
Low	69°	69°	69°	71°	73°	74°	74°	74°	74°	73°	72°	70°
High	83°	84°	85°	86°	86°	86°	86°	87°	88°	87°	86°	84°
Average	76°	76°	77°	79°	80°	80°	80°	81°	81°	80°	79°	77°
Days of Rain	19	15	15	13	18	21	22	22	20	19	20	19

LOCATION ... One of the largest islands in the Lesser Antilles, Martinique is situated halfway between Puerto Rico and Trinidad. Fort-de-France is 278 air miles from Trinidad.

CHARACTERISTICS ... Martinique, "where it is always summer," is known in the Caribbean as Madinina, queen of the Antilles. It is a place to enjoy tennis, swimming, sailing, fishing, water skiing and relaxing in an atmosphere of tropical beauty. The natives are friendly toward tourists and will do their best to be helpful. There is practically no night life and by midnight most places are quiet.

POPULATION ... More than 320,000, of which approximately 230,000 are West Indians.

SIZE ... Approximately 50 miles long and 19 miles wide, Martinique has an area of 425 square miles.

CAPITAL ... Fort-de-France, a city of 92,000.

GOVERNMENT ... The former colony of Martinique became a department of France in 1947.

HOW TO GET THERE ... By Pan American Clipper, 3 hours from San Juan, Puerto Rico (which in turn is 3½ hours from New York), including island stops; and 2¼ hours from Trinidad. By ship from New York about 8 days, and from Trinidad 2 days.

ACCOMMODATIONS ... Space is limited, particularly during the winter season. The new *Hotel Cap Est,* on a superb beach 22 miles from Fort-de-France, has 15 air-conditioned cottages, each containing 2 double rooms; $28 single, $42 double in winter, Modified

American Plan (2 meals). Other hotels include the *Lido,* 4 miles from town, same rates; the smart, very new *Hotel Bakoua;* and the *Auberge de L'Anse Mitan* situated on the beach across the harbor from Fort-de-France, $13 single, $23 double, American Plan (3 meals). The hotels offer very good French cuisine and excellent French wines. Some smaller hotels have rates from $10 single, $20 double American Plan.

ARTS ... Museums and native crafts: Museum of Saint-Pierre, birthplace of Empress Josephine, at Trois-Ilets; native pottery, straw hats and baskets, Martinican dolls, woodcarving ... Museum of Fort Saint Louis, Caribbean Art Center.

BANKS ... Bank of Martinique, a private bank, represents the French-American Banking Corporation; Credit Martiniquais represents the First National City Bank of New York; Banque Nationale pour le Commerce et l'Industrie (private bank); Royal Bank of Canada.

CALENDAR OF HOLIDAYS ... All Catholic holy days, plus Bastille Day on July 14; November 11, Armistice Day; May 1, Labor Day; the famous carnival on Mardi Gras; the funeral of Carnival King on Ash Wednesday, the only spectacle of its kind, with the entire population mourning. Stores are closed on all these days and usually on Saturday afternoon and Sunday.

CIGARETTES AND TOBACCO ... American and English cigarettes are available but expensive, about 55¢ a pack. French tobacco and cigarettes are available. No local brands.

CLIMATE ... The climate is like summer all the year round. Fort-de-France is rather hot but the nights are cool. See weather chart.

CLUBS ... Fort-de-France clubs open to tourists: the Cercle de Fort-de-France, the Fort Royal and the Yacht Club.

COMMON COURTESIES AND LOCAL CUSTOMS ... Every time people meet or leave each other, they shake hands. Men need not wear coats and ties in restaurants. One can wear beach dresses for shopping in town, but shorts are seldom worn.

COMMUNICATIONS ... A 3-minute phone call to the U.S. costs from 37.05 to 59.25 francs; a 10-word cablegram is 23.16 frs. Airmail postage to the U.S. is 70 centimes for a 5-gram letter, 50 for a postcard.

CURRENCY ... There are 5 new francs to the U.S. $1.

CUSTOMS REGULATIONS AND DOCUMENTS REQUIRED FOR UNITED STATES CITIZENS ... Proof of citizenship showing photograph and continuation or return ticket are the only documents required for a stay up to 10 days. Passport is needed for longer stays —cholera and yellow fever certificates if coming from infected areas. Duty-free imports: 1,000 cigarettes, 1 bottle of liquor.

DRUGSTORES ... French drugstores sell only drugs.

ELECTRIC CURRENT ... At present, both 110 and 220 volts, 50 cycles, A.C. Plug adapters are needed.

FAUNA ... In certain villages, cockfights and fights between snakes and mongooses are arranged as a tourist attraction, if you can take that sort of thing.

FLORA . . . There is a great variety of flowers in Martinique: hibiscus, wild orchids, bougainvillaea, Chinese hats, anturiums, lauriers, ixoras, and many others. The vegetation is very dense and tropical (arborescent ferns). The main plantations raise sugar cane, bananas, pineapples.

FOOD . . . Martinique has French cooking and good native dishes, such as *colombo,* made with Indian seeds comparable to curry and saffron, cooked with pork or beef and eaten with rice. A delicious dish is stuffed crabs. Crayfish, the size of a small lobster, are also very good. Try calalou soup made from greens, and gumbos eaten with rice and fried codfish. A delightful dish is the yam baked in its own skin with cheese and butter. You must taste the wonderful salad of palm heart; coconut heart; and the snails ("escargots de Bourgogne") that you can eat at any of the best restaurants. Milk here is safe.

LANGUAGE . . . French is the official language, but you will have little difficulty if you speak only English.

LAUNDRY AND DRY CLEANING . . . Dry cleaning is expensive, but good laundry service is provided by hotels.

LIQUOR . . . The chief native drink is the famous rum punch, which is inexpensive, as are American drinks—whiskies (no bourbon), imported and local beers, Coca-Cola, Pepsi-Cola and other soda drinks. Daiquiri is a popular drink. Bally is one of the most popular rums. Hotel bars and others are open till midnight.

MEDICAL FACILITIES . . . There are no American hospitals. The Clinics St. Paul and Roseau are about the best private clinics.

MOTION PICTURES . . . There are five motion-picture theaters in Fort-de-France, including a modern air-conditioned theater, showing mostly French and American films with French sound track.

MUSIC . . . Martinique is renowned as the home of the béguine. Native orchestras and dancers excel at it.

NIGHT CLUBS . . . Dances in many places during Carnival season and on Saturday nights most of the year. *La Bananaraie,* about 6 miles from Fort-de-France, has dancing from 9 P.M. to 2 or 3 A.M.

PHOTOGRAPHY . . . Cameras, movie films, black-and-white or color, and photo equipment are all available. Prices are about the same as in the United States. Developing takes 2 days.

RELIGION . . . Martinique is almost entirely Roman Catholic; however, other denominations are represented.

RESTAURANTS . . . *Hotel de l'Europe, Chez Gerard* and the *Lido* are very good. *Manoir,* situated on a hill, 5 minutes from town, also has good food. Ask for snails, pâté de foie gras, and crayfish bouquet. A good meal will cost $6, apéritif and wine included.

SHOPS AND STORES . . . The shopping district is close to Pan Am's office. Watches, silver, crystals can be purchased at low prices. 20% discount on items bought with travelers checks. Roger Albert's free-port shop specializes in French perfumes, crystals, local souvenirs. Beaufrand has perfumes, Martinique dolls and other colorful items. Mad has native crafts and home furnishings. La Malle des Indes sells antiques. The Caribbean Art Center is popular. Prices are very reasonable. Shops are open from 8:30 A.M. to noon, and from 2:30 to 5 P.M. Beaufrand has a free-port shop at the airport that sells perfumes, liquors, local art and souvenirs.

SPECTATOR SPORTS . . . Football every Sunday at the Stadium. Cockfighting is popular.

SPORTS . . . Tennis, water skiing, football and basketball.

THEATERS . . . A troupe from France comes every year in February.

TIME . . . Noon in Martinique is 11 A.M. in New York.

TRANSPORTATION . . . Buses are used mostly by the natives. Better take a taxi that will drive you for a very reasonable rate. Hertz and Shotta auto rentals are available at around $9 per day, plus mileage. A Government launch makes frequent runs daily across the bay to Trois-Ilets.

WATER . . . Drinking local water is safe, and good; inexpensive locally bottled mineral water is plentiful (Didier water).

WHAT TO WEAR . . . Only washable summer clothes. Don't forget your swimming suit, dark glasses, raincoat and a light jacket.

WHERE TO GO—SIGHTSEEING . . .

Martinique . . . is world famous for the eruption of Mt. Pelée in 1902, which wiped out the entire population (40,000) of the former capital city of St. Pierre in three minutes. There was only one survivor, a prisoner held in an underground dungeon, who died soon after, it is said, from the effects of radioactivity. Ruins of the city, called the "Pompeii of the New World," afford an interesting climax to a trip along the spectacular west coast of the island, with its fishing villages, tropical beaches, cliffs and coves. The volcanic museum at the foot of Mt. Pelée vividly impresses the visitor with the violence of this catastrophe.

Martinique is also renowned as the birthplace of Napoleon's Empress Josephine, whose marble statue stands in the center of the Savanna, the public park in Fort-de-France. Across the beautiful Bay of Fort-de-France, at Trois-Ilets, near a native pottery factory, a small museum commemorates Josephine's birthplace. In Fort-de-France, ancient Fort Royal (now Fort St. Louis) was the scene of fierce battles among the Dutch, French and English as the island changed hands during the 17th and 18th centuries.

Off the southwest coast of the island rises the great Diamond Rock, which was commissioned as a ship by the British Navy in the 18th century. For over 10 years, H.M.S. Diamond Rock held out against the French. This is also the location of the island's most beautiful beach, Diamond, facing Diamond Rock.

SOURCES OF FURTHER INFORMATION . . . Martinique Tourist Bureau, Fort-de-France. L. de la Houssaye & Cie, 1 rue Liberté (Tel. 66-66), specializes in tours and sightseeing. Pan Am's office is at 62 Avenue Duparquet (Tel. 65-52 and 65-53).

NASSAU
AND THE BAHAMAS

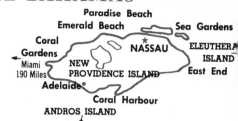

WEATHER IN NASSAU—Lat. N25°05'—Alt. approx. sea level

Temp.	JAN.	FEB.	MAR.	APR.	MAY	JUNE	JULY	AUG.	SEPT.	OCT.	NOV.	DEC.
Low	67°	67°	68°	69°	72°	75°	76°	76°	76°	75°	71°	69°
High	76°	77°	78°	80°	83°	86°	88°	88°	87°	85°	80°	78°
Average	72°	72°	73°	75°	78°	81°	82°	82°	82°	80°	76°	74°
Days of Rain	3	4	2	4	9	10	15	12	13	15	7	6

LOCATION ... Scattered over more than 70,000 square miles of sea, the Bahamas are composed of nearly 700 islands and about 2,000 cays. The islands extend from a point 60 miles east of Palm Beach to the north of Haiti in a 760-mile arc stretching in a southeasterly direction. Important islands include New Providence, site of Nassau, Abaco, Andros, the Biminis, Berry Islands, Eleuthera, Exuma, Grand Bahama, Harbour Island, San Salvador, Spanish Wells, Inagua, Cat Island and Long Island.

CHARACTERISTICS ... The Bahamas form a chain of beautiful semi-tropical islands that have a charming atmosphere and some of the finest beaches and sea bathing anywhere. Nassau, the most sophisticated and modern of the resorts in the Bahamas, is quaintly British, decorous and utterly lovely. Spend your days basking on world-famous Paradise Beach. Spend the evening dancing under the Bahamian moon on the terrace of one of Nassau's famed resort hotels, later making the rounds of the native night clubs and cabarets. Nassau offers its visitors a royal welcome and goes all out to make them comfortable.

POPULATION ... Estimated at 130,721, with Nassau and New Providence Island totaling well over half of that figure.

SIZE ... The total land area of the group is approximately 4,405 square miles, about half the area of Massachusetts. The island of New Providence is 21 miles long and 7 miles wide at its widest point.

CAPITAL ... Nassau, population about 80,822.

GOVERNMENT ... Since 1718 the Governor of the Bahamas has been appointed by the British Crown, but the Colony is self-governing with a Premier and two-chamber Legislature.

HOW TO GET THERE ... By Pan Am Clipper, Nassau is only 1 hour from Miami, and 2¾ hours from New York. Pan Am Jet flights to Rock Sound on Eleuthera take 25 minutes from Nassau; 3¼ hours from New York. By ship, overnight from Miami, 2½ days from New York.

ACCOMMODATIONS ... Nassau has some of the most luxurious and beautiful hotels to be found anywhere. Apartment houses, private homes (with rooms for rent), seaside villas and magnificent Bahamian homes (for rent complete) also provide seasonal accommodations. Typical guest houses include: *Gleneagles House, Harbour View, New Providence*, and the *Colonial House and Garden Apartments*. Rates, without meals, average around $12 per person in winter.

The winter season is the most fashionable and formal time of the year in Nassau, and hotel rates vary widely. Typical rates for Modified American Plan (room, breakfast and dinner) are: *Balmoral Club*, $18-$36 single, $28-$60 double. *Sheraton British Colonial Hotel*, $30-$47 single, $40-$55 double. *Carlton House*, $18-$20 single, $27-$30 double. *Coral Harbour Club*, $30-$50 single, $42-$65 double. *Montagu Beach Hotel*, $25-$45 single, $35-$55 double. *Emerald Beach Hotel*, $32-$55 single, $42-$65 double. *Nassau Beach Hotel*, $30-$40 single, $40-$50 double. *Nassau Harbour Club*, from $26 single, $38 double. *Pilot House Club*, $24-$36 single, $34-$46 double. *Dolphin Hotel*, $22-$26 single, $30-$40 double. On the Continental Plan (room and breakfast), the *Ocean Club* on Paradise Island, $55 single, $70 double; *Cumberland House*, $15 single, $20 double; *Olympia Hotel*, $12-$22 single, $18-$36 double. Representative of European Plan rates (no meals included) are the *Prince George Hotel*, from $12 single, $15 double; *Royal Victoria Hotel*, $16-$30 single, $22-$40 double; *Towne Hotel*, $10-$16 single, $16-$18 double. *Sapphire Waters Apartments*, $17 (efficiency apt.) to $60 a day for 3-bedroom beach house apartment. All these rates are reduced substantially from April 15 to December 15.

ARTS ... Nassau has a permanent painting exhibition at the Nassau Art Gallery. Art exhibitions are also staged at charity benefits.

BANKS ... Chase Manhattan Bank and First National City Bank of New York, among many, many others. Banking hours 9 to 1 on weekdays and 8:30 to 11 on Saturdays.

CALENDAR OF HOLIDAYS ... New Year's Day; Constitution Day, January 7; Good Friday; Easter Monday; Whitmonday; May 24, Commonwealth Day; the Queen's Birthday (celebrated by Proclamation); Labour Day, first Friday in June; August Bank Holiday (first Monday); October 12, Discovery Day; Christmas Day; December 26, Boxing Day.

CIGARETTES AND TOBACCO ... Nearly all American brands at Stateside prices. Fine English pipes and tobaccos.

CLIMATE ... The weather is warm and sunny and ideal for visiting any time of the year, although by tradition the social season is Christmas to Easter. Some winter evenings are cool.

CLUBS ... (Residential) Balmoral Club; Pilot House Club; Racquet Club; Coral Harbour Club; New Moon Club; Nassau Harbour Club and Loft House Club. (Non-residential) Bahamian Club; Nassau Yacht Club; Royal Nassau Sailing Club, Kiwanis, Lions and Rotary. For golf and tennis clubs, *see* SPORTS.

COMMON COURTESIES AND LOCAL CUSTOMS ... Abbreviated sundresses, very short shorts, and bra and halter ensembles should not be worn on the public streets. As in Britain, all traffic moves on the left-hand side of the road.

COMMUNICATIONS ... Nassau has 24-hour telephone service to every part of the globe. A 3-minute call to the U.S. costs from $4.50 to $7.50. Radio station ZNS broadcasts on 1540 and 1240 kc/s, and provides service to visiting yachtsmen by regularly scheduled bulletins. Airmail rate to U.S., one shilling (14¢) per half ounce.

CURRENCY ... The Bahamian pound based on the British sterling system is currently worth about $2.80 U.S., but American and Canadian dollars are acceptable generally.

CUSTOMS REGULATIONS AND DOCUMENTS REQUIRED FOR UNITED STATES CITIZENS ... No passports or visas are required, but you will need some proof of nationality. You may take in 200 cigarettes and 1 quart of liquor, unrestricted amounts of dollars, but not more than £25 in Bahamian, Bermudian, Jamaican or Bank of England notes.

DRUGSTORES ... Plentiful and modern, similar to those in the United States, but without soda fountains.

ELECTRIC CURRENT ... 115 volts, 60 cycles, A.C. All plugs and electrical appliances are the same as U.S. equipment.

FAUNA ... Raccoon on New Providence; wild hogs, wild horses, donkeys, cattle, sheep and goats on some of the islands; the iguana on Andros; many birds, including the flamingo, which is considered the national bird. For fish, *see* SPORTS.

FLORA ... Many varieties with never a time when some flowers are not in bloom. Peak blossom time is early summer with royal poinciana trees, Easter lilies, passion flowers. Poinsettias at Christmastime. Radiant hibiscus, oleander, bougainvillaea and other exotic flowers.

FOOD ... With the exception of some vegetables and fish, most food is imported from other countries. Meat from the United States, Canada and Australia. Bahamian specialty dishes include turtle soup and turtle pie, conch chowder, fish chowder, baked Nassau grouper with peas and rice, broiled native crawfish, or fillets of any of the famous Bahamian food fish, such as kingfish and dolphin. Be sure to try soursop ice cream and mango ice cream. Other desserts include coconut pie, pudding and ice cream, and guava duff.

GAMBLING ... During the winter season a Government-supervised Casino operates at Nassau's Bahamian Club, and a new casino has opened in the Lucayan Beach Hotel on Grand Bahama Island.

LANGUAGE ... English, of course, with British undertones.

LAUNDRY AND DRY CLEANING ... Excellent, modern.

LIQUOR ... All brands are available at prices much lower than at home. Scotch, for example, is about $3.50 a fifth, rum $1.50.

MEDICAL FACILITIES ... Modern hospitals, fine doctors.

MOTION PICTURES ... The *Shirley Street Theatre, Savoy* and the *Capitol* with first-run American pictures.

MUSIC ... There's a wealth of native music in the form of Bahamian folk songs, goombay and calypsos, heard nightly at the hotels, or in the night clubs and cabarets, or over the local radio station. During the winter season, well-known guest artists perform.

NIGHT CLUBS AND CABARETS ... On Bay Street are *Blackbeard's Tavern, Dirty Dick's Bar, Junkanoo Club* and the *Big Bamboo*. Native "over the hill" night spots include: *The Cat and the Fiddle Club, The Conch Shell, The Confidential Club, La Fin, The Silver Slipper Club, Drumbeat Club* and *Goombay Club*.

PHOTOGRAPHY ... Nassau is an excellent place to buy cameras and photo equipment. All types of film are available, also 24-hour developing service. Selling Japanese, Swiss and German cameras and equipment are Toogood's International Camera Store, John Bull, Moseley's Camera Shop and the Lightbourne Pharmacy.

RELIGION ... There are churches of 28 denominations in Nassau.

RESTAURANTS ... Nassau restaurants serve European, American and Bahamian foods. Try *Café Royal* in the world-famous gardens of the Royal Victoria Hotel, *The Buena Vista, Cumberland House* and *Sun-And*. Also worth trying: the *Red Lion Pub, Floridita, Grand Central, Poinciana, Riviera, The Golden Dragon, Rice House,* or *Harbour Moon* (for Chinese and American dishes). *Blackbeard's Tavern, Ba Ma Supper Club, The Big Bamboo, Howard Johnson's Restaurant* at the Nassau Beach Hotel, *Esquire Club Lounge, Ben Warry's, Purple Onion, Seven Seas. Black's Candy Kitchen* and the *Shell Restaurant,* two American-style soda fountains, also have restaurant service.

SHOPS AND STORES ... Nassau has many wonderful shops where you can buy top quality merchandise from the world over. Nassau prices are substantially lower than United States prices for such items as: U.S. golf balls, china, Irish linen, British tweeds, French perfume, Scottish plaids and tartans and German and Japanese cameras.

Shops selling some or all of these items are: Nassau Shop, West of England Store, Barry's, Park Store, Stewart's, Ambrosine, Mademoiselle, Sally and Vera's, Treasure Traders, Scottish Shop, Moseley's (books), Sue Nan Shop, Chinese Emporium, Paris Shop, Vanite, City Pharmacy, John Bull, General Hardware, Island Woodcrafts, Cole-Thompson Pharmacies, Stanley Toogood's International Camera Store, Vanity Fair, Linen Shop, Carousel, Lightbourne's Perfume and Camera Centre, Mayflower, Kelly's Hardware, Caprice, Sun 'n Sea, Island Shop, English China House, Moseley's Camera Shops, John S. George, Coral Reef, Sir Francis Peek, Dorothy McNab, Melita, Francise, The General Hardware, The Perfume Shop, Natcha's, Belinda, Johnson Brothers' Tortoise Shell Shop, Solomon's Mines, The Brass and Leather Shop, and Amanda Furs. Branches of many of these shops are found in Nassau hotels.

SPECTATOR SPORTS . . . Yachting regattas, local and international; championship-caliber golf and tennis tournaments; Bahamas-wide fishing tournaments; horse racing every Tuesday and Friday in winter at Hobby Horse Hall; boxing and wrestling at Nassau Stadium; cricket; soccer; rugby football; basketball; softball; water-skiing exhibitions. Champion sports car racing during Bahamas Speed Weeks in December.

SPORTS . . . Golf at the Nassau Golf Club; 18-hole course also at Coral Harbour; tennis at Racquet Club, Emerald Beach Hotel, Montagu Beach Hotel, British Colonial Hotel; badminton at the Nassau Stadium; spear-fishing; water-skiing; helmet diving conducted tours; sailboats, bicycles, motor bikes and cars for hire.

Fishing . . . The principal fighting game fish are amberjack, barracuda, bonefish, bonito, dolphin, grouper, jack, kingfish, mackerel, mako, blue marlin, white marlin, permit, sailfish, shark, snapper, tarpon, albacore tuna, Allison tuna (the mighty bluefin tuna which run off Bimini and Cat Cay each May and June), and the fighting wahoo, a game fish which, pound for pound, puts up the scrappiest fight of any fish. There are also crawfish and three different kinds of turtle. Throughout the year, visitors may compete in fishing tournaments.

TIME . . . Same as Eastern Standard Time.

TIPPING . . . Luggage porters are tipped 2/– (2 shillings) a bag; chambermaids from 3/– per day; 2/– for room service. If no service charge is included, tip waiter 15%-20% of the bill; 10% if charge is included. Beauticians are tipped 15% of the bill; 1/– for a barber. 1/– for gas-station attendant; from 5% of the fare for taxi drivers. Sixpence for shoeshine boy, washroom attendant, hat check.

TOURIST TAXES . . . $2 per person for air departure, children from 3 to 12 years $1. Same amounts for sea arrivals.

TRANSPORTATION . . . In U.S. currency: taxis, 56¢ for the first half mile and 17¢ each additional half mile for three persons or less; 49¢ each additional passenger; children under 10 half fare. Seven-passenger taxis rent for about $5 per hour; five-passenger taxis, about $4 per hour—half-price for each additional half hour. Picturesque horsedrawn carriages, 28¢ per mile or $2.80 per hour. Bicycles, $1 per hour, $2 per day, $10 per week. Motor scooter, $8 to $10 per day, $50 per week. Cars, $14 to $20 per day, $75 to $90 per week. Traffic moves on the left.

WATER . . . Excellent, but bottled waters available.

WHAT TO BUY . . . Woolens, tweeds, silver, doeskin gloves and doeskin fabric, English brushes, pipes, cameras and leather goods. Belgian, Irish and German crystal. French perfumes, cosmetics and lingerie, liquor, china and porcelain, tortoise-shell articles and, of course, the colorful native straw and sisal goods and shell jewelry.

WHAT TO WEAR . . . Lightweight summer clothes. Sports shirts and shorts or slacks for men; washable spectator dresses or sundresses for women; shirt-type blouses and shorts are quite acceptable for women, but no abbreviated dress is worn on public thoroughfares in Nassau. Bring swimsuits of course. Formal dress can be necessary for winter season from December 15 through Easter.

WHERE TO GO—SIGHTSEEING ...

Nassau ... You can take conducted sightseeing tours or go around on your own. A trip to Nassau's forts should be included. Fort Charlotte, with its eerie dungeons, about 1 mile west of Rawson Square, is the largest. It commands the western entrance to the harbor. Nassau's streets are lined with historic old churches and beautiful colonial houses and there are some interesting public buildings on Bay Street.

Blackbeard's Tower, now the ruin of an old watchtower, overlooks Tower Heights Village, 4 miles east of Nassau. Queen's Staircase, Elizabeth Avenue, is a flight of 66 steps said to be hewn out of solid rock by hand, and it leads to Fort Fincastle. Nearby on Bennett's Hill is the Water Tower, 126 feet high. Visitors may go to the top by elevator, where they will get a wonderful view of the city and harbor. See the flamingos at Ardastra Gardens. Paradise Beach, a 10-minute boat ride from Prince George's Wharf, is one of the most elegant and complete resort communities. Here are bath houses, cabañas, bar and restaurant. Visit the famous Sea Gardens, too.

Out Islands ... Island settlements scattered throughout the Bahamian archipelago are rapidly emerging as miniature resorts in their own right. There are scheduled and chartered air services, as well as regular mail boats from Nassau to the Out Islands. Unless otherwise noted, all rates given are winter rates.

Abaco ... Great and Little Abaco, northernmost of the Bahama Islands, are growing in popularity with both sportsmen and tourists. Unless otherwise stated, the following are American Plan (room and all meals). At Green Turtle Cay are *Bluff House,* $25 single, $45 double; *New Plymouth Inn,* $20 single, $32 double. Hopetown: *Elbow Cay Club,* single $20, double $39; *Coral Cottage,* $75 a week, no meals. Treasure Cay: *Sun-n-Sand Marina Hotel,* single $28, double $40; *Treasure Cay Inn,* $26-$34 single, $40-$46 double. Walker Cay: *Walker Cay Club,* single $20, double $40 with meals.

Andros ... The largest island of the Bahamas, 35 miles southwest of Nassau. Accommodations at Andros Town are: *Lighthouse Club,* $30-$40 single, $50-$60 double, American Plan.

Bimini ... Bimini, the nearest Bahamian island to the U.S. mainland, is regarded as "the gateway to the Bahamas" by the thousands of yachtsmen who make it their port of entry. Bimini is also famous for its big-game fishing, notably the annual tuna and marlin fishing, for its splendid bonefishing and fighters. Additional information on Bimini fishing can be obtained from the Executive Secretary of the Bimini Big Game Fishing Club. Accommodations include: *Anchors Aweigh Hotel,* $20-$30 single, $25-$35 double, European Plan. The new *Sunshine Inn* is $10-$12 single, $12-15 double. *Bimini Club and Hotel,* single $10 up, double $15 up. *The Compleat Angler,* $12 single, $16 double; *Seacrest Hotel,* $6 single, $8 double; *Brown's Hotel,* $8 single, $12 double; all European Plan.

Governor's Harbour, Eleuthera . . . This lovely Out Island town was the site of the first British attempt, in 1648, at a permanent settlement in the Bahamas. Today, Governor's Harbour is one of the most progressive of Out Island resorts, and is a year-round delight for visitors. Winter rates are: *Buccaneer Club,* $15 single, $30 double, with meals; *French Leave,* $35 single, $56 double, MAP.

Harbour Island, Eleuthera . . . This historic old settlement, known for its Pink Beach of coral sand, is just off the northeast tip of Eleuthera and offers modern accommodations in an ideal resort atmosphere. Winter American Plan rates are: *Little Boarding House,* $15 single, $30 double; *Pink Sands Club,* $20-$26 single, $40-$60 double; *Runaway Hill,* $18-$35 single, $35-$55 double; *Sunset Inn,* $14 single, $28 double; all AP.

The Current, Eleuthera . . . This picturesque settlement is adjacent to the cut where the tide boils through at a fast clip between Eleuthera and Current Island. *Current Club* rates $35 single, $48 double, with meals.

Rock Sound, Eleuthera . . . An old settlement is the site of the modern *Rock Sound Club,* a tiny resort on its own. Here are a saltwater swimming pool, golf course, tennis courts, guest cottages with private baths and fine food. Modified American Plan winter rates are: $30 single, $42-$50 double. Rock Sound's airport has a new 7,200-foot jet runway.

George Town, Exuma . . . Great and Little Exuma are the scene of the Bahamas' annual Out Island Regatta. Accommodations: *Club Peace and Plenty,* $30 single, $50 double; *Hoopers Bay Club,* $22 single, $42 double; both American Plan. Cottages are also available.

Grand Bahama . . . Only 68 miles east of Palm Beach, Grand Bahama is developing rapidly. The luxurious *Lucayan Beach Hotel* at Freeport features golf, golden sandy beaches and a smart gambling casino; from $44 single, $54 double, MAP. *King's Inn* at Freeport, adjoining an 18-hole golf course and sand beaches, is part of a developing community; doubles $16-$24, EP. At West End, the *Grand Bahama Hotel* is a complete vacation paradise, $27-$29 single, $38-$40 double, MAP.

Spanish Wells . . . A small scenic community just off the northern tip of Eleuthera. *St. George's Hotel,* $15 single, $30 double, and the new *Lloyds,* $42 single, $56 double; both American Plan.

SOURCES OF FURTHER INFORMATION . . . The Bahamas Ministry of Tourism is on Bay Street, Nassau. Pan American's office is on Mathew Ave. (Tel. 2-3394). Information also from the Bahamas Ministry of Tourism at 620 Fifth Ave., New York, N.Y., 10020; 1230 Palmolive Bldg., Chicago 60611; 1701 First National Bank Bldg., Miami 33131; 1406 Adolphus Hotel Arcade, Dallas 75202; 510 West 6 St., Los Angeles 90014; 707 Victory Bldg., 80 Richmond St. W., Toronto 1; and 5 Vigo St., Regent St., London, W.1, England.

NETHERLANDS ANTILLES

Oranjestad
ARUBA ISLAND
St. Nicholas

NETHERLANDS ANTILLES

CARIBBEAN   **Boca Tabla**
CURAÇAO
SEA   **BONAIRE ISLAND**
WILLEMSTAD
Piscadera Bay
Plesman   **Kralendijk**
Airfield

WEATHER IN CURAÇAO—Lat. N12°15′—Alt. approx. sea level

Temp.	JAN.	FEB.	MAR.	APR.	MAY	JUNE	JULY	AUG.	SEPT.	OCT.	NOV.	DEC.
Low	74°	74°	75°	76°	78°	78°	78°	78°	78°	77°	76°	75°
High	84°	85°	85°	86°	88°	88°	88°	88°	90°	89°	88°	88°
Average	79°	80°	80°	81°	83°	83°	83°	83°	84°	83°	82°	82°

LOCATION ... The territory of the Netherlands Antilles (formerly Netherlands West Indies) consists of the islands of Curaçao, Aruba and Bonaire off the coast of Venezuela and a group of small islands at the north end of the Leeward Islands 500 miles away.

CHARACTERISTICS ... Curaçao has the quaint fairytale charm of The Netherlands itself. The gabled houses and bridges are all part of the illusion. This is a wonderful spot to buy perfumes and other luxury items. Tiny Aruba combines shopping with heavenly beaches.

POPULATION ... Approximately 200,000, of which 130,000 live on the island of Curaçao. Aruba has about 60,000; Bonaire 6,000; and the three Windward Islands together, 4,000.

SIZE ... Curaçao is 38 miles long and 2½ to 7 miles wide. Aruba is 19 miles long and about 5 miles wide.

CAPITAL ... Willemstad, population about 50,000.

GOVERNMENT ... Formerly a Dutch colony, the Netherlands Antilles has been autonomous since 1954, an integral part of the Kingdom of The Netherlands with complete freedom in its internal affairs.

HOW TO GET THERE ... By Pan Am Jet Clipper nonstop to Curaçao, 6 hours from New York; Aruba is 7 hours by Pan Am direct from New York. By ship about 4 days from New York.

ACCOMMODATIONS ... Built above Curaçao's ancient waterfort with spectacular view is the fabulous air-conditioned *Curaçao Intercontinental* in the center of Willemstad, with beautiful terraces, gardens, dining rooms and a split-level swimming pool with portholes for spectators. Rates are from $23 double without meals between mid-

December and mid-April, about $4 less other times. Other good hotels include the *Americano,* which faces the harbour, rates $10-$13, double, without meals; *Hotel San Marco* in the business center, $12 double, without meals; *Park Hotel,* $10 per person, including meals. The *Avila* offers Old World charm with complete modern conveniences; has pool and private beach; $12 double, without meals. *Piscadera Bay Club,* which offers sea bathing, $17 double with breakfast. *Coral Cliff Hotel* on Santa Martha Bay features deep-sea fishing, $17 single, $25 double, without meals. *Hotel Biana* at the airport, $9.50 single, $14 double, with breakfast. In fast-developing Aruba there are complete luxury-resort facilities at the *Aruba Caribbean Hotel,* which has a casino, a night club with big-name performers, swimming pool, 1500-foot beach, all water sports, tennis and shuffleboard; $23-$27 single, $28-$32 double. The *Basi Ruti Hotel* on Palm Beach is also an atmospheric resort featuring water sports; $14-$20 single, $20-$26 double. The *Strand Hotel,* only 5 minutes from Oranjestad's shopping center, overlooks the Caribbean and has a pool, beach and night club; from $14 single, $22 double. Above rates are all European Plan and apply from December 16 to April 15; they are from $6 to $10 lower the rest of the year. There are also commercial hotels.

ARTS... The Curaçao Museum, housed in a restored building of old Dutch architecture, contains beautiful paintings, furniture, decorations and other antiques of past centuries, as well as exhibits of recent history of the island. Specimens of all trees and plants found on the island grow in its spacious gardens.

CIGARETTES AND TOBACCO... Same as at home.

CLIMATE... The sun shines almost continually and cool breezes prevail. The ideal time to visit is the whole year round.

COMMUNICATIONS... Telephone calls to continental U.S. are from 5 to 8 guilders per minute; less on Sunday. In local currency, airmail postage to the U.S. is 20¢ for letters, 15¢ for postcards.

CURRENCY... There are 100 cents in a guilder, which is worth about U.S. 53¢. Most stores accept United States currency.

CUSTOMS REGULATIONS AND DOCUMENTS REQUIRED FOR UNITED STATES CITIZENS... Birth certificate or naturalization papers and ticket to leave. Re-entry permit for resident aliens. No passport, no visa. Smallpox vaccination certificate required on entry. Visitors who stay 24 hours or less need no documents except proof of nationality. Small quantities of tobacco products and liquor for personal use allowed in duty free.

DRUGSTORES... Modern as at home. Soda fountains.

ELECTRIC CURRENT... 120 volts, A.C., 50 cycles (60 in Aruba).

FOOD... Creole food is served on request, but mostly you'll find Dutch, Spanish, Oriental and American food.

GAMBLING... There's a casino in Curaçao's Intercontinental Hotel, and in the Aruba Caribbean Hotel.

LANGUAGE... Dutch, Spanish and English. Also a native language called *papiamento.*

LAUNDRY AND DRY CLEANING... Modern and good.

LIQUOR . . . Curaçao is the famous local liqueur. There are also Holland gin, Holland beer, Antillian beer and imported whiskies to be had at more reasonable prices than at home.

MEDICAL FACILITIES . . . Completely up to date.

MOTION PICTURES . . . American and European films.

NIGHT CLUBS AND CABARETS . . . Entertainment at the larger hotels in both Curaçao and Aruba.

PHOTOGRAPHY . . . Large choice of cameras and photo equipment (European, Japanese and American) at prices lower than in the United States.

RELIGION . . . Protestant, Roman Catholic churches and Jewish synagogues, one of which is the oldest in the Americas.

RESTAURANTS . . . The award-winning *Fort Nassau Restaurant* overlooking harbor for excellent food. The *Curaçao Intercontinental* for elegant international cuisine. The *Avila Hotel* also has fine food. The *Lido* for quick lunches. The *Lam Yuen* and *Formosa* for Chinese dishes. *Piscadera Bay Club* for luncheon and dinner in a seabreeze, and *San Marco Hotel* for Italian food.

SHOPS AND STORES . . . Curaçao and Aruba, because of a low import duty of 3.3% on nearly all goods, are among the greatest shopping centers in the Western Hemisphere. *See* WHAT TO BUY.

SPECTATOR SPORTS . . . Tennis, basketball, softball and baseball. Soccer at Curaçao's Rif Stadium and many club fields.

SPORTS . . . In Curaçao, golf at the Shell Golf Club, tennis and basketball at the Kwiek Club, Curaçao Sport, Van Engelen Club and Piscadera Bay Club. Also fishing, horseback riding, soccer, baseball and sailing. Scuba and snorkeling equipment and fishing tackle may be rented. In Aruba, golf at the Aruba Golf Club.

TIME . . . 1 hour later than Eastern Standard Time.

TIPPING . . . About the usual 10 to 15%.

TRANSPORTATION . . . Before taking a taxi it is wise to know whether the driver is quoting the fare in American currency. Ask the driver for a copy of the official tariff. For all rides in town, taxi fares increase 50% between 10 P.M. and 6 A.M. For all trips out of town, fares are 25% higher between 10 P.M. and midnight and 50% higher after that. Station-wagon fares are lower than taxi fares, but you should arrange the fare with the driver before starting off. There is good bus service, too. Self-drive cars from $8 per day; no mileage charge.

WATER . . . Water is safe to drink right from the tap.

WHAT TO BUY . . . European cameras and photographic accessories, jewelry, liquor and liqueurs (among them the locally made Curaçao Liqueur). Swiss watches can be purchased here cheaper than any other place in the world. French perfumes (all the famous makes) are very cheap. Silk and carved ivory from the Orient, Brazilian and Argentine leather goods, Portuguese embroideries and laces, Spanish shawls, Irish linen, Panama hats. Delft Blue porcelain, silverware and brassware. Dutch dolls are good for souvenirs.

WHAT TO WEAR . . . Lightweight summer clothing all year.

WHERE TO GO—SIGHTSEEING . . .

Curaçao . . . Willemstad, with its gabled roofs and narrow buildings, looks like The Netherlands. There are many ancient buildings to be seen in the city itself. You should go to see the oldest Protestant church on the Islands, built in 1769, located on the square right behind Government House. The synagogue dates back to 1732. You will be interested in seeing Franklin D. Roosevelt House, the mansion and offices of the American Consul, located on the top of Ararat Hill, from which you get a magnificent view of Willemstad and the sea.

The business as well as the old residential section of the city have magnificent examples of Dutch colonial architecture; the suburbs of Willemstad and the housing projects adjacent to the oil refinery have strikingly modern residences amidst well-kept gardens.

Less than 2 miles from Willemstad's shopping center is the swank resort of Piscadera Bay. Here is beautiful *Piscadera Bay Club*.

Take a trip across the pontoon bridge called the Queen Emma to Punda, the oldest section of Willemstad, and see the floating market, small Caribbean schooners filled with fruits and vegetables from the neighboring Latin-American republics. Next you are in Fort Amsterdam, where the official residence of the Governor of The Netherlands Antilles is located. Fifteen minutes from town by car is the historical Jewish Cemetery. You should take a trip (55 minutes by car) to the famous coral cavern of Boca Tabla. Atmospheric dining at *Jan Kock,* old colonial house, 20 minutes from Willemstad.

Aruba . . . The island of Aruba, though smaller than Curaçao, is an important oil-refining center. The capital, Oranjestad, is typically Dutch. Aruba's Palm Beach is 3 miles long and one of the finest in the West Indies. Bathing and sailing here are excellent. This is also one of the great fishing centers of the island. Oranjestad, as well as Willemstad, has a wonderful shopping center and a beautiful residential section of modern homes, club buildings, etc., painted in the gayest of colors. There are sightseeing tours around the island. The *Bali* and *Trocadero* restaurants on the harbor are excellent; try *Olde Molen,* too.

Bonaire . . . Bonaire, the island of the flamingoes, is virtually a virgin playground for skindivers and *the* island for people who desire real rest and relaxation in unspoiled surroundings. *Flamingo Beach Club Hotel,* a bungalow resort hotel, and *Bonaire Hotel,* with a new casino, are recommended. There are also guest houses. Fishing is excellent here and a sightseeing trip is worthwhile.

SOURCES OF FURTHER INFORMATION . . . The Curaçao Tourist Bureau, Willemstad, Curaçao; the Bonaire Tourist Bureau, Bonaire; the Aruba Tourist Bureau, Oranjestad, Aruba, S. E. L. Maduro and Sons in Aruba, Bonaire, Curaçao and St. Maarten are agents for Pan Am. In New York: the Curaçao (and Bonaire) Information Center, 1270 Ave. of Americas; Aruba Tourist Bureau, 609 Fifth Avenue.

PUERTO RICO

WEATHER IN SAN JUAN—Lat. N18°28′—Alt. 20′

Temp.	JAN.	FEB.	MAR.	APR.	MAY	JUNE	JULY	AUG.	SEPT.	OCT.	NOV.	DEC.
Low	70°	69°	70°	71°	73°	74°	75°	75°	75°	75°	73°	71°
High	80°	80°	81°	82°	84°	85°	85°	85°	86°	86°	84°	81°
Average	75°	75°	75°	77°	79°	80°	80°	81°	81°	80°	79°	76°

LOCATION . . . Puerto Rico lies between the Atlantic Ocean and the Caribbean. Santo Domingo is about 45 miles to the west, and St. Thomas, Virgin Islands, is 75 miles to the east of San Juan.

CHARACTERISTICS . . . The sun shines all year, the beaches are wonderful, the hotels among the most luxurious, the food familiar or exotic depending on your taste. Yet you have a wonderful feeling of being at home in Puerto Rico despite the fact that chaperones are still the fashion and coffee and banana trees flourish before your eyes. Fishermen will be particularly happy there.

POPULATION . . . 2,600,000.

SIZE . . . 100 miles long and 35 miles wide, Puerto Rico has an area of 3,435 square miles, about 1½ times the size of Delaware.

CAPITAL . . . San Juan, with a population of 600,000.

GOVERNMENT . . . The island became a possession of the United States after the Spanish-American War of 1898. In 1948, the Hon. Luis Muñoz Marín became the first elected governor. Puerto Rico became a Commonwealth in July 1952, with a Constitution giving the island full autonomy. A Resident Commissioner in Washington has a voice but no vote in Congress.

HOW TO GET THERE . . . By Pan Am Jet nonstop from New York, 3½ hours; from Miami nonstop, 2¼ hours. Service also from Boston, Philadelphia and Baltimore-Washington, and direct flights from Europe, Central and South America.

ACCOMMODATIONS . . . San Juan offers a wide range of accommodations from luxurious beachfront hotels to attractive, modestly priced guest houses. The 460-room *Caribe Hilton* offers a balcony and ocean view with every room; $25-$37 single, $29-$41 double. Also in the Condado section are the new *San Jeronimo Hilton* facing its sister hotel across the waters of an inlet, same rates; the new *Da Vinci,* truly elegant and charming, is $20 single, $26 double; the colorful new *Flamboyan* overlooks the sea and Condado Lagoon, single $27-$33, double $32-$34; the Spanish-style *Condado Beach,* $20-$34 single, $24-$39 double; the *Puerto Rico Sheraton* on the ocean, $16-$34 single, $21-$39 double; and the dramatic *La Concha* with its shell-shaped night club, $25-$35 single, $30-$40 double. In the Isla Verda section are the 400-room *Americana,* $25-$38 single, $29-$42 double; *El San Juan Hotel* on 15 ocean-front acres, $27-$37 single, $26-$42 double; and the attractive *Holiday Inn,* $17-$25 single, $22-$36 double. These hotels are air-conditioned, have bars, restaurants, their own beaches or pools, evening entertainment and sports facilities. In the heart of Old San Juan is the beautiful *El Convento,* a restored 17th-century Carmelite convent furnished with lovely antiques, $20-$30 single, $25-$35 double. *La Rada,* on the edge of San Juan's Condado Lagoon, has 100 rooms and suites, some with kitchenettes, $20-$32 single, $25-$35 double. *El Miramar Charterhouse* is equidistant from beaches and commercial centers in San Juan and offers spectacular views of the capital from its rooftop restaurant, $15-$21 single, $22-$28 double. The *Pierre Hotel,* Swiss-operated, has rates of $19 single, $25 double; the *Normandie,* near Muñoz Rivera Park, is $14-$18 single, $16-$20 double. Smaller tourist hotels in San Juan include the *Condado Lagoon,* $17-$19 single, $21-$23 double. Twenty miles west of San Juan are two lavish hotels that are complete resorts in every way. The *Dorado Hilton* has an 18-hole golf course, among other facilities for sports and entertainment; MAP rates are $45-$55 single, $55-$65 double. The *Dorado Beach* has two 18-hole golf courses, all kinds of entertainment including movies and a Fiesta Jíbara every Wednesday evening; MAP rates are $50-$75 single, $60-$85 double. San Juan also has some 30 guest houses, many of which are on the beachfront. Others are in residential areas close to good public beaches. *See* SOURCES OF FURTHER INFORMATION. Hotels "out on the island" are listed under WHERE TO GO. Hotel rates quoted are for December 15-May 1; lower the rest of the year.

ARTS ... In Rio Piedras, the University of Puerto Rico has a good museum on the main quadrangle. In Old San Juan are the Galería Colibrí, Galería Campeche and Casa del Arte. The Institute of Puerto Rican Culture is interesting, and there is a notable collection of rare books in La Casa del Libro.

BANKS ... Besides several Stateside representatives, such as First National City and Chase Manhattan, there are good local banks.

CALENDAR OF HOLIDAYS ... The same as ours, plus such celebrations as January 6, Three Kings Day; January 11, Hostos' Birthday; March 22, Abolition of Slavery; July 17, Muñoz Rivera's Birthday; July 25, Commonwealth Day; November 19, Discovery of Puerto Rico. The Christmas festivities are famous.

CIGARETTES AND TOBACCO ... Well-known brands are available, but prices are a little higher than at home.

CLIMATE ... There are no extremes of heat or cold. The hills and mountains are always several degrees cooler than San Juan. With about 355 sunny days a year, Puerto Rico is ideal for vacationing the year round. December through May is especially recommended.

CLUBS ... Rotary, Lions, Elks, American Legion, Propeller Club, Exchange Club, Knights of Columbus, besides a large number of private clubs such as *Club Equestre* which sponsors an annual horse show.

COMMON COURTESIES AND LOCAL CUSTOMS ... Some of Puerto Rico's newspapers are printed in Spanish but there are one daily and one weekly in English. Also, there is no color line or segregation in the sense that we know them at home. "Out on the island" means anywhere outside San Juan and its environs.

COMMUNICATIONS ... To call the U.S. or any other country, dial 128; dial 123 for Information. Airmail, 8¢ per ounce.

CURRENCY ... Same as in the United States.

CUSTOMS REGULATIONS AND DOCUMENTS REQUIRED FOR UNITED STATES CITIZENS ... You do not need passports or visa, but proof of nationality required for return home. Anything you buy in other Caribbean spots is declarable there as part of the United States. Vaccination certificate not required unless certain other areas are included in trip.

DRUGSTORES ... Same as at home.

ELECTRIC CURRENT ... Same as in the United States.

FAUNA ... Wonderful tropical birds, doves, mockingbirds, cuckoos, flycatchers.

FLORA ... All sorts of tropical flowers, orchids, bougainvillaea, hibiscus, mahogany trees, pineapple and other tropical fruits.

FOOD ... Puerto Rican food is definitely Spanish. Famous are *arroz con pollo; asopao,* a soupy dish of rice cooked with shrimp or chicken; *pasteles,* grated plantains with a meat filling wrapped in plantain leaves and boiled; *lechón asado,* a barbecued pig; *jueyes,* fresh land crabs, shelled and boiled; and *pastelillos,* thin dough filled with meat or cheese and deep-fat fried. Good American, French, Chinese, Hungarian, Jewish and Italian food, too.

GAMBLING ... State lottery drawings every Monday; gambling casinos in the larger hotels. There is horse racing with pari-mutuel betting.

LANGUAGE ... Although Spanish is the mother tongue, English is spoken and understood throughout the island.

LAUNDRY AND DRY CLEANING ... Good at the hotels and in principal cities.

LIQUOR ... Puerto Rico is the proud Rum Capital of the world, sending its fine, light-bodied rums to all parts of the globe. Among the best-known brands are Bacardi, Rum Superior Puerto Rico, Don Q, Ron Rico, Merito and Carioca; brandies and whiskies are also available.

MEDICAL FACILITIES . . . There are good American and Puerto Rican doctors and hospitals.

MOTION PICTURES . . . There are many good theaters showing the latest Hollywood, European and Mexican pictures.

MUSIC . . . Puerto Rican music is distinctive and ear-catching. The *danza, plena,* and *aguinaldos* are the most representative. They are usually heard at religious festivals, home gatherings, private parties and sometimes at night clubs. Records of this music are easily obtainable at record shops. Important musical events include the Casals Festival and the Puerto Rico Symphony Orchestra season.

NIGHT CLUBS AND CABARETS . . . You can find almost any sort of night life you want in and around San Juan, from the lavish clubs and restaurants of the luxury hotels to the native cabarets. Especially popular are the *Ocho Puertas, La Carreta, La Danza, La Botella, The Sands and The Sea, The Owl, El Patio del Fauno Zaragozana, La Copa, La Ronda, Caesar's Pad, Las Cuevas de Altamira* and *El Calypso.*

PHOTOGRAPHY . . . Camera equipment and all types of film are available at prices slightly higher than in the United States.

RELIGION . . . Although Puerto Rico is predominantly Roman Catholic, there are a number of Protestant churches; also a synagogue and Christian Science reading room.

RESTAURANTS AND BARS . . . Most famous and oldest is *la Mallorquina* in Old San Juan, noted for its delicious seafood and Spanish dishes. Be sure to have *asopao* here. Continental in atmosphere and food are the *Swiss Chalet, Zipperle's Bavarian Tavern, Top of the First, El Hato Rey, La Cueva, Mexico in Puerto Rico, Cathay Chinese Restaurant, Four Winds and Seven Seas* in El San Juan Hotel, *Salón Ruiseñor, Le Carrousel, Trader Vic's* and *Rotisserie Castillo* at the Caribe-Hilton, *Rib Room* atop the Miramar Charterhouse and *La Hacienda. Mago's Saxony Steak House* for excellent charcoal steaks. You'll find Italian food at *La Estrella de Italia, La Góndola* and *Italian Village.* For an intimate luncheon or dinner (American food) tiny *El Burrito* in Old San Juan is delightful. Hotels serve cosmopolitan as well as Puerto Rican cooking, but if you want native atmosphere and food drive to *Mario's* in Isla Verde; *Patio Español* downtown. Other favorites: *El Cotillón Steak House,* near the Hilton, *Fontville,* Isla Verde, Cobian's *Rancho Hotel* in Aguas Buenas, *Ladi's* in Salinas, *La Palma* in Mayaguez, *Hotel Meliá* in Ponce, *La Parguera* guest house at La Parguera and *El Mediterráneo* in Old San Juan. Try also *El Carioca* bar, the *Gaucho Room* and *El Nilo.* New and good are *Gatsby's, La Barrachina, A Spot in the Sun.*

SHOPS AND STORES . . . In addition to modern department stores and gift shops in the leading hotels, there are Martha Sleeper's Casa Cavanaugh, Mary Vela's, Triana's and other small stores that carry a variety of native-made sports clothes. Nancy Nance for needlework. Notre Dame Industrial School is especially good for fine embroidered linens. Imports are featured at Guisti Caribbean Shop and fine tropical furniture at Humphrey Associates. Saint-Amour Boutique near La Rada Hotel is also good. Out on the island there's the Doll House in San Germán, and the famous market in Ponce.

SPECTATOR SPORTS . . . On Saturday and Sunday, cockfights are held in San Juan and every little village. The Galleras (pits) Canta Gallo in Santurce are easily reached as is Tres Palmas Gallera on the Bayamon Road. Horse racing on holidays, Wednesday, Friday and Sunday afternoons at El Comandante; baseball at the new Estadio Municipal Hiram Bithorn is also very popular; tennis tournaments are held at Rio Piedras Tennis Courts, *Caribe Hilton, Condado Beach* and *Dorado Beach* hotels. Boxing, wrestling and basketball at Sixto Escobar Park and the new stadium.

SPORTS . . . There are two 9-hole golf courses: The Berwind Country Club and Fort Brook at El Morro, in the capital area. Guest cards are available upon request. The two courses at the *Dorado Beach* hotel rank with the world's finest. Out on the island there are 9-hole courses at some of the Sugar Centrals, where you may obtain permis-.sion to play. The big hotels have their own tennis courts, and guest privileges are accorded at some of the private baths.

Swimming, of course, is wonderful. There are pools and beaches at the hotels. Escambrón Beach Club in San Juan has cabañas; Luquillo Beach, one hour's drive from San Juan, is magnificent. Skeet and trap shooting is available at the Club Metropolitano de Tiro. Horses may be hired for trips out on the island.

Fishing, as you might guess, is excellent. In San Juan, charter boats are available through Captain Art Wills (Tel. 723-0616). The charge for a charter boat for deep-sea fishing, including crew, tackle and bait, is $75 a day. Off the east coast, boats are available at Las Croabas, a fishing village at the tip of the island, between Luquillo and Fajardo. Rental is about $30 a day. On the southern coast, complete facilities for deep-sea fishing are available at Villa Parguera.

THEATERS . . . Ballet and plays in Spanish at the old *Tapia Theater* in San Juan. The *Little Theater of Puerto Rico* puts on frequent productions.

TIME . . . Noon in New York is 1 P.M. in Puerto Rico.

TIPPING . . . About the same scale as at home.

TRANSPORTATION . . . All authorized taxis carry green license plates and are metered, with rates starting at 25¢ for the first 1/5 mile and 5¢ for each additional 1/5 mile. There is good bus service within the metropolitan area, but it is wise to avoid buses during the rush hours. There is also daily bus service between San Juan and Mayaguez. *Público* cars provide inexpensive transportation throughout the island. They are similar to the jitneys which used to be found in many cities in the United States. There are numerous car-rental agencies; rates as low as $5 a day plus 5¢ a mile.

WATER . . . Perfectly safe throughout the island.

WHAT TO BUY . . . Hand-made and embroidered blouses, lingerie, mahogany bowls and souvenirs; men's linen suits. Don't forget there's an internal revenue tax on rum which must be paid at the airport upon departure on direct flights to the United States. Woven baskets are inexpensive and beautiful. Bamboo products and furniture made of native woods are good buys.

WHAT TO WEAR . . . You never need heavy clothes in San Juan. Bring summer cottons and silks. Some summer dinner and evening things for hotel wear. If you are going into the hills, take a topcoat and some medium-weight clothes. Men will need tropical suits, sports jackets, slacks and beach attire. Black or white dinner jackets.

WHERE TO GO—SIGHTSEEING . . .

San Juan . . . Old San Juan itself is an islet, connected to the modern sections of Condado, Santurce, Hato Rey and Rio Piedras through a series of bridges. In San Juan visit El Morro (1539), one of the most interesting forts in the Western Hemisphere and actually a historic site; the old fortress of San Gerónimo, now housing the fascinating Museum of Military History; La Fortaleza (1533), built to protect the entrance of San Juan harbor and now used as the Governor's residence; the Cathedral of San Juan Bautista (1527), where the remains of Don Juan Ponce de León, the "Gran Conquistador," lie. San Cristobal Fort ends the land protection of the walled city of San Juan.

Trips Near By . . . You will want to go to Luquillo Beach, about 27 miles east of San Juan, and El Yunque, a tropical rain forest which is utterly beautiful. Luquillo, a wonderful beach, nestles at its foot. At Las Croabas, the sumptuous *El Conquistador Hotel* overlooks the village and bay from a height of 280 feet; there is a funicular to the beach. American Plan rates are $37 single, $58 double.

A 3-day tour of the island (with or without a driver-guide) takes in most of the highlights of Puerto Rico. Aside from the varied scenery, a trip around the island will turn up such piquant sights as the glimpse of a large goat perched on top of a post in a pretty plaza, or an unscheduled cockfight initiated by the fowl instead of their owners. Somewhat less off the beaten track are visits to rum distilleries, pineapple plantations and the world's largest radiotelescope near Arecibo.

Ponce . . . Here is the spectacular new *El Ponce Intercontinental,* a complete resort which overlooks a superb view; rates $14-$24 single, $18-$28 double. The *Meliá*, a good downtown hotel, has rates from $11 single, $15 double. A visit to Ponce is worth while if only to see its famous fire station: red-and-black striped and splashed with yellow and green designs. It has an opera bouffe quality that is almost unbelievable. Make a tour of the needlework center of Mayaguez, where the handsome new *Mayaguez Hilton* offers facilities for fine deep-sea fishing; year-round rates are $10-$12 single, $14-$17 double. Nearby is historic San Germán, with one of the oldest Christian chapels in the New World, and the Inter-American University.

Phosphorescent Bay, a short boat ride from Parguera on the south coast, turns to liquid diamonds at night. *Villa Parguera* ($5-$10 single, $7-$14 double) provides deep-sea fishing facilities and an unforgettable trip by motor launch over the glittering bay.

SOURCES OF FURTHER INFORMATION . . . Puerto Rico Visitors Bureau in San Juan and at 666 Fifth Avenue, New York. Pan Am's San Juan office is at Calle Recinto Sur, No. 307 (Tel. 723-8000).

ST. LUCIA

WEATHER IN ST. LUCIA—Lat. N13°55′—Alt. approx. sea level

Temp.	JAN.	FEB.	MAR.	APR.	MAY	JUNE	JULY	AUG.	SEPT.	OCT.	NOV.	DEC.
Low	71°	71°	72°	73°	74°	75°	75°	74°	74°	74°	73°	73°
High	83°	83°	84°	86°	87°	86°	87°	88°	88°	87°	86°	84°
Average	77°	77°	78°	79°	80°	80°	81°	81°	81°	81°	80°	78°

LOCATION ... St. Lucia, the second largest of the Windward Islands, lies south of Martinique and is directly in the path of the trade winds on the route of the sailing clippers of long ago.

CHARACTERISTICS ... This delightful island, one of the Lesser Antilles, is French in heritage, British in character. The towns of Castries and Soufrière have a quiet charm which appeals to the visitor who wants to get away from regular tourist attractions. There is splendid bathing on uncluttered white sand beaches, excellent fishing, some magnificent scenery and a combination of mountains and sea which is irresistible. Winter months are dry and sunny but not excessively hot. An ideal spot for a different vacation.

POPULATION ... About 100,000, of which 30,000 live in Castries.

SIZE ... 27 miles long and about 14 miles wide, the island has an area of 238 square miles and a coastline of 150 miles.

CAPITAL ... Castries, one of the most beautiful harbors in the West Indies, with its green hills on each side covered with flamingo trees, allamanda vines, hibiscus and other tropical shrubs. Hotels and residences are located on the sides of the hill overlooking the harbor.

GOVERNMENT ... A British colony.

HOW TO GET THERE ... By Pan American from New York to St. Lucia in 6 hours, via Puerto Rico and Antigua. Steamship lines make stops at principal Windward and Leeward Island ports and there is motor-vessel service available between the islands.

ACCOMMODATIONS ... Newest is the *St. Lucia Beach Hotel,* 6 miles from Castries, on a superb beach; air-conditioned rooms with private balconies; nightly dancing and entertainment; boating, fishing, water sports. Rates per person are $24 double, $28 single, American Plan. Other top hotels are the *Yacht Haven* and the *Marigot des Roseaux Club and Hotel* on Marigot Bay; average rates are $25 single, $35 double, AP. *Hotel St. Antoine* is located high on a hill with a magnificent view of the capital and the harbor; quiet, charming West Indies atmosphere and excellent food, including native dishes. Rates from $14 per person, American Plan. The *Villa Hotel,* also on a hill, is newer and closer to town, also with excellent food. Rates from $10 up per person, American Plan. About 2 miles from Castries on the beach is the *Blue Waters Hotel,* $12 to $20 per person, American Plan. Famous for its 1½-pound steaks, the new *Reef Hotel* has a marina and attracts yachtsmen; from $10 per person. A 10% service charge is added to hotel bills. Lower rates prevail between April 16 and December 15.

CLUBS . . . The Vigie Club and Castries Club are private but cards and tennis may be arranged upon proper introduction. (Inquire at your hotel.) Other clubs are Palm Beach Club, Blue Danube, Gaiety, The Club Calabash and the Seven Seas.

CURRENCY . . . British West Indies dollar, worth about U.S. 60¢. Travelers checks convert better than currency.

CUSTOMS REGULATIONS AND DOCUMENTS REQUIRED FOR UNITED STATES CITIZENS . . . Regulations are the same as for other British West Indies islands. Proof of citizenship required.

DRUGSTORES . . . Mostly British pharmaceuticals.

WHAT TO WEAR . . . Washable summer clothes, cotton; slacks and shorts. Evening clothes not essential. Lightweight topcoats.

WHERE TO GO—SIGHTSEEING . . .

Castries . . . Castries, the capital, is a good harbor flanked by the imposing hills of Vigie and Morne Fortuné. There are interesting drives, good beaches, splendid fishing. Drive to Gros Islet and take a launch to Pigeon Island. The drive to Soufrière is picturesque and includes a stop at Sulphur Springs, noted for their medicinal value.

Soufrière, the next largest town to Castries, is in the shadow of two peaks, Gros Piton and Petit Piton, which rise from the sea to more than 2,500 feet. The land rises behind the town to the live crater of the volcano for which the town is named, and you can go by car to within 50 yards of its bubbling sulphur springs. The Piton peaks may be climbed by experienced climbers. The view is magnificent and rewarding. Other things to see on this charming island include a drive to the top of Morne Fortuné, where a visit should be made to Fort Charlotte. Take a drive along Barre-de-l'Isle. There is wonderful scenery, beautiful tropical foliage, and a pervasive charm which make a visit to this spot memorable.

SOURCES OF FURTHER INFORMATION . . . There is a St. Lucia Tourist Board in Castries. Peter and Co., Ltd., are agents for Pan American there.

ST. MAARTEN

LOCATION ... In the Windward Islands, east of Puerto Rico and the Virgin Islands on the ever-summer latitude of 18 degrees.

CHARACTERISTICS ... In 1648, so the story goes, a walking contest decided how much of the island would be Dutch (St. Maarten) and how much would be French (St. Martin). Ever since then, the two nations have lived in complete compatibility, with only a modest marker to indicate when you're leaving one half and entering the other. This happy attitude is symbolic of all phases of life on "The Beach Island of the Caribbean."

POPULATION ... 3,700 in St. Maarten; 5,550 in St. Martin.

SIZE ... St. Maarten is 17 square miles; St. Martin is 20 square miles. The island's most distant points are only about 8½ miles apart.

CAPITAL ... Philipsburg, capital of St. Maarten, is uniquely situated on a narrow sandbar separating Great Bay and Great Salt Pond, and is overlooked by low, green mountains at either end of the bar. Marigot, capital of St. Martin, is on an open bay.

GOVERNMENT ... St. Maarten is a dependency of Curaçao; St. Martin is a dependency of Guadeloupe.

HOW TO GET THERE ... By Pan American Clipper, 5¾ hours from New York via St. Croix and St. Thomas; 35 minutes from St. Croix.

ACCOMMODATIONS ... Rates in all St. Maarten hotels include all meals, which are in the hearty Dutch tradition, and scrupulous Dutch cleanliness is noticeable everywhere. Winter rates apply from mid-December to mid-April. *Little Bay Hotel,* overlooking the Caribbean, is within walking distance of Philipsburg, and features a full program of dancing and entertainment, movies and beach parties. Also at the hotel are a gambling casino and gift shop. Deep-sea fishing and smaller boats and cars are on hand for rental. Winter rates about $30 single, $44 double; summer rates from $18 single, $30 double. The *Seaview Hotel,* on the beach in Philipsburg, provides excellent service; year around rates: single from $12, double from $22. The *Pasang-grahan,* formerly the Government Guesthouse, offers true West Indian atmosphere; winter rates from $16 single, $24 double. *Mary's Fancy,* in the valley of Cul-de-Sac, is a modernized old estate with a fresh-water swimming pool and transportation to beaches. Winter rates $22 single, $32 double; summer $14 single, $24 double. The smart new *Caravanserai* adjoins Maho Beach; $28 single, $40 double in winter; $20 single, $28 double in summer. The *Prince's Quarter Hotel*, on a pretty hill, from $15 single, $25 double in winter and $12 single, $17.50 double in summer. Good guest houses are *Hunter's House* and *Captain Hodge's*. Hotels add 10% service charges to cover tipping.

CURRENCY ... The guilder, valued at U.S. 53¢.

CUSTOMS REGULATIONS AND DOCUMENTS REQUIRED FOR UNITED STATES CITIZENS ... Proof of U.S. citizenship is required, and a through or return ticket; smallpox vaccination certificate.

LANGUAGE ... Dutch and French, but everyone speaks English, too.

SPORTS ... Year-round water temperatures range from 75 to 80 degrees, and the immense sandy beaches are ideal for swimming. Snorkeling and water-skiing gear may be rented. Game fishing is excellent, and sailboats, complete with crew, rent for only about $2.12 for the first hour, half that for each additional hour. Bicycles rent for around $2 a day. (There are taxis, too, of course, and cars for hire.) Cockfighting is a lively spectator sport on the French side of the island.

WHAT TO BUY ... At low free-port prices, shops in Philipsburg offer lovely Dutch silver and pewter, Delft china, sporting goods, perfumes, liquor, tortoise shell and wood items. In Marigot, free-port prices also apply to French brandies, champagnes, liqueurs and perfumes. Cigarettes cost $1.50 a carton.

WHERE TO GO—SIGHTSEEING ...

The picturesque ruins of 17th-century Fort Amsterdam recall a less peaceful era. Peter Stuyvesant, later to become governor of New York, lost his leg in a 1644 expedition to recapture the island, and is commemorated in a remarkable stained-glass window in the cocktail lounge of the Little Bay Hotel. Circling lovely Simpson Bay on the western side of the island near the airport is a luxurious housing development. The whole island is an idyllic panorama of soft valleys, colorful vegetation, green hills and magnificent beaches. Windward Islands Airways have twice-weekly trips to St. Eustatius and Saba, two even tinier Dutch islands nearby. During the American Revolution, St. Eustatius was the booming transshipment port where blockade runners picked up arms and supplies for the colonies. Saba, which consists in entirety of an extinct volcano, shoots straight up out of the sea, and approaching the island in a boat is something of an adventure, as passengers and freight must be lightered ashore. Saba's principal village, The Bottom, is actually 800 feet above sea level, and is an enchanting collection of tidy little houses set in brilliant gardens. Well worth a trip (by plane) to see.

SOURCES OF FURTHER INFORMATION ... Netherlands Windward Islands Information Center, 1270 Ave. of the Americas, New York, N.Y. 10020. S. E. L. Maduro & Sons, Inc., are agents for Pan American in Philipsburg (Tel. 2202).

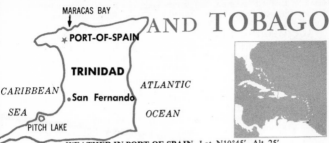

TRINIDAD AND TOBAGO

WEATHER IN PORT-OF-SPAIN—Lat. N10°45′—Alt. 25′

Temp.	JAN.	FEB.	MAR.	APR.	MAY	JUNE	JULY	AUG.	SEPT.	OCT.	NOV.	DEC.
Low	71°	71°	71°	73°	74°	74°	72°	73°	73°	73°	73°	72°
High	85°	86°	87°	88°	88°	87°	87°	87°	88°	88°	87°	86°
Average	78°	78°	79°	80°	81°	80°	80°	80°	80°	80°	80°	79°
Days of Rain	14	8	8	7	10	17	20	21	18	16	17	16

LOCATION ... Most southerly of the West Indies, the island of Trinidad is only about 10 miles from the Paria peninsula of Venezuela. The tiny island of Tobago lies about 20 miles northeast of Trinidad.

CHARACTERISTICS ... Trinidad is the most colorful and polyglot of all the West Indian islands. Here you may see an East Indian woman in a sari with a ring in her nose, Hindus in traditional dress, calypso-singing Negroes, Portuguese, Spaniards and Chinese. There are Moslem mosques, Hindu temples and bazaars. There are wonderful roads, beautiful scenery and some fine bathing beaches. The climate is splendid and the nights are cool.

The island of Tobago, sometimes called Robinson Crusoe's Island, is where you will find the magnificent Bird of Paradise Sanctuary, a whole coastful of wonderful beaches, small but modern hotels and an unspoiled quality which exists in very few places elsewhere in the Caribbean. Tobago can be reached by plane or boat from Trinidad.

POPULATION ... Trinidad has a population of 800,000. Tobago has a population of about 33,333.

SIZE ... Trinidad, 50 miles long and 30 miles wide, is about the size of Rhode Island. Tobago is 26 miles long, about 7 miles wide.

CAPITAL ... Port-of-Spain, with a population of about 93,950.

GOVERNMENT ... Trinidad and Tobago, independent members of the British Commonwealth, are combined for administrative purposes.

HOW TO GET THERE ... By Pan Am Jet Clipper, New York nonstop to Port-of-Spain, 5¾ hours elapsed time. Frequent Pan Am Jet service also from Miami, the West Coast, South American ports. By ship, about 4½ days from New York.

ACCOMMODATIONS ... The "upside-down" *Trinidad Hilton* hotel nestles against a steep hill, its entrance lobby on top and balconied guest rooms below looking out over the lush green expanse of the Savannah; winter rates from $21, double. The *Queen's Park Hotel* is on the opposite side of the Savannah, which is the setting for Port-of-Spain's sports activities; double from $9. A modern hotel, the *Normandie*, specializes in French cuisine and has a swimming pool; double from $13. Other good hotels are the *Pelican Inn, Bagshot, Bergerac, Simpsons Shorelands, Bretton Hall*—all with winter rates of about $13, European Plan. There are many guest houses in Port-of-Spain and the surrounding countryside. Most of them are charming, and all have very reasonable rates. The *Mt. St. Benedict Guest House* has a superb view. Pan American's *Piarco Guest House*, at the airport, is air-conditioned and has a swimming pool; double from $13. The *Bel Air Hotel* is also at the airport and also has a pool.

ARTS ... Royal Victoria Institute Museum; Trinidad Art Centre; National Museum and Art Gallery.

BANKS ... Barclay's Bank; Canadian Imperial Bank of Commerce; Royal Bank of Canada; Bank of Trinidad; Bank of Nova Scotia; Bank of London and Montreal; Chase Manhattan Bank.

CALENDAR OF HOLIDAYS ... New Year's Day; pre-Lenten Carnival; Good Friday; Easter Monday; May Day; Corpus Christi; Whitmonday; First Monday in August; Independence Day, August 31; Christmas; December 26 (Boxing Day).

Two important events of interest to tourists are the calypso season and the Moslem Hosein Festival. Calypso begins in early January and the Festival of Hosein takes place on the 6th, 7th and 8th day after the Mohammedan New Year. Other events of interest are: agricultural and horticultural shows and the Roman Catholic Feast of La Divina Pastora (*Siparia Fête*). Carnival is celebrated uproariously on the two days preceding Lent. It is one of the gayest and most colorful carnivals in the world.

CIGARETTES ... Most brands of American cigarettes are available. English cigarettes are plentiful, as are locally made brands. 200 cigarettes or equivalent allowed in duty free.

CLIMATE ... January to March is the ideal time in Trinidad. The weather is cooler then, but even in the hotter months the nights are cool. The rainy season is June to December; although the rains are heavy they are of short duration.

CLUBS ... Trinidad Yacht Club, American Women's Club, Canadian Women's Club, Rotary Club, the Trinidad Country Club (cards may be arranged; inquire of Pan American), the YWCA, the Palm Beach Aquatic Club. *See also* SPORTS.

COMMON COURTESIES AND LOCAL CUSTOMS ... Since Trinidad is in the British Commonwealth, afternoon tea is a ritual.

COMMUNICATIONS . . . In local currency, a 3-minute phone call to the States costs from $9 to $15 (U.S. $5.40-$9); airmail postage is 25¢ W.I. for a letter, 12¢ for a postcard.

CURRENCY . . . Trinidad's monetary unit is the W.I. dollar, worth about 58¢ U.S., or $1.71 W.I. to the U.S. dollar.

The Bureau de Change, at King's Wharf Passenger Center, issues W.I. currency in special envelopes in exchange for United States and Canadian currency at the prevailing official rate of exchange. The Bureau reconverts unspent balances of W.I. currency into United States currency provided that (a) *the original exchange transaction was made at the Bureau* and (b) surplus W.I. currency does not exceed the amount originally issued. *Original* envelopes *must* be presented when reconverting.

CUSTOMS REGULATIONS AND DOCUMENTS REQUIRED FOR UNITED STATES CITIZENS . . . No passports or visas, only proof of nationality for visits up to 6 months. Yellow fever inoculation required for entry from some areas. Smallpox vaccination certificate for re-entry to the United States. You may bring in 1 quart of spirits or wine. No more than $48 W.I. or £10 sterling in notes may be taken in or out. Departure tax is $2 W.I.

DRUGSTORES . . . Chemists' shops in Port-of-Spain carry well-known brands of merchandise.

ELECTRIC CURRENT . . . 115/230 volts, 60 cycles, A.C.

FAUNA . . . Wonderful birds, including the famous *"Qu'est-ce-qu'il dit"* (What does he say?) bird which repeats the question several times. There are deer and small game, too. The many species of hummingbirds have caused the place to be called "Land of the Hummingbird." There is a small zoo situated in the Emperor Valley, Royal Botanic Gardens, Port-of-Spain.

FLORA . . . The place is ablaze with flowers of all descriptions. In the wonderful Botanic Gardens there are cabbage palms, strychnine plants, flytrap flowers, orchids. All over the island there are lemon grass, bamboo trees, coconut palms, para rubber trees, Ceylon willows, century plants, red flowering immortelles which blaze all over the island during the early months of the year, *Poui* trees, which have golden and pink blossoms, and hundreds of brilliant tropical blooms. Anthurium lilies are beautiful here.

FOOD . . . Creole cooking is most popular in Trinidad. But it's possible to have international fare às well. Specialties include *sancoche* and *callalloo*, excellent soups, both of them. *Pastelles*, made of meat and cornflour dough, are wonderful. Crabmeat served in shells and tiny oysters are famous. Excellent Chinese food is available, and because of the large East Indian population, curries are famous, as are *roti* and other Indian dishes which are very hot and spicy. Of course, fresh fruit abounds; avocado pear, sapodillas, mangoes.

GAMBLING . . . Horse racing is very popular. Pari-mutuel and forecast betting and sweepstakes. There are 9 meetings throughout the year; December-January: 5 days—Queen's Park Savannah, Port-of-Spain. February-March: 2 days—Shirvan Park, Tobago. March-April

(Easter): 5 days—Union Park, San Fernando. May: 2 days—Arima. June-July: 5 days—Queen's Park Savannah, Port-of-Spain. August-September: 5 days—Santa Rosa, Arima. October: 2 days—New Union Park, San Fernando. October-November: 2 days—Shirvan Park, Tobago.

LANGUAGE . . . English, of course, is the native tongue. But French, Spanish, Hindi, Chinese and other languages are heard here.

LAUNDRY AND DRY CLEANING . . . Laundry is good. Dry cleaning good, with 8-hour service. Prices compare favorably with those in the United States. The Sanitary Laundry and the Trinidad Steam Laundry, both reliable, have branches throughout the island.

LIQUOR . . . Rum is the national drink. Trinidad is the home of Angostura Bitters. Many rum drinks cost about U.S. 20¢ and they are wonderful. Whisky, brandies and gins are available at prices lower than in the United States. British gin flourishes here, but Planter's Punch is the thing. Bar hours—8 A.M to 8 P.M. Hotel bar hours—9 A.M. to midnight.

MEDICAL FACILITIES . . . Excellent nursing homes are available. The General Hospital in Port-of-Spain is modern and the San Fernando hospital is one of the largest and most modern in the West Indies. Good English-trained doctors are available.

MOTION PICTURES . . . There are seven main cinemas: the *Astor;* the *Empire;* the *de Luxe;* the *Globe;* the *Strand;* the *Roxy, Hi-Way* and *Starlite* (drive-ins)—which show American and English films.

MUSIC . . . Trinidad is the home of the calypso, and the more recent innovation, the steel band, which consists of steel drums of varying tones beaten to all types of rhythm. The calypso singer, as everyone knows, takes a topical theme and weaves it into an extemporaneous song. In January, calypso tents spring up in the city and various calypso singers vie with each other in a "war."

NIGHT CLUBS AND CABARETS . . . Gaiety and individuality make Trinidad's night spots memorable. There is dancing nightly at the *Trinidad Hilton,* the *Penthouse, Miramar, Gay Cavalier, El Matador, Krab Hole Club* and *Tropical Hotel.*

PHOTOGRAPHY . . . Photographic equipment is in good supply in Port-of-Spain. Special 24-hour service for film developing may be had in Port-of-Spain at J. N. Harriman, 61 Independence Square; Chan's Photographers, 92 Frederick Street; Pereira and Co., Ltd., 24 Frederick Street; W. C. Ross and Co., Ltd., 27 Frederick Street.

RELIGION . . . Because of the polyglot nature of the population, one finds churches of almost all faiths here—Hindu temples, Moslem mosques, Jewish synagogues, Catholic and Protestant churches.

RESTAURANTS . . . Mostly in hotels, especially in Pan American's Piarco Guest House, and Normandie Hotel for French cooking. The *Pool Terrace* at the Trinidad Hilton is very smart for lunch; the *Inn-and-Out* cafeteria. For Chinese food: *Kimling, Kowloon, Ying King, Lotus.* Try the *Belvedere* on Lady Chancellor Hill overlooking Port-of-Spain, the *Hummingbird, Chez Paul* and the *Bongo Room* of the Tropical Hotel.

Trinidad and Tobago allow you to rest and relax. These tourists picnic amid Tobago's tropical beauty spots and excellent swimming conditions.

SHOPS AND STORES ... Frederick Street and Independence Square are the best places to find luxury goods at low prices collected from all over Europe and the Orient. Tailors in Trinidad's Syrian colony do good work on men's made-to-measure suits of fine imported materials for from $40 to $76. The market area in Scarborough, Tobago, has some fascinating little shops. Tourist Board offices on both islands can provide lists of stores that will send liquor and perfume purchases "in bond" to your plane or ship.

SPECTATOR SPORTS ... Horse racing at four racetracks. Boxing and basketball. Also cricket, soccer, hockey, water polo.

SPORTS ... Golf at St. Andrew's Golf Club; tennis at the Tranquillity Square Lawn Tennis Club; swimming and tennis at the Trinidad Country Club. There is good deep-sea and underwater fishing, yachting, and duck shooting in season. Special sports events at Eastertime.

TIME ... Noon in Trinidad is 11 A.M. in New York.

TRANSPORTATION ... There are motorbuses and taxis, as well as drive-yourself car services and round-island tours.

WATER ... Water is safe to drink at hotels.

WHAT TO BUY ... French perfumes, gloves, British woolens, leather goods, china, Swiss watches, Irish linens, German cameras, also jewelry, silver, native crafts. Liquors and Trinidad rum at half the usual price. Recordings of steel bands and calypso music.

WHAT TO WEAR ... Tropical clothes, cottons, beachwear. Take a raincoat in summer. Men will want summer light-weight suits, slacks, sports jackets, dinner jacket, and beach attire.

WHERE TO GO—SIGHTSEEING ...

Trinidad is one of the most colorful of the West Indies. Its population is a mixture of East Indian, English, Negro, Chinese, Spanish, French and Portuguese—which in itself makes the country fascinating. You will want to see the Pitch Lake (asphalt) which is said to be nearly 300 feet deep. You can walk on the lake without sinking. Trinidad asphalt has paved some of the most famous streets in the world. Take a drive over the beautiful North Coast Road and swim at Maracas Bay, and at Las Cuevas, 6 miles farther on. The return drive over "The Saddle" is famed for its bamboo groves. There are fascinating teak forests and thousands of scarlet ibis in the Caroni Bird Sanctuary open from July to October.

At Couva near the shore of the Gulf of Paria is one of the largest sugar factories in the British Commonwealth. There are good beaches in Trinidad, most of which are not within easy reach of Port-of-Spain. But the scenery everywhere is magnificent. Inland, the mountains rise to a height of 3,000 feet and afford wonderful views of the valleys and the sea. There are miniature waterfalls in the Diego Martin and Maracas Valleys.

Tobago . . . Tobago may be reached from Port-of-Spain by coastal boat or by plane. Allegedly the setting of the story of Robinson Crusoe, the island is famous for its tropical birds, particularly the bird of paradise, which is found on Ingram Island off the northern tip of Tobago.

Accommodations are all on the American Plan. (Winter rates per person quoted are in U.S. dollars.) The *Arnos Vale Beach Hotel,* situated on a 450-acre estate is 7 miles from Scarborough, the chief town on the island. It has a central house, cottages, swimming pool and beach house. Riding horses for hire, cabin cruiser and sailboat for fishing or exploring the coast, a coral beach. Rates from $25. *Bluehaven* also offers every comfort and convenience, first-class cuisine. There are a fishing launch and cruiser available to guests. Rates from $18. The *Robinson Crusoe,* on Rockley Bay, has its own beach, drive-yourself cars for rent. Rates from $12. *Bacolet Inn* consists of small bungalows surrounding the main building. Rates from $12. Others include the *Bird of Paradise Inn* ($15), at Speyside, 26 miles from Scarborough, and *Crown Point Hotel* (from $22), near Crown Point Airport and the *Castle Cove Beach Hotel* (from $10 MAP). Hotels feature beach barbecues, exuberant native orchestras.

You will want to drive to Man O'War Bay, a beautiful natural bay with hills reaching to the water's edge. Here is a wonderful sandy beach. Pigeon Point is one of the best bathing beaches in the West Indies. You may swim here at the *Aquatic Club.* There are cabañas, but cabañas thatched with palm leaves. It costs $1 W.I. to swim here, on introduction by a member. (Inquire of Pan American.) From a glass-bottomed boat, or equipped with sea goggles, you may see fascinating marine life in the Coral Sea Gardens at Buccoo Reef and enjoy a swim in the cool water of the *Nylon Pool.* Exciting game fishing with rod, net, or spear. The Easter goat races at Buccoo Point are an island tradition.

SOURCES OF FURTHER INFORMATION . . . Trinidad and Tobago Tourist Board at 56 Frederick St., Port-of-Spain; Administration Building, Scarborough, Tobago. New York office, 48 East 43 Street, New York, N.Y. 10017. Pan American's office is at 12 Abercromby Street, Port-of-Spain (Tel. 6161).

VIRGIN ISLANDS

ST. THOMAS I.   ST. JOHN I.

           CANEEL BAY

CHARLOTTE AMALIE

VIRGIN ISLANDS

CARIBBEAN SEA

ST. CROIX I.   **Christiansted**

Frederiksted

WEATHER IN ST. THOMAS & ST. CROIX—Lat. N18°20′—Alt. Approx. sea level

Temp.	JAN.	FEB.	MAR.	APR.	MAY	JUNE	JULY	AUG.	SEPT.	OCT.	NOV.	DEC.
Low	69°	70°	70°	71°	74°	75°	76°	75°	74°	74°	73°	70°
High	84°	84°	84°	85°	86°	87°	88°	89°	88°	87°	85°	84°
Average	77°	77°	77°	78°	80°	81°	82°	82°	81°	81°	79°	77°

LOCATION ... The Virgin Islands of the United States consist of the islands of St. Thomas, St. Croix, St. John and about 50 nearby islets. St. Thomas is 75 miles east of San Juan, Puerto Rico, St. Croix is 40 miles south of St. Thomas and St. John.

CHARACTERISTICS ... These perfectly delightful islands, which the United States acquired by purchase from Denmark, offer excellent vacation facilities. Since they are a "duty-free port," it is possible to purchase imports from all over the world at a fraction of their costs in the United States. There are new luxury hotels and older ones which are small but charming. The Virgin Islands have a delightful climate and a charm all their own. They are hay-fever free too.

POPULATION ... 36,000 inhabitants, 19,000 of whom live on St. Thomas, 16,000 on St. Croix and about 1,000 on St. John.

SIZE ... St. Thomas has an area of 32 square miles, St. Croix, 82 square miles, and St. John, 18 square miles.

CAPITAL ... Charlotte Amalie with 13,000 population is the capital of St. Thomas. Christiansted is the capital of St. Croix.

GOVERNMENT ... The islands are governed by a legislative assembly made up of 11 locally elected senators and a governor appointed by the President of the United States.

HOW TO GET THERE ... By Pan American Clipper nonstop to St. Croix, 3¾ hours from New York, 3½ hours from Miami via San Juan. For St. Thomas fly Pan Am to San Juan (3⅓ hours from New York, or 2¼ hours from Miami) with direct connections for the flight to St. Thomas. St. Croix and St. Thomas are about 25 minutes apart by air.

ACCOMMODATIONS . . . There are new hotels everywhere. Unless otherwise mentioned, rates quoted are the *minimum,* single and double, Modified American Plan (breakfast and dinner), December through April. They are lower the rest of the year. On St. Thomas: charming *Bluebeard's Castle,* $44 and $54, overlooks town and sea. The luxurious *Virgin Isle Hilton,* $44 and $54, has a beautiful pool, two cork tennis courts, dancing nightly, each room with private balcony. The *Water Isle Hotel and Beach Club,* on an island in the harbor, has fine facilities for snorkeling, sailing, spear fishing; $22 and $36. *Pineapple Beach Club,* on the east coast, offers both sea and pool swimming; $32 and $50. *Morning Star Beach Resort* has luxuriously appointed beach facilities; $20 and $25, European Plan. The elegant *Pelican Beach Club* is quietly secluded; $40 double, breakfast only. *Sapphire Bay Beach Club* is 5 miles from town; $22 and $26, EP. The new *Pavilions & Pools* offers complete apartments, each with its own swimming pool and maid service; $30 and $38, EP. *Shibui Hotel* is a colony of attractive Japanese-style cottages with a view; $50 double, EP. Downtown is the famous *Hotel 1829* with good food; $18 and $32. *Grand Hotel,* also central, is a commercial hotel on European Plan; from $10 single, $12 double. The *Caribbean Beach,* $26 and $38, is near the airport. Rates at *Yacht Haven Cottage Resort* are $33 and $45. There are also many very good guest houses, such as *Galleon House, Miller's Manor* and *Adams 1799 House,* which accommodate a limited number of guests from about $6, including breakfast. More expensive are the *Harbor View, Island Beachcomber* and *Dorothea Beach Club.*

St. Croix, Christiansted area: The *Buccaneer Hotel,* with beautiful beach, $24 and $42. *Hotel on the Cay* with main house and cottages, where guests are rowed in a boat from Christiansted wharf, $44 double. *Grapetree Bay Hotel & Villas* on a 750-acre estate; $30 and $42. *St. Croix by the Sea,* with beach and pool; $32 and $42. *St. Croix Beach Hotel* has air-conditioned beach-front lanai suites; $27 and $41. *Tamarind Reef Hotel;* $40-$45 double. *Cruzana Club* manor house; $16 and $20.

Christiansted Town: Newest hotels are the *Golden Roc,* $20-$25, and *Queen's Quarter,* $30-$40. Conveniently located is *King's Alley Hotel,* $25 and $32, EP. *Club Comanche,* $14 and $28. *Pink Fancy Apartments,* $100-$130 weekly. *Mahogany Inn,* $14-28 with breakfast; doubles only. Cane Bay on the north shore midway between the two towns has several small quiet cottage colonies with cooking facilities, such as *Cane Bay Plantation Cottages,* $30 and $42; *Estate Belvedere,* $100-$135 weekly; *The Waves,* $125 weekly; *Village at Cane Bay,* $20 a day double; and *Diamond Fancy,* $125 weekly.

Frederiksted area: Newest are the *Cottages by the Sea,* $95-$125 weekly; *Irvin Town House,* $150 weekly; *Liberty Hall,* $20 a day, EP; and *Royal Dane Hotel,* $24 and $38, MAP. Housekeeping facilities at *Sunset Beach Cottages,* $20-$30. *Estate Good Hope,* with beach, $44 and $52, MAP. *Clover Crest Hotel,* with pool, $26 and $42. *La Grange Guest House,* $34 and $40. *Sprat Hall,* with beach, $22 and $40, American Plan.

Caneel Bay Plantation, on tiny St. John, is completely de luxe; $38 and $50, American Plan. *Cruz Bay Cottages* and *Holiday Homes* have bungalows from $90 weekly. American Plan rates at *Lille Maho* guest house are $18 and $27.50.

Little Dix Bay, on Virgin Gorda in the British V.I., is excitingly new and unusual; from $45 single, from $60 double, American Plan.

ARTS ... St. Croix's collection of pre-Columbian Arawak and Carib Indian relics in Whim Great House. St. Thomas has a museum, in Beretta Center off Main Street, with interesting displays pertinent to the islands' 7 centuries of colorful history.

BANKS ... In both St. Thomas and St. Croix, the Virgin Islands National Bank, Chase Manhattan Bank, Bank of Nova Scotia.

CALENDAR OF HOLIDAYS ... Besides all the ones we observe at home, the Islands have a few of their own: March 31, Transfer Day (the day the Islands were taken over from the Danes), Carnival— 3 days of holiday (a real festival with street dancing, parades, floats, steel bands, calypso singers, crowning of king and queen). Carnival is usually celebrated during the last week in April. June 22, Organic Act Day; July 25, Supplication Day; two Thanksgivings, one the same as at home, the other October 25 in thanksgiving for the Islands' freedom from hurricanes (a hurricane has not been reported since 1928); November 1, Liberty Day; December 26, Christmas Festival.

CIGARETTES ... American cigarettes are only $1.60 a carton.

CLIMATE ... Not the usual tropical rainy seasons, but occasional sunshowers. The temperature averages about 80 degrees and varies little from day to night and season to season. Constant trade winds keep the humidity down.

COMMON COURTESIES AND LOCAL CUSTOMS ... Brief shorts are frowned upon. Walking shorts are accepted for men and women during day but ladies are more appreciated in female attire.

COMMUNICATIONS ... Telephone calls to the U.S. are $3 a minute; $2.10 for a 10-word cablegram. Postage rates same as U.S.

CURRENCY ... United States money is used.

DRUGSTORES ... Several on both St. Thomas and St. Croix.

FAUNA ... Wild deer, doves and mongooses.

FLORA ... Magnificently colored hibiscus, oleanders, bougain-villaea and orchids. Also tropical trees: banana, mamee, cocoa, papaya, orange, tamarind, lemon, lime, sapodilla, mahogany, turpentine.

ELECTRIC CURRENT ... 110 and 120 volts, A.C.; no problem.

FOOD ... In some places they serve native Creole and European dishes, but for the most part the hotels and the restaurants specialize in typical American food, charcoal-broiled steaks, and seafood.

GAMBLING ... There is a legal lottery with monthly drawing.

LANGUAGE ... English, of course. Some Spanish and Creole French are also spoken.

LAUNDRY AND DRY CLEANING ... There are several good

laundries and dry-cleaning places on both St. Thomas and St. Croix.

LIQUOR ... Any brand of liquor at the lowest prices: Scotch for $2.50 a fifth and up, excellent cognac for $3.75, rum about $1.25 a bottle. In the bars try a *Cruzan Morning* cocktail.

MEDICAL FACILITIES ... There is a Government-owned hospital with a capable staff on each of the 3 islands.

MOTION PICTURES ... In St. Thomas *Center Theater* is air-conditioned. Christiansted has the air-conditioned *Alexander Theater*.

MUSIC ... Native scratch bands, steel bands and calypso.

NIGHT CLUBS ... Leading hotels feature entertainment and dancing. Among the better known on St. Thomas are: *Virgin Isle Hilton, Bluebeard's, Yacht Haven.* Night clubs include: *The Loft, Katie's, The Fallen Angel, The Black Patch, The St. Thomas Club, Backstreet* and *Sebastian's*. On St. Croix, in Christiansted: *Buccaneer, Grapetree Bay, St. Croix by the Sea, Club Comanche, Queen's Quarters*. In Frederiksted: *Magic Isle Beach Club, Seven Flags, Persian Virgin*.

PHOTOGRAPHY ... Black-and-white and color film and photo equipment are available. Developing service is good and reasonable.

RELIGION ... While the Virgin Islands are predominantly Roman Catholic and Lutheran, there are churches of other denominations, and the second-oldest synagogue in the hemisphere.

RESTAURANTS ... The larger hotels offer buffet lunches and terrace dining, often with entertainment. Smaller hotels, guest houses and beach resorts all offer good dining with special dishes, barbecues, etc., on certain nights. In the center of Charlotte Amalie the air-conditioned *Left Bank* and the *Harbor View* (overlooking the town) are outstanding. The *Grand Hotel* gallery is fun for snacks. Among others along the waterfront, *Sebastian's* and *Carousel* have excellent cuisines. For country dining, *Lord Rumbottom's*, 3 miles from town, is excellent. All have bars. Dinner in the better places averages $5.50. See local "This Week" newspaper for details on these and other places. On St. Croix, Christiansted: *Pelican Cove Beach Club, The Office, The Stone Balloon* and *Duke's Manor*. In Frederiksted: *Magic Isle, Persian Virgin, The Yardarm*.

STORES AND SHOPS ... There are 102 enticing shops in Charlotte Amalie, most of them along Main Street and its quaint little side streets, especially Palm Passage and Beretta Center. *See* WHAT TO BUY.

In Christiansted go to International Shop for the Virgin Island Character Dolls. Try Continental, Inc., Island Sport Shop, Danish House, Compass Rose, Little Switzerland, Carib Cellars, Vickys, Cavanaugh, Island Imports and King's Alley with its many small shops. In Frederiksted, Florhall Gift Shop, Alexander Moorhead, Mary O'Neil's and Cavanaugh's Butik.

SPECTATOR SPORTS ... Baseball, cricket and basketball. Horse racing in St. Thomas and St. Croix and cockfighting in St. Croix.

SPORTS ... Deep-sea fishing, spear fishing; lobster diving; conch diving; sailing in yawls, sloops and schooners; motor cruises; yachting; horseback riding; tennis. In St. Thomas there's a 9-hole golf

Luxury goods from all over the world are sold at free port prices in quaint shops near the harbor in Charlotte Amalie.

Bluebeard's Hill provides a magnificent view of the harbor and colorful buildings of Charlotte Amalie, capital of St. Thomas.

course, swimming at Morning Star, Lindberg beach on the Caribbean, or Magen's Bay and Sapphire Bay Beach Club on the Atlantic. New on St. Croix is the spectacular Fountain Valley Golf Course, designed by Robert Trent Jones, and the beautiful, recently developed Davis Bay Beach. Also swimming at Cramer's Park, Fort Louise Augusta, Sandy Point and West End beaches, golf and tennis at Estate Carlton, tennis at Hotel Buccaneer.

TIME ... Noon in the Islands is 11 A.M. in New York.

TIPPING ... Same as at home.

TRANSPORTATION ... There are cars to hire with or without a chauffeur and conducted tours can be made by car.

WATER ... Hotels usually provide safer drinking water than the ordinary tap water.

WHAT TO BUY ... This is truly a shopper's paradise. Because it is a free port, you can buy things for much less than at home, such as: Danish, American, English and Scandinavian silverware; Peruvian, Mexican, Danish and Guatemalan silver jewelry; Scandinavian crystal and ceramics; French perfumes; Florentine, Mexican and Guatemalan leather goods; English woolen goods; mahogany, tortoiseshell, bead and sea jewelry; coral and cameos; liquors; bay rum; Italian linens and alabasters; knickknacks from Haiti, Puerto Rico and Tortola.

WHAT TO WEAR ... For women, light summer dresses, sports clothes, sweaters and maybe one cocktail dress; and if you are staying in one of the better hotels, a formal gown. For men, sports clothes, lightweight suits (hats are seldom worn), tropical shorts. Jacket and tie are required in certain restaurants.

WHERE TO GO—SIGHTSEEING ...

St. Thomas ... You'll want to visit the French Village, where the people are descendants of the early French settlers. Here is the beautiful shrine of St. Anne, which overlooks the village. Drake's Seat is another place to see. It is reported that this is where Sir Francis Drake, the famous navigator, sat while he was charting the channels and passages of the Islands. Take a trip up the street of 99 Steps on Government Hill, where Government House, the official residence of the Governor, is located, also, the magnificent administration building. There is an ancient Danish cemetery; the tombs were built of conch shells cemented together and in most cases brightly painted. Some of them even have the faces of the people sculptured on them. The dungeons of Old Fort Christian, built in 1671, are another historic sight. See St. Peter and St. Paul's Church with its magnificent altar, and All Saints Anglican Church, which has an organ over 100 years old. The District Courthouse in Emancipation Park is where the proclamation was issued freeing the slaves in 1848. There are many legends about Bluebeard's Hill and Castle. You can take a trip in a glass-bottomed boat that operates daily and get a wonderful view of marine life. Ride the new 1000-foot aerial tramway up Flagg Hill for a stupendous view of sea and distant islands.

St. Croix... The island of St. Croix is the largest of the Virgin Islands and fast becoming a major resort, although it is an agricultural island deriving its revenue principally from sugar cane, cattle ranches, and rum distillation. The Federal National Park Reserve includes on twice-daily free tours the following historical sites: the old Fort Christiansted dating back to 1760; the Steeple Building; the Lutheran Church with tombstones on the floor and in the walls (official Danish Government Church); Government House; the newly furnished Reception Hall with replicas of original Danish Government furnishings. You'll also enjoy the interesting archways and decorative architecture; the Christiansted Wharf and downtown business area; trading schooners at the wharf; the St. Croix Museum; Alexander Hamilton Store where Alexander Hamilton worked as a boy; Rachael Lavien Monument at Grange (mother of Alexander Hamilton); East End of Island, most easterly point in U.S.; the Bethlehem Sugar Factory; cane fields; windmills dotting the island; old ruins of sugar estates; Salt River, where Columbus first landed in the Virgin Islands and had his first battle with Carib Indians. Go to Buck Island with its beautiful beaches, and Butler's Bay. Here snorkelers follow the fantastic new Underwater Trail, 250 yards long, through coral reefs about 12 feet below the surface. See the old Frederiksted Fort. Sailing and fishing boats are available for a day's outing.

St. John... There are daily boats to the island of St. John (½ hour) and day package tours for visits to the Virgin Islands National Park and Trunk Bay, an outstanding beach, and to Caneel Bay.

SOURCES OF FURTHER INFORMATION ... The Chambers of Commerce and offices of the Department of Commerce Visitors Bureau, in St. Thomas and at Christiansted. Virgin Islands Government Tourist Information office at 16 W. 49 St., New York, N.Y. 10020. Pan American offices on both St. Thomas and St. Croix.

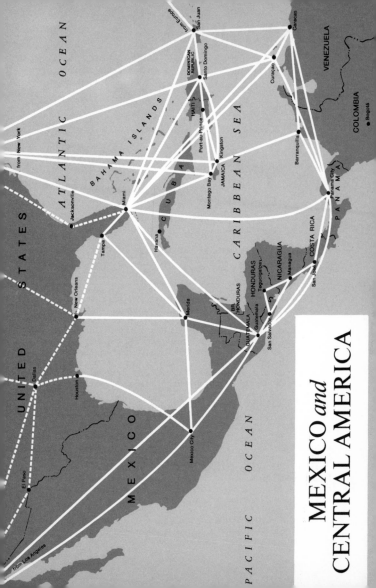

MEXICO *and*
CENTRAL AMERICA

COSTA RICA

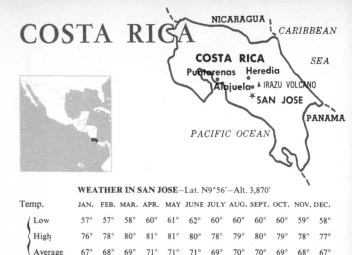

WEATHER IN SAN JOSE—Lat. N9°56′—Alt. 3,870′

Temp.	JAN.	FEB.	MAR.	APR.	MAY	JUNE	JULY	AUG.	SEPT.	OCT.	NOV.	DEC.
Low	57°	57°	58°	60°	61°	62°	60°	60°	60°	60°	59°	58°
High	76°	78°	80°	81°	81°	80°	78°	79°	80°	79°	78°	77°
Average	67°	68°	69°	71°	71°	71°	69°	70°	70°	69°	68°	67°
Days of Rain	2	2	2	5	19	21	19	20	24	24	18	7

LOCATION ... Costa Rica lies between Nicaragua and Panamá, bordered on the east by the Caribbean and on the west by the Pacific Ocean.

CHARACTERISTICS ... Its cleanliness, ideal climate, beautiful scenery, restful atmosphere and hospitality offer special attractions to the tourist. Its cities are quaint and friendly. The charm of the country lies mainly in its colorful countryside. Costa Rica has the highest percentage of literacy in the Latin American republics. In fact, it has more school teachers than soldiers. The people are friendly and helpful.

POPULATION ... 1,500,000 inhabitants.

SIZE ... 19,655 square miles. It is 288 miles long; from 75 to 175 miles wide.

CAPITAL ... San José City, with 115,669 inhabitants.

GOVERNMENT ... A republic. Its President is elected by the people for a four-year period.

HOW TO GET THERE ... By Pan Am Clipper direct from Houston via Mexico City and Guatemala in 6 hours or from San Francisco, Miami or New Orleans via Guatemala. About 1 hour by Clipper from Managua, 1 hour from Panamá. Airport bus fare is 1 colón, taxi 6.65 colones.

ACCOMMODATIONS ... San José has many good hotels; the largest is the *Gran Hotel Costa Rica* with 130 beautifully furnished rooms with private bath, located in the heart of the city. Rates are

$7-$10 single, $12-$16 double. *Hotel Europa,* recently rebuilt in modern design, has 50 rooms and is famous for its excellent cuisine. Rates start at $8.50. The *Balmoral* is located in the downtown section and has 80 modern, well-appointed rooms. Rates start at $7. The new *Royal Dutch Hotel* is conveniently located. Rates are from $7.50. Single rates at *Hotel Amstel,* which features a Dutch cuisine, start at $6. *Pensión Canada,* known for good food, and the *Hotel Plaza* have singles from $5.

ARTS ... The National Museum, located at the antique Bella Vista Fort in San José City, contains interesting collections of Indian relics in gold, pottery and stone from the ancient civilization which existed long before the Spaniards came to Costa Rica. Closed Mondays.

BANKS ... Banco Nacional de Costa Rica, Banco de Costa Rica and Banco Anglo Costarricense have affiliations with U.S. banks. Travelers checks may be cashed anywhere, and there are currency-exchange facilities at the airport.

CALENDAR OF HOLIDAYS ... The public holidays are: January 1, New Year's Day; March 19, Feast of St. Joseph; Thursday and Friday, Easter festivals; April 11, Anniversary of the Battle of Rivas; May 1, Labor Day; Corpus Christi, a Thursday in June; June 29, Feast of St. Peter and St. Paul; August 2, Feast of Our Lady of the Angels; August 15, Feast of the Assumption; September 15, Independence Day; October 12, Columbus Day (*Día de la Raza*); December 8, Feast of the Immaculate Conception; Christmas Day.

CIGARETTES AND TOBACCO ... American cigarettes are about 3.75 colones (55¢) a pack. Good cigarettes are manufactured in Costa Rica and cost about 2 colones (30¢) a pack. Try *Rex* and *Master.*

CLIMATE ... One of the greatest attractions of this country is its wonderful climate. Costa Rica, like other Central American countries, has only two seasons, the rainy season and the dry one. The ideal time to visit is during the dry season fom December to April, but the climate is agreeable all year around.

CLUBS ... Union Club, Costa Rica Country Club, Costa Rica Tennis Club, Rotary Club, Lions Club, Junior Chamber of San José (Jaycees).

COMMUNICATIONS ... Telephone and telegraph services are very well organized. All America Cables and Radio, Inc., the Tropical Radio Telegraph Co. and Compañía Radiográfica provide excellent radio telephone service to points all over the world. A 3-minute call to the States costs 71.60 colones (U.S. $10.71) to New York or New Orleans; rates vary to other cities. Variable also for cablegrams. Postage for airmail letter is 45 centimos.

CURRENCY ... The unit of currency is the colón worth about U.S. 15¢. The rate of exchange is 6.62 colones per U.S. $1.

CUSTOMS REGULATIONS AND DOCUMENTS REQUIRED FOR UNITED STATES CITIZENS ... For travelers carrying only clothing and personal effects, no declarations are necessary. Two bottles of liquor, about 1 pound of tobacco are allowed in duty free. No restrictions on currency. You need a Tourist Card (available for $2 at Costa Rican consulates or at Pan Am offices in the U.S.), and proof of citizenship. Air arrival or sea departure tax 5 colones.

DRUGSTORES ... The usual variety of medicines and drugs is available including practically all American products.

ELECTRIC CURRENT ... Electric current in San José is the same as in the United States, 110 volts, 60 cycles, A.C.

FAUNA ... There are special hunting zones with an interesting variety of wild life which includes puma, deer, bear, wild pig, squirrel, monkey, wild turkey, alligator, rabbit, jaguar, fox, pigeon, etc.

FLORA ... Many varieties of beautiful tropical flowers are seen everywhere in Costa Rica. The Guaria Morada (*Cattleya skinerii*), Costa Rica's national flower, as well as many other kinds of orchids, grow in the mountains and in beautiful gardens near the cities.

FOOD ... *Tamales, tortillas* and *gallo pinto* are the favorite native food. In addition all kinds of continental food are served in private homes and hotels. Local beef is both good and inexpensive.

GAMBLING ... All forms are prohibited with the exception of the Government lottery.

LANGUAGE ... Spanish is the official language, but a high percentage of people speak English fluently. At the airport, aviation companies, souvenir shops, hotels and better stores, the tourist will find employees who speak English.

LAUNDRY ... There are many good dry-cleaning establishments in San José City.

LIQUOR ... Here you will find all kinds of American and European liquors. The National Liquor Factory is one of the best in Central America, and some of its products are comparable to those from abroad. Prices are about the same as in the U.S.

MEDICAL FACILITIES ... There are many English-speaking doctors. The principal hospitals in the capital city are: San Juan de Diós Hospital, Seguro Social Hospital, Clínica Bíblica, Clínica Mater.

MOTION PICTURES ... American and European pictures are shown at the *Palace, Raventós, Lux, Coliseo, Roxy, Ideal, Center City, Rex, Variedades, Moderno, California, Cine Central, Metropolitan*. Showings are at set hours.

MUSIC ... There is a Symphony Orchestra which gives concerts at the National Theater weekly. There are also performances in the same theater by visiting artists. The Military Band offers concerts once a week in Central Park.

NIGHT CLUBS AND CABARETS ... Night clubs as known in the States and the Caribbean are not found in San José. However, there are several "boites" such as the *Maracas, Grill la Pampa* and the *Boite Europa,* the latter on the outskirts of the city; and the *Petite Chose* in the Balmoral Hotel.

PHOTOGRAPHY ... Black-and-white and color films are available in all photo stores in San José, as well as a complete line of cameras and equipment, both foreign and American made. Developing facilities are available and the work is of top quality.

RELIGION . . . The official religion is Roman Catholic, but other denominations are represented in the capital city and elsewhere.

RESTAURANTS . . . At the *Gran Hotel Costa Rica* and the *Gran Hotel Europa,* continental food; *Chalet Suiso; Vesuvio* and *El Principe,* Italian food. French specialties at *La Bastille* and *Le Gourmet.* Other good restaurants include the *Americano, Gina's, Holland House.* Good suburban Drive-Inns are: *El Roble, La Tranquera, El Ranchito, El Chicote, Winner Inn,* Bar-B-Q *Los Anonos.*

SHOPS AND STORES . . . The best stores are located along Central Avenue and around the Central Market of San José City.

SPECTATOR SPORTS . . . Soccer football, including games with foreign teams, is played on Sundays at the National Stadium. Basketball and baseball matches are played at the baseball stadium.

SPORTS . . . Swimming, horseback riding, golf, tennis and ping-pong. There's wonderful fishing for black marlin, Pacific sailfish, tuna, etc. Big-game hunters make guided safaris into Sarapiquí province northeast of San José to bag the huge *El Tigre* (jaguar), 6-foot iguanas, alligators, white-tailed deer and 600-pound tapirs. Guanacaste province is excellent for wild game birds.

TIME . . . Same as United States Central Standard Time.

TIPPING . . . Give porters 50 centimos per bag; tip 1 colón for room service, and to barber or beautician; 10% to waiters, taxi drivers.

TRANSPORTATION . . . San José is well equipped with taxis, for which the usual rate is about $1.30 per hour, for 1 to 4 persons. Excellent highways connect San José with all points of interest in the country. There are also bus services. Three international airlines serve Costa Rica, in addition to a local one. The Ferrocarril Eléctrico al Pacífico, owned by the Government, links San José with the port of

Oxen and carts are still an important means of transportation on the coffee fincas of Costa Rica.

Puntarenas. The Northern Railway Company is a private concern and connects San José with Port Limón. U-drive cars are available in San José.

WATER . . . You will find good drinking water anywhere.

WHAT TO BUY . . . Costa Rica has fine leather, wooden and tortoise-shell articles; handpainted skirts and blouses; unusual jewelry.

WHAT TO WEAR . . . In and around San José, the tourist ordinarily wears medium-weight clothes all year round. Evening dress is not essential in San José for the one-day visitor. For a trip to the volcanoes you need sweaters and coat, as it is very cold.

WHERE TO GO—SIGHTSEEING . . .

San José . . . When in San José, tourists should visit the National Theater, which has solid marble stairways, beautiful sculpture, beaten gold and bronze decorations, immense ceiling and wall paintings executed over sixty years ago. Other places worth visiting in town are: the National Museum, with interesting collection of pre-Spanish relics; the National Congress on Avenida Central, where the nation's laws are made; the Metropolitan Cathedral, principal church of the Roman Catholic faith; the National Stadium, where exciting international matches are frequently staged; the National University, University City, one of the most remarkable constructions of San José. Tourists are attracted to the promenade of the young people along Central Avenue during the evenings.

Side Trips . . . Near San José is the Costa Rica Country Club, which offers facilities for golf, tennis, bowling and swimming. Ojo de Agua, on the highway to Alajuela about 30 minutes by bus or taxi from San José, is a pleasant swimming pool. Go to Sarchi, where the country's brilliantly painted oxcarts are still lovingly decorated by hand.

La Catalina Holiday Cabins, on a coffee plantation, offer a beautiful vacation spot only 35 minutes from San José en route to the Poas Volcano; they have good facilities for swimming, tennis, riding. One of the most interesting sightseeing points in Costa Rica is the active crater of the Irazú Volcano at an altitude of 11,322 feet. It is only 1½ hours from San José on a good paved road that reaches the summit. Another interesting trip is to Poas Volcano, which has the world's widest geyser, a boiling lake of sulphur that erupts to a height of 2,000 feet. In the Province of Cartago, a short distance from the capital city, the beautiful valley of Orosi is well worth seeing, as are the ruins of Ujarrás, an old church located in the same province. From San José you may take a morning trip to Escazú, Santa Ana, Villa Colón, returning to the hotel for lunch. Another place of interest to visit is Puntarenas, on the Pacific coast, a 4-hour scenic ride by electric railroad. Puerto Limón is on the Atlantic coast, a 5-hour train ride from San José through magnificent scenery.

SOURCES OF FURTHER INFORMATION . . . Pan American office in San José is at Avenida Primera, Calle Primera (Tel. 4204). The Consulate General of Costa Rica is at 211 E. 43rd St., New York, N.Y. 10017.

EL SALVADOR

WEATHER IN SAN SALVADOR—Lat. N13°43'—Alt. 2,250'

	JAN.	FEB.	MAR.	APR.	MAY	JUNE	JULY	AUG.	SEPT.	OCT.	NOV.	DEC.
Average Temp.	73°	75°	76°	77°	76°	76°	76°	76°	75°	75°	73°	73°
Days of Rain	1	1	2	4	12	19	20	20	17	16	5	2

LOCATION ... El Salvador, smallest and most densely populated of the Central American republics, lies along the Pacific next to Guatemala and Honduras.

CHARACTERISTICS ... Silent volcanoes, beautiful lakes, lush tropical scenery and inviting Pacific beaches all lie within a few miles of San Salvador, the tiny republic's modern capital. The people are thrifty and industrious and welcome visitors to their fascinating country, which, like the rest of Central America, is one of the most accessible but least-traveled vacation spots. El Salvador abounds in sights to see and things to do—ranging from visiting hinterland villages, which still bear the mark of Spanish colonial times, to hunting alligators.

POPULATION ... The inhabitants number approximately 2,850,-000, born of the fusion of Spaniard and Indian.

SIZE ... 8,169 square miles with a maximum length of 160 miles and an average width of 60 miles.

CAPITAL ... San Salvador, population about 250,000. San Salvador in the last few years has grown to the point where it is called the most progressive city in Central America.

GOVERNMENT ... A democratic republic.

HOW TO GET THERE ... By Pan American Clipper 4 hours from Miami; 5¾ hours from Houston; 3¼ hours from Mexico City.

ACCOMMODATIONS ... The air-conditioned *El Salvador-Intercontinental,* only 10 minutes from the center of San Salvador, features an individual garden terrace or private balcony for every room, with a spectacular view of both the city and the famous volcano. There's an outdoor swimming pool too. Rates are about $10 and up single,

$14 and up double, European Plan. *San Salvador Gran Hotel* and *Hotel Nuevo Mundo* are two modern hotels in the heart of the city. Singles about $9.50, European Plan. There are smaller hotels and pensions with singles about $8, American Plan, among them *Hotel Internacional, Casa Clark* (American-owned and operated) and *Parker House.*

ARTS ... For Indian relics, the National Museum, the Mayan ruins of San Andres 20 miles from the capital, with ruins dating from the 6th century, the temple ruins of Tazumal.

BANKS ... Bank of London and Montreal, Ltd.; Banco Salvadoreño; Banco de Comercio, Banco Hipotecario, Banco Capitalizador and Banco Agrícola Comercial.

CALENDAR OF HOLIDAYS ... New Year's Day; Holy Week; May 1, Labor Day; August 5 and 6, Fiesta of the Patron of San Salvador; September 15, Independence Day; October 12, Columbus Day; November 5, First Cry of Independence; Christmas Day.

CIGARETTES ... American cigarettes are available but they cost 80¢ a pack. Local cigarettes of good quality cost 20¢.

CLIMATE ... El Salvador has a rainy season and a dry season. (See weather chart.) Climate is warm but not everywhere nor at all hours. Evenings are usually cool.

CLUBS ... The Club Campestre Cuscatlán has a 9-hole golf course, and there's an 18-hole course at Corinto, Lake Ilopango. The Círculo Deportivo Internacional is a favorite resort for swimming, tennis, volley ball. The Club Salvadoreño has good bowling alleys, billiards and excellent cocktail lounge. It also has a beautiful night club, for members and guests only. There are Lions, Jaycees and Rotary clubs here, too.

COMMUNICATIONS ... A 3-minute call to the U.S. costs C22.50 ($9); cablegrams 75 centavos a word depending upon city. 10-word cablegram, about C10. Airmail postage to the States is 20 centavos. Local phone calls are 10 centavos.

CURRENCY ... There are 100 centavos in a colón (C), which is worth U.S. 40¢. There are 2.50 colones to U.S. $1.

CUSTOMS REGULATIONS AND DOCUMENTS REQUIRED FOR UNITED STATES CITIZENS ... Tourist cards $2 are issued by airlines, shipping companies and consulates to all citizens of Western Hemisphere countries. Vaccination certificate. Firearms require permits. One kilogram of tobacco in any form (5 cartons of cigarettes, or 330 cigars or about 2 lbs. of tobacco), and 2 bottles of liquor allowed duty free.

DRUGSTORES ... American and European products available.

ELECTRIC CURRENT ... 110 volts, 60 cycles, A.C.

FAUNA ... Deer, wild pig, jaguar, and other tropical animals.

FLORA ... Balsam, carnation, rose, and, among many gorgeous tropical plants, maquilishuat, fir tree, orchid and gardenia.

FOOD ... Salvadorean food is less spicy than that of most Latin countries, but chile and other hot sauces are served if requested. Try *Gallo en Chicha. Tamales, tortillas, enchiladas, Pupusas, Chilate* and other local dishes may be ordered. Seafood and tropical fruits are good. Continental food is served at the best hotels and clubs.

GAMBLING ... There are three national lotteries a month.

LANGUAGE ... Spanish; English understood in larger towns.

LAUNDRY AND DRY CLEANING ... There are many laundry and dry-cleaning establishments in San Salvador.

LIQUOR ... All kinds of liquors are available and Scotch whisky costs as little as $6 per bottle. Local liquors are of good quality.

MEDICAL FACILITIES ... Doctors and specialists, many of them graduates of United States and European universities, are available.

MOTION PICTURES ... American, Mexican, Argentine and European films are shown at set hours. Recommended theaters are the *Caribe, Central, Apolo, Roxy, Fausto,* and *Deluxe.*

MUSIC ... American, European, Mexican, Cuban and Argentine music, all popular. Marimba music can be enjoyed, but the dance orchestras are composed mainly of American-type instruments. Serenades are still a lovely local custom.

NIGHT CLUBS ... Dancing and nightly floor shows in the *Rendezvous Room* of Hotel El Salvador Intercontinental. The *Gran Mirador, El Sótano, El Cisne* and *El Rancho* also have dancing and entertainment.

PHOTOGRAPHY ... Black-and-white still and movie film, color film, cameras and practically all other photo equipment available.

RELIGION ... Catholic, but most denominations are represented.

RESTAURANTS AND BARS ... Your best bets are the main hotels and clubs, where almost any type of drink or food can be had. The *Siete Mares* in San Benito, the *Monterey, Chez Balta, China Palace, La Parrilla, La Fonda* and *Pampa Argentina* are recommended.

SHOPS AND STORES ... The better shops are within a radius of about 10 square blocks. Also try shops in the Caribe Building, Silva's Building, the hotels and airport.

SPECTATOR SPORTS ... Soccer games (the national sport) are held nearly every Sunday and holiday at the National Stadium. Basketball during winter season only.

SPORTS ... Deep-sea fishing off the coast, also at the Estero de Jaltepeque and in the Gulf of Fonesca, off the port of La Union. Sailing along the wide channels of the Estero de Jaltepeque and Jiquilisco, the visitor is fascinated by the vistas of lush tropical vegetation, quiet waters, roaring surf and breathtaking sunsets. Surf bathing along the Litoral, or coastal highway, is another attraction.

TIME ... Same as United States Central Standard Time.

TIPPING ... Tip porters 25 centavos per piece of luggage; 25 also for doorman, shoeshine boy, hat checker, parking-lot attendant; tip taxi drivers 15% of the meter reading, 30 centavos minimum. Hotels and restaurants do not include service charges in bills; tip waiter 15%, tip chambermaid about C1 for each day's stay. Tip beauticians C1; 50 centavos for the barber.

TRANSPORTATION ... Taxi ride from airport to city about $3; from point to point within city limits 80¢. Taxis may be hired for tours, and several agencies offer guided tours.

WATER ... Hotels serve bottled water and there are soft drinks.

WHAT TO BUY ... Native handcrafts, hand-woven textiles, pottery, native dolls, leather goods, blankets and jewelry.

WHAT TO WEAR ... Sports clothes are everyday wear. Nights are cool enough for light worsteds. Topcoats not necessary at all. Hats should be lightweight. A raincoat for May to October.

WHERE TO GO—SIGHTSEEING ...

San Salvador ... Is a growing city and has been modernized since some of the principal buildings were destroyed by fire. Several old churches such as La Merced remain. A trip to the hills, called Planes de Renderos, will give you an "aerial" view of the city. Balboa Park, with its "Devil's Door" vantage point, crowns the summit. Because of the country's dense population, you'll find the land tilled even on the volcano slopes. Santa Ana, second largest city, is a coffee center.

Izalco ... Is a 6,300-foot volcano near the old colonial city of Sonsonate, about 40 miles from San Salvador. Of the 7 volcanoes which exceed 3,000 feet in height, Izalco is the country's most famous. A few remnants of the vanished aboriginal race may still be found in the villages near here. The best view is from Cerro Verde mountain top.

Panchimalco ... Beyond Planes de Renderos is the Indian town of Panchimalco. Low adobe houses with tile or thatched roofs, irregular streets paved with uneven blocks of stone, and an old colonial church attract tourists by their peaceful charm. Here women wear ample blouses, wide, long skirts made from material woven on their primitive looms. On their heads they wear bright-colored shawls, and they wear necklaces of red and blue decorated with old Spanish silver coins. Blankets, rugs and hand-woven textiles are irresistible here.

El Boquerón ... The crater of the Volcano of San Salvador may be reached from Santa Tecla. The crater is a mile wide and a half mile deep. At the bottom there is a smaller cone left by the eruption of 1917. From the northern edge a petrified stream of lava stretches for many miles down a slope, toward Quezaltepeque.

Lake Ilopango ... Of volcanic origin, this beautiful lake, 10 miles long, is the favorite resort of the Salvadoreans. There's a modern park at Apulo, with restaurants, bath houses and pier.

Lake Coatepeque ... One hour's ride from San Salvador is one of the loveliest lakes in Central America, its shores lined by beautiful private residences. The waters, the lake and Baños La Toma, a natural swimming pool, are highly medicinal and compare favorably with those of Vichy. Lake crabs here are a gourmet's delight.

Other places to visit include the National Parks of Atecozol and Ichanmichen, Apastepeque Lake, Los Chorros, Amapalupa, Cerro de Las Pavas and the 16th-century village of Cojutepeque.

SOURCES OF FURTHER INFORMATION ... National Tourist Bureau, Calle Rubén Darío No. 619, San Salvador. Pan American's office is in the Edificio Dueñas (Tel. 1225). The Consulate General of El Salvador is at 211 E. 43rd St., New York, N.Y. 10017.

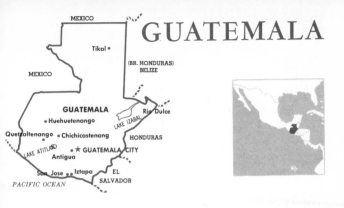

GUATEMALA

WEATHER IN GUATEMALA CITY—Lat. N14°37'—Alt. 5,000'

	JAN.	FEB.	MAR.	APR.	MAY	JUNE	JULY	AUG.	SEPT.	OCT.	NOV.	DEC.
Average Temp.	61.3°	62.8°	65.7°	66.2°	68.0°	66.2°	65.8°	66.0°	65.7°	64.8°	62.8°	61.3°
In. of Rain	0.3	0.2	0.5	1.3	5.6	11.5	8.0	8.0	9.2	6.7	0.9	0.2

LOCATION ... South and east of Mexico, Guatemala is the most northern country in Central America.

CHARACTERISTICS ... Guatemala is for the traveler who is seeking atmosphere rather than gay night life, local color rather than chic resorts. Part of Guatemala's charm is its unspoiled native life. Guatemala City has been rebuilt since the last earthquake in 1917; it is a clean, very progressive city with a cosmopolitan air. Guatemalans are friendly and glad to help the visitor. They are a quiet-spoken, well-educated, proud and patriotic people.

POPULATION ... Approximately 4,200,000.

SIZE ... 42,042 square miles, excluding Belize.

CAPITAL ... Guatemala City, with 572,937 inhabitants.

GOVERNMENT ... A republic, the Government is divided into three bodies: executive, legislative and judicial. The executive is represented by the President and ten cabinet ministers, the legislative by one congress composed of 66 members representing 22 states (called *departamentos*). Each state has a governor appointed by the President.

HOW TO GET THERE ... By Pan American Jet Clipper, 3 hours from New Orleans; 2½ hours from Miami; 1½ hours from Mexico city, 4½ hours from Los Angeles. By ship 3 days from New Orleans to Puerto Barrios.

ACCOMMODATIONS ... There are good hotels in Guatemala City and throughout the highlands. Rates quoted are double, European Plan (without meals) and apply year round. First-class hotels in the capital include: the new *Ritz Continental;* the *Palace* ($8 up); the *Guatemala-Biltmore* ($12-$19; has swimming pool); *Pan American* ($8 up); the *Maya Excelsior* ($8-$16); the *Motel Plaza* ($8 up). Good pensions include *Casa Shaw, Chez Bruna* and *Fernandez.* A 10% hotel tax is added to all rates.

ARTS ... Indian crafts and weaving. Many modern cultural groups in music, ceramics and painting. Guatemala City has fine museums, art academies, and exposition centers. Art treasures from ruined city of Antigua are displayed in the Cathedral and La Merced church.

BALLET ... Although there is no set season, the Ballet Guatemala and foreign groups perform from time to time in the capital.

BANKS ... In Guatemala City there are the Bank of London and Montreal, Ltd.; Banco Agrícola Mercantil; Crédito Hipotecario Nacional; Banco de Occidente; Bank of America; Banco Agrario Nacional; Banco Inmobiliano; Banco de Comercio é Industria; and Banco del Agro. All are affiliated with U.S. banks.

CALENDAR OF HOLIDAYS ... Stores and museums are closed on: January 1; Thursday and Friday of Holy Week; July 3; August 15; September 15 (Independence Day); October 20; and Christmas Day. There is a long roster of fiesta days; some of them are: March 19 at San José; Holy Week celebrated throughout the country; July 25 at Santiago de Atitlán; July 28-31 at Momostenango; August 14-16 at Guatemala City; November 1 and 2 throughout the Republic; December 8-12 at Escuintla; December 17-21 at Chichicastenango.

CIGARETTES AND TOBACCO ... American cigarettes of any popular brand are available but cost about 75¢ a pack. Local cigarettes such as *Victor, Viceroy, Club, Raleigh, Fleetwood* and *Altenses* are 20¢ to 28¢ a pack.

CLIMATE ... It is almost always balmy and pleasant, although there is a "showers" season and a dry season. See chart on page 315 for Guatemala City temperatures. In the highlands the days are warm, the nights cool.

CLUBS ... Guatemala Country Club, Mayan Golf Club, American Club, Lions Club, Rotary Club, Tennis Club and Guatemala Club. Visitors' cards can be arranged through your travel agent.

COMMON COURTESIES AND LOCAL CUSTOMS ... Since, as mentioned before, Guatemalans are softspoken and well bred, loudness in speech and manners and exaggerated dress are frowned upon. Men should always wear a jacket in restaurants and clubs.

COMMUNICATIONS ... Local dial telephone service (10¢ a call) in Guatemala City. Tropical Radio and Telegraph service and All American Cables. Radiograms to all parts of the world. A cablegram to the U.S. costs 37¢ per word; a 3-minute phone call is $9. Postal cards by airmail carry 6¢ postage; 7¢ for half-ounce letters.

CURRENCY ... The monetary unit is the quetzal, which is divided into 100 cents and is at par with the United States dollar with similar coin and bill denominations.

CUSTOMS REGULATIONS AND DOCUMENTS REQUIRED FOR UNITED STATES CITIZENS ... Tourist cards (dated within

60 days before arrival) may be obtained by U.S. and Canadian citizens through some offices of PAA, especially gateways (coastal cities), as well as through some travel agents. Cards cost $3. Documentary proof of citizenship and age are necessary to obtain them. All travelers must have a smallpox vaccination certificate. A logical amount and class of photographic equipment is allowed. Customs officials are instructed to conduct inspection of baggage of visitors very lightly. Specified duty-free limits are 200 cigarettes or 3½ ounces of tobacco. Air or sea arrival tax $1 unless you have a tourist card.

DRUGSTORES . . . European and U.S. pharmaceuticals and cosmetic products. French perfumes are good buys.

ELECTRIC CURRENT . . . In Guatemala City and throughout the tourist centers, it is 110 volts, A.C., as in the U.S.

FAUNA . . . Deer, wild boar, mountain puma, monkey, alligator, tapir, wild turkey, duck, crane. Guatemala's national bird is the quetzal, a rare species with beautiful feathers. The country is also well known for its variety of hummingbirds.

FLORA . . . Climatic conditions make Guatemala an ideal spot for an almost unlimited variety of flowers, such as the native orchid and hydrangea, hibiscus, violet and rose. A white orchid called *monja blanca* (white nun), indigenous to the country, is Guatemala's national flower.

FOOD . . . Most restaurants serve continental food, others specialize in native dishes. Here are some you may want to try: *gallo en chicha* (chicken in cider), *enchiladas, chiles rellenos* (stuffed peppers), *chojin* (minced, marinated radishes), *tamales, rellenitos de platano* (fried bananas stuffed with mashed black beans) and, of course, Guatemalan coffee, among the best. Pasteurized milk is served in the principal cities.

GAMBLING . . . Against the law except for national lotteries, bingo games. Private betting at cockfights and horse races is overlooked.

LANGUAGE . . . Spanish is the official language, but you will have no trouble being understood when speaking English.

LAUNDRY AND DRY CLEANING . . . Dry-cleaning establishments and hotels where you can get practically anything done—double tariff for rush orders—within 24 hours.

LIQUOR . . . Good local rums and gins cost around $2.50 a bottle. Scotch, bourbon and Canadian whiskies are sold in grocery stores for about $6 a fifth. Bars charge from 60¢ to 90¢ a drink for imported liquors. Local beer is excellent, and do try a fiery *aguardiente*.

MEDICAL FACILITIES . . . Practically all doctors speak English, and specialists exist in almost all phases of medicine. Most of the doctors and surgeons are ex-interns from famous institutions in the United States such as the Mayo Clinic, Johns Hopkins and others.

MOTION PICTURES . . . U.S., British, Italian, French, Mexican, German and Argentine films are shown by most movie houses. In the center of town are the *Lux, Capitol, Palace, Fox, Tikal, Capri, Lido, Cali* and *Paris.* In the residential district the *Reforma,* a plush, up-to-date theater. All foreign films have Spanish titles.

MUSIC . . . Guatemala's fine Symphony Orchestra performs throughout the year under local and guest conductors. The scheduled season is from July to November. Chamber-music concerts and performances by famous international artists are held at the National Conservatory of Music. Guatemala is noted for marimba music, and marimba bands are especially featured at *El Gallito.*

NIGHT CLUBS AND CABARETS . . . There isn't much night life in the capital; however, the few night spots are located in the downtown district. Since popularities flare and wane, ask at your hotel for the places currently the most entertaining.

PHOTOGRAPHY . . . All brands of American and European black-and-white and color films are sold throughout the country at prices similar to those in the States. 24-hour color-film developing service at Biener Tabush and Legrand. For camera repairs: Foto Muñoz.

RELIGION . . . The country is Catholic; however, Protestant sects such as Presbyterian, Seventh Day Adventists, Episcopalian, Lutheran, Church of England, and Baptist are represented. There is a synagogue. Most of the Protestant denominations have services in English, Lutherans in German.

RESTAURANTS . . . Besides the dining rooms of Guatemala City's firstclass hotels, there are the following specialty restaurants: for Spanish dishes, such as *paella, Hosteria Don Pepe, La Macia, La Puerta* and *Mediterraneo;* for Italian food: *Las Palmas, Las Vegas* and *La Dulce Vida;* for Argentine-style charcoal-broiled steaks; *Churrascos, El Palenque, La Tablita, La Parrillita, Bill's Brazer* and *El Gaucho;* for Chinese food: *Canton, Fu Lu Sho,* and *Chung King* are outstanding. For a continental cuisine: *Chez Lissette* and *El Patio,* the latter with a lovely Spanish décor. There are tempting French-style pastry shops, such as the *Corinne, Simon, Jensen, Austria, Bonbonnière* and *Palace.* Tops among many American-style soda fountains are the *Cafesa, Café de Paris, Reforma* and *La Plazuela.*

SHOPS AND STORES . . . Shopping district in the capital is along 6th Avenue; on 12th Street and 8th Street, as well as on 9th, 10th and 11th Streets. Stores generally open from 8:30 A.M. to 12:30 noon and from 2:30 P.M. to 6:30 P.M. Native curio shops are open until 8 P.M. Some of the main stores are: La Paquetería, La Ciudad de Paris, La Perla, La Marquesa, El Paje, Fru-Fru, El Cairo, Lazaro. These stores carry U.S. and European merchandise. Curio shops are: Maya Modern on 7th Avenue at 9th Street; La Tinaja, at 12th St., No. 4-80; Guatelandia, at 8th Avenue, No. 8-24; Jimmy Tex, Avenida Reforma, for materials in exclusive designs; souvenir shop at the Pan American Hotel; La Regional and several others at Central Market; and Rigalt's, Nelly's, La Dama and Regina Shop on 12th Street between 4th and 5th Avenues. Also Handtex, 12th Street and 6th Avenue.

SPECTATOR SPORTS . . . Soccer and basketball, both local and international games every Sunday and occasionally weekdays, held at the capital's Olympic Stadium and Gymnasium located at the Olympic City on 7th Avenue Colonia Lima; baseball at the Olympic Field, at Minerva Park at the end of Avenue Simeon Cañas.

SPORTS . . . Golf, tennis, swimming, water skiing and skin diving thrive all year round in Guatemala's mild climate. Shooting and skeet at the Club de Caza Tiro y Pesca. Good fishing on both coasts, and at Amatitlán and Atitlán lakes, the latter well-stocked with sportive black bass. There are special bridle paths for horseback riding in Guatemala City and Antigua. Hunting opportunities are abundant with duck, squab, quail, wild turkey, deer, cougar, lynx, and puma. A license for the importation of firearms may be obtained from any Guatemalan consulate; no hunting license is required.

THEATERS . . . Several groups stage monthly performances at *Conservatorio Nacional* and the *Gadem Theater,* where the American Little Theater Guild presents plays in English. Special performances by foreign artists at the *Capitol* and *Palace* theaters.

TIME . . . Central Standard Time is observed throughout the year.

TIPPING . . . Tip for the same services you would at home, but slightly less.

TRANSPORTATION . . . Taxis abound in Guatemala City. Bus lines run in all directions covering practically the whole city. To travel inland you can use the services of a tour operator or hire a car, about $25 a day for trips outside the city. There are railroad and local airline services throughout the country.

WATER . . . Tap water is safe for drinking, but hotels and restaurants also serve bottled water. All popular U.S. soft drinks are available.

WHAT TO BUY . . . Guatemala excels in colorful Indian weaving. Indian market and native curio shops offer a variety of these products. As an example, leather (hand-tooled) shoulder-strap bags cost from $3.50 to $10 in comparison with similar goods (imported from Guatemala) that sell in the United States for $24. Skirts in Mayan designs, shirts, blouses and sandals make wonderful and colorful sportswear.

WHAT TO WEAR . . . Medium-weight apparel, sportswear, light sweaters, walking shoes, topcoat and swimsuit are suggested. A light raincoat is advisable for travel during May to October and through the lowlands. A dark basic dress or suit is appropriate for evening.

WHERE TO GO—SIGHTSEEING . . .

Guatemala City . . . See the Church of Santo Domingo, which is whiter than white because milk and the whites of eggs were mixed into the mortar to give it greater strength. The Presidential Palace of light-green stone is attractive. A must for tourists is the relief map of Guatemala in Minerva Park, which gives a clear picture of the contours of the country. The Cathedral, which survived the 1917 earthquake, is beautiful. The National Museum is of interest, too. The markets, particularly the big one at the Mercado Central behind the Cathedral, and Mercadito are fabulous. Hayter Travel, Clark Tours, Agencia Liang and Eca Tours offer 4-, 5-, and 9-day tours which

In Chichicastenango, life centers around the colorful market place. In the background Indians burn incense on the steps of the Church of Santo Tomás.

cover the Mayan highlands and Guatemala City and include Chichicastenango, Antigua and Lake Atitlán. Other tours take you to such out-of-the-way places as the deep jungle, Rio Dulce and Lake Izabal.

Chichicastenango is delightful. Its great church is a pilgrimage center where Christian saints and pagan gods are comfortably intermingled. The *Mayan Inn* is Spanish colonial style furnished with genuine antiques. Barefoot Indian boys are house servants, and strolling marimba players entertain you. Rates are from $13 single, $21 double, American Plan. Schedule your visit for a Thursday or a Sunday when the huge Indian market fills the main plaza.

Antigua is the former capital of the country, and many fine old buildings still stand. The market is famous for hand-wrought silver. Stay at *Posada Belém,* or hotels *Antigua* or *Aurora.* Palin, south of the capital, holds its market under a gigantic ceiba tree.

Tikal was a magnificent Mayan ceremonial city 3,000 years ago, and has been recently rediscovered with many of its carvings intact. An hour's flight from Guatemala City lands you near the modern, comfortable *Jungle Lodge* ($16 single, $24 double, American Plan), which is less than a mile from the Great Plaza of Tikal. Guides and jeep services available.

Sayaxche, south of Tikal, is headquarters for visits to the country's remotest Mayan ruins, and for hunting trips in the Petén jungle where deer and jaguar roam freely. Hunting, fishing and camping equipment may be rented at the new *Rio Pasion Lodge,* reached by Aviateca on scheduled flights on Thursdays.

Lake Atitlán is 5,000 feet above sea level and three volcanoes overlook it. Hotels *Casa Contenta* and *Tzanjuyu* here are excellent. Indian villages ring the 85-mile shoreline. Other points of interest are: Quezaltenango, the country's second city, a mountain town with a cool, moderate climate and an interesting market and narrow streets; and Puerto Barrios, chief port of the Caribbean, which is 200 miles by train or paved highway through the jungles from the capital.

SOURCES OF FURTHER INFORMATION... The National Tourist Bureau at 6 Ave. No. 5-34 and the tour operators mentioned above have literature, maps and information. Pan Am's office is on 6a Avenue, No. 12-12 (Tel. 12-1-44). (Above addresses are in Guatemala City). In New York the Guatemala Consulate is at 1270 Ave. of the Americas (Rockefeller Center).

HONDURAS

WEATHER IN TEGUCIGALPA—Lat. N14°6'—Alt. 3,200'

	JAN.	FEB.	MAR.	APR.	MAY	JUNE	JULY	AUG.	SEPT.	OCT.	NOV.	DEC.
Average Temp.	65°	71°	73°	74°	73°	75°	73°	73°	73°	70°	71°	66°
In. of Rain	0.18	0.05	0.29	0.97	5.90	5.00	6.76	6.53	7.76	3.55	1.26	1.31

LOCATION ... The Republic of Honduras lies between Guatemala and Nicaragua in the Central American strip, with coastlines on the Caribbean and Pacific. El Salvador is its neighbor to the southwest.

CHARACTERISTICS ... Honduras, most mountainous of the Central American countries, offers the vacationist adventure difficult to match in any other Latin American country today. In this little republic—which jumped from the oxcart to the airplane in one prodigious leap—16th-century Spanish colonial atmosphere is superbly preserved. Here visitors can see the ruins of the ancient Maya city of Copan, which flourished about the time of Christ, and take a boat trip through a tropical jungle whose trees teem with brilliantly colored birds and hordes of chattering monkeys. All the larger cities of Honduras offer good hotel accommodations at a wide range in prices. Chief recreational pastimes include golf, tennis, hunting, swimming and fishing (both lake and deep sea). The people of Honduras are mostly Indian and *mestizo* (a combination of Spanish and Indian). They are a very friendly people. You'll enjoy this tropical country off the beaten tourist track.

POPULATION ... 2,100,000 inhabitants.

SIZE ... Approximately 43,277 square miles.

CAPITAL ... Tegucigalpa, D.C. (Central District), with a population of 170,000 including the neighboring city of Comayaguela.

GOVERNMENT ... An independent republic.

HOW TO GET THERE ... By Pan American Jet Clipper from

Miami, New Orleans, Houston, Mexico City, Los Angeles and San Francisco to Guatemala where connections are made with Pan American Clippers to Tegucigalpa. 6 hours from Miami; 6¾ hours from Houston. By ship from New Orleans, Houston, or New York.

ACCOMMODATIONS . . . Honduras is an economical country to visit. Rates quoted here include all meals and apply the year round. In Tegucigalpa, single rates at the *Gran Hotel Lincoln* and the *Prado* average $12 per day; at the *Savoy,* $8. Other hotels include the *Boston* and *Marichal,* with single rates from $4. In San Pedro Sula: the *Bolivar,* from $10, and *San Pedro,* from $8. In La Ceiba, *Hotel Paris,* $8. Bay Islands (Guanaja): *Lundy's Boat Motel,* $8.

CALENDAR OF HOLIDAYS . . . January 1; February 3, Honduras Virgin Day; May 1, Labor Day; September 15, Independence Day; October 3, Birthday of Morazán, Central American hero; October 12, Columbus Day; October 21; December 25; Holy Thursday, Friday and Saturday preceding Easter. Stores and museums close on all holidays.

CIGARETTES AND TOBACCO . . . American cigarettes and tobacco are available; cigarettes cost 40¢ to 60¢ per pack. Local cigarettes, such as Crown, Belmont and Paladin, cost 25¢. These are manufactured by a branch of American Tobacco Company. Honduras is famous for its excellent tobacco from Copan, where fine cigars are made.

CLIMATE . . . Honduras has a tropical climate, but in Tegucigalpa the climate is very pleasant throughout the year with the exception of March, April and May, when it gets warmer. It cools off, however, at night. The climate on both the north and south coasts is always hot; it averages about 85 degrees and at times it goes up to 100 and 105 degrees in some places.

CLUBS . . . Tegucigalpa Country Club, Casino Hondureño, Lions Club, Rotary Club, Club Tegucigalpa.

COMMUNICATIONS . . . A phone call to the U.S. costs about $3 a minute. Airmail postage to the States for postcards and airletters is 12 centavos, 24 centavos for a 5-gram letter.

CURRENCY . . . The monetary unit is the lempira, and the current rate of exchange is 2 lempiras for U.S.$1. There are 100 centavos in 1 lempira.

CUSTOMS REGULATIONS AND DOCUMENTS REQUIRED FOR UNITED STATES CITIZENS . . . Passport properly visaed is required; *or* a tourist card, which costs $2, may be obtained from any Honduran Consul, Pan American office, or upon arrival at the airport upon presentation of a valid identification document such as a birth certificate. A smallpox vaccination not over 12 months old is required. Tourist cards are valid for 90 days' stay from date of entry into Honduras. One carton of cigarettes, 2 bottles of liquor may be brought in duty free.

DRUGSTORES . . . American products, as well as European and others, are available but are expensive.

ELECTRIC CURRENT . . . The current in Tegucigalpa and most of the rest of the country is 220 volts, 60 cycles, A.C. Hotels will furnish transformers upon request to convert 220 to 110 volts.

FAUNA ... Among a variety of tropical animals, there are deer, jaguar, mountain lion or American puma, peccary or wild pig, wild turkey, monkey, alligator, tapir. Water fowl is abundant both on the north coast and Pacific coast lagoons, rivers, etc., especially from October to February. There are quail, whitewing pigeon, dove, parrot and many types of singing birds, such as *zorzal, jilguero, zensontle.* Opportunities for hunting are abundant.

FLORA ... There is a variety of flowers, among which are orchids of various types. Many hardwoods grow here: mahogany, primavera, *guenacaste, carreto,* and many others. Honduras has enormous sources of timber, especially pine. Ordinary and tropical vegetation is found most anywhere in Honduras due to the variety of altitude and climate.

FOOD ... Among the typical native foods there are *nacatamales, mondongo, tapado de carne salada, quesos blancos de Olancho y Choluteca, tortillas* and *enchiladas.* Chili is not used as much as in Mexico and Guatemala. Restaurants and hotel dining rooms serve continental food. Pasteurized milk is available and good. Meals at the best hotels and restaurants range from $1 to $1.25 for breakfast, $1 to $3 for lunch, $3 to $6 for dinner.

GAMBLING ... There are presently no casinos, horse or dog racing; the only legal gambling is the National Lottery, but casinos are now legal for touristic development.

LANGUAGE ... The official language is Spanish, but there is a large percentage of English-speaking people. Many Honduran people send their children to school in the United States. There are several American schools. The influence of large American companies established in the country for many years is causing the English language to be learned by all Hondurans.

LAUNDRY AND DRY CLEANING ... Laundry facilities cannot compare with those in the United States in either speed, quality or price. This applies also to dry cleaning. Although facilities are available, the service is only fair and rather expensive. Hotels will take care of customers' laundry within 24 hours, at double tariff for rush orders.

LIQUOR ... All kinds of fine liquors, both European and American, can be bought at lower prices than in the United States. Native liquors are *aguardiente* and *ron catracho.*

MEDICAL FACILITIES ... Almost all doctors speak English. In Tegucigalpa there are the following hospitals: Viera, Centro Médico Hondureño; La Policlínica. In addition, the United Fruit Company has its own up-to-date hospitals at La Lima and Tela.

MOTION PICTURES ... American movies are shown at *El Presidente, Variedades, Clamer* and *Palace* in Tegucigalpa; *Centenario* in Comayaguela. When you buy tickets, request the *palco* (box) section.

MUSIC ... The distinctive music is the native marimba bands.

NIGHT CLUBS AND CABARETS ... Night life in Tegucigalpa

at *El Faro, La Cabaña* and the *Duncan Mayan Club*. Dancing often, too, at *Hotel Lincoln*.

PHOTOGRAPHY ... Tourists can buy good photo equipment, black-and-white as well as color, still and movie film in Tegucigalpa and most of the north coast cities. Rivera & Cia. are the local Kodak dealers. European products are cheaper here than in the United States. Film-developing facilities are available within 24 hours. However, movie films have to be sent to the United States for developing.

RELIGION ... Principal local religion is Catholic. However, there are a few churches for Episcopalian and other Protestant denominations.

RESTAURANTS ... Aside from hotel dining rooms, the best places to eat in the capital are *La Cabaña* (international cuisine), *El Chico Club* (Spanish food), *Roma and Venezia* (Italian), and the *Riviera Drive-In*. The best restaurants in San Pedro Sula are *Vincente's, El Rincon Gaucho* and the *Country Club*.

SHOPS AND STORES ... The better-class shops are to be found on Avenida Paz Barahona in Tegucigalpa. Fresh American groceries are available at Tip Top Super Market, Bazar Union, and Linton's. Baskets and pottery can be found at the Los Dolores market near the Pan American office.

SPECTATOR SPORTS ... Football (soccer), basketball and baseball.

SPORTS ... Arrangements for golf and tennis can be made through the Pan American office or by contacting the president of the Country Club of Tegucigalpa. Information on how to make arrangements for hunting and fishing can also be obtained from Pan American.

TIME ... Same as United States Central Standard Time.

TIPPING ... Tip waiters 10% of the bill. Tip luggage porters 50 centavos per bag. Otherwise, there is not much tipping in Honduras.

TRANSPORTATION ... Taxis or cars may be hired for tours around the country. Train service is available throughout the north coast. There is bus service, but it is very poor. There is frequent scheduled air service throughout the country via SAHSA, Pan American's affiliate. Small planes may be chartered for 3 or 4 persons for special trips as well as larger planes for excursions.

WATER ... The water in Tegucigalpa and all other towns and cities must be boiled before it is safe to drink. Bottled water, also, and many U.S. soft drinks are available in Tegucigalpa.

WHAT TO BUY ... Excellent Panamá hats, known as *sombreros de junco,* made in Santa Barbara, are among the best buys; also beautiful handbags made of same material as Panamá hats. Baskets, pottery, native crafts carved in beautiful, unusual hardwoods. Imported French perfumes are cheaper than in the States.

WHAT TO WEAR ... Honduras, like all tropical countries, is informal, so take sports clothes—linen, cotton, for north and south coasts, and tropical worsted, palm beach, light clothes for Tegucigalpa, except in December and January, when it gets cool, especially at night. No topcoat is ever necessary for men; women may want one. Men will need slacks, sports jackets. Dark suit desirable for evening, as well as dark daytime and evening dresses for women.

WHERE TO GO—SIGHTSEEING ...

Tegucigalpa ... is a picturesque city where the colonial atmosphere is evident on every hand. Built on the side of Mount Picacho, 3,200 feet above sea level, its streets run in all directions and at all angles and grades, culminating in odd little plazas at unexpected places.

Four of the city's churches and many of its pastel-colored stucco residences and business structures date back to colonial times. The President's palace is a fortresslike structure with towers and turrets facing the steep-banked Choluteca River.

Principal show places in the city include Morazan Plaza, Concordia Park, the United Nations Park on top of Mt. Picacho, and the Peace Monument. The picturesque town of Santa Lucia, 20 miles from Tegucigalpa, is worth seeing, too.

Travel agents can arrange interesting tours around the city and to such places as Zamorano (magnificent tropical plants and flowers at the Pan American Agricultural School), to Comayagua, the ruins of Copan, and Yojoa Lake.

Copan ... can be reached in little more than an hour by chartered plane; also scheduled SAHSA flights to Copan via San Pedro Sula. In the days of their glory, the temples, palaces and courts of Copan—capital of the first Maya Empire—sprawled over 15 square miles. To-day many of these unique stone structures are still intact and may be easily inspected.

Comayagua ... Former capital of Honduras, this 16th-century city has been preserved in the tradition of the conquistadores, and is famous for its beautiful churches with altars of solid gold. See also the Padres Franciscanos Museum at the Casa Cural. Comayagua is 3 hours by car from Tegucigalpa.

Yojoa Lake ... lies between the capital and San Pedro Sula, 6 hours by car from Tegucigalpa. Excellent fishing; restaurant and cabins for overnight stays.

North Coast Area ... San Pedro Sula, Tela and La Ceiba are the principal cities and are reached by regularly scheduled SAHSA flights from Tegucigalpa. San Pedro Sula is highly industrialized but has some lovely residential sections. Superb beaches at Tela and La Ceiba, with suitable tourist accommodations. The old Spanish Fort at Omoa, near Puerto Cortes, also warrants a visit.

Bay Islands ... in the Caribbean off the North Coast. Ideal conditions for deep-sea fishing and skin diving near Guanaja and Roatan. The islands may be reached by scheduled flights from La Ceiba.

SOURCES OF FURTHER INFORMATION ... In Tegucigalpa inquire at Pan American's office, Edificio Marichal (Tel. 18-66); in San Pedro Sula the Pan Am office is in Hotel Bolivar. In New York City the Honduras consulate is located at 30 East 42nd Street.

MEXICO

WEATHER IN MEXICO CITY—Lat. N19°26′—Alt. 7,349′

Temp.	JAN.	FEB.	MAR.	APR.	MAY	JUNE	JULY	AUG.	SEPT.	OCT.	NOV.	DEC.
Low	42°	44°	48°	52°	54°	55°	54°	54°	54°	50°	48°	43°
High	66°	70°	75°	78°	79°	76°	74°	74°	72°	70°	68°	65°
Average	54°	57°	62°	65°	67°	66°	64°	64°	63°	60°	58°	54°
Days of Rain	3	4	6	11	15	19	25	24	20	12	6	4

LOCATION . . . Mexico lies between the United States and Central America. Mexico City is 1,560 air miles from Los Angeles, 1,275 air miles from Miami, 746 air miles from Houston.

CHARACTERISTICS . . . Mexico, land of the ancient Aztecs, has a wide range of attractions for everyone: fabulous beaches and world-famous resorts . . . modern cities flavored with the charm of Old Spain . . . volcanoes, snow-capped mountains, blooming deserts . . . thrilling bullfights, colorful fiestas . . . exquisite shops, luxurious hotels, the gayest of night clubs. You'll find all these and more in Mexico.

POPULATION . . . Mexico has a population of 40,000,000.

SIZE . . . 761,600 square miles. The U.S.-Mexican border is 2,000 miles long. Mexico has 3,759 miles of coastline on the Pacific; 1,709 miles on the Gulf of Mexico.

CAPITAL . . . Mexico City, officially Mexico D.F. (Federal District), has a population of 5,750,000.

GOVERNMENT . . . Mexico is a republic of 30 states, officially known as the United States of Mexico, two territories (South Lower California and Quintana Roo) and a Federal District.

HOW TO GET THERE . . . By Pan Am or connecting airlines, Mexico City is 1¾ hours from Houston; 3¼ hours from Los Angeles. By connecting airlines through Houston, elapsed time to Mexico City is 4½ hours from St. Louis; 5½ hours from Washington D.C. Non-stop service from New York and Chicago, 4¼ hours and 3½ hours, respectively. Mérida is 1½ hours from New Orleans and 1¾ hours from Miami. By train Mexico City is 3 days and 3 nights from New York.

ACCOMMODATIONS . . . There are hotels of every type available. You can live luxuriously or modestly, depending upon your budget. Here are some of the good hotels (all European Plan) in Mexico City:

The *Reforma Intercontinental,* famous hotel on the fashionable Paseo de la Reforma, is convenient to both shopping and entertainment spots. Operated by Intercontinental Hotels Corp., it is modern throughout, uses only filtered artesian well water, has modern sanitary kitchens, excellent cuisine, informal coffee shop and popular bar; average rates $12 single, $14 double. Other good hotels in a similar price range are the *Continental Hilton,* Reforma 166; *Alameda* (operated by Western Hotels), Juárez 50; *Del Prado,* Juárez 70; *Del Paseo,* Reforma 208; *Prado-Alffer,* Revillagigedo 18; *Bamer,* Juárez 52; *Plaza Vista Hermosa,* Insurgentes y Sullivan. Other luxurious hotels are the *Maria Isabel* at Reforma 325 and *El Presidente* at Hamburgo 135. Rates start at $14 single, $22 double. At the smart *Hotel Tecali,* at M. Escobedo 736, rates start at $28 single, $32 double. Good hotels in the moderate-rate class (about $8 single, $10 double) are the *Ambassador,* Humboldt 38; *Cristobal Colón,* Colón 27; *Monte Cassino,* Génova 56; *Premier,* Atenas 76; *San Francisco,* Luis Moya 11. Good hotels in the $6 single, $8 double range are the *Francis,* Reforma 64; *Geneve,* Londres 130; *Majestic,* Madero 73; *Metropol,* Luis Moya 39; *Regis,* Juárez 77; *Ritz,* Madero 30; and the *Romfel,* Revillagigedo 35.

There are many other good and convenient hotels throughout the city, some with rates as low as $4 single and $6 double. All the better hotels have good restaurants, bars, and some have beautiful rooftop dining rooms with music for dancing.

ARTS . . . There is so much art in Mexico City that it is difficult to decide what to see first. Musts are: the Palace of Fine Arts, with frescoes and murals by Rivera, Orozco, Siqueiros and others and exhibitions of many kinds. The National Museum of Plastic Arts, plus a theater with famous Tiffany glass curtain whose scenic design is beautifully illuminated. The new and truly magnificent National Museum of Anthropology and History with all the cultures of Mexico superbly represented. See the National Palace with frescoes by Diego Rivera; the Palace of Justice; the Museum of Flora and Fauna, filled with exotic specimens from all over the country; the beautiful and interesting displays in Chapultepec Castle; the Central Art Gallery; House of Anáhuac (Anahuacalli), housing the great Diego Rivera collection of prehispanic sculpture; the National Museum of Popular Art and Industries; ·Juárez Museum; Natural History Museum. Museums are open every day; galleries close Sundays and holidays.

BALLET . . . There is a gorgeous Mexican folklore ballet every

Sunday at 9:30 A.M. and at 5 and 8 P.M. and Wednesday evening in the Palace of Fine Arts. Opera is presented at the Palace of Fine Arts each summer (June, July, August and September).

BANKS ... All major hotels have branch banks in their lobbies. Banking hours are from 9 A.M. to 1 P.M., except Sundays and holidays. Most hotels and shops will change money at other hours. The First National City Bank of New York, Uruguay e Isabel la Católica; Banco Nacional de Mexico, S.A., Av. Isabel la Católica No. 44; Banco de Londres y Mexico, 16 de Septiembre y Bolívar; Banco de Mexico, 5 de Mayo No. 2; Banco de Comercio, V. Carranza 44.

CALENDAR OF HOLIDAYS ... There is scarcely a day in the year that there is not a fiesta in some province or town, but here is a list of national holidays celebrated by the entire country; January 1 and 6; February 5, anniversary of the establishment of the Constitution in 1857; Shrove Tuesday, celebrations like Mardi Gras; Easter week, when most business houses and all Government offices are closed; March 21, Birthday of Benito Juárez; May 1, Labor Day; May 5; Mexican National Holiday celebrating victory over French at Puebla, 1862; September 16, *El Grito* or Independence Day; October 12, Columbus Day; November 1 and 2, All Saints and All Souls Days, the days of the dead; November 20, Anniversary of the Revolution of 1910; December 12, Guadalupe Day; December 16 to 25, the *Posadas* to celebrate Christmas.

CIGARETTES AND TOBACCO ... Imported English and American cigarettes cost 40¢ to 50¢ per pack. Popular made-in-Mexico brands are *Del Prado, Raleigh, Kent, Viceroy* and *L & M,* which cost from 16¢ a pack and up. Local cigars are also inexpensive and good. American and English pipe tobaccos are fairly costly.

CLIMATE ... Mexico City, situated at 7,349 feet, has a wonderful springlike climate. Because of the altitude it is essential to take things slowly to avoid overfatigue. There are no sharply defined seasons, but there are light afternoon rains from June through October. Mornings are invariably sunny, even during the rainy season. Mexico City claims to have more sunshine than any other large city and is an excellent spot for asthma sufferers.

CLUBS ... American, French, Rotary, Lions, University, Variety, Women's International, American Legion, Skal, Kiwanis, YMCA, and YWCA. Cards are necessary for some and may sometimes be obtained from resident members or through a travel agency.

COMMON COURTESIES AND LOCAL CUSTOMS ... Bargaining is accepted practice in the markets and in small shops. The big stores have a one-price policy. Women in slacks and shorts are not permitted on the streets of Mexico City. Men should not remove their coats or ties. Women, unless they are in the heart of the city, should not be unescorted. Don't take pictures of people without asking permission. Everyone plays the national lottery. Residents call Mexico City merely "Mexico."

COMMUNICATIONS ... Depending upon city called, day rates for a 3-minute phone call to the U.S. are 40-80 pesos. A 10-word cablegram is 27.50 pesos. Airmail to the U.S. costs 80 centavos for each 10 grams.

CURRENCY ... The Mexican unit is the peso, designated by the dollar sign and worth 8 cents in United States currency. Official rate is 12.50 pesos to the United States dollar. Banks and money exchangers may accept dollars at a slightly lower rate.

CUSTOMS REGULATIONS AND DOCUMENTS REQUIRED FOR UNITED STATES CITIZENS ... Tourists are permitted to bring in anything for personal use duty free. 200 cigarettes, or 50 cigars, or 250 grams of tobacco, 12 rolls of film, 1 bottle of liquor permitted duty free. Evidence of citizenship should be carried. If you have valuable articles of foreign make, cameras, etc., register them with the U.S. Customs before leaving the United States. There are no restrictions on importation or exportation of money except for gold, so don't buy jewelry containing gold coins. Radios and TV sets are restricted. They are registered and must be taken out on departure.

Tourist cards, valid for 30 days, are issued free. Tourist cards valid for six months, costing $3, may be obtained from any Mexican Consulate or Tourist Commission office and from some Pan American offices. A multiple entry card, costing $5, is valid for various visits within 6 months. Passport, birth certificate or some other definite proof of citizenship is required. Smallpox vaccination certificate is necessary. Yellow fever and cholera certificates required if coming from an infected area.

DRUGSTORES ... You'll find a wide choice of U.S. and European products. Small drugstores are to be found in or near all the better hotels.

ELECTRIC CURRENT ... 110 volts, 50 cycle A.C. in the Federal District; 60 cycles in most of the rest of the country.

FAUNA ... Birds and animals native to southwestern United States are found in Mexico. Parrots of many types, tapirs, honey bears and several varieties of monkeys are native to much of Mexico.

FLORA ... Beautiful flowers and plants, spectacular flowering trees, cacti of all varieties, orchids of many kinds, and many exotic tropical plants abound.

FOOD ... *Tamales* are, of course, known to everyone, but equally famous is *mole de guajolote,* turkey in spicy chocolate sauce. *Tacos* and *enchiladas* are made of meat or chicken rolled in *tortillas* (maize pancakes) and are delicious. Mexico abounds in fruits and vegetables, and Indian dishes are found everywhere. *Chile, mole, tostadas* (toasted fried *tortillas* with chicken, beans and lettuce) are all Indian and good. Mexican beans (*frijoles*) appear in various dishes. Red snapper, Veracruz style (sautéed with pimientos and spices) is a famous fish dish. Fruits include a vast assortment of tropical types—avocados, bananas, pineapples, *zapotes,* pomegranates, guavas, limes and *mangos de Manila,* which are delicious. Many varieties of the above are unknown at home. Don't eat fruit unless you peel it, and avoid raw vegetables. Try *higos rebanados* (delicious fresh sliced figs), *guacamole* (a mashed avocado salad) and, of course, papaya, which you may or may not like. In most tourist areas you can get any type of food, and pasteurized milk. Mealtimes are later than in the United States. Luncheon is the main meal, served between 1 P.M. and 3 P.M. Dinner is late in the evening.

GAMBLING . . . Not allowed. There is horse racing at the Hipódromo de las Americas in Mexico City every Tuesday, Thursday, Saturday and Sunday from October 12 to September 16. Pari-mutuels here and at jai-alai games. Betting on cockfights outside of Federal District.

LANGUAGE . . . Spanish is the official language, but all the stores and hotels have English-speaking employees.

LAUNDRY AND DRY CLEANING . . . Better hotels have their own plants and offer special 24-hour service. There are other good plants throughout the city. Service outside the bigger cities is not recommended. Prices are about the same as in the United States.

LIQUOR . . . *Tequila,* distilled mainly in Jalisco, is potent. Tourists should be cautious. *Mezcal,* too, is far from mild. Mexican beer is famous; Bohemia, Carta Blanca, Superior, XX and Corona are all good. Imported whiskies and brandies of nearly every brand are available but more expensive than in the United States. Local rums, gin and wines are excellent, inexpensive. Drinks hit fast at high altitudes, so take it easy. Drunkenness is sternly frowned upon. Minimum legal age for drinkers is 18.

MEDICAL FACILITIES . . . English-speaking and American-trained doctors and dentists available, often as staff physicians in the best hotels. In Mexico City there is an American-British hospital (Bondojito 171, Tacubaya), a French hospital and many Mexican institutions.

MOTION PICTURES . . . Mexican movie industry makes its own pictures. Hollywood and British films are usually with English sound, dubbed-in Spanish text. French and Italian movies are popular.

MUSIC . . . The concert season is July and August. In Mexico City concerts are held in the Fine Arts Palace. Orchestras of the National Conservatory of Music and National University give concerts throughout the year. There are also native *mariachi* bands, whose music is famous throughout the country.

NIGHT CLUBS AND CABARETS . . . In Mexico City: *Señorial,* Hamburgo 188, international floor show; *Jacaranda* and *Can-Can,* Genova 44; *Los Globos,* Insurgentes Sur 810; *Normandie,* Niza 5; and many others, all with good shows. *La Fuente,* Insurgentes Sur 890, is Mexico's largest night club and always has outstanding entertainment. Most of the top hotels have night clubs. For colorful, out-of-the-way spots, take a guide with you.

PHOTOGRAPHY . . . All kinds of equipment are readily available. Prices are lower than in the United States on most articles, especially cameras. Color film may be developed in Mexico. American Photo Supply, Av. Madero 21, Foto Regis, Av. Juárez 80, Foto Rudiger, V. Carranza 11, are good places for equipment or film work.

RELIGION . . . Mexico is a Catholic country. Some of the cathedrals are world famous and should be visited. Services in English are held at Christ Church Episcopal, Artículo 123 #134; Union Evangelical Church, Reforma 1870; Lutheran Church of the Good Shepherd, Palmas 1910; St. Patrick's Church (Catholic), Bondojito 248, Col. Tacubaya; First Church of Christ Scientist, #21 Dante, Col. Anzures.

RESTAURANTS ... You choose your restaurants here, as you do at home, by what you want to spend. Here are some of the leading places in Mexico City: *Ambassadeurs,* Paseo de la Reforma 12 (swank and high priced); *Prendes,* 16 de Septiembre 12 (good European food, moderate); *La Cava,* Insurgentes 37 (excellent French food and steaks, lavishly decorated as an old French tavern, moderate); *Alfredo,* Genova 74 (good Italian food); the smart *Restaurant del Lago,* at the new extension of Chapultepec Park; *Chalet Suizo,* Niza 37 (very popular with tourists, specializes in Swiss and German food, moderate); *Shirley's Restaurant,* Sullivan 166 (real American food, moderate); *Focolare,* Hamburgo 87 (swank and high priced); *Rivoli,* Hamburgo 123 (a gourmet's delight, high priced); *Jena,* Morelos 110 (deservedly famous, à la carte, expensive); *Parador,* Calle de Niza 17 (Spanish specialties, expensive, good); *Sanborn's* four locations: del Prado Hotel Arcade, Paseo de la Reforma 45, next door to Pan Am, Madero 4 and on the Reforma next to the Maria Isabel Hotel. (American and Mexican food). Other recommended restaurants are *Delmonico's,* Londres 87; *Mauna Loa,* Hamburgo 172; *Derby,* Reforma 400; *El Paseo,* Reforma 146; *Normandie,* Niza 5; *Chipp's,* Genova 59; *Alex Cardini's,* Madrid 21, home of the famous Caesar Salad. All the top hotels have excellent cosmopolitan restaurants. Mexico City has many bars. Here are a few favorites: *La Cucaracha,* Gante 1; *El Jorongo* in Hotel María Isabel; *Bar Jardin* in the Hotel Reforma; *Muralto* atop Latino Americana tower; *Montenegro* and *Nicte-Ha* in Hotel Del Prado.

SHOPS AND STORES ... The parade of shops is endless. Mexico City's Avenida Madero is like the Rue de la Paix in Paris. Sanborn's is famous for textiles and handcrafts. There are also good shops on or near 5 de Mayo, 16 de Septiembre, Niza and Insurgentes. Mexican jewelry of handmade silver can be bought everywhere. Among the good silver shops are Sanborn's, Los Castillo, Prieto, and Vendome. Perfumes are lower priced than at home. There are also good buys in quality leather and suede articles. Be sure to visit the markets. There is one in every district. All sell pottery, glassware, textiles, serapes and jewelry. The National Pawn Shop turns up a bargain now and then, too. It's a national institution worth a look. Mexican tinware and Mexican lacquer are to be found everywhere.

SPECTATOR SPORTS ... Baseball; boxing and wrestling (Wednesday and Saturday in the Arena Coliseo or Arena Mexico); bullfights from October to March every Sunday at 4:30 P.M. *Charreadas* or rodeos every Sunday morning at Rancho del Charro. Football (soccer) in season at the new Estadio Azteca and the University City Stadium; horse racing from October 12 through July at Hipodromo de las Americas; jai alai daily, except Monday, at Fronton Mexico.

SPORTS . . . Golf at Chapultepec, Mexico, Churubusco and Hacienda golf clubs. Cards can be arranged. (Inquire at your hotel or travel bureau.) Hiking is a good sport in Mexico. Hunting and fishing permits may be obtained at the Departmento Forestal y Caza, Edison 145, Mexico City, and the Secretaria de Marina, Azueta No. 9, respectively. Permits are needed for inland and deep-sea fishing. Polo at Polo Club de Mexico. Riding horses may be hired from several stables, called *pensiones*. Tennis may be played at the Reforma and Churubusco Country Clubs. Public swimming pools (*balnearios*) are out along the Puebla road. Admission about 5 pesos.

THEATERS . . . Vaudeville houses include the *Lírico* and the *Blanquita.*

For those who understand Spanish, theater in Mexico City is most interesting. There is a large variety of musicals, comedies and dramas.

TIME . . . Same as United States Central Standard Time except in northwest states where Mountain or Pacific Time applies.

TIPPING . . . Tip luggage porters at least 1 peso per bag. 2 pesos is average tip for the attendant who opens your hotel room, services of bellboy or room service waiter, concierge, hat check. 1-peso tip for shoeshine boy, washroom attendant, parking-lot attendant, theater usher. Tip barbers, beauticians, bartenders and waiters 15% of the check.

TRANSPORTATION . . . Taxis are plentiful and cruise all over the city. Empty taxis carry a sign reading *libre,* meaning free. Meters are now used on all Mexico City cabs. Taxis from stands near hotels have the right to collect 1 peso surcharge. Fares are quite reasonable. Buses and streetcars serve the entire city. There is frequent inexpensive bus service all over the country. Drive-yourself cars may be hired from various car rental organizations including Hertz, Avis and Volkswagen. Rates from $36 per week. Even if driving your own car, take out local insurance; full coverage is slightly over $1 a day.

WATER . . . Is potable in most large cities; elsewhere it is not. Plenty of good bottled water available. For distant trips take a bottle of chlorine tablets just in case.

WHAT TO BUY . . . This depends on what you want to spend, what takes your eye and what you can't live without. Silver is, of course, a staple product. Careful shopping will turn up the unusual: Mexican glassware, pottery, handwoven textiles, lacquers, native baskets, fine leather goods and handcrafts of all types. If you go on side tours, various spots are famous for certain things: Taxco for silver, for instance, and beautiful tinware; Oaxaca for pottery and serapes, gold filigree and black pottery; Guadalajara for handblown glass and pottery. Each state has its own style of handcrafts. Perfumes are cheaper than in the United States, but patronize the stores, not street vendors. Take purchases through U.S. Customs yourself rather than have them sent by the store.

WHAT TO WEAR . . . Mexico City is very dressy. Dress here as you would in any large United States city. But never, never wear slacks or shorts in public places or on the street. High altitude makes for cool nights and some cool days. Bring a topcoat, raincoat. For coastal resorts, plenty of cotton frocks, sports clothes, bathing suits and pastel silks. Good walking shoes are a must. As there is little central heating, a warm robe is needed in winter. Bring dark glasses. Evening clothes depend upon you and the kind of gaiety you plan, but are not necessary in Mexico City night spots. Sweaters come in handy. Men should take seersucker or linen jackets and suits. Wool suits for Mexico City, light topcoat, swimming trunks, raincoat, bathrobe, sports shirts and slacks.

WHERE TO GO—SIGHTSEEING . . .

There is so much to see in Mexico that you have to take your choice unless you have a lot of time. Guides are available and the government requires all *bona fide* guides to be licensed. Don't take chances; hire them through hotels or tourist bureaus.

Mexico City . . . The museums are mentioned under ARTS. La Catedral on the Zócalo is the oldest church on the American continent; Chapultepec, a beautiful forest park with a castle (National Museum of History), dates from pre-conquest times. It contains a zoo and a lake; there are band concerts and promenades. The Franciscan Monastery at Churubusco is worth a trip. There are many short one-day trips from Mexico City. Among them consider: the Pyramids at San Juan Teotihuacan, and ruins of a sacred city (this is about 30 miles from Mexico City); Xochimilco floating gardens and flowery canals; beautiful church and monastery. City tour, including Chapultepec Castle, National Palace, museums and residential district, costs about $5 per person; Shrine of Guadalupe, Pyramids and Acolman Monastery tour costs about $6.50; one-day tour to Cuernavaca and Taxco, including lunch, costs about $13; two-day tour, including hotels and meals in Taxco, costs about $23 per person. See also snow-covered Popocatepetl, an easy car trip through interesting Amecameca to the 13,000-foot level.

Cuernavaca . . . 46 miles from Mexico City by a new super highway. A fashionable resort once favored by Cortés, Maximilian and Carlota. See Palacio de Cortés with Rivera murals donated by Dwight Morrow, Borda Gardens. There are pyramids, lakes, cathedrals, quaint streets, wonderful old houses, good shops. There are many good hotels, American Plan. Many have gardens, swimming pools, bars.

Taxco . . . 101 miles from Mexico City. Beautiful, picturesque town, surrounded by silver-rich mountains, Taxco is a national monument and has over 800 silver shops and workrooms. Good hotels are the *De La Borda, Victoria, Rancho Taxco* and *Posada de la Misión;* rates run $16 to $24 double, American Plan. Satisfactory, less expensive hotels are the *Santa Prisca, Melendez* and *Los Arcos.* Visit *Paco's Bar* and the famous *Barta's,* but take it easy on the *tequila* and wear low-heeled walking shoes on those steep, cobblestoned streets. Taxco's houses are attractive stucco or stone with delightful red tile roofs. Visit the lovely Borda Cathedral on the main plaza, and don't miss the Indian market.

Acapulco . . . 282 miles from Mexico City by road, about 60 minutes by plane. Magnificently beautiful coastal resort on the Pacific. The oval bay is surrounded by mountains and the scenery is fantastic. Hotels are numerous and range from super de luxe to modest. *Hotel Pierre Marques,* on Revolcadero Beach 12 miles from the city, is very swank with lavish entertainment; winter Modified American Plan rates from $22 per person. Also tops are the *Acapulco Hilton, El Presidente, Caleta, Ritz* and *Las Brisas* (has 70 swimming pools!) with winter rates averaging $30 double, European Plan. Excellent hotels with Modified American Plan rates include the *Playa Hornos, El Mirador* (dramatically perched on the Quebrada Cliffs), the *Costero, Las Hamacas, El Pozo del Rey* (AP), *Elcano* and *Majestic;* average MAP winter rate is $28 double. Many good lower-priced hotels: *Boca Chica, Club de Pesca, Maris, Papagayo, Del Monte; Motel Acapulco* and *Autohotel Ritz.* All rates lower in summer. Swim at Caleta in the morning, at Los Hornos Beach in the afternoon; see the spectacular diver at the La Perla Club. Hotels arrange fishing and hunting. Shops are filled with handicrafts.

Guadalajara . . . Second city of Mexico, was founded in 1530, is 5,248 feet above sea level and has a fine year-around climate. Good hotels such as the new *Guadalajara Hilton,* the *Fenix, Del Parque, Gran Hotel, Camino Real* and *Genova,* charge from $6.40-$16 double, European Plan. There's lots to see here. Nearby are Tlaquepaque, famous for pottery and *mariachi* music, Lake Chapala and the art colony of Ajijic, and the small town of Tequila where the native drink is made. There are many good buys in glass, ceramics and leather. See the cathedral and the state museum. Guadalajara is only 1¾ hours by plane from Mexico City, with flights daily.

Oaxaca . . . 330 miles from Mexico City, less than two hours by air. Very old, pre-Spanish city with year-round pleasant climate. Located in beautiful semitropical valley near jungle and mountains. Several good hotels: *Marques del Valle, Monte Alban, Margarita, Oaxaca Courts, Victoria,* with cottages, swimming pools. Rates average $8 to $12 double, European Plan. See the archaeological site nearby at Monte Alban; the ruins at Mitla, 45 minutes away; the church of San Felipe Neri with Churrigueresque altars; the Cathedral; the Church of Santo Domingo with its genealogical tree of the Virgin; La Soledad with the famous shrine of the Virgin. City market is picturesque, and on Saturday natives from surrounding villages come to buy. Serapes, black-glazed pottery, blankets, thin woven-straw mats, obsidian and jade idols are excellent here. Hunting is excellent.

Yucatán . . . 2½ hours by air from Mexico City, on the Gulf of Mexico. This is where the great Maya civilization flourished. All social classes speak Mayan and Spanish, and native men and women always dress in white. Women wear their hair in coiled braids piled on the head and tied with colored ribbon. The ruins of Chichen-Itza, Uxmal and Izamal are accessible from Mérida, the capital of the state of Yucatán. Mérida has several good hotels, such as the de luxe *Panamericana,* $10 double and up, European Plan. *Hotels Mérida,* the

A good place to make your headquarters in Mexico City is the Hotel Reforma Intercontinental, right in the center of all the activity that makes Mexico interesting.

Tropical Maya and *Colón* also have air-conditioned rooms; rates from $6 up, European Plan.

Chichen-Itza is an archaeological wonder. The ruins of the once-great Maya city are fabulous. The Temple of the Warriors, the Round Tower, the Great Temple of Kukulkan, all testify to the remarkable culture and progress of the Maya civilization. *Hotel Mayaland* ($22 single, $36 double, including meals) and *Hacienda Chichen-Itza* ($14 single, $24 double, including meals). Izamal is older than Chichen-Itza but is less frequently visited.

The ruins of Uxmal, 58 miles south of Mérida, are reached by bus or taxi. The Nunnery, the Governor's Palace, the House of the Prophet (a pyramid surmounted by two temples) are marvelous to see. Kabah, Sayil and Labna, in the Yucatán jungle, are easily reached from the *Hacienda Uxmal* resort hotel ($20 single, $34 double, including meals). It is possible to visit other Mayan ruins from Mérida but special arrangements are necessary. The weather in Yucatán is perfect from October to April. Summer days are hot, but nights are cool. It's advisable to wear sun glasses, for the light is blinding.

Of interest for their charm and fishing are Puerto Vallarta and Mazatlan on the Pacific Coast, Isla Mujeres and Cozumel on the Caribbean. All have excellent hotels.

SOURCES OF FURTHER INFORMATION . . . The Mexican Government Tourist Department, Reforma y Lafragua, Mexico City. Offices also in New York, Washington, Chicago, New Orleans, Miami, San Antonio, Houston, Dallas, San Diego, Tucson and Los Angeles.

Tickets for bullfights, jai alai, etc., may be obtained easiest through travel bureaus by paying a ticket-broker's fee. There are dozens including Cooks and American Express. Pan American's office (Tel. 46–46–60) is at Paseo Reforma 35.

English newspapers, the *Mexico City Times* and the *News,* are published daily. The *Daily Bulletin, This Week* and *The Gazer* are free tourist publications.

NICARAGUA

WEATHER IN MANAGUA—Lat. N12°8′—Alt. 150′

	JAN.	FEB.	MAR.	APR.	MAY	JUNE	JULY	AUG.	SEPT.	OCT.	NOV.	DEC.
Average Temp.	81°	82°	83°	86°	86°	82°	82°	83°	82°	82°	82°	80°
In. of Rain	0.12	0.02	0.02	0.50	5.64	8.24	5.11	4.74	8.38	11.58	1.70	0.41

LOCATION ... In the heart of Central America, bordered on the north by Honduras, on the south by Costa Rica, on the east by the Atlantic Ocean (Caribbean) and on the west by the Pacific Ocean.

CHARACTERISTICS ... Land of lakes and volcanoes, Nicaragua gives its aerial visitors a breath-taking introduction to its spectacular scenery with a view of some of the 20-odd volcanoes that line the western side of the largest Central American republic. Some of the volcanoes spout clouds of steam and smoking ash, others cradle sky-blue or peacock-green lakes in their craters. While black, congealed lava makes many of the peaks a forbidding spectacle, a luxuriant green mantle of tropical growth makes others a delight to see. Nicaragua is also a land of broad lowlands matted by rain forests and laced with swift-flowing rivers. But only the adventuresome explore this sparsely populated, little-developed region in the east. Most visitors head for the Pacific coastal plain, with its backdrop of volcanoes, where the bulk of the population, the principal cities, resorts and lakes are concentrated. Nicaraguans are noted for their friendliness.

POPULATION ... The inhabitants of the country number approximately 1,600,000.

SIZE ... 57,145 square miles, about the same size as Illinois.

CAPITAL ... Managua, with over 226,000 inhabitants.

GOVERNMENT ... A republic.

HOW TO GET THERE ... By PAA Clipper from Los Angeles, 7¼ hours; from San Francisco, 9¼ hours; from New Orleans, 6¼ hours; from Miami 7 hours, all via Guatemala; and also from Panama, 3 hours. By ship 12 days from New York. Taxi from the airport, if shared, costs 7 cordobas.

ACCOMMODATIONS... In Managua: *Gran Hotel* and *Lido Palace Hotel* are the most frequently visited. Both have their own swimming pools. Rates from $10 single, $16 double, European Plan (without meals). Other hotels: *Hotel Nicaragua, Estrella, Santa Maria Ostuma,* a mountain hotel, 81 miles from Managua; the *Hotel Barlovento,* located in San Juan del Sur, a beach resort on the Pacific coast near the Costa Rican border. Approximately 2½-hour drive from Managua.

BANKS... Banco Nacional de Nicaragua, Banco Nicaraguense, Banco Central de Nicaragua, Bank of London y Montreal, Ltd., Caley and Dagnal, Bank of America. Travelers checks may be cashed anywhere, but there are no currency-exchange facilities at the airport.

CALENDAR OF HOLIDAYS... The most important are January 20, San Sebastian, at Diriamba, 25 miles from Managua; Holy Week, during which all business houses are closed and almost the entire population goes to the beaches on the Pacific coast; May 1, Fiesta del Trabajo; August 1 to 10, Santo Domingo de Guzmán, celebrated in Managua with bullfighting and cockfighting. (On the first day of this fiesta, Santo Domingo de Guzmán is brought from "Las Sierras." On the last day, Santo Domingo de Guzmán is taken back to the Sierras in the same manner. It is the belief of the Indians that if Santo Domingo de Guzmán is not taken back to his church in "Las Sierras," he will disappear in Managua and will be found in his church.) September 14, Batalla de San Jacinto (Nicaraguan troops defeated the famous American Filibusters headed by William Walker); September 15, Día de la Independencia; November 29 to December 7, La Purísima, celebrated in the whole country in honor of Virgin Mary.

CIGARETTES... American cigarettes are available and cost around 42¢ a pack. The local brands are available for approximately 25¢ a pack; *Windsor* and *Esfinge* are popular with tourists.

CLIMATE... Nicaragua, like other countries in Central America, has two seasons: the rainy season, warm but fresh, the dry season, cool but very dry. The best time to visit is December to May.

CLUBS... Club Terraza, Club Managua, Club Internacional, French Club, Nejapa Country Club, Rotary, Lions International.

COMMUNICATIONS... Nicaragua is served by All America Cables and Tropical Radio for phone calls and telegraph messages to foreign points. A 3-minute call to the States costs from $3 to $5, depending upon city. Airmail postage for 5-gram letters or postcards is 45 centavos.

CURRENCY... The monetary unit is the cordoba, divided into 100 centavos. The rate of exchange is C.7.00 to $1 but market or street rate varies depending upon demand.

CUSTOMS REGULATIONS AND DOCUMENTS REQUIRED FOR UNITED STATES CITIZENS... Duty-free allowances: 2 cartons of cigarettes, 1 bottle of liquor. Native-born U.S. citizens may enter with a tourist card issued by Pan Am offices in the U.S.

DRUGSTORES ... Most all American drug products are available, and there are many excellent locally manufactured items.

ELECTRIC CURRENT ... Electric current is alternating and is rated at 110 volts, 60 cycles, as in the United States.

FAUNA ... Deer, wild turkeys, wild ducks, and other tropical animals and birds.

FLORA ... Carnations, dahlias, orchids, roses, gardenias, and a great variety of tropical vegetation.

FOOD ... There's a profusion of tropical fruits, and local meats are excellent. Nicaraguans do wonderful things to such staples as corn, rice and beans. *Tiste,* made with corn, is the national soft drink.

GAMBLING ... There is an official Government lottery and all the profits go to the hospitals.

LANGUAGE ... Spanish is the official language, but English is spoken by a large percentage of the population.

LAUNDRY AND DRY CLEANING ... All hotels furnish 24-hour service for laundry and dry cleaning at reasonable prices.

LIQUOR ... All kinds of imported liquors are available. There are several locally made rums, good beer, and *aguardiente.*

MEDICAL FACILITIES ... Most of the doctors in this area have been educated in the United States or Europe, and speak Spanish, English and one other language. Hospitals in Managua: the Hospital General, the Baptist Hospital, and Hospital Militar.

MOTION PICTURES ... There are many motion-picture theaters from the finest, air-conditioned houses to the outside unroofed theaters. Prices range from 35¢ to 90¢.

MUSIC ... Both American and Latin American music are played in all clubs.

NIGHT CLUBS AND CABARETS ... There are some small clubs and cabarets. The *Versailles* is popular, and guest cards are available for *Club 113,* a key club.

PHOTOGRAPHY ... Color film as well as black and white can be obtained in Managua and good quality developing of black and white can be obtained locally. Ektachrome can be developed in 24 hours. Robt. Teran & Cía. is the local Kodak dealer.

RELIGION ... The country is Catholic, but other sects are represented.

RESTAURANTS AND BARS ... There are several excellent restaurants in the center of town, such as *El Patio, Gambrinus, Guadalajara, Club 113* for steaks, *Mandarin* for Chinese food, *El Coliseo* for Italian dishes, *Salon, Rincón, Munich* and *El Colonial* (American style food). The average complete dinner costs about $4.

SHOPS AND STORES ... Most of the stores in Managua are located on Avenida Roosevelt and Calle Central, where you will find American merchandise of all kinds. Nicaragua is famous for hand work and filigree gold jewelry at reasonable prices.

SPECTATOR SPORTS ... Baseball, basketball, and cockfights are the outstanding sports. Managua has the most modern and largest stadium in Central America, with a seating capacity of 40,000. At present, there are 162 pro and amateur baseball teams in Nicaragua.

SPORTS ... Deep-sea fishing, sailing on the lakes, swimming, hunting, golf, tennis.

TIME ... Same as United States Central Standard Time.

TIPPING ... Tip porters C1 per piece of luggage. Service charges are not added onto hotel or restaurant bills; tip waiter 10% of the check; split 10% of your hotel bill between chambermaid and room-service boy. Taxi drivers are tipped 10% of the fare; C1 minimum tip. C2 is customary for a beautician; C1 for a barber; 25 centavos for shoeshine boy.

TRANSPORTATION ... Taxis. Cars may be hired for tours around the country. Bus trips also available.

WATER ... Bottled water is available, also soft drinks made with purified water.

WHAT TO BUY ... Native handicrafts, alligator goods, hand-embroidered articles, hammocks, guitars, shoes (very fine shoes are handmade in Nicaragua). Baskets and woven items. Gold jewelry.

WHAT TO WEAR ... Sports clothes and light clothing in general, as Nicaragua has predominantly a tropical climate.

WHERE TO GO—SIGHTSEEING ...

Managua ... The capital, Managua, is 28 miles from the Pacific. It rises gradually from the shores of Lake Managua and its red tiled roofs and pastel-colored buildings give it a pleasant effect of freshness. The Nicaraguan capital is a new city. In 1931 an earthquake followed by a fire destroyed a large part of it, and the city was rebuilt on the ruins.

The best way to see the city is to start at Central Park near the lake front. Across the street is the park dedicated to Rubén Darío, Nicaragua's immortal poet. In this vicinity tourists may visit the capitol (called the National Palace), the city hall (known as the Palace of the National District), and the Cathedral. In Parque Darío is the splendid monument dedicated to the poet. On the east side of this park is the Club Managua.

For an interesting tour of the city, hire a car and drive past the President's residence, built in Moorish style on a hill overlooking Lake Tiscapa in the crater of an extinct volcano. A stop should be made at Piedrecitas Park, loveliest spot in the capital. Here one may enjoy a magnificent view of three lakes—Asososca, Managua and Jiloa—with bald, smoking Mt. Momotombo in the distance.

In the southwestern section of Managua is one of the city's most unusual sights. Here are the footprints of people and animals made 2,000 to 5,000 years ago, according to foremost authorities. At some undetermined era they fled westward from a volcanic disturbance, leaving their footprints in a mudflow which later solidified.

From Managua, the tourist can make interesting excursions. Masaya, 27 miles southeast, features fine Indian handicrafts; fishing in Lake Masaya. A pleasant drive is that to Tipitapa, a spa on Lake Managua, 14 miles from the capital. The town is famous for its fish dinners. There's a "fisherman's retreat" here with boats and equipment.

Granada ... Nicaragua's oldest city is situated at the northwest end of Lake Nicaragua, 30 miles from Managua. Granada was founded by the Spanish conquistadores in 1524, and today it is still a charming and leisurely old town with many Spanish landmarks. Sharing the streets with modern cars are horse-drawn carriages and yoked oxen drawing high-wheeled carts.

Lake Nicaragua is 100 miles long, 45 miles wide, and dotted with islands. One, Ometepe is crowned by two volcano peaks. The lake is the only one in the world where sharks, sawfish and tarpon may be found in fresh water. Historians believe that ages ago Lake Nicaragua formed part of a Pacific Ocean bay; then, during one of the volcanic eruptions, the entrance to the bay was closed. Thus the salt-water fish were trapped, and as fresh-water streams gradually diluted the salt, they adapted themselves to the change and survived.

At San Carlos on the south side of Lake Nicaragua is a hotel. Arrange through Nicaragua Expeditions, Managua, for renting of fishing equipment and transportation.

Fifty miles north of Managua is Leon, a 17th-century Spanish city, which has one of the largest and oldest cathedrals in Central America. The church was built in the 18th century and contains the tomb of the poet Rubén Darío, as well as an exceedingly beautiful white topaz shrine, presented by Philip II of Spain, and the superb *Christ of Esquipulas* crafted in bronze. The University of Leon graduated students before the landing of the Pilgrim Fathers at Plymouth Rock. A short distance from Leon is the beach resort of Poneloya on the Pacific, with broad sand beaches. Corinto, just north of Poneloya, is the main port for cruise ships and is connected by railway with Managua, Granada and Leon.

A ride on the Inter-American highway takes you as far as the Costa Rican border, going through the coffee plantations and the city of Diriamba, where you will find the modern *Hotel Majestic,* located at an altitude of 3,000 feet above sea level. There are many beautiful beaches on the Pacific coast, such as San Juan del Sur, Casares, Boquita, Masachapa, Poneloya. All are connected by good roads.

The gold-mining district may be visited and is accessible by air.

SOURCES OF FURTHER INFORMATION ... The principal source is the Pan American office in the Gran Hotel, Managua, where tourist information and travel to the interior are available (Tel. 2351). The Junta Nacional de Turismo in Parque Central also will supply information. In New York, The Nicaragua Consulate is at 1270 Ave. of the Americas.

PANAMA
AND THE
CANAL ZONE

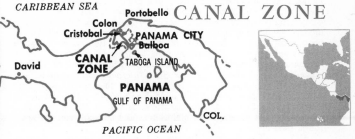

CARIBBEAN SEA
Portobello
Colon
Cristobal
PANAMA CITY
Balboa
CANAL ZONE
TABOGA ISLAND
David
PANAMA
GULF OF PANAMA
COL.
PACIFIC OCEAN

WEATHER IN PANAMA CITY—Lat. N8°57′—Alt. 40′

	JAN.	FEB.	MAR.	APR.	MAY	JUNE	JULY	AUG.	SEPT.	OCT.	NOV.	DEC.
Average Temp.	79°	80°	81°	82°	80°	79°	80°	80°	79°	78°	78°	79°
In. of Rain	.9	.9	.6	2.8	7.8	8.2	7.2	7.8	7.9	10.1	10.1	4.2

LOCATION ... The Isthmus of Panamá is geographically situated between Costa Rica in Central America and Colombia in South America. At its narrowest point, 50 miles wide, the Atlantic and Pacific Oceans are united by the world-famous Panamá Canal.

CHARACTERISTICS ... Here is a wonderful combination of old-world charm and modern comfort. The natural friendliness of its people, their gaiety and hospitality make Panamá a place to be visited and enjoyed. It is a paradise for sportsmen. Big-game fishing is famous here and hunting is excellent in the interior. There are luxury hotels and good beaches where swimming is delightful. Tourists are an old story in this colorful little country; they are very welcome.

POPULATION ... Estimated over 1,178,000.

SIZE ... 28,753 square miles.

CAPITAL ... Panamá City, population 273,440.

GOVERNMENT ... Panamá is an independent Republic of 9 provinces, except for the 10-mile-wide strip of land surrounding the Panamá Canal, land-leased to the U.S. Government and under its jurisdiction.

HOW TO GET THERE ... By Pan Am Jet Clipper from Miami, 2½ hours to Panamá City. From Los Angeles via Guatemala City, 7¼ hours. By National-Pan American-Panagra interchange 6¼ hours from New York. By ship, about 5 days. By land, via the Inter-American Highway.

ACCOMMODATIONS ... Hotels are all run on the European

Plan. The centrally located, luxurious new *Hotel El Continental* is air-conditioned, has a swimming pool, gambling casino, night club, several fine dining rooms and a coffee shop ˙open 24 hours a day. Double $12-$18 (December 16-March 31). The smartly decorated *Lux,* also in the center of town, has year-round double rates from $13. The lavish *El Panamá Hilton* is situated in the residential section of the capital and is one of the most spectacular buildings of its kind. Ultra-modern studio-style bedrooms with private balconies are designed for beauty and comfort. Featured are an outdoor patio, swimming pool, cabaña and tennis club, putting green, lovely roof garden for dining and dancing, and gambling casino. Rates from $15 up, double (slightly higher January 6-March 31). The *Hotel Internacional,* also quite new, has a roof garden and is in the heart of the theater and night-club section; year round from $10 double. The *Colón,* also in the downtown area, is $7-$15 double. *La Siesta Hotel,* at the airport, is a complete resort in itself with night club, pool and golf course. Year-round rates are $12 single, $16 double.

ARTS . . . The Panamá Museum in Panamá City contains a representative collection of native arts and crafts that have been influenced by Spanish and ancient Inca civilization. Fortunately, Panamá crafts have escaped overcommercialization. You will see fine examples of Panamanian taste and imagination in the art of these people.

BALLET . . . The Escuela Nacional de Ballet and private ballet clubs occasionally present ballets at the Nacional Theater. *El Tamborito,* the national dance, is colorful and enchanting. The folk dances may be seen particularly during the 4-day pre-Lenten Carnival period. Women dancers wear the *pollera* and heirloom jewels.

BANKS . . . In Panamá City, the National Bank of the Republic of Panamá, Panamá Trust Company, Chase Manhattan Bank of New York, First National City Bank of New York; these last two have branch offices in Balboa, C.Z., and Colón, R.P.

CALENDAR OF HOLIDAYS . . . Stores and museums close Tuesdays and for: Carnival Time, 4 days of fiestas before Ash Wednesday; New Year's Day; March 1, Constitution Day; May 1, Labor Day; November 3, Independence from Colombia; November 10, First Call of Independence; November 28, Independence from Spain; December 8, Mother's Day; Christmas Day.

CIGARETTES AND TOBACCO . . . Practically all brands of American cigarettes are sold in Panamá, and some are now made there. They cost from 20¢ to 35¢ a pack. Duty-free allowance 200 cigarettes, 50 cigars, or 1 lb. of tobacco.

CLIMATE . . . The temperature of tropical Panamá is remarkable for its uniformity throughout the year. The average temperature is about 80 degrees. Noon is the hottest part of the day. Most of the stores close for a 2-hour lunch period. Except for rainy October and November, Panamá is a pleasant place for visitors the year around, although it is at its best during the driest months, January through April.

CLUBS . . . The Union Club and Golf Club in Panamá City extend cards to visitors through the courtesy of their members. There are also the Rotary International of Panamá and Lions International. Beer-garden clubs, the Rancho, the Balboa and the Atlas, are open to the public.

COMMON COURTESIES AND LOCAL CUSTOMS . . . Panamanians are friendly and courteous to strangers, but have strict laws against littering the streets.

COMMUNICATIONS . . . A 3-minute phone call to Florida is $8.20; up to $11.80 for farther points. Airmail rate between Panamá and the States is 11¢ a half ounce.

CURRENCY . . . The balboa is on a par with U.S.$1.

CUSTOMS REGULATIONS AND DOCUMENTS REQUIRED FOR UNITED STATES CITIZENS . . . The Tourist Card ($2) is sold at transportation offices through the United States port of embarkation. Carry proof of citizenship for re-entry to the United States.

Smallpox vaccination certificate and transportation beyond Panamá required for tourist card and admission into Panamá. Sea arrival and air departure tax each $2.

DRUGSTORES . . . Well-stocked drugstores in all major centers.

ELECTRIC CURRENT . . . Same as in the U.S.

FAUNA . . . There are jaguar, puma, tigrillo, ocelet, mule, deer, wild boar, peccary and the *conejo pintado* (painted rabbit). The fowl include wild turkey, quail, partridge and pigeon. The name "Panamá" means abundance of fish. Panamanian waters off both shores offer all sorts of deep-sea, big-game fish. There are giant tarpon, marlin and sailfish, to mention a few. The mountain streams of Panamá have some of the best trout in Central America.

FLORA . . . The rich tropical vegetation and bizarre flowers of Panamá are often breath-taking in their beauty. Orchids grow in profusion all over the countryside. Majestic palms are everywhere, especially along the superb beaches. If you go up into the highlands, you'll see the huge coffee plantations of Panamá's large coffee industry. The entire Panamanian landscape is a riot of color.

FOOD . . . American, French, Italian or Spanish cookery. You will also enjoy the Panamanian food. Try a delicious *sancocho,* chicken soup with vegetables, the Panamanian tamales, which the natives boast are the best in Central America. *Arroz con pollo,* a universal dish in Latin America, is delicious made in the Panamanian manner. Try fish marinated in champagne. *Patacones de platano verde,* or fried plantains, are a cocktail-hour delicacy. Meals cost about the same as in the States.

GAMBLING . . . The National Lottery is universally popular. Drawings every Sunday at 11 A.M. Pari-mutuel betting every Saturday, Sunday and holiday at Presidente Remón Race Track. Gambling nightly at El Panamá Hilton and Continental hotels.

LANGUAGE . . . The official language is Spanish, but almost everybody speaks English too.

LAUNDRY AND DRY CLEANING . . . Available on a 24-hour service in most hotels or outside establishments.

LIQUOR ... All the regular brands are available in Panamá at prices lower than in the States. Panamanian beer is excellent.

MEDICAL FACILITIES ... American-trained English-speaking doctors are available in Panamá's modern hospitals and clinics. The Republic takes great pride in its high health standards.

MOTION PICTURES ... First-run American pictures are shown at the *Lux, Bella Vista* and *Central* theaters, which are the best. There's also a drive-in theater. All pictures are in English with Spanish titles. There are showings also of Spanish, French, and Italian films. *El Presidente* and *Tropical* are the most popular for Spanish-speaking pictures, made mostly in Mexico or Argentina.

MUSIC ... You'll hear all kinds of music all the time you are in Panamá. The combination of native music and the influence of jazz have given an individual slant to the Panamanian type of Latin music with its several kinds of drums for *El Tamborito,* Panamá's famous national dance.

NIGHT CLUBS ... Panamá City is a gay all-night town. Most hotels have music and dancing. Especially nice are the *Portobello Room* at El Panamá Hilton; and *El Sotano* and *Los Embajadores* at the Continental Hotel.

RESTAURANTS ... Panamá City's best restaurants are in the Panama Hilton and El Continental hotels. Wonderful food and drink are served under the stars—indoors when rains come. Also notable are the *Capri* and *La Fiorentina* (Italian food), *Panamar* (for sea-food), *Los Americos* (Panamanian dishes) and *La Gran Formosa* (Chinese). Meals in Panamá cost about the same as they do at home.

RELIGION ... Roman Catholic, but all creeds are represented.

SHOPS AND STORES ... Central Avenue is the great shopping center in Panamá City. Good shops include: American Bazaar, Dante's, Novedades Antonio, Quinta Avenida, Felix B. Maduro, Shaw's, Fastlich. Panamá is famous for its East Indian shops, and among the most famous is Casa Solomon. Panamá Bonito and Curio-sidades Panameñas specialize in souvenirs. Duty-free shop at the air-port and everywhere in the Colón Free Zone.

SPECTATOR SPORTS ... Horse racing Saturday, Sundays and holidays at the new Presidente Remón Race Track, with clubhouse available to tourists; baseball and the unique annual fishing rodeo that is increasingly popular with the world's best fishermen. Basketball is becoming very popular. Swimming races and golf tournaments draw crowds, too. Annual open golf tournament, with world-famous golfers participating, in January or February. Bullfighting during dry season.

SPORTS ... The fishing is marvelous, both in the sea and in the trout streams in the mountains. Exciting big-game fishing for marlin, tuna, dolphin, pompano and mackerel can be done at various seasons of the year. Boats complete with bait, tackle, food and crew are avail-able at reasonable rates on a 24-hour-or-less basis. The best trout streams can be found in Chiriquí, the southwestern province of Panamá. The interior is a hunter's wonderland. The mountain jungles abound with big game and wild fowl. Jaguar, puma, tigrillo and ocelot, mule deer, tapir and wild hog are among the principal animals. The fowl include wild duck, turkey, partridge and some quail. There are guides, horses, and all varieties of camping equipment for hire. There is open season all year round for both hunting and fishing. Panamá's beaches are beautiful, and the waters of the Pacific and Caribbean offer wonderful swimming and sailing. Panamá has fine golf courses, too. The Panamá Golf Club in Panamá City has an exceptionally fine course that is available to tourists. *Club de Pesca* is a deluxe new fishing resort at Piñas Bay, in the world's best game fish waters.

TIME . . . Same as United States Eastern Standard Time.

TIPPING . . . The 10% rule applies here on all tipping. Luggage porters get 10¢ per bag.

TRANSPORTATION . . . Some taxis are metered; others charge about 50¢ per person for each zone covered, and microtaxis charge about 35¢ per zone. Taxi fare from airport to Panamá City is $5; $1.50 in the limousine. There is good air service, also bus and railway systems. The 1-hour train trip from Panamá City to Colón parallels the Canal.

WATER . . . Uniformly excellent in cities.

WHAT TO BUY . . . Panamá hats are good. Leather goods, especially alligator skins, cameras and Swiss watches are other top buys. French perfume, English and Swedish china, Peruvian silver, Colombian emeralds, textiles of all kinds. Chinese silks and rugs, ivory and jade, English woolens and cashmeres and Italian and Irish linens are all good buys. The cities of Panamá and Colón are very fine shopping centers. You may have "liquor in bond" delivered to your plane, tax free, or buy it at the airport.

WHAT TO WEAR . . . Lightweight, comfortable clothes are essential in Panamá. Cool cotton and linen clothes during the day and lightweight black at night for women. Linen and seersucker suits for men. Formal clothes are worn for evening in the more lavish night spots. Have them cool and colorful. White jackets for men. The nights are cooler in the mountains where sweaters, jackets, or similar light wraps are needed after sundown.

WHERE TO GO—SIGHTSEEING . . .

Panamá City . . . Panamá City, like the entire Republic, is an interesting mixture of old Spanish culture and Western Hemisphere civilization with overtones of native Indian culture. The city is divided into three parts: the present city, Old Panamá (destroyed by the famous pirate Morgan in 1671), and the beautiful residential sections. Your sightseeing trips should include the San Francisco and the Cathedral, the largest churches in Panamá City, facing on the Plaza Catedral, and the Church of San José, with its famous Altar of Gold saved from the original church in Old Panamá City. The native market place is bustling and colorful. Here, native fishing boats bring their daily catch to be sold. See also the Presidencia, home of Panamá's presidents. The patios are very beautiful; plumed egrets wander through them. Bolívar Plaza contains a handsome monument of Simón Bolívar, one of Latin America's greatest heroes. Walking along

Las Bovedas Promenade you'll have a glorious view of the Bay of Panamá. The Palace of Justice, a fine example of Spanish colonial architecture, faces the Promenade. The Church of Santo Domingo on Calle 3A has the famous Flat Arch.

The King's Bridge is the first thing to see in Old Panamá. It marks the boundary of the old city. The best place to start your tour of the ruins is the plaza in front of the old cathedral. Stone pillars mark the site of the first administration building. Going toward the sea you will come to the great arch that was part of the original San José Church that housed the Golden Altar.

A 2-hour drive from Panamá City in the cool mountain climate of El Valle, the *Club Campestre* (country club) offers pleasant accommodations, $5-$8 double, without meals. *El Greco Hotel,* from $6 single and $8 double, is also near resort activities and attractions such as hard-to-believe square trees, golden frogs and Indian caves.

Colón and the Canal Zone . . . No one going to Panamá should miss seeing the busy Canal Zone and the Panamá Canal. You can watch the giant locks in action and the entire engineering masterpiece perform. Coming from Panamá City, you first reach the town of Balboa, headquarters of the Zone. The Administration Building has interesting murals depicting the history of the canal. The Orchid Gardens in Balboa are breathtakingly lovely. Ancon is the residential district.

On the Caribbean side are the twin cities of Cristobal and Colón. Cristobal is in the Canal Zone and Colón is in the Republic of Panamá. Cristobal is primarily a port city full of the colorful mixture of sailors of the nations of the world. Colón is a very cosmopolitan city, and its Free Zone offers unique opportunities for international trade. Dine at *Hotel Washington,* or *El Tropico Restaurant.*

Portobelo . . . Near Colón, Portobelo, the old fortress city, is an important sight to see. These interesting ruins are reached by rented launch, about $25 for the 22-mile trip.

Taboga . . . The Island of Flowers is one of the loveliest resorts in Panamanian waters. The fishing and swimming here are very fine. A new, partly air-conditioned 32-room hotel, *Taboga,* offers cool and pleasant accommodations for $8 single, $10 double.

The Chiriquí Highlands . . . Chiriquí Province, bordering on the Republic of Costa Rica, is the coffee and sugar district of Panamá. There's good hunting for wild game. Trout fishing in the streams of 11,000-foot El Volcan is the very best. There are guides and accommodations available at reasonable prices. Go by air, stay at the *Nacional* in David, or at *Dos Rios* or *Hotel Panamonte* at Boquete.

The San Blas Islands . . . Are a group of islands off the Atlantic coast where the colorful Cuna Indians live. The blue of the sea and the vivid costumes are a fantasy in color. Comfortable accommodations at *Kuna Inn* on Porvenir Island. Go by boat or plane.

SOURCES OF FURTHER INFORMATION . . . Panamá Government Tourist Bureau in Panamá City, Apartado 4421. Its New York office is at 630 Fifth Avenue. Pan American offices in Hotel El Panamá Hilton (Tel. 3-1660) and Hotel El Continental (Tel. 20670).

SOUTH AMERICA

ARGENTINA

WEATHER IN BUENOS AIRES—Lat. S34°16′—Alt. 45′

Temp.	JAN.	FEB.	MAR.	APR.	MAY	JUNE	JULY	AUG.	SEPT.	OCT.	NOV.	DEC.
Low	63°	62°	59°	53°	46°	41°	42°	43°	46°	50°	55°	60°
High	85°	84°	78°	72°	64°	58°	57°	59°	63°	69°	75°	82°
Average	74°	73°	69°	63°	55°	50°	50°	51°	55°	60°	65°	71°
Days of Rain	8	5	6	5	5	6	6	5	5	4	4	5

LOCATION . . . Argentina fills the southern point of South America except for the thin strip of Chile along the western border. It extends for 2,300 miles from Bolivia to Tierra del Fuego between parallels 22° and 55°, almost the distance across the whole United States.

CHARACTERISTICS . . . "B.A." is a modern city as cosmopolitan as any in the world. The theaters, shops, hotels, subways and public buildings are the last word in progress. You will do the same things here that you would do in New York, London or Paris; you will dress in the same way. There is much that is strange, new and exciting; and the Porteños, as residents of Buenos Aires are called, are highly sophisticated people with a wide range of cultural interests.

POPULATION . . . More than 22,186,000

SIZE . . . 1,072,749 square miles, approximately a third the size of the United States.

CAPITAL . . . Buenos Aires, the largest city of Latin America, with a population of over 3,226,900. Greater Buenos Aires has a population of 5,850,000.

GOVERNMENT . . . Argentina is a republic, with a constitution similar to that of the United States.

HOW TO GET THERE . . . By Pan Am's Jet Clipper nonstop to Buenos Aires, 10½ hours from New York. By National, Pan American and Panagra with no change of plane down the west coast 11¼ hours from New York via Miami. By ship 19 days from New York.

ACCOMMODATIONS...In Buenos Aires, the *Plaza,* on the Plaza San Martín, has top rating with Porteño society and much of the social life of the city revolves around it. Rates are from about $12.50 single and $15.70 double with bath, European Plan, plus service charge of 24%.

The *Alvear Palace* on the Avenida Alvear also has an excellent reputation. The rates are less than at the *Plaza.* Even less expensive are the *Continental,* in the business district, the *Lancaster,* accessible to the shopping district, the *City, Claridge, California, Dora, Nogaró* and many others. All of these hotels cater to an international clientele. Because of the hotel shortage, make reservations well in advance. There are various apartment hotels, if you plan to stay for a longer time. You may also find comfortable accommodations in the many boarding houses. The best way to find these is through advertisements in the local English newspapers.

ARTS...Buenos Aires' National Museum of Fine Arts at Avenida Libertador General San Martín 1473 (open daily except Mondays from 4 to 8 P.M.) is the largest and most important museum in the country. It contains not only paintings and sculptures of world masters, but also works of native Argentinean painters and sculptors. Also worth seeing are the Museum of Decorative Arts at Avenida Libertador General San Martín 1902 (open from Tuesday through Sunday), notable for its paintings, tapestries and antiques. The Museum of Spanish-American Art, Isaac Fernández Blanco, at Suipacha 1422 (open from Wednesday to Sunday), is a lovely reproduction of a colonial house and has an interesting collection of old silver, costumes and antiques. The Municipal Museum of Fine Arts is at Avenida Libertador General San Martín 2373. There are also a number of private art galleries, including Wildenstein, which have interesting exhibitions.

BALLET...There is a local ballet company which, during the season (May to September), performs at Buenos Aires' famous Teatro Colón. There is a short ballet season before and after the grand season, too. In addition to native artists many world-famous dancers appear in Buenos Aires during the season.

BANKS...In Buenos Aires (open from noon to 3:30 P.M., Monday through Friday), the First National City Bank of New York; First National Bank of Boston; the Bank of America; the Bank of London and South America; the Royal Bank of Canada.

CALENDAR OF HOLIDAYS...The officially recognized holidays are: New Year's Day; January 6, Día de Reyes; pre-Lenten Carnival; Holy Thursday; Good Friday; May 1, Labor Day; May 25, National Anniversary of the Cabildo Abierto of 1810; Corpus Christi; June 20, Flag Day; July 9, Independence Day; August 15, Assumption of the Blessed Virgin; August 17, Anniversary of San Martín's death; October 12, Columbus Day; November 1, All Saints Day; December 8, Feast of the Immaculate Conception; Christmas Day.

CIGARETTES AND TOBACCO...American cigarettes are not

hard to find but cost around 70¢ per pack. Bring in all you're allowed; *see* CUSTOMS REGULATIONS. American pipe tobacco is hard to obtain.

CLIMATE ... Buenos Aires has a mild climate. The seasons are reversed, of course. Winter begins in June and summer in December. The warmest months are January and February. It seldom freezes and never snows in winter, but it is chilly. There is no rainy season. All in all, October to December is the ideal time to visit Argentina.

CLUBS ... In Buenos Aires, the American Club, Viamonte 1133 (guest cards can be arranged; inquire of Pan American locally); the American Women's Club, Paraguay 755 (vistors are welcome); Automobile Club, Avenida Alvear 2759; Rotary International, Florida 229; Strangers Club, Bartolomé Mitre 430; Jockey Club, Cerritos 1353 (members and guests only); YMCA, Reconquista 439; YWCA, Tucumán 844; Lions. For sports clubs *see* SPORTS.

COMMON COURTESIES AND LOCAL CUSTOMS ... Office hours in Buenos Aires are from 9 to 12 and 2 to 6. Street doors to apartment houses are locked after 9 P.M. Cocktail parties are from 7 to 9. The dinner hour is from 9 on. It is appropriate to send flowers to your hostess after a dinner. Send them the day of the party if it's a dance or a large affair. Argentineans usually dine and entertain in their homes.

COMMUNICATIONS ... A 3-minute call to the States is about U.S. $11; day-rate cablegrams are around 48 pesos per word with a 7-word minimum. Airmail letters to the U.S. are 18 pesos.

CURRENCY ... The monetary unit is the peso written with the $ and worth approximately 170$ARP per U.S. $1, but it varies frequently. Check for current rates. It is impossible, however, to exchange pesos for dollars at the official rate.

CUSTOMS REGULATIONS AND DOCUMENTS NEEDED FOR UNITED STATES CITIZENS ... For visits up to 3 months, tourists need only a passport and smallpox vaccination certificate. Radios, typewriters, sports equipment and similar items which are not wearing apparel must be declared in customs. 500 cigarettes or 50 cigars and 3 quarts of liquor may be brought in duty free. Tourists may take as baggage when leaving the country leather articles (including shoes) and fabrics up to a value of U.S. $300 per person, exempt from export permit. There are airport taxes of 100$ARP to boundary countries and 200$ARP to non-boundary countries.

DRUGSTORES ... Argentine drugstores, or *farmacías,* sell drugs and toilet articles only. One of the largest drugstores is Franco Inglesa at Florida and Sarmiento, Buenos Aires. There are many others in every district, which alternate staying open all night.

ELECTRIC CURRENT ... 220 volts, 50 cycles, A.C. European continental-type plugs needed.

FAUNA ... Tourists may bring in fishing equipment and .22-caliber guns without restriction, but for any other gauge get entry information from Club Argentino de Caza Mayor, Viamonte 867, Centro de Cazadora de Buenos Aires, Maipú 370. Dove, duck and partridge hunting are good. Wild game like puma, jaguar and some deer are found in the mountains, Vicuña, smaller than the llama, provides wool for scarves, sweaters and ponchos; very warm. Fishing is excellent; lake-region trout and salmon are superb. Dorado, a river species and without doubt the fightingest fish in the world, is found in the Paraná River. National bird is the *hornero* (oven bird), small and gray; makes its own home of mud and straw with curving entrance which protects it from wind and rain; greatly admired and respected by Argentineans. In contrast to this little bird is the tremendous condor, inhabiting the lofty Andean peaks.

FLORA ... Argentina lies in three climatic zones, therefore its flora is varied. Jungle and forests lie to the north; *quebracho* wood, hard as steel, is abundant. National flower is the ceibo, reddish bud of the ceiba tree. Flower vendors have open-air shops along Buenos Aires' principal thoroughfares. Fruits are abundant; grape country is Mendoza, a famous wine-producing region. The Botanical and Zoological Gardens at Palermo are rated among the best in the world.

FOOD ... Steak, steak, steak is the thing most North Americans remember. It is wonderful and inexpensive. But it is not the only food in the Argentine. So after you've had your fill try some of the more exotic dishes, such as the *empanada,* a sort of meat pie eaten with the fingers. Some of these contain raisins, a hard-boiled egg and olives. *Chorizo* is a highly spiced version of the hot dog and worth a try. *Paella,* rice with chicken, is excellent. *Puchero de gallina,* chicken, sausages, corn, potatoes, and squash cooked together, is a fine dish. If you can't get away from steak, try *bife a caballo,* or steak on horseback. This is a steak with two fried eggs. *Dulce de leche* is a very sweet boiled milk and sugar sauce served on desserts and pancakes. Milk is available everywhere and safe to drink.

GAMBLING ... Horse racing at Palermo and San Isidro with pari-mutuels. There are lotteries every week. The Christmas lottery is the biggest. There are casinos in Bariloche, Mar del Plata, Necochea, Miramar and Mendoza.

LANGUAGE ... Spanish, with variations of pronunciation and vocabulary from Castilian. However, English is spoken to a considerable extent.

LAUNDRY AND CLEANING ... These are excellent. Among the dry cleaners in Buenos Aires: Sandoz, Avenida Libertador General San Martín 3556; Casa Alvarez, Piedras 1080. Laundries include: Aseo Billinghurst, Billinghurst 1560; Del Norte, Cavia 3581; Franco-Argentino, Ceriño 3373. Velco, Luís Maria Campos 201, has a special service for tourists—laundry and dry cleaning in 8 hours.

LIQUOR ... Scotch and other imported liquors (good Scotch, that is) are more expensive here than in the United States. Argentina produces a lot of wine, most of it good, some of it very good. Among those recommended are: Bianchi Cabernet, Casa de Piedra, Fond du Cave, Norton, San Felipe. Good domestic champagnes cost about U.S. $1.50 in restaurants. Try Federico de Alvear or Monitor. There is good local beer, too. American cocktails are served by name in all bars, but a martini is called a *San Martín.*

MEDICAL FACILITIES . . . There is an excellent British Hospital in Buenos Aires at Pedriel 74. There are also many private clinics or nursing homes. The Little Company of Mary, at San Martín de Tours 2952, has English-speaking sisters as nurses. There are many excellent doctors and dentists.

MOTION PICTURES . . . The big movie houses in Buenos Aires show American films with Spanish subtitles. There are also English, French and Italian pictures. Performances are at 4:, 6:, 8: and 10: o'clock. The big houses are around the Avenida Corrientes and La-valle, which corresponds in a manner to Broadway. *Ocean, Luxor, Iguazú, Opera, Gran Rex, Broadway, Metro* and *Normandie* are modern American-style, air-conditioned houses. For newsreels and shorts go to *Porteño, Novedades* or *Rotary.* Prices are about 50¢.

MUSIC . . . The *Teatro Colón* is said to be the largest opera house in the world. It is the pride of Argentina. The season starts May 25 with a gala performance attended by the President and his cabinet. The theater has a National Symphony Orchestra of 100 pieces and its own opera and ballet company. Internationally famous conductors, singers and dancers appear. Dress is a must on gala nights. There is a summer season from January to March in the outdoor theater *Anfiteatro Municipal* at Parque Centenario. There are three other symphony orchestras which are heard frequently during this time. It is interesting that during the opera season the French and Italian operas are presented first, the German favorites toward the end of the season.

Much serious music with a folklore background is played in this country. There are several native ballets, also, with folklore background. Then there is the typical Argentine music, including the tango.

NIGHT CLUBS AND CABARETS . . . Buenos Aires is a gay city and a big one, so you may find almost any kind of night life you prefer. There are dance halls, small boites, large brassy spots. The better spots include: *Gong,* Córdoba 630, with American and tango bands, always filled with smart Argentineans and Americans. *Rendezvous,* Maipú 854, is one of the smartest clubs, with excellent orchestra and usually a name singer. *L'Hirondelle* and *Reviens* in the Olivos section are tops, and *Tabaris* on Av. Corrientes is fun too. Don't overlook some of the folklore spots, such as the *Mi Rincón,* Cerrito 1050 and *Achalay Huasi,* Esmeralda 1040 with typical Argentinean music and dances. Night life doesn't get started in B.A. until after 10 P.M.

PHOTOGRAPHY . . . U.S. black-and-white and color film cost almost twice their U.S. price, but you can buy fine Argentine films and European brands very reasonably. Agfa color films can now be developed in Buenos Aires. Quality of work, good. All types of American and European cameras can be purchased at high prices. There are many good photo shops on Florida Street.

RELIGION . . . The religion of the country is Roman Catholic, but there are churches of all denominations to be found. American Church (Methodist Episcopal), Corrientes 718; Anglican, St. John's Pro-Cathedral, 25 de Mayo 282; Scottish Presbyterian, Perú 352;

Christian Science, Sargento Cabral 847; United Lutheran, Cuenca, 3285; Baptist, Bolaños 262; Disciples of Christ, F. Lacroze 2985; Seventh Day Adventist, Uriarte 2429; Mormon, V. del Pino 2120; Orthodox Church, Brasil 315; and Israelitic Synagogue, Libertad 785.

RESTAURANTS AND BARS ... The hotels all serve good food. The *Plaza Grill* is famous for its pepper steaks. *La Cabaña*, Calle Entre Ríos 431, has wonderful steaks cooked on an open grill, particularly baby beef. The *London Grill* specializes in curries. *Au Bec Fin*, 1211 Arrenales, for fine French food. Another nice place is the *Claridge* at Tucumán 535. For dining and dancing in the American manner, try *Amerio's* on the 10th floor of the Argentine Automobile Club; also *Bucking's* in Olivos, and *Winter Garden* in Belgrano. *Hostería del Caballito Blanco*, Charcas 479; *Coraggio*, Entre Rios 662, for good food at low prices and singing waiters. Also *Corrientes 11* at Corrientes 135. *Canton*, Córdoba 945, if you're in the mood for Chinese food. *La Emiliana*, inexpensive, for Italian food. *La Goleta* in the Boca section. Several good and pleasant night spots are located in the residential section, roughly 8 miles north of the center of town. These include *Erwin's*, *L'Hirondelle* and *Reviens*, to name a few, which offer fine dinners and dancing to recorded music. *El Pescadito*, Pedro de Mendoza 1475, in La Boca, or the Italian quarter, by the docks, is a tavernlike spot which serves fine fish. In Buenos Aires there is what is called the *bodegón*, or corner restaurant, which is comparable to that little out-of-the-way spot at home that you and a few others know about. Sometimes they are good; sometimes terrible. Worth a try if you come across one you think you might like.

There are hundreds of bars in the city, but take note of the *Plaza*, *City* and the *California Hotel Frisco Bar*. All the hotels have cocktail lounges, too. The *confitería*, or tearoom, occupies a unique place in Buenos Aires. Unlike our tearooms, these are very smart and are frequented by the best Argentinean society. They combine the best features of our cocktail lounge, soda fountains and tearooms. A visit is a must. Teatime (4:30 P.M.) is the fashionable hour. *Queen Bess McGregor's*, *Dover Coll*, *St. James*, *Confitería Ideal*, *Richmond* and *El Aguila* are tops.

SHOPS AND STORES ... The big stores are open from 9 A.M. to 7 P.M. Some of the smaller ones are apt to close for 2 or 3 hours for lunch. Shopping is an event of importance in Buenos Aires. In fact, the main shopping center, Florida Street, is closed to any but foot traffic for most of the day. The shops in the Argentine capital are among the finest in the world. Many of them are along Avenida Santa Fé. The two largest department stores are Harrod's and Gath and Chaves. For good dress materials and tailored suits visit any one of a number of fine shops, such as Warrington's, Rhoder's, Genovese, and Manchester's. For luggage and leather goods, Pisk, Mayorga, Mattaldi, Casa Henri and López. For handmade shoes, Ricardo, Lopez Taibo, Guante. For some interesting records of "camp" or gaucho music similar to our Western songs, go to Iriberri, on Florida. The city is a center for jewels and silver. Handsome alligator bags and suede coats are available all over town.

SPECTATOR SPORTS ... Horse racing at Palermo and San Isidro. At Palermo the grandstand seats 30,000; at San Isidro it seats 50,000. Polo matches are played at Hurlingham and at Las Tortugas Country Club and Palermo. Soccer is the national game. Matches at River Plate Stadium, which seats 100,000 people. *Pato,* a sort of basketball on horseback, is dangerous and exciting. Horse shows are the important social event at Club Hípico Argentino and at Exposicion Rural in July/August. Boxing and wrestling matches at Luna Park.

SPORTS ... There are many excellent golf courses at the clubs. You need a guest card which can be arranged through an introduction. (Inquire at local Pan American office.) The clubs include: the San Isidro, the San Andrés, the Hurlingham, the Ituzaingo, the Jockey Club of San Isidro, the Don Torcuato. A public golf course is nearby at Palermo. Tennis is played at Hurlingham, the Lawn Tennis Club of Buenos Aires, the Lawn Tennis Club Argentino. Cards are needed. There are public courts at Palermo. Horseback riding is popular and there are miles and miles of bridle paths in Palermo Park. Horses may be rented from Rustici's, among other stables. Some country clubs have swimming pools. Rowing is one of the favorite sports. At El Tigre, some 45 minutes from the capital, there are many boating clubs. There are also several sailing and yacht clubs for which cards may be arranged. (Inquire at Pan American office in Buenos Aires.) Fishing usually means a trip somewhere, to San Martín de los Andes, Nahuel Huapi, Traful, or Sierra de la Ventana, all of which are overnight trips at least. For dorado fishing you go up the Paraná River some 36 hours away. Ski season at Bariloche is July-October.

THEATERS ... Evening performances start about 10 P.M. But there is a before-dinner performance, called "Vermouth," on Saturdays at 6 P.M. The principal theaters are *Nacional Cervantes, General San Martín, Politeama, Ateneo* and *Liceo,* with varied repertories of modern and classic plays. At the *Maipo* you'll see slapstick and girls. At the *Odeón* visiting French companies perform, and internationally famous performers often stage Spanish versions of Broadway shows at the *Opera.*

There are also many so-called experimental amateur theaters, some of very high standards, like *Los Independientes, Teatro Caminito, Teatro del Pueblo* and *Máscara.*

TIME ... Noon in "B.A." is 11 A.M. in New York.

TIPPING ... Tipping has been ostensibly abolished by law in restaurants but waiters still expect it. A good rule of thumb is 10% of the total charge, although service is included on your bill. Hotels add 24% for service. A 10-peso tip is customary for cab drivers, doormen, movie ushers and porters.

TRANSPORTATION ... Taxis are identifiable by red license plates and red signals on meters. They are cheap but hard to get during the luncheon interval and at the end of the business day. Buenos Aires has 5 subway lines, which are closed between 1 and 5 A.M. There are buses which are comfortable and large, and buses which are uncomfortable and slow. Also many trolley buses. U-Drive cars are available. Bring an International Driver's License, obtainable through the AAA. There is frequent hydrofoil boat service from B.A. across the Plate to Uruguay. Internal air lines are excellent and very inexpensive.

WATER ... Safe in large cities and resorts. Use boiled water in rural areas and small towns.

WHAT TO BUY ... Alligator bags and other articles made of alligator leather are much cheaper here than at home. A good bag can be bought for $30. Handmade shoes are less expensive in Argentina, too. Furs are excellent. Nutria of the finest quality is grown in Argentina, and a nutria coat costs much less than in the U.S., as do steamer rugs and ponchos made of vicuña and guanaco fur. The antique shops sometimes turn up a bargain. *Bombachas,* the baggy trousers worn by gauchos, are fun to bring home. Most popular souvenir is the bowl used for drinking *yerba maté* and the *bombilla,* or silver tube, that goes with it. Don't be tempted by aigrettes, birds of paradise or ostrich. You can't bring them through our customs. Kid gloves are a good buy. Hand-embroidered blouses are excellent. Antelope suede jackets and sleeveless pullovers are also good values.

WHAT TO WEAR ... Dress in Buenos Aires exactly as you would in any large city. In their winter you'll need a fur coat or a winter wool coat, suits, afternoon dresses. In their summer, linens and cottons, sheer dark crepes. Evening clothes, of course, if you are going to be social. You dress for the opera galas, not for the theater. Men dress conservatively in Buenos Aires, so dress as you would in a city at home. Argentinian men *always* wear a coat in Buenos Aires, even in midsummer. You may wear slacks and a sports jacket if you like. Light suits are correct in summer. Take a topcoat and a heavier coat in winter. Dinner clothes if you plan to go out much. Keep in mind that the farther south you go in Argentina, the colder it gets; the farther north, the warmer—but keep the reversed seasons in mind.

WHERE TO GO—SIGHTSEEING ...

Buenos Aires ... The Calle Florida is the main shopping street, Avenida Corrientes is the Broadway. The Avenida 9 de Julio is said to be the widest avenue in the world. It has 5 lanes for traffic, separated by grass plots, and parking space underneath for 1,000 cars. One of the best ways to see the city is by taxi or hired car. Here are some suggested rides: out the Avenida Alvear to Palermo Park, from the Plaza de Mayo to Plaza Congreso, then along the Avenida General Paz. La Costanera is a drive along the waterfront. Palermo Park has everything: a rose garden, a race course, miles and miles of beautiful walks, drives, and paths. Hire a horse-drawn coach and see it. There are few old buildings in the capital, as it is essentially a modern, rebuilt city. The quarter of the city known as La Boca is atmospheric, mostly Italian and by the waterfront. Interesting if you like local color. Take a look at Casa Rosada, the pink house, housing the President's offices. The Hall of Congress is worth seeing, too. Among the old churches, visit Nuestra Señora de la Merced (Our Lady of

On the border between Chile and Argentina stands the famous statue of "Christ of the Andes."

Mercy), the Cathedral on Plaza de Mayo, Santo Domingo and Nuestra Señora de Pilar. See the uniquely ornate Recoleta Cemetery. El Tigre, the delta of the Paraná River, is a region of 320 canals and islands. Take a launch trip for views of handsome estates.

Museums: In addition to the various museums listed under ARTS, the National Historical Museum, Defensa 1600 (open Sundays, Thursdays and holidays), is worth seeing for its exhibitions of historic flags, uniforms, documents and arms from the period of Argentine struggle for independence. Also very interesting is the Argentine Museum of National Sciences, Avenida Angel Gallardo 470 (open Tuesdays, Fridays and Sundays), and the Ethnographic Museum, Moreno 350 (open Thursdays and Sundays).

Luján is a typical rural town about 1½ hours out of the city. There is a magnificent Gothic cathedral, where pilgrims flock each year. The Virgin of Luján is the patron saint of Argentina. There is also a famous museum, the Cabildo, which is an old town hall preserved from colonial times.

La Plata, about an hour's trip from Buenos Aires, is the university city of Argentina. The Natural History Museum has a wonderful collection of prehistoric animals. The city also has a fine race track.

Mar del Plata, on the Atlantic Ocean, about 250 miles from the capital, is Argentina's leading beach resort. Here is the famous *Casino,* the largest in the world, next to the luxurious *Hotel Provincial.* There are many beaches here. Cabañas may be rented at Bristol Beach. St. James Beach is filled with private clubs. There are about 1500 hotels at the resort. The *Riviera* is open the year round; the others during the season. Among the best are: the *Horizonte,* the *Hermitage,* the *Nogaró* and the *Royal.* Apartments may be rented, too.

Buenos Aires' "Ninth of July" Avenue (said to be the widest in the world) and the Obelisk, which commemorate the 400th anniversary of the founding of the City of Buenos Aires.

Plaza del Congreso in Buenos Aires, Argentina.

Nahuel Huapi National Park offers wonderful vacation opportunities and good facilities, such as Hotel Llao Llao, surrounded by 12,000-foot peaks.

Fishing is fine here and the seafood is famous. From Mar del Plata you can make trips to the *estancias* at Chapadmalal and Ojo de Agua, where two of the famous breeds of Argentine race horses originated. Necochea, south of Mar del Plata, is the second largest beach resort. Still farther away is Tandil, in the hills, a favorite summer resort.

Iguassú Falls on the Brazilian border, about 1,300 miles from the capital, 5½ hours by plane or 6 days by boat, is one of the most magnificent sights in the world. The falls are greater than Niagara or Victoria Falls, and have 275 separate cataracts. The season is May to November. *Hotel Cataratas* is on the Brazilian side, the new *Hotel Iguazú* is on the Argentine side. Gambling casino open May-September.

Argentine-Chilean Lake District ... Go by plane (twice weekly jet service) in only 2 hours to (San Carlos de) Bariloche, which looks like a Swiss village and in fact was originally settled by the Swiss. This is in Nahuel Huapi National Park, which has several distinct regions. The popular spot is Lake Nahuel Huapi where there are the *Hotel Llao-Llao* (pronounced yao-yao) and the *Tunquelen;* also good are the *Tres Reyes, Bellonista* and *Cristal.* The lake is at an altitude of 2,000 feet and is surrounded by mountains which point some 12,000 feet upward. During the winter season (July to October) there is excellent skiing (equipment can be rented), and the *Cathedral Hotel* provides first-class lodging. Game is protected, but you may get a permit to shoot wild boar. Fishing is wonderful at Lake Traful, 4 hours from Bariloche. You can climb the peaks, too. *Club Andino Bariloche* arranges things and furnishes guides. The hotel is excellent, the food very good. Take the boat trip (motor launch) to Puerto Blest at the end of a 10-mile fjord. You pass Cascada Blanca, a huge waterfall from the great glaciers. From Puerto Blest you can go to Puerto Alegre on the Chilean border and continue into Chile or return to Bariloche and Buenos Aires. If you go on into the Chilean lake regions, you will cross the border at Puerto Alegre. In Chile head for Lake Todos Los Santos as far as Villarica Lake. Here you stay at Pucon at the *Pucon Hotel,* where there is a golf course, good salmon fishing and swimming. For further information on Chilean lake region, *see* CHILE.

Other Side Trips ... While in Argentina you should visit Mendoza, Argentina's great wine center, and beautiful Córdoba. Córdoba is the second-oldest city on the continent and, though now industrialized, it is one of the two cities in this part of Latin America which still bear traces of Spanish colonial rule. The other is lovely, sleepy Salta in northwestern Argentina.

SOURCES OF FURTHER INFORMATION ... Pan American has a tourist corner, offices at Avenida Roque Saenz Pena 788 (Tel. 45-0111), and at the Plaza Hotel. An English-language newspaper, *The Buenos Aires Herald,* is published daily in Buenos Aires. In New York, the Consulate General of Argentina is located at 12 West 56 Street.

BOLIVIA

WEATHER IN LA PAZ—Lat. S16°29′—Alt. 12,200′

Temp.	JAN.	FEB.	MAR.	APR.	MAY	JUNE	JULY	AUG.	SEPT.	OCT.	NOV.	DEC.
Low	43°	43°	42°	40°	35°	36°	34°	35°	38°	40°	42°	43°
High	64°	64°	64°	66°	66°	60°	61°	62°	62°	65°	67°	64°
Average	54°	54°	53°	53°	51°	49°	48°	49°	50°	53°	55°	54°
Days of Rain	25	16	15	7	1	6	1	6	12	11	10	24

LOCATION ... Bolivia is the only country in South America, except Paraguay, without a seacoast. While much of the country consists of low plains which are humid and hot, the principal cities are located on the high, cool plateau.

CHARACTERISTICS ... La Paz, highest capital in the world, is over 12,000 feet above sea level. The city itself is in the bottom of a deep, narrow gorge entirely surrounded by mountains. It is a city of steep streets with houses built on inclined surfaces. The airport, at 13,358 feet elevation, is the highest commercial airport in the world. The plateau is studded with snowy peaks that reach another 8,000 feet into the sky.

POPULATION ... The estimated population of the country is 3,850,000, with an average density of only 8 people per square mile.

SIZE ... Estimated 424,162 square miles; 932 miles at its widest and longest points.

CAPITAL ... La Paz, with over 375,000 inhabitants, is the administrative capital. Sucre, 40,000, is the constitutional capital. Cochabamba's population is about 89,000.

GOVERNMENT ... A republic with a President, Senate and House of Deputies.

HOW TO GET THERE ... By National, Pan American and Panagra interchange to La Paz, 12¾ hours (elapsed time) from New York via Miami. By Panagra 1¾ hours from Lima, Peru. Cochabamba is an hour's flying time from La Paz. By ship from New York, 14 days to Arica, Chile; then about 9 hours by Swiss-built diesel train that leaves Arica twice a week for La Paz.

ACCOMMODATIONS... Best hotels in La Paz are the *Crillon,* the *Copacabana* and *Grand Hotel Sucre Palace,* where rates start at about $5 single, European Plan. It is advisable to get confirmed reservations in advance.

ARTS... The Tiahuanaco Museum houses a significant collection of pre-Inca relics and is well worth a visit. Also the historical museum, Casa de Murillo, with colonial furniture and paintings.

BALLET... There is a local ballet company.

BANKS... The First National City Bank of New York has a branch in La Paz.

CALENDAR OF HOLIDAYS... New Year's Day; 3-day pre-Lenten Carnival; Easter; May 1, Labor Day; Corpus Christi in June; August 5, 6, 7, National Festivities; October 12, Columbus Day; November 1, All Saints Day; November 2, All Souls Day; Christmas Day. There are frequent photo-worthy, costumed fiestas.

CIGARETTES AND CIGARS... American cigarettes are available and cost about 40¢ per pack.

CLIMATE... A dry, sunny climate, extremely pleasant during the dry season. Some foreigners find the high altitude difficult for the first few days. They are advised to walk as little as possible and to hire cabs for any destination until they become acclimated. The weather is cool all year around in the western part and cold in winter, but sunny most days. Even in summer you need blankets at night.

CLUBS... Anglo-American Club; Bolivian-North American Business Council; Club Alemán; Círculo Francés and Círculo Peruano; Club de La Paz; Club Tennis La Paz; Club Tennis Sucre; Club de Caza y Pesca; Yacht Club; International branches of Rotary and Lions; Automóvil Club; Club 16 de Julio; Club Arabe; Club Social Chileno; Mallasilla and Los Pinos Golf Clubs; Círculo de la Unión; Club Hípico Los Sargentos. Guest cards are available (inquire at your hotel or at the Panagra office).

COMMUNICATIONS... A 3-minute phone call to the U.S. is $b119.80 (U.S. $14.38). Day cable rate is $b4 per word. Airmail postage is $b2.80 for 5 grams; $b4 for 10 grams.

CURRENCY... The peso boliviano ($b), in circulation since November, 1963, is the equivalent of 1,000 bolivianos, in which prices are still often quoted. The exchange rate is $b12 to U.S. $1. Exchange for tourists is at a free-market rate.

CUSTOMS REGULATIONS AND DOCUMENTS REQUIRED FOR UNITED STATES CITIZENS... Passport but no visa for tourist visits up to 90 days, but tourist cards (free) are required. Good health and vaccination certificate. Inquire of Pan Am about business travelers' requirements. Personal effects such as cameras and typewriters are allowed, but for all other articles, passengers must secure special permission. Two quarts of liquor, 100 cigarettes, or 25 cigars, or 2 tins of tobacco allowed duty free.

DRUGSTORES... Almost all have American products. Many good European pharmaceuticals are available, too.

ELECTRIC CURRENT ... Generally 110 volts, 50 cycles, A.C.; 220 volts, A.C., is also available. Hotels are generally adapted for U.S.-type plugs.

FAUNA ... Llama, vicuña and alpaca on the plateaus; fresh-water fish in mountain streams. Wolf, American tiger, bear and game birds are in the forests; monkeys, parrots and alligators in the tropical regions. Salmon trout in Lake Titicaca.

FLORA ... The vegetation of the valleys of Bolivia is lovely with ferns, orchids, banana and coffee trees. There are virgin forests in eastern Bolivia.

FOOD ... Truly native food is highly seasoned with an extremely hot pepper (*aji* or *locoto*). Among favorite dishes are *humintas* (corn meal steamed with raisins and nuts inside corn husks); *salteñas* (small meat pies with raisins and olives); *plato paceño* (resembles a boiled dinner of corn on the cob, potatoes, cheese and beans); *picante de pollo* (chicken in pungent tomato sauce); *chicharron* (crisp fried pork); *fritanga* (pork stew in hot sauce). International-style food is served in hotels, and in some restaurants, too.

LANGUAGE ... Spanish; but in the better hotels, restaurants and shops, English is spoken and understood.

LAUNDRY AND DRY CLEANING ... Panba is the best, where all clothes can be well cleaned. Fast service.

LIQUOR ... Most imported liquors are reasonably priced but try the local *Pisco*. Bolivian beers are excellent.

MEDICAL FACILITIES ... The American Clinic is one of the best, with a North American director. There are also the Clínica Alemana, Clínica Santa-Isabel and Clínica Muller.

MOTION PICTURES ... *Universo, Cine 6 De Agosto, Monje Campero, Tesla, Cine La Paz,* the new *Cine Scala* and others.

MUSIC ... There is the Bolivian Symphonic Orchestra. Particularly exciting is the native music of bands, called out to make a fiesta of almost any event at unexpected times.

NIGHT CLUBS AND CABARETS ... Best in La Paz are the *Oasis, Club 21, Flamingo, Maracaibo* and the *boite* in Hotel Crillon. All have dance orchestras.

PHOTOGRAPHY ... Black-and-white still film as well as color film are available. Cameras and equipment are now also available in local shops. Developing facilities are of good quality.

RELIGION ... There are many Catholic churches, all beautiful. Don't miss seeing the Church of San Francisco, which is over 400 years old and magnificent with colonial carvings and paintings. There are synagogues in larger cities, and a number of Protestant mission denominations. For English-speaking Protestants, there are interdenominational services in the La Paz Community Church at Landaeta and 20th de Octubre.

RESTAURANTS ... In La Paz, the *Daiquiri* is known for its *parillada* (mixed grill cooked over charcoal). Also recommended are the *Pasapoga, Chinese Restaurant, Shorton Grill, Club Alemán;* and hotels Grand Sucre Palace, Crillon and Copacabana.

SHOPS AND STORES . . . The shopping center in La Paz is in Calle Loayza and Calle Comercio. Shops offer vicuña rugs, alpaca, gold and silver jewelry, filigree work. Camacho, Lanza and Sopocachi markets are held daily. The markets are run by native women who wear those amazing derby hats. Calle Sagarnaga is the Street of the Indians, and here everything imaginable is for sale; don't miss the winding street of stores selling Indian magic. Everywhere you will find Ekeko, the Indian god of good luck. He comes in plaster and silver, with a load of household items on his back, and wears a bright knitted cap.

SPECTATOR SPORTS . . . Soccer and football in Miraflores Stadium; basketball in new Coliseum; horse shows at Club Hípico Los Sargentos.

SPORTS . . . There are fine trout streams. Lake-trout fishing here is gaining world renown for some of the world's biggest salmon trout; Glaciar Lake is especially rewarding. Skiing is excellent near La Paz, but is over 17,000 feet above sea level. There is a new golf course, Mallasilla Golf Club, with grass greens and fairways, about ½ hour from downtown La Paz. Tennis is popular. Hunting and shooting are good in the Yungas and near Cochabamba. There is big-game hunting in the wilds of eastern Bolivia around Santa Cruz and Beni; air service and safari arrangements are available.

TIME . . . Noon in La Paz is 11 A.M. in New York.

TIPPING . . . No tipping for taxis. There is a 23% charge added to your hotel bill and 10% added to restaurant bills to cover service.

TOURIST TAXES . . . International fares are taxed 3%; all national fares are taxed 2%.

TRANSPORTATION . . . City taxis are plentiful and inexpensive. The fare from the airport into La Paz, with several sharing the car, is about U.S. $1.50 per person. There are several bus lines operating between La Paz, Oruro, Cochabamba and Santa Cruz. City buses, however, are too crowded for comfort. Internal air services, affording views of spectacular scenery, are operated by Lloyd Aéro Boliviano. The Bolivian railways are miracles of engineering: the train from La Paz to Potosí, for instance, crosses the Paso del Cóndor at an elevation of 15,816 feet, and the train to Arica, Chile, goes through scenery like that on the moon. The passenger steamers which cross Lake Titicaca, connecting Peru and Bolivia, were made in England and carried up in sections to the lake, 12,500 feet above sea level.

WATER . . . It is advisable to drink only bottled water.

WHAT TO BUY . . . Vicuña, alpaca, hand-knit sweaters, gold and silver jewelry, the jointed silver fish (regarded as a fertility charm!), hand-loomed blankets and rag dolls in native costumes, gold filigree, the little god Ekeko, colored shawls, rugs and woven hats.

WHAT TO WEAR . . . In La Paz it is cool in the morning and the late afternoon. Take suits and dresses such as those worn in the United States in the fall. A topcoat is necessary; and take it along when starting out for a day's trip. The mercury is temperamental in this city in the Andes and takes frequent and unexpected dives, so have a warm bathrobe, bedroom slippers. A hot-water bottle is a good idea, too. The same rules of dress apply to men; wool suits, topcoats, sweaters. Raincoat season is November through April.

WHERE TO GO—SIGHTSEEING . . .

La Paz . . . The home of the Executive Government and Congress, and the most important Bolivian city. In and around La Paz the Indian markets, fiestas and life in general are fascinating. The cathedral is one of the largest churches in all South America. A trip around the city is interesting for seeing different architectural styles of various eras. You don't have to go anywhere to see snow-capped Illimani, the mountain which towers over the city. From el Montículo, a small park in residential La Paz, you get a magnificent view of the city. The Prado (Avenue 16 de Julio) is exquisitely landscaped with colorful flowers, and its promenade is the pride of the city. City tours include many fine projects built by Alliance for Progress and a view of Moon Valley.

Cochabamba . . . Is a popular resort city located in a garden valley, and is an agricultural center. The old Spanish houses have overhanging tiled eaves. Best hotels are the *Gran Hotel Cochabamba,* with swimming pool, tennis courts; and the delightful motel-style *Hotel Beverley,* with pool. Also good are *Hotel Colón* and the *Capitol.* Cochabamba was the home of the late Simon Patiño, the Tin King of Bolivia. He built *Los Portales,* a palace with solid copper roof, near the edge of the city, now a museum. *El Cortijo* is a lovely spot, with excellent bar and restaurant, swimming pool and tennis courts. Fifteen miles from the city is Pairumani, a beautiful estate of 5,000 acres, with model farms, gardens, and a magnificent house. The shopping center of Cochabamba is comparable to that of La Paz. The Indian market is especially interesting. The magnificent climate here is the main feature. From the top of San Sebastian hill in the middle of the city, you have a wonderful view of the town with its pink churches and red tile roofs.

Copacabana . . . This is a famous shrine visited every August by pilgrims from all parts of the country. Its main feature is the church that has the Virgin of Copacabana which was carved in the 16th century. There is a hotel operated by the Government and one run by Compañía Hotelera Boliviana.

Copacabana is 4 hours or so from La Paz on Lake Titicaca, the world's highest lake. Spend the night there; see the sun rise across those strange waters, and the straw boats, wild ducks and geese.

Santa Cruz . . . This 16th-century city, now connected to Cochabamba by a good paved highway that cuts through deep rain forests, is Bolivia's boom town. Isolated for centuries, Santa Cruz has suddenly come alive with oil wells, sugar mills and modern cowboys in jeeps. The pre-Lenten Carnival here is one of the longest and most spectacular in all South America. Set at an elevation of only 1,400 feet, Santa Cruz has a semitropical climate, with marvelous citrus fruits and pineapples. Stay at the new *Drive-In Motel.*

Indian fishermen put out in their balsa boats on Lake Titicaca, about 60 miles from La Paz.

Palacio Legislativo is one of the government buildings in La Paz, capital of Bolivia.

Sucre . . . The former, and still official, capital of Bolivia and seat of the Supreme Court, is known as the white city because all its churches have white towers. It has a beautiful 17th-century university, interesting buildings and an air of quiet charm. See the fabulous, carefully guarded treasures of the Virgin of Guadalupe in the Cathedral.

Potosí . . . The city whose silver gave the Spanish conquerors fame and glory. In the 16th century, it was densely populated. Notable for its colonial churches and buildings, old paintings. The superbly designed *Casa Real de la Moneda* has been a mint since 1572. *Las Cajas Reales,* the old treasury, is now the courthouse. *Potosí,* built around a veritable mountain of silver, retains most of its ancient beauty.

The Yungas are deep, narrow tropical valleys descending sharply from the high plateau. The climate is subtropical. The drive (3 hours from La Paz) gives you a close-up view of Indian farms and villages.

SOURCES OF FURTHER INFORMATION . . . Grace y Cía (Bolivia) at Mercado 1085 (Tel. 12100) are the Panagra agents. The Consulate General of Bolivia in New York City is at 10 Rockefeller Plaza.

BRAZIL

WEATHER IN RIO DE JANEIRO—Lat. S22°54′—Alt. 30′

Temp.	JAN.	FEB.	MAR.	APR.	MAY	JUNE	JULY	AUG.	SEPT.	OCT.	NOV.	DEC.
Low	74°	76°	75°	73°	69°	67°	65°	66°	66°	69°	71°	73°
High	82°	83°	81°	81°	75°	74°	73°	73°	74°	75°	78°	81°
Average	78°	80°	78°	77°	72°	71°	69°	70°	70°	72°	75°	77°
Days of Rain	13	11	12	10	10	7	6	7	11	12	12	14

LOCATION ... This huge country, larger than continental United States, occupies the east-central section of South America and includes several climatic regions—the tropical Amazon basin near the equator, the subtropical central section, and the temperate mountainous regions facing the southern coast.

CHARACTERISTICS ... Rio de Janeiro is a city of beauty, of white buildings, mosaic walks, blue, blue water, purple mountains. It is a city of gaiety, a carnival city, ready to amuse you. Its Copacabana Beach and its hotels are world famous. You can have fun in Rio. The hotels are superb, the scenery fabulous. São Paulo is a fast-growing industrial center, where tourists are treated wonderfully.

POPULATION ... Estimated approximately 80,000,000.

SIZE ... 3,286,470 square miles; 2,600 miles long and equally wide.

CAPITAL ... Brasilia, a brand-new city already with a population of over 300,000. Rio de Janeiro, the former capital, has a population of 3,900,000 and São Paulo has over 5,000,000.

GOVERNMENT ... A federation of 22 States, a Federal District and 3 Territories, with a President, a Federal Senate and a Chamber of Deputies.

HOW TO GET THERE ... By Pan Am Jet Clipper 8¾ hours from New York to Brasilia, 10 hours to Rio, an hour more to São Paulo. By ship from New York, about 11 days.

ACCOMMODATIONS ... Rio de Janeiro has many excellent hotels. On Copacabana Beach, the brand new *Leme Palace,* the *Copaca-*

bana Palace, Trocadero, Excelsior, Lancaster, Miramar, Ouro Verde, Olinda and *California* all enjoy a magnificent view of the ocean. The *Copacabana Palace* has a swimming pool and night club. The *Excelsior* and *Miramar* have excellent restaurants. The *Gloria,* closer to town, best of the older hotels, has been thoroughly modernized with air conditioning. It also has a pool. The view of Rio's harbor from the *Gloria* is magnificent. Top hotels charge $6-$14 single, $10-$21 double, European Plan. Other hotels in Rio are the *Serrador, Ambassador, Guanabara Palace* and *San Francisco.* Most luxurious hotels in São Paulo are the *Jaraguá* and *Othon Palace.* Single $8-$15 with breakfast. Other good hotels are the *Excelsior, Comodoro, Maraba, Terminus, Cá D'Oro, Danubio, Lord Palace, Principe* and *São Paulo.*

ARTS ... The Museum of the Indian, located in front of Gate No. 15 of the Maracaña Stadium, is the newest and most modern museum in Rio. It consists of a series of expositions, agreeably organized, about different themes of the life of Brazilian Indians. The National Museum in Rio's Quinta da Boa Vista Park, one of the oldest in Brazil and once the residence of Dom Pedro I and Dom Pedro II, has interesting collections of mineralogy and ethnography. Natural Historic Museum, on Praça Marechal Ancora, has a superb collection of historical objects, silver, porcelain, paintings, etc. National Museum of Fine Arts, Avenida Rio Branco, houses collections of old paintings and sculpture and also has a gallery showing contemporary artists. The Museum of Modern Art exhibits modern painting and sculpture. Museum of Historical and Geographical Institute, Praça Mahatma Gandhi, has interesting collections from the period of the monarchy. In São Paulo see the Ipiranga Museum for historical objects, and the excellent Museum of Modern Art.

BALLET ... Foreign and local ballet companies appear in both Rio and São Paulo during the winter season (May to August).

BANKS ... In Rio and São Paulo: First National City Bank of New York, First National Bank of Boston, Royal Bank of Canada. American Express Co., Rua Mexico 74, Rio.

CALENDAR OF HOLIDAYS ... New Year's Day; January 6, Epiphany; pre-Lenten carnival; Holy Week; April 21, Tiradentes; May 1, Labor Day; Corpus Christi; June 29, St. Peter's Day; September 7, Independence Day; November 1, All Saints Day; November 2, Memorial Day; November 15, Republic Day; Christmas.

The Carnival in Rio is one of the gayest in the world. All business stops for 4 days. There are costume balls, among them the famous Copacabana Palace and Municipal Theater Ball. There are also galas at hotels, clubs, and private homes, dancing in the streets, lavish costumes, fireworks, music, pretty girls and everything it takes to make a carnival. By Ash Wednesday, everyone is totally exhausted. New Year's Eve is exciting with mystic candlelit African rites performed by *Macumbeiros* on Copacabana and other beaches.

CIGARETTES AND TOBACCO ... Brazilian cigars are among the world's finest mild cigars. Suerdick Co. makes the best. American cigarettes cost about 3 times as much as local brands.

CLIMATE ... It's always summer in Rio. During the winter season, June to September, the nights are quite cool, but temperatures below 50 degrees are almost unknown. It's often hot during the daytime in Rio's summer. São Paulo is 2,500 feet above sea level with an ideal climate. Local winter and spring are the best times to visit.

CLUBS ... In Rio: A.B.I. Brazilian Press Association (no cards needed) has a separate section for non-member guests; American Chamber of Commerce and American Society at Av. Rio Branco, 80, 19th floor; American Club, Ave. Rio Branco, 80, 20th floor, is an American businessmen's luncheon club, excellent food and bar service (card needed); University Club (for graduates and students of North American universities), Avenida Graça Aranha, 182; American Legion, Avenida Graça Aranha, 182; YMCA and YWCA; Rotary Club, Avenida Nilo Peçanha, and Lions Club. For golf and yacht clubs *see* SPORTS. Principal clubs in São Paulo are the Automobile (businessmen's luncheon) Club, Jockey Club for lunch, the Scandinavian Club, American Chamber of Commerce, São Paulo Athletic Club, Rotary.

COMMON COURTESIES AND LOCAL CUSTOMS ... Beware of the traffic—South Americans drive with more abandon than we do. The dinner hour is from 7 to 10 P.M. Cocktails are at 6. Local businessmen stop between appointments for a *cafezinho* (demi-tasse) at one of the innumerable cafés. For "Thank you," men say *Obrigado;* ladies say *Obrigada.*

COMMUNICATIONS ... A 3-minute phone call to the States costs about $19; a 10-word cablegram is about $5.50. In local currency, airletters and airmail postcards are CR$120; 5-gram airmail letters are CR$200.

CURRENCY ... The monetary unit is the cruzeiro. You get best value in exchange at the cambios (money exchange shops). The latest market rate, which fluctuates widely, is CR$1850 to U.S. $1.

CUSTOMS REGULATIONS AND DOCUMENTS REQUIRED FOR UNITED STATES CITIZENS ... You may bring in a camera, 3 bottles of liquor, and cigarettes in limited quantities. You need passport, smallpox vaccination certificate, tourist card issued by Pan Am, 2 passport photos, and return or through ticket.

DRUGSTORES ... Most American pharmaceuticals are available.

ELECTRIC CURRENT ... 110 volts, 50 cycles, A.C. in Rio, Recife and Natal; 220 D.C. in Manaus; 220 A.C., 60 cycles in Santos. Elsewhere, 110 volts, 60 cycles, A.C., as in the U.S.

FAUNA ... Rich and varied in species of birds and wild animals.

FLORA ... Orchids; bougainvillaea; 100,000 different species of plants and trees can be seen at the Botanical Gardens.

FOOD ... Naturally, coffee is plentiful, for Brazil is the world's largest producer of coffee. All the hotels serve international food if you don't want to sample the native dishes. If you do, however, try *feijoada,* made of meat, black beans and rice, cooked separately and spiced with herbs. The Brazilians do well by fish of all sorts. If you like hot food try *vatapá,* a fish porridge which contains several varieties of fish and shrimp mixed with local vegetable oil called *dendê,* then sprinkled with pepper and paprika, served very hot. Try *camarões á Grega* (shrimps on a spit) at the Copacabana. Local beef dishes are superb. Try *churrasco*, barbecued beef, pork and sausages.

GAMBLING... There is racing at Rio's Jockey Club track on Thursday, Saturday and Sunday, with pari-mutuel betting.

LANGUAGE... Portuguese. English is understood in tourist centers and by many businessmen, especially in São Paulo.

LAUNDRY AND DRY CLEANING... Can be arranged through your hotel. Two-day delivery if requested.

LIQUOR... Excellent native wines. The best with local dishes are white *Precioso*, rosé *Bernard Taillan* and red *Granja Union*. There are good Brazilian rum and gin. Scotch and other imported liquors are expensive. Brazilian beer is fine and costs about 25¢ a quart. *Pilsen Extra* and *Brahma Extra* are recommended. Draft beer is called *Chopp* (pronounced "shóppy").

MEDICAL FACILITIES... Hospital dos Estrangeiros, Rua Passagem 188, Rio, is staffed with English-speaking doctors and nurses, as is Hospital Samaritano, Rua Conselheiro Brotero 1486, São Paulo.

MOTION PICTURES... There are many fine cinema houses. Fairly new Hollywood movies are shown in the big ones.

MUSIC... The *Teatro Municipal* in Rio is the mecca of music lovers who from June to September hear world-famous singers and conductors. The late Heitor Villa-Lobos, the composer, was a Brazilian. Brazilian folk songs and chants are famous. There is a National Symphony Orchestra. Fine concerts are given at the National School of Music. The samba and bossa nova are Brazilian. São Paulo offers fine concerts and Italian opera.

NIGHT CLUBS... In Rio: *Sacha's* and *The Top Club* are the swankiest Copacabana Beach spots. Expensive but nice. Excellent food and soft music for dancing. *Fred's* has a good Brazilian floor show. The best known hotel night club is the *Midnight Room* in the *Copacabana. Corridinho* and *Elbodegon* are also very smart night spots. Others feature dancing and entertainment usually with a moderate cover or minimum charge. Some of the better known, quiet, more intimate places are the *Scotch Bar, Michell's, The Drink, Kilt Club* and *Crazy Rabbit.* Leading São Paulo night clubs are *Quitandinha* with folklore shows; *Stardust* and *Zum-Zum* for fine dining and atmosphere; and the new *Le Club.* All are reasonably priced.

PHOTOGRAPHY... There are camera dealers in all major cities.

RELIGION... In Rio: Union Church, Protestant nondenominational, Rua Paula Freitas, 99. Our Lady of Mercy Chapel, for English-speaking Catholics, Rua Visconde de Caravelas. Jewish Synagogue, Rua Tenente Possolo. Christ Church (Anglican), Rua Real Grandeza. First Church of Christ Scientist, Av. Churchill. São Paulo, while principally Roman Catholic, has most denominations.

RESTAURANTS... Around Copacabana and Leme beaches, *Ouro Verde* and *Excelsior* restaurants are considered the finest. Restaurants specializing in French cuisine are very popular. *Le Bistro* and *Le Bec Fin* are the best. For those who like Italian food, *Al Pap-*

pagallo and *Cantina Sorrento* are well recommended. The *Cabaça Grande* and *Rio Minho* serve wonderful seafood Brazilian style. Go to *Corridinho's* and *Galo's* for Portuguese specialties. *Churrascaria Gaucha* and *Recreio* for barbecued meat. *Restaurant Mesbla* serves fine food and offers a magnificent view of Sugar Loaf and the famous Rio bay. The better hotel restaurants in the city are the *Gloria*, *Ambassador* and *Serrador*. For international cuisines, the *Terasse* in the Avenida Central skyscraper building, and the restaurant in the Museum of Modern Art. For Russian food, *Doubianski*. For Chinese food, *Hong Kong Restaurant* and *Kin Wah*.

In São Paulo the best restaurants are *La Cassarole, La Popote* and *Freddy* for French cuisine and atmosphere. *A Baiuca*, international cuisine. *Don Fabrizio*, Italian food. *Excelsior* on the 23rd floor of the Hotel Excelsior (50 choices for U.S. $1.50) including a huge smörgåsbord. *Cá D'Oro* for international cuisine, nice atmosphere. The *Airport Restaurant* is very good. *Zillertal* and *Brahma* for German food. *Fasano* in the fabulous Conjunto Nacional building is a must. The *Hungaria* serves central European and Balkan specialties. *Cabeça, Chata, Rubaiat* and *La Cabana* serve superior Brazilian food; and *Os Viking* features an authentic Scandinavian smörgåsbord.

SHOPS AND STORES... In Rio: H. Stern, Av. Rio Branco, 173, Amsterdam, Rua Mexico, 41, and Maximino, Rua Santa Clara, 27–B, for set and unset precious stones. Curiopan, Avenida Rio Branco 175, Casa Hugo, Rua Buenos Aires, 91, and Zitrin, Rua Buenos Aires, 110, for jewels, fine curios; and Casa do Folclore, Rua Chile 16, for antiques and Portuguese silver; Imperial Modas, Rua Gonçalves Dias 56, for lingerie and wonderful handmade blouses; Henrique Liberal and Cia, Praia do Flamengo 284, excellent antiques and wood carvings; Casa Sloper, Rua Uruguaiana 55, Mesbla, Rua do Passeio 42, Sears Roebuck, Praia do Botafogo 400 are the best department stores in the city. Perfumarias Carneiro, Rua do Ouvidor, 103, and Casa Hermanny, Rua Gonçalves Dias, 50, for French perfumes (but they're expensive). For gloves, shoes, bags, Marketa's, Zita's and Lilian's. Don't be tempted by street peddlers of perfumes or stones. Also see WHAT TO BUY.

Shops and stores in São Paulo include the Mappin Stores, Mesbla, Sears Roebuck, Casa Sloper and several other good stores. Rua Barão de Itapetininga, Rua Augusta and Ave. São João are the main shopping streets. R. Simon, at Praça da República, 146, and H. Stern, at Praça da República, 242 (largest, has guided tours) for Brazilian precious stones and handmade jewelry.

SPECTATOR SPORTS... Soccer is Brazil's most important sport. Around Rio, horse races at the Jockey Club (Thursdays, Saturdays and Sundays). The races are important in the social life of Rio. The *Grande Premio Brasil* race held the first Sunday in August draws everyone who is anyone. Soccer at Maracanã Stadium, world's largest (150,000 seats). Boxing, basketball and other matches at Maracanazinho Gymnasium. International tennis matches. In São Paulo soccer is played 3 days a week at the Pacaembu Stadium (70,000 capacity), horse races at the Jockey Club on Saturdays and Sundays.

SPORTS . . . In Rio golf at Gávea Golf and Country Club in the midst of orchid-bearing trees, sensational scenery; card necessary. Itanhangá Golf Club at Lake Jacarepaguá is another scenic marvel; good course, card necessary. The Yacht Club of Rio de Janeiro is host to the Buenos Aires-Rio annual ocean yacht race. Nice restaurant, good drinks. Card necessary. Sociedade Hípica Brasileira for horseback riding, card necessary. There is fine salt- ·and freshwater fishing around Rio. In the highland lakes there are plenty of fish to be caught. The Rio Country Club has a swimming pool and tennis courts, card needed. Swimming, of course, is a national sport. If you want to climb mountains, you can do it right in Rio. There's golf at the São Paulo Golf Club (card necessary), underwater fishing at Ubatuba near Santos, numerous tennis clubs (cards necessary). Hunting is excellent in the interior: boar, alligator, jaguar, wild buffalo, tapir; game fish and game birds. Conducted trips are organized by Brazil Safari Tours of Rio.

THEATERS . . . There are several theaters in Rio. During their winter you see foreign companies as well as local ones. Most of the plays are in Portuguese, but even if you don't understand it, you'll enjoy the experience. For those who enjoy musical reviews *type français* there are usually good shows at the *Recreio, João Caetano* and *Carlos Gomes.* Times of performances 8 P.M. and 10 P.M., except Mondays. In São Paulo performances start at 9 P.M. and are in Portuguese except for those of foreign companies.

TIME . . . Noon in Brazil is 10 A.M. U.S. Eastern Standard Time.

TIPPING . . . A service charge of 10 to 15% is added onto your hotel and restaurant bills, but it is usual to tip 10% additional. Taxi drivers, beauticians, etc., are also tipped 10%.

TRANSPORTATION . . . City taxis have red license plates. They cruise the streets, or you can telephone the nearest taxi stand for a cab. Pay only what the meter reads and for no "extras" except luggage. Carry small denomination cruzeiro notes, for drivers can seldom make change.

For getting about this huge country, using local airlines is the best way; shuttle flights between Rio-São Paulo-Brasilia. Long-distance bus and railway service are good in the states of São Paulo, Rio de Janeiro and Minas Gerais.

WATER . . . It is advisable to drink only bottled water. *Água Lindoya* is noncarbonated; *Agua Magneziana* is mildly carbonated and *Agua Caxambu* is highly carbonated. All are good.

WHAT TO BUY . . . The best buys in Brazil are precious gems, both set and unset. Topazes, amethysts, aquamarines and tourmalines are the more popular stones. Alligator bags and other leather goods are handsome. Wood carvings, antique silver, handmade lingerie, swimsuits, sportswear and blouses are all good buys here. Note: Shipping packages out of Brazil is complicated and expensive.

WHAT TO WEAR . . . Women will want lightweight spring or summer clothes, plenty of beachwear. A great deal of black is worn in cities during the winter, especially evenings, so some good little black dresses will come in handy. Jewels are worn after 6 P.M. Fur jackets and stoles are seen in the evening. A lightweight woolen suit is always nice to have along. Slacks and a topcoat may come in handy. Evening and dinner clothes for the season. Men will want linen suits, lightweight wool suits, beachwear, dinner clothes, if you are there during the Brazilian social season, June through September. Highly recommended are seersucker suits or wrinkle-proof synthetics for men during Brazilian summers, heavier suits for winter. Keep sports clothes on the conservative side.

WHERE TO GO—SIGHTSEEING ...

Rio de Janeiro ... Rio is full of things to see. You can scarcely miss the magnificent Copacabana Beach section with its serpentine mosaic walk famed the world over. Neither can you miss Sugar Loaf Mountain and Corcovado (Hunchback Mountain) which tower over the city. Sugar Loaf is a huge granite cone at the entrance of the bay. Take the cable car to Sugar Loaf and a cog railway to Corcovado. The summit of Corcovado is crowned by the famed statue of Christ the Redeemer. The views from these two spots are fabulous. Visit the Gavea district by car; it affords some of the most beautiful scenery anywhere. This is where the racetrack is, too. Among the many churches, be sure to see the Church of Nossa Senhora da Glória do Outeiro with its Bible scenes in blue tile. The São Bento Monastery is interesting, but only men are allowed in the cloisters. The Guanabara Palace, now housing the Governor's office, is at Rua Pinheiro Machado, was once the residence of Princess Izabel. The São Joaquin Palace, Praça da Glória, is the official residence of the Archbishop.

The largest park in Rio is the Quinta da Boa Vista, containing the National Museum, once the residence of two emperors. It has zoological gardens, a small tropical-fish aquarium. Botanical Gardens are situated near Lake Rodrigo de Freitas and the Jockey Club. Here is a great avenue of palms 2,200 feet long. Tijuca Forest is fine for a day's excursion.

A trip to Paquetá, an island at the far end of the bay, is a delight. You may hike, cycle or hire a carriage for a drive from one end of the island to the other. There is a ferry trip from Praça 15 de Novembro and a shorter ferry ride to Niteroi, a picturesque town across the bay, which is the residential section for the English colony. There are pleasant beaches at Icarai and Imbui for a quiet day's jaunt. Now famous Ipanema is within Rio's city limits.

Petrópolis ... Is a leading summer resort. It is about an hour's ride from Rio and boasts of the *Hotel Quitandinha,* now a private club but with a restaurant and public rooms open to visitors. It is set in the middle of fantastic tropical scenery, including orchid-draped trees on the edge of a small lake. There are 20-foot bird cages, indoor Roman pools, a theater, a marble entrance hall and almost anything else you can imagine. Nearby is the royal palace built by the last emperor of Brazil, Dom Pedro II. The palace is now the Imperial Museum. You may see the royal jewels on Thursdays and Sundays.

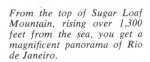

From the top of Sugar Loaf Mountain, rising over 1,300 feet from the sea, you get a magnificent panorama of Rio de Janeiro.

Rio de Janeiro's world-famous Copacabana Beach is flanked by luxury hotels and purple mountains.

Another popular resort nearby is Terezópolis, which is about 1½ hours from Rio by a new scenic highway. Best hotels there are *Fazenda da Paz* and *Pensão Pinheiros*.

São Paulo ... South of Rio is São Paulo, the greatest industrial city in South America. It can be reached in 1 hour by air, or 7 hours by bus. Travel agents will arrange sightseeing tours, and you'll be fascinated with all the beautiful modern buildings and fabulous garden apartments. The famous Snake Institute Butantan is a leader in antibiotic research. Also interesting are the Museum of Modern Art and the permanent industrial exhibition at Parque Ibirapuera.

Santos ... Only an hour south of São Paulo is Santos, the world's largest coffee port. This is a resort center with beaches and excursions to nearby mountains. The *Parque Balneario* and the *Atlantic* are good hotels. See the orchidarium and Guarujá across the bay. The drive or cog railway trip from São Paulo to Santos is exciting. Buses run very frequently between the two points; the ride takes about an hour.

Campos do Jordão (Fields of Jordan) ... The leading mountain resort for the São Paulo area. Delightful Swiss-style hotels serve excellent food. Golfing, horseback riding and a relaxed holiday atmosphere in a fine climate.

Iguassú Falls ... On the Argentine border is one of the sights of the world. They can be reached in about 3 hours by plane from São Paulo. Larger than Niagara, they are 2½ miles wide. Eight miles away are the falls of Sete Quedas (more on Iguassú Falls in section on ARGENTINA. See also under PARAGUAY.) *Hotel Cataratas* on the Brazilian side is first class.

Belo Horizonte . . . Capital of the state of Minas Gerais and center of steel and mining industries. Single rates at *Hotel Normandie* are $6 to $10. From the city, take the day-long tour to Ouro Prêto. A gem of colonial art and architecture, the town is preserved as a valued national monument and is famed for its sculptures by *Aleijadinho,* "The Little Cripple," a genius of the late 18th century.

Recife . . . "The Venice of America" is laced with waterways crossed by numerous graceful bridges. The city was founded about 1535 and is rich in magnificent churches. Hotels: the new *Plaza,* the *Boa Viagem, Guararapes, Grande.*

Belém . . . The capital city of the State of Pará at the mouth of the Amazon, way north of Rio, looks like the setting for an adventure movie. *Hotel Grande* is air-conditioned and lively.

Manaus . . . For the adventurous looking for something different off the tourist path, there are frequent flights from Rio and Belém to Manaus, 1,000 miles up the Amazon in the heart of the jungle. The center of the rubber boom of 50 years ago, Manaus has an astonishing Opera House and a fabulous history. You can take river trips, fish for *tucunaré,* one of the world's great game fish, and buy an alligator hide or jaguar skin for a very few dollars. The *Hotel Amazonas* is new and modern, with some rooms air-conditioned. Rates are $10-$14 double, European Plan. Sightseeing and fishing are organized by the *Hotel Amazonas* at moderate rates.

Salvador . . . Called "Bahia" by Brazilians, Salvador (in the state of Bahia) is the royal capital port and the fourth-largest city in Brazil. *Hotel de Bahia* and *Plaza* (about $5 single) are the best. The market, native costumes, colonial churches and buildings, fabulous beaches, rainbow-tinted houses make it well worth a visit.

Brasília . . . The new capital of Brazil, an architectural and city planning wonder, stands on a high plateau 580 miles northwest of Rio de Janeiro. Among outstanding buildings designed by Brazil's famed Oscar Niemeyer are the President's Residence and the Plaza of the Three Powers. Among hotels are the beautiful *Brasília Palace* (from $8 single) and *Nacional* (from $12 single with breakfast). Advance reservations advisable.

Pôrto Alegre . . . Rich, busy river port in the heart of the gaucho country where spit-roasted beef reaches the heights of gustatory supremacy. The *Plaza* is among several good hotels.

SOURCES OF FURTHER INFORMATION . . . The Rio tourist commission office at Rua São José 90 has folders, maps, lists of events. The *Brazil Herald* is an English-language newspaper. The Pan American office is at Avenida Presidente Wilson, No. 165A (Tel. 52-8070) in Rio. At Rua São Luiz 29 (Tel. 36-0191) in São Paulo. In New York the Brazilian Consulate General is at 630 Fifth Avenue.

BRITISH GUIANA

VENEZUELA

ATLANTIC OCEAN

GEORGETOWN
Bartica
BRITISH GUIANA

KAIETFUR FALLS

BRAZIL

ESSEQUIBO RIVER

SURINAM

WEATHER IN GEORGETOWN—Lat. N6°49′–Alt. below sea level

	JAN.	FEB.	MAR.	APR.	MAY	JUNE	JULY	AUG.	SEPT.	OCT.	NOV.	DEC.
Aevrage Temp.	79°	79°	80°	80°	80°	80°	80°	81°	82°	82°	81°	80°
Days of Rain	20	17	19	17	23	25	24	17	8	7	13	22

LOCATION ... British Guiana lies along the northeast shoulder of South America between Venezuela and Surinam.

CHARACTERISTICS ... For vacationists who like to get off the beaten track, British Guiana offers picturesque towns, strange peoples and odd customs, spectacular scenery and untamed jungles; and in the center of the country is one of the wonders of the world, Kaieteur Falls, five times higher than Niagara. Sometimes called the "land of six peoples"—Africans, Amer-Indians, Chinese, East Indians, Portuguese and other Europeans—British Guiana has a reputation for overwhelming hospitality shared by all.

POPULATION ... 624,000 inhabitants, 90% of whom live on the flat coastal belt. Owing, among other things, to improved health conditions, the population is expected to double in the next decade.

SIZE ... 83,000 square miles, about the size of Great Britain.

CAPITAL ... Georgetown, "The Garden City of South America," population 112,000.

GOVERNMENT ... Colony, with internal self government.

HOW TO GET THERE ... By Pan American Jet Clipper 7¾ hours from New York via Barbados and Trinidad. 1 hour from Trinidad by jet.

ACCOMMODATIONS ... Georgetown's *Hotel Tower,* with swimming pool, has rates from $11.20 single, $17.80 double for air-conditioned rooms; less for non-air-conditioned. Similar rates at the *Park Hotel, Woodbine* and *Belvedere.* Hotel rates include breakfast in the

British fashion. Electric current is 110 and 220 volts, 50 cycles, A.C.

CURRENCY ... The B.W.I. or British Caribbean dollar, worth about 58¢ in United States currency. £1 equals $4.80 B.W.I.

CUSTOMS REGULATIONS AND DOCUMENTS REQUIRED FOR UNITED STATES CITIZENS ... Passengers are required to make only an oral declaration. Passports are not required of any Canadian or American citizen who satisfies a member of the Immigration Service of his citizenship; that he is in possession of a return ticket; and that he intends to remain in the Colony for a period not exceeding 3 months from the date of his entry.

RESTAURANTS AND BARS ... All hotels in Georgetown have dining rooms and are equipped with bars. For variety, try the *Cactus Club* in Hotel Tower; *The Moonglow* at Hotel Woodbine for juicy steaks; delicious Chinese food at *The Bamboo Gardens;* the *Palm Court* is also famous for steaks. Among others are the *Belvedere* (Indian dishes); *Oasis,* chicken-in-the-rough; *Farm Fresh Inn* and *Golden Lotus,* curries and barbecued chicken. 10% of the bill is the usual tip. Dancing on Saturday evenings at most restaurants.

WHERE TO GO—SIGHTSEEING ...

Georgetown ... Is a garden city with many sights of interest. It extends for 2 miles along the Demerara River front, and has excellent roads, wide and straight, and shady, tree-lined avenues. A visit to the Botanical Gardens is of first importance, quiet, cool and beautiful, a wonderland of tropical verdure, the plant population ranging from exquisite tropical flowers to experimental rice fields. Miniature diamond and gold mines are displayed in the British Guiana Museum. The Zoological Park in the Botanic Gardens contains a collection of local fauna set in picturesque surroundings. Daytime taxi fares are about 60¢ B.W.I. to any place in town; 75¢ at night.

Kaieteur Falls ... The fabulous Kaieteur Falls, with a sheer drop of 741 feet, is one of the world's highest "bridal" falls. If you leave Georgetown at 9:30 A.M., the falls can be reached in a delightful hour's flight over the jungle and up the gorge of the Potaro River. A short walk to the brink of the falls for a picnic lunch and a view of the falls from various vantage points is a memorable experience. A plane which carries 6 passengers (for $57.50 B.W.I. each) can be chartered through the Guyana Airways Corporation, but this service is not run on a regular schedule. However, full day tours to Kaieteur may be arranged through Guiana Travel Tours; charter of a 4-seater Cessna is $140.

SOURCES OF FURTHER INFORMATION ... Government Information Service in Georgetown. Bookers Shipping (Demerara), Ltd., at 23 Main St., are agents for Pan American in Georgetown. In New York contact Mr. Felix Cummings, Government of British Guiana Public Relations and Information Office, 310 E. 44 St.

CHILE

PERU
Arica
Tocopilla   BOLIVIA
Antofagasta
ARGENTINA
CHRIST OF THE ANDES   MT. ACONCAGUA
Viña del Mar   Portillo
Valparaiso   SANTIAGO
Concepcion
Villarica
Osorno   Puyehue
Puerto Montt   Puellao
PACIFIC   CHILE
OCEAN
ATLANTIC
OCEAN
Punta Arenas

WEATHER IN SANTIAGO—Lat. S33°27'—Alt. 1800'

Temp.	JAN.	FEB.	MAR.	APR.	MAY	JUNE	JULY	AUG.	SEPT.	OCT.	NOV.	DEC.
Low	52°	52°	50°	46°	43°	42°	43°	43°	43°	48°	49°	53°
High	83°	83°	84°	77°	67°	58°	59°	61°	66°	74°	79°	84°
Average	67°	66°	64°	62°	55°	47°	48°	51°	54°	60°	63°	66°
Days of Rain	0	0	0	2	4	5	4	4	3	2	1	0

LOCATION ... A narrow strip between the Andes and the South Pacific, Chile extends from Peru 2,600 miles along the west coast of South America—farther than from New York to Los Angeles.

CHARACTERISTICS ... The capital of Chile has a different atmosphere from most of the capitals in its sister countries. Somehow Santiago is less Latin. Many of the people have English, Irish or German ancestry. You will see many blond people who speak only Spanish but look as though they should speak English. The city itself is beautifully located on a high plain. The Mapocho River runs through the city; the peaks of the Andes are to the east. Commanding the city is Cerro San Cristobal, whose terraced slopes rise high above the town. Santiago is modern and there are few old buildings.

POPULATION ... Estimated at about 8,394,000.

SIZE ... 286,396 square miles, a larger total area than Texas, but most of the country is barely 100 miles wide.

CAPITAL ... Santiago, population 2,100,000.

GOVERNMENT ... A Republic with a President and National Congress elected by universal suffrage.

HOW TO GET THERE ... By National, Pan American and Panagra without change of plane down the west coast of South America, 14 hours (elapsed time) from New York, 10¼ hours from Miami. Stopovers if you wish en route. By Pan Am Jet Clipper down the east coast, 12½ hours to Buenos Aires from New York. Then by Panagra, Santiago is 1¾ hours from Buenos Aires. From the United

States West Coast, flights for South America connect at Miami or Panamá City. By ship about 18 days from New York to Valparaiso and about 30 days from the United States West Coast.

ACCOMMODATIONS... Hotels in Santiago are marvelous, have good food and smart European-style service. The *Carrera Hilton,* a 17-story hotel with rooftop swimming pool and garden, is one of the finest hotels on the continent. Single rates from $9, double from $11, European Plan. Other first-class hotels in Santiago are the *Emperador, Crillón, Panamericano, Grand, Palace, Carlos V* and *Santa Lucia,* with rates considerably less than at the Carrera. The *Kent, Lido, Ritz, Savoy* and *City* hotels are comfortable and inexpensive. Hotels add up to 21% to your bill to cover service and taxes.

ARTS... The Museum of Natural History, the Museum of Fine Arts, the Museum of Modern Art, and the huge National Library.

BALLET... There is a native ballet company which performs at the Teatro Municipal. Visiting ballet companies appear occasionally.

BANKS... First National City Bank of New York, Bank of London and South America Ltd.

CALENDAR OF HOLIDAYS... Stores and museums are closed on January 1; Good Friday; May 1, Labor Day; May 21, Battle of Iquique; Ascension Day; Corpus Christi; June 29, SS. Peter and Paul; August 15, Feast of the Assumption; September 18, 19, Independence Day; October 12, Columbus Day; November 1, All Saints Day; December 8; Christmas. Museums are also closed Mondays.

CIGARETTES... *Lucky Strikes* and *Viceroys* are made in Chile. Best local brands are *Liberty, Capstan* and *Hilton*. Local pipe tobaccos are not the best; take your own supply.

CLIMATE... The name of the country is derived from an Indian name meaning "cold." Santiago, however, is mild the year round. The climate is similar to that of Southern California. It grows colder as you go south, warmer toward the north. Their summer season is our winter. Andes ski season is June through September.

CLUBS... Cards may be arranged for most of the Santiago clubs through members or if you are a member of a comparable club at home. Club de la Unión is famous and very good, with an excellent restaurant and fine wine cellar; Club Hípico (racetrack) is exclusive and swank; Los Leones Golf Club; The Prince of Wales Club for golf; the Polo Club has tennis courts and swimming pool. Also Lions, Stade Française, Estadio Italiano, Estadio Español, Paper-Chase, Rotary.

COMMON COURTESIES AND LOCAL CUSTOMS... The chaperone is a thing of the past in Chile. The dinner hour is late, after nine. Tea around five is a local custom. Cocktail parties begin around seven and guests are apt to drift in late unless the host specifies *hora Inglesa* (English time), which means you should be punctual.

COMMUNICATIONS... A 3-minute phone call to the States costs $12 for first 3 minutes, $4 for each additional minute. A 10-word cablegram is $4.92. Airmail postage is E°0.250 (8¢).

CURRENCY ... Since 1960, the escudo (E°), equal to 1,000 pesos, has been the Chilean currency, but old peso notes and coins are still in circulation. There are 100 centésimos in an escudo, which is valued at about E°3.80 to U.S. $1, but the tourist rate of exchange frequently fluctuates.

CUSTOMS REGULATIONS AND DOCUMENTS REQUIRED FOR UNITED STATES CITIZENS ... Passport, and smallpox vaccination certificate required. No visa required, but you'll need a Tourist Card, issued free to U.S. citizens, and valid for 90 days. You may bring in all articles of personal use. No restrictions on cameras and small restrictions on liquor (about 3 bottles per person). 500 cigarettes, 200 cigars and 1 lb. of tobacco allowed duty free. Air departure taxes from E°0.30 (10¢) to E°2 (61¢), depending upon airport and destination.

DRUGSTORES ... Almost no American products are available, but there are U.S.-licensed substitutes.

ELECTRIC CURRENT ... 220 volts, A.C., 50 cycles.

FAUNA ... Among Chile's larger wild animals are the puma (mountain lion), guanaco (larger version of the llama), Andean wolf and huemul (a large deer). The chinchilla, becoming very rare, still exists in the mountains. The pudú, smallest species of deer, may be found in South Chilean forests. The Chilean bullfrog is an edible delicacy. Lakes are stocked with trout imported from North America.

FLORA ... Flowers are abundant; a great variation in all the length of the territory. There are some exclusively national specimens in the south, where you will also find some unexplored woods. *Copihue,* beautiful specimen of Chilean flora, is the national flower.

FOOD ... Seafood is famous in Chile; lobster dishes are especially delicious. Try *caldillo de congrio,* a fish soup, crab (*jaibas*), shrimp (*camarones*) and the delectable baby crawfish called *langostinos. Chupe de Mariscos* is a superb shellfish plate. *Chupe de locos* is an abalone soup. *Corvina* is delicious, here, and so are swordfish steaks. There is, of course, excellent and inexpensive beef, too. National dishes are usually highly spiced. Try *cazuela de ave*—rich chicken soup with green vegetables cooked in broth. *Pancho Villa* is a dish made of local *bayo* beans cooked with *chorizos* (pungent smoked sausages) and fried eggs. *Pastel de choclo* is fresh green corn stew with ground-up meat and vegetables. *Humitas* (Chilean hot tamales), must be tasted. *Empanadas* (meat pies) vary in every native restaurant. Desserts are cool and imaginative; pineapple with champagne, for instance, is one favorite.

LANGUAGE ... Spanish, of course, is the official language, but most people in tourist centers speak and understand English.

LAUNDRY AND DRY CLEANING ... Hotels will furnish the information required and some of them have their own service. Two good dry-cleaning companies in Santiago are Lavandería Manchester and Sandrico, which will give you 24-hour service for a 50% surcharge. The ordinary service is 5 days for suits and shirts.

LIQUOR ... The native wines are the thing to buy and drink.

Tops are *Santa Carolina,* a white wine; *Tarapacá ex-Zavala* and *Tocornal* in the burgundy class. Some Chilean Rieslings are well-known in the States and there are many more brands available. Chilean champagnes are dry and splendid. All the wines are inexpensive.

MEDICAL FACILITIES . . . There are several hospitals, and English-speaking doctors are available. Two of the good ones in Santiago are Clínica Santa Maria and Clínica Alemana.

MOTION PICTURES . . . Most films shown in the States are shown in the Santiago theaters with only the difference that titles are Spanish. The best theaters in Santiago are: *Windsor, Metro, Bandera, Central, Plaza, Lido, Rex, Ducal, Astor, Pacifico* and *Gran Palace.* For films in Spanish, you can go to the *Teatro Santiago* and *Continental.*

MUSIC . . . There are concerts at Santiago's Teatro Municipal with local conductors and frequently with big-name guest conductors from the States and Europe. Guitar music is popular.

NIGHT CLUBS, CABARETS . . . The *Boîte* in the Hotel Carrera is very swank, as is the *Hideaway;* also the *Tap Room* and *Waldorf.* Interesting out-of-town spots are *Las Brujas, Lo Curro, La Pirámide, Las Tres Carabelas* and *Las Perdices.*

PHOTOGRAPHY . . . Supplies are somewhat limited. Take plenty of film with you.

RELIGION . . . Roman Catholic. There are other churches, however, some with services in English.

RESTAURANTS AND BARS . . . Dining in Chile is marvelous and cheap. In Santiago the hotels *Carrera* and *Crillón* have superb continental food. English is spoken at *El Parrón,* famous for meat and mixed grills, Chilean dishes. It also has an outdoor patio. The *Waldorf* has American and French cuisine, a good orchestra. *El Escorial, Nuria* and *Chiaranda* for continental food. The *Due Torri* specializes in Italian dishes; *El Danubio Azul* in Chinese food. Also try *Langen's Bar, El Santiago, Shorton Grill* and *Mervilles* for Chilean specialties. *El Pollo Dorado* is excellent for chicken and beef served in a typically Chilean atmosphere. Try *Parrilla de Vanancio* for barbecues.

SHOPS AND STORES . . . Among the best stores in Santiago are Los Gobelinos, Falabella, Almacenes Paris, Casa Garcia, Rosenblitt, Flaño and Ville de Nice. Chilean Arts, a block from the Carrera, is a fine new store with local handicrafts. Stores are closed Saturday afternoons and all the feast days; during the week they are open from 9:30 to 1 and 3:30 to 8 P.M.

SPECTATOR SPORTS . . . Around Santiago there is racing on Sundays and feast days at the Club Hípico and Hipódromo de Chile. Pari-mutuel betting, of course. There is racing in season at Viña del Mar, too. Here the Derby, a big social event, is held. Soccer is a favorite sport and there are international matches throughout the summer season; National League the rest of the year. There are ski tournaments in the Chilean Andes and lots of rodeos.

SPORTS . . . This is the one country in South America where sports take precedence over almost everything else, including sightseeing.

Skiing . . . From June through September, skiing in Chile is the finest in the world. From Santiago you travel by rail or auto to the area of deep snow in just a few hours. Here you'll find the most famous ski resorts in South America. The slopes are gentle or swift, as you prefer, and there is a choice for every skier's ability.

Portillo is the country's ski center. Special ski trains take you on a spectacularly scenic ride in 5 hours from Santiago to the *Hotel Portillo,* at 9,300 feet, which is an 8-story building with a movie theater, night club and hospital, all centrally heated. Single rates $18.50, double $35, American Plan. At Portillo there are magnificent trails, tows, chairlifts and a 6-mile ski run. Some of the top instructors in the world are on hand in season. Try a 1-day excursion to nearby *Christ of the Andes,* with skiing all the way back to the hotel.

The ski center of Farellones is 32 miles from Santiago. Accommodations are in *refugios* and private lodges. Two miles from Farellones is La Parva. Llaima and other fine resorts are in southern Chile.

Fishing . . . Chilean rivers and lakes, glittering like jewels amid intensely colorful scenery, are currently the world's finest fly-fishing waters. From Lake Panguipulli to Lake Llanquihue, trout average at least 3 pounds. All-inclusive fishing trips can be arranged in Santiago. Take an 8'-9½' fly rod adapted for a spinning reel. Best season, October 15 to April 15.

Other Sports . . . Favorite sport of the Santiago social set is wild-dove shooting near Santiago. Tennis, golf, riding, polo, skin diving and swimming are all possible in and around Santiago. The Prince of Wales Country Club and Los Leones Golf Club have fine golf courses. Cards are needed. The Polo Club has tennis courts and a swimming pool.

THEATERS . . . In Santiago the *Atelier,* the *Petit Rex,* the *Cariola, Camilo Henriquez, Antonio Varas* and the *Municipal,* which also has musical performances. All plays are in Spanish.

TIME . . . Noon in Santiago is 11 A.M. in New York.

TIPPING . . . Tip porters 20 centésimos per bag. Tip 10 centésimos for all small services performed by everyone from the hotel attendant who opens your room to parking lot attendants; 10 centésimos to movie and theater ushers; 10% of the bill to waiters, and 30 centésimos per day to hotel chambermaid, despite service inclusion in hotel and restaurant bills. Taxi drivers, however, need not be tipped.

TRANSPORTATION . . . Taxis are plentiful and reasonable.

WATER . . . It is advisable to drink bottled water. Puyehue, bottled at the resort of that name, is one of the best. Panimavída and Cachantún are also good. For noncarbonated water, specify *"agua mineral sin gas."*

WHAT TO BUY . . . Shopping is not the major sport here, but handcrafts are the thing to buy. Black pottery jars can be bought at the Market. Hand-wrought copper trays and candlesticks. *Choapinos,* soft-napped wool rugs, are handsome. The Chilean wines are good buys.

WHAT TO WEAR . . . Depends a great deal upon where you are planning to go in Chile and at what time of year. It is colder toward the south; warmer toward the north.

For skiing in the Chilean Andes, June-September, you'll wear the same kind of ski togs you would in Switzerland or in the United States. Santiago has climate similar to that of Southern California. It never gets very hot or very cold. Wear the same sort of thing you would at home in spring. A fur jacket and topcoat come in handy.

Cocktail parties are dressy, so pack afternoon dress and your newest and gayest hat. In fact, Chilean women are world famous for always being beautifully dressed in the latest, smartest styles.

Men can wear sports jackets and slacks in town, but regular business suits are more appropriate. A topcoat is a necessity. Evening clothes are not necessary, as dark suits are the accepted dinner attire.

WHERE TO GO—SIGHTSEEING ...

Santiago ... Santiago is a beautiful modern city surrounded by snow-capped mountains. You will get the best view of it from Santa Lucia Park, a picturesque hill covered with terraces, gardens and walks high in the middle of the city. The first Spanish fort in Chile, it is open to the public from 7 A.M. till midnight, and can be reached by car. There are gardens and a small museum. Cerro San Cristobal rises about 1,000 feet above the city. There is a funicular to the summit, from which you get a magnificent view; you can lunch here at the *Restaurant Casino*. The road to the top is lined with gardens and promenades. Be sure to include a visit to Government House, *La Moneda*, the residence of the President; well worth seeing. The beautiful Avenida O'Higgins, best known as the Alameda, is the widest street in the city, with pedestrian walks in the center. The main square is the Plaza de Armas.

Try to get invited to a *fundo*, or farm, for a sample of Chilean life, where your host may stage a rodeo for you. Chilean rodeos are different from American ones. You should try to see one if you are around in November or December. The cowboys, called *huasos*, play guitars and sing typically Chilean cowboy songs. The national dance of Chile, the *cueca*, is danced to guitar music.

Valparaiso ... Chile's second city and the principal port on the west coast of South America, Valparaiso was founded in 1536 by Juan de Saavedra. It is 116 miles from Santiago by train and 91 miles by bus (both very modern and comfortable), but a lovely way to approach Valparaiso is by sea. The city's great semicircular bay is circled by tall hills, all covered with buildings which at night, with their myriad lights, make an unforgettable scene from the harbor.

The downtown area is very smart, and the public walks and streets are beautiful. The *Condell* is the best hotel. *Castillo Fornoni* and *Torreén* are restaurants outstanding for seafood.

Viña del Mar ... The famed beach resort is about 90 miles from Santiago and right next to Valparaiso. It is reminiscent of Monte Carlo, Juan-les-Pins and Nice on the French Riviera. The season at this highly fashionable spot is January through March. *Hotel Miramar*, open all year, has a private swimming pool and beaches, also facilities for water sports; single from $9.50, double from $12.50. The *O'Higgins* is another first-class hotel, older and somewhat larger. The *San Martín* and *Alcázar* are also good. There are many fine restaurants in addition to hotel dining rooms. A new one is *Chez Gerald*. For Italian food, *San Marcos;* try lunch at *Los· Lilenes,* on the road to Concon.

The Casino is world famous. It is municipally run, and thousands of people can be found at the gaming tables—14 roulette and 19 *punto y banca* (chemin de fer). Hours of operation are 6 to 9 P.M. and 10 P.M. to 3 A.M. from September 15 to March 15. There are also a cabaret theater, a *boîte* and a large dining room surrounded by magnificent gardens.

Other points of interest are Parque Vergara and Parque del Salitre. Take a ride along the sea to Concon, a beach resort; the scenery along the way is breathtaking. It is about 20 minutes by car from Viña del Mar, and there are good restaurants along the way.

There are races every Sunday during local summer at the Sporting Club, and good golf at the Granadilla Country Club. Viña del Mar is very smart, and you'll want to wear your most fashionable clothes. Rates for single rooms at hotels are from $4.50 to $10.50 a day, European Plan.

Chilean Lake Country ... The Chilean Lake country is˜ one of the most picturesque lake regions anywhere. It's a land of magnificent scenery and fine sports. You can tour the Lake Country by train, bus, and boat ... traveling south from Santiago. Pucon is probably your first stop on a typical itinerary. It is on Lake Villarrica, which offers incredibly good rainbow- and brown-trout fishing. Villarrica volcano, 9,000 feet high, is nearby. The *Hotel Pucon,* here, is fine and the *Hotel Antumalal* is marvelous for good fishing and a rest.

Traveling on by train, you reach Osorno—one of the most beautiful towns and volcanos on your route. It rises in a perfect cone on the edge of a placid lake. Best hotel is the *Gran Hotel Osorno,* quite moderate in price. The luxurious *Puyehue Springs Hotel* has both thermal hot springs and superb trout fishing.

Leave Osorno by train for Puerto Varas through scenery very much like the blue-grass country of Kentucky. From Puerto Varas, on the southern tip of Lake Llanquihue (pronounced "Yankee-way"), visit Puerto Montt and its picturesque fishermen's wharf at Ongelmo. Spend the night at the *Gran Hotel Puerto Varas* or *La Playa.* Leave by bus for Ensenada, still on Lake Llanquihue, and then go inland to Petrohue, along the Petrohue Falls, reaching lovely Lake Todos los Santos. (You can also make a direct, but less scenic, trip by bus from Osorno to Ensenada and Petrohue.)

From Petrohue a small steamer will take you across Lake Todos los Santos to Peulla where you can spend the night in a comfortable hotel patterned after a Swiss chalet. While here, you can take day excursions to Cayutúe and Rio Blanco. You clear customs at Peulla and, shortly after leaving by bus, you arrive at Casa Pangue and enter Argentina.

If you enter Chile from Argentina, go by way of Bariloche and enter the Lake Country at Peulla. By a combination of bus, train and boat go to Villarrica, where the scenery is as fine as the fishing and skiing. The trees, the forests, the snow-capped mountains, the crystal lakes, the views, the fishing, the magnificence of the scenery will entrance you. In Villarrica stay at the *Hotel Antumalal* which has a beautiful golf course and facilities for water skiing. You should really have two weeks to devote to this lake trip. For more on the Lake Country, see Argentina chapter.

Antofagasta ... A province becoming of great importance to archaeologists. Antofagasta City is unique—not a twig or a blade of grass; water is piped in from the Andes. Earth in the city square came as ballast from England. The brand new *Hotel de Turismo* is first rate. If you're game for the fantastic trip to "Chuqui"—world's largest open-pit copper mine—first get permission from Anaconda. If granted, make arrangements through the local Panagra agent (Tel. 22072). You may also visit old ruins, or the Indian Museum of Father LePage at San Pedro de Atacama in the interior of the province.

SOURCES OF FURTHER INFORMATION ... Panagra has offices in Santiago at the Hotel Carrera (Tel. 82011) and at Morande 341 or Huerfanos 1189 (Tel. 81961). The Chilean Consulate General is at 61 Broadway, New York, N.Y. 10006.

The church of San Francisco, built in the 16th century, blends well with modern structures on Santiago's Alameda Bernardo O'Higgins.

COLOMBIA

WEATHER IN BOGOTA—Lat. N4°36'—Alt. 8,600'

Temp.	JAN.	FEB.	MAR.	APR.	MAY	JUNE	JULY	AUG.	SEPT.	OCT.	NOV.	DEC.
Low	45°	45°	46°	50°	50°	49°	48°	48°	46°	48°	48°	46°
High	71°	70°	71°	68°	67°	67°	67°	67°	67°	68°	68°	69°
Average	58°	57°	58°	59°	58°	58°	57°	57°	57°	58°	58°	57°
In. of Rain	2.14	1.12	2.93	4.03	4.08	2.65	1.86	1.28	2.60	6.33	7.20	3.83

LOCATION ... Colombia lies in the northwest corner of South America. It is the only country on the continent that fronts both the Atlantic (Caribbean Sea) and Pacific Oceans.

CHARACTERISTICS ... Colombia is very Spanish in its culture and traditions. This can be seen in its churches, its old public buildings, and its mountain towns. Bogotá, the capital, has often been called the Athens of South America because it has been a cultural center since the time of the Spanish viceroys.

The main shopping center in Bogotá is on Carrera 7a between Calles 10 and 25. In this area too are the fine hotels, clubs and theaters of the city. In the northern part of the city is another important shopping district, Chapinero, on Carrera 13 between Calles 54 and 63. The national flower of Colombia is the orchid. It grows everywhere, but it is one of the sights of Medellín. Colombia is a country of infinite variety, from skiing in Manizales to jungle hunting and fishing along the Amazon River in Leticia.

POPULATION ... Estimated at more than 15,434,000.

SIZE ... 439,512 square miles.

CAPITAL ... Bogotá, with a population of 1,488,000.

GOVERNMENT ... A republic governed by a President.

HOW TO GET THERE ... By Pan Am Jet 4½ hours from New York to Caracas which in turn is 1½ hours from Bogotá. Miami-Barranquilla 4½ hours. Panamá to Bogotá nonstop 1¼ hours; Quito-Bogotá 1¼ hours; Panamá-Barranquilla 1½ hours; Panamá-Medellín

1½ hours; by Panagra, Panamá-Cali 1¾ hours; Quito-Cali 1¼ hours.

ACCOMMODATIONS . . . Tops in Bogotá is the *Hotel Tequendama,* which, like all Intercontinental hotels, is beautifully equipped, and operated by American standards. It has studio-type rooms with a view of the mountains and city. Singles from $14.50, doubles from $18. The *Hotel Continental* is also new and good. Small, but new and modern, are the *Cordillera* and the *Presidente.* Also good: *Residencias Santa Fé* and *Residencias Steves.*

ARTS . . . A must for the tourist in Bogotá is the *Quinta de Bolívar,* which was given to the Libertador, Simón Bolívar, by the first vice-president of Colombia in 1820. It is a perfect example of Spanish colonial architecture. Also of interest is the Museum of Colonial Art located in front of the Palacio San Carlos, the actual residence of the President of the Republic. This museum contains Spanish colonial painting, sculpture and furniture. In a special vault of the Banco de la República is the Gold Museum, a collection of emeralds, pieces of jewelry and amulets made by primitive Indian tribes living in Colombia before the Spanish Conquest. The National Museum is devoted to archaeology and the history of the country.

BALLET . . . Visiting ballet groups appear frequently. There are several ballet academies in Bogotá.

BANKS . . . The Banco Commercial Antioqueno, Banco de Colombia, Banco de Bogotá, Banco Popular, First National City Bank of New York, Royal Bank of Canada, Bank of London and South America.

CALENDAR OF HOLIDAYS . . . January 6, Epiphany; March 19, San José; Holy Week; May 1, Labor Day; Ascension; Corpus Christi; June 29, San Pedro, San Paulo; July 20, Independence Day; August 7, Battle of Boyacá; August 15, Asunción de Nuestra Señora; October 12, Columbus Day; November 1, All Saints Day; November 11, Independence of Cartagena; December 8, Immaculate Conception; Christmas and New Year's Day. Stores and museums close on holidays; banks close from December 24–January 2.

CIGARETTES AND TOBACCO . . . All American brands of cigarettes and tobacco. Cigarettes are 30¢-45¢ U.S. per pack. There is also a variety of local cigarettes, cigars and tobacco at much lower prices. All very good.

CLIMATE . . . Bogotá has an altitude of 8,600 feet. The city is cool throughout the year, similar to spring in the United States.

CLUBS . . . In Bogotá, the Jockey Club, Gun Club, Anglo-American Club, Club Médico, Lawyers' Club, Lions and Rotary. Country Clubs are the Bogotá Country Club, Los Lagartos, San Andrés Golf Club, Military Club, American Sport Club.

COMMON COURTESIES AND CUSTOMS . . . A mixture of Spanish, European and American. Dinner can be as late as 10:30. Colombian society enjoys visiting the hotels and night clubs for dining and dancing. Social life is dressy, but seldom formal.

COMMUNICATIONS . . . In local currency, a 3-minute phone call to New York costs 57.60 pesos; a 10-word cablegram is 41 pesos. Airmail postage to the U.S. is 60 centavos for airletters and postcards, 80 for a 5-gram letter.

CURRENCY . . . There are 100 centavos in 1 peso. Exchange rates fluctuate but are currently about 16 pesos (written with a $) to U.S. $1.

CUSTOMS REGULATIONS AND DOCUMENTS REQUIRED FOR UNITED STATES CITIZENS . . . Proof of citizenship, 2 photos and tourist card issued by Pan Am, and smallpox vaccination certificate are required. Commercial travelers may obtain business visas or transit cards. Ticket to a point outside Colombia also required. You may bring in, duty free, 200 cigarettes or 50 cigars, and 2 bottles of liquor for personal use.

DRUGSTORES . . . Everywhere. All U.S. products available.

ELECTRIC CURRENT . . . 150 volts A.C., 60 cycle in Bogotá except at the Hotel Tequendama, which has 110 volts, A.C. Transformers should be 110-150 volts, A.C., 60 cycle with U.S. flat-prong plugs. Other cities have 110-120-volt current.

FAUNA . . . Colombia is filled with wildlife. Jaguars, pumas, tapirs, armadillos, partridge and many exotic birds are waiting for the hunter, but arrangements should be made in advance. Excellent fishing on the seacoast and in Tota Lake, 4 hours by car from Bogotá.

FLORA . . . Every variety of tropical flower, particularly orchids in Medellín.

FOOD . . . Native dishes, such as *ajiaco, puchero, sancocho, ternera a la llanera,* are highly spiced and marvelous. Try a *piquete,* which is a popular Colombian meal combining potatoes, *platanos,* meat, *yuca,* and *ají,* a very highly seasoned sauce. Try frijoles and pigs knuckles and corn bread, too. Restaurants and hotels in Bogotá serve more international food than those in any other city in South America.

LANGUAGE . . . Spanish is the universal language, but English and German are widely spoken. The traveler from the United States has no trouble making himself understood.

LAUNDRY AND DRY CLEANING . . . Available in every section of the city. 24-hour service in hotels if desired.

LIQUOR . . . In every bar and restaurant the popular drink is Scotch, but try the native drink, *aguardiente,* a fiery liquor. All liquors are available, but expensive. *Ron Caldas,* a rum made in Manizales, is comparable to Jamaica rum, *Ron Medellín* is lighter.

MEDICAL FACILITIES . . . There are many English-speaking doctors and nurses who have had U.S. training and experience.

MOTION PICTURES . . . There are large, comfortable movie houses. Largest in Bogotá are the *Teatro Colombia,* the *Coliseo,* the *Cid,* and the *Olympia;* Cinerama at *Teatro Escala.* Most of the movie theaters in town are good. The open-air theater, *La Media Torta,* located near the Quinta de Bolívar, presents free plays, musical shows, and native dancers almost every Sunday.

MUSIC . . . Bogotá has a conservatory of music and a National Orchestra. Bands play Sunday mornings in the Parque Independencia. Famous artists occasionally perform at the *Teatro de Colón.*

NIGHT CLUBS AND CABARETS ... Bogotá society prefers the *Monserrate Room* at the Hotel Tequendama and the *Grill Europa* in the Continental, with floor shows usually at both. Others are the *Casino delle Rose, La Zambra, Torre de Oro, Kyreos* and *La Pampa.*

PHOTOGRAPHY ... Supplies available at Kodak Colombiana Ltd., Carrera 13, No. 18–66, Bogotá, and in other major cities.

RELIGION ... Colombia is a Catholic country and has 17 cathedrals. In Bogotá the Protestant Church attended by the English-speaking colony is the Union Church on Calle 24 No. 5–43; St. Alban's, the Episcopal Church, on Calle 69 near Carrera 7.

RESTAURANTS ... The food at the top hotels is excellent. A continental cuisine is featured at Bogotá's *Monserrate* and *Grill Europa,* noted above. They have cocktail lounges, too. *Gran Vatel* is a first-class restaurant serving European dishes. *La Zambra* is popular for its Spanish food, music and atmosphere. *Pollo Dorado,* downtown and in El Chico suburb, is famous for chicken dinners; *La Réserve* and *La Table Duroy* for French food and wine. Also try *Luigi's, Agustino's,* the *Koster* and the *Balalaika.* Hotels and private clubs also serve good food, and several *churrascos* serve marvelous Argentine steaks for about $1.

SHOPS AND STORES ... Some of the many good Bogotá shops are: A. Pamp, Aglaya, Valdiri, Sandra, Picadilly, Almacén Bogotá, Jennie, Camacho Roldan, Gregory, Salon Margarita. Sears has two branches in Bogotá and is the largest department store in the city. Many shops offer emeralds, jewelry, silver and other items at much less than prices at home.

SPECTATOR SPORTS ... In Bogotá horse racing Sundays at the *Hipodromo,* pari-mutuel betting as in the U.S. Bullfights Sundays February and March at the Plaza Santamaria. Polo matches at the Polo Club at Bogotá, Polo Club de Santa Fé. Soccer is the national sport. Baseball is played in Barranquilla and Cartagena. Bullfighting in Cali at Christmas time. Cockfighting is popular.

SPORTS ... There are many golf courses in Bogotá, among them the Bogotá Country Club (cards required, two 18-hole courses), Los Lagartos, and San Andres. Tennis courts at all three clubs. All the country clubs have pools. Hunting and fishing expeditions to various parts of the country can be arranged. There is excellent duck shooting. Good marlin fishing is to be found at Barranquilla. Lake Tota, about 160 miles from the capital, in the mountains, offers the best trout fishing in Colombia.

THEATERS ... The *Colón* is the capital's opera and concert house, the *Colombia* also has stage shows from time to time.

TIME ... Same as United States Eastern Standard Time.

TIPPING ... Usually 10%, no more. Hotels add 20% to cover service. Tip porters 1 peso per bag. Taxi drivers are not tipped.

TRANSPORTATION ... There are many taxi fleets and cars for hire; they are very cheap. Aerotaxi (affiliate of Avianca) has air service to areas otherwise difficult to reach. Helicopter service is also available through Helicol (Helicopteros Nacionales de Colombia, another Avianca affiliate).

WATER... Safe in all the big cities.

WHAT TO BUY... Bogotá is the world center for the best emeralds (Chivor Emerald in the Tequendama Hotel, Bauer and Kling are the leading jewelry shops). There is the usual handwrought silver, copper and bronze ware, fine leather goods, Indian rugs, blankets and infinitely practical *ruanas*. The figurines sculptured from crude rubber, then tinted, are unusual; these are available in Cartagena.

WHAT TO WEAR... For Bogotá and Medellín, women will need lightweight wool suits and dresses, sweaters and skirts, and fur jacket or topcoat. A raincoat is recommended wherever you go. Men need a topcoat and light wool suits for mountain cities. Summer sports clothes for the coastal cities.

WHERE TO GO—SIGHTSEEING...

Bogotá... There are many old Colonial buildings in Bogotá dating from the pre-Bolívar era. The Palace of San Carlos, where the Libertador once lived, is now the President's home. Also the Teatro de Colón and the churches of La Veracruz, San Ignacio, San Agustín, La Tercera, San Diego, and San Francisco. All of these are very old. There are at least 60 churches in the city. The cathedral on the Plaza de Bolívar was originally built in 1572. Also don't fail to see the Quinta de Bolívar. Bogotá's seats of learning are many. You should see the University City, the Universidad de los Andes, the Gimnasio Moderno and the Colegio Nacional de San Bartolomé, founded in 1604. Near the capital is Monserrate, a peak that may be ascended by funicular or cablecar. There is a famous chapel on the summit. The Salto de Tequendama is a spectacular waterfall 20 miles from the city. It was an Indian shrine, and there are many legends connected with it. Las Salinas de Zipaquirá, 30 miles from the city, are salt mines which are also spectacular. (It's cold underground; take a coat.) Entering through a portal, one can drive for 3 miles underground. At the end of the largest gallery is a full-sized cathedral. By car or horseback go on to Laguna de Guatavita, 35 miles from the capital, a lagoon rimmed by high mountains, which was held sacred by the ancient Chibchas.

Barranquilla... A bright modern city of 500,000 near the mouth of the Magdalena River. September to March are the best months for a visit. *Hotel El Prado,* singles from $8.80, has a swimming pool and gorgeous gardens. Its *Patio Andaluz* night club is known for good food. Nearby *Brande's* restaurant and *Alfredo's* have European cuisines. The Yacht Club has fishing boats for rent for the excellent deep-sea fishing. The Country Club has an 18-hole golf course, swimming, tennis, and dining facilities. Santa Marta, a 15-minute flight or 2½-hour drive from Barranquilla, may soon be the *in* resort with the Jet Set. Lovely beaches, good fishing.

Cartagena... only 20 minutes by air from Barranquilla, is a wonderful old walled city which lies on a sandy peninsula. There are many interesting old buildings and fortifications dating from the 16th century, especially San Felipe fortress, the clock tower and Fort Boca-chica. There is good swimming at Boca Grande Beach. The *Hotel del Caribe,* on this beach, is fine and so is the new *Hotel Americano,* which is on top of Colombia's only gambling casino. Also the *Flamingo* and the small *Bahia,* in the city, are good.

Cali . . . is a city in the rich Cauca Valley with altitude of 3,000 feet and pleasant year-round climate. The *Alferez Real* and the *Hotel Menendez* are on the Cali River; another good hotel is the *Aristi.* Good restaurants are *Restaurante Hostal, Hosteria Madrid* and *Don Carlos. La Bella Nápoles, El Cortijo* and *Goyescas* are also good restaurants with very reasonable prices. The *Club Campestre de Cali,* which now occupies a specially designed million-dollar building, is the most important social center of Cali and among the best in Latin America. Among its attractions, an 18-hole golf course, seven tennis courts, a riding school, private lake for boating and fishing, and an Olympic-size swimming pool. The *Club La Ribera* is also a very interesting place, offering facilities for all sports.

Medellín . . . is the second city of Colombia. Famous for orchids, it is situated about 150 miles northwest of Bogotá and has the climate of late spring. It is an industrial center. The *Nutibara* is the leading hotel and compares with the best. The *Medellín Country Club* has excellent food, golf courses, tennis courts and swimming pool. (Invitation by a member required.) Be sure to visit the beautiful Cathedral of Medellín, fronting on Plaza Bolívar, said to be the largest brick building in the world. There are many interesting excursions out of Medellín, such as the orchid plantation at *la finca El Ranchito,* just outside of the city, and the estate owned by Mr. Ospina Pérez, which has 70,000 orchid plants of more than 300 varieties.

Manizales . . . Built on a ridge of the Cordillera Central at an altitude of 7,062 feet, Manizales is a comfortably cool city, an important coffee center, and has the largest cathedral in the country. The people are extremely hospitable. Every tourist is welcomed with a free bottle of *Rum Caldas.* The city goes in big for fiestas and corridas de toros (bullfights) the last week in January. The best hotel is the new *Ritz.*

At *El Nevado del Ruiz* (16,000 feet) there is year-round skiing, with ski lift and ski lodge.

SOURCES OF FURTHER INFORMATION . . . National Tourist Office in Bogotá with branches in principal cities. Pan Am offices in Bogotá at Carrera 10, No. 16-39 (Tel. 420-720). In Barranquilla at Carrera 45, No. 34-20 (Tel. 11-610). In New York, the Colombia National Tourist Board is at 608 Fifth Avenue.

ECUADOR

WEATHER IN QUITO—Lat. S0°12'–Alt. 9,248'

Temp.	JAN.	FEB.	MAR.	APR.	MAY	JUNE	JULY	AUG.	SEPT.	OCT.	NOV.	DEC.
Low	46°	47°	47°	47°	47°	45°	44°	44°	45°	46°	46°	46°
High	69°	69°	69°	69°	69°	70°	71°	71°	72°	70°	70°	70°
Average	55°	55°	55°	55°	55°	55°	55°	56°	56°	55°	55°	55°
Days of Rain	17	18	21	22	20	11	6	7	13	19	17	16

LOCATION ... Ecuador is on the northwest coast of South America between Colombia and Peru, occupying a region where the Andes split into two ranges, and divide the country into three regions: the inter-Andean valleys or "sierra," producers of cereals, potatoes, fruits and pastures; the "costa" or littoral, with great plantations of coffee, cocoa and bananas (Ecuador is the world's largest banana exporter); and the east low plains, where the fabulous Amazon jungle begins.

CHARACTERISTICS ... In Quito the sun rises at about 6 A.M. every morning because the city is so near the equator. Quaintly beautiful, Quito is filled with wonderful Spanish colonial architecture and art. Its streets are colorful, and some are steep. The country descends from the grandeur of the Andes to the tropical city and busy port of Guayaquil (over 511,000 inhabitants) on the Guayas river. Ecuador is a miniature world: sea, beaches, desert and jungle; snow-capped mountains, pastures and valleys. For wonderful scenery, a taste of ancient civilization, a touch of deep-sea fishing, try Ecuador, where North Americans are extremely welcome.

POPULATION ... 4,732,930, about half that of Texas.

SIZE ... 105,684 square miles, about the size of Colorado.

CAPITAL ... Quito, a city of 392,962.

GOVERNMENT ... A republic of 19 provinces and one insular territory, with a President, Vice President, Senate and Chamber of Deputies, temporarily replaced by a de facto military junta.

HOW TO GET THERE ... On the interchange flight of National, Pan American and Panagra, New York to Quito is 9 hours, to Guayaquil 9 hours. From Miami to Quito the time is 4¾ hours, 5¼ hours to Guayaquil. Flying time between Quito and Guayaquil is only 45 minutes. By ship about 9 days from New York to Guayaquil.

ACCOMMODATIONS ... Luxurious *Hotel Quito,* with spectacular view of the Andes, has swimming pool, night club, gambling casino, coffee shop and elegant dining room. Single from $8, double from $12. *Hotel Humboldt,* centrally located, has singles from $5.60, doubles from $8.35. *Hotel Savoy,* also central, has rates from $4 single, $6 double. The *Colón,* 10 minutes from the center of town, has a friendly atmosphere and very good food. Rates from $6 single, $10 double, including American-type breakfast. American Plan rates available, too. The *Embajador,* 12 minutes from the center of town, has comfortable rooms and good service. Rates from $4 single, $8 double, European Plan. The *Majestic* and *Crillón* are commercial hotels in the center of Quito. *Residence Lutetia* is a very clean, comfortable boardinghouse with rates (including all meals) from $5.50 single, $11 double. Other hotel listings appear under individual cities. All hotel bills are subject to 10% service charges and 10% tax.

ARTS ... Quito, during colonial times, was the art center of South America. There are churches and museums containing centuries-old paintings and sculptures. Quito's magnificent churches like La Compañía, San Francisco, La Merced, Santo Domingo, San Augustín, etc., with altars carved like lace, famous old paintings and sculptures —sparkling baroque jewels of the Moorish art—are wonders without equal elsewhere in the Southern Hemisphere.

The Museum of Colonial Art and Municipal Museum exhibit fine collections of Ecuadorian paintings and sculptures of the last four centuries. The Franciscan Museum and the Museum of the Monastery of Santo Domingo have valuable collections of colonial religious art.

The Casa de la Cultura Ecuadoriana has a gallery of antique and modern Ecuadorian art and a museum of musical instruments, the Museo Musical Traversari, one of the most complete in the world.

BANKS ... Banco de Descuento,, La Previsora, Bank of London and Montreal. The First National City Bank of New York has branches in Guayaquil and Quito.

CALENDAR OF HOLIDAYS ... New Year's Day; 2-day carnival on Monday and Tuesday preceding Lent; Maundy Thursday and Good Friday; May 1, International Labor Day; May 24, Battle of Pichincha; July 24, Bolívar's Birthday; August 10, Ecuador's Independence Day; October 9, Anniversary of Guayaquil; October 12, Columbus Day; November 1, All Saints Day; November 3, Anniversary of Cuenca; December 6, Foundation of Quito; Christmas Day.

CIGARETTES AND TOBACCO ... American brands of cigarettes cost 25¢ to 30¢ a pack. There is a variety of local cigarettes. American pipe tobacco is also sold.

CLIMATE ... Don't think of Ecuador as a hot country. The coast is tropical, but the sierra with its snow-capped mountains is cool. Quito is called the City of Eternal Spring, but it is apt to be a little colder than spring as we think of it. June to October (the dry season time) is the best to visit Quito or Guayaquil. Temperatures in the mountains, at that time, range from 50° to 65°. Next to La Paz, Quito is the highest capital in the world.

CLUBS . . . Club Pichincha for bridge and other card games. Rotary, Jaycees and Lions. Cards may be arranged. For golf and tennis, *see* SPORTS.

COMMON COURTESIES AND CUSTOMS . . . Bargaining is accepted practice in small shops or with street vendors. Women in slacks are not seen on the streets. Office hours in Quito are from 9 A.M. to 12:30, and 2:30 to 6 P.M. Afternoon tea is ritual in Quito's social life. Cocktail parties begin around 7 P.M.; dinner is 8 to 10 P.M.

COMMUNICATIONS . . . All America Cables and Radio Inc., International Telephone and Telegraph and Radio Internacional del Ecuador. Airmail rates to American countries: letters 2 sucres, Ecuadorian currency; postcards, 1.20 sucres, Ecuadorian currency.

CURRENCY . . . The monetary unit of Ecuador is the sucre, divided into 100 cents. It is worth about 5 U.S. cents; 18.50 sucres to U.S. $1. Banks, travel agencies or money-exchange houses will exchange at the rate fixed by the Central Bank of Ecuador.

CUSTOMS REGULATIONS AND DOCUMENTS REQUIRED FOR UNITED STATES CITIZENS . . . No restriction on currency, cameras or films; 1 liter liquor, 300 cigarettes, or 50 cigars, or 7 ozs. pipe tobacco may be brought in duty free. No visa required, only tourist card issued by air carrier, with 4 front-view photos attached (fee $2); valid for 4 years. Certificates of smallpox vaccination and health certificate stating that you have no contagious or incurable disease. Business travelers should check regulations about bringing in samples.

DRUGSTORES . . . There are modern stores where most United States and European medicines are sold. However, bring your own special prescriptions, already filled, with you.

ELECTRIC CURRENT . . . 110 volts, A.C., as in the U.S.A.

FAUNA . . . The most imposing is the condor, the giant bird that lives in the highest altitudes of the Andes. It appears on the Ecuadorian National Seal, symbolizing strength. Birds of fantastic plumages —from the small hummingbird to the large-beaked *huacamayos*—can be found in the mountains. There are also herons, flamingos, ibis. In other zones of Ecuador there are monkeys, pumas, wildcats, bears, tapirs, deer, alligators. The waters of Ecuador are rich in many types of fish. The coast of the Galapagos Islands 600 miles west of Guayaquil, and Isla de la Plata, near the coast of Manta, afford excellent deep-sea fishing. The Galapagos are also famous for the big tortoises that abound there, as well as for large lizards that have been classified as antediluvian.

FLORA . . . Among the native species the most important are: the balsa tree (Ecuador produces over 90% of the world's supply of balsa wood), the cinchona tree (quinine), kapok tree, guayacan tree, fan palm tree. *Naranjilla* is a fruit grown only in Ecuador.

FOOD . . . Typical native dishes are well spiced and fairly exotic for the American palate. Try *llapingachos*—fried mashed potatoes with cheese—or *locro,* a stew soup of potatoes and cheese; both are served with an avocado on top. *Humitas* are tamales made of sweet corn, more delicate than the Mexican type. *Chocolo* is corn on the cob. If you are in a bar at noon, try *ceviche de corvina* or *ceviche de langostinos* or *cocktail de camarones.* They are native dishes; hot, but very good with a glass of beer. Try *naranjillada,* a fruit-juice drink. Pasteurized milk is available in bottles. Food prices in restaurants are lower than in the United States; meals run from $2 up. *See* LIQUOR.

GAMBLING ... There is a weekly national lottery. Gambling also at the *Bim Bam Bum* restaurant-swimming pool-casino in Guayaquil year round; at Playas *Casino* from May through December.

LANGUAGE ... Spanish, although English is spoken and understood in the tourist centers, hotels and better shops.

LAUNDRY AND DRY CLEANING ... La Qúimica and Luxor are among the best in Quito. 24-hour service, good quality, prices below those in the United States. Your laundry can always be arranged for through your hotel.

LIQUOR ... Pilsener and Victoria are 2 native beers famous throughout South America. American drinks (about 70¢, or 12 sucres) are available in hotels and restaurants, as are French and Chilean wines. Aguardiente and rum drinks are less expensive.

MEDICAL FACILITIES ... Hospital Vozandes (the Rimmer Memorial Hospital); Clínica Santa Cecilia; Clínica Pichincha; Clínica del Niño (for children only); and Isidro Ayora Maternity. All are modern hospitals and have English-speaking doctors.

MOTION PICTURES ... All movie houses in Quito show American films with titles in Spanish. The best theaters are: *Bolívar, Atahualpa, Pichincha, Variedades, Central* and *Alhambra,* in the center of town; *Teatro Universitario, Cine Fenix, Colón, Mariscal* and *Capital* in the residential zone.

MUSIC ... *Pasillo, San Juanito, Albazo, Fasacalle* and *Yaraví* are the native dances. Military bands give Sunday concerts in the principal squares. Internationally famous artists play at the Sucre Theater in Quito.

NIGHT CLUBS AND CABARETS ... Quito is not much of a night-club town. There are the *Rincón Quitiño* and the *Rondador* in Hotel Quito. Also *Le Toucan.* Prices are about 20% above those in the U.S.

PHOTOGRAPHY ... Black-and-white and color still and movie film are available as well as cameras and photo equipment. Prices slightly higher than in the United States. Developing of still films takes 24 hours. Kodak Ektachrome and Ansco color film can be developed locally.

RELIGION ... Ecuador is a Catholic country. Quito has about 60 churches. There are also Protestant (several denominations) churches and Jewish synagogues.

RESTAURANTS ... *Normandy* (French food); *Rincón de Sicilia* (excellent Italian cooking); *Mesón Andaluz* for Spanish food. Other good spots in Quito are the *Hotel Colón, Bodegón del Quijote*

Wonder Bar, La Cueva de Luis Candelas, El Cid, Pio Pio, Los Quitus (good Ecuadorian food) and *Le Toucan*. International cuisine at Hotel Quito, where there is a magnificent view of the city from the 7th-floor dining room.

SHOPS AND STORES ... Shopping center in Quito is on Venezuela and Guayaquil streets. You must see "Fábrica AKIOS," Gorívar 326 (Barrio Obrero), which has a varied stock of typical women's wear and mañy local curiosities. Folklore (Av. Colón 274) makes very fine handwoven rugs, two of which adorn the floor of the U.N. Building in New York. The shop is also tops for women's wear, leather goods and silver jewelry. *Silver shops:* Hamilton, Chile 1065; Joyería Bolívar, Espejo Street (inside the lobby of Teatro Bolívar); and Diamond Club, Venezuela 858. *Book Shops:* (books in English), Librería Científica, Venezuela 645; Su Librería, Chile 1160 (Plaza Grande); and Librería Selecciones, Venezuela 589. Shops are open from 9 A.M. to 1 P.M. and from 2:30 to 6:30 P.M.

SPECTATOR SPORTS ... Horse racing at the Hipódromo Santa Cecilia in Guayaquil. Pari-mutuel betting, 25¢ (5 sucres) a ticket. Polo matches are played in Quito, Guayaquil and Riobamba. In Quito and in several towns in the uplands a local sport called *Pelota de Guante* (glove ball) is played skillfully with a very heavy bat and ball, on Saturday afternoons and Sunday at Estadio Mejía (Mejía College's sport ground). No admission charge. Soccer and basketball are very popular sports. Soccer is played Saturday afternoons and Sunday mornings at Estadio Olímpico Municipal, Estadio de la Concentración Deportiva and Estadio Universitario. For basketball and indoor sports: the Coliseo Bullfights are scheduled occasionally, and are a regular feature during the week of the Quito Fair, beginning December 6.

SPORTS ... The Quito Tennis y Golf Club is a de luxe country club in Quito, on the way to the airport, 15 minutes from town. It has a good golf course, a lovely swimming pool and tennis courts. (Members and their guests only.) Near Quito are thermal swimming pools at Alangasí, Tingo and Cununyacu. For hunting wild game, arrangements may be made through local travel agencies. In Guayaquil, the Golf Club, Tennis Club and Yachting Club are all fine. Fishing is varied and abundant here, too. There is big-game fishing for bonito and marlin on the coast at Playas, Salinas, and farther north, at Manta. The fishing club at Salinas has boats which visitors may rent.

THEATERS ... Principal theater in Quito is *Teatro Sucre.* Plays in Spanish only. Also concerts and ballet.

TIME ... Same as United States Eastern Standard Time.

TIPPING ... In hotels and restaurants tip 10%. Tip porters 5 sucres (25¢) for all luggage. No tips for taxi drivers.

TRANSPORTATION ... Taxis are available everywhere in Quito. Fare from downtown to the residential zone, or vice versa, is 50¢ (10 sucres). Buses are always crowded. *Colectivos* (station wagons) offer fairly good service, fare 5¢ (1 sucre). Auto rental with driver

$1.60 (30 sucres) per hour in the city. The rate between airport and the city is $1.65 (30 sucres) per person. Prices should be settled in advance. Cars may be hired for about $12 (200 sucres) per day. Local travel agencies have exceptionally good sightseeing tours.

WATER . . . Bottled water is advised. Güitig and Mercedes are the best.

WHAT TO BUY . . . Panamá hats are the best buy in Ecuador. Properly called Montecristi, they are woven here, and not, as you might think, in Panamá. Montecristi and Jipijapa hats, famous the world over, may be bought for as little as $12, but we recommend advice by an expert or a travel-agency guide. Beautiful antique silver Indian ornaments. Indian costumes, hand-carved wooden chests, handbags and cigarette cases woven of palm fiber. Native rugs, shawls and tweeds woven by Indians, beautiful and colorful native embroideries and paintings, pottery, all kinds of articles, such as bookends, plates, and salad bowls made out of shiny guayacan wood.

WHAT TO WEAR . . . Quito is cool (see chart page 390). For women woolen suits and dresses with fur jacket or topcoat. Men need woolen suits and topcoats. For places on the coast of Ecuador like Guayaquil and Playas, you'll need tropical clothes and swimming gear.

WHERE TO GO—SIGHTSEEING . . .

Quito . . . There is a lot to see in the capital itself. Quito is full of excellent examples of colonial art. Any of its churches is rewarding to the tourist. The Church of San Francisco is famous for its art treasures and cloisters. Women may not enter the cloisters without permission. La Compañía, the church of the Jesuits, was built by Moslem workmen. The façade is so delicately carved it resembles lacework, and the interior glows with gold leaf. All the churches have magnificent displays of gold, silver and jewels, exquisitely carved altars and vaulted ceilings brilliant with gold leaf. The Church of La Merced and the Chapel of the Virgin of the Rosary in the Church of Santo Domingo must be seen. Don't miss Quito's museums. *See* ARTS.

Quito is a city of steep streets, white houses and red-tiled roofs. Climb Panecillo (The Little Loaf of Bread) for a breath-taking view of the city. Walk through La Ronda street—one of the most typical in town—and go to Paseo Escénico (Scenic View) in the residential zone. In the Chillos Valley, about 1 hour away from Quito by car, are the thermal swimming pools of Alangasí and Tingo. Sightseeing tours: City tour (2½ hours); Equatorial Monument (marking the divide between the Northern and Southern Hemispheres) tour (2½ hours); Valley of Chillos tour (3 hours). Rates $4.80 per person.

Side Trips . . . The Indian Fair at Saquisilí, on Thursdays only, is an interesting sight. The trip takes you by the snow-capped volcano of Cotopaxi. Saquistilí is 1¾ hours from Quito by car; the tour takes the whole day. A 2-day trip by car to Otavalo for the Indian Fair early Saturday morning, one of the largest in Ecuador, is fun. The Otavalo Indians weave wonderful woolen cloth not unlike Scotch tweed. Ambato, known as the garden city of Ecuador, is in the interior on the way to Baños, where the Amazon jungle starts. Baños is something of a summer resort and a spa. There are small but comfortable hotels with good food. Go to Riobamba for market day if you can. It is 110 miles south of Quito and well worth seeing. Santo Domingo is a little village of the Colorado Indians who paint their bodies red and comb their hair into a helmet shape which tourists find fascinating. Sightseeing trips by train or car should be arranged through Quito travel agencies.

Guayaquil ... The rail journey from Quito to this principal port and commercial city descends from the Andes into the heart of the jungle. Guayaquil lies about 60 miles from the ocean on the Rio Guayas, a river floating with boats, ships and hyacinths, and has a pleasant tropical climate. The *Humboldt International Hotel* on the riverfront offers rooms with private balconies, and there's a swimming pool. Rates from $6 single, $11 double, European Plan. The new *Palace Hotel* in the center of the city is air-conditioned and has good dining facilities. The *Hotel Continental* near the heart of the city is modern and comfortable, good food. Other hotels are the *Majestic* and *Crillón*. There are several good restaurants, including *Salón Rex* and *Melba,* (soda fountain) and *La Maison Dorée*. There is a golf and country club, also a tennis club, yacht club, and English-American Phoenix Club. Cards are needed for all of these. (Inquire at your hotel.)

Playas ... is a beach resort 2½ hours from Guayaquil. The *Hotel Humboldt* here has rates from $7.25 single, and from $10 double, European Plan. You may swim in the sea or in a pool. There is deep-sea fishing in the Humboldt current. Guests have Shangri-la Golf and Country Club privileges, and use of all sports equipment.

Salinas ... Only 2½ hours from Guayaquil, this beach resort has the new air-conditioned *Hotel Miramar*. There are the Yacht Club and Club de Pesca with boats for deep-sea fishing. Horse racing every Sunday at the Hipódromo from February to April, which is also the rainy season.

Cuenca ... Was founded in 1557 and still is genuinely colonial; located on a beautiful flowery plain, 8,517 feet in the Andes. Cobbled streets. Old buildings with lavish use of marble. The patios of houses are painted with murals, often with old Spanish proverbs inscribed. Here you can see the famous Panamá hats made of toquilla straw. Go there on Thursdays for the Fair.

SOURCES OF FURTHER INFORMATION ... Travel agencies such as Metropolitan Touring, Ecuadorian Tours in Guayaquil and Quito, and Turismundial in Quito have folders and maps and will provide tour guides. Panagra in Quito is at Avenida 10 de Agosto 255 (Tel. 10145). In New York the Ecuadorian Consulate is at 1270 Avenue of the Americas. Also in New York, at 535 Fifth Avenue, is the Ecuadorian American Association, Inc., a nonprofit organization designed to increase trade, travel and cultural relations between the U.S. and Ecuador.

This charming building is the Museum of Colonial Art, containing Ecuadorean paintings and sculptures dating from the era when Quito was the greatest cultural center in the Western Hemisphere.

Graceful Spanish baroque architecture beautifies Independence Square in Quito, which ranked as a Spanish provincial capital from 1541 until the end of colonial rule in 1822.

At an elevation of 9,248 feet, Quito's air is very clear and always cool enough for sightseeing explorations on foot.

FRENCH GUIANA

ATLANTIC OCEAN

St. Laurent

CAYENNE

SURINAM **FRENCH GUIANA**

BRAZIL

WEATHER IN CAYENNE—Lat. N4°50′—Alt. 25′

Temp.	JAN.	FEB.	MAR.	APR.	MAY	JUNE	JULY	AUG.	SEPT.	OCT.	NOV.	DEC.
Low	75°	75°	75°	77°	75°	75°	73°	75°	73°	75°	77°	75°
High	84°	84°	84°	84°	84°	84°	86°	88°	90°	90°	88°	84°
Average	80°	80°	80°	81°	80°	80°	80°	82°	82°	83°	82°	80°
Days of Rain	25	23	19	18	27	24	18	9	2	6	8	27

LOCATION . . . French Guiana is situated on the northeast coast of South America between Surinam (Dutch Guiana) and Brazil.

CHARACTERISTICS . . . Wild and primitive, French Guiana is a relatively undeveloped country, unspoiled by modern trends, and the least explored of the three Guianas. It is known around the world for its formerly infamous Devil's Island Penal Colony, now deactivated. The country is rich in unexploited minerals and hardwood timbers.

In Cayenne the visitor sees enormous palms and trees loaded with wild orchids; a trip up-river in a motor-powered dugout canoe reveals the lush jungle with its multicolored birds and butterflies.

POPULATION . . . 35,000 of whom 18,000 reside in Cayenne.

SIZE . . . The country has an area of 35,135 square miles. It is 250 miles long, 190 miles wide, and has a coastline of 200 miles.

CAPITAL . . . Cayenne, at the mouth of the Cayenne River, whose population is composed of the native Guyanese and numerous French governmental employees and Chinese.

GOVERNMENT . . . French Guiana is now a Department of France over which a Prefect named by the French ministry presides.

HOW TO GET THERE . . . Cayenne is 10½ hours from New York. Check on latest Pan Am service. Or fly by Jet Clipper direct to Trinidad (4½ hours) or to Paramaribo, Surinam, and make connections.

ACCOMMODATIONS... There's an excellent new *Hotel Montabo* located 5 minutes' drive from the center of Cayenne. It's on top of Montabo Hill about 200 feet above the sea, with a view of Devil's Island to the northwest. The hotel has 30 rooms, each with bath and twin beds. Food and service are very good. Single rates from $6; higher with air-conditioning. Electric current is 127 volts A.C., 50 cycles.

CURRENCY... Official rate, 5 new francs to U.S. $1, but old rate of 500 to U.S. $1 is also used.

CUSTOMS REGULATIONS AND DOCUMENTS REQUIRED FOR UNITED STATES CITIZENS... United States citizens must have a valid passport, ticket to leave, yellow fever inoculation if coming from infected area and a smallpox vaccination certificate.

RESTAURANTS... The best international food is at the *Hotel Montabo* and at *Guilbaud's* and *Montjoly* bar-restaurants, which, in the French fashion, add 1 fr. cover charge for bread. Authentic Chinese food at *Yee Kong Chung's* and *Chung Fat's*. Vietnamese cuisine at the new *Dragon d'Or*. Rum and Scotch are much cheaper than in the States.

WHERE TO GO—SIGHTSEEING...

Cayenne... In the center of town is the Place des Palmistes, which beckons to the visitor in the heat of the day. It is a park of green grass, cool and inviting, with giant palms overhead. A stroll through the palm-lined walks reveals well-kept tennis courts. To the north the visitor may see the official residence of the Prefect which was built by the Jesuits, the hospital and offices of the Principal public services. To the east are the Sports Stadium and the Botanical Gardens.

A taxi can be hired which will carry the visitor to see the summer homes along the beach. Another tour will take the visitor through the jungle, where trees and foliage are so dense that the sun never penetrates and where bamboo grows in huge clumps that form an archway over the road. A complete taxi tour of the city and island of Cayenne costs about $7 (35 frs.).

A trip up-river is well worth taking, although it is not usually possible to return the same day. Unless one likes "roughing it," better not attempt a river journey—but for those with a zeal for adventure, by all means, don't miss it!

Devil's Island... Off the coast of French Guiana is a rocky, palm-covered little tropical island that one day may become a delightful tourist resort with a fascinating appeal all its own: Ile au Diable—Devil's Island.

The Iles de Salut—of which Devil's Island is one—are situated 6 miles off the Guiana coast, and are one of the sights pointed out to passengers by captains of Clipper flights to Cayenne.

SOURCES OF FURTHER INFORMATION... J. Ste. Claire and Co., 6, Avenue du General de Gaulle, are agents for Pan American in Cayenne. In New York contact the French Government Tourist Office, 610 Fifth Avenue.

PARAGUAY

WEATHER IN ASUNCION—Lat. S25°16'—Alt. 253'

	JAN.	FEB.	MAR.	APR.	MAY	JUNE	JULY	AUG.	SEPT.	OCT.	NOV.	DEC.
Average Temp.	80°	80°	78°	72°	67°	63°	64°	66°	70°	72°	76°	80°
In. of Rain	5.4	5.1	4.2	5.1	4.6	2.8	2.2	1.6	3.1	5.5	5.8	6.2

LOCATION ... An inland country, Paraguay is crowded between Argentina, Brazil and Bolivia in central South America.

CHARACTERISTICS ... Paraguay, once off the beaten track, is now becoming the Jet Age crossroad for transcontinental air services. It is not for the tourist who wants to find everything comparable to things at home. But it is definitely for those who like the colorful, the picturesque and a spot not yet wholly overrun by tourists. Asunción, the capital, is a port on a river, in which the native women still wash their clothes and beat them on stones.

POPULATION ... Estimated at about 1,817,000.

SIZE ... 157,047 square miles.

CAPITAL ... Asunción, a city of 350,000.

GOVERNMENT ... A republic, founded in 1811.

HOW TO GET THERE ... By Pan American Jet Clipper, elapsed time is 10¼ hours from New York, 5 hours from Caracas, 1½ hours from Buenos Aires. Asunción offers the fastest route to Iguassu Falls, reached by Brazilian Varig Airline or good highway. By ship from New York, about 19 days to Buenos Aires, then 4 days by river steamer.

ACCOMMODATIONS ... The splendid new *Guaraní Hotel,* with a magnificent view of the city, is air-conditioned, has a swimming pool, underground theater and top-floor night club. Single rates from $10.50; add $5 to include all meals. Asunción's traditional *Gran Hotel* *del Paraguay* was once the residence of Eliza Lynch, paramour of Lopez, who practically held court there. The murals in the hotel dining room, which was once her private theater, are strange and provocative. Single rates from $10, including meals. Other air conditioned hotels in the city are the *Plaza,* the *Colonial* and the *Asunción Palace Hotel.* Electric current is 220 volts, A.C., 50 cycles.

CURRENCY . . . The guaraní (G), divided into 100 centimos, is currently valued at G100 to U.S. 70¢. The First National City Bank of New York and Bank of London have branches in Asunción.

CUSTOMS REGULATIONS AND DOCUMENTS REQUIRED FOR UNITED STATES CITIZENS . . . Passport, smallpox certificate required. Duty-free allowances: 200 cigarettes, 1 bottle of liquor.

WHERE TO GO—SIGHTSEEING—

Asunción . . . Although the 20th century is definitely apparent, shawl-wrapped women carrying umbrellas and riding donkeys side-saddle can still be seen around the markets, and a few ox carts still plod picturesquely into town amid buses, taxis and imported cars. Some of Asunción's older buildings are distinctively Italianate, for the elder Lopez, Don Carlos, imported an Italian architect to design the National Palace, but the Pantheon is patterned after Les Invalides in Paris. Genuine Spanish colonial houses may still be seen, and the Casa de la Independencia is delightful. The shopping district is centered on calles Palma and Estrella. Local drugstores carry American, German and Swiss pharmaceutical items. The famous Paraguay lace and shirts and blouses of *aho-poí* embroidered cloth make the most unique souvenirs; shop around, too, for recordings of Paraguayan music featuring guitars, singers and small *guatambu* harps.

Two of the capital's best restaurants are *La Preferida* and *La Pergola del Bolsi.* Outstanding for Paraguayan meat dishes are *El Jardin de la Cerveza, La Calandria* and *Club 74.* Best for night life are the *Boite* atop Hotel Guarani and the *Rancho Bar* in Gran Hotel del Paraguay. Try a cocktail made of *caña,* native rum. Tap water is safe to drink in Asunción; drink bottled *agua mineral* outside the city.

San Bernardino . . . This is Paraguay's summer resort, set on Lake Ypacaraí an hour's drive from the capital. During the hottest season (December through February), this little place is alive with gay young people from Asunción's society. There are the smart *Hotel del Lago, Hotel Playa,* and the very swank private club, *Club Nautico de San Bernardino.*

Iguassu Falls . . . Although located on the Argentina-Brazil frontier, the easiest way to each the falls is from Asunción, and local travel agencies can arrange one-day round trips by air. A good paved highway now also cuts the automobile trip to 4 hours from Asunción to Puerto Presidente Stroessner, beyond which a new International Bridge over the Paraná River links Paraguay and Brazil at Foz do Iguassu. *Hotel Cataras,* on Brazilian side, overlooks falls.

SOURCES OF FURTHER INFORMATION . . . The *Dirección Nacional de Turismo,* Asunción. The Pan Am agents, A. y C. Abente Haedo, are at Calle Independencia Nacional 571.

PERU

WEATHER IN LIMA—Lat. S12°03'—Alt. 501'

Temp.	JAN.	FEB.	MAR.	APR.	MAY	JUNE	JULY	AUG.	SEPT.	OCT.	NOV.	DEC.
Low	63°	65°	64°	62°	58°	57°	56°	56°	56°	57°	60°	63°
High	83°	83°	84°	80°	76°	70°	67°	67°	69°	69°	74°	79°
Average	72°	74°	74°	71°	67°	64°	62°	62°	63°	63°	67°	71°

LOCATION ... Peru, on the west coast of South America along the Pacific, contains some of the highest peaks of the Andes.

CHARACTERISTICS ... Peru is one of the most astonishing countries in the world. Archaeologists have still not fathomed the mysteries of its vanished civilizations which go back to prehistoric times. The magnificent Inca ruins at Cuzco and Machu Picchu are awe-inspiring. Today the outstanding feature of Peru is the blending of its Indian and colonial past with its 20th-century present. Peruvians are among the most traditional and conservative people in South America, but withal, extremely sophisticated. The women are ultra-chic. The rural Indians are still primitive and colorful.

POPULATION ... Estimated 11,854,000.

SIZE ... Roughly the shape of California, Peru is 3 times as large —496,223 square miles.

CAPITAL ... Lima, a city of 1,800,000, is larger than Detroit.

GOVERNMENT ... A republic with a President, assisted by a cabinet, and two legislative chambers.

HOW TO GET THERE ... By National, Pan Am and Panagra one-plane service to Lima, 10¼ hours from New York. Flight time from Miami is 6½ hours; from Los Angeles, 9¾ hours.

ACCOMMODATIONS ... Lima's *Gran Hotel Bolívar* has everything, including a night club. Rates range from about $11 single, $15 double, European Plan, plus 22% for service and taxes; all rooms fully air conditioned. The *Crillón* is air-conditioned, is popular for conventions and meetings, and has Turkish baths. Grill serves excellent European food; smörgåsbord featured. Rates from $7 single, from $11 double, European Plan. *Hotel Maury* is one block from the Plaza de Armas. Formerly old-fashioned and picturesque, it has been renovated in modern style; from $6 single, from $8.50 double. New and fully air-conditioned, the *Savoy* has singles from $6, doubles from $9. Other fine hotels are the *Riviera* and *Alcazar*. All Peruvian hotels add from 17¼% to 22% to bills for service and taxes.

The *Lima Country Club,* which is really a top-flight hotel, is in San Isidro, a 5-mile taxi ride from the city. This is one of the finest places to stay in Peru, with tennis courts and swimming pools, near the golf course. Rates are from $10 single, $15 double, plus taxes, European Plan. Lovely view, quiet, good food, wine, service. The numerous pensions offer comfortable accommodations at modest rates. These pensions are usually charming villas with gardens and many servants to take care of you. Rates run from about $30 a week, including meals.

ARTS ... National Museum of Archaeology (Inca Museum) in a Lima suburb houses a fabulous collection of specimens of Inca and pre-Inca cultures. Open every day 10-12 and 3-6. The Pinacoteca Municipal Merino is devoted to the works of Peruvian artists. The "Museum of the Republic" houses colonial collections of Lima. The beautiful Rafel Larco Herrara Museum contains treasures from 2,000 B.C. to the Inca period. These stunningly displayed artifacts are a must-see for everyone. The Quinta Presa, now a museum, is a 17th-century villa with many relics of La Perichole, the actress whose story is told in Thornton Wilder's *Bridge of San Luis Rey*. Nearby is the Bullfighters Museum.

BANKS ... In Lima, First National City Bank of New York, Royal Bank of Canada and Bank of London and South America, Ltd., are affiliated with U.S. banks.

CALENDAR OF HOLIDAYS ... New Year's Day; Holy Week, which consists of Thursday (afternoon) and Friday before Easter; May 1, Labor Day; June 29, SS. Peter and Paul; July 28, 29, Independence of Peru; August 30, Santa Rosa de Lima; November 1, All Saints Day; December 8, Immaculate Conception; Christmas Day. June 24, Amancaes in Lima, Indian Day holiday celebration; June 24, Inti-Raymi in Cuzco, Indian Day celebration to ancient Sun God. Monday before Easter Sunday, religious festival of "Our Lord of Earthquakes," in Cuzco.

CIGARETTES AND TOBACCO ... American cigarettes cost about $5 a carton. Popular local brands—*Inca, Presidente* and *Country Club*—are 3 soles a pack. A passenger may bring in 200 cigarettes, 25 cigars or ½ lb. of tobacco.

CLIMATE ... Spring begins in September. Summer starts in December. It hardly ever rains, but in winter a heavy overcast prevails, with cool, damp weather from May through October. The Humboldt current off the coast keeps it from ever becoming unbearably hot.

Because of its moderate climate, a visit to Lima at any time is enjoyable.

CLUBS . . . Lima's clubs are delightful, but guest cards are required and can be requested through members only. There are the Club Nacional, Club de la Banca y Comercio, the Club Phoenix, Country Club de Villa, Santa Maria del Mar, Lions and Rotary Clubs. *See* SPORTS.

COMMON COURTESIES AND LOCAL CUSTOMS . . . Lima is proud of its traditions and conserves many old customs. Life goes on at a comparatively leisurely pace and social activities are often on the formal side. Tea, from 5:30 to 7, is an important daily event. Cocktail parties usually begin about 7:30 and the dinner hour is from 9 on. In the summer, stores and offices are closed for 3½ hours at noon, to give everyone an opportunity to go to the beach, and in the winter are closed for 2½ hours for lunch.

Do not address taxi drivers, waiters or other servants familiarly. Peruvians are very formal, very polite; they resent casualness. As in most Latin American countries, both men and women shake hands on meeting and on saying goodbye.

COMMUNICATIONS . . . Day-rate cables to New York are S/11.49 per word; 3-minute phone call is S/221 ($8.84). Rates vary to other U.S. cities. Airmail to U.S. is S/3.

CURRENCY . . . The sol is the monetary unit of Peru. It is worth about 4¢, but check first because rates often fluctuate.

CUSTOMS REGULATIONS AND DOCUMENTS REQUIRED FOR UNITED STATES CITIZENS . . . Valid passport; visa (free), or tourist card (fee $2) good for 90 days; you will also need a smallpox vaccination certificate; onward transportation. Air departure tax 180 soles (about $6.80). Sea arrival tax $10.

DRUGSTORES . . . Along Jirón de Unión, Lima's main shopping street, there are many drugstores including Antigua Botica Francesa, Botica Inglesa. On Calle del Correo, Botica del Correo (in front of the Post Office); Botica El Inca (Plaza San Martín). Most well-known American products available here.

ELECTRIC CURRENT . . . 220 volts, A.C., 60 cycles. U.S. appliances can be used only with transformers or resistor cords.

FAUNA . . . The llama, indispensable beast of the highlands, is the most notable animal in Peru. Vicuña, mountain lions and condors in the sierra, and all sorts of animals such as tigers, snakes, alligators, monkeys, sloths, etc., as well as the greatest variety of birds in the jungle region of the interior. There are organized tours to the jungle.

FLORA . . . All kinds of flowers (orchids, roses, geraniums, violets, cactus, etc.).

FOOD . . . The cuisine here is more interesting than any other in Latin America. Peruvian seafood from the cold, teeming waters of the Humboldt current is exceptional. *Ceviche* is raw fish marinated in lemon juice and served with onions and hot peppers; delicious. *Corvina* (sea bass) is prepared in many ways. One of the most interesting local dishes is *anticuchos,* squares of beef heart (corvina and shrimp are also used) on skewers broiled over charcoal, served with hot sauce. Hot chili pepper (*aji*) is widely used as seasoning. *Camarones* are big, freshwater shrimp. Chinese food, served in "Chifa" restaurants, is almost as traditional as Spanish food in Lima.

Fruits, including pineapple, bananas, oranges, papaya and cherimoya, are varied and excellent. Avocados (*paltas*) are plentiful. *Pachamanca* is a local feast consisting of chickens, pork, sweet potatoes, corn and yucca cooked in a pit over hot stones. Corn originated in Peru, and there are hundreds of varieties. *Chicha morada* is a soft drink made from purple corn. Pasteurized milk is available in Lima, but be sure to ask for *Maranga* or *Plusa,* and have it served directly from the bottle.

GAMBLING...Everyone here plays the various lotteries, but tourists are warned to watch drawing dates. There is horse racing Saturdays, Sundays and holidays the year round at the beautiful Hipódromo de Monterrico. Cockfighting in several arenas.

LANGUAGE...Spanish, of course, but English is spoken and understood in the hotels, shops and other places you will frequent.

LAUNDRY AND DRY CLEANING...American Dry Cleaners; Lima Dry Cleaners; Peter Moll; Giesman; Hotel Bolívar Dry Cleaning. All of these take from 24 hours to 3 days and give good results.

LIQUOR...Pisco, a native grape brandy, is inexpensive and served in a variety of drinks. Most popular is the pisco sour, made with lemon juice and given a frothy topping of egg white. Good beer is brewed in Peru. All well-known cocktails and brands of liquor are obtainable at about the same cost as in the United States. Good local wines including champagne are available.

MEDICAL FACILITIES...Anglo-American Hospital in San Isidro, also Clínica Loayza (English spoken). If you need a doctor, inquire at Panagra or at your hotel.

MOTION PICTURES...Lima's best movie theaters charge only about 50¢. Principal theaters are the *Tacna* on avenida Tacna, *Metro* on Plaza San Martín, *City Hall,* avenida Venezuela; *Biarritz* on Jirón de la Unión; *Le Paris,* on avenida Nicolás de Piérola; *Teatro Central* on Jirón Ica; *El Pacífico* in Miraflores; *Alcázar* in San Isidro; *Roma* on Teniente Fernandez Street. Most of the pictures are in English.

MUSIC...The National Symphony Orchestra frequently plays at the outdoor auditorium of the Campo de Marte during the summer, at the Municipal Theatre in winter. Visiting artists perform in Lima too. The "Entre Nous" cultural institution presents Peruvian folklore programs of music and dancing in native costumes every Thursday at 7 P.M. Two local radio stations have programs in English.

NIGHT CLUBS AND CABARETS...The *Aquarium* at the Lima Country Club; *Sky Room* at Hotel Crillón; *The Grill* at Gran Hotel Bolívar; *Embassy* on Plaza San Martín. But Lima is not much of a night club town. There are also cocktail lounges, such as *The Sunset, Ed's Bar, Candlelight Room,* the *Planetarium* and *Mon Cheri.*

PHOTOGRAPHY...All types of films are available in Lima at prices about 20% higher than those in the United States.

RELIGION . . . The most important Catholic church in Lima is the Cathedral on the Plaza de Armas (what is said to be Pizarro's body can be seen in a glass coffin in the right nave of the cathedral); La Merced on Jirón de la Unión; San Agustín on Plateros de San Agustín; Santo Domingo on Santo Domingo Street; and St. Francis church with catacombs. Other denominations include the Church of England and Union Protestant Church.

RESTAURANTS . . . Lima's citizens like their food highly seasoned, and if you like yours that way, we suggest the *Pildorín, La Toscana, Karamanduka, Rosita Ríos, Piselli* restaurants for their authentic Peruvian dishes. The *Bolívar, Crillón* and *Lima Country Club* hotels have excellent restaurants. Others in downtown Lima that you will enjoy are: *Le Pavillon* (French); *Chalet Suisse; Tony's* (German); *Club 91, Giannino's, Grotta Azurra* (Italian); *Kuo Wa, Chifa El Pacífico, Chifa Wilson* (Chinese). For visitors who want to experience a real Spanish-Colonial atmosphere with delicious foods and drinks, the *Trece Monedas* is a must. In the suburbs, you'll like the *Key Club* (steak and lobster), *Todo Fresco* (seafood), *Canela Fina* in San Isidro; *Gambrinus Pizzeria, Bavaria,* and *Burgomaestre* in Miraflores; and *El Suizo* on the beach at Herradura (November-April). Also on the beach is the *S.O.S. Restaurant,* serving fine food in attractive surroundings. No visit to Lima is complete without a drive up the side of the Andes, 20 miles from town, to the *Granja Azul,* one of the most superb settings on the west coast, for spring chicken, spit-roasted—all you can eat for $4—also steaks and crêpes Suzette. *Crem Rica,* a chain of sandwich and soda-fountain-type restaurants, has one on Lima's Jirón de la Unión and one on the Plaza San Martín. There's a *Todos* snack bar in San Isidros. These and the *Domino* serve very good, inexpensive meals.

The average price at most of the restaurants listed above is about $2.50 for luncheon and $4 for complete dinner with beer, but not with wine. The *Club 91, Trece Monedas* and *Pavillon* are more expensive, but worth it for atmosphere and quality of food.

SHOPS AND STORES . . . Lima's main shopping thoroughfare is the Jirón de la Unión. It starts at the Plaza San Martín. The main store for men and women is Oeschle's on the Plaza de Armas, which is lined with silver shops, big and little, full of bargains in tea sets, jewelry and almost anything else you can think of that comes in silver. Well-known silver shops are Welsch, Kohler, Old Cuzco, Murgia, Piaget; visit Lima's major silverwork plant, the Camusso factory on avenida Colonial. For leather goods: Pedro P. Díaz on Jirón de la Unión. For men, Crevani and Cambana on Jirón de la Unión. For antiques and Incaic curiosities, Casa Más is tops. The Souvenir Shop at Camaná 828 has a fascinating collection of Indian costumes, pre-Inca pottery. Fluffy llama slippers, fur rugs and all sorts of souvenirs, such as hand-tooled leather coffee tables, are for sale in shops close to the fascinating Plaza San Martín. For high quality modern *objets d'art* of Indian inspiration, see Graciela Laffi's workshop near Plaza Mexico. The Art Center at Av. Ricardo Palma 246, Miraflores suburb, has outstanding handicraft items.

SPECTATOR SPORTS . . . Horse racing Saturdays and Sundays at Hipódromo de Monterrico. The "polla," a horse-racing pool, rivals the lottery in popularity. There are bullfights in March at the Acho Bull Ring, but the real season is October and November.

Cockfighting at the Coliseo de Sandia usually Saturdays, Sundays and holidays. There are automobile races, fencing, cricket matches, yacht races, bicycle races. Soccer at the Estadio Nacional. Basketball is quite popular. Horse shows at the Club Hípico Peruano. Polo matches at the Polo Club. Boxing at Luna Park.

SPORTS . . . There is excellent swimming and bathing along the coast at the many beach resorts. At the Herradura beach little cabañas may be rented by the hour, also at some of the other beaches such as Lobo del Mar. Surfboarding in the Hawaiian manner is popular at the Waikiki Club (on invitation). Swimming in local summer only.

The Lima Golf Club and the Los Incas Club offer excellent golfing facilities. Visitors must obtain guest card from a member. Greens fees are in the $2 to $3 range. There are bowling clubs in San Isidro and Miraflores suburbs. The Lawn Tennis Club also has facilities for swimming and other sports besides tennis; serves food.

Peru offers some of the world's finest deep-sea fishing at Cabo Blanco (Talara), and fine rainbow-trout fishing in the rivers flowing into Lake Titicaca. Facilities are limited, and information should be obtained in advance of your trip. Panagra's Traffic and Sales office in the Hotel Bolívar, Lima, will assist you.

THEATERS . . . There are performances at 7 P.M. at *Teatro Municipal* and *Teatro Segura*, Lima's leading theaters.

TIME . . . Same as United States Eastern Standard Time.

TIPPING . . . Most Peruvian hotels add a large service charge to your bill, but it is customary to give the chambermaid S/5. Where no service charge is added, give waiters 5% of the bill. Porters get S/4 per bag, or a minimum of S/5. Tip beautician S/5; barber S/3; shoeshine boy S/1; hatcheck girl S/2. Taxi drivers are not tipped.

TRANSPORTATION . . . Taxis are plentiful and inexpensive. The usual rate for a taxi trip anywhere in the central part of Lima is 6 soles per cab, not per person. The rate from Lima to San Isidro is 15 soles and to Miraflores 18 soles, with all rates doubled after midnight. The rate per hour is from 50 to 60 soles, depending on the type of cab and where the cab is to be used. Agree on rate with driver in advance. Cars may be hired for about $7.50 to $15 per day.

WATER . . . It is best not to drink tap water in Peru. Bottled waters: Viso, San Antonio and San Mateo. If you want noncarbonated water specify "sin gas." Also Coca-Cola, Pepsi-Cola, Crush, etc.

WHAT TO BUY . . . Silver, of course. Jewelry, tea sets, antique silver all cost less than at home. Indian textiles hand-loomed and hand-spun. Peruvian Indian costumes, llama and alpaca slippers, rugs, etc. Dolls dressed in Indian costumes are a tourist favorite. Lima's market on the Jirón Ucayli is one of the city sights. The better shops have fixed prices, but in the market bargaining is accepted practice;

don't pay the first price asked.

WHAT TO WEAR . . . Take lightweight clothing to Peru, suitable for spring and autumn in the States—unless you intend to go into the mountains, in which case you will also need woolens and tweeds. Tropical clothing is not practical except in Peruvian summer (U.S. winter). Lima is sophisticated and formal.

WHERE TO GO—SIGHTSEEING . . .

Lima . . . Lima's Plaza de Armas is one of the most historic spots in South America. On one side is the Presidential Palace, a gleaming white baroque building erected on the site of Pizarro's original palace. A fig tree planted by Pizarro over 400 years ago is in one of the patios. The Torre Tagle Palace, now the foreign ministry, is an excellent example of Lima's golden age of architecture.

The room where the trials of the Inquisition took place can be visited on the Plaza de Bolívar. Oldest university in the Americas (founded 1551), the University of San Marcos, is located near the Plaza San Martín. Avenida Arequipa, a long, shaded boulevard, leads to Miraflores and San Isidro. *See also* ARTS.

The Chosica Valley, an hour's drive east from Lima, has sunshine the year round and has pleasant stops for luncheon or tea. Ancón is a summer beach resort on the Pan American Highway, and is also the site of interesting archeological discoveries believed to be 2,000 years old. Visit the nearby artificial satellite observatory. Try to see an Inca festival at the Ruins of Puruchuco.

Callao . . . Is the port of Lima, about 7 miles from the city, reached by streetcar or taxi. In early morning or late afternoon the pier is busy with fishing boats. The famous guano islands can be seen offshore. The Real Felipe Fortress is now a military museum.

Pachacamac . . . About 20 miles south of Lima are pre-Inca ruins such as the Temple of the Creator-God which predates by a long, long time the Inca Temple to the Sun which was erected near it. Allow about 3 hours for this trip. Go by guided tour.

Huancayo . . . Can be reached by a spectacular rail trip over the highest standard-gauge railway in the world, 15,805 ft. Excellent tourist hotel. Purchase rail ticket Friday, $9 round trip, leave Saturday, see Sunday market, return Monday. Oxygen is carried for passengers who may need it. Huancayo is an ancient Inca center. Every Sunday the Indians crowd the streets with their wares. They utter almost no sound. The silence is the striking thing about the market.

Cuzco . . . This ancient capital of the Incas is 11,444 feet above sea level; take warm clothes. The city is a mixture of Spanish and Inca civilizations. The Cathedral on the Plaza de Armas is the most interesting of the many churches in the city. The altar is of silver, and there is a dragon carved from a single emerald. Cuzco is 2 hours by air from Lima. *Hotel Cuzco* and the new *Hotel Savoy-Cuzco* are excellent. Reserve well in advance for both hotel and plane space.

Machu Picchu . . . is probably the most awe-inspiring sight in South America, an absolute must on any trip to the southern continent. A mountain-top sanctuary used by the Inca rulers in times of distress, it was so well hidden that its existence was hardly dreamed of until its discovery in 1911 by Hiram Bingham, one-time Senator from Connecticut. There are magnificent ruins with temples, houses, a cemetery. A strangely cut stone altar, where the priests "tied the sun" at the times of the equinoxes, overlooks the beautiful Sacred Valley. Three hours by train from Cuzco. Minimum time for Cuzco-Machu Picchu trip is 3 days. Nearby towns are interesting too.

Puno ... There is very good service on the 12-hour train ride southeast through the Andes from Cuzco to Puno on Lake Titicaca, highest navigable lake in the world. Stay at *Hotel Puno.* Note the superb artistry of carved stone on so many old buildings; the incredible richness of the Church of Pomata. Visit the floating reed islands built by Uros Indians, who still wear striking attire; fish for immense trout. During the dry season you can drive around Titicaca to Guaqui near La Paz in Bolivia. The famous steamer trip across the lake, at an elevation of 12,664 feet, is made only at night.

Arequipa ... Peru's second city, lies in the shadow of cone-shaped volcano, El Misti. It is called the "white city" because most of the buildings are made of a white volcanic stone, and has many interesting houses and churches dating from colonial times. One of Arequipa's chief claims to fame is its dry climate with sunshine practically all the time. Llamas wander the streets. At 7,500 feet above sea level, Arequipa is an ideal stopping point to get accustomed to the altitude before continuing to La Paz or Cuzco. The *Hotel Arequipa* here, one of the Peruvian national chain, is excellent. Arequipa is 2½ hours by air south of Lima. There's train service from Arequipa to Cuzco or La Paz via Puno.

Trujillo ... Northwest 315 miles from Lima is Trujillo, a typical Spanish colonial city. The *Hotel Trujillo* is good. There are many ruins nearby, most of them dating back to the Chimus, a pre-Inca race. The once imperial city of Chan-Chan covers 11 square miles.

Talara ... An oil center on the northern coast of Peru, is becoming an important game fishing center. The *Cabo Blanco Fishing Club,* a private organization, has facilities at Cabo Blanco, about forty miles from Talara. Request information at Cabo Blanco Fishing Club, Room 1616, 247 Park Ave., New York, N.Y. 10017.

Iquitos ... The fabulous jungle of the Amazon is only 3½ hours from Lima by plane. The flight across the Andes is $50, round trip. Stay at *Hotel Turistas de Iquitos,* which is very comfortable; single from $6.50, double from $13.50. The highlight of any trip to Iquitos is a day cruise on the Amazon River by launch, visiting the primitive little Indian villages along the way. Local travel agencies can also organize hunting trips into the vast green jungle where Yagua tribesmen still use curare-tipped darts, blown through a long *cerbatana,* to capture wild monkeys.

SOURCES OF INFORMATION ... For information on sightseeing tours, tickets or immigration matters contact PAA's affiliate, Panagra, in the Hotel Bolívar (Tel. 75-810).

In New York, the Peruvian Consulate is at 10 Rockefeller Plaza.

SURINAM

WEATHER IN PARAMARIBO—Lat. N5°50'

	JAN.	FEB.	MAR.	APR.	MAY	JUNE	JULY	AUG.	SEPT.	OCT.	NOV.	DEC.
Average Temp.	79°	80°	80°	80°	80°	80°	80°	82°	83°	83°	82°	80°
In. of Rain	8.4	6.3	6.7	9.0	12.3	12.0	8.2	6.3	3.0	3.0	4.7	8.4

LOCATION . . . Surinam (or, as it formerly was called, Dutch Guiana) lies along the northeastern coast of South America, between British and French Guiana and north of Brazil.

CHARACTERISTICS . . . The traveler with an eye for unusual places will find great delight in Paramaribo, the surprisingly cosmopolitan capital of this wild and primitive land. Surinam, however, has recently become very tourist conscious, and tours can now be made in comfort and safety to remote jungle villages. Government officials are cooperative, and friendly citizens provide a ready pipeline for information on such events as Javanese birthday parties, Hindu weddings and Creole processions, or *winti* (fire) dances, which may be of interest to the visitor.

POPULATION . . . 358,000; Creoles, Hindustanis, Indonesians, Bush Negroes, Amerindians, Chinese, Dutch and others.

SIZE . . . 63,251 square miles, smaller than Washington state.

CAPITAL . . . Paramaribo, with over 122,000 inhabitants.

GOVERNMENT . . . A self-governing member of the Kingdom of the Netherlands.

HOW TO GET THERE . . . By Pan American Jet Clipper from New York in 9 hours, elapsed time.

ACCOMMODATIONS . . . Set amid orchid gardens and flower-filled pools, the new, luxurious *Surinam Torarica* is completely air-conditioned, has a night club and one of the most modern gambling casinos in South America. Winter rates: single $15-$19, double $19-$23, European Plan; less in summer. The older hotels also have air-conditioned rooms. *Hotel Vervuurt* has a cocktail lounge and roof garden; single $7-$9, double $10-$12. *Palace Hotel,* with casino and night club, is $7-$8 single, $11-$12 double, American Plan (all meals included). Also operated on A.P. are *Alexandra Pension, Kersten Hotel, Hotel Lashley;* single rates $5 to $10. In the districts you'll find Governmental *pasanggrahans* (boarding-houses), clean and spacious, with good food. Prices, meals included, about $5 a day.

CALENDAR OF HOLIDAYS ... January 1, fireworks and dances; pre-Lenten Carnival; April 30, Queen Juliana's birthday celebrations; July 1, Freedom Day, commemorating abolition of slavery with parades, *Kotto Missie* show; August-September, *Konfriejarie* Week of festivals with a fair, sports events, shows; October, Surinam Trade Fair; October 10, Founding of Nationalist China; December 5, St. Nicholas Day; December 25. Exuberant Hindu and Moslem holidays are also observed. There's something colorful going on most of the time.

COMMUNICATIONS ... In local currency, a 3-minute phone call to New York costs SF 24 ($4.56) on weekdays, SF 18 on Sundays; cablegrams are SF 0.52 per word to New York, SF 0.66 elsewhere. Airmail postage to the U.S. is SF 0.20 for letters, SF 0.10 for postcards.

CURRENCY ... The Surinam florin, or guilder, is divided into 100 cents.

CUSTOMS REGULATIONS AND DOCUMENTS REQUIRED FOR UNITED STATES CITIZENS ... American passports; return or through ticket; smallpox vaccination. Permits for any sort of shotgun are needed.

ELECTRIC CURRENT ... 127 volts, 50 cycles, A.C. in Paramaribo and Nickerie; 115 volts, 60 cycles, A.C. in Moengo and Paranam.

FOOD ... Good food and fine service are traditional in Paramaribo, and the local cuisine is highly varied. Best restaurants are *Iwan's Hong Kong* and *Bali-Lunapark.* Among popular Dutch dishes is *hot pot,* a sturdy casserole of pork chops and potatoes. Indonesian *rijsttafel* is rice garnished with a variety of spicy tidbits. *Satee boemboe* is barbecued meat with a curry tang. *Pisang goreng* is fried plantains. *Ajam-koening* is the highly seasoned local version of fried chicken. Peanuts (*katjang*) are widely used in soups and sauces. All sorts of drinks are available, but Holland gins, beers and liqueurs predominate, naturally. Tap water is pure and safe to drink.

SPORTS ... Excellent tarpon and piranha fishing. Hunting for such wild game as deer, alligators, crocodiles, wild boar. Swimming in pools and rivers. Golf, lawn tennis. Soccer, basketball and cricket.

WHAT TO BUY ... Native handicrafts by the Bush Negroes and Amerindians. The intricately carved wood items are unique, and shops in Paramaribo offer a wide range, as well as native necklaces of odd seeds and kernels. Exquisite gold and silver jewelry at modest prices, even gold nuggets, are for sale. Javanese-style bamboo and wicker-work. East Indian saris; oriental goods. Drugstores carry familiar American pharmaceuticals. American cigarettes cost from SF 0.95 to SF 1 per pack; local brands half as much.

WHERE TO GO—SIGHTSEEING ...

Paramaribo ... Paramaribo looks as if it could be in Holland despite being within the proverbial stone's throw of a dense tropical jungle where Indians still hunt with poisoned arrows and Bush Negroes in loincloths still practice the ceremonial rites of their African tribal ancestors and maintain their own jungle villages.

The city's heterogeneous population includes Javanese as comely as those of Bali, Hindus, Moslems and Chinese with the cultures and customs of their native countries. Yet in appearance, the immaculate city is Dutch to the core.

The city's marketplace is a riot of color, dominated by the *Kotto Missie,* or native market women, who are noted for their great dignity. Oranje Square is the center around which life in Paramaribo revolves. Adjacent to the square are the Governor's House and other Government buildings; the beautiful Park Club; the city's principal business district; and the river waterfront, serving alike ocean-going steamers, riverboats and dugout canoes used to transport produce. Many of the city's streets are lined with magnificent mahogany trees, poincianas, tamarind trees and royal palms.

There are interesting sightseeing possibilities for even transient visitors. In one day a real Bush Negro village can be reached by car and launch; in one day you can visit an Amerindian dwelling in the jungle. In fact, in one day it's possible to see the town, go shopping, visit modern factories (plywood) and old plantations (citrus fruits) and have a look at the agricultural experimental station or botanical gardens. With 2 or 3 days, you can take the beautiful jungle trip by steamer to the Moengo bauxite mines. Moengo is an inland river port, deep in forests inhabited by primitive Djukas, descendants of African slaves who escaped into the jungle some 200 years ago. With advance notice, they'll stage an eerie voodoo fire dance that looks genuinely suicidal, but they'll emerge unscathed. You won't see this show anywhere else, not even in Paramaribo. Tour operators can arrange hunting trips and excursions of all kinds to the interior, providing English-speaking guides for out-of-this-world visits to remote villages accessible only by native canoes. Despite the very primitive surroundings, overnight stops are made in clean, comfortable rest houses. For the traveler who thinks he has seen everything, Surinam offers the wild, rapids-foaming beauty of the Maroni River where, deep in the interior, the luxurious guest house on Stoelman's Island provides modern accommodations and fine food. This is an area of unusual beauty, of thrilling waterfalls and immaculate Amerindian and Bush Negro villages.

SOURCES OF FURTHER INFORMATION ... Surinam Tourist Bureau, 10 Rockefeller Plaza, New York. In Paramaribo, the Surinam Tourist Development Board, Kerkplein 10. Pan American's office is at Malebatrumstr. 5 (Tel. 2718/2719).

URUGUAY

WEATHER IN MONTEVIDEO—Lat. S34°53′—Alt. 30′

Temp.	JAN.	FEB.	MAR.	APR.	MAY	JUNE	JULY	AUG.	SEPT.	OCT.	NOV.	DEC.
Low	62°	62°	60°	54°	49°	45°	44°	44°	47°	50°	54°	59°
High	83°	82°	78°	71°	66°	61°	59°	60°	64°	68°	74°	80°
Average	73°	72°	69°	62°	57°	53°	51°	52°	55°	59°	64°	69°

LOCATION ... Uruguay, the smallest of the South American countries, lies between Brazil and Argentina on the Atlantic coast. Montevideo is less than 150 miles from Buenos Aires.

CHARACTERISTICS ... This delightful little country is one of South America's famous playgrounds. Montevideo, the charming, gracious capital, is situated on the Rio de la Plata. A chain of beach resorts which extends for some 200 miles up the coast provides an unparalleled vacation land. Uruguay is famous for its excellent hotels, its casinos, its wide stretches of sandy beaches. Punta del Este is known as the Riviera of South America and is the gathering spot for wealthy South Americans who enjoy yachting, water skiing, gay night life (at the casinos), and the luxury of the cabaña-dotted beaches.

POPULATION ... Estimated at 2,592,563, nearly half of it in Montevideo. Largest cities of interior are Salto (92,216) and Paysandú (87,229), both on the banks of the Uruguay River.

SIZE ... 72,172 square miles, about the size of North Dakota.

CAPITAL ... Montevideo, with a population of 1,202,890.

GOVERNMENT ... A republic with a "pluripersonal executive," that is, instead of a President there is a Council of nine men. Otherwise, Uruguay's government is exactly like that of any other republic with advanced social legislation (Uruguay was called "the first welfare state").

HOW TO GET THERE ... Through Pan Am Jet Clipper 12 hours from New York or 35 minutes from Buenos Aires. Buenos Aires is only 10½ hours from New York via Pan Am Jet. By ship from New Orleans or New York, 13 days.

ACCOMMODATIONS ... Best in Montevideo is the fine air-conditioned *Victoria Plaza,* one of the Intercontinental hotels. Single $11 to $15, double $14 to $18, plus 26%. Other Montevideo hotels downtown include the brand-new *Columbia Palace,* the *Nogaró,* the *Alhambra,* the new, low-priced *Crillon,* the *Lancaster, Oxford, London Palace, California* and the *Residencial Uruguay.* On Ramirez Beach: *Parque Hotel,* which has a casino. On Pocitos Beach: the *Ermitage.* On Carrasco Beach, 12 miles up the coast: *Hotel Casino Carrasco* (open only during the season, December 8 to March 24), *Cottage Hotel.* Hotels add 15% to 26% service charges in lieu of tipping.

Hotels at Atlántida Beach, 35 miles up the coast: *Atlántida* and *Casino Golf Palace.* Also, small hostels like *Chalet, Remanso, Mi Cielo, Los Angeles.* At Balneario Solís Beach, 62 miles up the coast: *Hotels Solís* and *Alción.*

At Piriápolis Beach, 72 miles up the coast: the big French-style *Argentino Hotel* and the small pension-like *Embassy, Juvencia, Rex, Italia, Atlántico, Perla, Rambla, Explanada, Josesito, La Cumbre, Petit Pension, San Sebastian.* At La Paloma, center for salt- and fresh-water fishing, 160 miles up the coast: Hotel *Cabo Santa María.* At nearby La Pedrera, *Hotel La Pedrera.*

At Punta del Este, famous glamour spot 90 miles from the capital, are the *Cantegril Country Club, San Rafael* and the *Oxford Hotel.* For description and listing of other hotels here, *see* WHERE TO GO.

Rates at all of the above resort hotels range from about $3 at the smaller ones to $10 single, European Plan, plus service charges.

All over the interior of the country where no first-class hotels are available, the National Tourist Commission maintains a chain of *paradores,* or inns.

ARTS ... Museum of Fine Arts, at Park Rodó, contains works of the most outstanding Uruguayan sculptors and painters. Historic Military Museum, at the top of the hill, overlooks Montevideo Harbor. At the many private galleries good paintings can be bought at bargain prices ($25 to $100).

BALLET ... There is the National Ballet Corps. European and American troupes come to Montevideo regularly.

BANKS ... Bank of London & South America, agent for American Express checks. Wagons-Lits/Cook for Cook's travelers checks. First National City Bank of New York also handles travelers checks.

CALENDAR OF HOLIDAYS ... The Carnival held in Montevideo (usually in February) is gay and has a color and atmosphere all its own. There's a colorful parade, music, dancing. There are masked balls, fiestas, and merrymaking everywhere you turn. *Semana Criolla* takes place in March or early April. This is similar to a rodeo. The gauchos, or local cowboys, come from all over the country. They wear the traditional gaucho costume, which includes the *bombachas,* or full, baggy pants, the sign of the gaucho today. Exhibitions of riding, breaking of broncos, horse shows, are part of the show. Guitar playing is a gaucho accomplishment and their songs are similar to our Western folk songs. New Year's Day is gala with displays of fireworks. Corpus Christi (in June) is the biggest Catholic celebration, with a parade (sometimes held in the better weather of October) down the main avenues. December 8 is Day of the Beaches, start of the summer season.

CIGARETTES, PIPES AND TOBACCO . . . American cigarettes are available at about 34¢ a pack, all brands of pipe tobacco at correspondingly higher prices. The local "blond" cigarettes, made with American tobacco, are good. Local people prefer "black" cigarettes or roll their own. This practice is most common in the interior, where the gauchos sometimes deftly roll corn husks instead of paper. It is quite an art to cut and dry the leaf, thin it out with a knife and crop it to the size of cigarette paper. Best local brands (blond, or *rubio*) are: *Coronado, Master, Richmond, Union, Buffs, Poker, Nevada.* The best blacks, or *negros*, are: *La Paz* and *Republicana.* A pack of *rubios* of local manufacture costs half as much as United States cigarettes; *negros* cost a little over 10 U.S. cents a pack.

CLIMATE . . . Seasons in Uruguay are the opposite of ours. Their summer is our winter and vice versa. The season is December until March, usually considered the best time to visit Uruguay, although their autumn and spring are delightful too. It's exceedingly windy in the spring and children go to the beaches to fly kites. The climate is bright, dry and invigorating; snow is unknown.

CLUBS . . . The Jockey Club has a fine restaurant, but tourists must be guests of members. Golf Club, Automóvil Club and Yacht Club are open to visitors. The Golf Club, with excellent food, is considered one of the best in Latin America. Rotary, Lions Club and Junior Chamber of Commerce. At Carrasco: Polo Club, Cricket Club, Lawn Tennis Club, Carrasco Bowl.

COMMON COURTESIES AND LOCAL CUSTOMS . . . Dinner hour is very late, from 9 P.M. to 11 P.M. There is a central information number to dial in Montevideo: "214," which informs you on train, airplane and bus schedules, weather reports and anything else you might like to know about the city.

COMMUNICATIONS . . . A 3-minute phone call to the States costs about 288 pesos (about $5.75); day-rate cablegram is 9 pesos per word. Airmail postage to the U.S. is 1.50 to 2.60 pesos.

CURRENCY . . . Montevideo is a free market where all world currencies can be exchanged at the best available rates. The monetary unit is the peso, written with a $ sign and worth about U.S. 2¢. There are $50URP (pesos) to U.S. $1. Best exchange rate is obtainable at one of the *cambios*, or money exchanges, such as Wagons-Lits/Cooks, Exprinter, COT, CEVI and many others located all over Montevideo.

CUSTOMS REGULATIONS AND DOCUMENTS REQUIRED FOR UNITED STATES CITIZENS . . . Smallpox vaccination certificate and valid passport for visits of 90 days or less. Yellow fever and cholera certificate required if coming from infected areas. For short stays you may bring in 1 opened carton of cigarettes or 50 cigars or 3 small opened tins of tobacco, 1 opened bottle of liquor.

DRUGSTORES . . . Drugstores are modern and stock most things you need, although items other than drugs must be bought at department stores or shops. Dialing "214" will tell you where the nearest drugstore is located and what hours it is open.

ELECTRIC CURRENT . . . Electric power in Uruguay is 220 volts, 50 cycles, A.C. Ordinary American plugs are used in the Hotel Victoria Plaza; in other hotels, adapters are necessary. Transformers for appliances using 110 volts are easily available.

FAUNA . . . Pumas and jaguars are almost extinct now, but deer and boar exist in the western part of the country. Partridge, quail, parakeets and hares are plentiful. American ostriches may also be seen. Most interesting is the *hornero* (oven bird), who builds his sturdy two-room home (one for himself and wife, another for the eggs) of mud and straw, on roofs, telegraph poles and fences. He is loved as a symbol of work and homemaking. Another interesting bird: the *terutero* or *tero,* which is an expert at attracting the attention of trespassers to the place where his nest is *not* to be found; he is also a fine weatherman, announcing rain in advance.

FLORA . . . Acacia, willow, pine, eucalyptus trees. Scarlet and white verbena brighten the prairies. Bougainvillaea and other semitropical flowers grow in profusion. Beautiful roses and carnations are plentiful in the spring and early summer, and are sold in the streets. Because of the spring wind Uruguay is a country of few trees. Local species are the *ombu* with soft wood that crumbles in your fingers and *ceibo* with wood as light as balsa and bright red flowers.

FOOD . . . Beef is practically the national dish. You get steak such as you have never eaten, for very reasonable prices. Other specialties include barbecued pig, grilled chicken in wine, meat pie, grilled fish. Two good native dishes are *carbonada* (a stew of meat, rice and believe it or not, peaches, pears and raisins) and *parrillada* (assorted grilled meats). These are served at the Victoria Plaza. *Dulce de leche* (milk jam) is a local delicacy for dessert.

Maté, made with a unique herb, is the favorite drink. Native wines are excellent. The pastries are wonderful to look at and marvelous to eat. Leading hotels are the fashionable places to eat, and are excellent. There are many restaurants serving international food. Because of the large Italian population there are many fine Italian restaurants.

Sanitation standards are on a par with those in the United States. It's perfectly safe to drink the milk and water and to eat fresh fruits and salads.

GAMBLING . . . There are many gaming casinos. The Park and Carrasco Hotels in Montevideo and the smart beach resorts have their own. There is horse racing Thursdays, Saturdays and Sundays at Hipódromo de Maroñas and Hipódromo de las Piedras with parimutuels. Uruguay has a national lottery.

LANGUAGE ... Spanish is the native tongue, but English, Italian and French are also widely spoken.

LAUNDRY AND DRY CLEANING ... Excellent. Laundry prices are lower than in the United States; dry cleaning, higher. The Victoria Plaza Hotel has its own laundry and dry-cleaning plant, offering 24-hour, first-class service.

LIQUOR ... Local wines are fine and inexpensive; try Chablis (white) and Cabernet (red) Santa Rosa; the whites of San Borja, La Cruz, Mil Botellas; Pinot and Claret Cerros de San Juan; Fond de Cave and Faraut champagne. Local beer (made of barley) is delicious, more body and flavor than at home. Like cigarettes, beer can be either *rubia* or *negra*, depending on malt content; black beer is preferred in winter. *Malta* is a nourishing beverage for children, and the usual American soft drinks are also available. Local vermouths are good. Hard liquors of local manufacture include *caña* and *grappa*. Scotch is about $10 a bottle; bourbon is practically unknown; French and Spanish cognac are relatively cheap. Since most business people work until 7 P.M., the cocktail hour is late by U.S.A. standards. Minimum legal age for drinkers is 18. As you know, the practice of drinking wine with meals is very popular; no ice water is served unless you ask for it.

MOTION PICTURES ... Several excellent movie theaters showing American films and also French, English, Italian, Argentine, Mexican, Swedish, German, Russian, Japanese and other films, all in their original versions, with printed subtitles in Spanish. No stage shows. No popcorn.

MUSIC ... Aside from symphony concerts (*see* THEATERS), there is little classical music. Popular music: tango, *milonga, vidalita,* and *Candombe,* a contagiously rhythmic folk music.

During the Carnival, tourists have a chance to hear the *comparsas de negros* (most of them white boys in blackface) beating the real, authentic jungle drums. It is so phony that it has a charm of its own. In the summer, the Government sponsors native fiestas at the open-air theaters in the Parque Rodó and the Parque Rivera, where *pericón,* the stately and lovely old Uruguayan dance, may be enjoyed by the public. Also, during *Semana Criolla* (April), tourists can hear native songs and see native dances. All of these are similar to the Argentine folklore. Open-air symphony concerts are given, free, at Parque Rodó on Sunday mornings in summertime.

NIGHT CLUBS AND CABARETS ... Night life does not flourish in Uruguay. What there is centers around the casinos in the summer. *Victoria Plaza Hotel* is a popular spot for dinner music and dancing. Night clubs offering floor shows include the *Pinar del Rio* and *Bonanza.* In Carrasco, *Marecchiare, Orfeo Negro, Chez Carlos, Squire, Dominique* and the *Country Club;* at Pocitos, the *Ermitage;* at Solymar, the *Parador Solymar.* Although restaurants add a service charge, night spots usually don't. A tip of 15% of the bill is considered sufficient.

PHOTOGRAPHY ... Black-and-white still and movie film is available; color film is sometimes in short supply. Cameras and all other equipment are available, but not cheap. Film development and printing (Ektachrome and Ansco color) are excellent; black-and-white films take 24 hours; color, 3 to 5 days; prices, moderate.

RELIGION ... Cathedral at Plaza Matriz, Montevideo; many other Catholic churches in different parts of town and in all interior cities. Two Methodist churches, 1 Anglican, 1 Baptist, 2 Adventist, 1 German church, 6 synagogues.

RESTAURANTS ... You can find all types of restaurants in Montevideo. The *Victoria Plaza* has an excellent dining room serving local and American dishes in air-conditioned comfort. Italian food and music at *Ana Capri*. Swiss cuisine at *El Bungalow*. Restaurants specializing in Uruguayan barbecued meats include the *Mitio, Tahiti, Las Tahlitas, La Azotea* and *La Sombrilla. Morini's* has fine filet Chateaubriand and *entrecôte* and fish (*corvina a là parrilla*); this is a nice, traditional place with sawdust on the floor, and efficient service which belies its appearance. *El Aguila,* next to Teatro Solís, is a superb restaurant, and its *gâteau águila* dessert is famous. A dinner at any of these places will cost from $3 to $4, including fine local wines. Also recommended is the *Golf Club,* overlooking scenic Punta Carreta lighthouse on the River Plate, a five-minute ride from downtown. A specialty: *perdices en escabeche* (partridge boiled in oil with spices). This is an elegant place for lunch, preferred by businessmen and diplomats. Other first-class restaurants and their specialties: *Automóvil Club* (chicken pie with mushrooms); *Catari* (Italian green noodles); *Chino* (Chinese food); *Brotola* (Normandy-style fish); *El Pollo Dorado* and *El Malecón* for chicken.

For typical Uruguayan dishes, aside from the *Victoria Plaza,* try *Facal, Stradella* or *Sirocco* for *chivitos* (steak on a roll).

SHOPS AND STORES ... Leading shops are: London Paris, Caubarrere, La Madrileña, Introzzi, Casa Soler, La Opera, Angenscheidt, Casa Rim, which are department stores. Specialty shops include: Bazar Colón for old silver, Casa Schiavo for leather goods. Bargaining is not an accepted practice. The Sunday street fair is worth seeing and often has bargains. Most stores are open from 9 A.M. to 6:30 P.M. There are branches of top Montevideo stores in Punta del Este, and many beach resort hotels maintain delightful shops.

SPECTATOR SPORTS ... Soccer, played in their fall and winter, is by far the most popular attraction; watching a game in the big (80,000 seats) Centenario Stadium is an experience. There's horse racing Thursdays, Saturdays and Sundays; *pelota vasca,* similar to jai alai; basketball, yacht races, golf and tennis tournaments.

SPORTS ... Golf at Montevideo Club, which has a championship course. Hotel guests of the Victoria Plaza, Parque, and Carrasco granted guest cards. There are excellent courses at the beach resorts. Punta del Este has the Cantegril Country Club and Punta del Este Yacht Club. Cards may be arranged. (Inquire at your hotel).

Fishing for dorado is one of the great sports of the country. Salto Grande (Great Falls) is a happy hunting ground for this colorful fish. There is superb deep-sea fishing at Punta del Este.

Horseback riding is, of course, available; horses may be hired. Sailing and yachting are national sports. You may hire boats at beach resorts. Aquaplaning is possible if you have the skill. Tennis at all beach resorts and in Montevideo, too.

THEATERS . . . *Solís, Cervantes, Sodre, Odeón, Sala Verdi.* Legitimate plays staged during winter season (United States summer months) by the *Comedia Nacional* (National Theater Company). Good Spanish, Argentine, Italian and French theater, ballet, opera and musical-comedy groups play Montevideo during winter season. In summer there are outdoor performances at the *Parque Rodó* and *Parque Rivera* theaters. Several good little-theater groups, including a theater in the round (*Teatro Circular*). Also, fine symphony concerts by the National Symphony Orchestra at the *Sodre,* featuring world-famous conductors. Big shows and sports take place at the *Palacio Peñarol.*

TIME . . . Noon in Montevideo is 10 A.M. in New York.

TIPPING . . . Hotels add a 26% service charge to your bill, and restaurants add 10 to 15%, but it is customary to add a little, such as 5% for a waiter; 5 pesos for room service, 5 for doorman and chambermaid after several days' stay. Luggage porters are tipped 3 pesos. Movie and theater ushers 1 peso; cloakroom and washroom attendant, shoeshine boy and taxi driver, 1 peso.

TOURIST TAXES . . . There is a 10 peso (about 20¢ U.S.) landing tax on arrival at airport.

TRANSPORTATION . . . In Montevideo buses and trolley buses are plentiful but crowded. Taxis plentiful too and rates are low: 15 pesos for a crosstown ride or 80 pesos per hour. Private cars are available for rent but at a minimum cost of $14 per day with limited mileage. Tours through travel agencies are recommended for sightseeing.

WATER . . . Perfectly safe to drink. Fine bottled mineral waters, Salus and Matutina, are also available.

WHAT TO BUY . . . Woolen goods are excellent and inexpensive. Amethyst, topaz and aquamarine stones are available at reasonable prices ($50 for a gold ring with large amethyst). Uruguayan specialties include: suede and *nonato* (unborn calfskin) bags, jackets, belts and other articles; also alligator bags, shoes, belts, billfolds. Prices are about the same as in Buenos Aires. Uruguayan nutria is the best in the world, with thicker, longer, softer hair and better color; a full-length coat costs from $300 to $400; a three-quarter coat from $200 to $300; a stole from $120 to $200. Furs can be bought in "blankets" (about 35 furs) to be styled at home. Price: $6 to $12 per fur. Another bargain: *alparagatas* and "ballerina" slippers, made of canvas with rubber soles, the most comfortable footwear for home and travel. Souvenirs: silver *maté* cups and *bombillas;* knives with silver handle and sheath (price from $5 to $15); gaucho dolls (about $3); *boleadoras,* the stone balls wrapped in leather used by gauchos to catch wild ostriches; *bombachas,* the baggy gaucho trouser; wide leather belts with pockets and silver buckle. Colorful wool ponchos are an ideal gift for children. Note: Shipping purchases out of Uruguay is complicated and expensive.

WHAT TO WEAR... During the season (their summer) you'll want the same type of summer clothes you would wear at home. For beach wear, the newest, smartest sports and beach togs are needed. You won't really need evening clothes, for life is informal, but some short dinner dresses in cotton or light color are appropriate. Take a light topcoat, a sweater or two. If you go in their wintertime, take clothes for an average fall day at home. Same requirements apply to men. Linen, cotton or lightweight wools for summer. Beach clothes, slacks, sports shirts. A topcoat. Life is very informal at Punta del Este and other summer resorts, where neckties are "banned."

WHERE TO GO—SIGHTSEEING...

Montevideo... Montevideo is a charming city, modeled to some extent on Paris. Its avenues are broad and tree-shaded. Plaza Independencia is surrounded by the sidewalk arcades. Montevideo is a café town and the streets are lined with sidewalk cafés filled with people drinking *café expreso*. There are numerous things to see in Montevideo itself, and many short excursions within city limits. See the Legislative Palace of Uruguayan marble and pink granite, topped with gold. The beautiful drive along the Rambla follows the beaches to Carrasco. The Planetarium in Park Pereira Rossell (home of the city zoo) is one of the most modern to be found anywhere.

The COT travel agency offers a wide choice of sightseeing tours to the summer resorts (Atlántida, Piriápolis, Punta del Este, La Paloma, La Coronilla) and to places in the interior, in comfortable buses, at very reasonable rates. (A full day's excursion to Punta del Este, including lunch, costs only 120 pesos ($2.50).) Rental of self-drive cars not advised: too expensive, too many restrictions.

From Montevideo to some 200 miles up the coast there is a chain of beaches and beach resorts, all of which are delightful, all worth seeing. An interesting 3-day excursion is to La Coronilla on the Brazilian border. At Santa Teresa National Park, near the Brazilian border, there is a picturesque inn, *Parador San Miguel*.

Punta del Este... The choice place here is the *Cantegril Country Club*. It is a delightful vacation spot which has been compared with Boca Raton in Florida. Cantegril is not a hotel, but a private club, where PAA passengers are welcome visitors. Guests rent lovely bungalows at a flat rate of about $6.50 per day, without meals. Sometimes during the local summer season, the bungalows are restricted to club members, so check with PAA. Accommodations are also crowded during the annual International Film Festival. A new motel and *Cantegril House,* a small hotel, are near the club.

Cantegril is also a residential area, where some of the finest homes in Punta del Este have been built. It boasts all kinds of sports activities. The Lido district has the largest and prettiest garden in Punta del Este.

The only hotel in Punta del Este of the large, luxurious type is

The Victoria Plaza, a favorite of society in Montevideo, offers the finest of accommodations and a conveniently located center for all your vacation activities.

the Tudor-style *San Rafael Hotel,* facing the beach of the same name, which has a casino and night club. Rates are $8 to $10 American Plan. There's a government-operated casino and night club in the former Hotel Nogaro; open approximately December 15 to April 18.

Punta del Este has smaller and less expensive establishments, such as the charming *La Cigale,* which features French cooking, *Playa, Floreal* and many others, where a double room with meals costs $6 per person (plus the usual 26% service charge).

There are also tourist attractions in the interior of the country. Dorado fishing is popular at Salto Grande in the Uruguay River (*see* SPORTS) and in the Rio Negro, near the Rincón del Bonete hydroelectric dam. Minas (80 miles north of Montevideo), with a Renaissance church and a fine little inn, *Parador Salus,* 8 miles out of town (where food and lodging cost $4), is a quiet spot for fall vacations, as is the region of Colonia Suiza (80 miles west of Montevideo), an interesting place founded by Swiss colonizers. Try also to visit a ranch in the cattle country. Finest ocean fishing (shark, skate, black corvina) is found at La Coronilla, near Brazilian border. Several good inns here: *Parador La Coronilla, Costas del Mar, Oceania, El Pescador* and *Las Cholgas.*

SOURCES OF FURTHER INFORMATION ... The National Tourist Commission Information Bureau at 18 de Julio and Andes Street, Montevideo (Tel. 8-6201). Pan Am office, Avenida 18 de Julio 945 (Tel. 8-9787). In New York the Uruguayan consulate is at 17 Battery Place.

VENEZUELA

CARIBBEAN SEA

CURACAO MARGARITA ISLAND

Puerto Cabello CARACAS Barcelona
Maracaibo
Barquisimeto Maracay
Valencia ORINOCO Maturin
RIVER Ciudad Bolivar
TRINIDAD
VENEZUELA
BR.
GUIANA
COLOMBIA

BRAZIL

WEATHER IN CARACAS—Lat. N10°30'–Alt. 3164'

Temp.	JAN.	FEB.	MAR.	APR.	MAY	JUNE	JULY	AUG.	SEPT.	OCT.	NOV.	DEC.
Low	56°	56°	57°	60°	62°	62°	61°	60°	61°	61°	60°	58°
High	75°	77°	78°	80°	80°	78°	77°	78°	79°	79°	77°	75°
Average	66°	67°	68°	70°	71°	70°	69°	69°	70°	70°	69°	67°
Days of Rain	6	2	3	4	9	14	15	15	13	12	13	10

LOCATION . . . At the very top of South America, the coast of Venezuela is only about 10 miles from Trinidad.

CHARACTERISTICS . . . Caracas, the birthplace of the great Liberator, Simón Bolívar, has a lot of authentic charm to offer the visitor. The city is a composite of modern and Spanish colonial architecture, but the intense building boom of the last 15 years has changed the face of the city so that its historical aspect is tending to disappear.

Its accommodations vary from the simplest pensions to the most modern hotels. Its social and sporting clubs are magnificent. The city as a whole reflects the fact that it has become one of the wealthiest capitals in the world. There is lots to see and do and the fine climate makes it all very pleasant.

POPULATION . . . Venezuela's growing population is now estimated at over 8,426,000, with an average density of 19 people per square mile, excluding the hard-to-count tribal Indians.

SIZE . . . 352,150 square miles; 950 miles wide, 807 miles long.

CAPITAL . . . Caracas, a growing city of 1,589,411.

GOVERNMENT . . . A constitutional republic made up of one Federal District, 20 states and 2 territories.

HOW TO GET THERE . . . By Pan Am Jet Clipper, only 4½ hours from New York to Caracas. Flights from Miami, 2¾ hours. Direct service also from Los Angeles and San Francisco. Caracas is 2 hours from Panamá, where connections are made with Pan Am flights from other points. One hour nonstop from Trinidad. By ship, about 5 days with stops, from New York.

ACCOMMODATIONS . . . In Caracas, the *Hotel Tamanaco,* with its superb view of the city, luxurious studio bedrooms, attractive night club *Naiguatá,* extra large swimming pool, many shops, good bars and lounges, is a resort in itself, and makes a convenient headquarters. Rates from $16 single and $19.50 double. The *Hotel Avila* is another luxury hotel. Others are *Comercio, El Conde, Mara, Potomac, Tiuna* and *Waldorf.* The luxurious new *Macuto-Sheraton* is on the beach, 20 miles from Caracas, with rates from $13.50 single, $17.75 double. The Venezuelan government has built a chain of hotels across the nation including the elaborate *Hotel Maracay* with golf course, swimming pool and movie theater at Maracay. Other hotels in this chain (CONAHOTU) are the *Bella Vista* at Porlamar on the Island of Margarita, and in the Venezuelan Andes the *Aguas Calientes,* the *Prado Rio,* the *Tama* and the *Trujillo.* Good hotels, many of them with air conditioning, can be found throughout the nation. Most first-class hotels operate on the European Plan and rates average about $10 single and $15 double.

ARTS . . . The Museum of Fine Arts has an excellent collection of historical paintings, especially by the national artist Michelena; Bolívar's Museum is an important national shrine with relics of the War of Independence.

BANKS . . . The First National City Bank of New York has two branches here; Royal Bank of Canada; Anglo-South American Bank. There are also several important Venezuelan banks with U.S. connections, among them Banco Mercantil, Banco de Venezuela, Banco de Caracas and Banco Unión.

CALENDAR OF HOLIDAYS . . . Major holy days of the Roman Catholic Church. Other holidays include New Year's Day; Carnival Monday and Tuesday before Ash Wednesday; April 19, Declaration of Independence; May 1, Labor Day; June 24, Battle of Carabobo; July 5, Independence Day; July 24 Bolívar's birthday; October 12, Columbus Day; December 17, Anniversary of the death of Bolívar.

CIGARETTES . . . Locally made American brands are 45¢ a pack.

CLIMATE . . . Caracas (altitude 3,164 feet) is springlike all year. Weather is perfect even in the rainy season, June to December. Venezuela has every kind of climate depending on the altitude.

CLUBS . . . Rotary, Lions and Junior Chamber of Commerce are extremely active throughout Venezuela. Private clubs include the exclusive Caracas Country Club, Valle Arriba Golf Club and Altamira Tennis Club in Caracas and the Caraballeda Golf and Yacht Club on the coast. Club Paradise and Club Venezuela are old social clubs patronized by the finest Venezuelan families. *See also* SPORTS.

COMMON COURTESIES AND LOCAL CUSTOMS . . . Caracas, because of its cool climate, has an unusual amount of formality. Shorts are not seen in the streets but are restricted to the beaches and country clubs. All the best local restaurants and bars require men to wear coats. Dinner even in private houses is likely to be 8:30 to

9 P.M. ... often much later. *"Gracias"* is "Thank you."

COMMUNICATIONS ... A 3-minute phone call to the States costs 40 bolívars (U.S. \$8.80); day-rate cablegram is 1.04 bolívars per word. Venezuelan postage for airmail to the U.S. is 40 céntimos.

CURRENCY ... There are 100 céntimos in a bolívar, which is worth 22 cents in U.S. money, or, conversely, 4.54 bolívars make one dollar. There are no exchange restrictions. U.S. paper currency and traveler's checks may be easily changed at hotels and shops.

CUSTOMS REGULATIONS AND DOCUMENTS REQUIRED FOR UNITED STATES CITIZENS ... For stays up to 8 days, tourist card from PAA, for which you need proof of citizenship, smallpox vaccination certificate, 4 photos, and onward transportation; or tourist card from Venezuelan Consulate, good for 30 days. Otherwise passport and visa. Only 2 bottles of liquor and 200 cigarettes permitted. Cameras may not be used from aircraft flying over territory, nor may airports be filmed without prior permission.

DRUGSTORES ... Caracas, Maracaibo and other sizable towns have stores which carry United States toilet goods, patent medicines and staples. Prices higher than at home.

ELECTRIC CURRENT ... In Caracas, 110 volts, 50 cycles, A.C. Elsewhere in Venezuela it is 110 volts, 60 cycles. Before importing electrical appliances one should check on the specific local condition.

FAUNA ... The country is particularly rich in birds, from the smallest hummingbird to the huge herons and condors. In the extensive unexplored areas of the country there are many types of mammals and reptiles. Hunting for jaguars, crocodiles, tapirs and other wild game can be arranged.

FLORA ... Within a short distance of Caracas there are forest areas, including 200,000-acre Rancho Grande National Park, that are alive with a variety of orchids and bromelias. Venezuela probably has the largest variety of tree species of any area of comparable size.

FOOD ... There are restaurants offering every style of cuisine. In Caracas, especially, one can find a host of international-type restaurants, as well as national cuisine. *Criollo* (native) dishes famous in Venezuela are *hallacas* (a type of tamale of corn, meat, eggs and olives, cooked in banana leaves). *Sancocho* is a stew of meats, chicken, roots and vegetables. Eating small oysters and clams with lemon juice is a custom to be found on all public beaches.

GAMBLING ... There are no casinos but everybody plays the horses at the Hipódromo in Caracas on Saturdays, Sundays and national holidays. Try your luck at the "5 y 6," a 6-horse parlay every Sunday with fabulous prizes. There are municipal and state lotteries several times weekly. Cockfighting may be seen in the country only a few miles out of Caracas.

LANGUAGE ... Spanish is the official language but an increasing number of people understand English. Among nationals the common greeting is *"Qué hubo?"*

LAUNDRY AND DRY CLEANING ... Good fast service in all

hotels. Prices on par with those in the United States.

LIQUOR . . . Some good native rums. Try *Ponche crema,* a not-too-potent cream eggnog. Imported liquors cost about the same as at home. Legal minimum age for drinkers is 18.

MEDICAL FACILITIES . . . Most hospitals are privately owned and operated. Many doctors speak English.

MOTION PICTURES . . . American films are shown everywhere in Venezuela, always with Spanish subtitles. Films from many nations are shown regularly, and, of the Spanish language films, those from Mexico are predominant. Movies are very popular and one can find some excellent theaters, including the *Canaima, Broadway, Cine Caribe, Lido, Paris, Radio City, Metropolitano, San Bernardino; Teatro Altamira, Teatro del Este, Cine California,* and *Cine Olimpo.* Admission charges run about $1 to $1.50.

MUSIC . . . Just two blocks west of Plaza Henry Clay in Caracas is the *Municipal Theater,* a little old-fashioned but plushy opera house. First-class concerts, opera with visiting stars, good symphony concerts, too. The Venezuelan Symphony Orchestra gives frequent concerts which are generally free to the public. Open air concerts are given occasionally at the *Concha Acústica* (acoustic shell).

NIGHT CLUBS . . . The majority of the cabarets are new and entertainers are usually imported. Prices are high and it is best to inquire ahead as to what one is likely to receive in the way of a check. The best known are the *Naiguatá* in the Hotel Tamanaco; *La Chismosa,* on Plaza la Castellana, is famous for jazz and floor shows; *Key Club,* Calle Recreo, Sabana Grande; *Zebra,* la Castellana; *Bagatelle,* near Hotel Tamanaco; *Mon Petite* on Plaza Altamira. *Pasapoga* on Avda. Urdaneta; *Le Mazot, Tony's* and *Hector's* are night spots without a floor show. A few miles out of Caracas on the Baruta road there is a French night club strangely called *Mi Vaca y Yo* with the unusual feature of a cow being made to walk through the dance floor every hour or so to remind the clients that milk is also available. There's also *Montmartre* in Baruta and *Hippocampo* in Altamira.

Hotel bars are open until 2 A.M., night clubs until 4 A.M.

PHOTOGRAPHY . . . Black-and-white and colored movie and still films are available. American and European cameras can also be purchased at prices which compare favorably with the U.S. Developing and printing of black-and-white film is done rapidly—24-hour service—at prices only a little higher than the U.S. Ansco and Kodak Ektachrome color film can be developed in 36 hours.

RELIGION . . . Venezuela is a Catholic country, but there is complete freedom in religious matters. The Caracas American Church is located at Avenida La Arboleda 54, El Bosque; English Church in Los Caobos; Episcopal in San Roman; a synagogue in San Bernardino.

RESTAURANTS . . . Among the many good ones to be found in Caracas are *Hector's, Chicote, Monseigneur, Rossini's, Anatole, Tarzilandia, Tyrol, El Molino, Dragón Verde, El Palmar* (Chinese), *Vert Galant, Casa Italia, Lee Hamilton's Steak House, Rincon Bavario.*

For Argentine-style steaks: *La Estancia, Shorthorn Grill, Zig-Zag, El Caney*. For seafood: *El Mar, Porlamar, Rio Chico*. For French cuisine: *Henry IV, Biarritz Abadie, Ambassador, La Cascada*. One of the most expensive is the exclusive *La Belle Epoque* in Colinas de Bello Monte.

SHOPS AND STORES . . . Caracas has many shopping districts; one of the most popular is along the Avenida Sabana Grande. Store hours are usually 8 A.M. to 12 noon and 2 P.M. to 6 P.M. Stores of the department store type are VAM on Avenida Andres Bello, and the Sears, Roebuck stores located at Bello Monte and San Martín in Caracas, as well as in Maracay, Puerto la Cruz, Barquisimeto, Maracaibo and Valencia.

SPECTATOR SPORTS . . . Every Saturday and Sunday horse racing at the new *La Rinconada* racetrack in El Valle attracts many thousands of people. This racetrack, located in the suburbs of Caracas, is one of the most elaborate racing plants in the world. Bullfights in the arenas in Caracas and Maracay are held on Sundays during the winter season, November through March. Baseball is the popular sport during the winter months and big-league players from the U.S. are to be seen with the various Venezuelan teams. Night games are well attended, but Sunday mornings are the most popular. In Caracas these games are played at the University City Stadium. Tennis is becoming an increasingly popular spectator sport with annual visits by champions from all over the world. Cockfighting is popular but more so in the interior towns of Venezuela.

SPORTS . . . Golf at the Caracas Country Club, Valle Arriba in Caracas; Junko in the mountains 30 minutes from Caracas; and at Carabelleda on the seacoast. Tennis at Altamira Club in Caracas and swimming at the Tamanaco, Casablanca and Paraíso. As all are strictly private clubs, special arrangements will be made for visiting tourists on a temporary basis, for use of certain of these facilities. Game hunting is available in the areas in the interior of the country and deep-sea fishing can be arranged at coastal boating clubs.

THEATERS . . . The *Teatro Municipal* and *Teatro Nacional* are in operation the year round with a variety of entertainment, including Spanish-speaking drama and comedy, opera, musical comedy, ballet and world-famous visiting artists. The Caracas Theater Club presents several works annually in the English language and the Caracas Sports Club presents a limited number of works each year.

TIME . . . Noon in Caracas is 11:00 A.M. in New York.

TIPPING . . . Tip Bs. 1 or 2 for most services. Average tip in restaurants is 15% of the bill; 10% is included and you leave 5% more. Taxi drivers are not tipped.

TOURIST TAXES . . . Aliens traveling on a passport with visa pay Bs. 20 (U.S. $4.40) at entrance and Bs. 83 (U.S. $18.45) on exit. There is no entrance or exit tax for visitors with tourist cards.

TRANSPORTATION . . . Share-the-ride taxis are known as *"por puestos."* Regular taxi rates are not much higher than in any large city in the United States, although it is best to establish the fare before taking a long ride or tour. The ride from the airport up to Caracas costs $7.50. Intercity bus service is fairly frequent. Rental cars are available and Venezuela has over 3,800 miles of paved roads.

WATER ... Although the city water system supplies abundant potable water it is recommended that bottled water be used, particularly during a stay of short duration. Mineral waters are available in most restaurants and hotels. In the interior, drink sealed bottled waters.

WHAT TO BUY ... Many articles of daily consumption in Venezuela are imported and shopping opportunities are limited, but duty on imported Swiss watches is much lower than in the United States. The jewelry stores in Caracas specialize in gold articles made of *cochano* gold, this being the pure gold that is still found in the Guayana country. Recommended are Joyería Metropol and Joyeria El Arte in Sabana Grande and the two shops of Peters Brothers. Perhaps the most varied shopping is on the Isle of Margarita. There are natural pearls and a variety of mother-of-pearl articles, native hats, sandals, fine hammocks and other straw goods. Look into the handicraft shops the Ministerio de Fomento has opened in El Silencio in downtown Caracas for examples of souvenirs handmade in the interior by skilled artisans, and the utensils made by the Indians of the Orinoco forest. Also see the large selection of gifts and jewelry at the Folklore Shop on Conde a Principal, or at Plaza Chacaito Askain near Hotel Tamanaco.

WHAT TO WEAR ... In Caracas summer wear the year around for daytime. This applies as well to the interior area of Venezuela, with the exception of places in the Andes Mountains, such as Mérida and Trujillo. In the evening in Caracas fur jackets are worn and for almost all social occasions custom requires high-style, if not formal, clothes. Coldest months are December through February.

WHERE TO GO—SIGHTSEEING ...

Caracas ... A six-lane highway from the Maiquetia airport carries the traveler into Caracas in about 20 minutes. Only a few years ago it was an hour and a half over a rather spectacular, sharp-turn road.

In the city of Caracas one finds drastic contrasts between the ultra-modern styling and the old colonial architecture. Casa Natal, the house of Simón Bolívar's birth, is a fine example of the old Colonial. It is located near Plaza Bolívar, exactly in the center of old Caracas. Only a few blocks north of Plaza Bolívar is the Pantheon, site of the tomb of Bolívar. This is another example of graceful Colonial architecture, far different from the 20-story twin towers of the Civic Center Simón Bolívar.

For the most impressive sight of the city, take the cable car (*teleférico*) to the top of Mt. Avila. Take a drive to see the Circular Militar and the Avenida de los Proceres, with its line of statues, monuments and well-arranged shrubs and flowers; or to the botanical gardens atop El Calvario. Throughout the city one finds dozens of plazas, and of interest to the North American visitor are the Plaza Henry Clay just north of the Santa Teresa Church and Plaza Washington in El Paraíso. University City, with its many buildings, and beautifully landscaped Parque del Este are of interest.

Maracay . . . *Hotel Maracay*, probably the most luxurious of the Conahotu chain of hotels, has an 18-hole golf course, giant swimming pool and riding stables. The *Hotel Jardin* in Maracay is not a first-class hotel but is of considerable interest for the beautiful mosaic tiles and patio gardens inside the old Colonial structure. It was originally one of the many homes of the dictator Gomez. Only 60 miles from Maracay is the old Colonial town of Valencia. Today, Valencia is an industrial center, with active manufacturing plants of world-famous tires, paints, plastics and cables. Good hotels include the *Grand Hotel Valencia* and the *Hotel Carabobo*. Not far away is the Rain Forest and nearby is the battlefield of Carabobo where the struggle for Venezuelan independence was won. A 1-hour ride down the mountain from Valencia to the sea is the old port town of Puerto Cabello.

Maracaibo . . . One hour and 20 minutes by air, to the west of Caracas, is the wealthy, fantastically fast-growing city of Maracaibo. Built on the shores of Lake Maracaibo, its activity fed by the more than 2 million barrels of oil pumped daily from its hundreds of wells drilled into the lake, it has a completely international population. In one of the most tropical climates, air-conditioning has changed the pattern of living in this area. Here one finds air-conditioned book stores, barber shops, theaters, restaurants, offices, and almost all hotels offer this pleasant retreat from warm weather. The *Hotel Del Lago*, of the Intercontinental Hotels Corporation group, offers everything the traveler needs. Good restaurant, pleasant bar and outstanding night club, swimming pool and conference rooms. Rates are from $13.50 single, from $18 double, European Plan. Other good hotels are *Detroit, Fitzwater, Shamrock, Chama* and *Hotel Peters*.

Mérida . . . Lovely mountain city, a 2-hour flight from Caracas, is site of world's longest cable railway that goes up Pico Espejo (15,380 feet) in 5 stages. The *Prado Rio* and *Belenzate* hotels are first class.

Angel Falls . . . The world's highest waterfall, with a total drop of 3,212 feet, is south of Ciudad Bolívar and is reached by air tours. The beautiful Canaima area, also here, overlooks setting for Sir Arthur Conan Doyle's *The Lost World*.

Orinoco River . . . The Government operates interesting 5- and 6-day trips on the river. Check locally with PAA for details.

SOURCES OF FURTHER INFORMATION . . . The *Caracas Daily Journal,* an English language newspaper that is sold throughout Venezuela, is a good source of information for movies, sports and local events. Club de Turismo (Tel. 81-02-66) will arrange tours and sightseeing. Avensa has a special tour to Canaima and other air tours. The new American Embassy and Consulate building is in La Floresta. The PAA office is at Puente Urupal on Avenida Urdaneta in San Bernardino (Tel. 55-81-01 and 54-70-46), in Hotel Tamanaco and on Ave. Miranda, opposite the U.S. Embassy. In New York the Venezuelan Government Tourist Bureau is at 445 Park Avenue.

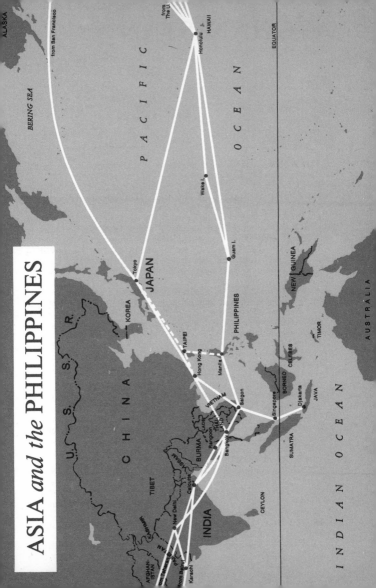

ASIA *and the* PHILIPPINES

AFGHANISTAN

LOCATION ... This legendary land of high mountain ranges and fertile plains and valleys lies in the heart of Central Asia.

POPULATION ... Estimated at 15,000,000, of which about 400,000 live in Kabul. Afghans are practically all Moslems.

SIZE .... 250,966 square miles, roamed by nomadic tribes.

CAPITAL ... Kabul (altitude of 6,200 feet) in the Hindu Kush Mountains, has both picturesque clutter and splendid spaciousness.

GOVERNMENT ... A constitutional monarchy.

HOW TO GET THERE ... Kabul and Kandahar are served by local and international airlines. From the U.S. connections can best be made at Teheran, New Delhi or Beirut from Pan American Round-the-World Jet flights. Elapsed time from New York 31 hours.

ACCOMMODATIONS ... *Hotel Kabul* and the new *Spinzar* (both from $6 single, American Plan) are the only really modern hotels in Kabul. Service charges and taxes extra. Make advance reservations.

CIGARETTES ... American, English and German brands available at reasonable prices.

CLIMATE ... Summer (except for Jalalabad and Kandahar) and fall offer the best weather. Go in autumn for grapes and melons.

CURRENCY ... The afghani is divided into 100 puls. Free market exchange rate is approximately 45 Afs to the dollar.

CUSTOMS REGULATIONS AND DOCUMENTS REQUIRED FOR UNITED STATES CITIZENS ... Personal effects, 200 cigarettes and 1 open bottle of liquor can be imported duty free. You will need a valid passport, visa (from Afghan embassy or consulate), eight photos, exit permit. Tetanus and typhoid inoculations in addition to the required smallpox vaccination are recommended.

DRUGSTORES ... American and European drugs available.

ELECTRIC CURRENT ... 220 volts, 50 cycles, A.C.

FOOD ... Continental food is available at the *Khyber Restaurant, Spinzar* and *Kabul* hotels. Afghanistan is known for its *pilaus* (rice cooked with meat and chicken); Afghan kabob; large variety of delicious fruits, especially Afghan melons of 40 known varieties, and 63 varieties of grapes. No pork. Average price for a meal is $1.

LANGUAGE ... Pushto and Dari (Afghan Persian). English, French and German are widely understood.

LIQUOR ... Not sold in stores. Beer is available at Kabul's International Club, the hotels and Khyber restaurant.

MEDICAL FACILITIES ... American and European trained doctors are readily available in Government hospitals.

SPECTATOR SPORTS ... Most unusual is *Bozkashi* in which large teams of competing horsemen try to retrieve a beheaded calf and carry it to the goal. Polo, invented here, is also played.

SPORTS ... Fishing, hunting, rugby, volley ball, tennis, hockey, golf, skiing, horseback riding.

TIME ... Noon in Kabul is 3:30 A.M. in New York.

TIPPING ... Tip 5 or 10 Afs for usual services.

TRANSPORTATION ... Ariana Afghan Airline provides service to principal cities. The Afghan Tourist Bureau can furnish private cars for local sightseeing and excursion tours. Taxis are also available, and there are two-wheeled horsedrawn carriages called *Tangas* or *Gadis*. Afghanistan has no railroads.

WATER ... Always ask for boiled water.

WHAT TO BUY ... Afghan carpets and rugs, Karakul ("Persian" lamb) skins, hand-woven fabrics, carved trinkets, Afghan musical instruments, old coins, old postage stamps, old type of colored Afghan guns, Afghan shoes, marble bowls, plates, boxes and lapis lazuli jewelry. Bargaining is expected.

WHERE TO GO—SIGHTSEEING ... Kabul, the old city with its colorful bazaars, is interesting as are the tribal nomads with their camel caravans that delight all tourists. Kabul is full of historical relics, vestiges of Buddhist period (A.D. 2nd and 3rd centuries). Of special interest in or near Kabul are Babur's garden as well as Chilstoon and Rishkhor gardens; Kabul museum with Greco-Buddhic statuary and art; unique Bagram ivory carvings; the valley of Kohdaman with famous grape vineyards; Karezmir, the king's property open to the public; and various historical Buddhist sites. Istalif, 30 miles away, is one of several picturesque villages. Paghman is a summer resort 15 miles from Kabul.

Other places of interest afield are the famous Khyber Pass, route between Afghanistan and Pakistan; Bamyan, the great center of Buddhism from A.D. 1st to 4th century with its gigantic statues of Buddha carved in the face of a cliff; the awe-inspiring mountain scenery of the Band-i-Amir lakes region; Guilbahar, a summer resort lying at the confluence of the Panjsher and Sheetul rivers; and the picturesque Panjsher valley which extends to the lofty Hindu Kush mountains.

The most interesting cities from a historical and archaeological point of view (served by Ariana Afghan Airlines) include Balkh (old Bactria, the mother of cities), beautiful Mazar-i-Sharif north of the new Salang Tunnel, Ghazni, Kandahar, Herat, Ghor, Jam, Hadda (Jalalabad) and Nooristan.

SOURCES OF FURTHER INFORMATION ... Afghan Consulate, 122 West 30th St. New York, N.Y. 10001; or the Sales Manager, Ariana Afghan Airlines, Kabul. Afghan Information Bureau, 1875 Connecticut Ave., N.W., Washington 8, D.C.

BURMA

WEATHER IN RANGOON—Lat. N16°46′—Alt. 55′

	JAN.	FEB.	MAR.	APR.	MAY	JUNE	JULY	AUG.	SEPT.	OCT.	NOV.	DEC.
Average Temp.	72°	75°	85°	92°	84°	76°	75°	76°	78°	80°	75°	70°
Days of Rain	1	1	1	2	13	23	25	24	20	11	4	1

LOCATION ... Burma forms part of the Indochina peninsula of Southeast Asia, 638 air miles southeast of Calcutta and 362 air miles northwest of Bangkok.

CHARACTERISTICS ... Burma is one of the most interesting and colorful independent republics in Asia. The people are of Tibeto-Mongolian stock, with brown, cheerful faces; they dress in bright, vivid attire. They are both hospitable to visitors and generous in spirit. Burma is a land of vast expanses of rice fields, and rich teak forests stretch up the hills. Burma is also known as the land of pagodas, where the dominant feature of any scene is the golden Buddhist pagoda. In this land of precious stones, rubies, jades and sapphires are of distinctive interest.

POPULATION ... 22,351,131; Burmans, Shans, Chins, Kachins, Indians, Chinese, Indo-Burmans, and others.

SIZE ... 261,789 square miles; about 1,000 miles long.

CAPITAL ... The city of Rangoon, situated on the Hlaing, or Rangoon, River, is about 21 miles from the sea and is the main port of entry into the country by sea or air. There are no overland routes into Burma. Rangoon has a population of nearly 900,000.

GOVERNMENT ... A republic with a Revolutionary Council headed by a chairman.

HOW TO GET THERE ... Rangoon is a regular stop on Pan America's Round-the-World routes. It is 1¼ hours from Calcutta,

1 hour from Bangkok, approximately 27 hours (elapsed time) from San Francisco, 27 hours from New York by Pan Am's Jet Clippers. Connections also available from other East and West Coast cities. By ship to Rangoon from New York via Britain takes about 40 days.

ACCOMMODATIONS... There are only two really first-class hotels in Rangoon. The *Inya Lake Hotel* is new, fully air-conditioned, and overlooks a lovely lake 12 minutes from the center of the city. The hotel provides free transportation into town. Single from $11, double from $17. The hotel has a swimming pool. The *Strand,* near the downtown business and shopping area, has singles from $7.35, doubles from $10.50, including breakfast. Hotels add 20% for taxes and service. Tip luggage porters 50 pyas per bag. It is important to reserve rooms well in advance.

CIGARETTES... Only local brands available.

CLIMATE... Like most other semitropical countries, Burma has only three seasons. The "hot season" from March to May is uncomfortable, with temperatures reaching about 100 degrees at noon; during the "rainy season" from June to October, the weather is moderately cool, but the rain may stretch out into days; and the "cool season" from November to February has temperatures around the 70s. Humidity is high during the rainy season; the best time to visit is during the cool season.

CLUBS... Rotary and Lions.

CURRENCY... The unit of Burmese currency is the kyat, which is divided into 100 pyas. The exchange value of the kyat is about U.S. 21¢ or K 4.76 to U.S. $1. Currency is controlled and exchange may be made only at authorized banks or money changers.

CUSTOMS REGULATIONS AND DOCUMENTS REQUIRED FOR UNITED STATES CITIZENS... Passport and visa required. Also health certificate; cholera and yellow fever if coming from infected area and smallpox vaccination. Exit permits are required from those staying 30 or more days. Currency and travelers checks must be declared. No Burmese currency allowed. Guns and a limited amount of ammunition are allowed into the country upon a payment of duty and after all entry formalities have been complied with. Radios may be brought in after payment of duty. Travelers are also allowed to bring in or take out, duty free, 200 cigarettes, 50 cigars or ½ pound tobacco, and 1 quart of liquor.

ELECTRIC CURRENT... 220 volts, A.C., 50 cycles.

FOOD... Burmese food is strikingly similar to Indian, Siamese and Malay food and consists of rice and curry. Curry dishes are generally meat or vegetables or a mixture, cooked with a liberal admixture of spices, pepper, onions and sesamum oil. *Ngapi* (dried fish paste) smells terrible but tastes good. *Mohinga* and *khowswe* are delicious national dishes. Most hotels and restaurants serve Western food as well as Chinese and Indian dishes.

RESTAURANTS... In Rangoon the *Strand Hotel, Inya Lake Hotel* and *Envoy* are the most popular Western-type restaurants. *Aye Nanda* on Phayre Street, *Hai Yuan* on University Ave. and *Nam Sin* on Prome Road (8 miles) provide excellent Chinese food. Food is not expensive in Burma. Usual rates are not more than $2 per person.

WHAT TO BUY ... Jade, sapphires and rubies at well-established jewel shops; locally-woven cottons and silks, lacquerware, silver, ivory, carved wood items.

WHAT TO WEAR ... For men, dacron or any other light-material suits are recommended; for women, washable linen, cotton or dacron dresses. Rangoon is not a "dressy" place, but it is a good idea to bring your tropical formals along. Sunglasses are indispensable. Light suits will do fine for any weather in Burma; raincoats are essential.

WHERE TO GO—SIGHTSEEING ...

Rangoon ... The capital of Burma, situated in the low hills about 24 miles from the sea, Rangoon is one of the most distinctive cities in the East. It combines the mystery and religious aura of the East with the modern facilities of the West. It is well laid out, with pleasant tree-lined streets, parks and gardens; there are two fine lakes, Royal Lake and Inya Lake, on the edge of the city. The people are friendly and cheerful and highly attractive in their gay and colorful *longyis*. Sightseeing tours are available. A 3-hour group tour costs about $6. Here are the main sightseeing places in Rangoon:

The gleaming, gold-coated spire of Shwedagon Pagoda towers about 326 feet from the summit of a hill near the heart of the city and is a welcoming landmark that greets every traveler, by sea or air, to Burma. It is the largest pagoda of its kind in the world and every year attracts many Buddhist pilgrims from all over the world. Remove all footwear before entering any pagoda; floors are kept very clean. Also in Rangoon is the picturesque Sule Pagoda, situated exactly in the heart of the city. See the World Peace Pagoda and Great Cave built for the Sixth Buddhist Synod, held 2,500 years after the death of Gautama Buddha.

Other attractions include the colorful bazaars bustling with activity; the cigar-rolling center where Burmese girls may be seen wrapping and rolling the tobacco leaf; umbrella shops, where skillful workers produce gorgeous umbrellas of silk and bamboo; workshops that produce silverwork or wood and ivory carvings; the National Museum; the State Library; the State Institute of Fine Arts; Burmese costume drama, dancing, or puppet shows which can be seen frequently in just about any quarter of the city.

Burmese marriage ceremonies, the *Shinpyus* of young Burmese males when they are initiated into monkhood, and earring-boring ceremonies for young Burmese girls are other occasions of immense interest; the Rangoon Zoo and the occasional snake-kissing show, featuring the king cobra and the snake charmer; the busy port and teeming wharves; the campus of the University of Rangoon; the religious buildings. All are interesting.

SOURCES OF FURTHER INFORMATION ... Feel free to inquire of Pan American's representative of 186 Phayre Street, Rangoon, for tourist information. The U.N. Mission of the Union of Burma in New York is located at 10 East 77th Street.

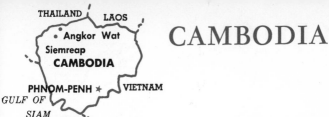

CAMBODIA

LOCATION ... Bounded by Thailand, Laos, Vietnam.

CHARACTERISTICS ... Cambodia is an exotic, picturesque country of rice paddies, sugar and rubber plantations, set against a background of ancient temples and monuments. Exchange rate at Angkor Wat is 60 riels to U.S. $1; elsewhere, 35 riels per $1.

POPULATION ... Estimated at about 6,000,000.

CAPITAL ... Phnom-Penh, population over 600,000.

HOW TO GET THERE ... By Pan Am Jet Clipper to Bangkok, Hong Kong or Saigon, then by connecting airlines to Phnom-Penh.

ACCOMMODATIONS ... In Phnom-Penh there's the new air-conditioned *Monorom* Hotel. Others are the *Raja Palace, Le Royal* (with swimming pool) and the partially air-conditioned *Sukhalay, Mondial* and *International*. Rates for air-conditioned rooms are $7-$12 single, $10-$17 double. The *Rajah Palace* is best for French food. Other restaurants are *La Taverne, Lotus d'Or, Mondial, Café de Paris*.

DOCUMENTS REQUIRED FOR UNITED STATES CITIZENS ... Passport and visa (available upon arrival and valid 30 days). You need smallpox vaccination, and if coming from an infected area, yellow fever and cholera inoculations, ticket to leave.

WHAT TO SEE ... In Phnom-Penh, visit Jayavarman II Museum; the Royal Palace with throne hall, silver pagoda, museum; Botum Vaddey Monastery; colorful Central Market; and the Art School.

ANGKOR WAT ... Located at Siemreap, a 1-hour flight from Phnom-Penh, the ruins of Angkor are among the greatest tourist attractions in Southeast Asia. This architectural wonder of Angkor Wat (temple) and many other ornamental monuments, temples and palaces with 200-foot towers, covering an area over 60 square miles, was built by the Khmer warrior kings more than a thousand years ago. Hidden by jungle growth, the ruins were rediscovered only within the last century and are still in process of being restored. A program of Cambodian classical dances is performed on the temple terrace (adm. $4.20), and you can take an elephant ride to Bakeng Hill ($2.50). Hotels include the de luxe *Villa Princière*, $11.10-$18.30; *Auberge Royale des Temples* and the *Grand Hotel d'Angkor,* single $4.70-$8.20, double $6.40-$9.90 including tax and services. Lunch/dinner $2.50, breakfast 70¢. There are organized excursions to the ruins for $4 per person per day. Car with driver can be hired for about $22 a day.

SOURCES OF FURTHER INFORMATION ... Pan American address in Phnom-Penh is care of Denis Frères Air Service, 219 Quai Sisowath (Tel. 3256 and 2928).

CEYLON

PALK STRAIT
Jaffna

▲ NATIONAL RESERVE
Trincomalee

Anuradhapura • • Mihintale
• Polonnaruwa
Dambulla • Sigiriya
CEYLON
Negombo • • Kandy
COLOMBO ★ • Nuwara Eliya
• Ratnapura
Bentota •
Hikkaduwa • • Hambantota
Galle
INDIAN OCEAN

WEATHER IN COLOMBO—Lat. N6°55′—Alt. 55′

	JAN.	FEB.	MAR.	APR.	MAY	JUNE	JULY	AUG.	SEPT.	OCT.	NOV.	DEC.
Average Temp.	79°	79°	81°	82°	82°	81°	81°	80°	81°	80°	79°	79°
Days of Rain	10	4	11	16	21	20	18	14	17	22	19	12

LOCATION . . . Ceylon is in the Indian Ocean, separated from the southeastern tip of India by the 20-mile-wide Palk Strait.

CHARACTERISTICS . . . A lovely island, fragrant with flowers and spices, that has been a major junction between East and West for centuries. Occupied by the Portuguese and Dutch for nearly 300 years, and ruled by the British from 1802 to 1948, Ceylon has both an international sophistication and an exotic individuality.

POPULATION . . . Estimated at more than 11,000,000.

SIZE . . . 25,332 square miles; 270 miles long, 140 miles wide.

CAPITAL . . . Colombo, with a population of over 511,700.

GOVERNMENT . . . A self-governing member of the British Commonwealth.

HOW TO GET THERE . . . By Pan American Jet Clipper from New York to Karachi with connections to Colombo in 26¼ hours elapsed time. Connections also from Calcutta and Singapore.

ACCOMMODATIONS . . . Top hotels in Colombo are the *Taprobane* (formerly *Grand Oriental*), in the city, from $10.21 single, $18.50 double; *Galle Face,* on the sea, from $11.63 single, $22 double; and the *Mount Lavinia,* a complete resort hotel 7 miles from the city on a lovely beach, from $11.30 single, $19 double. Rates include all meals. Air conditioning extra. Throughout the island in rural spots of special interest there are Government-owned rest houses of considerable charm; American Plan rates here are only $6.31 per person a day.

ARTS . . . Colombo has a gallery of contemporary local art and a museum of treasures from the 2000-year-long reign of the Sinhalese kings. The island is famed for its ceremonial dances performed at Kandy in a gorgeous panoply of costumes and masks, and for the devil dances performed (especially at full moon) in the villages. Puppet shows are another island art form.

CLIMATE . . . Always comfortably cool in the hills, and Nuwara Eliya has an average temperature of 55°. Except from November to February, the coastal plains can be very warm. December to April are the most popular tourist months, but Ceylon is a year-round resort spot.

COMMUNICATIONS . . . Airmail postage to the United States is Rs. 1.60 for a letter, 80¢ for a postcard, 60¢ for an air letter form.

CURRENCY . . . There are 100 cents (c) to the rupee, and the Ceylon rupee is valued at 21¢ American. U.S. $1 is valued at Rs. 4.65.

CUSTOMS REGULATIONS AND DOCUMENTS REQUIRED FOR UNITED STATES CITIZENS . . . Valid passport, but no visa needed for a visit of a month or less. Smallpox vaccination certificate required; yellow fever and cholera certificates needed if coming from an infected area. 200 cigarettes, or 50 cigars, or ½ lb. tobacco and 1 bottle of wine or ½ pint of spirits admitted duty free. No restrictions on U.S. currency, but no rupees of Pakistan, India or Ceylon may be taken into or out of the country. Entry tax 50¢ per person.

ELECTRIC CURRENT . . . 230 volts, 50-cycle, A.C.

LAUNDRY AND DRY CLEANING . . . One-day service possible, but expensive.

LIQUOR . . . Most kinds of imported liquors are available; much less expensive are the excellent local beer, gin, and refined *arrack* distilled from the juice of the coconut flower.

PHOTOGRAPHY . . . Ektachrome film can be processed in Colombo. Other color films must be developed abroad.

RESTAURANTS . . . Sinhalese food is very highly seasoned, but hotels for the most part serve Westernized meals. There are also some very good Chinese restaurants in Colombo. Evening entertainment, with dinner, at the *Blue Leopard* in the Taprobane Hotel, the *Mascarilla* in the Galle Face Hotel, and the *Little Hut* at the Mount Lavinia.

SHOPS AND STORES . . . Major shopping district in Colombo is the "Fort" area around Chatham, Prince and York Streets, but don't miss the teeming, colorful Pettah Bazaar where you can bargain vigorously. Stores close at 4:30, the bazaar at 6. Everything closes early on Saturday and all day Sunday unless a cruise ship is in the harbor. Ceylon is the world's largest producer of gem stones, and this is *the* place to shop for everything from amethysts to zircons; get a list of reputable jewel merchants from the Ceylon Government Tourist Bureau. Other good buys are lacquerware, inlaid brass, silver, decorative ivory and ebony pieces, tortoise shell, exquisite laces and hand-loomed textiles. Price-controlled handicraft shops in Colombo are the Ceylon Products Depot, in Chatham Street, and the Cottage Industries Department on York Street.

SPORTS ... Swimming, skin-diving (visitors may get temporary memberships in the Ceylon Reefcombers Club), deep-sea and fresh-water fishing, tennis, golf (the course at Nuwara Eliya is about the best in the East). Hunting is excellent from November 1 to April 30, and licenses are easily obtainable from the Warden, Department of Wild Life, Colombo.

TIME ... Noon in Colombo is 1:30 A.M. in New York.

TRANSPORTATION ... Take metered taxis; rates are only about U.S. 17¢ per mile, slightly higher after midnight. English-speaking driver-guides, with cars, may be hired from numerous agencies for U.S. 21¢ to 31¢ per mile. Government-owned bus and railroad lines are modern and comfortable. Air Ceylon has regularly scheduled flights to Anuradhapura, Batticaloa, Gal Oya, Jaffna and Trincomalee.

WATER ... Safe to drink, but bottled waters are available.

WHERE TO GO—SIGHTSEEING ...

Colombo ... Ride through Cinnamon Gardens, lovely residential section, and note the lavishly decorated Asokharamaya Buddhist temple. The whole city is dotted with temples and mosques of great beauty. Colombo's Dehiwela Zoo is one of the best in the East. The Kelaniya Temple, 6 miles from the city, is the setting for a great procession of dancers and elephants on the full moon day in January.

Anuradhapura ... Site of the holy Bo-Tree, under which Gautama Buddha attained Supreme Enlightenment, transported from India in 245 B.C. Magnificent ruins of palaces and dagobas recall an era of grandeur when Anuradhapura was Ceylon's capital for 1,000 years.

Kandy ... Only 72 miles northeast of Colombo, beautiful Kandy is 1600 feet above sea level. *Queen's Hotel* overlooks Kandy Lake, and across the lake is *Chalet Guest House*. *Peak View Hotel* is 2 miles from town. Most famous landmark is the ornate Temple of the Sacred Tooth. Buddha's Tooth is carried during the Kandy Perahera, 10-day festivities in July/August, a stupendous pageant and procession of unforgettable costumes and extraordinary dancing accompanied by the throbbing of Kandyan drums. Peradeniya Botanical Gardens, among the finest in the world, and the University of Ceylon are about 4 miles from Kandy.

Nuwara Eliya ... Ever-cool resort at an elevation of 6,250 feet. Ideal for golfers and fishermen. *Grosvenor* and *Grand* hotels.

Sigiriya ... Famous 5th-century frescoes are painted in the pocket of a huge rock. Modern resthouse nearby.

SOURCES OF FURTHER INFORMATION ... Ceylon Government Tourist Bureau, Chaitya Road, Colombo 1. Ceylon Embassy, 2148 Wyoming Ave., N.W., Washington, D.C. Pan Am's Colombo agents are Shaw, Wallace & Hedges, Ltd., 363 Kollupitim Road (Tel. 78271).

HONG KONG

New Territories
Airport
KOWLOON PENINSULA
★VICTORIA HONG KONG
Aberdeen
BIG WAVE BAY
SHEK-O
THE LIDO RESORT
REPULSE BAY

WEATHER IN HONG KONG—Lat. N22°16′—Alt. 25′

Temp.	JAN.	FEB.	MAR.	APR.	MAY	JUNE	JULY	AUG.	SEPT.	OCT.	NOV.	DEC.
Low	56°	55°	60°	67°	73°	78°	78°	78°	77°	73°	65°	58°
High	64°	63°	67°	75°	81°	85°	87°	87°	85°	81°	74°	67°
Average	60°	59°	64°	71°	77°	82°	83°	83°	81°	77°	70°	63°
Days of Rain	6	8	11	12	16	21	19	17	14	8	6	5

LOCATION ... Hong Kong Island, Kowloon Peninsula and the New Territories in southeast China are about 90 miles south of Canton. Its correct designation is "Hong Kong, British Crown Colony" or "Hong Kong, B.C.C."—*not* China.

CHARACTERISTICS ... This busy port offers the traveler a chance to see a thrillingly colorful Chinese city. Tourists are enchanted with its contrasts, its beauty, bargains and food. Nearby Macao, province of Portugal, provides an interesting experience, too.

POPULATION ... Estimated 3,800,000, mostly Cantonese (South China); the balance, northern Chinese, European and American.

SIZE ... The island of Hong Kong is 11 miles long with an area of 29 square miles. The total area of the colony is 398 square miles.

CAPITAL ... Victoria, often referred to as Hong Kong, with a population of over 1,005,000.

GOVERNMENT ... A British Crown Colony, the Queen represented by a Governor.

HOW TO GET THERE ... By Jet Clipper from the United States West Coast about 21 hours (elapsed time) via Honolulu and Tokyo, about 2 hours from Manila, 2¾ hours from Bangkok, 4½ hours from Tokyo. Hong Kong is on Pan Am's Round-the-World Routes. By ship about 18 days from San Francisco.

ACCOMMODATIONS ... On Hong Kong Island, the *Mandarin,* an Intercontinental hotel, is one of the most luxurious hotels in the Far East. It is centrally located, exquisitely decorated, is fully air conditioned and has a rooftop swimming pool. Each room has a private balcony overlooking either the harbor or Victoria Peak. Rates $13-$21 single, $17-$26 double. The completely de luxe *Hong Kong Hilton* towers over the fascinating harbor and also has a swimming pool; $10-$18 single, $14-$21 double. Less expensive hotels on the island are the *Repulse Bay* on the beach, 20 minutes from Victoria; the *Victoria, Carlton* and *Sunning House;* $6-$12 single, $7-$12 double. In Kowloon, on the mainland, are the long-famous *Peninsula,* the *Park Hotel,* the *Ambassador,* the *Empress, President, Merlin* and *Miramar;* average rates $10 single, $14 double. Also good are the *Astor, Clover, August Moon* and *Imperial;* $6-$8 single, $8-$12 double.

ARTS . . . The City Hall contains a museum, art gallery, exhibition halls, theater and auditorium for visiting international artists.

BANKS . . . The First National City Bank of New York, Chase Manhattan Bank, Bank of America, Hong Kong and Shanghai Banking Corp., The Chartered Bank, Bank of Indo-China, Bank of East Asia, Netherlands Trading Society. The American Express Co. also has a banking section.

CALENDAR OF HOLIDAYS . . . Added to all the British holidays are the gorgeously colorful Chinese New Year (January-February), which culminates in the Lantern Festival; Ching Ming Festival (April 5), pilgrimages to ancestors' tombs; Tin Hau Festival (March-April), honoring the goddess of fishermen; Cheung Chau Bun Festival (April-May), three days of parades and festivities; Dragon Boat Regatta (June); Mid-Autumn Festival (September-October); Founding of the Republic of China (October 10).

CIGARETTES . . . British, European and American cigarettes are readily available at prices much lower than in the United States.

CLIMATE . . . The best season is from September 15 through March 1; the wet season is from April through June; the warm months are from the end of June into September.

CLUBS . . . Royal Hong Kong Golf Club; Jockey Club; American Club; The Country Club; Rotary; Lions; Junior Chamber of Commerce; Hong Kong Club; Royal Hong Kong Yacht Club; Foreign Correspondents' Club. Ask about visitors' cards at local Pan Am offices.

COMMUNICATIONS . . . A 3-minute call to the States costs HK$48 a 10-word cablegram is HK$17.50. Airletter forms HK50¢.

CURRENCY . . . The open market rate of exchange for the Hong Kong dollar is about HK$5.71 to U.S. $1. Legal money exchange houses often give better rates than hotels or banks.

CUSTOMS REGULATIONS AND DOCUMENTS REQUIRED FOR UNITED STATES CITIZENS . . . Passport. Visa required if staying over 7 days. Get a multiple-entry visa if you plan to go to Macao. Smallpox vaccination; cholera inoculation certificate officially stamped by your city or state medical association is required for Macao entry. Duty-free allowances: 200 cigarettes, or 50 cigars or 8 ounces of tobacco, and 1 quart bottle of liquor. Hotels can supply lists of shops which issue Certificates of Origin required for clearing Chinese-type purchases in U.S. customs.

DRUGSTORES . . . Chemists' shops are numerous and have name-brand pharmaceuticals from the States and Europe.

ELECTRIC CURRENT . . . Voltage in Hong Kong is 220, 50 cycle A.C.; two-prong transformer plugs required.

FOOD . . . No other city can offer such varieties combined with exquisite taste. The Chinese have been famous for centuries for their cooking, and their methods have been handed down from generation to generation. Principal dishes are: fried rice, sweet-and-sour pork, sharkfin soup, birdnest soup, suckling pig, sweet almond cream, and dozens more. Many northern delicacies such as Szechuan and Peking duck are available. Milk is safe to drink.

GAMBLING . . . Hong Kong has no casinos, but there is a wonderful racetrack at Happy Valley with pari-mutuel betting.

LANGUAGE . . . The official language is English, but the city is populated almost entirely by Chinese. Cantonese is heard mostly on the streets. English, however, is readily understood in hotels, restaurants and shops. In Chinese, Hong Kong means "fragrant harbor."

LAUNDRY AND DRY CLEANING . . . Laundry is good. Dry cleaning is not too reliable. Be sure your room-boy understands *dry clean*, not *wash*, if you want something dry cleaned.

LIQUOR . . . All drinks are available at moderate prices. Chinese prefer locally produced rice wine, which they drink warm.

MEDICAL FACILITIES . . . The University of Hong Kong, Matilda Hospital, Queen Mary Hospital and new Queen Elizabeth Hospital all have excellent equipment. British and Chinese doctors.

MOTION PICTURES . . . Numerous first-class air-conditioned theaters in the city show first-run American films. A few theaters show locally made Chinese films which would be of interest to tourists.

MUSIC . . . Native music can be heard at performances of Chinese opera, which runs constantly. Hong Kong has a choral group and a symphony orchestra composed of amateur musicians. International performers are at the City Hall auditorium.

NIGHT CLUBS . . . *Button Supper Club* (Mandarin), *Eagle's Nest* (Hilton), *Siamese Starlight Roof* (President), *Bayside, Crown, Highball, Gaddi's, Paris, Maxim's, Golden Phoenix, Carlton, Princess Garden, Paramount* and *Marco Polo Room;* most have Filipino orchestras, floor shows. Newest are the *Latin Quarter, Show Boat, Gaslight, Grotto.*

PHOTOGRAPHY . . . Fine bargains in all types of cameras and film. Camera supplies are available almost everywhere.

RELIGION . . . In addition to religions of the Far East: Church of England and Roman Catholic churches; most American Protestant missions represented; Jewish synagogue.

RESTAURANTS . . . Some of the best are the Mandarin Hotel's *Saddle and Sirloin;* Hilton's *Grill Room;* President's *Starlight Room; Parisian Grill,* French and Russian dishes; *Dairy Farm* for ice cream, sodas; *Jimmy's Kitchen* for steaks; *Champagne Room,* with music;

Tai Tung and *Kam Ling,* Cantonese style; *Hoover (Sky) Restaurant, Peking (Touring Hing Lau), Princess Garden,* Peking style; and *Winter Garden* for Szechuan or Shanghai style. Continental food at *Gaddi's* and *Lido* or *Repulse Bay Hotel.* Others include *Café de Paris, Kowloon Restaurant, Maxim's, Dateline, Diamond Horseshoe.* The *Tai Pak* and *Sea Palace* floating restaurants in Aberdeen. There are Russian, Indian and Indonesian restaurants, too.

SHOPS AND STORES . . . Bargaining is practiced in small corner shops catering to tourist trade, but not at leading stores that are members of the Hong Kong Tourist Association, identified by the HKTA insignia on their windows. Linens and embroidered articles on On Lan Street; carved camphorwood boxes, ivories on Queen's Road, East; silks, smoking jackets, lingeries, carved rosewood beads on Wyndham Street. You can get wonderful bargains in British woolens. Fast, excellent tailoring at many shops.

SPECTATOR SPORTS . . . Horse racing, soccer, tennis, hockey.

SPORTS . . . At the numerous beautiful beaches there's good swimming June through October, tennis (arrangements can be made for the use of courts at some clubs), golf by arrangement with the club. There's also boating, water skiing and lawn bowling.

THEATERS . . . Chinese opera in Cantonese.

TIME . . . 16 hours later than the United States Pacific Coast Time. Daylight Saving Time from late March to early November.

TIPPING . . . Some hotels and restaurants include a service charge of 10%; otherwise tip 10-15%. Luggage porters are tipped HK$1 per bag. Barbers and beauticians are tipped 20% of their bills.

TRANSPORTATION . . . Metered taxis, rickshaws (establish fare first), trams, self-drive cars, buses, transport coolies. Frequent, very inexpensive ferry service between Kowloon and downtown Hong Kong. Ferries also to Cheung Chau, Lantao, Peng Chau and Lamma islands.

WATER . . . Good drinking water now flows 24 hours a day.

WHAT TO BUY . . . Because Hong Kong is free of import duty on everything except liquor and tobacco, it is much cheaper to shop here for perfumes, cameras, woolens, radios, jewelry, watches. Oriental items require a Certificate of Origin for entry into the States.

WHAT TO WEAR . . . For summer, clothing should be as light as possible. Sunshades and shady hats will be comfortable, too. A topcoat may be required during the winter months.

WHERE TO GO—SIGHTSEEING . . .

Hong Kong . . . A visit to such districts as Sai Ying Pun and Wanchai is fascinating. Here are the "ladder streets," narrow lanes with steep flights of stairs and typically Chinese markets. On Wing On Street you can get bargains in woolen, cotton goods, real and artificial silk. There are curio dealers in this district, tailors, grocers and restaurants. There are open-air bookshops where you see Chinese ranging from small tots looking at picture books to adults poring over books of learning. You should try to visit the Tiger Balm Garden and take a drive through the beautiful residential district. Sightseeing tours to the New Territories or around the city start at about $5. Night tours, about $10, include several drinks at various spots. The Hong Kong Tourist Association can recommend the best tours of the Colony.

Hong Kong has 4 very popular bathing beaches. Repulse Bay can be reached from Hong Kong in 20 minutes by car. Another beach resort is *Shek-O* in the old village of Dragon's Back Peninsula. Deep Water Bay and Big Wave Bay also have splendid bathing beaches. The fishing village of Aberdeen is one of the most picturesque places in Hong Kong. Junks gather here by the hundreds, and two have been converted into the famous floating restaurants. Take a ride on the Peak Tram to the top of Victoria Peak; visit the Chinese temples; see outer islands by rented cruise boat or ferries.

New Territories . . . Consist of 355 square miles leased from China on the mainland; terrace farming and typical Chinese villages can be seen on conducted tours which take about 4½ hours, including stops for lunch and taking pictures at the walled villages of Kam Tin, built during the Sung dynasty.

Macao . . . (or Macau), is a Portuguese province on the peninsula of Chung Shan, Kwangtung, with first-class hotels and luxurious casinos. Tourists are intrigued by this city, which is a mixture of Chinese and Portuguese atmosphere. Air-conditioned hydrofoil boats make the trip in about 1¼ hours; four 15-minute flights daily.

Aside from the famous gambling houses, there are many points of interest in this small province: the Praia Grande, gardens and grotto of Portugal's immortal poet, Camões, who composed part of his epic *The Luisads* here. There are many lovely Chinese temples to be seen, and beautiful gardens; the Guía Lighthouse, the oldest on the China Coast; the famous façade of the Cathedral of St. Paul, which is centuries old; Penha Hill; the Barrier Gate between this colony and the Chinese territory. Take in the Avenida Almeida Ribeiro, the main shopping center of Macao. Kun Iam Tong, the Temple of the Goddess of Mercy, is where the first treaty between the United States and China was signed in 1844. Lin Fung Miu is another ancient Chinese temple, as is the 600-year-old Ma Kok Temple, after which Macao is named. Other places of interest to see are: the yards for junks—all types are seen here, fishing junks, sampans and other wooden vessels; a trip to a match factory—the manufacture of matches is one of the important industries. There are some good hotels and restaurants here, such as the *Villa Taiyip, Bella Vista, Hotel Riviera, Grand Hotel,* the new *Estoril Hotel* and the *Macau Inn* (Portuguese atmosphere); *Fa Siu Lau* (Laughing Buddha Restaurant, famous for roast pigeon), and *Nan Lau* Restaurant. The *Melco Club,* which is the Macao Electric Light Company's staff club, is open to visitors.

SOURCES OF FURTHER INFORMATION . . . Hong Kong Tourist Association, 4 Yun Ping Road (Tel. 776211). Pan American offices: Public Relations Dept., Prince's Building (Tel. 243081) and Peninsula Hotel (Tel. 664319).

INDIA

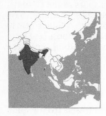

WEATHER IN CALCUTTA—Lat. N22°30′—Alt. 85′

Temp.	JAN.	FEB.	MAR.	APR.	MAY	JUNE	JULY	AUG.	SEPT.	OCT.	NOV.	DEC.
Low	56°	60°	69°	76°	78°	79°	79°	79°	78°	75°	65°	56°
High	77°	82°	91°	95°	95°	91°	89°	88°	88°	87°	82°	77°
Average	67°	71°	80°	86°	87°	85°	84°	84°	83°	81°	74°	67°
Days of Rain	1	2	2	3	7	13	18	18	13	6	1	0

LOCATION ... Topped by the Himalaya Mountains, India juts into the Indian Ocean between the Arabian Sea and the Bay of Bengal.

CHARACTERISTICS ... This is a colorful country undergoing what amounts to a revolution in its social and economic life. Its fabulous temples, magnificent mosques, exotic bazaars and shops, its world-famous Taj Mahal are in themselves reason enough to visit India. Delhi, the capital; Calcutta and Bombay, thriving industrial centers and major ports of India; Jaipur, the pink capital of Rajasthan; the holy city of Varanasi (Benares); the ancient rock-cut caves of Ajanta and Ellora, and the temples of South India are some of the major tourist attractions of this fascinating land. The Indian Government is eager to have the outside world know more about the country.

POPULATION ... Estimated at over 461,300,000.

SIZE ... 1,259,992 square miles; about 2,000 miles long, as much as 1,855 miles wide.

CAPITAL ... New Delhi, which, together with Delhi City, has a population of 2,660,000.

GOVERNMENT ... Republic framework with a Parliament (Council of States and House of the People). The Cabinet consists of a Prime Minister and Council of Ministers.

HOW TO GET THERE ... By Pan Am Jet Clipper, through-plane service from New York to Calcutta, 24½ hours; to Delhi 24 hours (elapsed time); Delhi is 1½ hours by air from Karachi, 2¼ hours from Calcutta. Bombay is 1½ hours from Karachi via Middle East Airlines. By ship, 25 to 45 days.

ACCOMMODATIONS... In Calcutta the top hotels are the *Oberoi Grand* (about $10 single, $15 double, European Plan—without meals); the new *Park Hotel* in the same price range; the *Great Eastern* and *Spence's* (about $10 single, $19 double, American Plan—with meals). All have bars, restaurants and orchestras. Best in Delhi are the Oberoi chain's *Maidens* and *Swiss*. In New Delhi is the luxurious new *Oberoi Intercontinental* ($10.50-$17.75 single, $18.90-$24.15 double, EP). Also the new *Hotel Rajdoot*, $7.35 single, $10.72 double, EP. Single American Plan rates at the *Imperial* and *Claridge's* average $12; about $2 less at *Ashoka, Janpath* and *Ambassador*. Best hotels in Bombay are the *Taj Mahal, Ambassador, Nataraj* and *Ritz*, averaging $12 single, $20 double, AP; the *West End, Airlines* and *Grand* average $9 single, AP. *Sun-n-Sand* on Juhu Beach near Santa Cruz Airport is excellent; from $7.35 single, AP. These hotels provide European meals as well as local dishes, and have cabarets. Hotels in Agra are *Laurie's*, the *Imperial* and *Clark's-Shiraz* overlooking the Taj Mahal ($12 single, $19 double, AP). In Jaipur, the *Jaimahal* and the *Rambagh Palace*, former home of the Maharajah of Jaipur; rates average $10 single, $20 double, AP. Hotels add a 10-12½% service charge, plus extra for taxes and air conditioning. The Government maintains picturesque and often luxurious circuit houses and dak bungalows in out-of-the-way places; rates about $4, including all meals.

ARTS... Outstanding are the Indian Museum and Victoria Memorial Museum in Calcutta; National Museum, National Art Gallery in New Delhi; Prince of Wales Museum in Bombay; Government Museum and National Art Gallery in Madras.

BALLET... There is no ballet as we know it, but dancing occupies a unique place among the arts, combining action, song, melody, rhythm and harmony and is an integral part of Indian life, having both spiritual and social significance. There are four major schools of dancing in India: the classical Bharata Natyam of South India, the Kathakali of Kerala, the Kathak of North India and the Manipuri of Assam. The last three may be regarded as the counterpart of the ballet in the West. Folk ballet is entirely different. Try to see Bharatiya Kala Kendra, Indian National Theater, and the Students of Viswabharati (Santiniketan) and Kalakshetra, Madras.

BANKS... The First National City Bank of New York, Thos. Cook's and the American Express Co. have branches in a number of the larger Indian cities. Money exchange facilities at airports.

CALENDAR OF HOLIDAYS... Hindu and Moslem festivals are governed by the lunar calendar, hence within a certain period their dates vary from year to year. January 26, Republic Day celebration; March, Holi (Spring Festival); August 15, Independence Day; April-May, Muharram (Moslem holiday); September-October, Dussehra; October-November, Diwali (Festival of Lights).

CIGARETTES AND TOBACCO... Indian and British. American brands, when obtainable, cost 50¢ and up per pack.

CLIMATE ... Being a vast country, India has varied climates. In Calcutta, for example, the winter months (November-February) are bright and sunny. The summer months (April-October) are quite warm and humid. Delhi experiences extremes of climate. In summer (mid-April to July) the temperature rises to about 110 degrees and it is hot and dusty; the rainy season (July, August and September) is warm and humid and the temperature ranges between 70 degrees and 90 degrees. In winter (mid-November to February) it is cold and bracing, the temperature at times touching 40 degrees or less. Delhi has a short spring (March to mid-April). The best time to visit Bombay is November to March, when temperatures are around 80 degrees. April and May are hot and June, July and August are the monsoon months of torrential rains.

CLUBS ... Rotary Club in most major cities. Guest members are welcome. In Calcutta there are a number of good clubs, including the Calcutta, the Bengal, the Royal Calcutta Golf Club and an active Chamber of Commerce, which foreign businessmen like to visit. There is also an American Club, which meets once a month and is composed of the majority of the American community.

In Delhi, Delhi Gymkhana, the Chelmsford, Delhi Golf Club, National Sports Club of India (N.S.C.I.) and the Roshanara Club have arrangements for transient memberships. Bombay and Madras have also several European and Cosmopolitan Clubs.

COMMON COURTESIES AND LOCAL CUSTOMS ... Visitors should take off their shoes before entering an Indian temple or mosque.

COMMUNICATIONS ... A 3-minute phone call to the States costs Rs 54; a 10-word cablegram is Rs 12. Airmail postage to the U.S. is Rs 1.40 for up to 10 grams, Rs .55 for an airletter, Rs .45 for a postcard.

CURRENCY ... There are 100 paise in one rupee, which is worth U.S. 21¢. Rs. 4.76 equals U.S. $1. Many prices are still quoted in annas; 8 annas equal 50 paise, 16 annas equal one rupee.

CUSTOMS REGULATIONS AND DOCUMENTS REQUIRED FOR UNITED STATES CITIZENS ... Passport and visa are required. If you're going to India only on a visit, get the special tourist visa with country-wide liquor permit and other special privileges, including 3 entries during 3-month stay. There is a duty-free limit of 200 cigarettes, 50 cigars, or ¼ pound of tobacco; 1 bottle of whiskey; perfumes and cosmetics limited to a reasonable amount for personal use. Three hunting guns per adult may enter duty free; license may be obtained upon arrival. You must make a currency declaration (including travelers checks) but there is no restriction except that import or export of Indian currency is absolutely prohibited.

DRUGSTORES ... Chemists, druggists or pharmacists can be found in the shopping and business centers and in most of the hotels. In large cities there is special night and Sunday service. American products are scarce and expensive, but there are some locally made equivalents that are U.S.-licensed.

ELECTRIC CURRENT ... In most areas, 220 volts, A.C., 50 cycles.

Various kinds of resistors and converter plugs are required. Check at your hotel before using U.S. electrical appliances.

FAUNA . . . In its variety of wildlife few regions of the earth are as interesting as India. There are more than 500 species of animals. Typical are the wild elephant, lion, tiger, panther, leopard, cheetah, *nilgai* (blue bull) bison, wild buffalo, rhinoceros, camel, sloth bear, wolf, fox, antelope, *sambhar,* gazelle, wild pig, monkey, and spotted, barking and swamp deer. There are zoological gardens in Delhi, Calcutta, Lucknow, Jaipur, Baroda, Madras, Mysore and Trivandrum. Photographs of wildlife can be taken at the wildlife sanctuaries in the states of Assam, Gujarat, Madras, Mysore, Kerala and Uttar Pradesh. There is a large variety of birds, among which the peacock, *bulbul,* myna and *sarus* crane are typical. As for game, pheasant, duck, partridge and geese are plentiful. Hunting excursions can be arranged.

FLORA . . . The better-known botanic gardens are in Calcutta, Darjeeling, Bombay, Poona, Ootacamund, Coonoor, Bangalore, Madras and Trivandrum. Among the flowers, lotus, varieties of jasmine, orchid, rose lily, *champa, gulmohr* and laburnum are typical. The mango, banana, banyan, *neem, pipal,* cassia, tamarind, coconut casuarina, sandalwood, rubber, teak, *sheesham,* bamboo, cinchona and eucalyptus are some of the tropical trees found in various areas.

FOOD . . . Some of the specialties are: in Calcutta *rossagolla* and *sandesh* (desserts); fish curry and rice; *shinghara* (meat or vegetable patties); in Delhi *tanduri* chicken and *nan* (oven-baked chicken and bread); *rogan josh* and *paratha* or *chapatti* (mutton and wheat pancakes); *Pulao* or *biryani* and *korma* (rice and mutton curry); *murgh* curry (spiced chicken); *kabab;* desserts—*kulfi, gulab jaman, halva.*

LANGUAGE . . . In dealing with managers and key personnel of hotels, you will encounter no difficulty when using English but Hindi is the official language.

LAUNDRY AND DRY CLEANING . . . Dry cleaners are available. Domestic launderers (*dhobis*) pick up and deliver your laundry. Quick service is available in good hotels, but check price list first.

LIQUOR . . . Tourist liquor permit is valid throughout the country; but of India's 343 districts, only 109 are "dry."

MEDICAL FACILITIES . . . There are many good doctors, surgeons, hospitals and nursing homes. Inquire at your hotel.

MOTION PICTURES . . . There are a number of movie theaters in Bombay, Madras, Calcutta and Delhi which are air-conditioned and comfortable. Shows are at set hours, and seats should be reserved.

MUSIC . . . Indian music on All-India Radio. Performances of Indian music are held during winter in larger cities.

NIGHT CLUBS AND CABARETS . . . Only Bombay, Calcutta and New Delhi have real nightclubs; however, many of the leading hotels have Western-style ballrooms and cabarets.

PHOTOGRAPHY . . . Supplies and facilities are available in the big cities. A tourist can bring in 12 plates or 25 rolls of film with a camera and 8 reels of film with a small movie camera, duty free.

RELIGION . . . Hindu, Jain and Sikh temples, Moslem mosques,

Catholic and Protestant churches, and in some areas Jewish synagogues.

RESTAURANTS ... In addition to the hotel dining rooms and bars, the following are the recommended restaurants: In Calcutta, *The Blue Fox, Moulin Rouge, Firpo's, Nanking, Mocambo, Sky Room, Amber, Kwality, Magnolia, Ferrazini, Prince's Lido, Trimcas, Maxims, Le Gourmet, Peiping* and *Waldorf*. In New Delhi, *Gaylords, Volga, Laguna, La Cabana, Standard, Kwality, York, La Boheme, Gufa, Mikado, Embassy, Wenger's*. In Delhi, *Moti Mahal, Khyber*; in Bombay, the Ambassador's *The Other Room*, Taj Mahal's *Rendezvous* and Ritz's *Little Hut* are best. Also good are *Gaylord, Airlines, Moka Bar, Bombelli's, Volga, Astoria's Venice, Napoli, Gourdon, The Horse Shoe* and *Tea Centre*. Specializing in Indian dishes are *Green's Gulmohr, Berry's, Khyber, Ali Baba* and *Kwality*.

SHOPS AND STORES ... In Calcutta, New Market, Bengal Home Industries Association, West Bengal Government Emporium, Handloom House, Kashmir Government Arts Emporium; in New Delhi, Central Cottage Industries Emporium, Handloom House, Kashmir Government Arts Emporium, U.P. Government Handicrafts Emporium, Rajasthan Government Handicrafts Emporium, Madras Handicrafts Emporium, Khadi Gram Udyog and shops in Connaught Place, Janpath and Chandni Chowk; in Bombay, Government fixed-price shops, Khadi and Village Industries Emporium, Handloom House, Kashmir Government Arts Emporium, Cottage Industries Emporium, U.P. Government Handicrafts Emporium; in Madras, Victoria Technical Institute, Cottage Industries Sales Emporium, Handloom House, Kashmir Government Arts Emporium.

SPECTATOR SPORTS ... Wrestling, hockey, soccer, cricket, football and tennis. Important tournaments held in all large cities attract big crowds. Horse racing in Calcutta, Bombay, Bangalore, Madras, Ootacamund and Poona.

SPORTS ... Golf, tennis, badminton, soccer, hockey, polo, cricket, swimming, *shikar* (hunting—big-game hunting trips can be arranged) and fishing. Some sports clubs have temporary memberships open to visitors. For swimming, India has some fine beaches, and there are a few good pools in Calcutta, Delhi, Bombay and Madras.

TIME ... Noon in Calcutta is 1:30 A.M. in New York.

TIPPING ... Tip luggage porters Rs .50 per load; Rs .50 per day to room boy; Rs .50 is usual tip for most small services. Rs. 25 to shoeshine boy. Keep plenty of small change handy for *baksheesh*. Taxi drivers are not tipped.

TRANSPORTATION ... There are metered taxis in most cities, but establish the fare before setting out in an unmetered taxi, a gharry or a rickshaw. Rates are low. Chauffeured private cars and guides may be hired in major cities, where there are also modern sightseeing bus tours. Air-conditioned buses run between Delhi and Agra (round trip $8.40). Indian Airlines flies to most tourist centers, but the most luxurious way to see most of India is with the special $118, 30-day railway ticket which permits unlimited travel in luxurious air-conditioned trains with sleeping accommodations and a choice of Indian or European meals (not included in fare) served in your compartment or in the dining car.

WATER ... It is wise to drink only boiled or bottled water.

WHAT TO BUY ... Silks, brocades, woven and printed textiles, jewelry, costume jewelry, ivory, wood carving (sandalwood, rosewood and walnut wood), articles made from horn, brass and copperware, silverware, *bidri* and other inlaid work, leather articles, lacquer work, toys, gold-and-silver-thread embroidery, lace, handbags, Jaipuri embroidered slippers. Government-controlled establishments, department stores and other well-known shops have fixed prices; you are expected to bargain briskly in the smaller shops.

WHAT TO WEAR ... Daytime dress is casual because of the high temperatures during all but the winter seasons. Seersucker, light cottons, dark or light linen—in short, washable fabrics. During the summer these are comfortable day or night. In winter, light tweed and flannel for Calcutta and heavy woolen clothing for Delhi are necessary. For the rainy season (mid-June to mid-October) you will need a good umbrella. In Bombay, light clothing is suitable the year round; Calcutta is quite formal, so men may find a dinner jacket useful.

WHERE TO GO—SIGHTSEEING ...

Calcutta ... Long the capital of British India, Calcutta is still the commercial metropolis of modern India. It has a population of 5,000,-000 and is a huge, sprawling, noisy city, teeming with life. The nerve center is Dalhousie Square, where tall, imposing buildings, Government offices and mercantile houses stand in a quadrangle around the placid waters of the reservoir. But the center of attraction is the famous Chowringhee, the wide avenue flanked on one side by shops, cinemas and fashionable restaurants, and on the other by the Maidan, which stretches as a vast expanse of green dotted with reservoirs, monuments and clusters of trees. Here are the playing fields where crowds gather to watch a hockey or football match. Here too are the Eden Gardens, famed as the cricketer's paradise.

Rising from the Maidan and overlooking the Chowringhee is the marble Victoria Memorial, built by the British. In its galleries are many objects of interest relating to British-Indian history, historical documents and paintings. The Hooghly, like the Thames, has lost some of its natural beauty due to the smoke of the factories that sprawl on its banks, but it is still appealing. Dakshineshwar Temple, where the great saint and yogi of the 19th century, Ramakrishna Paramahamsa, lived, and Belur Math, the monastery founded by his great disciple, Swami Vivekanand, are both on the banks of this river. A little farther away are the Botanical Gardens, which are well worth a visit. Among the sights in these gardens is an ancient banyan tree which has so spread itself that several hundred people can sit in its shade. Connecting the two banks of the river is the new Howrah Bridge, the third largest cantilever bridge in the world.

Among other sights of interest are Fort William, begun by Lord Clive in 1757; the Zoological Gardens; the Museum, the biggest in

India; the seemingly bejeweled Jain Temple, standing in a fascinating garden; and the Kalighat Temple, the oldest temple of Calcutta, which was there long before the city was founded. Trained guides are available at the Government Tourist Office, 13 Old Court House Street. Several companies offer sightseeing tours.

Delhi ... Delhi's most ancient sites and monuments, dating from India's epic age, emphasize the dynamic change in modern India's way of life and thought. The city has continuously been the seat of imperial power since the 10th century. Here many cities have risen and fallen; only their ruins mark the sites where they once stood. Old Delhi has many architectural masterpieces. The Red Fort, built 300 years ago, dominates the city and stands as a symbol of Mogul glory. Inside it are the relics of what was once the Imperial Palace of Shah Jahan, builder of the Taj Mahal. From the Fort to the Fatehpuri mosque runs the Chandni Chowk, once famous as the richest street in the world. A little to the south towers the famous mosque Jama Masjid, one of the largest in the world, and one of the noblest buildings in India. Conducted sightseeing bus tours are available.

New Delhi ... has a circular Parliament House and an imposing Central Secretariat, which stands at the approaches to the residence of the President of the Republic. On the right bank of the Yamuna is a hallowed spot—Rajghat, where the body of Mahatma Gandhi was cremated in 1948. The monument has become a national shrine. Prime Minister Nehru was cremated on the banks of the Yamuna in 1964. The modern Lakshmi Narayan Temple, opened by Mahatma Gandhi in 1937, and Jantar Mantar, an observatory with a unique set of 200-year-old-stone astronomical instruments, are also of interest. Trained guides are available at the Government of India Tourist Office at 88 Janpath. South and southwest of the city are the Tomb of Humayun, built in the 16th century of red sandstone inlaid with white marble; the Cyclopean ruins of 13th-century Tughlakabad, the capital of warrior kings, with its massive fort and the founder's imposing tomb; and the Qutb Minar, dating from the 12th century, another tower of victory, beautifully fashioned out of 700-year-old red sandstone, regarded as one of the most perfect towers of the world. Nearby is the famous rustproof Iron Pillar, dating from the 4th century A.D. Other points of interest are Isa Khan's tomb (15th century in style); Nizamuddin, the burial place of saints, princes and poets for over 3 centuries; Nawab Safdar Jung's tomb, the last Mogul monument of note (18th century); Haus Khas, fascinating ruins of a once-important university, and a 14th-century water reservoir.

Eastern India ... Santiniketan, 93 miles northwest of Calcutta, is the home of famous Visva Bharati, the international university founded by the poet Rabindranath Tagore. Darjeeling is a Himalayan hill station from which Mt. Kanchenjunga, the third highest peak in the world, and sometimes Mt. Everest, can be seen. Bhubaneswar, a city of ancient temples, is the new capital of Orissa. Nearby are the Jain and Buddhist rock-cut caves of Khandagiri and Udaygiri, and Asoka's rock edict (2nd Century B.C.) at Dhauli. Puri is well known for the Jagannath Temple and the annual Juggernaut car festival held in June or July. Fifty-one miles from Puri is Konarak, famous for the Sun Temple.

Nepal . . . See details on page 473.

Northern India . . . South of Delhi, about 3 hours by road or rail through extremely interesting country, is Agra, the city of the Taj Mahal. Besides this fabulous edifice of extraordinary beauty, other important sights are the Agra Fort, Emperor Akbar's magnificent mausoleum at Sikandra, the tomb of Itmad-ud-Daulah and Dayal Bagh. The new air-cooled hotel, *Clark's-Shiraz,* offers a view of the Taj from its sixth-floor terrace. Twenty-six miles from Agra on the way to Jaipur is Fatehpur Sikri, the abandoned Mogul capital city of palaces, which is in an excellent state of preservation. All of these date back to the 16th and 17th centuries. Benares (Varanasi), half-way between Delhi and Calcutta, is a Hindu pilgrim center, with the famous bathing and burning *ghats* along the Ganges. It is also the home of a famous university. About 6 miles from Benares is Sarnath, one of the great Buddhist centers, where the Buddha preached his first sermon. The pink city of Jaipur, an hour's flight from Delhi, is the capital of Rajasthan, in the heart of India's princely states. Udaipur is 2¼ hours from Delhi. Colorful scenes, picturesque vistas of elegant buildings, dream-palace rooms, elephant and camel processions—it's a page out of an Eastern fairy tale. Udaipur's *Lake Palace Hotel* is the luxurious, completely modernized former summer palace of the Maharana of Mewar. It stands on an exquisitely landscaped island in a lake. Single rates $15-$18, double $23-$28, including meals. Amber, 7 miles from Jaipur, is a picturesque medieval capital containing fabulous palace ruins amid lovely scenery.

About 150 miles northwest of New Delhi lies the much-publicized new capital of the Indian state of Punjab at Chandigarh. The first phase of this superbly designed city has risen out of the jungle at the foot of the Shiwalik range in only a few years and represents the collaboration of some of the world's foremost architects, including Le Corbusier of France. Sixty-four miles away is Bhakra Nangal Project, India's biggest multipurpose construction plan. The dam at Bhakra, when completed, will be the world's highest straight gravity dam.

Southern India . . . Madras has a beautiful beach on the Bay of Bengal, a good museum and attractive public buildings. Thirty-seven miles from Madras is the 7th-century seaport of Mahabalipuram, famous for its monolithic rock-cut temples. Madura to the south is noted for the great Meenakshi Temple, and Tanjore for the Brihadeswara Temple and Art Gallery. Ootacamund is known as the "Queen of Hill Stations." The enchanting Brindavan Gardens are only 13 miles from Mysore. Nearby is Srirangapatnam, the former capital of Mysore State, with Tippu Sultan's fort, mosque, and palace. Belur and Halebid, about 120 miles west of Mysore, are famous for their elaborately sculptured temples. Hampi is the ruined capital of the famous Vijayanagar Empire. Jog Falls is one of the highest waterfalls in the world. Trivandrum has a lovely beach, a famous art gallery and

India's modern railways and highways make shooting locales easily accessible but then elephants take over for stalking tigers deep into the jungle.

In New Delhi, the Lakshmi Narayan Temple, a modern blend of Eastern and Western styles of architecture, was opened by Mahatma Gandhi in 1937.

museum, and is well known for its ivory work. Ernakulam, across the harbor from Cochin, is famous for its backwaters, fringed by Hindu, Moslem, Christian and Jewish settlements. At the Periyar Wild Life Sanctuary are wild animals in their natural surroundings. Kanya Kumari (Cape Comorin) is the southernmost tip of India, where the waters of the Arabian Sea, the Bay of Bengal and the Indian Ocean meet.

Bombay... Known as Mumbai hundreds of years ago, this city on the Arabian Sea is called the Gateway of India. There is an actual gateway built on the waterfront to commemorate the visit of King George V and Queen Mary in 1911. It is now used for ceremonial landings and departures. The island of Bombay is one of the most important centers in India and is linked with the world by its modern harbor, the Santa Cruz airport, and good overseas communication. Since the division of India and Pakistan in 1947, when many Hindus moved from Pakistan, Bombay has grown rapidly so it is now nearly 5,000,000. Reported to be the most cosmopolitan city in the East, Bombay has much appeal for the tourist. Places of interest include the Prince of Wales Museum, a stately, domed building with sections featuring arts, archaeology and natural history; the Jehangir Art Gallery; the Raja Bai Tower of the Bombay University Library, with a splendid view of the city; Marine Drive, in the modern residential area, leading to Malabar Hill, which faces the Arabian Sea. The view from here, popularly called "The Queen's Necklace," is magnificent—especially at night, when it reminds one of the French Riviera. The Hanging Gardens and Kamla Nehru Park on the slopes of Malabar Hill are most attractive. The Terrace Garden is noted for its fine example of topiary art—the trees and shrubs have been trained and trimmed into the shapes of a variety of animals. The Mahalakshmi Temple, dedicated to Lakshmi, goddess of wealth and plenty, is a popular place of Hindu pilgrimage. Near the temple is a Moslem shrine built 500 yards from the mainland on rocks which are completely submerged at high tide.

Other points of interest in Bombay: The Mahalakshmi Race Course, one of the finest in the East, where races are held on weekends and holidays from October to March; the Victoria Gardens with the Bombay Zoo, 20 minutes by car from Hotel Taj Mahal; Crawford Market for fresh fruits, vegetables and fish on Dadabhoy Naorojee Road, with dozens of nearby shops selling everything from pots and pans to expensive jewelry; the Pherozshah Mehta Road and the Colaba Causeway, also shopping areas for Indian goods. Most shops have fixed prices, but bargaining goes on in pavement-shops. It is advisable to go out shopping with someone who knows the city.

Near Crawford Market is a fascinating part of Bombay, with Hindu and Jain temples and Moslem mosques in the midst of narrow lanes and teeming with people of varied origin—Parsees, Gujaratis, Maharashtrians, Tamils, Malayalis, Sikhs, Bengalis and others. Each retains his regional individuality of dress, language and customs. Conducted sightseeing bus tours are available in Bombay. Except during monsoon, there is regular ferry service to the island of Elephanta, 6 miles southeast of Bombay. Here are the fabulous 8th-century cave temples containing huge rock deities. The Ajanta and Ellora rock-hewn temple caves may be reached by weekend bus excursions out of Bombay; no trip to India is complete without seeing these astonishing sculptures. Good rest houses at both sites.

Kashmir ... Although disputed territory politically, this paradise for tourists is a perfect jewel bordering India, Pakistan and Tibet. The capital city of Srinagar (population 284,753) is a 3-hour flight from Delhi. From mid-May through October is the best time for a visit.

The incredibly lovely Vale of Kashmir lies at an elevation of 6,000 feet. It is 80 miles long and no more than 25 miles wide, and is completely surrounded by snow-capped mountains. Srinagar lies nearly in the center of the valley on the Jhelum River and Dal Lake. American Plan hotels are *Nedou's* (from $6 single, $11.60 double) and the *Oberoi Palace Hotel*, modernized former home of the Maharaja of Kashmir, with its own golf course and view of Dal Lake; single from $9.50, double from $15.80, American Plan. Enchanting Kashmiri houseboats can be rented completely furnished. The largest models, which can accommodate 6 adults and 4 children, cost about $5 per person a day, which includes meals and the services of 4 servants. *Shikaras* (taxi-boats) are fun for sightseeing on the lake and river, and some also carry provisions and handicrafts to the houseboats like floating shops. Mosques and fairy-tale gardens of Mogul emperors beautify Srinagar, and idyllic Shalimar, "the abode of love," is only 10 miles from the capital. Lovely wood carvings, embroideries, silverware and Kashmiri shawls are sold at fixed prices at the Government-supervised Kashmir Arts Emporium and the Central Market. Srinagar has both a Catholic and a Protestant church. Movies in English at the *Regal Cinema*. Guest memberships are available at the Srinagar Golf Club.

Kashmir's superb hunting and fishing are major attractions. Licenses may be obtained from the game warden in Srinagar, where tents and equipment may be rented from several different agencies. Buses provide adequate transportation to resort centers. Gulmarg, 8,700 feet above sea level and 29 miles from Srinagar, has 3 fine golf courses, is in ideal mountain hiking country; skiing from Christmas to Easter. The *Golf View* and *Nedou's* are modern hotels; about $5 single, including meals. Pahalgam (elevation 7,000 feet) is 60 miles from Srinagar, in lovely Liddar Valley, and a favorite with campers.

SOURCES OF FURTHER INFORMATION ... Government of India Tourist Offices with qualified guides are located in principal Indian cities. There are information offices at 19 East 49th St., New York; 685 Market St., San Francisco; and 177-179 King St., Toronto, Canada. Pan American offices at 42 Chowringhee Road, Calcutta (Tel. 44-3251), Imperial Hotel, New Delhi (Tel. 4-8717), Taj Mahal Hotel, Bombay (Tel. 21-1063).

A blend of Persian and Indian design makes the marble Taj Mahal at Agra one of the world's loveliest buildings.

INDONESIA

SOUTH CHINA SEA

Singapore BRUNEI SABAH *PACIFIC OCEAN*
Medan SARAWAK
Padang BORNEO
SUMATRA CELEBES
Palembang
DJAKARTA Djogjakarta WEST IRAN
Bandung
INDIAN OCEAN JAVA
BALI

WEATHER IN DJAKARTA—Lat. S6°10′—Alt. 25′

	JAN.	FEB.	MAR.	APR.	MAY	JUNE	JULY	AUG.	SEPT.	OCT.	NOV.	DEC.
Average Temp.	79°	79°	80°	81°	81°	81°	80°	80°	80°	81°	81°	80°
Days of Rain	20	19	16	12	9	8	6	4	6	9	13	16

LOCATION ... This group of more than 3,000 islands extends along the equator between Asia and Australia south of Malaysia.

POPULATION ... Estimated at over 104,366,000.

SIZE ... The land area is 575,893 square miles.

GOVERNMENT ... A republic.

CAPITAL ... Djakarta, population about 3,000,000.

HOW TO GET THERE ... By Pan American Jet Clipper across the Pacific, via Singapore, to Djakarta (also spelled Jakarta). Elapsed time counting stopovers about 26¾ hours from Los Angeles.

ACCOMMODATIONS ... The luxurious, air-conditioned Intercontinental *Hotel Indonesia* has a swimming pool, night club, Indonesian and European specialties in its 5 restaurants; single from $12, double from $16, in dollars only, European Plan. Other Djakarta hotels are the *Hotel Duta Indonesia* and the *Transaera*, with single rates from $7. People traveling alone may have to share rooms in hotels in smaller towns. Hotels add 20% to bills for service and taxes.

ARTS ... Don't miss visiting Djakarta's Museum, the finest of its kind of Southeast Asia—a wonderful ethnographical collection of arts and crafts from the islands, and old Chinese porcelains.

BALLET ... The world-famous Balinese dances and ballet are a delight of exotic costumes and gamelan music. The great Ramayana classical dance drama is given near Djogjakarta annually from June through October.

BANKS ... Currency exchange facilities banks, at Kemajoran airport and Hotel Indonesia.

CIGARETTES ... *Commodore* cigarettes are popular with tourists, and cost about 1/6 as much as American brands.

CLIMATE . . . The tropical heat throughout the islands is tempered by frequent showers and sea breezes. Mountain resorts such as Bandung are delightfully cool.

COMMUNICATIONS . . . Rates change, but current costs are Rps. 64 per word for a day-rate cablegram to the U.S., and Rps. 2500 for a 3-minute phone call. Airletters are Rps. 75.

CURRENCY . . . There are 100 sen in 1 rupiah. The rate of exchange, which fluctuates, is presently Rps. 4000 to U.S. $1.

CUSTOMS REGULATIONS AND DOCUMENTS REQUIRED FOR UNITED STATES CITIZENS . . . You will need a passport, visa, and smallpox and cholera vaccination certificates. Duty-free allowances are 200 cigarettes, 50 cigars, or 2 lbs. tobacco, 2 bottles of liquor (one partially consumed). Be sure your foreign currency (limit U.S. $100) is properly recorded to avoid difficulty in taking it out.

DRUGSTORES . . . Mostly European pharmaceuticals.

ELECTRIC CURRENT . . . 110-130 volts, 50 cycles, most places.

FAUNA . . . Varying with the island, there are tigers and panthers, elephants, single and twin-horned rhinoceros, monkeys, orangutans and gibbons, wild bear, the unique dwarf deer, crocodiles and giant lizards up to 9 feet long; parrots, birds of paradise and the curious casuaris bird.

FLORA . . . Flowers grow in great profusion, notably the fragrant frangipani, scarlet hibiscus, many varieties of orchids; banyan trees, coconut and bamboo. The Botanical Gardens in Bogor have one of the largest and finest collections in the world.

FOOD . . . European, Indonesian and Chinese foods are served in the big restaurants. Indonesian dishes include *gado-gado* (a mixture of all kinds of vegetables with peanut sauce), *nasi goreng* (fried rice with exotic spices, slivers of ham, shrimp and chicken), *gudeg* (jackfruit with eggs, chicken and bean cakes) and *rijsttafel*. Mangoes, mangosteens, papayas, bananas, pineapples and *djeroeks* (oranges) are among local fruits.

LANGUAGE . . . Indonesian is the national language, derived from Malay. English is spoken by hotel and restaurant personnel.

LAUNDRY AND DRY CLEANING . . . Excellent at Hotel Indonesia; quality and speed elsewhere are not the best.

LIQUOR . . . In the big cities most foreign brands are available, not expensive. Bars are open from 10 A.M. until midnight.

MEDICAL FACILITIES . . . No American hospitals, but fully equipped hospitals with good doctors and surgeons in all major cities.

PHOTOGRAPHY . . . Equipment and film are available, developing only fair.

RELIGION . . . The national religion is Islam although Buddhism and Hinduism are prevalent in some areas. There are also many Catholics and Protestants.

RESTAURANTS . . . *Seno Restaurant, Chez Mario, Duta Bar and Restaurant* (air-conditioned), *Atase, Wisma Nusantara, Airport Restaurant* have European food. There are also good restaurants for Chinese food. Hotel Indonesia has the *Java Room* (American-style coffee shop), *Ramayana Room* (international cuisine), *Nirwana Supper Club*, the *Orientale* (Chinese and Asiatic specialties).

SPECTATOR SPORTS ... Football, tennis, badminton, swimming.

SPORTS ... Fishing, golf, yachting, hunting, surfing.

TIPPING ... 500 rupiahs for average load of luggage. A pack of American cigarettes is a welcome tip for other services.

TRANSPORTATION ... Airline, air-conditioned trains, taxis, auto rentals. Travel agencies have trips all around Java and Bali.

WATER ... Generally safe in cities and resort hotels.

WHAT TO BUY ... Javanese and Balinese woodcarvings. Silverware and batik. Alligator and snakeskin goods, paintings.

WHAT TO WEAR ... One should wear very lightweight clothing.

WHERE TO GO—SIGHTSEEING ...

Bogor ... An hour's drive from Djakarta, has a famous botanical garden with hundreds of thousands of varieties of tropical vegetation. Thirty miles from Bogor is the Puntjak area (4,800 feet with invigorating climate) where Hotel Indonesia operates the *Riung Gunung* restaurant. The area is Djakarta's playground, studded with small hotels, restaurants and swimming pools.

Bandung ... The capital of West Java, a half hour by air from Djakarta, is one of the most delightful cities of the Far East (population 952,000), beautifully laid out on a high plateau surrounded by mountains covered with rice fields, cinchona and tea plantations and forests. The local people (Sundanese) are noted for their infectious gaiety and colorful dress. Visit one of the markets, and see the remarkable building which houses the technical school of the University of Indonesia. Among the hotels are the *Savoy Homan* and the *Preanger*. The 6,300-foot Tangkuban Prahu volcano is nearby.

Island of Bali ... "The Paradise of the Pacific" should be included in your ticket before you leave home. This densely populated little island has all the charm and spectacular beauty associated with it. The 10,000-foot Gunung Agung (Peak of Bali) is the island's Mt. Fuji. Bali-Hinduism, the important factor in the people's lives, is evident in their wide variety of colorful ceremonies and celebrations, and the omnipresent temples. In the capital of Denpasar is the *Bali-Hotel*. The hotels *Bali Beach, Segara Beach* and *Sindhu Beach* are on the sea, 20 minutes from town. Single rates average $5 a day with meals.

Djogjakarta (Djogja) and Solo ... Are the most typically "Javanese" cities of Java, known for their exquisite silverware and batik. Visit the magnificent Borobudur, one of the world's greatest Buddhist sanctuaries, 24 miles from Djogja. Two miles from Borobudur is the Mendut Temple, which contains an indescribably beautiful statue of a seated Buddha, flanked by Boddhisatvas. The 9th-century Prambana Temple is the elaborate background for the dance and drama festival.

SOURCES OF FURTHER INFORMATION ... Pan American in Hotel Indonesia (Tel. 40020). The Indonesian Consulate is at 5 East 68th St., New York, N.Y. 10021.

JAPAN

WEATHER IN TOKYO—Lat. N35°42'—Alt. 30'

Temp.	JAN.	FEB.	MAR.	APR.	MAY	JUNE	JULY	AUG.	SEPT.	OCT.	NOV.	DEC.
Low	30°	31°	36°	47°	54°	63°	69°	72°	66°	54°	43°	33°
High	47°	47°	53°	63°	70°	76°	83°	85°	79°	69°	60°	51°
Average	39°	39°	45°	55°	62°	70°	76°	79°	73°	62°	52°	42°
Days of Rain	7	8	13	14	14	16	15	13	17	14	10	7

LOCATION . . . Japan consists of 4 islands and over 3,000 small islets which lie in the North Pacific Ocean off the coast of China.

CHARACTERISTICS . . . Japan welcomes tourists, and gives them a wonderful opportunity to see fascinating glimpses of Japanese culture, arts and architecture. The people are eager for friendly relationships with the Western world. A wide variety of tours for visitors are packed with wonderful things to see and do.

POPULATION . . . 97,190,000.

SIZE . . . A curving archipelago, 1,300 miles long, roughly the shape of California but slightly smaller in area (142,726 square miles).

CAPITAL . . . Tokyo, population 10,695,593.

GOVERNMENT . . . A constitutional monarchy ruled over by an Emperor and a Cabinet. There is a Parliament of two chambers.

HOW TO GET THERE . . . By Pan American Jet Clipper to Tokyo from United States West Coast via "Great Circle" route 13 hours; via Honolulu, about 14½ hours (elapsed time); 4 hours from Hong Kong. Tokyo is on Pan American's Round-the-World Route. By ship the journey from the United States West Coast takes about 12 to 14 days.

ACCOMMODATIONS . . . There are excellent western style hotels, which the average tourist may prefer. In Tokyo, there are the famous *Imperial Hotel, New Otani, Tokyo Prince, Hotel New Japan, Tokyo*

Hilton, Nikkatsu, Palace and *Okura,* with rates averaging $10.50 single, $16 double. Less expensive westernized hotels include the *Daiichi, Marunouchi, Shiba Park, Ginza Tokyu, Kokusai Kanko.* Rates average $7.80 single, $11 double. Rates are for European Plan (meals not included), exclusive of 10% service charge and 10% tax. Foreign visitors are often delighted with *ryokan,* Japanese-style hotels, in which rooms are usually entire suites with private verandahs; interior walls are sliding paper screens, beds are thick, soft floor mats, and meals are served in your suite. Rates $9-$17 for one, including breakfast and dinner, plus 15% service charge and tips.

ARTS . . . Japanese art is too vast a subject to discuss in detail. Japanese paintings and sculptures are admired the world over. The Japanese Art Academy in Tokyo holds an exhibit every autumn. Nihon Bijutsu-in (Institute of Japanese Art) holds private exhibitions, as does the Nika-kai, or modern, group. The Tokyo National Museum, which has branches in Nara and Kyoto, houses wonderful treasures of Japanese and Oriental culture. The Tokyo Metropolitan Fine Art Gallery, the National Museum of Modern Art and the Bridgestone Gallery are also noteworthy. Exhibitions are also held at the city's leading department stores. Many national treasures may be seen at the temples and shrines. Also interesting are the Memorial Picture Gallery in Meiji Shrine Outer Garden and the Folkcraft Museum at Komaba, Tokyo. The Kamakura Art Museum, one hour by electric train from Tokyo, is visited by many.

BALLET . . . Several local ballet troupes perform from time to time. Western ballet performances by visiting foreign artists are immensely popular.

BANKS . . . In Tokyo: First National City Bank, Chase Manhattan Bank, Bank of America, American Express, Hong Kong and Shanghai Banking Corp., The Chartered Bank, Netherlands Trading Society, Bank of Tokyo, Dai-ichi Bank, Fuji Bank, Sumitomo Bank, Mitsui Bank, Mitsubishsi Bank, among others.

CALENDAR OF HOLIDAYS . . . Japan puts its heart into festivals. Of national importance are: New Year's Celebration, January 1 to 3; Adults' Day, January 15; Spring Equinox Day, March 21 or 22; Emperor's Birthday, April 29; Constitution Day, May 3; Children's Day, May 5; Autumn Equinox Day, September 23 or 24; Culture Day, November 3; Thanksgiving Day, November 23. Other traditional events include: Bean Throwing Ceremony, February 4; Doll Festival, March 3; Floral Festival, April 8; Boys' Festival, May 5; Star Festival, July 7 or August 7; Feast of the Lanterns, honoring the dead, July 13 to 15.

CIGARETTES AND TOBACCO . . . Some American brands of cigarettes are available at about 50¢ a pack. *Hilite* (20¢) is a good Japanese filter brand. Cigars are available in limited supply.

CLIMATE . . . Similar to that of the middle belt of the United States, although it seldom gets either as hot or as cold. Spring and autumn are the busiest tourist seasons, but fine winter resorts lure skiers.

CLUBS... Rotary and Lions Clubs are very active in Japan and it is possible to attend in all the main cities.

COMMON COURTESIES AND LOCAL CUSTOMS... All traffic moves on the left. Remove your shoes before entering a Japanese-style hotel, private home or temple. *Arigato* is "thank you." The Japanese never use soap in the bathtub. The custom is to lather, then rinse, after which comes a long, hot soak in tub or big open bath.

COMMUNICATIONS... A 3-minute phone call to the States costs 4.320 yen on weekdays; 3.240 yen on Sundays. A 10-word cablegram is 1.200 yen. Airmail postage rates to the U.S. are 40 yen for a postcard, 50 yen for an airletter form, 80 yen for a 10-gram letter. Local phone calls are 10 yen.

CURRENCY... The monetary unit is the yen. The basic rate of exchange is 360 yen to one United States dollar. Foreign currency can be exchanged at the airport, stores, hotels and designated banks. There is no limit on the amount of foreign currency that may be brought in, but only 36,000 yen ($100) may be reconverted into dollars.

CUSTOMS REGULATIONS AND DOCUMENTS REQUIRED FOR UNITED STATES CITIZENS... Passport, smallpox vaccination certificate. No visa needed for tourist visit under 72 hours with *onward* transportation from same airport; visa required for all U.S.-Japan-U.S. roundtrips and business trips. Cholera vaccination required of visitors from infected local areas. 200 cigarettes, or 50 cigars, or ½ lb. tobacco, 3 quarts of liquor permitted duty free. See under WHAT TO BUY regarding tax exemption forms.

DRUGSTORES... Aside from many Japanese drugstores, there are the fully stocked American Pharmacy and the Rexall Drug Co., both located in Tokyo, where you can obtain American products.

ELECTRIC CURRENT... 100 volts, A.C., in local hotels and homes. There is no need to use special transformer plugs.

FAUNA... Boar, deer, pheasant, quail, snipe, wild geese.

FLORA... Cherry and plum blossoms, tea, persimmons, loquat, figs, and thousands of flowers including the lotus, wisteria, azalea, camellia, chrysanthemum (which forms the crest for the Imperial Family). Japan is the land of flowers, and flower arrangement is a fundamental accomplishment of Japanese women. In Japan it is a high art, called *ikebana*, and there are special *ikebana* classes for foreigners.

FOOD... Daintiness is the characteristic of a truly Japanese meal. Japanese cooks take great pride in having the table and the food look appetizing and attractive. There are many excellent Western-style restaurants, and Japanese beef is considered among the best to be found anywhere. The main native dishes to try are *sukiyaki,* which is beef and vegetables cooked at the table; *tempura,* deep-fried sea food and vegetables; and *chawanmushi,* chicken, fish and vegetables steamed with egg custard. Fresh raw fish, broiled mushrooms, dried seaweed, bean curd are also worth trying. Green tea is the national nonalcoholic drink. *Kabayaki,* boiled eels, is considered a delicacy.

GAMBLING ... Horse racing from March to December. The most noted track is Tokyo's Fuchu, with Yodo race course at Kyoto being next largest. Bicycle racing and motorboat racing are also popular.

LANGUAGE ... English is understood in hotels, restaurants and stores. Excellent guide service is available, but you can get around on your own with very little trouble.

LAUNDRY AND DRY CLEANING ... Readily available and of good quality. Laundry service is fast; dry cleaning ordinarily takes about two days, but can be expedited.

LIQUOR ... *Sake,* a rice wine, is the national drink. Japanese beer is excellent. *Suntory* is the admirable local equivalent of Scotch. *Tory* and other lower proof whiskies are also good and even cheaper. Imported liquors are abundant, but expensive.

MEDICAL FACILITIES ... There are fine hospitals all over Japan, as well as fully qualified American and British doctors.

MOTION PICTURES ... There are theaters which show American and European films besides the native productions. The *Yuraku-za, Hibiya Eiga Gekijo* and *Piccadilly Theater* are some of the important theaters in Tokyo showing pictures with original sound tracks. *Theater Tokyo* shows Cinerama films, and the *Nichigeki* and *Kokusai* feature attractive girls' revues.

MUSIC ... The Japanese are very much interested in all types of Western music. Symphony orchestras hold regular concerts in the winter season. Instrumental and vocal recitals are daily occurrences, and there are frequent visits by foreign artists of international stature. The Fujiwara Opera Company is the pioneer of Japanese opera troupes. Popular dances and jazz bands are numerous. Indigenous Japanese music differs greatly from Occidental music, but the skill of the instrumental performers may still be appreciated. In Tokyo, such performances usually take place at the *Nissei Theater, Sankei Hall,* or *Bunkakaikan Hall.*

NIGHT CLUBS AND CABARETS ... Tokyo has hundreds of cafés, bars and many very good night clubs such as *New Latin Quarter, The Queen Bee, Crown,* among others. There is a cover charge of from 1,000 up to 3,000 yen, depending upon the elaborateness of floor shows, plus a 10% waiter's charge and 15% entertainment tax. Hostess charges average 1,000 yen per hour. Some of the larger hotels have dance orchestras, too. *Ochaya,* or tea houses, are where to find performances by geisha girls, the delightful professional entertainers.

PHOTOGRAPHY ... Both black-and-white and color film are manufactured locally, and American brands may be obtained at leading stores. Prices of Japanese films are roughly equivalent to the film prices in America, but imported film may cost 30 to 40% more. Black-and-white and color film processing is available almost anywhere. Many shops (identified by "DPE" signs) offer 24-hour service.

RELIGION ... There are many religious denominations. The three major religions are Buddhism, Shintoism and Christianity.

RESTAURANTS ... All major hotels have dining rooms that

serve familiar western food. Besides these, the following are among the best places to eat in Tokyo: *Tokyo Kaikan Prunier* for seafood; the *Suehiro Steak House, Crescent, Frank's* for steaks and chops; *Okahan, Yugiri* for *sukiyaki* dinners; *Chinzanso* (with lovely garden) and *Fujino* for Japanese barbecue dinners; *Inagiku, Ten-ichi* for *tempura* dishes; *China House, Sun-ya,* or *Liu Yuan* for Chinese food. Prices vary widely, but range from under $1 in locally-popular spots to well over $10 in touristy places.

SHOPS AND STORES ... Japan is a shopper's paradise. Ginza Street in Tokyo is the main shopping center. Principal department stores are: Matsuya, Mitsukoshsi, Matsuzakaya, Shirokiya, and Takashimaya. There are many small shops, too. Interesting ones are Watanabe Woodblock Prints and Mikimoto Pearl Store, both on the Ginza. Fabulous shopping arcades in the Imperial and other hotels. Large stores are open from 10 A.M. to 5.30 P.M.; small shops to 10 P.M. Department stores close one day a week, but not all on the same one. See under *What to Buy.* Make sure that you carry your "Record of Purchases of Commodities Tax-Exempt for Export," obtained from the Japanese Customs office when you enter Japan.

SPECTATOR SPORTS ... *Sumo,* Japanese wrestling, *Judo* exhibits, baseball (tremendously popular—games are played in Tokyo at the stadium at Meiji Shrine grounds and the Korakuen Stadium), horse racing (notably at Fuchu track in suburban Tokyo and Yodo track in Kyoto), swimming meets, football, tennis matches and archery. There are numerous annual meetings and tournaments.

SPORTS ... There are golf, tennis, yachting, swimming, skiing, hunting, skating, fishing and bowling in various parts of the country.

THEATERS ... Japan's native theatrical art is centuries old. The traditional theater is divided into Noh, Kabuki and puppet drama. The Noh, originally a religious dance in the 14th century, developed into a highly stylized dramatic form dealing with historical and Buddhist subjects. The actors in the chief roles wear masks and elaborate costumes as they perform one of the 242 Noh plays which survive. There are 5 schools of Noh actors in Japan. The Kabuki—unlike the Noh, which was for the aristocracy—was for the people. Kabuki plays are similar to European drama except that dialogue is accompanied by musical instruments or an orchestra, and all the women's roles are played by men. You can see Kabuki at the Kabuki Theater in Tokyo. An all-puppet theater, the Bunrakuza, is at Osaka. In April the Cherry Dance presentations at the theaters are worth seeing. There is modern Japanese theater, too; revues and light opera are popular and who could resist the Shochiku or Takarazuka Girls Troupes?

TIME ... 17 hours later than United States Pacific Standard Time.

TIPPING ... 50 to 100 yen per bag for the boy who carries your bags. The 10 to 15% that restaurants, hotels and *ryokan* add to your bill is sufficient tip. Japan is unique in that only bar girls and geishas expect—or even want—tips!

TRANSPORTATION ... There are modern tramways, streetcars, motor buses, and subways in Tokyo and other cities, and superb electric trains to major places, such as the 125 m.p.h. Tokyo-Osaka run. Taxis and cars for hire, are readily obtainable. Rates are less than those in the United States. The Japanese National Railways, Japan Air Lines and All Nippon Airways operate throughout the country.

WATER . . . Safe to drink in cities and resorts.

WHAT TO BUY . . . Tortoise shell from Nagasaki, porcelain and cloisonné from Nagoya, lacquerware from Kyoto, silk, cultured pearls, embroidered kimonos and obis, ceramics, Japanese prints and wood-cuts, wonderful silk damasks and many other things. Tourists in possession of a "Record of Purchase of Commodities Tax Exempt for Export" form, which may be obtained on entry to Japan, may buy the following articles free of tax at designated shops: pearls and articles decorated with pearls; articles made of precious metals; ivory and cloisonné ware; furs; cameras; articles used for room decoration; lighters and other smoking articles made of metal or lacquer work; ceramic ware; personal ornaments made of metal or lacquer work; woodblock prints; dolls.

WHAT TO WEAR . . . Let the season of the year determine this. In winter women want furs, men will need overcoats. In spring, lighter weight clothes and in summer, cottons, sports clothes. Be sure to take a raincoat. You won't need evening clothes unless you are being entertained by diplomatic society.

WHERE TO GO—SIGHTSEEING . . .

Tokyo . . . Everything is so different, so novel, that just going out into the streets of Tokyo is a sightseeing tour in itself. You will want to see the Imperial Palace even though the inner enclosure is not open to the public except on January 2 and April 29. Walk or drive through Hibiya Park opposite the Imperial Hotel where the azaleas bloom in May and the chrysanthemums in November. In Shiba Park is the famous Zojo-ji Temple and 1,092-foot Tokyo Tower. The National Stadium at Meiji Shrine Outer Garden was the site of the 1964 Olympic Games. Ueno Park, noted for its cherry blossoms, contains the National Museum, the Zoological Gardens, the Metropolitan Fine Art Gallery, the Imperial Library and a monument to General Grant. City sightseeing buses with English-speaking guides run morning, afternoon and night tours. You can make arrangements through travel agencies to visit families in such cities as Tokyo, Yokohama, Kyoto and Kobe. These people welcome foreign visitors into their homes, and it is a memorable way for you to know the Japanese way of living.

Side Trips . . . There are packaged tours which cover parts of Japan which are most interesting to foreigners. For example, starting at Tokyo you can go to Fuji-Hakone-Izu National Park and Atami Hot Springs Resort. You pass through Kamakura, site of the shrine of the Great Buddha, or Daibutsu. You may climb to shoulder level inside the Buddha. A little farther on is Hachiman Shrine in a grove of cherry trees. If you are on a tour you will proceed to Hakone Mountains to the *Fujiya*, one of Japan's most elegant hotels, at Miyanoshita, high in the mountains; or to the *Hakone* on the shores of Lake Hakone; or the new *Mt. Fuji* resort on Lake Yamanaka. Then on to Atami over the Ten Provinces Pass, from which you get a wonderful view of Mt. Fuji. The *Atami Hotel* and *Atami New Fujiya Hotel* are good here.

Kyoto . . . Known as the "classic" city of Japan, Kyoto is reached by air or express train from Tokyo. Western hotels are the *Kyoto* in the central shopping district, *Kyoto International* near Nijo Castle, and *Kyoto Station Hotel* near the railway station; the *Miyako Hotel* overlooks the city from a hill. Kyoto's fabulous shrines and temples, "Teapot Lane," bazaars and shops are famous. Visit the Imperial Palace, where emperors were crowned. The Higashi and Nishi Honganji are among the country's most elaborate Buddhist temples. The vermilion-lacquered Heian Shrine in Okazaki Park is set in a superb garden. Every October, this is the site of festivals, and endless processions of Shintoists, dressed in historical costumes, pay homage here. Nijo Castle is known for the elegance of its decorations and its garden. Daigoji Temple retains a 5-storied pagoda built in 907.

Nara . . . This gem of a city is considered the cradle of Japanese art and culture. Visit the Kasuga Shrine, hung with metal lanterns; Todaiji Temple, housing the immense bronze Buddha (71½ feet high) that was cast in 749; Horyuji Temple, founded in 607 and probably the world's oldest wooden structure, which contains a priceless collection of art treasures; the Kofukuji Temple, with the 13th-century wooden image of the Muchaku-Bosatsu; the lovely Deer Park where tame deer roam. Stay at the *Nara Hotel*.

Osaka . . . Near Nara and Kyoto, Osaka is host to the annual spring International Music and Arts Festival. Shinsaibashisuji and Midosuji Boulevards will enchant you with fine stores, colorful bazaars and amusement places. Osaka Castle, illuminated at night, is an amazing structure with walls of huge granite pieces, and tiny bridges spanning its moat. For remarkable puppetry, visit Bunrakuza Theater; Kabuki plays are at the Shin-Kabukiza Theater. Osaka's Shitennoji Temple and Sumiyoshi Shrine are both regarded as national treasures. The largest commercial and industrial city, next to Tokyo, Osaka caters to foreign guests and has special night tours of the sights. Excellent hotels include the *New Osaka, Osaka Grand, New Hankyu, Osaka Royal, International Hotel*. Rates average $8 single, $13 double.

Nikko . . . A mountain resort, about 90 miles north of Tokyo, Nikko is a National Park famous for its lovely lakes and waterfalls, and its Toshogu Shrine rich in gold and silver leaf and lacquer. The Yomeimon Gate, leading into the shrine, is one of the most exquisite structures in Japan. Notice the carvings of the famous Three Wise Monkeys on the stable beyond the gate. A few miles from Nikko is Lake Chuzenji (4,194 feet above sea level), which spills in a sheer, 330-foot drop to form the Kegon Waterfalls. The lake offers the best trout fishing in Japan, and good swimming, too. In autumn, the scenery here is incomparable. In winter, this is a lively ski resort. The *Nikko-Kanaya* hotel has a swimming pool and ice-skating rink. The *Lake-Side* and *Nikko-Kanko* are also year-round resort hotels.

Kobe . . . on the Inland Sea, 20 miles west of Osaka, is a city backed by the Rokko Mountain Range. There is an 18-hole golf course at the top of Mt. Rokko. Within easy reach of the city are the beautiful Suma, Maiko and Akashi beaches. The *Oriental, New Port* and *Kobe International* hotels are convenient; rates about $6 single, $11 double. From Kobe (or Osaka) take a comfortable Kansai Kisen cruise ship through the lovely Inland Sea National Park with its thousand pine-green islets.

Miyajima . . . "Shrine Island," a perfect jewel of the Inland Sea, is famous for cherry blossoms and the vermilion-lacquered Itsukushima Shrine. Its airy galleries, at high tide, seem to float in the sea. You can stay at the *Iwaso* or *Kamefuku ryokan*. One hour from the island, by train and ferry, is the rebuilt atom-bombed city of Hiroshima. There are guides for sightseeing tours.

Beppu . . . Southern terminus of the Osaka-Beppu Inland Sea route, Beppu is the gateway to the southernmost island of Kyushu, and is a sensationally lovely resort on a hill sloping to the Sea. Hot spring mineral baths are piped into hotels, and there are hot sand baths on the beach. Motorbuses make tours around the many steaming "hells" (boiling ponds). Visits to volcanic Mt. Aso, Nagasaki, oldest international trading port in Japan, and many other points of interest on Kyushu are recommended.

Nagoya . . . 75 miles east of Kyoto, Nagoya is the center of Japanese porcelain-making, and the Noritake chinaware factory may be visited. The picturesque Nagoya-jo (castle) has two valuable golden dolphins. The *Hotel New Nagoya, Miyako, International* and *Nagoya Kanko* are the most modern hotels. Ise Jingu, Japan's most sacred Shinto shrine, and Shima Peninsula, dotted with pearl culturing farms, are just a few hours by train from Nagoya or Osaka. Toba's Pearl Island, owned by the Mikimoto Pearl Co., welcomes thousands of foreign visitors every year. Gifu, about 30 minutes from Nagoya by electric train, draws visitors to see the unique cormorant fishing, which takes place on the Nagara River from May 11 to October 15. Besides many fine Japanese inns, Gifu has the western style *Nagaragawa Hotel*.

Hokkaido . . . On this sparsely-populated, northernmost Japanese island, you'll find the Ainus, aborigines who have no racial affiliation with the Japanese. From October to April, the mountains of Hokkaido attract ardent skiers. Sapporo, the major city, has the de luxe new *San-ai Hotel,* as well as the popular *Sapporo Grand* and *Royal* hotels.

SOURCES OF FURTHER INFORMATION . . . In New York, the Japan National Tourist Organization is at 45 Rockefeller Plaza. Other offices are in Chicago, Dallas, San Francisco, Honolulu and Toronto. In Tokyo, the Japan Travel Bureau is at 1, 1-chome (Tel. 211-3211), the airport, Imperial Hotel and other locations. Pan American offices in the Imperial Hotel, and the Mitsubishi Shoji Bldg. on Chiyoda-Ku (Tel. 211-2441). In Osaka, Pan Am is in the Osaka Grand Hotel (Tel. 202-0061).

MALAYSIA
AND SINGAPORE

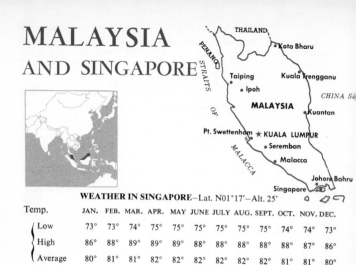

WEATHER IN SINGAPORE—Lat. N01°17′—Alt. 25′

Temp.	JAN.	FEB.	MAR.	APR.	MAY	JUNE	JULY	AUG.	SEPT.	OCT.	NOV.	DEC.
Low	73°	73°	74°	75°	75°	75°	75°	75°	75°	74°	74°	73°
High	86°	88°	89°	89°	89°	88°	88°	88°	88°	88°	87°	86°
Average	80°	81°	81°	82°	82°	82°	82°	82°	82°	81°	81°	80°
Days of Rain	16	11	14	15	14	14	13	14	13	16	18	19

LOCATION . . . On the tip of the Malay Peninsula, bounded on the north by Thailand, on the west by the Malacca Straits, on the south and east by the Indonesian Spice Islands and South China Sea. The mile-wide Straits of Johore separate the independent island of Singapore from mainland of Malaya. The former territories of Sarawak and North Borneo (now Sabah), members of the Malaysian Federation, lie along the northwestern strip of the island of Borneo.

CHARACTERISTICS . . . These exotic lands have always been the symbol of the color and romance of the East, where new discoveries await the traveler. The Malays, Chinese, Europeans, the Kadazans, the Dusans, the Land and Sea Dyaks, the Muruts, Indians, Pakistanis, Eurasians and others who make up the population staunchly retain their individual cultures, traditions, festivals and national dress. Shops and bazaars are filled with fascinating goods from all over the world, and Singapore and Penang are free-port bargain paradises. In these lands of perpetual summer, something gay is always going on.

POPULATION . . . 7,232,000 in Malaya; 1,800,000 in Singapore; 475,000 in Sabah (North Borneo) and 780,000 in Sarawak. Total is 10,237,000.

SIZE . . . Malaya, with 50,690 square miles, is 465 miles long, 200 miles wide. Singapore island, 224 square miles, is 27 miles long, 14 miles wide. North Borneo, approximately 1,000 miles from Singapore, is 29,338 square miles, much of it mountainous. Sarawak has about 48,250 square miles.

CAPITAL ... Kuala Lumpur, with about 500,000 population, is the capital of Malaysia. Singapore is a separate nation.

GOVERNMENT ... Malaysia and Singapore are self-governing members of the British Commonwealth.

HOW TO GET THERE ... By Pan American Jet Clipper, Singapore is 24¾ hours from San Francisco, with stopovers in Honolulu, Manila and Saigon. There are regular Malaysian Airways flights to Malaca, Kuala Lumpur and Penang in Malaya; to Kuching, Jesselton, Sondkan and Brunei Town in Borneo.

ACCOMMODATIONS ... In Singapore, the luxurious new *Singapura Intercontinental* is completely air-conditioned, and each room has a private balcony; Olympic-size swimming pool with cabanas and snack bar; music, dancing and entertainment in main dining room. Single rates $13.50-$16.75, double $20-$23.50, suites from $30. Also in Singapore are the famous old *Raffles, Prince's, Adelphi* and *Goodwood Park;* average single rates $10-$17, doubles $14-$21. Good, and less expensive, are the *Ocean Park, Cathay, Cockpit* and *Biltmore,* with singles from $7, doubles from $10. Hotels generally add 10% for service charge.

In Kuala Lumpur, best hotels are the new *Malaysia* (single from $6, double from $8.50), the *Federal* ($9-$16 double) and the *Merlin* ($9-$10 double). The *Station* is exotically Moorish in style; single rates from $7, double from $10. Government-owned rest houses, much like motels, are found in many of the Peninsula's towns and hill stations. They provide car shelters, rooms with or without bath, and Malaysian or Western-style meals at very reasonable rates. The *Aurora* and *Borneo* hotels in Kuching, Sarawak, have the most suitable tourist accommodations, outside of Jesselton (page 472), on Borneo.

ARTS ... All the larger communities have a Malaysian handicrafts center where you can buy true works of art—Malaysian silverware, hand-engraved pewter, lovely wood carvings, hand-printed batiks, brocades, silks, straw work of all kinds and pandanus leaf articles. The new National Museum in Kuala Lumpur, housed in a lovely, typical Malaysian building, devotes its large galleries to cultural, historical and natural-history displays. There are exhibits of Chinese, Malay and Indian dances and costumes; shadow plays; furnishings; ancient religious artifacts.

BANKS ... Among the many are the Chase Manhattan, First National City Bank of New York, the Bank of America, the Chartered Bank, Eastern Bank, Ltd., and the Hong Kong and Shanghai Bank.

CALENDAR OF HOLIDAYS ... Almost every day is a festival day somewhere in Malaysia, but the major holidays are: Thaipusam (Hindu), February: Chinese New Year, January or February; Hari Raya Puasa (Moslem), January; Hari Raya Haji (Moslem), March; Wesak Day (Buddha's Birthday), May 18; Birthday of the Supreme Head of State, June 6; Birthday of the Prophet Mohammed, August 12; Independence Day, August 31; Deepavali (Hindu), October, November; Christmas, December 25. Hindu, Moslem and Chinese holidays and religious activities are governed by the lunar calendar, falling on a different date each year.

CIGARETTES AND TOBACCO ... English cigarettes are about U.S. 80¢ for a tin of 50. Most American brands are available for about U.S. 35¢ a pack. Local brands are quite good and cheap.

CLIMATE ... All regions have a fairly even temperature with very little seasonal variation. Days are very warm, sunny and humid, but evenings are usually pleasantly cool. There is no distinct wet or dry season, and any time of year is a good time for a visit.

CLUBS ... In Singapore: the Tanglin Club, Singapore Island Country Club, Singapore Swimming Club, Polo Club, American Club, Flying Club, Gun Club, Rotary, Junior Chamber of Commerce. Guest cards for the American Club may be obtained from the Pan American representative. In Kuala Lumpur: Selangor Golf Club, Selangor Club, Kuala Lumpur Flying Club. Visitors' cards arranged through the courtesy of members. Kuala Lumpur also has branches of Lions, Rotary and Junior Chamber of Commerce.

COMMON COURTESIES AND LOCAL CUSTOMS ... The gracious, good-natured politeness of the East helps visitors to feel accepted and at ease, despite all the exotic sights, sounds and aromas. Nearly the only constriction is that you must remove your shoes before entering a mosque. The most common phrase for "Thank you" is *Trema kaseh.*

COMMUNICATIONS ... A 3-minute phone call to the U.S. is M$42; a 10-word cablegram is M$9.50. Airmail postage to the States is M$1.20 per ½ ounce. Airletter forms are M$.30.

CURRENCY ... The Malaysian dollar, written M$, is worth about U.S. 33¢. Money can be exchanged at any bank or hotel, and by both licensed and unlicensed professional money changers.

CUSTOMS REGULATIONS AND DOCUMENTS REQUIRED FOR UNITED STATES CITIZENS ... Passport and international smallpox vaccination certificate are required. If arriving from an infected area, you must also have proof of immunization against cholera within the last 6 months. You may bring in 200 cigarettes, or 50 cigars or ½ lb. of tobacco, duty-free. You may also bring in 1 quart each of malt liquor, wine and spirits. Visitors may bring in Malaysian currency up to M$500.

DRUGSTORES ... Many American products are available in chemist shops.

ELECTRIC CURRENT ... This may be a real problem for the traveler, as both alternating and direct current are supplied at 230 volts, depending upon the area. There are no fewer than 18 different types of electrical plugs in use, also depending upon location and the whims of the contractors.

FAUNA ... The Malay jungles teem with wild life, and you'll find elephants, seladangs, tapirs, tigers, monkeys, leopards and other large cats, strange deer and even bear; also a variety of colorful game birds.

FLORA ... Brilliant hibiscus, orchids, gardenias and flame trees. Tropical fruits include mangosteens, durians, rambutans, pomeloes, mangoes.

FOOD... Western food is served in hotels, but wonderful Chinese dishes are also available, and Malaysian curries are superb. Try *satay* —meat or chicken grilled on bamboo skewers over charcoal and served with a chili and peanut gravy. Grilled turtle is delicious, and local pork is excellent. Pasteurized milk may be found in larger cities.

GAMBLING... There are no gambling casinos as such, but the Turf Clubs in Singapore, Kuala Lumpur, Ipoh and Penang each have race meetings 4 or 5 times a year and there is lively betting.

LANGUAGE... The official language is Malay, but English is widely understood. Singapore policemen who are especially fluent in English wear red shoulder tabs.

LAUNDRY AND DRY CLEANING... Services are inexpensive. Be sure to emphasize the type of cleaning you want, and when you need it back. All hotels do good work.

LIQUOR... "Whisky" is always Scotch, although bourbon is available. A Stengah is a mild ½-ounce of whisky with soda. You may have to ask for ice, omitted through long British tradition. The famous Singapore Sling is a blissful blend of dry gin, cherry brandy and Benedictine, topped with club soda and a twist of lime peel. Try to find *samsu,* a local beer brewed from rice. Malaysia's Tiger and Anchor brands of beer have won international awards. All bars close at midnight, but some clubs have later hours.

MEDICAL FACILITIES... The United States Seventh Day Adventist Hospital in Singapore is excellent, and the General Hospital is the best-equipped in the Far East for treating tropical diseases. There are many excellent doctors in practice all over Malaysia.

MOTION PICTURES... Generally American or British films are shown in the larger air-conditioned, comfortable theaters. Chinese and Malays prefer the noisier and more action-packed pictures.

MUSIC... Chinese opera in September and October. People's Variety Concerts are frequently staged outdoors. Concerts, recitals and plays are given at the Singapore Cultural Center Auditorium, the Victoria Theater, Memorial Hall and the National Theater.

NIGHT CLUBS AND CABARETS... In Singapore and all the other principal cities of Malaysia are amusement parks known as "Worlds" where you will find numerous native cabarets, complete with hostesses and taxi dancers. More conventional places for dining and dancing in Singapore are the new Singapura Intercontinental Hotel's *Four Lions Restaurant, Arundel Room* in the Goodwood Park Hotel, *Prince's Restaurant, French Restaurant* in the Cockpit Hotel, and the *Cathay Restaurant.* Good spots for dining and dancing in Kuala Lumpur are the *Elfin* and *Dragon Court* (Merlin Hotel), and the *Mandarin Palace* (Federal Hotel).

PHOTOGRAPHY... All kinds of film are available, and Singapore has good processing. There is 1-day service for Kodacolor, but Kodachrome is sent to Honolulu to be developed. Fine German, Swiss and Japanese cameras and equipment are very inexpensive in the free ports of Singapore and Penang.

RELIGION... There are churches of all denominations, as well as temples, mosques and pagodas.

RESTAURANTS ... American-style coffee shop and an international restaurant in the new Singapura Hotel. *Prince's* on Orchard Road is excellent and features air-conditioned dining and dancing as well as a cocktail lounge. The *Adelphi Grill* in the Adelphi Hotel has Swiss chefs and is very popular. The *Elizabethan Grill* in famed Raffles Hotel is a Singapore landmark. The *Cathay Restaurant* in Cathay Building specializes in Chinese food. Albert Street is lined with marvelous Chinese restaurants where you can overeat for about U.S. $1. Aside from the hotel dining rooms in other Malaysian towns, there are countless street vendors selling really delicious native cookery that is safe even for tourists.

SHOPS AND STORES ... In Singapore, Helen Ling's for all kinds of Eastern art; Malaysian-Javanese arts and curios; C. K. Tang's for Chinese and Javanese wood carvings, Bali heads. Stamford Road for alligator and snakeskin accessories; High Street for Indian saris; English silverware and china from Robinsons and John Little's. B. P. Silva for star sapphires, jade and other precious stones; Thaicraft for hand-woven Siamese silks. Malay Handicraft Centers are fine sources for local workmanship in all the larger towns. Before a foreigner can send out unaccompanied shipments of purchases, he must obtain an export permit. Contact the Pan American representative for assistance in getting permits. Chinese articles require a Certificate of Origin to enter the United States; at present this can be obtained only in Hong Kong.

SPECTATOR SPORTS ... Soccer, hockey, badminton, football and basketball.

SPORTS ... Golf, tennis, fishing, swimming, water skiing, yachting, sailing, badminton, squash. On the Peninsula, no license is needed to hunt tiger and leopard in the states of Pahang, Trengganu and Perak, but you'll need one for elephant, seladang (bison) and bear. Guides, trackers and porters are available for U.S. $2 a day per man.

TIME ... 15½ hours later than U.S. Pacific Standard Time. Tuesday noon in Singapore is 8:30 P.M. on Monday in San Francisco.

TIPPING ... If service is not included, tip water 10% of the bill. Tip luggage porters M$1 for the average load of baggage. Otherwise, almost no tipping is expected.

TOURIST TAXES ... At the Singapore airport there is an embarkation charge of M$5 ($1.65) for international flights, and M$1 (33¢) for domestic flights.

TRANSPORTATION ... Lots of metered taxis in cities, but trishaws are more of a novelty, and rates are the same as for taxis. See Singapore's busy waterfront from a sampan water-taxi (about U.S. $2.50 for the tour). Air-conditioned chauffeured limousines are available, and self-drive cars rent for as little as U.S. $6.50 in Singapore; slightly higher on the Peninsula, which is well covered with good highways. Air-conditioned express trains connect Singapore with Johore, Kuala Lumpur, Ipoh and Penang. Long-distance bus services and Malaysian Airways also reach major points.

WATER . . . Tap water is safe in all tourist centers.

WHAT TO BUY . . . Transistor radios, cameras, British woolens, Swiss watches, jewelry and similar imports from far away are found in fixed-price department stores and shops in Raffles Place, High Street and Orchard Road. Leather goods found near the National Museum are good buys. You can bargain the low prices even lower in bazaars devoted to silks, batiks, rugs; and don't miss Change Alley where native Singapore residents shop. In Kuala Lumpur, Montbatten Road, Batu Road and Petaling Street are the places to go. All of Penang is an exciting free port, long known as the "Warehouse of the East."

WHAT TO WEAR . . . You'll need lots of lightweight clothing because of the heat. Evening dress is nearly extinct; tropical-weight dark suits for evening for men, cocktail styles for women. Woolens are needed in hill resorts such as the Cameron Highlands where the temperature can drop to 36°.

WHERE TO GO—SIGHTSEEING . . .

Singapore . . . Numerous places have been named for, and built in memory of, Sir Stamford Raffles, who rediscovered the island in 1819: Raffles Institution, Raffles Hotel, Raffles Place, to name a few. Splendid reminders of Singapore as an "outpost of the British Empire" may be seen in the old government buildings; St. Andrew's Cathedral; the garrison on Fort Canning Hill where Sir Stamford Raffles lived; lovely Queen Elizabeth Walk along the sea; the National Museum. Singapore's temples and mosques are world-famous. Major Hindu places of worship include the Subramanian and Sri Mariamman temples. Highly photogenic is the Moslem Holy Sultan Mosque, where a muezzin in the minaret calls the faithful to prayers 5 times a day. Chinese temples are especially delightful—The Temple of Heavenly Happiness, The Monkey God Temple, the Lotus Mountain Temple. Singapore's Botanic Gardens have a fabulous display of orchids, and the Van Kleef Aquarium has a remarkable collection of tropical fish and sea animals. On a hill overlooking the sea is the Haw Par Villa with its weird collection of sculptures and artifacts from the days of Chinese warlords. The House of Jade has a priceless collection of all kinds of jade and Chinese art. Take the scenic drive over the causeway to Johore where, from the hill topped with government buildings, you get a vast, panoramic view of Singapore and the surrounding seas. There are several storybook palaces in Johore, and the Sultan's private zoo is open to the public. At sundown, take a ride up Singapore's Mount Faber, 350 feet high with a view of most of the island and harbor. After dark, explore the city's Chinatown, fragrant with joss sticks, tinkling with music and jostling with vendors and shoppers.

Kuala Lumpur . . . Distinguished for its graceful, Moorish-style architecture, the capital city also has picturesque streets of thatched *kampongs* (houses) on stilts. Visit the National Museum of sculptures, textiles and porcelains, and the Art Gallery. Merdeka Stadium is the largest sports arena in the East. See the exquisite new National Mosque in which ultra modern design combines with traditional

Islamic architecture. Several miles from the city is Petaling Jaya, a newly constructed town with an unusually good Malaysian handicrafts shop. Also within easy reach of the capital are the cathedral-like Batu Caves containing a Hindu shrine; Templar Park in a virgin jungle setting; a tin mine and rubber plantations.

Penang . . . This historic free port is 250 miles north of Kuala Lumpur. At unbelievably low prices you'll find Chinese ivory and jade, Indian and Thai jewelry, Indonesian wood carvings, Malaysian curios of all kinds, as well as European and Japanese goods sold for much less than in their countries of origin. Penang Island (regular 15-minute ferry service from the mainland) mounts to a steep crag in the center. There is a funicular railway to the top where, from an elevation of 2,272 feet, you get a superb view. Other places of interest (aside from the shops) include the Kek Lok Si Temple, the Ban Hood Pagoda of 10,000 Buddhas, Waterfall Gardens, the Snake Temple, and the many beautiful bathing beaches. Good places to stay are the *Eastern & Oriental Hotel*, the new *International* and the *Town House*, with rates averaging $7 single, $9 double.

Cameron Highlands . . . In the cool hills, 135 miles from Kuala Lumpur. Tennis courts, a golf course, and interesting tea plantations nearby. Hotels include the *Cameron Highlands, Eastern, Federal, Smoke House Inn* and *Town House*.

Malaysia National Park . . . You can reach it only by plane or by riverboat. An out-of-this-world paradise for jungle hiking and stalking big game with a camera; boating through rapids, fishing, mountain climbing. Rest house, bungalow accommodations and campsites.

Jesselton . . . The clean, pretty little capital of North Borneo was founded in 1899, and has been almost entirely rebuilt since World War II bombings. The population is largely Chinese, with colorful tribal people represented, too—Dusans from the rice fields, seafaring Bajaus, and Muruts from almost inaccessible mountains of the interior. But the flavor of Jesselton is still British, and there are modern movie houses and air-conditioned hotels such as the *Jesselton* ($10 single, $13.50 double) and *Ang's* ($8 single, $12 double), both Modified American Plan (2 meals). The little city looks out over the South China Sea and is backed with a mountainous jungle. North Borneo is a land of mountains, plateaus, wildly rushing rivers and lush jungles. Travel to Sarawak is almost entirely by air. The climate on Borneo is balmy and pleasant, and you'll never eat better birds' nest soup or turtle eggs, two gourmet delicacies that originated here. If you visit a longhouse, leave shoes, socks or hose on the ground; the ladders and bamboo pole floors were made for bare feet.

SOURCES OF FURTHER INFORMATION . . . Tourist Promotion Board, Raffles Place, Singapore 1. Pan Am's office is at 13/15 Robinson Road (Tel. 70081). In Kuala Lumpur, the Department of Tourism, P.O. Box 328. Pan Am's office in Kuala Lumpur is in the A.I.A. Building, Jalan Ampang (Tel. 24341/2).

NEPAL

Lying on the southern slopes of the Himalayas between Tibet and India, this country, isolated by its former rulers for centuries, has recently been opened to tourists, cordially received, and can now be reached easily by daily air service from either Calcutta (3¼ hours) or New Delhi (3¾ hours) both on Pan Am's round-the-world routes.

Only 530 miles long and 95 to 150 miles wide, Nepal has a population of 9,700,000, of whom about 195,000 live in the capital city of Kathmandu. The government is a constitutional monarchy. Spring and autumn are the best times to visit, when weather and views are excellent. To enter Nepal you need your passport, a visa (valid 7 days; extendable) from the Royal Nepalese Embassy, 2131 Le Roy Place, N.W., Washington, D.C., or the Consulate General in New York; smallpox and cholera vaccination certificates. 100 cigarettes allowed duty free; no duty-free liquor allowances. The rupee exchange rate is about Rs. 7.60 Nepalese to U.S. $1. No Indian rupees may be imported. Departure tax 5 Nepalese rupees.

Hotels with approximate rates per person including meals are the *Snow View*, $7.90; *Royal Hotel*, $9.45; the *Coronation*, $7.25; *Shanker Hill*, $8.50; *Green Hotel*, $7.25; and the *Imperial*, $5.26. Always drink boiled water. A 10% service charge is added, but additional tipping is expected. Elsewhere the usual tip is one Nepalese rupee (also called *mohur*). Since taxi rates are not fixed, usual procedure is to bargain. Pedicabs charge about Rs. 3.50 per hour. Bicycles can also be rented. Bring plenty of camera film.

WHERE TO GO—SIGHTSEEING ...

Nepal's culture dates back thousands of years and the country is a veritable museum of artistic treasures, magnificent shrines and temples and other lavishly decorated edifices, images and carvings of exquisite design all competing with scenic mountain grandeur unequaled anywhere, exotic flora and the richest sanctuary of wild life. Kathmandu lies in a fertile valley, 15 miles long by 20 miles wide, surrounded by the highest peaks in the world ranging from 17,000 to 26,502 feet—Makalu, Gaurishankar, Annapurna among them. Several tours covering principal sights are available at about $3.50 per half day per person in private car including guide. Don't miss Swayambunath, 3,000-year-old Buddhist Temple overlooking the city from a hill groved with trees in which monkeys chatter amiably. Cities of principal interest to tourists are shown on map above.

SOURCES OF FURTHER INFORMATION ...

Royal Nepalese Consulate General, 300 E. 46th St., New York, N.Y. 10017. Tourist Information Center, Basantapur, Kathmandu (Tel. 11293).

OKINAWA

Okinawa, largest of the 72 islands in the Ryukyu archipelago, is about 2 hours from Hong Kong, Tokyo and Manila, and may be included in jet itineraries at no extra travel cost. As if its lush, semitropical beauty were not enough, the island now has air-conditioned hotels with room television, and city shops sell luxury goods at prices often lower than in Hong Kong. Okinawa has a population of over 800,000, half of whom live in the capital city of Naha. The friendly, easygoing islanders maintain a delightful blending of ancient Okinawan traditions with those of China and Japan, but the Western influence is noticeable in that English is widely understood, U.S. money is used and the electric current is the same as in the States. American citizens need only passport and smallpox vaccination certificate to visit this balmy Pacific paradise that is just 65 miles long and 2 to 16 miles wide.

The *Ryukyu Tokyu Hotel,* on a promontory overlooking Naha and the China Sea, is $9 single, $13 double. The *Royal Hotel,* in downtown Naha, is $5 single, $7 double. The 10% service charge added to bills covers tipping. The island's drinking water is pure, and locally grown fruits and vegetables are equally safe. The Okinawan cuisine is both exotically Oriental and familiarly Western. Be sure to dine in an Okinawan teahouse, where you can see a performance of ancient dances in exquisite costumes.

Of the many World War II memorials, perhaps the favorite is the Ernie Pyle Memorial on the small offshore island of Ie Shima (Jima). The "turtleback" tombs, scattered throughout the whole island, are a unique form of local architecture. Be sure to visit the University of the Ryukyus, located at the site of 700-year-old Shuri Castle atop a hill overlooking both the Pacific and the China Sea. Taxis for sightseeing are very inexpensive.

Pan American's office is in Awase Meadows Business Center, Koza (Tel. 077-3411).

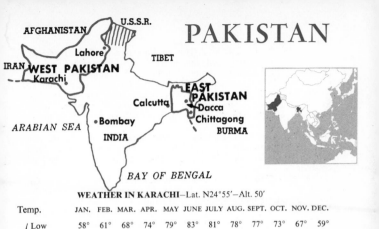

PAKISTAN

WEATHER IN KARACHI—Lat. N24°55'—Alt. 50'

Temp.	JAN.	FEB.	MAR.	APR.	MAY	JUNE	JULY	AUG.	SEPT.	OCT.	NOV.	DEC.
Low	58°	61°	68°	74°	79°	83°	81°	78°	77°	73°	67°	59°
High	76°	78°	82°	85°	89°	91°	88°	85°	86°	88°	85°	78°
Average	67°	70°	75°	80°	84°	87°	85°	82°	82°	81°	76°	69°
Days of Rain	1	1	1	0	0	1	2	2	1	0	0	1

LOCATION ... Two widely spaced units, East and West Pakistan are separated by approximately 1,000 miles of foreign territory, much the same as Alaska is separated from Continental United States. West Pakistan adjoins India, Iran, Afghanistan and the Chinese province of Sinkiang, whereas East Pakistan abuts India and Burma.

CHARACTERISTICS ... While the name Pakistan is a new one, the land is both ancient and colorful. The terrain of East Pakistan is flat, covered with rivers, and very verdant. The landscape of West Pakistan is extremely varied, consisting of snow-capped hills and green valleys, with abundant food and industrialization; in fact, skilled irrigation and "manufacturing" existed at Mohenjo-Daro in the Indus Valley nearly 5,000 years ago. You will find the people of Pakistan friendly and hospitable to visitors, especially Americans.

POPULATION ... Nearly 110,000,000 inhabitants.

SIZE ... About 365,529 square miles, which is larger than the combined areas of California, Oregon and Washington.

CAPITAL ... Temporarily shifted from Karachi to Rawalpindi pending the building of a new capital to be called Islamabad, on the nearby Potwar Plateau, which has an altitude of 2,500 feet.

GOVERNMENT ... A president and 11 ministers administer a federal form of government for both wings of the country.

HOW TO GET THERE ... By Pan American Jet Clipper, about 21 hours elapsed time from New York; 31½ hours from San Francisco. Karachi is on Pan American's Round-the-World jet route. By ship, about 23 days.

ACCOMMODATIONS ... The de luxe new *Karachi Intercontinental* has a swimming pool, numerous shops, dining rooms and supper club; single $12-$15, double $16-$19. Other hotels are the *Metropole,* $13.25 single, from $20 double; the *Beach Luxury,* from $10 single, $14.50; double and the *Palace,* single from $10, double from $15.75. The reliable Oberoi chain operates hotels in Lahore, Murree, Peshawar and Rawalpindi. Hotel rates are subject to 26% additional for service and taxes.

ARTS ... National Museum, Karachi. The real center of art, however, is perhaps Lahore, where the Museum, Chunghtai's Studio, School of Modern Art and several other institutions have valuable collections.

BANKS ... In Karachi: Bank of America, First National City Bank of New York, American Express Company, Bank of India, National and Grindlay's, Eastern Bank, Ltd., Chartered Bank and the Netherlands Trading Society. Exchange facilities at leading hotels.

CALENDAR OF HOLIDAYS ... Fixed-date national holidays are March 23, June 30, August 14, September 11, October 27, and December 25. There are also a number of Muslim holidays with variable dates based on the lunar calendar.

CIGARETTES AND TOBACCO ... Pakistan and British cigarettes and tobacco are plentiful, but American cigarettes are not available.

CLIMATE ... East Pakistan from November to mid-March is generally delightfully cool with low humidity and little rain. The rest of the year generally has higher humidity and temperatures. Mean temperature in cold months is 60 degrees and in the hot season 83 degrees. West Pakistan, except for the coastal strip of Sind, is subject to extremes, from freezing night temperatures in January and February to the 70's in the daytime, making a very healthy winter climate. In summer, the days can be very hot, though the nights generally are cool. Karachi enjoys a pleasant climate with invigorating sea breezes except for April, May, June and October.

CLUBS ... In Karachi, Sind Club, Rotary International Club, Junior Chamber of Commerce International, Lions Club International, Gymkhana, Boat Club and Race Club. Inquire locally.

COMMON COURTESIES AND CUSTOMS ... Shoes or sandals should be taken off before entering a mosque. Don't be surprised if men do not take off their Pakistani caps in social gatherings, as it is not customary to do so. *"Shukria"* is "Thank you."

COMMUNICATIONS ... A 3-minute phone call to the U.S. costs Rs. 75.62 ($15.88). Cablegrams are R. 1 per word. Airmail postage to the States is Rs. 1.25 per ½ ounce. Airletter forms only 60 paisas.

CURRENCY ... The Pakistani rupee is worth U.S. 21¢; or, Rs. 4.76 to U.S. $1. One rupee equals 100 paisas (formerly 16 annas).

CUSTOMS REGULATIONS AND DOCUMENTS REQUIRED FOR UNITED STATES CITIZENS ... A passport and visa are required. Certificates of smallpox vaccination and inoculation against cholera are recommended. Yellow fever inoculation certificate required if you are coming from Africa or South America. No duty is charged on 1 quart of whiskey, 200 cigarettes and jewelry up to Rs. 5,000 (about $1,000). There is no limitation on personal effects within reasonable limits. Limit of Rs. 80 Pakistan currency. Foreign currency must be declared upon arrival and departure, and may be exchanged only through authorized dealers and banks. Air departure tax $1.05.

DRUGSTORES... Found in all the shopping and business centers and in most hotels. American products are scarce and expensive.

ELECTRIC CURRENT... In Karachi, 220 volts, 50 cycles. Alternating and direct current are found in different parts of Pakistan.

FAUNA... The Zoo Gardens on Garden Road, near Karachi, present a picturesque scene. You'll see camels everywhere.

FOOD... Pakistanis are fond of spicy but tasty food. There are numerous varieties of curries, *pulaos* (specially cooked meat and rice), and *kebabs* (fried and broiled meat), *shami kebab* (fried meat cakes). *Kofta* (meat balls); *murgh-i-mussalam* (stuffed fried chicken); and *shahi tukra* (sweetbreads cooked in milk and honey) are a "must." Milk is available in Karachi but should be boiled.

LANGUAGE... English is used extensively in Government and generally in commerce and is also widely understood and spoken throughout Pakistan. Other languages widely used are Urdu, Bengali, Pushtu, Gujarati, Punjabi and Baluchi.

LAUNDRY AND DRY CLEANING... Laundries and dry cleaners are available almost everywhere.

LIQUOR... In the main centers of Pakistan many foreign brands of liquor are available, but expensive. However, few Muslims drink. Hotel bars, mostly patronized by foreigners, are open every day until midnight except on Fridays, when they close at 10 P.M.

MEDICAL FACILITIES... Fully equipped hospitals are to be found in all the leading cities. English is understood by hospital staffs. There is a good Seventh Day Adventist American hospital in Karachi. Holy Family Hospital run by American Medical Mission Sisters has hospitals in Karachi, Rawalpindi and Dacca.

MOTION PICTURES... Movie theaters, showing both American and English films, run shows at set hours. Seats are reserved at the box office. Five film studios are in operation in Lahore.

MUSIC... Radio Pakistan, which is semi-commercial, devotes most of its programs to Pakistan classical and folk music.

PHOTOGRAPHY... Photographic equipment, including cameras and still and movie film, black-and-white and color film are available, but prices are higher than in America. Color and movie films are sent abroad for processing; 24-hour local service on black-and-white film. Inquire at your hotel or Pan American office for recommended camera stores. Ask permission before photographing Pakistani women.

NIGHT CLUBS AND CABARETS... Night clubs, as we know them, are not found in Pakistan. However, all the leading hotels have

Western-type barrooms and cabarets. There are floor shows at the *Karachi Intercontinental, Beach Luxury, Metropole, Palace* and *Excelsior.*

RELIGION ... The majority of the people are Muslim. Others are Christians, Hindus and Zoroastrians. Most faiths have established places of worship in Karachi and the principal cities of Pakistan. There is complete freedom of worship in Pakistan.

RESTAURANTS ... Most tourists dine at their hotel, but better Karachi restaurants include *Aga's Tavern, Sabrina, Chicken Inn. Shezan,* an air-conditioned restaurant, is also recommended. The air-conditioned *Hotel Farooq* is popular for Chicken Tikka (chicken barbecue), and there are some Chinese restaurants.

SHOPS AND STORES ... In Karachi the shops around the Metropole Hotel offer all varieties of goods. Elphinstone Street is also a big shopping center. Prices on some items are high because of restricted imports.

SPECTATOR SPORTS ... Hockey, cricket and football (soccer), are popular national games. Tournaments are held in the big cities. Horse racing on the week ends in winter season in Karachi, Dacca and Lahore with pari-mutuel betting.

SPORTS ... Swimming, sailing, water skiing, tennis, badminton, golf, horseback riding and fishing. Carry sporting equipment with you. Fishing is mostly deep-sea. Hunting is good, and you can take your own guns and a reasonable supply of cartridges into Pakistan.

TIME ... Time in Karachi and West Pakistan is 10 hours later than United States Eastern Standard Time. East Pakistan time is 11 hours later.

TIPPING ... Tip luggage porters 50 paisas per bag; 25 for shoeshine boy, hat-check, washroom attendant. There is no need to tip waiters, barbers, beauticians or taxi drivers.

TRANSPORTATION ... State-owned railroads in both West and East Pakistan and air services provide access to most of the principal cities. Much of the track is 5′6″ gauge, widest in use anywhere. For local transportation, taxis, buses, *victorias* (horse and carriage) and rented automobiles are available as are economical auto rickshas and baby taxis. East Pakistan has the world's widest helicopter services.

WATER ... Safe to drink only at Karachi Intercontinental, which has its own filter plant. Elsewhere use special water flask in your hotel room.

WHAT TO BUY ... Ivory and brass articles admired for their delicacy; products of papier-mâché and pieces of embroidery, brocades, fur caps, Baluchistan carpets, Sindhi glasswork and other handmade goods. Items are sold at leading hotels, at the Cottage Industry Sales and Display Center, Preedy Street in Karachi; and at similar centers in Lahore, Dacca and Chittagong. There is a duty-free shop at the Karachi airport for departing and transit passengers.

WHAT TO WEAR ... In winter (November to March), tropical worsted; in summer, dacron, cotton and other washable fabrics. Winter nights sometimes become suddenly cold. Take a light topcoat. Men

About 3 hours by air from Karachi at Lahore is Pakistan's famous Badshahi (the Royal) Mosque, one of the largest in the world.

Lahore's beautiful Shalamar Gardens were built in 1637 by the Shah Jehan who also built the Taj Mahal.

wear dark suits and ladies wear cocktail dresses for evening functions.

WHERE TO GO—SIGHTSEEING . . .

Karachi . . . In Karachi sightseeing tours are limited, but you can get about the city by cab or *gharry* (a horse-drawn vehicle) the driver of which will act as your guide. About 3 miles from the town of Karachi is the Clifton Beach on the Arabian Sea. On moonlight nights the charm of the surroundings is intensified. About 14 miles from Karachi is fertile Malir, which, with swimming pool and the *Grand Hotel,* offers a fine spot for relaxation. West of Karachi is the little island of Manora, which offers an excellent view of the city and interesting sights such as a pilot station, a lighthouse and a fishermen's camp attract many visitors. From Manora, westward about 12 miles, is Cape Monz. Boat transportation and rental automobiles are available for these sightseeing trips.

Four and a half miles from Manora is Sandspit, accessible by boat up the creek, at this point separated from the sea by a narrow strip of beach. Spend a day there. Another such holiday resort is Hawk's Bay, about 12 miles from Karachi. Manghopir (11 miles north from Karachi), well-known shrine of a saint, is built on a rock and is famous for its hot sulphur springs. Children are especially interested in a pool that is full of crocodiles bred from two originally tamed by the saint. A trip to Bund Murad Khan is good for lovers of fish and sport. Another place worth visiting is Thatta, 64 miles from Karachi, full of historic ruins of the Mogul and pre-Mogul period.

Lahore ... Roughly 3 hours by air from Karachi, Lahore is the second largest city of Pakistan, with a population slightly over 1 million. It is the cultural and academic center of Pakistan, the location of over 40 colleges and institutions, including Punjab University. One of Lahore's great treasures is the exquisite Shalimar Gardens, a masterpiece of the great Mogul Emperor, Shah Jahan, who was also the builder of the Taj Mahal. The beautiful tomb of Jahangir, the father of Shah Jahan, is also well worth a visit.

The famous Badshahi (Royal) Mosque, one of the largest mosques in the world, is also located in Lahore. Among the many monuments of interest, you'll see a plaque in the office of the *Civil and Military Gazette,* on the Mall, recording the fact that Rudyard Kipling once worked there. Kim's gun, Zam Zama, still stands outside the Museum where Kipling's father was curator. The *Ambassador, International Park* and *Oberoi Faletti's* hotels are modern and comfortable.

Lahore's famed Horse and Cattle Show (usually held February 15-March 10) is staged in an enormous stadium patterned after a Mogul fortress, and has all the excitement of a medieval Asiatic rodeo, with polo, trick riding, camel fights and acrobatic displays.

A visit to the northern areas of West Pakistan is strongly recommended. A round trip to the Khyber Pass can be made from Peshawar in half a day, via air-conditioned buses. In Peshawar, stay at *Oberoi Dean's Hotel.* Visit the attractive new city of Islamabad about 60 miles south of Peshawar.

Ancient Cities ... Visitors should not miss seeing the archaeological excavations of Mohenjo-Daro in Sind and Harappa in the Indus Valley, in Punjab Province, dating to about 3,000 B.C., and other places of historical interest, such as Taxila in the Punjab and Bhambhore in Sind. There are rest houses at many sites.

East Pakistan ... Principal places of interest: Sylhet is headquarters of the tea-growing area. Dacca, the capital, historically known for its silk and Dacca cotton muslin, has many historical monuments, including the Lal Bagh Fort, Bibi Pari's tomb, Bara Katra, Husani Dalan, Churihata Mosque, Satgumbad (seven domes) Mosque and Dhakeswari Temple, as well as modern structures and interesting museums. Places of archaeological interest include Mahasthan Garh, Rajshahi and Mainamati. The scenic Chittagong Hill Tracts is a region of picturesque towns, thick forest and wild animals and a quiet seaside resort, Cox's Bazaar.

SOURCES OF FURTHER INFORMATION ... In Karachi the Government Tourist Bureau is on Club Road. Pan American office in the Metropole Hotel (Tel. 50281). In Lahore contact Pan Am on Egerton Road (Tel. 68868); in Dacca the Pan Am office is in Karim Chambers (Tel. 80689). Consulate General of Pakistan is located at 12 East 65 Street, New York.

PHILIPPINES

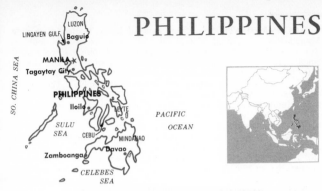

WEATHER IN MANILA—Lat. N14°36′—Alt. 25′

Temp.	JAN.	FEB.	MAR.	APR.	MAY	JUNE	JULY	AUG.	SEPT.	OCT.	NOV.	DEC.
Low	70°	71°	75°	75°	76°	76°	74°	75°	76°	75°	72°	71°
High	80°	81°	84°	87°	88°	87°	85°	85°	83°	84°	82°	81°
Average	75°	76°	80°	81°	82°	82°	80°	80°	80°	80°	77°	76°
Days of Rain	5	3	3	4	10	16	21	22	21	17	12	9

LOCATION . . . This group of 7,109 islands (only 2,773 of which are named) lies in the Malay Archipelago. Borneo lies to the southwest and Formosa less than 100 miles to the north.

CHARACTERISTICS . . . History has made the Philippines a unique blend of Eastern and Western civilizations, which visitors find intriguing. The roads, highways and hotels are excellent. Beach resorts, within an hour's drive from Manila, are splendid. English is generally spoken and the average American feels at home even though the scenery, the people and customs seem foreign.

POPULATION . . . Over 31,293,000.

SIZE . . . The total land area is 115,601 square miles; 1,152 miles long, 688 miles wide. The islands are spread over an area as large as Mexico. Luzon, with 40,420 square miles, is the largest island.

CAPITAL . . . Quezon City, a suburb of Manila, is now the official capital, although the seat of the national government remains in Manila, which has a population of about 1,339,000.

GOVERNMENT . . . A republic of 56 provinces and 6 subprovinces, with a President and a bicameral legislative body. It was granted its independence on July 4, 1946, by the President of the United States.

HOW TO GET THERE . . . By Pan Am Jet Clipper from San Francisco via Honolulu, about 18½ hours (elapsed time) to Manila. From Saigon it is 2¼ hours and from Singapore another 2½ hours. By ship from San Francisco, 17 to 21 days.

ACCOMMODATIONS... On beautiful Roxas Boulevard skirting Manila Bay are the *Manila Hotel* ($9 single, from $12 double), *Bay View Hotel* ($7.90 single, $9.25 double), *Filipinas Hotel* ($8.70 single, $10 double), *Shellborne Arms Hotel* (single $6-$10, double $10-13), *Swiss Inn* ($4.35 single, $6.38 double), *Hotel Mabuhay* is in an uptown shopping district ($7 single, $8.10 double). The *Luneta* overlooks Luneta Park ($4.50 single, $7.10 double). An hour's drive from Manila is the *Taal Vista Lodge,* a completely equipped resort in Tagaytay City, where weekly rates are from $1.74 single, $2.90 double; rates nearly double on weekends. Fine hotels, comparable to those in Manila, are the *Pines* in Baguio City in northern Luzon, the *Apo View* and *Davao Insular* at Davao City on Mindanao, the *Capitol Hotel* and *Magellan Hotel* in Cebu City on Cebu; and the *Bayot* in Zamboanga on Mindanao. Hotels generally add a 10% service charge in lieu of tipping.

ARTS... The National Museum displays interesting collections of weapons, art, local costumes and literature dating back several centuries. See, too, the museum in the ancient University of Santo Tomás. Philippine handicrafts are world famous. Local art industries include shellcraft, *piña, jusi* and other textile weaving, wood carvings, handmade silver filigrees, buntal hats, reptile belts and other accessories and, of course, exquisite Philippine embroidery. Galleries of Philippine paintings are in the Ermita district.

BALLET... Ballet school and professional ballet performances are held frequently in Manila. Filipino dance troupes which have won international acclaim are the Bayanihan and the Filipinescas.

BANKS... The First National City Bank of New York and the Bank of America have branches in Manila. The American Express Co. is on United Nations St. and Florida. Banking hours are from 9 A.M. to 2:30 P.M., Monday through Friday. The Philippine Commercial and Industrial Bank has a branch on the second floor of the Manila International Airport for the convenience of flight passengers.

CALENDAR OF HOLIDAYS... Banks, stores and museums are closed on January 1 and 6; Maundy Thursday; Good Friday; May 1, Labor Day; June 12, Philippine Independence Day; June 19, Birthday of Dr. José Rizal, national hero; July 4, Philippine-American Friendship Day; August 19, President Quezon Day; August 26, First Cry of Balintawak, commemorating the beginning of the Philippine Revolution against Spain; November 1, All Saints Day; Thanksgiving Day, last Thursday in November; November 30, National Heroes Day; Christmas Day; December 30, commemorating execution of Dr. José Rizal. The Philippines have an extended Christmas season, beginning with the Dawn Masses, called *Misas de Aguinaldo,* on December 16 (and every morning thereafter until *Misa de Gallo,* or Midnight Mass on December 24) and continuing up to the Feast of Three Kings on January 6.

CIGARETTES AND TOBACCOS... American cigarettes are not too hard to find, but they cost about 70¢ a pack. The Filipinos are now manufacturing comparatively good brands of blended cigarettes, which sell for only 12¢ a pack. Choice Corona cigars make ideal gifts to friends abroad; a good brand of cigars will cost $4 for a box of 50. Monogrammed, Philippine mahogany gift boxes may also be made to order for a reasonable price.

CLIMATE ... The most pleasant season in Manila is around Christmas, when the temperature is 75 to 80 degrees. The rainy season is from June to November; however, rains are generally interspersed with good sunny weather. April and May are warm months and sometimes uncomfortable for foreigners from cold countries.

CLUBS ... There are many clubs in Manila, which include the Army and Navy Club, Manila Overseas Press Club, Club Filipino, the Elks Club, Yacht Club, the Casino Español, Manila Club, Wack Wack Country Club, the Manila Golf Club and the Manila Polo Club, with all modern facilities for sports, recreations and social functions. Guest cards may be arranged with members.

COMMON COURTESIES AND LOCAL CUSTOMS ... Filipinos are noted for their hospitality, especially in the provinces. During the day, men generally dress informally with long- or short-sleeved shirts of cotton, silk or rayon, with plain or Hawaiian prints. Coats and ties are generally worn in offices, in exclusive hotels and night clubs in the evening. During the summer months and also throughout the year, the local version of evening apparel for men is the *barong tagalog,* a shirt made of piña cloth, derived from the pineapple fiber, or *jusi,* woven from silk and piña fiber. For strictly formal wear, the *barong tagalog* is worn with tuxedo, black evening shoes.

COMMUNICATIONS ... A 3-minute phone call to the States costs P46.20 on weekdays, P34.65 on Sundays. A cablegram (minimum 7 words) is P1.52 per word. Airmail postage to the U.S. is 50 centavos for an airletter, 70 for a postcard or 5-gram letter.

CURRENCY ... There are 100 centavos in a peso, valued at from 3 pesos, 90 centavos (P3.90) to P4 to U.S. $1, free market rate.

CUSTOMS REGULATIONS AND DOCUMENTS REQUIRED FOR UNITED STATES CITIZENS ... Valid passport; no visa needed for a stay of less than 17 days if you have onward transportation. Smallpox certificate; also yellow fever and cholera vaccination certificates if coming from an infected area. Tourists may bring in an unlimited amount of foreign currency. The following will be allowed in duty free: wines or spirits, 1 quart; 300 cigarettes, 50 cigars or 2.2 lbs. of pipe tobacco; coffee prohibited. No restrictions on cameras or films. Only military areas are banned from the photographer. Chinese-type articles are either prohibited or require a Certificate of Origin for entry into the United States. Consult the nearest U.S. Consul for latest requirements. Air departure tax $1.30.

DRUGSTORES ... Manila is literally dotted with drugstores, but the bigger ones are the Botica Boie, Mercury Drugstore, Dolor's Pharmacy, Metro Drugstore, Oro, Central, Occidental, Rubi, Quinta, Lexal Laboratories, Modern Pharmacal, Yucuanseh Drug Company and the Oceanic Commercial. All kinds of medicines and drugs are available.

ELECTRIC CURRENT ... Voltage in Manila is 220 volts, A.C. but the Bay View, Filipinas, Mabuhay, Manila, Luneta, and Shellborne hotels also have 110-volt outlets.

FAUNA ... The carabao, or water buffalo, is indigenous. There are several varieties of birds that are exported to the United States. Large shipments of monkeys are also shipped to U.S. zoos and research laboratories. Geckos are ubiquitous and harmless.

FLORA ... The flowers are beautiful; they are smaller but more fragrant than American flowers. In June and July you can get quantities of gardenias for practically nothing. The *sampaguita,* a small, white, multipetaled and exceedingly fragrant blossom, is the national flower. Orchids grow in abundance. The vanda sanderiana species, or *waling-waling,* is the most famous of all Philippine orchids. This highly esteemed flower has large brown-and-purplish-tinted blossoms which survive more than 30 days.

FOOD ... Rice, corn and *camotes* (like sweet potatoes) are staples. Native dishes include: *adobo* (a mixture of chicken, pork and beef, and lots of garlic), *lechon* (a whole roasted pig), and *sinigang* (stewed fish or meat with vegetables). The mango is the best liked of all Philippine fruits and is available from May till late October. Papayas and bananas are also excellent. Good American, Spanish, Filipino, Chinese and European meals are available at $2 up. There is plenty of pasteurized milk produced by sanitary dairies.

GAMBLING ... The most popular form of gambling among Filipinos is cockfighting (two gamecocks fight with sharp leg spurs), which is held on Sundays and holidays in the suburbs of Manila, and horse racing on Saturdays and Sundays at the San Lazaro and Santa Ana racetracks. Jai-alai is played nightly except on Sundays at the Jai-Alai Building on Taft Avenue, where one may also enjoy excellent music and food in its *Sky Room.*

LANGUAGE ... Tagalog, which is spoken in Manila and in the surrounding provinces, is the national language, better known as the Filipino language. English is taught from grade school up; the Filipino language is similarly taught. The Philippines has one of the highest rates of literacy in the Far East. English is spoken and understood in any part of the Archipelago. *Mabuhay* is the Philippines' welcome to the Philippine soil for tourists and friends. It means "Welcome," "long life," "Farewell" or "Good-by and Godspeed." Because the Philippines were under Spanish sovereignty for almost 400 years, Spanish culture and language are still dominant. (The Philippine Islands were named after King Philip II of Spain, who at the time of their discovery was the ruling monarch of that country.)

LAUNDRY AND DRY CLEANING ... There are excellent laundries and dry-cleaning establishments, where work is done in a few hours. In a hotel, your roomboy will make the necessary arrangements. Rates are moderate.

LIQUOR ... *Tuba,* a native drink, is made from the fermented juice of the palm. Philippine beer is exceedingly popular among Filipinos, alien residents and visitors alike. A great quantity of Philippine rum is also manufactured and exported. Philippine and imported liquors are always available. Hotel bars are open from 8 A.M. in the morning to about 12 midnight. Other bars are open later. The price of a drink of Scotch ranges from 50¢ to $1.50, depending on quality and the prestige of the establishment. Minimum legal age for drinkers is 21.

MEDICAL FACILITIES ... There are numerous excellent public and private hospitals. A few American private hospitals are the Manila Sanitarium, Waterous Clinic, Mary Johnston Hospital, Manila Doctor's Hospital, and St. Luke's Hospital. There is also an excellent Chinese hospital, whose medical staff has been trained in the best American hospitals.

MOTION PICTURES ... In Manila the *Roxan, Ideal, Lyric, Capitol, Avenue, State, Galaxy, Odeon, Ever, Cinerama* and *Universal* are first-class air-conditioned theaters, as is the *Rizal;* in Makati suburb. There are also a great many second-class, air-conditioned theaters all over the city. These theaters show second-run films and double features. Movie theaters, or *cines* as they are commonly called, start at 8:30 in the morning. Last screening starts about 9 in the evening. Hollywood, British, Italian and Spanish films are shown, although Hollywood films are the most popular. Foreign films with dialogue other than English are shown with English subtitles.

MUSIC ... The *kundiman* is a distinctive native music. This type of music almost always has a plaintive and amorous air. Several *kundimans* composed by great Filipino composers have won fame all over the world. Native *rondallas,* or string bands, are regularly heard over the radio. Filipinos are expert with the guitar and other stringed instruments. Excellent bands play nightly in many of the night clubs. The Manila Symphony Orchestra and the Filipino Youth Symphony periodically play concerts in school auditoriums. There are also the University of Philippines Symphony and the National Philharmonic.

NIGHT CLUBS AND CABARETS ... Among the most patronized are the Manila Hotel's *Champagne Room, El Dorado, Alba's, Bayside, Nautilus, D'Wave, Safari* and the *Sky Room* in the Jai-Alai Building. These are all air-conditioned. Americans bands, artists and other musical troupes occasionally give performances in these night clubs.

PHOTOGRAPHY ... Photo equipment, black-and-white and color film are available in Manila and other principal cities, but prices are much higher than in the United States. Developing and printing of black-and-white film within 24 hours, color in 3 days.

RELIGION ... While the country is predominantly Catholic, there are churches of all denominations, including the Philippine Independent Church and the Iglesia Ni Cristo, which are modified forms of Catholicism and Protestantism respectively. In Manila there are numerous American churches, such as the Central Church on T. Kalaw Street, the Ellinwood Church on Wright Street, the Knox Memorial Church on Rizal Avenue, the Holy Trinity (Episcopal) on T. Kalaw, the newly reconstructed Manila Cathedral (Roman Catholic), and many others.

RESTAURANTS ... In Manila the *Bulakeña* Restaurant and the *Aristocrat* Restaurant on Roxas Boulevard specialize in native foods. *New Europe,* the *Keg Room,* the *Swiss Inn,* the *Petal* and *Moon Gate* at the Manila Hotel, the *Golden Lotus* at the Hotel Filipinas, *Bay View House* at the Bay View Hotel and *Boie's* on the Escolta serve Filipino, Spanish, American, Chinese, European and Indonesian foods. *Max's* on Roxas Boulevard and its main restaurant in Quezon City specialize in fried chicken and have delighted many tourists. *Guernica's* on M.H. del Pilar for Spanish dishes; *Casa Marcos* and *Alba's Supper Club* for steaks; *Madrid Restaurant* for Spanish and international cuisines. *Di'Mark's* on Menlo Road has excellent Italian food. *The D & E Restaurant* and *Aristocrat* in Quezon City are also recommended. Newest in the suburbs is the *Sulô* in Makati. Prices in these eating places are not any higher than American prices. For low-budget but very good food, try *Taza de Oro* on M.H. del Pilar, *Kentucky Tavern* on San Vicente St., and the *Jade Vine* on United Nations Avenue. Popular new places for an informal meal are the *Omelet House, Chuck Wagon, Brick House* and *Gourmet's Inn.*

SHOPS AND STORES ... The principal shopping places in Manila are on the Escolta, Rizal Avenue, Dasmariñas, Quezon Boulevard, Carriedo and Echague. Native articles, especially souvenirs, are also available in native stores on the Escolta and in Ermita and Malate Districts. Most of the merchandise sold in fixed-price stores is American. Stores are open from 8 A.M. to 12 noon and from 2 P.M. to 6:30 P.M. or later, evenings. On Sunday some stores are open only in the morning. Prices are slightly higher than those in the States. Local products are inexpensive.

SPECTATOR SPORTS ... Polo, baseball, soccer, basketball, boxing, yachting regattas. Baseball and basketball are now the most popular sports. Basketball games are held 12 months a year at the Rizal Coliseum. Araneta Coliseum, Cubao, Quezon City, is a huge domed auditorium for sports. Tickets are sold at the gamesite or at some of the larger stores in Manila.

SPORTS ... There are superb beaches on all the islands, and facilities for skin diving, water skiing and deep-sea fishing. Outstanding golf courses in Manila, Baguio and Cebu City; numerous tennis courts.

THEATERS ... Amateur dramatic societies stage plays and operettas, and visiting opera companies and theatrical troupes give performances occasionally. The price of admission ranges from $1.35 to $5. While most of these plays are in English, some are in Spanish.

TIME ... Manila is 16 hours later than U.S. Pacific Standard Time. Tuesday noon in Manila is 8 P.M. Monday in San Francisco.

TIPPING ... Tip luggage porters 35-50 centavos per bag. Waiters, barbers, beauticians and taxi drivers are tipped 10%.

TRANSPORTATION ... Good taxi service, buses, jeepneys, trains and steamers. There are over 72 daily interisland air trips to all points of interest. Chauffeur-driven cars for hire are available for as low

The famous volcanic peak, Mt. Mayon, rises near the city of Legaspi.

as $2.50 an hour in Manila or suburbs. Trips to outlying tourist spots in the provinces may be arranged through local tour operators.

WATER . . . Water in Manila is excellent and safe to drink.

WHAT TO BUY . . . Embroidery, buntal hats, delicate piña bags, handkerchiefs, bags, rattan art, silver filigrees, linens, textiles, wood carvings, cigars, shellcraft, beautiful wooden salad bowls, canapé trays, fruit bowls, paintings and many other items.

WHAT TO WEAR . . . Both men and women should take clothing of wrinkle-resistant materials. In the evenings at the clubs and best hotels, men wear black trousers and white dinner jackets or the cool *barong tagalog*. Recommended materials for men and women are dacron, cotton, and other light materials. Bring sportswear, too.

WHERE TO GO—SIGHTSEEING . . .

Manila . . . In Manila you should see the Malacañang Palace, the official residence of the President of the Philippines; Santo Tomás, founded in 1611, one of the oldest universities in the world; Intramuros, the Spanish Walled City, now in ruins; Fort Santiago, an old dungeon built by the Spaniards and used by the Japanese as a prison in World War II; Rizal Stadium, Manila's sports center, and the new University of the Philippines at Quezon City. A short drive from Manila over an excellent highway is cool Tagaytay Ridge, overlooking beautiful Lake Taal. The Manila Hotel maintains a guest house at the ridge. On the way, at the church in Las Piñas, is the famous Bamboo Organ, reputed to be the only one in the world.

Other interesting day trips from Manila include visits to the Balara Filters, Pagsanjan Falls, Clark Air Force Base, the beautiful white sand beaches at Batangas and Bataan, historical Corregidor at the entrance to Manila Bay, and the day cruise to the island of Mindoro.

One hour by air from Manila is Baguio, picturesque summer capital in the mountains. North of Baguio in Banaue one sees huge rice terraces carved from the mountainsides, a marvel of primitive engineering. If you have the time, you'll find it interesting to visit the Bicol provinces in southeastern Luzon and the southern islands of the Visayas, Mindanao and Sulu groups (2 hours by air from Manila).

SOURCES OF FURTHER INFORMATION . . . The Philippine Tourist and Travel Association, with offices in the Shurdut Building, Intramuros, Manila; at 15 E. 66th St., New York, N.Y. 10023; and at 212 Stockton St., San Francisco. Pan Am's Manila office is at 204 Escolta (Tel. 31981); and in the Magellan Hotel in Cebu City.

TAIWAN
(FORMOSA)

EAST CHINA SEA

TAIPEI ✱ Chilung

FORMOSA STRAIT

Wuchi ● Taichung
Changhua ●

PESCADORES

TAIWAN
(Formosa)

● Tainan

Kaohsiung ○

LUZON
STRAIT

WEATHER IN TAIPEI—Lat. N25°2′—Alt. 21′

	JAN.	FEB.	MAR.	APR.	MAY	JUNE	JULY	AUG.	SEPT.	OCT.	NOV.	DEC.
Average Temp.	60°	59°	63°	69°	76°	80°	83°	82°	80°	74°	68°	62°
Days of Rain	16	16	17	15	16	16	14	14	14	15	15	16

LOCATION ... The Taiwan Straits separate Taiwan from the Chinese mainland, 100 miles to the west.

CHARACTERISTICS ... Called "Ilha Formosa" (Beautiful Island) by Portuguese explorers, Taiwan (Terraced Bay) is one of the loveliest islands on earth, and is one of the few places in the free world where you can savor genuine Chinese culture, atmosphere and the wide, wonderful gamut of Chinese provincial cookery. The friendliness and hospitality of the islanders, as well as a hotel-building boom, have made Taiwan a must for travelers to the Far East.

POPULATION ... 11,884,000, of which 210,000 are aborigines.

SIZE ... Comprising 13,808 square miles, Taiwan is about 250 miles long, 85 miles wide. In addition, there are 64 small islands of the Pescadores group and 14 other outlying islands.

CAPITAL ... Taipei (pronounced Tie-bay), population 1,108,284.

GOVERNMENT ... A republic, founded in 1912.

HOW TO GET THERE ... By Pan American Jet Clipper to Hong Kong, then 1½ hours by jet to Taipei; or to Tokyo, then 4½ hours by jet; or to Manila, then 1¾ hours by jet. By ship, about 21 days.

ACCOMMODATIONS ... The *Grand Hotel,* long a tradition in the East, is outside Taipei on a hill overlooking city and river. Grandly Oriental in design, very Western in comfort, rates at this de luxe hotel are $10 single, $12.50-$15 double. New hotels opened in 1962 are the *Astar, China, Nanking* and *First;* rates average $6.50 single, $10 double. In 1963, the *New Taipei* and *Hotel Taiwan* were added; in 1964: the 400-room *President Hotel* and the 300-room *Ambassador:* in 1965, the 330-room *Mandarin Hotel*. Less expensive are the *Prince Hotel, Hotel Oasis,* the *Green Garden, Queen, Paris, Lucky, Park Hotel* and *Stone House;* rates about $5 single, $7.50 double. All hotels listed have air conditioning; European Plan rates, exclusive of 10% service charges. Charming, comfortable hotels are located throughout the island at scenic spots.

CALENDAR OF HOLIDAYS... New Year's Day; Youth Day, March 29; Confucius' Birthday, September 28; National Day, October 10; Restoration Day, October 25; Dr. Sun Yat-sen's Birthday, November 12; Constitution Day, December 25. Of the many colorful festivals governed by the lunar calendar, the most elaborate are: Chinese New Year (January or February), followed by the Lantern Festival; Buddha's Birthday (April); Dragon Boat Festival (May or June); Moon Festival (September or October).

CIGARETTES AND TOBACCO... American brands not readily available. Popular local cigarettes are *Paotao, Long Life, Suang Shi, President* and *Jade Mount.*

CLIMATE... In the north, the warm and humid summer season lasts from May to October. January and February can be chilly. The average rainfall is 101 inches, with regional variations. Southern Taiwan is warmer, less humid—like southern California. Typhoons can occur from late August to mid-October.

COMMUNICATIONS... Overseas radio and radiophone services. Airmail postage rates to the U.S. are NT$10 (equivalent to U.S. 25¢) for letters, NT$6 for airletters and NT$5 for postcards.

CURRENCY... There are NT$40 (40 New Taiwan dollars) to U.S. $1.

CUSTOMS REGULATIONS AND DOCUMENTS REQUIRED FOR UNITED STATES CITIZENS... Passport and smallpox and cholera vaccination certificates. Apply for a transit or tourist visa at any Chinese consulate; readily obtainable. Personal effects, 1 bottle of liquor and 200 cigarettes enter duty free.

ELECTRIC CURRENT... Same as in the United States.

FOOD... A number of hotels and restaurants serve Western food, but Taiwan is the place to revel in genuine Cantonese cookery; to try the sweet and salty dishes of Shanghai; peppery-hot dishes in the style of Szechuan; crisp meats à la Peking; all-around Chinese dishes of Hunan; real Mongolian barbecued meats; Shensi- and Soochow-style breakfasts; Foochow shrimp balls; Hangchow vinegared fish. You'll speedily grasp the art of eating with chopsticks. Food prices are very modest by Western standards. This is truly a gastronomes' paradise. Pasteurized milk is available in Taipei. The better hotels and restaurants serve distilled water; elsewhere drink hot tea. Local beers, rice wine and plum liquors are good, and imported liquors are served at bars.

LANGUAGE... English is widely understood. Mandarin Chinese is official.

LAUNDRY AND DRY CLEANING ... Efficient services.

MEDICAL FACILITIES ... Several American hospitals.

SPORTS ... A fine 18-hole golf course and scenic beach at Tamsui, north of Taipei. Green Lake, 6½ miles south of the city, is ideal for boating.

TIPPING ... Very little goes a long way. A really "big" tip is NT$10 (25¢), but you get willing service with no tipping at hotels where the 10% service charge is included. In first-class restaurants, tip 10%. Taxi drivers are not tipped.

TRANSPORTATION ... Taxi rates are NT$6 for the first mile; NT$2 for each additional ⅓ mile. Pedicabs are fun and can be hired for NT$40 an hour. The air-conditioned Bienvenue tourist express train runs the length of the island in 6 hours. Sleek, modern buses link all cities, and Civil Air Transport (CAT) planes reach major centers.

WHAT TO BUY ... Lovely embroideries and drawn work; jewelry of coral, semi-precious stones, pearls; lacquerware and ceramics; carved wood, bamboo and rattan furniture. Recommended shops are identified by the insignia of the Taiwan Visitors Association (TVA), but you'll also enjoy bargaining for curios in Haggle Alley.

WHERE TO GO—SIGHTSEEING ...

Taipei ... There are numerous travel agencies in Taipei that will send a car and English-speaking guide to your hotel to take you on tours of the city; escorted all-day tours cost about $10. Guides, for very reasonable fees, will also accompany you on trips around the island by train, plane, bus or car. In Taipei, major sights are the Botanical Gardens, within which are the National Historical Museum (magnificent Chinese arts of all kinds) and the National Science Hall. See the charming Provincial Museum; the Taiwan Handicraft Center; the gorgeously ornate Lungshan Temple; Confucius Temple; the night market. On the outskirts of the city is Grass Mountain, a lovely resort area famed for its hot springs, pretty waterfall and exotic vegetation. Be sure to see at least one Chinese opera; visit the China Pottery Factory near Peitou.

Taichung ... A ¾-hour flight from Taipei, this typically Chinese city is the provincial capital, with the fabulous National Palace Museum (closed Mondays) on the edge of town. Here are displayed priceless treasures from the Peiping Palace, one of the world's greatest collections of Chinese arts. At Changhua, 10 miles south, is the 72-foot Buddha, largest statue in the Far East. In cool hills, 45 miles from Taichung, is exquisite Sun-Moon Lake at an elevation of 2,508 feet. An incomparably beautiful place, where you can enjoy the singing and dancing of pretty aborigine girls and take cruises on the lake. Stay at the popular *Evergreen Hotel*. In eastern Taiwan, Taroko Gorge is one of the greatest natural spectacles in the Orient.

SOURCES OF FURTHER INFORMATION ... Taiwan Visitors Association, 158 Sinsheng N. Road, Section I, Taipei (Tel. 44537). Pan American is represented by Taiwan Trading Corp., 103 Chung Shan N. Road, Sec. II (Tel. 46935; 48284-7).

THAILAND
(SIAM)

LAOS
BURMA
Chiengmai
Vientiane
Lopbori
BANGKOK
Ayudhya (Ayuthia)
Angkor Wat
Hua Hin
Ruins (Seamreap)
CAMBODIA
THAILAND
BAY
OF
Songhla
SOUTH CHINA
BENGAL MALA
SEA

WEATHER IN BANGKOK—Lat. N13°45′—Alt. 40′

Temp.	JAN.	FEB.	MAR.	APR.	MAY	JUNE	JULY	AUG.	SEPT.	OCT.	NOV.	DEC.
Low	67°	70°	73°	76°	76°	76°	76°	76°	75°	75°	71°	67°
High	92°	93°	95°	97°	95°	93°	92°	92°	91°	91°	89°	89°
Average	80°	82°	84°	87°	86°	85°	84°	84°	83°	83°	80°	78°
Days of Rain	1	3	4	6	17	18	19	19	21	17	7	3

LOCATION ... In the southeast corner of Asia between Burma on the west and Laos, Cambodia and Vietnam on the east.

CHARACTERISTICS ... Thailand is pronounced Tie-land. The people in the north and northeast are much fairer in color than those in the south. Thai rice is really the wealth of the country. Tourists will be impressed by the pleasantness and almost childlike cheerfulness of the Thai people. "The Land of Smiles" will best describe these pleasant people. "Mai Pen Rai," which means "never mind," is one of the popular Thai sayings.

POPULATION ... Estimated 28,835,000.

SIZE ... 198,247 square miles; 960 miles long, 540 miles wide at its widest point.

CAPITAL ... Bangkok, including the city of Thonburi, directly across the river, has a population of over 2,000,000 inhabitants.

HOW TO GET THERE ... By Jet Clipper, Bangkok is 3½ hours flying time from Hong Kong and approximately 26½ hours eastbound from New York. By ship 50 to 60 days from New York.

ACCOMMODATIONS ... One of the best hotels in Bangkok is the air-conditioned *Erawan* with swimming pool and 3 dining rooms. The new air-conditioned *Rama Hotel* also has a pool and a shopping center. *Oriental Hotel,* with its new swimming pool and Tower Wing, located on the river, and *Trocadero Hotel* and Annex are in a central location. Average rates are $12 single, $16 double. The *Princess* ($8-$13 single, $10-$15 double) and *Plaza* ($10 single, $14 double) are also central. The *Royal* (with swimming pool) and the *Palace*

Hotel are located near the Grand Palace but are not in the main business area. Other hotels: the *Rex, Imperial, Federal, Amarind, Thai, Grand Hotel,* and *Kings;* average $8 single, $10 double. Check on the availability of the luxurious *Bangkok Intercontinental Hotel.*

ARTS . . . The National Museum in Bangkok has an extensive collection of sculpture, textiles and porcelains. Bangkok has some 350 Buddhist monasteries, many of which contain fine examples of Thai frescoes and sculpture. The two most important are the Chapel Royal or Wat Phra Keo in the old palace, in which is housed the Emerald Buddha, and Wat Benjamabopit (Marble Temple).

BALLET . . . There is no ballet as we know it, but the world-famous Royal Thai classical dancing is a must for tourists. Enchanting performances at the Rama, Erawan and Royal hotels, at Phakavali Institute and the National Museum.

BANKS . . . Bank of America; Chase Manhattan Bank; Hong Kong Shanghai Bank; the Chartered Bank; Bank of China; Banque de L'Indo-chine; Indian Overseas Bank, Ltd., Mercantile Bank of India, Ltd. Travelers checks may be cashed at banks, with licensed money changers and at many shops.

CALENDAR OF HOLIDAYS . . . Holidays are variable depending upon lunar calendar. Shops and museums usually stay open.

CIGARETTES AND TOBACCO . . . U.S. cigarettes cost 10 baht (50¢). Good Thai brands cost 6 baht (30¢).

CLIMATE . . . December, January and February are the best months to visit Thailand. It's hot but not humid during the day, and cool at night. March, April and May constitute the "hot season"; June through October, with refreshing monsoon showers, is a delightful time; and November through February is the "cool season."

CLUBS . . . American Chamber of Commerce, American Women's Club, Rotary, Skal Club and Lions. Also private clubs, such as the Royal Bangkok Sports Club, Polo and Riding Club, Turf Club, and Cosmopolitan Club.

COMMON COURTESIES AND LOCAL CUSTOMS . . . The word *"Sa-wat-dee"* is an all-occasions greeting. *"Korb-jai"* is "Thank you." Thais are lively, easy-going people and very tolerant, but even foreigners are asked to remove their shoes before entering Buddhist temples, and Thais have an aversion to being nudged or back-slapped.

COMMUNICATIONS . . . Long-distance calls to the States cost 275.5 baht for 3 minutes; 70 baht for a 10-word cablegram. Postage for a 5-gram letter is 4.80 baht. Airletter forms are only 3 baht.

CURRENCY . . . The baht (also called tical) is divided into 100 satangs, and is worth about 5¢, or 20–21 to U.S. $1.

CUSTOMS REGULATIONS AND DOCUMENTS REQUIRED FOR UNITED STATES CITIZENS . . . You must have a passport but no visa necessary for visits up to 15 days. Smallpox vaccination and cholera inoculation certificates required. Yellow fever inoculation if coming from infected areas. You may bring in 200 cigarettes or 50 cigars and 1 bottle of liquor duty free. No more than $500 in U.S. currency, the rest in travelers checks. Up to 500 baht may be taken in or out. Chinese-type articles are either prohibited or require a certificate of origin for entry into the United States. Consult the nearest U.S. Consul for latest requirements. Air departure tax $1.

DRUGSTORES ... There are drugstores with the usual pharmaceuticals, both American and European.

ELECTRIC CURRENT ... Voltage 220, A.C., 50 cycles. British-style plugs (round prong) are used for some electrical fixtures.

FAUNA ... Tigers, serpents, crocodiles, bears, boars, deer (Asiatic varieties), rhinoceros, monkeys and gibbons, tapirs, porcupines, hares, leopards, seladang (wild buffalo), wild dogs, elephants, big lizards, peacocks, parrots, myna birds and many other varieties of birds as well as domesticated and pet animals. Siamese cats, of course, including the Korat cats, which are gray.

FLORA ... Every variety of orchid, gardenias, hibiscus and other exotic tropical plants; flame trees, teak forests; huge assortment of tropical fruits: mangoes, rose apples, bananas (20 varieties), papaya, durians, oranges, pomeloes, very tender pineapples, mangosteens, lichee-like rambutans, enormous jack-fruits.

FOOD ... Chinese delicacies, such as bird's-nest soup and shark's-fin soup. Thai rice is considered the best in the world and Thai curries are excellent. Rice birds, *plakapong* (a large but delicate fish), superb prawns, are delicacies. Thai dishes are often explosively seasoned, many with *nam prig* (shrimp and pepper juice), but most hotels and many restaurants serve European foods (*see* RESTAURANTS).

GAMBLING ... No organized gambling, except legal betting at the horse races, and Government lottery held weekly.

LANGUAGE ... Thai (pronounced "Tie") is the national language. Personnel in the first-class hotels and shops understand some English, so don't worry about not speaking Thai.

LAUNDRY AND DRY CLEANING ... There are adequate laundry facilities. Dry cleaning is available, and is fairly satisfactory.

LIQUOR ... All the better known wines and spirits are available at bars and restaurants as well as in grocery stores. Try some *mekong,* a local Thai whisky made from rice.

MEDICAL FACILITIES ... The Bangkok Nursing Home, Bangkok Christian Hospital, Seventh Day Adventist Hospital, Red Cross Hospital, Siriraj Hospital and Chulalongkorn Hospital. There are American- and European-trained doctors.

MOTION PICTURES ... Air-conditioned movie theaters showing pictures in English. Shows at set hours; seats reserved.

MUSIC ... Only in connection with dancing and drama, mentioned elsewhere, at the fights, and on radio and TV.

NIGHT CLUBS ... European-type: *Tropicana Room, Ambassador Club, Club Keynote, Dewdrop Inn, Sida, Domino, Moulin Rouge* and *Orchid Room.* With hostesses: *Lido, Luna Club, Sani Chateau, Champagne Room, Naturist, Starlight.*

PHOTOGRAPHY ... Film is available but expensive and color developing very expensive. There is a Thai dance show every Saturday morning at 9, November through May, at the National Museum where, for a $3 fee, shutterbugs can snap pictures of exotic dancers.

RELIGION ... The national religion of Thailand is Buddhism. There is a Protestant Episcopal church on Convent Road in Bangkok; the Protestant International Church; and numerous Roman Catholic churches in Bangkok.

RESTAURANTS ... *Erawan Hotel, Oriental Hotel, Rama Hotel, Trocadero Hotel, Princess Hotel, Nick's Hungarian Inn, Mizu's, Trader Keith's, Palms Restaurant and Club Keynote,* and numerous very good Chinese ones such as *Hoi Thien Lau* or *Golden Dragon; Plaza Hotel* for Thai food, also the *Sabai Thong, Tip Pre Cahr Thai Sala* and *Salinee* restaurants.

SHOPS AND STORES ... Hours same as in the United States; Chinese shops are open on Sunday. *See* WHAT TO BUY.

SPECTATOR SPORTS ... Kite-flying contests are held every afternoon in the hot season on the Pramain Ground near the Royal Palace (February through May). Boxing with native music, a must, takes place Sundays and Thursdays at 5 P.M. in the Rajadamnern Stadium. There's also boxing at Lumpini Stadium on Tuesdays and Saturdays. Horse racing every Saturday afternoon at the Sports Club and Sunday at the Turf Club with pari-mutuel betting except during August and September. *Takraw* is one of the oldest Thai games. It is a kind of static soccer. The object of the game is for players, who form a circle, to send the hollow wicker ball across to one another by hitting it with any part of the body without its hitting the ground. *Takraw* may be seen all year round and is in the nature of a "pickup" game rather than an organized sport.

SPORTS ... Fishing: There is a tremendous variety of fish in the rivers and the Gulf. Fishing trips can be arranged on the Chao Phraya River and in the Gulf of Thailand. There is fine duck shooting up the Chao Phraya and good rice-bird shooting in the rice paddies outside of Bangkok. Squash at the Sports Club. Tennis: There are both grass and clay courts as well as many private courts. Golf: There are courses at the Royal Air Force Golf Club, Sports Club and Turf Club, but guest cards are necessary. Swimming: Most of Bangkok's best hotels have pools, and there is fine sea bathing in the Gulf of Thailand. Water skiing and yachting at Pataya Beach, a 2½-hour drive from Bangkok, and at Hua Hin, 4½ hours away. Hunting: Licenses are required for firearms and hunting. Equipment may be hired locally through travel services.

TIME ... Twelve hours later than U.S. Eastern Standard Time.

TIPPING ... Bangkok hotels add a 10% service charge to your bill, which covers everything but 2 to 5 baht for luggage porter. There is no need to give extra tips to waiters and taxi drivers.

TRANSPORTATION ... Automobiles with a chauffeur may be hired at any hotel. Self-drive cars may be rented, but are not advised because of traffic conditions. Taxis are plentiful, but even if your taxi has a meter, bargain for the fare before starting. Avoid expensive hotel and night club taxi ranks; hail a passing cab down the block. Regular air service to all parts of the country.

WATER ... Drink bottled water (*Polaris*).

WHAT TO BUY ... There are many jewelers and silversmiths in Bangkok where fine semiprecious stones and antique jewelry, among other items, can be purchased. Try Ainslee on New Road, Zerner's at Rama Hotel, Alex's on Oriental Avenue, Oriental Jeweler's in Oriental Lane, T. Seng in Banmoh area and Jonny Siam. For very fine hand-woven silks and brocades try Star of Siam in the Erawan Hotel. Thai silk hand-weaving factory opposite the Trocadero Hotel and Thai Silk Company, Ltd., 430 Suriwongse Road. For made-to-measure dresses try Star of Siam in the Erawan Hotel. Go to Thai Nakorn, Kwang Ann, E. Seng Chong, Pratib on New Road for Neilloware and silverware. Attractive and unusual are temple stone-rubbing designs on rice paper. Nakorn Kasem is the antique dealer's area. Also, the Monogram Shops in Erawan and Oriental Hotels for antiques. Crocodile and snakeskin bags, shoes, belts and wallets at Crocodile Store on New Road. Bronze flatware with horn handles is a bargain.

WHAT TO WEAR ... In Bangkok wear the same type of clothing that you would in Nassau or Hong Kong. Lightweight suits, a light sports jacket and slacks for men; washable dresses for women. Bangkok is not a "dressy" place. Women should not wear shorts except in private clubs or pool areas.

WHERE TO GO—SIGHTSEEING ...

Bangkok ... Is a breath-taking vista of exquisite temples and lovely palaces. The city is interlinked by canals, called *klongs,* and the main river, called the Chao Phraya. The floating market is the highlight of a visit to Thailand—go out at 7 A.M. by boat and come back at 10 A.M. The Temple of the Reclining Buddha (Wat Po) and the Temple of Dawn (Wat Arun), whose tower offers a fine view, are both fantastic. *See also* ARTS. Other sightseeing possibilities include; the royal barges; Suan Pakkad Palace; the colorful weekend market on the Pramain Ground, the "thieves" market located in the Nakorn Kasem section of Bangkok; Pasteur Institute on Rama IV Road with its Snake Farm.

Chiengmai ... The northern capital of Thailand is the second largest city in the country. Chiengmai is easily reached by air in about 3 hours by daily service from Bangkok, 20 hours by train. Tourists immediately will enjoy a complete change of scenery. While the surroundings of Bangkok are flat and extend into seemingly endless rice fields, Chiengmai has pleasantly hilly countryside, and teak forests. Air-conditioned rooms with bath at *Chiengmai, New Railway* and *Suriwongse* hotels.

Hua Hin ... Thailand's best sea resort, with a fine beach, good swimming, tennis, golf and sailing. The main season is from December to May. Hua Hin is about 5 hours from Bangkok. The *Hua Hin* hotel features European food.

Ayudhya ... The former capital of Thailand, founded in 1350, is noted for the ruins of its former palaces and temples, where a vast seated Buddha may be seen. Ayudhya (Ayuthia) can be reached by river from Bangkok in 6 hours and by road in approximately 2 hours.

Lopburi ... The ruins of this very old city are located 100 miles

You'll be fascinated by the bizarre statues and temple architecture in Bangkok. Precious stones, gold and brightly colored tiles go into the elaborate designs of religious significance.

Charming Siamese girls in beautiful ornate costume do their intricate classical dances for tourists. The Siamese Classical Theater is a must in Bangkok.

north of Bangkok. Legend has it that Lopburi was founded in 468 A.D. as the town of Lavo, by King Kalavarhadi. Under King Narai the Great, Lopburi became the capital of Siam and one can see in the ruins what was perhaps an attempt to emulate the Hall of Mirrors at Versailles. Lopburi may be reached by train in 8 hours, by riverboat in about 10 hours or by car in 6 hours.

Nakorn Pathom ... Half-day trips are available to Thailand's oldest city, 30 miles west of Bangkok, which dates from 150 B.C. Pilgrims throng to the glittering-spired Phra Pathom Chedi shrine, decorated with very ancient stone figures.

Angkor Wat, Cambodia ... Check with Pan American regarding the availability of tours by air to these fabulous ruins.

SOURCES OF FURTHER INFORMATION ... Tourist Organization of Thailand, 20 E. 82 St., New York, N.Y. In Bangkok, Pan American is opposite the Trocadero Hotel (Tel. 38901) and at the Erawan Hotel. The Tourist Organization of Thailand is on Rajadamnern Ave. (Tel. 20043).

VIETNAM

WEATHER IN SAIGON—Lat. N10°47′

	JAN.	FEB.	MAR.	APR.	MAY	JUNE	JULY	AUG.	SEPT.	OCT.	NOV.	DEC.
Average Temp.	79°	83°	83°	86°	86°	84°	84°	82°	83°	82°	80°	79°
Days of Rain	0	0	0	6	7	18	25	24	21	15	7	3

LOCATION ... In the extreme southeast corner of Asia, bordering the South China Sea.

CHARACTERISTICS ... Saigon is one of the most attractive cities of the Orient, characterized by a combination of French and Oriental cultures and tastes. It has many fine buildings, wide, tree-lined boulevards, and some of the prettiest women in the world. Adjoining is Cholon, the Chinese city and commerce center with all the exotic charms of the East.

POPULATION ... Approximately 15,317,000 in South Vietnam.

SIZE ... 66,280 square miles; 900 miles of coastline.

CAPITAL ... Saigon, with Cholon, has 2,000,000 people.

GOVERNMENT ... South Vietnam is a Republic.

HOW TO GET THERE ... By Pan American Clipper, 2¼ hours from Manila, 1¾ hours from Singapore, 2½ hours from Hong Kong, 21¼ hours from San Francisco. Saigon may be easily included in a Round-the-World itinerary.

ACCOMMODATIONS ... Best hotels in Saigon are located on Tu-Do Street in the main shopping area. The new, fully air-conditioned *Caravelle,* from $13.83 single, $18.42 double, including breakfast; the air-conditioned *Majestic,* $10-$12 single, $14-$15.20 double, including light breakfast and choice of lunch or dinner; *Continental Palace,* $9.59-$12.33 single, $13.50 double, including breakfast and taxes. Non-air-conditioned rooms in all hotels are considerably cheaper. Hotels add a 12% service charge in lieu of tips, and most also add 10% tax.

CLIMATE ... The climate is tropical with only slight temperature variations. There are two seasons in Vietnam, the dry season from October to May and the rainy season from May to October.

CURRENCY ... The monetary unit is the piastre (dông). Tourist rate of exchange is 73 to U.S. $1. Money should be exchanged at banks, at the exchange bureau in the airport or at leading hotels.

CUSTOMS REGULATIONS AND DOCUMENTS REQUIRED FOR UNITED STATES CITIZENS ... American citizens who have a passport and onward transportation, if traveling as tourists, are exempt from visas if their stay in Vietnam will not exceed 7 days. All other persons remaining more than 72 hours and those going to Cambodia (Angkor) require a visa. Smallpox vaccination is required and yellow fever and cholera inoculations are required if coming from infected area. Visitors on business should make visa applications early through Vietnamese Legations. 400 cigarettes, one opened bottle of liquor may be brought in duty free. No more than 500 piastres allowed.

ELECTRIC CURRENT ... 110/220 volts, A.C., 50 cycles.

FOOD ... Fine French foods and wines are served in hotels, but the rich fragrance surrounding the street vendors will make you want to try Vietnamese foods, too. Westerners particularly like *phong tom* (large shrimp chips), *cha-gio* (similar to Chinese egg roll), *cha tôm* (omelet with pork and shrimps), and the intricate "beef in seven dishes." *Nuoc mam,* a much-used fish paste, tastes better than it smells.

WATER ... Avoid drinking water that hasn't been boiled. Bottled drinks are available.

WHAT TO BUY ... Textiles in exotic patterns, lacquerware of all kinds, ceramics, tortoise-shell ware. Visit the Handicraft Center on Tu-Do Street. Ladies will be tempted to buy an *ao-dai,* the wonderfully becoming costume of Vietnamese ladies, and a conical straw hat. Don't miss the fascinating hodgepodge in the huge Central Market. You are expected to bargain everywhere except in department stores, where French imports are good buys.

Saigon ... You'll want to browse around in the Central Market, the Flower Market, the many lovely Chinese and Vietnamese pagodas, the superb Botanical Garden and zoo. The National Museum has a good collection of Oriental art, and there is an unusual display of palanquins and 18th-century war gear at the temple of Marshal Le Van Duyet. Local travel agents can arrange motor boat trips down Saigon's river teeming with junks and sampans.

Angkor Wat ... One of the great sights of the Orient; several flights weekly from Saigon to Siem Reap, Cambodia. *See* CAMBODIA chapter.

SOURCES OF FURTHER INFORMATION ... Pan American's representative is located at 23 Duong Ngo Duc Ke, Saigon, care of Denis Frères, General Agent (Tel. 22618 and 22522).

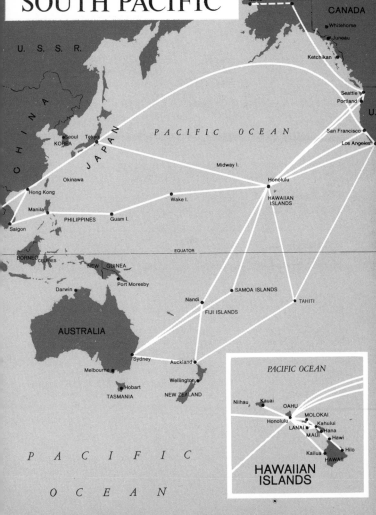

ALASKA, HAWAII *and the* SOUTH PACIFIC

U. S. S. R.

ALASKA

Nome Fairbanks

CANADA

Whitehorse

Juneau

Ketchikan

Seattle
Portland

U.

San Francisco

Los Angeles

CHINA

Seoul
KOREA Tokyo

JAPAN

PACIFIC OCEAN

Okinawa

Midway I.

Honolulu

Hong Kong

Wake I.

HAWAIIAN
ISLANDS

Manila

PHILIPPINES Guam I.

Saigon

EQUATOR

BORNEO
CELEBES

NEW GUINEA

Port Moresby

Darwin

Nandi

SAMOA ISLANDS

TAHITI

FIJI ISLANDS

AUSTRALIA

Sydney Auckland

Melbourne

Wellington

Hobart

NEW ZEALAND

TASMANIA

P A C I F I C

O C E A N

HAWAIIAN ISLANDS

PACIFIC OCEAN

Niihau Kauai

OAHU

Honolulu

MOLOKAI

LANAI Kahului

Hana

MAUI Hawi

Kailua Hilo

HAWAII

ALASKA

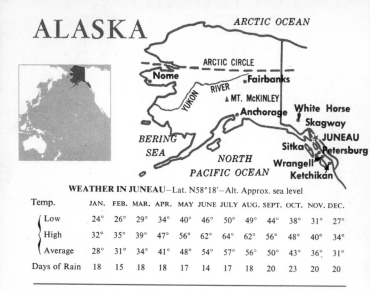

WEATHER IN JUNEAU—Lat. N58°18′—Alt. Approx. sea level

Temp.	JAN.	FEB.	MAR.	APR.	MAY	JUNE	JULY	AUG.	SEPT.	OCT.	NOV.	DEC.
Low	24°	26°	29°	34°	40°	46°	50°	49°	44°	38°	31°	27°
High	32°	35°	39°	47°	56°	62°	64°	62°	56°	48°	40°	34°
Average	28°	31°	34°	41°	48°	54°	57°	56°	50°	43°	36°	31°
Days of Rain	18	15	18	18	17	14	17	18	20	23	20	20

LOCATION ... Alaska, our 49th state, lies in the far northwest corner of the North American continent and includes the Aleutian Islands. The Alaska mainland is due north of Honolulu. The Aleutians extend as far west as New Zealand.

CHARACTERISTICS ... The name "Alaska" was derived from an Aleut word meaning "great land," and every inch of Alaska lives up to its name, with the highest mountains on the North American continent (Mt. McKinley, 20,300 feet) and rivers long and mighty (Yukon, 2,300 miles). It's a big and beautiful country from the steepwalled fjords of the southeast to the wide horizons of the Bering Sea coast. In the summer the sun shines 18 to 24 hours. In winter it's a Jack Frost wonderland awesomely illuminated by the Northern Lights. It's also a sportsmen's favorite, with big fish and big game.

POPULATION ... Alaska's total population is 250,000, of which about 33,000 are military and about 43,000 are Indian, Aleut and Eskimo.

SIZE ... 586,400 square miles—more than twice the size of Texas.

CAPITAL ... Juneau, with a total population of 13,000.

GOVERNMENT ... A U.S. state since January 3, 1959.

HOW TO GET THERE ... By Pan Am Jet Clipper, nonstop service from Seattle to Fairbanks, 3 hours flying time. Service also from Portland. Fairbanks to Juneau by Wien Alaska Airlines, 1½ hours; Fairbanks to Nome, 2 hours via Wien Alaska. Anchorage is 2½ hours flying time beyond Juneau via Pacific Northern Airlines.

Cruise ships operate during the summer. The Alaska Highway, now partially paved, is reached through Alberta, Canada, or the Hart Highway through British Columbia.

ACCOMMODATIONS ... The *Baranof-Western* in Juneau is one of the favorite hotels in Alaska and has music nightly in the Latchstring; single $14, double $21-$35. In Anchorage the *Anchorage-Westward* is distinctive and features The Top of the World restaurant overlooking city, mountains and harbor; single $12-$22, double $15-$26. Top hotels in Fairbanks are the new *Fairbanks Inn*, single $14-$18, double, $20-$24; *Travelers Inn*, single $16-$18, double $22-$24; and *Sullivan*, single $13.50, double $18. In Ketchikan, the *Ingersoll*, single $11-$12, double $15-$16; *Stedman* and *George*, about $8 single, $11 double. All rates are European Plan. Fairbanks and Juneau hotels add 3% sales tax; in Anchorage they add 2%. Inns and motels charge about the same rates.

ARTS ... In Juneau, the museum in the State Capital Building, and in Fairbanks, the University of Alaska museum on the campus, contain collections of Alaska Indian, Eskimo and Aleut artifacts.

CALENDAR OF HOLIDAYS ... In addition to U.S. national holidays, there are Seward's Day on March 30, and Alaska Day, October 18. Opening days of the Salmon Derby in Juneau and Ketchikan are usually declared a civic holiday.

CIGARETTES AND TOBACCO ... All American brands.

CLIMATE ... In the Arctic and in the area around Fairbanks, it is dry and cold with subzero temperatures in the winter, but quite warm and sunny during the summer months. Anchorage and the Kenai Peninsula area have weather comparable to the Midwestern states of the United States. The southern coastal areas are warmed by the Japanese current. The days of rain on the chart above are for southeastern Alaska only, and do not reflect the weather conditions in the interior. Best months to visit are May through October.

CLUBS ... Rotary, Lions, Kiwanis, Elks, Moose, Eagles, Toastmasters, Toastmistress, Soroptomists, Quota, Business and Professional Women, and National League of American Penwomen, among others. Cards required for Elks, Moose and Eagles.

COMMUNICATIONS ... Same as in other states.

CURRENCY ... United States currency used throughout Alaska. In southeastern cities Canadian currency is generally accepted.

COMMON COURTESIES AND LOCAL CUSTOMS ... You'll see familiar stores along Main Street, although civilization may appear to stop abruptly at city limits, because of the sparse population. An old timer is known as a *sourdough*, a tenderfoot is a *cheechako*.

DRUGSTORES ... All the usual products are available.

FAUNA ... Big game includes brown, black and grizzly bear, mountain goat and sheep, moose, deer and caribou. Other wildlife includes mink, beaver, marten, lynx, muskrat, wolf and wolverine. Waterfowl are abundant. The beautiful Husky dog is used for transportation in the Arctic during the winter months.

FLORA ... Alaska is a blaze of color during the summer months with beautiful wildflowers and wild rosebushes. A heavily wooded country, the principal trees are spruce, birch, hemlock, cedar, alders, cottonwood and mountain ash.

FOOD . . . During the summer, restaurants and hotel dining rooms serve freshly caught salmon and halibut. Various types of shrimp dishes are a specialty; tender, succulent crab is another northern treat. In Nome and Kotzebue reindeer is available. Almost all other foods are imported. Prices are slightly higher than in Seattle.

GAMBLING . . . Gambling is prohibited.

LANGUAGE . . . English is spoken throughout Alaska.

LAUNDRY AND DRY CLEANING . . . Same as at home.

LIQUOR . . . Same as in the rest of the United States.

MEDICAL FACILITIES . . . Excellent hospitals and clinics.

MOTION PICTURES . . . First-run pictures shown everywhere.

MUSIC . . . Opera and concert artists appear in major cities during the winter season.

NIGHT CLUBS AND CABARETS . . . A variety of night clubs in the principal cities. Visiting U.S. bands and floor shows are featured.

PHOTOGRAPHY . . . Black-and-white still and movie film and color film are available. Prices slightly higher than in the other states.

RELIGION . . . Virtually all churches represented.

RESTAURANTS . . . For the sportsman: most restaurants will cook freshly caught fish if requested. Full-course meals cost about the same as in the rest of the United States. Short orders slightly higher. Steaks are excellent in most of the better eating places.

SHOPS AND STORES . . . Modern, well-lighted, well-stocked establishments carrying all nationally advertised brands.

SPORTS . . . June through August are the best months for huge trout, pike and salmon. Hunting safaris bag bighorn sheep, moose, deer, caribou, walrus, grizzly and polar bears from early August until mid-December. There are also bowling, curling, skiing, outboard motorboat racing, sled dog racing, stock car racing, horseback riding. Baseball, basketball and tennis are featured locally. Golf at the Fairbanks Golf Club; in Anchorage at the Forest Park Golf Club; in Juneau at the Sand Blasters Golf Club.

TIME . . . There are four time zones in Alaska: Juneau and southeastern Alaska on Pacific Standard Time; Yukon Standard Time, 1 hour earlier; Fairbanks and Anchorage on Alaska Standard Time, 2 hours earlier; Nome on Bering Sea Time, 3 hours earlier.

TIPPING . . . Same as in the rest of the United States.

TRANSPORTATION . . . Taxi firms, bus lines and limousine service in all of the principal cities. Car-rental services in Juneau, Anchorage, Ketchikan and Fairbanks. Local airlines, charter planes.

WATER . . . Excellent in all places.

WHAT TO BUY . . . Fur and cloth parkas, caps and gloves, wood and ivory carvings and jewelry, exquisite jade and black-diamond jewelry, totem poles, whalebone baskets and various other woven trays and baskets. Beautiful reindeer and other leather goods in hats, jackets, bags, shoes and clothing. Tanned salmon- and halibut-skin wallets and bags. Fur and leather moccasins and *mukluks* (Eskimo boots). Fur garments should be bought only from established firms.

WHAT TO WEAR ... The same weight and type of clothing as you would wear in the rest of northern U.S. in season. Slacks are in order. Wool suits, tweeds, sweaters and rainwear are recommended. Dress clothes are not needed.

WHERE TO GO—SIGHTSEEING ...

Juneau ... In Alaska's beautiful capital city, among the buildings of interest are the State museum, Governor's Mansion and a number of interesting curio and leather shops. A 13-mile bus trip on Glacier Highway will take you to Mendenhall Glacier, a vast receding river of ice. (Price of round trip, $6.50.) In late July the Golden North Salmon Derby, a 3-day contest featuring prizes for big fish, attracts sportsmen from all over the United States. America's northernmost Catholic shrine, the Shrine of St. Theresa, is about 23 miles north of Juneau.

A Gray Line bus tour goes up Mt. Roberts to Gold Creek and the Alaska-Juneau Gold Mine (world's largest deposits); then a tramway and miners' cars take you through the hard rock tunnel.

Taku Lodge, a modern resort, is one of the scenic highlights of Alaska. About a half hour by air, or 3 hours by boat from Juneau, the Lodge features trout fishing and swimming in warm springs. Rates $20 a day American Plan. *Tongass Lodge* at Excursion inlet is 20 minutes by air from Juneau; rates $21 per day per person, AP.

Adjacent communities offer much of interest to the visitor. The charm of the old Russian days is still alive at Sitka, where the old Cathedral of St. Michael, with its rich oil paintings and fabulous ikons is located. A large collection of restored totems comprise the Sitka National Monument, open to visitors at no charge.

Haines is 70 miles north of Juneau at Lynn Canal. Excellent trout fishing. In the background is the scenic Chilkat range. The annual Fourth of July celebration and Strawberry Festival here features native Indian war dances. Stay at *Hotel Halsingland,* noted for its Swedish cuisine. Rates $8 single, $14 double, European Plan.

Skagway, terminus of White Pass and Yukon narrow-gauge railroad, retains its gold-rush atmosphere with original buildings, "gambling" saloon, annual Days of '98 Festival. Rates at new *Sourdough Inn* are $10 single, $16 double. From Skagway there are tours to Lake Bennet and Carcross.

Anchorage, Alaska's largest city, is the site of huge Army and Air Force bases. It is constantly throbbing with activity.

Stellar attraction of the area is Mount McKinley's National Park, habitat of wild animals and colorful birds. There are many beautiful lakes; excellent fishing. *McKinley Park Hotel* is a modern, modern inn. Park tours are available over the 90 miles of road within the reserve. For hikers and mountaineers *Camp Denali* offers limited facilities for the more adventurous. Mt. Alyeska, 38 miles south of Anchorage, is the site of the National Alpine Ski Championships. The *Tiger's*

Den is a cozy lodge here.

Katmai National Monument, on the far-flung Alaska Peninsula, where volcanos dot the terrain, is another of the colorful trips available from Anchorage. Accommodations and fishing camps are operated by Northern Consolidated Airlines. Large rainbow and grayling trout lakes are found at the various camps. Trips are $131.50 plus tax and up. Sightseeing flights are also available.

The romantic fur-seal islands in the Bering Sea can now be reached. Here 4 million seals and sea lions arrive annually to raise their young. Tours operated by Reeve Aleutian Airlines, $160 plus tax for 2-day round trip; meals and housing included.

Anchorage Fur Rendezvous, a week-long festival held in February, includes sports tournaments, ski contests, Eskimo pageants, parades and balls.

Fairbanks, heart of the gold-mining industry in the new state, is Alaska's second-largest city. Points of interest include the huge Ester Creek gold operation, the University of Alaska and its museum, and the University experimental farm. There are Husky dog kennels, a log-cabin town, and many unique restaurants and night clubs. Seasonal events in Fairbanks are: the Winter Carnival, a week-long pageant which includes the North American dog-racing derby, held in March; Golden Days, colorful celebration of discovery of gold, held in July; midnight baseball game on June 21, longest day; Tanana Valley Fair, August.

One of the most exciting trips out of Fairbanks is the 2-day all-expense tour with Wien Alaska Airlines to Kotzebue, on the Bering Sea, and Nome (about $150). Eskimo dances, skin-boat rides, reindeer-steak dinners are all part of planned entertainment. En route you cross the International Date Line and see the East Cape of Siberia. There's auto sightseeing in Nome, and a visit with the King Island Eskimos, whom you can watch carving ivory under their skin boats called "oomiaks." Another excellent tour is to Barrow, largest Eskimo village, where you see whaling in season, huge arctic ice packs, primitive sod houses, and take a short trip to the farthest north village site of the continent, where visitors can dig for artifacts.

Ketchikan has many famous old Indian totems at Saxman Park, 2 miles out, and more Indian poles and houses are located at Mud Bight, about 11 miles from the city. The Ketchikan Salmon Derby, held in early June, is the most spectacular event of the season.

Information on trout fishing and the many excellent lakes is available from Alaska Coastal-Ellis Air Lines, Ketchikan.

Kodiak is headquarters for the big-game hunter in search of a Kodiak bear, the world's largest carnivorous animal. Guides are available. In the town itself there are fish canneries and much lore of the old Russian days. Nearby is the Kodiak Naval Air Base.

SOURCES OF FURTHER INFORMATION . . . Alaska Travel Division, Alaska Office Building, Juneau, Alaska. Also local Chambers of Commerce. Pan American office at 511 Second Ave. (Tel. 452-2118), Fairbanks.

WEATHER IN SYDNEY—Lat. S33°52′—Alt. 138′

Temp.	JAN.	FEB.	MAR.	APR.	MAY	JUNE	JULY	AUG.	SEPT.	OCT.	NOV.	DEC.
Low	65°	65°	63°	57°	52°	48°	46°	47°	51°	56°	60°	63°
High	78°	78°	76°	71°	67°	61°	61°	63°	68°	71°	74°	77°
Average	72°	72°	70°	61°	59°	55°	53°	55°	59°	64°	67°	65°
Days of Rain	13	12	13	14	12	11	12	10	11	11	11	13

LOCATION . . . Australia lies in the South Pacific in the temperate zone except for parts of the north which reach into the tropic zone. The Island state of Tasmania lies about 140 miles off the south coast.

CHARACTERISTICS . . . This is the "sunshine continent," an open, smiling land of beautiful beaches, wonderful fishing, fine skiing and good golf. Australians spend most of their lives out-of-doors. They are marvelous sportsmen. Australians and Americans are alike in many ways. You'll find yourself quite at home "down under." There is, of course, no language barrier, although you will find some of their terms unfamiliar. Australia has something for everyone who enjoys new sights, new experiences. The cities are cosmopolitan, the roads good, the people hospitable. Much of Australia is wild and uncultivated, but the parts the average American tourist visits have most of the comforts of home with the advantage of being different.

POPULATION . . . 11,500,000.

SIZE . . . 2,974,576 square miles; 2,500 miles east-west, 2,000 miles north-south. Tasmania is slightly larger than West Virginia.

CAPITAL . . . Canberra, a fast-growing city of 100,000.

GOVERNMENT . . . A member of the British Commonwealth of Nations, Australia consists of six states (New South Wales, Victoria, Queensland, South Australia, Western Australia and Tasmania) which are self-governing on local matters, the Capital Territory and the Northern Territory. The country as a whole is governed by a Federal Parliament. A Governor-General represents the British sovereign.

HOW TO GET THERE ... By Jet Clipper via Honolulu, and the Fiji Islands, Sydney is 17¾ hours (elapsed time) from San Francisco and Los Angeles; via Auckland, 18¾ hours. Melbourne is about 1¼ hours from Sydney by air. By ship about 21 days from the U.S. west coast.

ACCOMMODATIONS ... Hotels in Sydney include: the smart *Chevron* and the new *Menzies,* both designed for the international tourist, rates from $13 single, $20 double; the *Australia,* also in the center of the city, from $9 single, $14 double; the *Carlton-Rex,* opposite the Australia, from $10.70 single, $15.20 double; the *Metropole,* convenient and comfortable, single from $8.75, double from $13. *King's Cross Rex,* in the heart of the night-club district, is 2 miles from the business section, double from $11.15. *Hotel Manly* is 7 miles from the city near a Pacific surf beach, single from $5.60, double from $11.20. *Astra Hotel,* overlooking Bondi surf beach, is 5 miles from the city, $9.50 single, $17 double; the *Coogee Bay,* handy to a surf beach, 6 miles from the city, from $4.75 single, $9.50 double.

Hotels in Melbourne (with single rates given) include: the luxurious new *Southern Cross,* an Intercontinental Hotel that is completely air-conditioned and encompasses 9 restaurants and bars, and an open plaza with 70 specialty shops and a 300-car underground garage, single from $9.40; the *Australia,* also conveniently located, $9; *Ress Oriental,* handy to shops and theaters, $9.50; *Menzies,* $9.50; *Savoy Plaza,* $8.40; *Windsor,* $9.50; *Chevron* (10 minutes from city center), $10.35. In suburban Melbourne, the *Prince of Wales* is near shops and beach, $6.50 single, $10.50 double; *St. James,* in a smart shopping and night club district, $6.30 single, $10.50 double, including breakfast. Hotel reservations should be made well in advance, particularly during spring racing season from September to November, and during the March racing season. American-style motels are springing up all over Australia. Rates for two average $11 per night.

ARTS ... In Sydney, the National Art Gallery contains a good collection of Australian and foreign paintings and statuary. Australian Museum, College Street and Hyde Park, specializes in aboriginal life and natural history. Macquarie Galleries, the Hungry Horse and other private galleries have exhibitions by leading Australian artists.

In Melbourne, the National Museum on Swanston Street carries a very fine selection of native crafts, as well as the stuffed and mounted "Phar Lap," the wonder horse. The National Art Gallery, Swanston Street, contains some of the finest works of art in the southern hemisphere, many acquired through the famed Felton Bequest. A noteworthy attraction in addition to the old masters is a collection of paintings by Australian artists.

BALLET ... Touring American and European companies appear from time to time. There is a national company too.

BANKS ... Representatives of banks meet every incoming plane to convert overseas travelers' funds and cash travelers checks, regardless of the arrival time of the aircraft. Thos. Cook & Son is at 350

George Street in Sydney, 159 Collins Street in Melbourne. American Express is at 87 King Street, Sydney.

CALENDAR OF HOLIDAYS ... New Year's Day; Good Friday; Easter Monday; Queen's Birthday (in June); January 26, Australia Day; Anzac Day, April 25; Labor Day, date varies in each State; Christmas Day; December 26, Boxing Day.

CIGARETTES AND TOBACCO ... About a dozen different U.S. brands of cigarettes are made in Australia. Imported American cigarettes are available at 30% above U.S. prices. Most Australian cigarettes (about 35¢ a pack) are American type; pipe tobacco is very good.

CLIMATE ... Australian seasons are the reverse of ours; summer starts in December; autumn in March; winter in June; spring in September. Climates vary greatly, and it is always perfect weather somewhere on the continent. April through November is the best time on the Great Barrier Reef, and October through April is best for seeing picturesque Tasmania.

CLUBS ... Sydney Turf Club; Lions; Rotary; Australia Jockey Club; American National Club. Tourists must be sponsored by a member at The Athenaeum, Melbourne and Green Room, all on Collins Street, Melbourne; The Australian, William Street, and R.A.C.V., Queen Street. For sports clubs, *see* SPORTS.

COMMON COURTESIES AND LOCAL CUSTOMS ... Australians are rather like Americans in their habits. Except when attending official functions and balls, most Australians dress quite informally. Beachwear is the same as in the United States. Modern public buildings, restaurants, hotels and motels are air-conditioned.

COMMUNICATIONS ... Cable, radio and airmail service and Trans-Pacific telephone service. Airmail rates are: postcards, 10 cents; letters, 20 cents per half ounce; airmail letters 8 cents.

CURRENCY ... Australia has changed from pounds and shillings to dollars and cents. After February, 1966, U.S. $1 equals $A.89, and $A1 is worth U.S. $1.12. Old currency is still in circulation, however, and prices are quoted in both old and new money.

CUSTOMS REGULATIONS AND DOCUMENTS REQUIRED FOR UNITED STATES CITIZENS ... Passport and visa. Vaccination certificate. You may bring in duty free 400 cigarettes, or 1 lb. of tobacco or 1 lb. cigars, 3 quarts of liquor per adult; unlimited foreign currency (except only £5 English Sterling allowed in, $A50 (Aust.) out). No more allowed out than declared on entry.

DRUGSTORES ... Known as chemist's shops here. They carry pharmaceuticals, cosmetics and photo supplies and service. Most American pharmaceuticals and cosmetics are available.

ELECTRIC CURRENT ... 220–240 volts, 50 cycles, mostly A.C.; some D.C. in country areas. Transformer plugs needed.

FAUNA ... The animals of Australia are known the world over: the kangaroo, koala, wallaby, platypus, anteater, and giant turtles. Among birds, count the fascinating kookaburra, which allegedly laughs instead of singing; the huge emu; the lyre bird, which imitates its feathered colleagues; cockatoos and parrots; penguins; bower birds and love birds. All these animals and birds won't be found around or in the cities, but are native to the country and may be seen in Sydney's Taronga Park or Melbourne's Zoological Gardens or at nearby fauna reserves such as the Healesville Wild Life Sanctuary outside Melbourne, and the Lone Pine Sanctuary near Brisbane.

FLORA... New South Wales is famous for its vegetation. Distinctive to the section is the waratah, a rosette of red; the flannel flower, which has green-tipped white petals; the red Christmas bush. These and many others may be seen at Botanic Gardens. In Melbourne, a very fine selection of Australian flora is usually on display in the Botanic Gardens. In September and October, southwestern Australia is carpeted with 7,000 species of wild flowers.

FOOD... Australians are great meat eaters. Beef and lamb are very popular. There is also a plentiful supply of fish, together with most types of international food, introduced by European immigrants. Prices in restaurants are quite reasonable by American standards. Pasteurized milk is available and of course is safe to drink.

GAMBLING... No casinos, but there is frequent horse racing and dog racing at various courses with pari-mutuels (known as totalisators) and legal bookmakers.

LANGUAGE... English and Australian slang.

LAUNDRY AND DRY CLEANING... Facilities compare favorably with the United States in speed, quality and price.

LIQUOR... Beer is inexpensive and the most popular drink. Good but stronger than ours. Whiskies, imported liqueurs, popular American cocktails are all readily available at prices about the same as at home. Bourbon and rye are available in leading hotels. Try Australian wines, especially still dinner wines. Resident hotel guests and diners are not subject to the licensing laws which close public bars at 10 P.M. in some states and at 6 P.M. in others. Minimum legal age for drinkers is 21.

MEDICAL FACILITIES... Medical facilities are comparable to those in the United States. Doctors and dentists are excellent.

MOTION PICTURES... There are a number of theaters in both Sydney and Melbourne which show first-run Hollywood and British films, several that show foreign films with English subtitles.

MUSIC... The world-renowned Sydney Symphony Orchestra gives concerts at Town Hall, Sydney, from early March till October, also open-air orchestral concerts. Visiting ballet companies, opera and concert singers appear frequently.

Symphony and other concerts, as well as visiting artists from overseas are also heard regularly in the Melbourne Town Hall. During the summer months Hollywood-Bowl-type performances are held in the Myer Music Bowl in the Domain.

NIGHT CLUBS AND CABARETS... Among many night spots in Sydney: the *Silver Spade Room* at the Chevron; *Emperor Room* at the Menzies; *Chequers* at Pitt and Goulburn St. In Melbourne it's *Mario's*, Exhibition St., and *The Troika* in Hampton, with dinner and supper dancing to 2 A.M. Surfers Paradise, Queensland, rivals Miami Beach for night life.

PHOTOGRAPHY . . . Still and movie film, including color, is available at reasonable prices. Also a wide variety of cameras and accessories, mainly German and Japanese brands. Kodak has its own laboratories and stores in Sydney and Melbourne. Same-day developing service. Allow 2 weeks for color developing.

RELIGION . . . In Sydney: St. Andrew's Cathedral (Anglican), George Street; St. Mary's Cathedral (Roman Catholic), College Street; St. Stephen's (Presbyterian), Macquarie Street; Wesley Chapel (Methodist), Castlereagh Street; Central Baptist Church, George Street; First Church of Christ Scientist, Forbes and Liverpool Streets; the Great Synagogue, Elizabeth Street.

In Melbourne: St. Paul's Cathedral (Church of England), Swanston and Flinders Streets; Baptist Church, Collins Street; Christian Science, St. Kilda, Kilda Road and Dorcas Street; Congregational, Latrobe Street; Jewish Synagogue, Toorak Road, South Yarra; Lutheran, 22 Parliament Place; Wesley Church (Methodist), 148 Lonsdale Street; Scots Church (Presbyterian), Collins and Russell Streets; St. Patrick's Cathedral (Roman Catholic), East Melbourne.

RESTAURANTS . . . Luncheon and dinner hour are early by our standards. Some restaurants are licensed to sell hard liquor only until 10 P.M. So if you want to sit around all evening, pick your spot. Among the good places to eat in Sydney are the *Caprice* on the pier at Rose Bay; *Pruniers* and the *Weinkeller* at Double Bay; *Romano's, Le Trianon* and *Chelsea* which have good food and smart clientele; while the *Rhinecastle Bistro* (very popular for lunch) provides good Australian wine in a gourmet atmosphere. For vintage Australian atmosphere, *The Coachman*. Also good are the *Villa Franca, Beppi's* and the *Angus Steak Cave.* The *Cahill* chain is reasonable and good.

In Melbourne, the best restaurants are the *Mayfair* at the Southern Cross Hotel, with dancing and floor shows; in the same hotel is the *Club Grill* with an open rotisserie; *Molina's,* Bourke and Spring Streets; *Florentino* (Italian), Bourke Street; the *Oxford Hotel,* Swanston Street; the *Ritz* (continental), Lonsdale Street; *Capers,* Collins Street; *Beefeater,* Carlyle Street. *La Popotte* (French), *Madrid* (Spanish), *Balaclava* (English inn atmosphere) and *Mario's* (Italian and French). *Maxim's* and *Antonio's,* both in Toorak Road, South Yarra, feature international cuisine. Medium-priced restaurants are the *Russell Collins,* corner of Russell and Collins Streets; *Fanny's,* 243 Lonsdale Street, a cozy continental restaurant; *The Bistro,* next door to the Florentino; and *The Balzac* (French cuisine with wine *en carafe*) in East Melbourne. Dinner-dancing nightly until 10:30 at the *Southern Cross Hotel, Menzies, Australia, Savoy Plaza, Federal, Chevron, Mario's, Top of the Town* and *Oriental;* to 2 A.M. at the *Troika* and *Tarantella.*

Eliza's, which has dancing nightly, and *Rob's Drive-In* are in Albert Park, 2 miles away, and easily reached by public transport.

SHOPS AND STORES . . . In Sydney, Cornelius Furs in King

Street features delightful garments of kangaroo skin. Aboriginal crafts available at the Church Missionary Society Book Shop, 93 Bathurst St.; toy koalas at the Koala Bear Shop, 43 Park St.; the Continental Bag Co., 283 Elizabeth St., specializes in made-to-order lizard and crocodile bags; House of Prouds for opals, for which it is famous. For woolens and blankets, shop at David Jones, Ltd., Elizabeth Street. Farmers, George Street, caters to the well-dressed man and woman. Grace Brothers of Broadway is one of the largest department stores.

In Melbourne, Myer's Emporium is the biggest of many fine stores. Georges, Collins Street, is a top woman's specialty store which carries large stocks of imported and local goods. There are many other stores, including Buckley and Nunn, Henry Buck Pty. Ltd., a first-class man's shop. Aboriginal crafts at the Aboriginal Enterprises, Belgrave. In addition, there are lots of interesting, small shops in Melbourne's numerous arcades. Merchandise is not expensive.

SPECTATOR SPORTS . . . There are four race courses in Sydney's metropolitan area: Randwick, which accommodates 100,000 people; Canterbury; Rosehill, which has a 2-furlong stretch. Trotting races are held Friday nights at Harold Park Race Course; greyhound racing on Saturday nights. There is a tote at all courses, and legal bookmakers, too. All tracks have restaurants and bars. Meets are held Saturday and Wednesday afternoons and on public holidays.

Cricket matches are played at Sydney Cricket Ground. Football is popular during their autumn and winter season. Tennis, of course, is the national pride. Matches are played at the Lawn Tennis Association courts at White City, Rushcutter's Bay. Boxing and wrestling matches at Rushcutter's Bay or Leichhardt Stadiums. Midget car and motorcycle racing at Sydney Sports Grounds. Yachting regattas at Sydney and its nearby coastal resorts. Colorful surf lifeguard carnivals at major beaches, November through March. Golf tournaments at the various golf clubs. The Royal Sydney Golf Club at Rose Bay is world famous.

Horse racing is also the favored spectator sport in Melbourne. Races are held at least every Saturday. The principal courses are Flemington, Caulfield, Sandown and Moonee Valley. The Flemington race course is so large that it has a straight 6 furlongs, for 6 furlong races. The Melbourne Cup, Australia's premier horse race, is run at Flemington on the first Tuesday in November. Trotting races, during the season, are held at the Royal Show Grounds. During their winter months, Australian Rules Football attracts crowds of up to 110,000 spectators. Baseball, soccer and softball are also gaining popularity.

Visitors in Melbourne may also see top-ranking tennis stars in action at Kooyong at the end of November, when the Victorian Championships are played with entrants from all States. Boxing and wrestling matches are popular and are held on Friday nights at Festival Hall, West Melbourne. Cricket is regularly played at the Melbourne Cricket Ground and other ovals in the greater Melbourne area every Saturday during the summer months. From time to time test matches are played between Australia and overseas countries, such as England, South Africa and India.

SPORTS . . . There are many good municipal golf courses in Sydney at which visitors are welcome, or you may arrange for cards at the various private golf clubs. (Check with Pan American.) Royal Sydney Golf Club is the largest. Municipal courses at Moore Park, Randwick and Bondi. There are horses for hire and many bridle paths. Swimming is wonderful at the beaches to the north and south of the city. There are many indoor pools, too. Visitors may play tennis at many private tennis clubs upon application. Squash courts also available for hire. Inquire at the Tourist Bureau about game shooting and about the new Prince Alfred Swimming Pool and Ice Skating rink (Olympic hockey size, 185 by 85 feet). Big-game fishing is a favorite sport in New South Wales, where tuna and shark are plentiful. Inland streams are well stocked with trout and bass, and there are special excursions from Sydney to trout-filled Encumbene Lake near Cooma.

In and near Melbourne, visitors may play golf on a number of fine public courses, one of the best being Yarra Bend National Park and Public Golf Course, a few miles from the city. They may also play on a private club course if they are introduced by members. Some of the better-known clubs are Metropolitan, Royal Melbourne, Commonwealth, Kingston Heath and Huntingdale. The St. Kilda Tennis Club opens its courts to the public, but visitors must be introduced by members at Kooyong courts. Private tennis courts are also available for hire. Horseback riding around the Botanic Gardens and Government House is pleasant.

Indoor swimming is available at the Melbourne City Baths, Swanston Street, YMCA, and Richmond Baths, where the water is heated. During Melbourne's summer months, you may swim at one of the nearby beach resorts, such as St. Kilda, Frankston, or, for those who like surfing, Portsea, which is 60 miles from Melbourne. Regular train and bus services operate to these resorts. Ice skating is available at St. Moritz, St. Kilda. Boating on the Yarra River is a pleasant pastime; boats may be hired at Macauley's new Boat Shed, day or evening. Squash courts are available for hire at Findlay's Health School, 279 Little Collins Street, Flinders Lane Squash Courts, 237 Flinders Lane, St. Kilda Courts (squash), Canterbury Road, St. Kilda. The Oasis, 13-23 George Parade, off Collins Street, features Turkish bath, gym, and squash for men and women. Fees are moderate.

THEATERS . . . In Sydney big musicals, opera and spectacular shows usually appear at *Her Majesty's,* while smaller dramas play at the *Royal;* theater-in-the-round at the *Ensemble,* and the *Independent* has a repertory stock company. The *Tivoli* and the *Phillip Street Theater* specialize in vaudeville and revues.

In Melbourne, *Her Majesty's Theater,* Exhibition Street, and the *Princess,* Spring Street, show all types of stage productions, from musical comedy to grand opera. The *Comedy Theater,* located at Exhibition Street, is well known for its first-class stage plays. The *Tivoli Theater,* Bourke Street, specializes in variety shows and stars both local and imported artists. There are also a number of little theaters in and around Melbourne, such as the *Union Theater* (University), *Russell Street Theater, National Theater,* East Melbourne, opposite St. Patrick's Cathedral, and the *Little Theater,* South Yarra.

TIME . . . Time in Sydney and Melbourne is 18 hours later than Pacific Coast Standard Time. There are 3 time zones within the country. No Daylight Saving Time.

TIPPING . . . Tip luggage porters 20 cents per bag. Waiters, taxi drivers, barbers and beauticians are tipped 10%. Except in Sydney and Melbourne, tipping is less common than in the U.S.

TRANSPORTATION . . . There are electric trains, buses, trams and ferries. These last are important in Sydney, which is a harbor city. Cars for hire are reasonable; traffic keeps to the left. Cross country jet air travel is very highly developed and fares are low.

WATER . . . As safe to drink as at home.

WHAT TO BUY . . . Australian woolens and opals are the finest in the world. Blankets and sheepskin rugs are a good buy. Crocodile and lizard bags and shoes are cheaper here.

WHAT TO WEAR . . . Depends entirely on when you go and where. Remember the Australian seasons are the reverse of ours. In their summer season, you will need beach clothes, sports attire and going-out clothes. Formal dress is necessary only for official functions and gala balls. For Melbourne, Sydney and the other large cities, dress as you would at home. Light-colored clothes are fine in summer. Medium or light-weight suits for women are always practical. Take a topcoat and raincoat. Men need slacks and sports jackets. White suits for the tropics, warmer clothes for other areas.

WHERE TO GO—SIGHTSEEING . . .

Sydney . . . Sydney, often called the Harbor City, is cosmopolitan and gay. Located on the coast of New South Wales, it is surrounded by beach resorts which stretch for hundreds of miles in each direction. It is a fast-growing city of tall buildings and parks. Its port is one of the world's busiest. Hyde Park, almost in the center of the city, is worth seeing. It contains war memorials, flower gardens and attractive walks. The underground (subway) traverses its length. Very near by are the Botanic Gardens, on the edge of which stands the residence of the Governor of New South Wales. The gardens contain wonderful examples of Australian flora. At the Zoological Gardens, which are reached by ferry from Circular Quay or by bus over the famous Sydney Harbor Bridge, there is a fine assemblage of indigenous Australian animals which are shown in surroundings that resemble their native haunts. Centennial Park, reached by various bus lines, is enormous and has magnificent flower gardens and lakes. Visit Fort Denison, a little island in Farm Cove off Sydney Harbor, which was once used to detain convicts. Kurnell, on Botany Bay, is where Captain Cook landed. Incidentally, the frequent harbor ferry excursions are one of the best ways to see Sydney. The view from the top of the AMP Building at Circular Quay is magnificent.

Bondi Beach, about a half hour from Sydney, is one of the most popular resorts on the coast. There are a beach pavilion, restaurants, swimming pool. Manly, another resort across the harbor, is 7 miles to the northeast of Circular Quay, the main ferry station. It is reached by ferry in half an hour. There is fine surf bathing, a promenade and, on the bay side, a swimming pool. Cronulla, on the coast, is 17 miles away and has a fine beach and esplanade. Coogee, Dee Why and Palm Beach are other beaches particularly well known.

The Blue Mountains, about 2 hours from Sydney, are well worth a trip. There is a full-day planned tour from the city which takes you there or you may go on your own. The mountains range about 3,500 feet above sea level and fringe the Hawkesbury Basin. The scenery is magnificent and there are several towns with hotels for tourists. One of the sights is the Jenolan Caves, a series of limestone caverns lighted by electricity, giving an eerie and beautiful effect. There are guided tours daily. The *Jenolan Caves House* has good hotel accommodations convenient to the beautiful, unusual countryside. Near the caves is a bird and wildlife sanctuary which is well worth a visit. Katoomba is one of the main towns in the region. From there you may visit the Wentworth Falls and Leura Falls, all interesting. There are two National Parks within a comparatively short distance from Sydney: Kuring-gai Chase and Royal National Park. Each is a sanctuary for animal and bird life and each features indigenous flora. They are both worth seeing. The Hawkesbury River has magnificent fjordlike scenery, and launches may be hired for day or week trips in these vast protected waters. Try to visit a sheep or cattle "station" (ranch).

Mount Kosciusko . . . Not far from Sydney is Mt. Kosciusko National Park, a mountain reserve in the Great Dividing Range. Here some of the world's best skiing is enjoyed from July to October. Trout fishing at nearby Lake Encumbene is the world's best. Six miles below the summit is the *Chalet*, an extraordinary-looking hotel with a round tower entrance. It has modern accommodations, central heating and other attributes, including a resident surgeon on hand for ski injuries. *The Man From Snowy River Hotel* and the *Sundeck* are completely modern resorts, all-inclusive weekly rates, $60 per person. In addition, there are a number of smaller lodges in nearby Thredbo Valley. Ski lifts and ski classes are available. There is a good motor road from Jindabyne to the summit. Mt. Kosciusko is a summer resort, too. There are tennis courts, excellent trout fishing in well-stocked streams, riding and mountain climbing.

Melbourne . . . Melbourne is popularly described as being like Boston in temperament and atmosphere. Its citizens are conservative and rather aloof. But once they know you, they are hospitable in the extreme. The city's streets are broad and airy. The center of the city is busy and crowded, but in the outlying sections there are beautiful gardens and parks. The city is situated on the Yarra River, and from the riverbanks you get a lovely view of the skyline (sightseeing boats operate during Melbourne's summer months from Prince's Bridge). Collins Street is the pride of the town, a broad tree-lined street with shops, cafés and coffeehouses. At the top of Collins Street is the Treasury Building, surrounded by the Treasury Gardens. An avenue of elms leads into Fitzroy Gardens, where you will see Captain Cook's cottage, miniature village, and the carved fairy tree. Enter from Spring Street or Wellington Parade. The Botanic Gardens to the southeast of the city feature the wonderful flowers for which this land is famous. Government House, residence of the State Governor, is near here. Take a trip to the zoo in Royal Park. There is a miniature railroad and an elephant ride for the children. You'll enjoy a drive along St. Kilda Road, a boulevard lined with triple rows of trees which runs from Prince's Bridge to St. Kilda, where you will find Luna Park, an amusement spot like Coney Island. There are restaurants, cinemas, skating rinks and roller coasters. At Village Belle, adjacent to the park, are night clubs and restaurants. Other points of interest include the Geological Museum, Gisborne Street; the Museum of Applied Science, next to the National Art Gallery, Swanston Street.

Less than an hour by electric train from Flinders Street Station and well worth while is the trip to Upper Fern Tree Gully with connecting bus to Olinda, Sassafras, Belgrave and Monbulk, resort towns which are noted for their beautiful fern gullies, forests and picturesque mountain walks. Readily accessible by train is Geelong, 45 miles from Melbourne, on Corio Bay. This progressive city is the gateway to Victoria's rich western district. Two other interesting day trips well worth taking from Melbourne are to Ballarat, one of Victoria's leading provincial cities, with beautiful gardens and statuary, and the Eureka Stockade; and to Bendigo, a charming provincial center in northern Victoria.

Cowes (Phillip Island) is a delightful seaside resort noted for its remarkable mutton-bird rookeries, evening parade of penguins, seal colony and koalas. Frankston is another popular seaside resort, with panoramic views across the bay and pleasant inland walks. It's one hour from Flinders Street Station, Melbourne. Also take a day's trip to the favorite seaside resorts of Sorrento, Portsea, Flinders and Mornington, all on Mornington Peninsula; and Torquay, Anglesea and Lorne—all on the ocean.

Canberra . . . The federal capital of Australia, Canberra, is midway between Melbourne and Sydney. Chicago architect Walter Burley Griffin was responsible for the overall design, and its wide boulevards, garden settings and modern buildings are a tribute to his vision. The center of Australian Parliamentary and diplomatic life, Canberra's government buildings are well worth seeing. The Australian Academy of Science, the National War Memorial Museum and the National University are also here. Newest hotel is the *Rex at Canberra*. Also recommended are the *Canberra* and *Ainslee-Rex;* single rates from about $8.50.

Brisbane . . . The capital of Queensland is a modern subtropical city with a population of more than half a million spread out as is Los Angeles. The hotels include *Lennons* (from $8.95 single, $15.80 double), the *Majestic,* the *Carlton,* the *Canberra* and the *Gresham.* Sixty miles away is the "Gold Coast," a tourist area covering more than 20 miles of surfing beaches. Surfers Paradise here is a town of

Cruises and tours of all kinds are available to the vast vacation area of Great Barrier Reef.

30,000 people which increases to almost 100,000 in summer. Hotels in the area include *Lennons on Gold Coast* and *Chevron-Paradise*.

Great Barrier Reef ... This great coral reef stretches for about 1,200 miles along the Queensland coast. It is reached by plane from Sydney in about 3 hours. Here you will find hundreds of small islands and coves almost completely unspoiled. For the most part, this is a paradise for fishermen, surf lovers and people who like to laze in the sun. At some points the reef is only about 20 miles from the mainland; at the widest it is 150 miles off. There are several fine resorts. Outstanding are the *Hayman, Lindeman* and *Brampton Islands* in the Whitsunday Group off the mainland towns of Mackay and Proserpine. At these resorts, fishing trips, visits to the Outer Reef and all kinds of outdoor activities are arranged. The 5-day boat cruise from Mackay to the islands and Reef is very popular. Other islands, such as Heron and Green Island, are part of the reef proper and are actually coral cays. Heron Island, about 300 miles north of Brisbane, has a magnificent beach, a green lagoon, wonderful trees and flowers. The sea here is so clear that you can see marine vegetation from an ordinary boat. Green Island, 17 miles out from Cairns, has excellent facilities for viewing the color wonderland of the Reef from an underwater observatory. The island, reached by daily launch services from Cairns, also has a remarkable tropical aquarium. All along the Great Barrier Reef you can take glass-bottomed boats or motor launches along what the Australians call "the great canal." This is a superb vacation spot, a paradise for the sportsman and an escape for everyone tired of cities, night clubs and too many people. Even though modern resorts have been developed, people who want peace and quiet are still able to find it.

Northern Territory . . . Is really the world's "largest frontier," and home of the Flying Doctor service. There are huge cattle ranches here, the true wide-open spaces. Much of the Territory is undeveloped, but year after year civilization encroaches a little more, and safaris to bag buffalo, crocodile and other game are becoming popular. Darwin is the capital of the Northern Territory but Alice Springs, known to Australians affectionately as "The Alice," marks virtually the geographical heart of the country and is a growing tourist attraction. In the area are Ayers Rock, the biggest single rock in the world, the Macdonnell Ranges, inspiration to artists, all set in some of the most rugged but most colorful country in the Commonwealth. If you want to see Australian aborigines in their native habitat this area of Central Australia is your starting point. The season is April through September. Best hotels in Alice Springs are the new *Stuart Arms* ($6) and *Alice Springs Hotel* ($6.60); bed and .breakfast.

Adelaide . . . The capital of South Australia, is in the center of sheep-and-cattle-grazing country. It is a well-planned city, with broad straight streets and avenues set at right angles. The city has been planned so that the beaches and hill resorts are no more than a half hour's trip from the capital. The newest hotel is *Hotel Australia*. Rates with bath from $8.50 single, from $16 double. All European Plan. Other good hotels are the *South Australian,* $9 single, $15.70 double; the *Earl of Zetland;* and *Oriental*.

Places of interest: Botanic Gardens, entrance from North Terrace, opposite East Terrace; Koala Bear Park in Parklands, between Walkerville car line and Zoological gardens; Torrens Lake, King William Street. Boats for hire. Bordered by Elder Park (south bank) and Memorial Drive (north bank). Suburban seaside resorts (within half an hour's journey by rail, tram or bus from the city) include Largs, Glenelg, Marino and Kingston Park (a national pleasure resort). Long stretches of clean, shelving sand and good bathing facilities are features of these modern seaside resorts.

Seven miles from Adelaide, in the Mount Lofty Ranges, and connected with the city by bus, is Morialta Falls Reserve, with a winding path which leads through magnificent mountain scenery to the waterfalls. Waterfall Gully, also in the Mount Lofty Ranges, is reached by following the Burnside bus route to the terminus, then about 3 miles along a winding road of exceptional beauty. Refreshments are obtainable at a kiosk. On Sundays and holidays buses run from the Burnside tram terminus to the Falls. The National Park abounds in shady gullies, magnificent trees and luxuriant foliage. Much of it has been preserved in its virgin state, but ample conveniences, such as refreshment rooms, cricket pitches, tennis courts, and golf links have been provided. Adelaide is the gateway to the Barossa Valley vineyards to the north, and the intensely colorful Flinders Ranges; game fishing resorts on Kangaroo Island to the south, and Yorke Peninsula to the west.

The beaches are excellent in Australia. This one is 60 miles from Brisbane, capital of Queensland.

Tasmania . . . South of Melbourne is the heart-shaped island of Tasmania, smallest of the 6 Australian states. It is separated from the continent by 140 miles of the Bass Strait. A verdant, misty spot, it is rather like Ireland. Hobart, its capital, nestles in the shadow of Mt. Wellington, the summit of which is about twelve miles from the center of the city. The *Wrest Point Hotel* at Sandy Bay, Hobart, is excellent. *Hadley's Hotel* and *Travellodge Motel* are also recommended. Hobart, one of Australia's most historic cities, is today a metropolis with theaters, shops, offices and factories. There are ferries and electric streetcars and trolley buses to the main suburbs. Among the attractions of Tasmania are the wildflowers in the spring. Mountain climbing, fishing, including trout fishing, and sailing are among the sports this island has to offer.

Tasmania has an excellent road system so you can tour the island in comfort by car or bus, or make your headquarters at a selected center and undertake from there day trips to the ruins of the old penal settlement at Port Arthur and the scenic Huon Valley. Routes to the summits of mountains, easily accessible from Hobart and Launceston, give you impressive panoramic views. Here are two interesting trips:

Hobart to Launceston via east coast (2 days): the east coast provides a series of resorts of scenic interest. The tour covers 274 miles, with an overnight stop on the way. Leave Hobart via Hobart Bridge and pass by Cambridge and Sorell. Be sure to see the magnificent window in the century-old church at Buckland. Then to Orford, Triabunna and Swansea. During the afternoon proceed through Bicheno, St. Marys and Scamander to St. Helens. From St. Helens the tour leaves the coastline and turns inland through Pyengana, Weldborough Pass, Derby, Branxholm, to Scottsdale and over Meredith's Siding to Launceston.

Hobart to Launceston via west coast (2 days): this trip, almost in direct contrast to the east coast, consists of bold, mountainous and forest scenery, commencing with the Derwent Valley and passing through Ouse. Tarraleah to the Hydro-Electric Works at Butler's Gorge. In the afternoon the tour continues along the West Coast Road, from which extensive panoramas of the beautiful ranges of mountains can be seen, on the way to Queenstown. Returning over the same road on the second day to Lake St. Clair, then via Bronte Park and Great Lake to Launceston.

Launceston ... In the north of the state is Launceston, charmingly situated where the North and South Esk Rivers merge to form the River Tamar. This "garden city" is famous for its beautiful parks. Among hotels are the *Tasmania* (single $6.75) and the *Launceston* (single $8).

Several large tracts of Tasmania have been reserved for pleasure purposes. The Mount Field National Park (about 40,000 acres), 50 miles from Hobart, includes Mount Field mountain range, with skiing and skating on the plateau. The scenery is superb. A still bigger national park is Cradle Mountain Lake St. Clair (about 525 square miles), where there are mountains, wild canyons, forests, waterfalls, and lakes galore.

Perth ... Capital of Western Australia, fringes the banks of the beautiful Swan River and enjoys the distinction of being Australia's sunniest capital. The Post Office and Commonwealth Bank in Forrest Place—a broad, though short, thoroughfare opposite the entrance to the Central Railway Station—are among the finest buildings in Australia and dominate the city's architecture. There are many others of striking architectural design.

Among the places of interest are the Art Gallery and Museum, Beaufort Street; Parliament House, Harvest Terrace; the Observatory, Havelock Street; the University of Western Australia; and King's Park. King's Park, set aside in 1871, now comprises about 1,000 acres, most of which are in bushland state and grow a large variety of indigenous flora that bloom profusely from August to November. There are good roads from which you get a magnificent panorama of Perth, the Swan River and the Darling Ranges. Within easy reach of the city are numerous ocean and river beaches available to visitors. Hotel accommodations are good at the *Esplanade* (single $8); the *Riverside Lodge* ($8); the *Palace* ($10); the *Savoy* ($5.50); and the *Adelphi* ($9.50).

SOURCES OF FURTHER INFORMATION ... Government Tourist Bureaus in major cities will gladly supply information on attractions and activities of interest. Pan American's Sydney office is at Berger House, 82 Elizabeth St. (Tel. BW 2252). In Melbourne, Pan Am is in the Southern Cross Hotel and at 133 Exhibition St. (Tel. 63 9077).

Australian National Travel Association, 636 Fifth Ave., New York; 350 Post St., San Francisco.

FIJI ISLANDS

WEATHER IN SUVA—Lat. S18°08′—Alt. Approx. sea level

Temp.	JAN.	FEB.	MAR.	APR.	MAY	JUNE	JULY	AUG.	SEPT.	OCT.	NOV.	DEC.
Low	74°	74°	74°	73°	71°	69°	68°	68°	69°	70°	71°	73°
High	86°	86°	86°	84°	82°	80°	79°	79°	80°	81°	83°	85°
Average	80°	80°	80°	79°	77°	75°	74°	74°	75°	76°	77°	79°
Days of Rain	21	19	24	20	17	14	10	12	14	14	16	17

LOCATION . . . This group of 300 Melanesian islands, totaling over 7,000 square miles, lies in the South Pacific, 2,000 air miles from Sydney in southern Australia.

CHARACTERISTICS . . . All of Fiji is rather like a picture postal card. The colors are brilliant; the flowers vivid and ever present; even the uniforms of the Fijian police are picturesque. There are now more East Indians in Fiji than native Fijians and they, too, add color to the scene. Duty-free shopping makes Fiji a bargain paradise to rival Hong Kong. All in all, it's a delightful dream spot with all the relaxed comforts and charms associated with South Sea islands.

POPULATION . . . Estimated at about 456,400.

SIZE . . . 7,083 square miles. Viti Levu, the largest island, with 4,011 square miles, is 138 miles wide.

CAPITAL . . . Suva, population 46,000.

GOVERNMENT . . . The islands in the group constitute the British Crown Colony of Fiji.

HOW TO GET THERE . . . By Pan American Clipper from the United States West Coast via Honolulu about 13 hours (elapsed time) to Nandi. Actually the time becomes a day later when you cross the International Date Line. Air service between Nandi or "Nadi" and Suva by Fiji Airways. By ship, Fiji is reached in 14 days.

ACCOMMODATIONS . . . The *Mocambo,* 5 minutes from Nandi Airport, is an air-conditioned resort hotel with swimming pool, horseback riding, tennis, nearby golf course, sightseeing facilities; from $9 single, $14.50 double. The *Skylodge,* adjacent to the airport, has swimming pool, 9-hole golf course; single $8.95, double from $11.45. In Suva, a 40-minute flight from the airport, is the *Grand Pacific Hotel,* set in tropical gardens on the edge of the harbor; air-conditioned rooms from $8.75 single, $14.40 double. The *Club Hotel* is completely air-conditioned; single from $5.35, double from $14.05. *Hotel Suva,* $8.65 single, $11.45 double. Tipping in Fiji is not obligatory.

CURRENCY . . . The Fiji pound is valued at 2.51 to U.S. $1.

CUSTOMS REGULATIONS AND DOCUMENTS REQUIRED FOR UNITED STATES CITIZENS . . . Valid passport and vaccination certificate are required. Continuation or return ticket also required. 200 cigarettes, 50 cigars or 8 ounces of tobacco and 1 quart bottle of liquor for personal use are allowed, duty free.

FOOD . . . Added to a British cuisine are such local delicacies as *ika vakalolo* (delicious marinated fish), prawns cooked in coconut milk, yams, taro, and superb local fruits and fish. Indian curries and Chinese dishes have a special Fijian touch. Tap water is safe to drink, and imported liquors are very inexpensive. *Yaqona* (kava), a muddy-looking Fijian beverage, is not alcoholic but has a stimulating effect similar to that of strong tea or coffee.

TRANSPORTATION . . . Buses are very inexpensive (85¢ from Suva to Korolevu, 65 miles), but taxis are preferable and rates are low. Self-drive cars rent from $5.60 per day, plus 7¢ per mile.

WHAT TO BUY . . . Imported goods from all over the world at low, duty-free prices. Local souvenirs include wood carvings, shell jewelry, tapa cloth, coral, grass skirts, recordings of Fijian music.

WHAT TO WEAR . . . Summer clothes are worn all the year round. During the winter a woolen cardigan is useful. Formal dress is required only at special functions. Bring sunglasses, too.

WHERE TO GO—SIGHTSEEING . . .

Suva . . . A Maughamesque South Sea port with a lovely harbor where luxury liners lie alongside island schooners trading in copra and bananas. The streets are colorfully cosmopolitan with Fijians, Indians, Sikhs, Chinese, Europeans and islanders from all around the South Pacific. Particularly photogenic are the Fiji policemen in dark jackets and scalloped-hem *sulus* (skirts), and the memorable band of the Fiji Military Forces. Rare island arts and crafts are displayed in the Fiji Museum in beautiful Suva Gardens. Explore the exciting polyglot markets, Walu Bay, Tamavua Heights, Reservoir Lookout, Samabula, Lauthala Bay, Suva Point. Even the Suva Cemetery, abloom with brilliantly colored crotons, is interesting and different. Suva is especially filled with color and excitement during the annual Hibiscus Festival, the third week in September. There are weekly dinner dances at the *Club* and *Grand Pacific* hotels, and the *Golden Dragon* night club features island music and floor shows. To view an underwater wonderland of jewel-colored fish and fantastic coral formations, take a cruise of Suva harbor in the glass-bottomed launch *Oolooloo.*

Lautoka ... On Viti Levu's northern (King's) highway, Lautoka is a handsome modern town in the heart of the sugar cane district. Golf, tennis. The famous Vatukoula Gold Mines, 47 miles away, may be visited on tours out of Lautoka. Modern air-conditioned hotels are the *Lautoka* and *Cathay.*

Korolevu ... Amid true Polynesian atmosphere with all the modern conveniences, the *Korolevu Beach Hotel* on the south shore, about 75 miles from the airport, is a place to Get Away From It All. Taxi fare from the airport is $15, whether there are 1 or 4 passengers. Accommodations are in airy native *bures,* each with private bath. A Polynesian trio plays nightly; war dances and native ceremonial entertainment on Saturdays; skin diving, deep-sea fishing, boating, tennis, horseback riding; sightseeing trips arranged. Rates, depending upon room, suite, or *bure,* from $5.35-$13 per person, EP. East of Korolevu on the southern (Queen's) road is the deluxe *Reef Lodge* with superb beach, fishing, skin diving amid coral reefs; single from $6.65, double from $10.45, including breakfast.

Beachcomber ... A ranch-style resort near Deuba between Korolevu and Suva; beautiful beach, deep-sea fishing, unique boat trip up the Navua River through tropical wilderness; single from $8.45, AP.

On your island drives you will see picturesque South Sea villages, with thatched huts, palm-lined beaches, magnificent views of surf breaking on the coral reef. Along the roadside you'll see native Fijians with wiry bushy hair which practically stands on end, and children who wave to you happily. In the East Indian settlements you will find women wearing the traditional saris and some of the men wearing white turbans. The Fijians and East Indians live in separate communities, rarely intermingle, but manage to live peacefully.

Ovalau ... Reached by inter-island boat from Suva. The little seaside town of Levuka was Fiji's former capital. You can relax completely at the *Royal Hotel;* $7.65 per person, including meals.

Vanua Levu ... Second largest of the islands, Vanua Levu is reached by Fiji Airways or inter-island trading vessels. This island, rich in copra, sugar and cocoa plantations, also offers such holiday attractions as fine fishing, reef explorations, water sports and an assured warm welcome by the islanders. On the ocean in the town of Savusavu is the *Hot Springs Hotel,* single with bath $6.50, including breakfast; spear and deep-sea fishing facilities. On a beach 9½ miles from town is *Muanicula Estate Reefside Resort;* accommodations in *bures* with private baths, from $6.30 per person, including meals.

SOURCES OF FURTHER INFORMATION ... The Fiji Visitors Bureau, P.O. Box 92, Suva, and at Nandi Airport, has tickets for local events and information on tours, local sightseeing and cruises; literature in English on Fiji, maps of Suva, Viti Levu and the Fiji Islands. The Pan American Sales Office, opposite Suva General Post Office, can provide similar information (Tel. 2641).

HAWAII

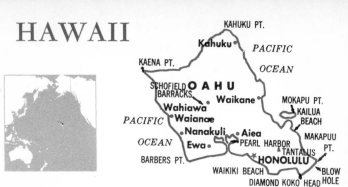

WEATHER IN HONOLULU—Lat. N21°18′—Alt. 25′

	JAN.	FEB.	MAR.	APR.	MAY	JUNE	JULY	AUG.	SEPT.	OCT.	NOV.	DEC.
Average Temp.	71°	71°	72°	73°	75°	77°	78°	79°	78°	77°	75°	73°
Days of Rain	14	10	13	12	11	11	13	13	13	13	14	15

LOCATION ... The Hawaiian Islands lie approximately 2,400 miles southwest of San Francisco. Honolulu is nearly the same distance north of the equator as Havana, Cuba.

CHARACTERISTICS ... Wonderful beaches, tropical flowers, hula dancers and flower leis are part of the fiber of the Hawaiian Islands. Here you have the additional delight of being on home territory, yet finding it as different as anything you have ever imagined. You can swim at the perfect beaches, luxuriate at wonderful hotels, go deep-sea fishing, learn to ride a surfboard, and enjoy the wonderful climate. It's a romantic spot, ideal for a vacation.

POPULATION ... 720,580 on the 8 main islands of Hawaii, Kahoolawe, Maui, Lanai, Molokai, Oahu, Kauai, and Niihau.

SIZE ... The area of the island group is 6,435 square miles, of which the largest island, Hawaii, is over 4,000 square miles, approximately the size of Connecticut and Rhode Island together, Honolulu's island of Oahu is 40 miles long and 26 wide.

CAPITAL ... Honolulu, with a population of 337,385.

GOVERNMENT ... Hawaii became the 50th U.S. state on August 21, 1959.

HOW TO GET THERE ... By Pan American Jet Clipper from San Francisco, Los Angeles, Portland or Seattle. Flying time from San Francisco 4¾ hours. By ship from San Francisco, 4½ days.

ACCOMMODATIONS ... The *Royal Hawaiian* (Sheraton) on Waikiki Beach, the best-known hotel in the Islands, has everything; rates about $22 to $37 double. The *Halekulani*, also on the beach, is quiet and pleasant; $16 to $45 double. Other good hotels on Waikiki, all European Plan, (with double rates quoted), include the *Moana,* $14 to $17.50; the huge *Hawaiian Village* (Hilton) with cottages and hotel rooms from $16 to $35; the *Reef,* $12 to $18 and the *Surfrider,* $17.50 to $28. There are a number of excellent new hotels: the *Kahala Hilton,* overlooking Waialae Golf Club, $24 to $37; the *Reef Tower,* $10 to $24; the *Princess Kaiulani,* $14 to $21; the stunning new *Ilikai,* $12 to $27; and the lovely *Waikikian,* with its authentic Polynesian atmosphere, $12 to $24. There are also many small hotels and apartment hotels which are available by the day, week or month. Rates given apply the year around; make reservations in advance.

ARTS ... Honolulu Academy of Arts contains interesting collections of Oriental and Western art, and special exhibitions of Pacificana and modern art. Bishop Museum houses one of the finest collections of Pacificana and crafts of the entire Pacific, birds, animals, famous feather work of the Hawaiians and historic relics. Queen Emma Museum is the beautiful home of the former Queen and contains many collections of personal and household relics of the era in which she lived. Archives, next to Iolani Palace, contains important and valuable Hawaiian documents, relics and old photographs of early island history. The Iolani Palace has the only throne room on U.S. soil.

BALLET ... Polynesian water ballet weekly at the *Reef Hotel,* and there is always the hula.

BANKS ... Banks have many branches throughout the islands.

CALENDAR OF HOLIDAYS ... All Mainland holidays are observed, plus Chinese New Year; Lei Day (May Day); June 11, Kamehameha Day; March 26, Prince Kuhio Day (Hawaii's first delegate to Congress). Aloha Week, which is held during the third full week of October, is similar to Mardi Gras.

CIGARETTES, TOBACCO ... Same as on the Mainland.

CLIMATE ... Like spring or early fall on the Mainland. There are frequent but short showers. Generally, it's "short-sleeved" weather.

CLUBS ... Rotary, Lions, Y.M.C.A., Kiwanis, Junior Chamber of Commerce, American Legion, Pilot, Soroptomist, Zonta, Altrusa and Civitan. For golf and tennis clubs, *see* SPORTS.

COMMON COURTESIES AND LOCAL CUSTOMS ... You will find that the Hawaiian people are extremely friendly and will go out of their way to make your stay enjoyable. Newcomers are called *Malihinis,* old timers, *Kamaainas,* and warm friends, *Aikanes. Aloha,* of course, is the traditional expression of greeting or farewell. The Hawaiian lei can be made of any one of a number of native flowers, but each island has its own lei and every flower lei has a different meaning. Hawaiians refer to the rest of the U.S. as the Mainland.

COMMUNICATIONS ... Same as on the Mainland.

CURRENCY ... Same as on the Mainland.

DRUGSTORES ... Many of them the same as on the Mainland.

ELECTRIC CURRENT ... Same as in most of the rest of the U.S., 120 volts, A.C., 60 cycles.

FLORA ... Hibiscus blooms the year round. Bougainvillaea is everywhere, as is the famous night-blooming cereus. The fabulous Bird of Paradise is guarded preciously when it blooms. Orchids are everywhere and are even sold in the dime stores. Hawaii's flowering trees are wonderful to see. The African tupil tree, the jacaranda, the shower trees, and Pride of India, the poinciana and many others are all indigenous to the Islands and add to their charm.

FOOD ... There are many restaurants and hotels where you can get international food. And, of course, there are wonderful Chinese and Japanese restaurants. The luau, which is a Hawaiian feast, features the Hawaiian dish *poi,* a paste made of the root of the taro plant. You must try it, along with the local fruits and juices, such as pineapple, papaya, guava nectar, passion-fruit juice and papaya juice.

LAUNDRY AND DRY CLEANING ... All modern facilities.

LIQUOR ... All the usual brands are available at regular prices. There are exotic local drinks with floating Vanda orchids, such as Moana Banyan Court Punch.

MEDICAL FACILITIES ... Same as on the Mainland.

MOTION PICTURES ... Same as on the Mainland.

MUSIC ... The Honolulu Symphony, under the direction of George Barati, is the leading musical organization of the Islands. Visitors can enjoy good music presented by the finest visiting artists. There is also the Hawaiian music so familiar on the Mainland.

NIGHT CLUBS AND CABARETS ... There is a tremendous variety of night life in Hawaii, although the typical night club is in the minority. At most night clubs you can see a good hula, and many places feature Tahitian and Samoan entertainment.

PHOTOGRAPHY ... All types of film and photo equipment are sold throughout the Islands. Overnight film-developing services.

RELIGION ... There are churches of all denominations.

RESTAURANTS ... Outstanding in Waikiki are *The Captain's Galley, Canlis' Broiler* and *Michel's* in the Colony Surf Hotel. Relatively new but already well accepted are *La Ronde,* a revolving restaurant high atop Honolulu's tallest building, and *Beau Rivage* in the new Ilikai Hotel. For steaks, try the *Colonel's Plantation, Beef Steak and Coffee House* in the International Market Place. Two of the best-known and most popular among the many fine Chinese restaurants are *Lau Yee Chai* in Waikiki, and *Wo Fat's* in downtown Honolulu. There are a number of picturesque Japanese teahouses. Reservations should be made in advance. Be sure to attend a Hawaiian luau, a combination of the best native food and Polynesian entertainment. Some of the places which feature these are *Duke Kahanamoku's, Queen's Surf* (home of the justly famous Barefoot Bar) and the *Royal Hawaiian.* Luaus are by reservation only, except for luau luncheons at *The Tropics Restaurant.* Among the best places for cocktails in the Waikiki area are the *Royal Hawaiian Hotel,* the *Captain Cook* bar in the Surfrider, *Michel's* at the Colony Surf, the *Kamaaina Bar* at the Moana, the *Shell Bar* and *Makahiki Room* at the Hawaiian Village, the *Queen's Surf,* the *House Without a Key* at the Halekulani and *Top of the Ilikai,* with a gorgeous view of Honolulu and the mountains.

SHOPS AND STORES . . . Honolulu is a wonderful place to buy Chinese and Japanese *objets d'art* and other oriental goods. The many fine stores in downtown Honolulu, as well as in Waikiki, have wide selections of hand-blocked linens, silks, carved Hawaiian woods, imported teak items, etc. Waikiki's International Market Place has many interesting shops—open evenings. Another worthwhile place to visit is the Ala Moana Shopping Center, where some of the Islands' outstanding firms have shops; a good place to look for imports from Japan and the Philippines.

SPECTATOR SPORTS . . . Polo, wrestling, boxing, baseball, football, watching the surfboarders.

SPORTS . . . Expert instructors and all the necessary equipment can be hired for scuba and skin diving, water skiing and, of course, surfboard riding. Equally exciting, but less strenuous, are outrigger canoe rides and catamaran cruises. Fishing is sensational, whether you spear reef fish, learn native net casting, or go out for marlin in a fully equipped charter boat. Of the many yacht clubs, several sponsor weekly sailing competitions. There are public tennis courts at Ala Moana Park, and racquets may be rented. There are fine hiking trails on all the islands, with numerous camp sites on mountain slopes and at beach parks. Superb bird and game hunting in the mountainous regions of Hawaii, Kauai, Lanai, Maui, Molokai and Oahu islands; guides are available. For those who prefer archery, some areas permit game hunting with bow and arrow, and targets are always standing in Kapiolani Park in Honolulu. The city has bowling alleys, too. Hotels can arrange guest cards so you can play at the many fine golf clubs in the Islands. The Ala Wai in Waikiki and Pali are public courses.

THEATERS . . . Stage plays are produced by the Honolulu Community Theater, Magic Ring Theater and University of Hawaii.

TIME . . . Noon in California is 10 A.M. in Hawaii.

TIPPING . . . About the same as on the Mainland.

TRANSPORTATION . . . Modern buses, taxis. Private cars can be rented easily. Frequent airline service between islands.

WATER . . . Both water and milk are safe to drink.

WHAT TO BUY . . . Hawaiian perfumes, native jams and jellies, textiles, coral jewelry, jades and oriental goods. You may want to take home an *holoku,* the traditional Hawaiian gown with long train for formal wear, and a *muumuu,* which makes a fine housecoat or hostess gown. Also Hawaiian wood crafts.

WHAT TO WEAR . . . Sportswear is worn on more occasions here than on the Mainland. You'll need sweaters for the higher altitudes of Hawaii and Kauai. Evening clothes are seldom required.

WHERE TO GO—SIGHTSEEING . . .

Honolulu . . . The Hawaii Visitors Bureau on Waikiki Beach can supply you with all kinds of information, maps, guides and a calendar of what is going on; there is a festival of some sort nearly every day somewhere on the Islands. Free entertainments include a hula show every evening and on Tuesday and Thursday mornings at the International Market Place; the new Wax Museum; the Concerts by the Sea in the Banyan Court of the Moana Hotel; attendance at the famous *Hawaii Calls* radio show, which is broadcast on a rotating basis on Saturdays at the Moana, Reef and Hawaiian Village hotels. Go to the Aloha Tower for a panoramic view of Honolulu Harbor, the city and its hills. The Hawaiian Village in Ala Moana Park near the Ala Wai yacht channel is an exact replica of ancient Hawaiin homes. There are guided tours through pineapple canneries, and Honolulu's fish markets are fascinating, with colorful piles of squid, octopus and brilliantly hued fish. Sampans that do most of Hawaii's deep-sea fishing gather picturesquely at Fishermen's Wharf. Honolulu's Chinatown is an enchanting, exotic jumble of apothecary, jade and food shops. There are special hibiscus drives and walks along the streets of the lei makers. Also, Foster Gardens, with all the flowers, trees and shrubs which grow in the Pacific tropics.

Try to see Upside-Down Falls, a phenomenon that occurs when a heavy rain dashes over cliffs and is blown upward instead of falling downward. Glass-bottomed boats make regular trips over the fantastic coral reefs at Kaneohe on the coast beyond the falls. Other Oahu Island attractions are: the new Sea Life Park at Makapuu Point, featuring underwater walking tours through glass tunnels, a Porpoise Theater and other marine spectacles; a drive through a luxuriant forest to the famous Nuuanu Pali, where from the lookout you get an impressive view; particularly interesting is the cruise on a yacht through Pearl Harbor; the Navy Yard, open to the public on Saturdays and Sundays (for United States citizens only). Diamond Head, a part of Honolulu and the city's greatest landmark, and Diamond Head Crater are at the eastern end of Waikiki.

Forty miles north of Waikiki is the new Polynesian Cultural Center at Laie, where six authentic, lived-in native villages from Samoa, New Zealand, Fiji, Tahiti, Tonga and rural Hawaii are reproduced; also shops, entertainment, interesting food. Open daily except Sunday; 7-hour motorcoach excursions from Waikiki to the Center cost $10, including admission fee. Also evening excursions for $13.50, which includes admission, a luau and spectacular Polynesian show.

Island of Hawaii . . . The Island of Hawaii, known as the "big island," is dominated by the spirit of Pele, the fire goddess who, it is said, causes the volcanoes Mauna Loa, Kilauea and recently active Makaopuhi to erupt. It's a thrilling sight to see. You will want to go to Kilauea and Halemaumau, the fire pit thought to be Pele's home. Make your headquarters in the city of Hilo, the second-largest city in the Islands. The chief hotels are the *Hilo* and the *Naniloa,* both excellent. In the National Park section, about 25 miles from the city, is *Volcano House,* situated on the very edge of Kilauea's crater.

Among other things to see on Hawaii are Akaka Falls at the end of magnificent tropical gardens; Kalapana Beach, which has black sand churned from the lava of the volcano. Paradoxically, there is skiing in winter on the slopes of the volcano. Hunters shoot wild goats there. Visit Parker Ranch. On the Kona coast of the island there is marvelous fishing. The charming *Kona Inn, Waiaka Lodge, Hotel King Kamehameha, Kona Hukilau, Kona Palms* and the elegant new *Mauna Kea Beach Hotel* are here.

Maui ... Villages at various altitudes rise from sea level to Haleakala, world's largest dormant volcano, whose cinder cones in brilliant colors stand among the unique Hawaiian silversword flowers. You can descend to the floor of the crater on horseback. Among the island's luxury hotels, are the *Hana-Maui, Sheraton-Maui, Kaanapali* and *Royal Lahaina Beach Hotel* (about $26.50 double). More moderately priced is the very good *Maui Palms Hotel* in Wailuku. *Napili Kai Beach Club* has very nice studios with kitchens for $16 double. The *Hale Napili* is also popular. For a step into the storied past, visit the *Pioneer Inn* on the Lahaina waterfront. The road from Wailuku to Lahaina is noted for its spectacular scenery. Lahaina has an outstanding golf course, the biggest banyan tree in the Islands and the oldest American school built west of the Rockies (1831). While on Maui, try to see a *hukilau*, or community fishing party, at Hana.

Kauai ... is known as the Garden Island because of its foliage. Captain Cook landed there. The *Coco Palms Hotel* and *Kauai Surf Hotel* at Lihue are modern and excellent. They have everything from swimming pools to Saturday-night hula shows. The *Waiohai* is more restful. Less expensive are the *Seven Seas* and *Prince Kuhio*. This is an island where you will do well to hire a U-Drive car or a private car, for you will have more fun and see more that way. Hanalei on Kauai is one of the finest beaches on the Islands; the luxurious *Plantation* overlooks the *South Pacific* movie setting. There are also, on the lee side, the Barking Sands, with 5-foot coral and lava dunes. The sand, when rubbed, sounds like a dog barking.

There is the sliding bathtub, where falls spray down a natural chute into a freshwater swimming pool. Here, too, is the Wailua River, near the mouth of which is the *Coco Palms Hotel*. You may go by hired boat up a river filled with water hyacinths to the Fern Grotto, where ferns hang from the rocks.

Molokai ... This island is almost completely unspoiled. There are ranches here and pineapple plantations. Wild deer roam all over the island and hunting is permissible. Some of the finest game fishing is to be found here. The hotel, *Seaside Inn,* offers relaxation here.

All the above islands can be reached via Hawaiian or Aloha Airlines at one-way fares from $9 to $20.

SOURCES OF FURTHER INFORMATION ... Hawaii Visitors Bureaus at 2051 and 2285 Kalakaua Avenue (Waikiki); 609 Fifth Avenue, New York, N.Y. 10017. Room 809, 3440 Wilshire Blvd., Los Angeles and at 400 N. Michigan Avenue, Chicago 11. Pan Am offices are at 2342 Kalakaua Ave., and Alexander Young Hotel (Tel. 570-011).

NEW ZEALAND

BAY OF ISLANDS

Auckland
Rotorua
NORTH ISLAND
LAKE TAUPO
WELLINGTON
Picton
NEW ZEALAND
SOUTH ISLAND
Christchurch
MILFORD SOUND
MOUNT COOK
Queenstown
Dunedin
SO. PACIFIC OCEAN

WEATHER IN AUCKLAND—Lat. S36°53′—Alt. approx. sea level

Temp.	JAN.	FEB.	MAR.	APR.	MAY	JUNE	JULY	AUG.	SEPT.	OCT.	NOV.	DEC.
Low	59°	60°	58°	55°	51°	48°	46°	47°	49°	51°	54°	57°
High	73°	74°	72°	68°	62°	59°	57°	58°	61°	63°	67°	70°
Average	66°	67°	65°	62°	55°	54°	52°	53°	55°	57°	61°	64°
Days of Rain	10	10	11	13	19	20	21	19	17	17	15	10

LOCATION ... New Zealand consists of two large islands (North Island and South Island) and numerous small islands, of which Stewart Island, just below South Island, and the Chatham Islands, 500 miles to the east, are the largest. Auckland is about 1,300 air miles east of Sydney, Australia, and about the same distance south of the Fiji Islands.

CHARACTERISTICS ... New Zealand is unique—a wonderland of scenery, a sportsman's paradise, and a delightful spot for a completely different vacation. The Government Travel Bureau sponsors a wide range of tours, and costs are moderate.

New Zealanders have much in common with Americans. On first acquaintance they appear reserved, but they are naturally friendly and hospitable. European New Zealanders live in harmony with native New Zealanders, the Maoris, whose arts and traditions have contributed much to the culture of the country.

POPULATION ... Estimated at 2,590,787 for the country. Auckland, the largest city, has a population of 500,000 inhabitants.

SIZE ... 103,740 square miles; 1,000 miles long, 300 miles wide.

CAPITAL ... Wellington, with a population of 255,700.

GOVERNMENT ... A member of the British Commonwealth of Nations, New Zealand is politically independent and governed by its own Parliament. The Queen is represented by a governor-general.

HOW TO GET THERE ... By Clipper from San Francisco, Los Angeles, Seattle or Portland, to Auckland via Honolulu, 14¾ hours elapsed time. From the Pacific Coast, 18½ hours via the Fiji Islands. 4¾ hours from Fiji. By ship about 17 days from San Francisco.

ACCOMMODATIONS ... There are no hotels of the super-deluxe class in New Zealand, but in most main tourist spots there are good, comfortable ones. Lodges provide excellent accommodations for sportsmen. Private bathrooms are limited and are not always available. Prices for food and accommodations are very reasonable and hotels are spotlessly clean. In Auckland, the *White Heron Lodge, Royal International* and the *De Brett* are the most modern hotels. Single from $10, double from $15, European Plan. Rates at the *Great Northern,* including breakfast, are from $11 per person. The *Star Hotel,* known for good food, charges $12.25-$14 per person, American Plan. The long-established *Grand,* overlooking the harbor, is $10 to $11.50 per person, American Plan. *El Cortez Motel* is from $8.50 per person, EP. There are also a number of less expensive hotels, motels and attractive guest houses (usually unlicensed for drinks).

ARTS ... The War Memorial Museum at Auckland contains one of the finest collections of Maori and Polynesian exhibits in the world. The Art Gallery features works by New Zealand artists. Christchurch has outstanding museums, and there are museums and art galleries in other cities.

BALLET ... A local ballet company has been formed in Auckland. Visiting companies appear occasionally in local theaters.

BANKS ... There are a number of trading banks, all of which have branches throughout New Zealand. Travelers checks can be cashed at any branch. Representatives of various banks meet every incoming aircraft in order to convert overseas travelers' funds, even when visitors arrive outside normal banking hours.

CALENDAR OF HOLIDAYS ... Christmas Day; December 26, Boxing Day; January 1 and 2; Anniversary Day (January 29 for Auckland); April 25, Anzac Day; Good Friday; Easter Monday; Queen's Birthday (early June); Labor Day (late October). There are special race meetings on the first 4 holidays mentioned; on Anniversary Day Auckland holds its famous yachting regatta. Most stores are closed from 9 P.M. Friday to 9 A.M. Monday.

CIGARETTES AND TOBACCO ... New Zealand cigarettes and tobacco; also locally made English and American brands.

CLIMATE ... North Island to the north of Auckland is moist and semitropical. Situated below the equator, it is warmer in the north and colder in the south. South Island is slightly cooler and higher. September to April is the ideal New Zealand season, as their seasons are the reverse of ours. July, August and September are best for winter sports. Because you are never far from the sea in New Zealand, the climate is moderate.

CLUBS ... Rotary International, Lions International, Overseas League, Victoria League, Royal Commonwealth Society, Travel Club, English Speaking Union. (Admission to the racing or trotting clubs can sometimes be arranged. Inquire at your hotel.)

COMMON COURTESIES AND LOCAL CUSTOMS . . . Tea is a ritual here; morning and afternoon. When you are invited to come to tea it probably means "supper." Traffic moves on the left.

COMMUNICATIONS . . . A 3-minute phone call to the States costs £3-6-0; a cablegram is 1/10 per word. Airmail postage to the U.S. is 8d for an airletter, 9d for a postcard, 1/6 for ½-ounce letter.

CURRENCY . . . The New Zealand pound is worth about U.S. $2.80. Decimal-system currency is due in mid-1967.

CUSTOMS REGULATIONS AND DOCUMENTS REQUIRED FOR UNITED STATES CITIZENS . . . Passport and visa. Ticket to leave. Smallpox vaccination certificate. For one customs declaration 200 cigarettes may be brought in free of duty, or 50 cigars, or ½ lb. of tobacco. Also 1 bottle of liquor.

DRUGSTORES . . . American pharmaceuticals, among others, and cosmetics are sold at chemists' shops.

ELECTRIC CURRENT . . . In most city hotels, the voltage is 230 A.C., 50 cycles; a double-wound transformer is required to reduce the voltage for American appliances, but this will not work in all places.

FAUNA . . . New Zealand is famous for its birds. Chief among them, and the emblem of the country, is the kiwi, which cannot fly. Other indigenous birds include the parakeet, long-tailed cuckoo, kingfisher, woodhen, kaka, pukeko—all rare and beautiful. The tuatara is a prehistoric reptile, sole survivor of the age of dinosaurs. Most of these native birds and tuataras can now be seen in captivity at the Auckland Zoological Gardens.

FLORA . . . Flowers are fabulous. The *houhere* (lace-bark) with its masses of snow-white clusters blooms in the autumn and varies in height from 10 to 45 feet. The *kowhai* shrub with its pendulous yellow flowers grows 40 feet high; *kaka's beak,* dainty and scarlet, is a beautiful plant, as are the climbing clematis and the red *rata.* The *pohutukawa,* the New Zealand Christmas tree, blooms along the coast in a profusion of red flowers during late December and early January. There are many other flowering shrubs, as well as the mountain lily and edelweiss. *Totara, rimu* and the giant *kauri* are among native timbers. Imported Monterey pines from California have flourished to the extent that their products are now forming an important industry.

FOOD . . . Seafood is good. Rock oysters are a delicacy in season. *Toheroas,* New Zealand clams, are a delicacy but somewhat rare. Crayfish and whitebait abound. Trout and game are not sold commercially, but in sporting areas they are served frequently. Beef, pork and bacon are excellent, lamb is superb. Dairy products of all kinds are very good. Natural-flavored cooking predominates, and meal prices are very reasonable.

GAMBLING . . . There is horse racing throughout the country with pari-mutuel betting. Almost any weekend or holiday, race meetings take place within easy distance of the larger towns. Bets can be placed on any race in New Zealand through the Totalisator Agency Board which has representative offices in all towns.

LANGUAGE...The language is English. American colloquialisms are readily understood, some adopted.

LAUNDRY AND DRY CLEANING...These services are available at leading hotels and are on a par with similar services in the United States, although perhaps not so speedy.

LIQUOR...Alcoholic beverages are sold to non-residents in licensed hotels between the hours of 9 A.M. and 6 P.M. Guests living at licensed hotels are served at any time. Minimum legal age for drinkers is 21. Local wines, beers and ales are excellent; imported whiskies available, too.

MEDICAL FACILITIES...There are good hospitals and doctors.

MOTION PICTURES...Current American and British films. Shows are at set hours; seats are reserved.

MUSIC...There is a New Zealand National Symphony Orchestra, which tours the country regularly. Maori singing is very melodious and can be heard at concerts in Rotorua.

NIGHT CLUBS AND CABARETS...In Auckland, an increasing number of restaurants feature dinner dancing and floor shows. Included are the *Colony, Sorrento, The Dutch Kiwi, Pinesong, Gourmet, La Boheme* and the *Ranchhouse*. In Wellington are the *Normandie, Orsini's* and *Zodiac*. In Christchurch, dinner and dancing at the *Malando*. Licensed restaurants may serve drinks up to 11:30 P.M.

PHOTOGRAPHY...Cameras and equipment are available and film is in reasonable supply. Prices are higher than in the United States. Black-and-white stills can be developed in a day, color less than a week. Or you can take undeveloped film back home.

RELIGION...This is a predominantly Protestant country, but you will also find Catholic churches and synagogues.

RESTAURANTS...Tops in Auckland are the *Gourmet* in Shortland Street, *La Boheme* in Wellesley Street, *Lutece* in Lorne Street, *The Rib Room* in Queen Street, *Forte* in Fort Street; *Tai Tung* in Swanson Street for Chinese specialties. In Wellington, the *Zodiac, Orsini's* and *Le Normandie*.

SHOPS AND STORES...Milne and Choyce, Ltd., Queen Street, Auckland, is one of the largest department stores in New Zealand. Manufactured goods are usually expensive, but woolen goods are superior and worth buying. There are a number of souvenir shops which specialize in Maori handicrafts.

SPECTATOR SPORTS...All cities and larger towns have racing and some trotting races. National sports are Rugby football in winter, cricket in summer. Tournament tennis and golf, women's basketball, soft ball, swimming meets, regattas, soccer football, wrestling and boxing matches. The biggest 1-day yachting regatta in the world is on January 29 at Auckland.

SPORTS...All cities and towns, even small ones, have good golf courses. There is excellent skiing at Tongariro National Park, Mt. Cook and Coronet Peak near Queenstown. There are broad sandy beaches in the North and South Islands. There are miles of beaches stretching north and south of Auckland. On the west coast, about thirty miles from Auckland, there is magnificent surf bathing in the Tasman Sea. There is yachting, sailing, boating. This is a sportsman's heaven.

Fishing . . . Many world-famous sportsmen claim that New Zealand's big-game fishing and angling for trout are the best in the world. Before starting on a fishing tour of New Zealand, ask for the folder "Sportsman's Guide to New Zealand."

Big Game Fishing . . . Some of the best big-game fishing in the world is found at Bay of Islands in the "northland" of North Auckland. There are a number of charter boats available with competent captains. Modern tackle is usually provided by the launchmaster. Best months are from mid-December through April. There are comfortable fishing lodges at the main areas. No license fee required.

Fishing in North Island . . . The North Island is famous for the rainbow trout-fishing districts of Taupo, Tongariro and Rotorua. In some of these spots you can actually see the trout in great numbers. The Lake Taupo region is accessible from all parts of the island. The famous Tongariro River is at the southern end. The *Tokaanu Hotel* and *Bridge Lodge* in Turangi provide accommodations. Overlooking the lake is the *Lake Hotel,* and the fine *Wairakei* is nearby.

Fishing in South Island . . . Quinnat salmon and brown trout abound in the inland waters of the South Island. The streams in the Canterbury section between Christchurch and Timaru offer the best and easiest dry-fly fishing in the country. The Selwyn, Rakaia, Rangitata and Waihao Rivers are particularly good.

Hunting . . . There are unlimited numbers of deer to be hunted in New Zealand. Red, fallow, wapiti, Virginian, sambur and chamois may be stalked. The best season is New Zealand's autumn. You may also hunt wild pig. There is no license fee, but opportunities vary in different districts, so it is well to inquire in advance. All rifles brought into New Zealand must be registered with the Arms Officer of the Police Department on arrival. No revolvers, automatics or pistols allowed. For game, 12- and 14-gauge shotguns and .22 rifles are commonly used. For birds, double-barreled 12-gauge shotguns are popular.

THEATERS . . . Visiting companies appear from time to time in Auckland, Wellington, Christchurch and Dunedin, but as a rule most performances are presented by local companies. Don't expect anything very spectacular in this line.

TIME . . . 10 A.M. Tuesday in Auckland is 2 P.M. Monday in San Francisco, a difference of 20 hours.

TIPPING . . . Only for special services.

TRANSPORTATION . . . Air services are good. Transport by motor coach is comfortable and reliable. Trains are not up to American standards. The most pleasant way of traveling through the country is by chauffeur-driven limousine. Auto rentals are also available. You can bring your own car in for 6 months or more if you take it out again. For local use taxis are plentiful; also buses.

WATER . . . You can safely drink the water.

WHAT TO BUY . . . Woolens, blankets, English pipes. Maori carvings and dolls dressed in native Maori costumes. Paua-shell novelties.

WHAT TO WEAR . . . This depends upon where you are going and what you are going to do. You'll need medium- and lightweight clothes for the North Island in their summer and heavier weight clothes in the winter. You will want beach clothes, raincoat, topcoat, slacks, sweaters and sports clothes. For walking through the Milford Track on South Island, you'll need boots and sports clothes and rucksack. (Rain capes and rucksacks are procurable at the Te Anau Hotel.) For fishing you'll need whatever you always need. The same goes for skiing. In Auckland dress as you would in any medium-sized city at home. You won't need evening clothes particularly, but you certainly need a variety of sports clothes plus topcoat, sweaters and the like.

WHERE TO GO—SIGHTSEEING . . .

Auckland and Environs . . . Auckland was founded in 1840, so don't expect to find anything very old. But you will find a pleasant city located on two oceans, the Pacific and the Tasman Sea. Within the city itself there are 31 parks and reserves. Waitemata Harbour is famous the world over and there are beautiful beaches which stretch to the north and south of the city. Take a drive over the new harbour bridge. You will want to see the view of the city from One Tree Hill, an extinct volcano cone in Cornwall Park. There are, by the way, 65 extinct volcanoes in and around Auckland. Drive to Ellerslie Gardens, through the Kauri and Rimu forest to Titirangi and Atkinson Parks. Take a trip to the top of Mount Eden for another gorgeous view. The scenic drive in the Waitakere Ranges gives you a good idea of the New Zealand Bush. Waiheke Island, about 13 miles from the city in the Hauraki Gulf, has some wonderful beaches; take a speedy hydrofoil boat. Kawau Island, also in the Gulf, is about 30 miles away. There is a hotel there, the *Mansion House.* Take a sightseeing bus for the waterfront drive which goes to Mt. Eden, Tamaki Heights and Ellerslie Racecourse. Forty-five miles north of Auckland is Helensville, famous for its mineral hot springs.

Waitomo . . . No tour of North Island is complete without a trip to Waitomo Caves, about 133 miles from Auckland. Here is the famous and unique Glow-worm Grotto. It must be viewed in silence, for the glow-worms extinguish their lamps at the slightest sound. There are other beautiful caves here. The Cathedral, the Fairy Walk, the Crystal Palace are all lovely to see. There is a pleasant hotel here, too, the *Waitomo;* $12 to $15 per person, including meals.

Rotorua . . . Is in North Island, in the center of an area of thermal activity. There is everything here: boiling mud baths, spouting geysers, alkaline and sulphuric waters. The waters are famous for bathing and drinking. Rotorua is the center of Maori life. To visit New Zealand without having seen these New Zealanders is unthinkable. Whakarewarewa is a Maori village in which the Maoris live their own easy, pleasant lives in their carved and thatched huts. Maori carvings are wonderful. During the summer season Maori concerts are given at Rotorua. If you are fortunate enough to be there at that time, be sure to attend. Maori girls sing and do a dance reminiscent of the Hawaiian hula. *Grand Hotel;* $12.50 per person, including meals.

There are 2-day trips of great interest which may be taken from Rotorua: the Waimangu round trip and the Rotorua-Okataina trip, and others. The first of these takes you to Earthquake Flats, site of a vanished lake, down the Waimangu Track, across two lakes to Lake Rotomahana. Cross the lake in a launch and walk to Lake Tarawera, which you cross by launch, to the buried village of Te Wairoa. Beyond are the Blue and Green Lakes. The Rotorua-Okataina trip takes you through 6 lakes, including picturesque and beautiful Lake Rotoiti.

Five miles from Lake Taupo there is the modern *Wairakei Hotel*, which is centrally heated by steam that is drawn from the nearby thermal area. The hotel has its own mineral swimming pool, golf course, tennis courts and bowling green. Trips are run several times each day to the Wairakei Valley thermal area, which is spectacularly thrilling and easily accessible. Other sightseeing trips include the Karapiti Blowhole, called the "Safety Valve of New Zealand;" Huka Falls; Aratiatia Rapids and Lake Taupo. Trout fishing is fine here.

Tongariro National Park and Egmont National Park ... There are two national parks in the North Island that are well worth a visit if you have time. Tongariro National Park is in the center of the island just south of Lake Taupo. There is a splendid modern hotel here, the *Château Tongariro*—a golf course, tennis courts, etc. Also wonderful fishing here in the mountain streams, and some breathtaking scenery. You will see three volcanic cones, two of which erupt spectacularly but harmlessly from time to time. Much of this park is untouched forest. Egmont National Park, about 100 miles to the west of Tongariro, is dominated by snow-topped Mt. Egmont, an extinct volcanic peak, which rises from the plains. Here, too, are a forest preserve and some interesting drives.

Wellington ... The capital (about 1½ hours by air from Auckland) is built on steep hills overlooking a beautiful harbor. The hills may be climbed by cablecars rather like those in San Francisco. The best hotels are the *White Heron Lodge, Royal Oak, St. George, Grand* and *Waterloo*. There are interesting drives through the mountains which form a backbone for the capital, and a good highway which follows the coastline north. In Wellington there are, of course, all sorts of public buildings, a National Art Museum, Gallery and Dominion Museum, Alexander Turnbull Library, with unique Pacific literature collection, and the Botanical Gardens. Visit Hutt Valley too.

South Island ... The South Island has some of the most marvellous scenery in the world—high mountains, majestic fiords, wide plains, lovely lakes and unspoiled forests. Starting point is usually Christchurch, "the most English town outside England" (population 227,000). Hotels include the *United Service, Warners, Clarendon, Russley* and *Shirley Lodge*. Tours of spectacular South Island by bus, air or self-drive car may be arranged in Christchurch.

Hanmer Springs ... Luxurious thermal resort, 82 miles north of Christchurch; jet boating through the gorge, hunting, fishing, riding, swimming, excellent golf, winter skiing. *Hanmer Lodge,* $9.80 per person, including meals.

Mt. Cook... Dominating the long chain of the Southern Alps is Mt. Cook (12,349 ft.), which towers over nearly a score of snow-clad peaks reaching 10,000 ft. There are accommodations at the newly built *Hermitage Hotel.* There are magnificent alpine views along the route from Christchurch.

Queenstown... On a sheltered arm of S-shaped Lake Wakatipu. Hotels include *Eichardts, O'Connell's Hotel* and *Fosters.* There are many sidetrips and launch excursions on the lake, and in winter nearby Coronet Peak is a popular skiing resort.

Lake Te Anau... Second largest New Zealand lake, it has delightful fiords to explore by launch and its own special glow-worm cave. Nearby is lovely Lake Manapouri.

Milford Sound... Star of New Zealand's fiordland is Milford Sound, reached through some of the world's finest forest and mountain scenery and through the ¾-mile-long Homer Tunnel, blasted through the solid rock of a mountain range. Milford Sound's rugged grandeur is often ranked with the fiords of Norway. Sheer and bush-clad, the tall mountains drop straight down into the deep sea. Mile-high peaks surround *Milford Hotel* at the head of the fiord; $17.75 per person, including meals. Here, too, is the famous Milford Track, a 33-mile 3-day walk often described as "The loveliest walk in the world." Hundreds walk it every year, but you need to be physically fit.

The Glaciers... On the west coast of South Island the main tourist attractions are the Franz Josef and Fox glaciers, which descend about 8,000 feet in 8 miles into lowland forest less than 700 feet above sea level. Visitors can reach these glaciers from the *Franz Josef* or *Fox* hotels, and there are daily guided excursions onto the ice itself. The west coast is reached by railroad through the Otira Tunnel, longest railroad tunnel (5½ miles) in the British Commonwealth, or by road through Arthur Pass, Lewis Pass, or the great Haast Pass highway.

Dunedin... Established by Scottish pioneers, is the nearest city to Queenstown. Hotels are *Wains,* the *City* and the *Grand.*

SOURCES OF FURTHER INFORMATION... New Zealand Government Travel Commissioner at 153 Kearny Street, San Francisco 8; at 510 W. 6th St., Los Angeles; and at 630 Fifth Avenue, New York, N.Y. 10020. In New Zealand, the New Zealand Government Tourist Bureau is on Queen Street, Auckland; Mercer Street, Wellington; Cathedral Square, Christchurch. Also the Tourist and Publicity Department 125 Lambton Quay, Wellington. The Public Relations Office, Achilles House, Customs Street (Tel. 31-825), specializes in services for Auckland visitors. Pan American's office is in Shortland Street, Auckland (Tel. 23249).

SAMOA

The Bay of Pago Pago is one of the most beautiful in the South Pacific, and Samoans are a friendly, generous people well known for their splendid physiques, love of ceremony and happy dispositions. The seven islands that make up American Samoa lie 2,300 miles southwest of Hawaii. By Pan American Clipper, Samoa's Airport is 11¾ hours from the U.S. west coast via Honolulu. Western Samoa is less than an hour's flight farther. Only passport, smallpox vaccination certificate and ticket to leave are required of U.S. citizens on American Samoa, but a visa is also needed to visit Western Samoa. U.S. currency is acceptable in both Samoas.

Tutuila Island is breathtakingly lovely, with steep green mountains dropping into the sea, with bays and fjord-like harbors. The new *Pago Pago Intercontinental* is air conditioned and luxurious; single $15 to $22, double $18 to $25, European Plan. Plans with meals also available. The *Rainmaker,* named for Tutuila's favorite mountain, is Pago Pago's famous old hotel. Rates per person $8 and up, including meals.

Western Samoa, independent since January 1, 1962, is famous as the last home and the burial place of Robert Louis Stevenson—at Vailima, several miles from the port capital of Apia. The island of Upolu, a lushly forested island bright with tropical flowers, rivers and waterfalls, has two hotels: the very atmospheric *Aggie Grey's* and the *Casino* ($9.80 per person, public bath, American Plan).

American food is served generally; Polynesian dishes served on request. Tap water is safe in Western and American Samoa. Liquor is served in hotels; also at night clubs in Western Samoa and *Goat Island Club* in Pago Pago.

For recreation: Pago Pago offers sightseeing tours, boat trips, excellent deep-sea fishing, skin diving amid colorful coral reefs, taxi rides along the beautiful coasts, hiking along primitive trails to outlying communities. There are television and movies, and Pago Pago has several taverns. Best are the *Island Moon,* with Friday night floor shows, and the *Kava Kupp,* with a magnificent view of Rainmaker Mountain.

SOURCES OF FURTHER INFORMATION ... The Samoan Industry Building; the Government Office Building; Pan Am's District Sales Office in Pago Pago. In Western Samoa: Goldstar Travel Bureau, Union Steamship Co., and Burns Philip (South Sea) Co., Ltd.

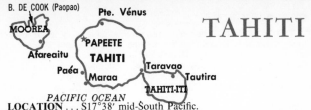

TAHITI

PACIFIC OCEAN

LOCATION . . . S17°38′ mid-South Pacific.

CHARACTERISTICS . . . The combination of French sophistication and unquenchable Polynesian gaiety, the carefree existence of these happy, handsome people and the unspoiled scenic splendor are guaranteed to enchant you. This is the most beautiful, most casual, relaxed and easy-going place in the world, and at the same time, it has all the modern conveniences for comfort.

POPULATION . . . About 85,000 in French Polynesia.

SIZE . . . Tahiti is 402 square miles; smaller than Los Angeles.

CAPITAL . . . Papeete (pah-peh-ay-teh), population 20,000.

GOVERNMENT . . . A French Overseas Territory.

HOW TO GET THERE . . . Tahiti is 7½ hours from Los Angeles, 5½ hours from Honolulu, 4 hours from Fiji, and can be included in Round-the-World itineraries. Upon arrival, taxi to your hotel, convert your currency to francs and then pay driver. Fare into Papeete is about 250 francs. There is a departure tax of 400 francs (U.S. $4.58).

ACCOMMODATIONS . . . For the most part, hotels, which are strung along the coast on both sides of Papeete, feature well-spaced guest bungalows in luxuriant gardens, with office, restaurant and bar centered in a thatched-roof, Tahitian-style main building. Most hotels front on their own beaches, or have swimming pools. Those listed below operate on European Plan. *Hotel Tahiti,* single $9.50-$25, double $12.50-$25; *Moana Nui,* $12.50-$25 per person; *Royal Tahitien,* $10-$20 per person. Less expensive are the *Matavia, Bel Air-* and *Taone.* Hotel Tahiti requires a 25% deposit the year round; other hotels request it June-August. The *Faratea,* 40 miles from Papeete, is convenient for island excursions and specializes in water sports; $10 single, $12 double, EP. Best hotels on other islands are the *Bora Bora* on that island; *Bali Hai* and *Aimeo* on Moorea; and *Bali Hai Raiatea* on Raiatea.

CLIMATE . . . During the cool, dry season of March through November, the temperature ranges from 68° to 87°; from 72° to 88° the rest of the year.

CURRENCY . . . French Pacific franc, valued at 87 to U.S. $1 for currency; at 88 to the dollar for travelers checks.

CUSTOMS REGULATIONS AND DOCUMENTS REQUIRED FOR UNITED STATES CITIZENS . . . Passport; no visa required for a stay of 10 days or less; smallpox vaccination certificate, a continuing or round-trip ticket. 400 cigarettes and 1 bottle of liquor allowed duty free.

ELECTRIC CURRENT . . . Mostly 110 volts, 60 cycles, A.C.; American type plugs. A few places have 220-volt current.

FOOD ... Hotels and some restaurants serve very good French food and wines. Recommended are the *Chapiteau* and *Bougainville* restaurants in Papeete, the *Moana Nui* and the *Faratea* (halfway round the island). Tahitian meals, served on request, might include marinated raw fish, roast suckling pig, yams, curried shrimp, wild pigeons, *taioro* (seafood and coconut). There is fine Chinese food, too, at such restaurants as the *Golden Dragon, Waikiki, Ah Tschoun* and *Arahiri Hotel.* Dinner in one of the top restaurants runs from $4-$6.50. Chief native drinks are *Hinano,* a local beer, and rum. All kinds of imported liquors are available, too. Tahiti's drinking water is excellent.

LANGUAGE ... French, Tahitian; English is widely understood.

NIGHT CLUBS AND CABARETS ... Unlike most dreamy Pacific islands, Tahiti comes very much alive after dark. There is dancing every night at *Hotel Tahiti,* on weekends in other large hotels. Traditional bistros in Papeete, all fairly throbbing with Maughamesque South Seas atmosphere, are the famous *Quinn's, Au Col Bleu* and *Bar Léa,* noted for its exceptional dancing. New and lively are the *Bounty Club, Zizou Bar* and *Whisky à GoGo.* There is an 11:30 curfew, but spots out of town, such as the *Lafayette,* keep going as long as the customers do. All this revelry is not limited to tourists; the Tahitians themselves are on a perpetual holiday spree, and gaiety is equally unconfined on Bora Bora and Moorea.

SHOPS AND STORES ... There are American-type drugstores for necessities. Chic little shops sell French swimming suits, perfumes, crystal, silver, lingerie, purses and fabrics for half the price in the States. Chinese dressmakers whip up smart frocks almost overnight, and local tailors are adept at turning out suits and handsome Tahitian sport shirts. The brightly colored *pareu* cloth is used for everything from clothes to curtains. Shop at the Cosiete Manuia for Tahitian war clubs, tikis, spears, drums, all kinds of wood carvings and basketry, and gorgeous dance costumes from Bora Bora. Tahitian music on records, generally unobtainable elsewhere, is well recorded in Papeete.

SPORTS ... Swimming, skin diving, fishing in ocean and swift mountain rivers, paddling outrigger canoes. Papeete's Diving Center of Polynesia rents out boats and all kinds of equipment.

TIPPING ... Strictly prohibited by law in French Polynesia.

TRANSPORTATION ... A good road circles Tahiti and its little appendage, Taiarupa, but the interior is wildly mountainous and uninhabited (Mt. Orohena—7,339 feet—was first climbed as recently as 1953). Both Hertz and Avis Rent-a-Car have agencies; daily rates from $7.50, weekly from $48.20. Taxis are expensive. There are flights to Bora Bora and the Tuamotu Islands, and a comfortable launch to Moorea, 12 miles from Tahiti. Schooner trips may also be arranged.

SOURCES OF FURTHER INFORMATION ... Office du Tourisme de la Polynésie y Française, Box 65, Papeete, Tahiti. The Pan American agent is Air Tahiti, 113 Quai Bir Hackeim (Tel. 870).

AFRICA

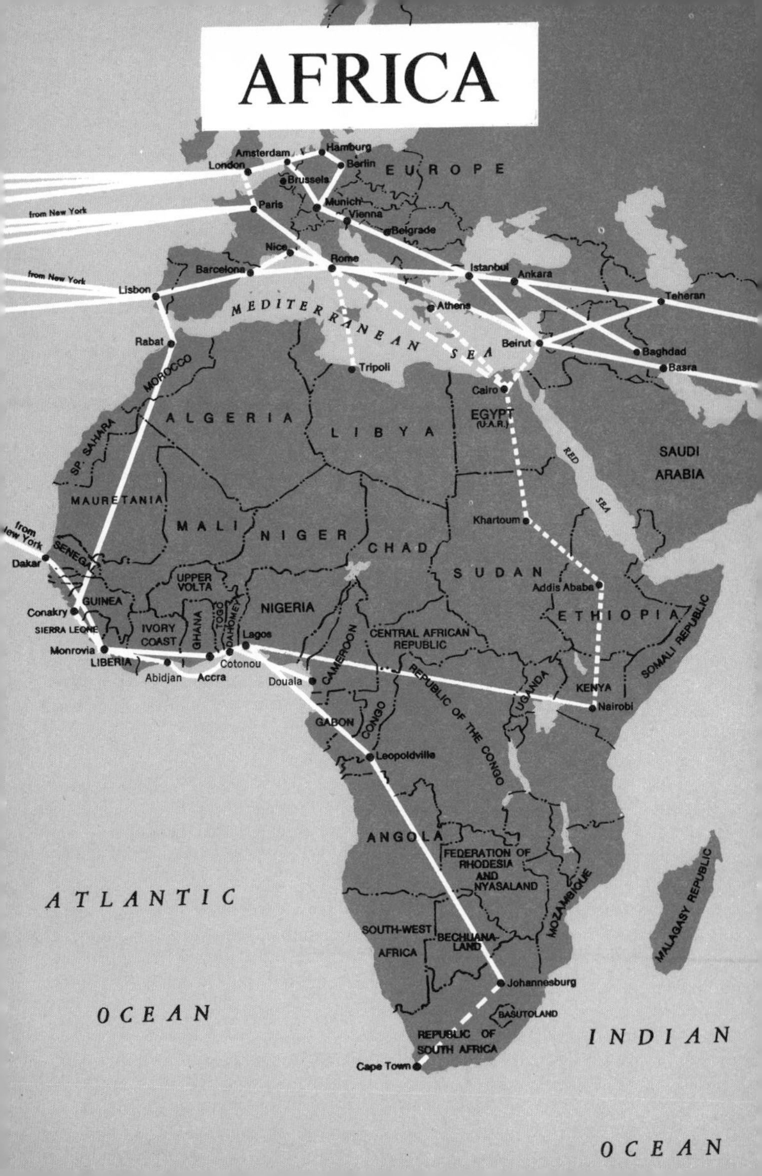

EUROPE
Amsterdam
Hamburg
London
Berlin
Brussels
from New York
Paris
Munich
Vienna
Belgrade
Nice
Rome
Barcelona
Istanbul
Ankara
from New York
Lisbon
Teheran
MEDITERRANEAN SEA
Athens
Rabat
Beirut
Baghdad
Basra
Tripoli
MOROCCO
Cairo
ALGERIA
EGYPT (U.A.R.)
LIBYA
SP. SAHARA
RED SEA
SAUDI ARABIA
MAURETANIA
Khartoum
MALI
NIGER
from New York
SENEGAL
Dakar
CHAD
SUDAN
UPPER VOLTA
Addis Ababa
GUINEA
NIGERIA
ETHIOPIA
Conakry
TOGO
DAHOMEY
SIERRA LEONE
IVORY COAST
GHANA
Lagos
CENTRAL AFRICAN REPUBLIC
SOMALI REPUBLIC
Monrovia
LIBERIA
Cotonou
Abidjan
Accra
Douala
CAMEROON
REPUBLIC OF THE CONGO
UGANDA
KENYA
Nairobi
GABON
CONGO
Leopoldville
ANGOLA
FEDERATION OF RHODESIA AND NYASALAND
MOZAMBIQUE
MALAGASY REPUBLIC
ATLANTIC
SOUTH-WEST AFRICA
BECHUANA-LAND
Johannesburg
OCEAN
BASUTOLAND
REPUBLIC OF SOUTH AFRICA
INDIAN
Cape Town
OCEAN

CONGO (LEOPOLDVILLE)

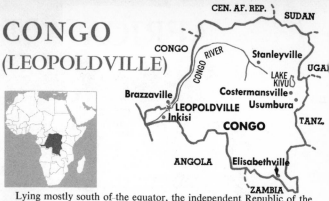

Lying mostly south of the equator, the independent Republic of the Congo is very much on businessmen's itineraries again and is hoping to attract tourists, too. June through September are the pleasantest, driest months, with cool evenings. Via Pan Am Jet, Leopoldville is 17¾ hours, elapsed time, from New York. U.S. citizens require passport and visa; yellow fever and smallpox certificates; police and good health certificates; 3 photos; onward transportation ticket. One opened bottle of liquor, 200 cigarettes allowed duty free, but cameras are subject to duty. The Congo franc (CFR) is 180 to U.S. $1. Electric current is 220 volts, 50 cycles, A.C.

The capital city of Leopoldville (population about 500,000) has several air-conditioned hotels: *Regina Hotel,* from $8 single, $10 double; *Memling Hotel,* from $7 single, $8 double. Rates quoted are European Plan (without meals). Advance reservations necessary. Each hotel has a cocktail lounge and restaurant where mainly European-style meals are served, with the addition of superb locally grown fruits. Tap water must be boiled, but bottled waters are available. Hotels and restaurants add a 10% service charge. Tip luggage porters 20 to 50 CFR per bag.

Lightweight, washable clothing is worn year-round. Formal occasions are few, but golf and tennis are popular, and Leopoldville has three beautiful swimming pools. Get up early and take your camera to the native market, which is at its teeming, colorful best from 7 to 10 A.M. A city tour should include the de Bock Park and the Zoological Garden, the Museum of Native Life, St. Anne's Cathedral, King Albert Monument, Pioneers Monument and Stanley Monument. In Old Leopoldville are the navy yard, the old camp of Stanley, from whose time the discovery of the area dates. The road along the Congo River gives you views of the Stanley Pool, the rapids, the Belvedere, the quay of boats which cross the river to Brazzaville (about 20 minutes), Point Kalina and the Cristal Mountains.

SOURCES OF FURTHER INFORMATION ... Congo (Leopoldville) Mission to the U.N., 211 E. 43rd St., New York, N.Y. 10017. Pan Am's office is in the Regina Hotel in Leopoldville. (Tel. 3371).

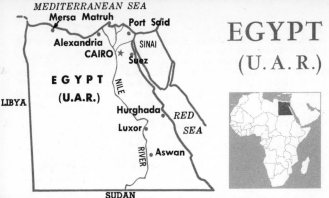

EGYPT
(U.A.R.)

EGYPT
(U.A.R.)

WEATHER IN CAIRO—Lat. N30°3'

Temp.	JAN.	FEB.	MAR.	APR.	MAY	JUNE	JULY	AUG.	SEPT.	OCT.	NOV.	DEC.
Low	45°	47°	51°	56°	62°	67°	70°	71°	67°	63°	56°	49°
High	67°	70°	76°	83°	89°	94°	96°	94°	89°	86°	79°	70°
Average	56°	59°	64°	70°	76°	81°	83°	78°	78°	75°	68°	60°
Days of Rain	3	2	2	1	0	0	0	0	0	0	1	2

LOCATION ... Egypt occupies the northeastern corner of Africa, with the Mediterranean on the north and the Red Sea on the east. Libya and the Sudan are border countries on the west and south. Egypt's northeastern corner, the Sinai peninsula, is separated by the Gulf of Suez and the Canal.

CHARACTERISTICS ... The banks of the Nile have witnessed the passing of many civilizations, which tourists may observe in remains dating from the dawn of history to Pharaonic Egypt, in the Pyramids at Giza, the Sphinx, Luxor tombs and temples, and those of Sakkara, Kena, Edfu, Kom Ombo, Nubia and Aswan. Alexandria has valuable remains of the Greco-Roman period in a new open-air museum. Early relics of Christendom in the Nile valley may be seen in the Sinai peninsula and along the coast of the Red Sea.

POPULATION ... Egypt has a population of about 28 million, 95% of whom live along the banks of the Nile.

SIZE ... 386,101 square miles; about 660 miles long.

CAPITAL ... Cairo, with a population of about 3,858,000.

GOVERNMENT ... A republic, known as the United Arab Republic, with a President and Presidential Council.

HOW TO GET THERE ... By Pan American Jet Clipper to Rome, about 8 hours from New York. Then by connecting airline, about 2¾ hours to Cairo. For Middle East travelers, Cairo is one hour via Middle East Airlines from Beirut, and may be included at no extra cost if you purchase a ticket in advance covering your full itinerary. By ship to Alexandria 13 to 17 days from New York.

ACCOMMODATIONS . . . In Cairo: *Nile Hilton Hotel*, overlooking the river, has 400 air-conditioned rooms (from $10.35 single, $12.65 double) and a floating annex on the Nile—the *Isis Boat*—$8 single, $10.30 double. *Shepheard's Hotel* has 290 air-conditioned rooms; $7.65-$11.10 single, $9.95-$13.35 double. The old, yet charming, *Semiramis* and the new *Cleopatra Palace*, *El Borg* and *The Nile* (on the Nile) and the *Scheherazade Hotel* are from $6 single, $9 double; all EP (European Plan—without meals). The new *Sphinx, Continental-Savoy* and *Mena House* (6 miles from the center of Cairo, overlooking the Pyramids of Giza) and *Cosmopolitan* hotels are from $4.50 single, $6 double, including breakfast. The *Omar Khayyam* has 28 rooms in a converted palace ($16) and 190 bungalows ($11.40, including breakfast). All hotels add a 10% service charge. In Alexandria: *Beau Rivage, Windsor, Cecil, Montaza Palace, San Stefano*; average rates are $7 single, $10 double, European Plan. At Luxor: *Winter Palace* and *New Winter Palace* ($8.55-$10.85 single, $10.85-$13.15 double) and *Luxor Hotel* ($7.45 single, $12.65 double, American Plan). At Aswan: *Cataract Hotel, New Cataract* and *Kalabsche* average $11 single, $18 double, American Plan (3 meals). The *Amun* is $7 single, $9.30 double, EP. Fine new hotels now extend along the Egyptian Riviera from Alexandria to the Libyan border.

ARTS . . . Covering over 7,000 years of history are: the Egyptian Museum (superb Tutankhamen collection), Roman Museum, Coptic Museum, Islamic Art Museum, Anderson Museum, Abdine Palace Museum, Gawhara Palace Museum, Al-Manial Palace Museum. Also Modern Arts, Egyptian Civilization, Geological museums.

BALLET . . . Occasional performances November through March.

BANKS . . . Money may be exchanged only at banks and at such authorized outlets as: American Express Co., 15 Kasr El Nil St.; Thomas Cook & Sons, 4, Champollion St., and in major hotels.

CALENDAR OF HOLIDAYS . . . Sham El Nessim in late April or early May, Anniversary of the Revolution on July 23, the Flooding of the Nile, 2nd fortnight in August, the Hegira New Year, End of the Fasting Month (Ramadan), Bairam Feast, Islamic New Year. Moslem holiday dates vary, depending upon lunar calendar.

CIGARETTES AND TOBACCO . . . Egyptian cigarettes are made of the best qualities of Turkish and American tobaccos and cost 41¢ a pack; *Belmonts* are popular. American cigarettes cost $1 a pack.

CLIMATE . . . In Cairo, summer days are hot and often humid, but evenings are cooler. Air conditioning advisable. In winter Egypt enjoys a warm temperature, although it can get as low as 40° in Cairo. Port Said and Alexandria temperatures are similar but with less variation between summer and winter.

CLUBS . . . The important clubs in Cairo are: the Automobile Club, Cairo Yacht Club, Fishing and Shooting Club, Gezira Sporting Club, Heliopolis Sporting Club, Maadi Sporting Club, Maadi Yacht Club, National Club, Rowing Club, Touring Club and Rotary

Club (meets every Tuesday at the Nile Hilton).

COMMUNICATIONS ... Phone calls to the U.S. are made between 4 and 11 P.M. A 3-minute call costs L3.300 (U.S. $7.55); a cablegram is 23 piastres (52¢) per word. Airmail to the United States is 8.5 piastres for postcards, 11.5 piastres for letters.

CURRENCY ... The Egyptian pound (L) is divided into 100 piastres (P.T. 100), or 1,000 milliemes (1,000 mills). The American dollar corresponds to 43.5 piastres. Currency may be exchanged at airports on arrival. Keep a record of all exchange transactions on official customs forms to be presented upon departure.

CUSTOMS REGULATIONS AND DOCUMENTS REQUIRED FOR UNITED STATES CITIZENS ... Passport and visa required, also smallpox certificates and others if coming from Eastern, yellow-fever or cholera areas. Check with Pan American. Personal effects are admitted duty free, although some need to be declared. 100 cigarettes or 25 cigars or ½ lb. tobacco and 1 opened pint of liquor allowed. No Egyptian currency is allowed into or out of the country.

DRUGSTORES ... Some American pharmaceuticals can be found.

ELECTRIC CURRENT ... In central Cairo it's 220 volts, A.C. In Heliopolis and elsewhere it varies, but is usually 110-120 volts, A.C.

FAUNA ... The camel can be ridden around the Pyramids and the Sphinx, but not in the towns. In the Egyptian deserts, the desert rabbits, the gazelle, and the fox. Hunting excursions can be organized through the Hunting and Fishing Club or the Touring Club of Egypt.

FOOD ... Most hotels serve European meals, but visitors enjoy *maza* (assorted hors d'oeuvres) that include *tahina dip,* stuffed grape leaves, *babaghanous* and *tamiya,* followed either by *kibab* (ground or in chunks), or couscous of steamed meat and vegetables on a farina-like cereal. Follow with dessert of *mahlabiya, eish el saraya,* or *kounafa* and, of course, a cup of strong Turkish coffee (*mazbut*—sugared; *sada*—without sugar). Milk should be boiled. (Powdered and canned milk, however, are sometimes available.)

GAMBLING ... Betting on horse races in winter in Cairo and in summer at Alexandria. Bets are also authorized at the Shooting Club. There are gambling casinos in Cairo and Alexandria.

LANGUAGE ... The tourist can make himself understood in English in most of Egypt. Among the various expressions in Arabic, the most used are: *Salam Aleikum* (Good day), *Ahlan wa sahlan* (Welcome), *Shukran* (Thank you) and *baksheesh* (tip).

LAUNDRY AND DRY CLEANING ... Dry cleaning in Cairo and Alexandria is available at major hotels and some shops.

LIQUOR ... Egypt produces a good quality of beer as well as some kinds of wine. Imported liquors are expensive, but the usual mixed drinks are served at bars, hotels and restaurants.

MEDICAL FACILITIES ... There are private and Government hospitals with English-speaking doctors in attendance. Some Egyptian hospitals use American equipment and methods.

MOTION PICTURES ... Many Cairo theaters show American films. The most important ones are: *Metro, Kasr el Nil, Radio, Rivoli,*

The celebrated Sphinx and the famous Pyramids of Gizeh form a traditional view of the Cairo area of Egypt.

Ramses and *Cairo Palace*. All first-class theaters are air-conditioned.

MUSIC ... There are concerts of both Arabic and European music to be heard at concert halls, dancing places and on the radio.

NIGHT CLUBS AND CABARETS ... The most renowned night clubs are: *Auberge des Pyramides, Sahara City, Pearl of Sahara* and the *Caravan Tent* at the Nile Hilton. Supper clubs with dancing are found on the roof gardens of several hotels.

PHOTOGRAPHY ... Egypt has branches of the leading firms dealing in photography and film of various kinds. Developing and printing are good and fast. Tourists are requested not to take pictures of military installations, factories and public works.

RELIGION ... The official religion is Islam. In addition to the mosques, there are churches of every sect, as well as synagogues.

RESTAURANTS ... The best are the *Kursaal, Aladdin's, Omar Khayyam* (in an exotic houseboat), *Estoril, Regent, Groppi's, Le Grillon, St. James,* as well as restaurants in the larger hotels. All serve Continental food and some examples of the local cuisine.

SHOPS AND STORES ... Fixed prices at Westernized stores; prolonged bargaining in *souks*. On Cairo's Musky Road and at the fabulous Khan Khalil bazaar, vendors peg prices 200% higher than they expect you to pay.

SPECTATOR SPORTS ... A great number of sporting events are held in Egypt, such as horse races at Cairo and Alexandria; soccer matches with foreign teams. Championship matches take place among the various teams in the Mediterranean as well as between the Arab nations in several sports such as swimming, tennis and basketball. Regattas and sailboat races are held on the Nile.

SPORTS ... The tourist can participate in tennis, golf, swimming, horseback riding at sporting clubs and at hotels. Ain Sokhna and Hurghada on the Red Sea are picturesque new water-sports resorts.

THEATERS ... Most notable are the Sound and Light performances, nightly in summer, at Cairo's Citadel and at the Pyramids.

Check local papers for special events featuring folk dancers, choral groups, play productions and, in winter, opera performances.

TIME . . . Noon in Cairo is 5 A.M. in New York. Daylight saving is observed from May 1 to October 31.

TIPPING . . . Hotels and restaurants add a 10% service charge. Tip luggage porters 5 piastres per bag. Tip pt.5-10 for small services.

TOURIST TAXES . . . Only at Luxor and Aswan, where a tax of 5% is added to hotel bills. Airport departure tax pt.50 ($1.15).

TRANSPORTATION . . . Taxis are inexpensive. De luxe air-conditioned express trains and United Arab Airlines for quick transport. But if you have the time, Nile steamers are recommended for travel from Cairo to Luxor, Aswan and Abu Simbel.

WATER . . . Tap water is safe in cities and tourist resorts.

WHAT TO BUY . . . Wooden objects encrusted with ivory and ebony, silver and gold jewelry, and copper plates encrusted with different metals; leather objects; camel-saddle ottomans; cotton textiles.

WHAT TO WEAR . . . Lightweight, crease-resistant clothing in light colors is best both winter and summer; a jacket for cool evenings, sunglasses, of course, and a lightweight hat.

WHERE TO GO—SIGHTSEEING . . .

Cairo . . . To get the most out of your sightseeing in Cairo you will probably need a dragoman (guide-interpreter). A brief checklist of principal places of sightseeing interest includes, of course, a visit to the Pyramids and the Sphinx at Giza, by camel if you wish. The Great Pyramid of Cheops is 446 feet high, 740 feet long on each side of the base, covers 12 acres, contains well over 2 million blocks of stone averaging 2½ tons each in weight. King Cheops' tomb composed of huge slabs of granite, is in the center. Other places of interest are: the Citadel and Mohammed Ali Mosque, with a wonderful view of Cairo and the Nile, the historical dwellings and mosques (especially Ibn Tulun, Al Azhar, Sultan Hassan and Kait Bey), the Babylon Citadel, Churches Kasr el Shamh (ancient churches), the ex-king's palaces and the Barrage, north of Cairo. Sakkara, ¾ hour's drive from Cairo, has the world's oldest stone buildings, including the Step Pyramid and the newly discovered Aesculapion, probably leading to Imhotep's tomb.

Side Trips . . . In Alexandria, 113 miles northwest by air from Cairo, are the ports, the Corniche, Kait Bay Fort, Antoniades Garden, the historical sights of Kom El Shogafa, the Catacombs, Pompey Pillar, the Greek Museum, Ras El Tin Palace and Montaza.

At Luxor, 316 miles by air south of Cairo in the heart of ancient Egypt, are the Luxor and Karnak temples, the Valley of the Kings and Queens, Queen Hatshepsut Temple and Memnon Colossi. Aswan, the High Dam site, has the Exotic Gardens and Elephantine Island fortress. South, at Nubia, is famed Abu Simbel.

SOURCES OF FURTHER INFORMATION . . . The United Arab Republic Tourist Administration, 5 Adly Pasha Str., Cairo, for information. For hire of Pan Am's official guide, Pan American's office: Continental Hotel, Cairo (Tel. 911233). In New York the United Arab Republic Tourist Office is at 630 Fifth Avenue.

ETHIOPIA

Ethiopia, in northeastern Africa, is a mountainous land of 457,142 square miles, gateway to the safari country of East Africa. Its Lake Tana is the source of the Blue Nile. Most of the thinly scattered population of 22 million are farmers and herdsmen. Much of the country is highland; the best time to visit is October to March. Addis Ababa, the capital (450,000 population), is overnight from Frankfurt, Madrid, Rome or Athens on Ethiopian Airlines jets. The city is at an always-cool elevation of 8,200 feet. You need a passport and visa (obtainable on arrival), smallpox and yellow fever certificates and onward ticket. Personal effects are admitted duty-free; also 1 quart of liquor, 50 cigars, 100 cigarettes or ½ lb. of tobacco.

Best hotels in Addis Ababa are the *Ethiopia, Ghion* and *Ras.* (The electric current is 220 volts, 50 cycle, A.C., with European type plugs.) Rates per person are U.S. $8-$14, American Plan, plus 10% service charge. (The Ethiopian dollar is worth U.S. 40¢.) *Injera,* an unleavened bread, and *wot,* a highly seasoned stew, are the main native dishes. Chief native drinks are *tej* (honey-sweet liquor) and *tala,* a local beer. American drinks are available. Water is usually boiled and filtered. Bottled water is available.

There are several night clubs and weekly dances at the Ghion and Ras hotels. Ethiopians love music and play unique instruments.

Amharic is the national language although English is widely spoken and understood. The Ethiopians are a proud and aristocratic people, most of whom are Coptic Christians.

SIGHTSEEING ... There are a number of tours of Addis Ababa which include Africa Hall, home of the United Nations Economic Commission for Africa; the New Market, where you can buy handwritten Bibles, old shields, swords and knives, silver ornaments and incense lamps quite cheaply; the imperial lions; the Palace of Emperor Menelik II; Parliament, Trinity and St. George's Churches; Massacre Victims Monument; and Mount Entoto. One-day excursions include the volcanic lakes at Debre Zeit; the thermal baths and the sources of hot springs at Ambo; the town of Nazareth; Koka Dam and Galela Palace at Koka; and the sugar plantation and refinery at Wonji.

SOURCES OF FURTHER INFORMATION ... Calvert-Stearns, Inc., 1 East 53rd Street, New York, N.Y. 10022.

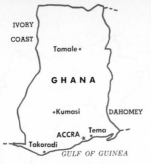

GHANA

A coastline of waving palms, superb sandy beaches and exhilarating surf ... a magnificent forest background ... and in the north, rolling plains make this Commonwealth republic interesting. Ghana is a land of contrasts: of ancient castles built by early European traders (who coined the name "Gold Coast" after the precious metal found there) and of modern buildings in industrialized cities.

Accra ... A city of 490,000, is a regular stop on Pan American's African service, 13 hours elapsed time from New York. There are several good hotels. Most modern is the *Ambassador*—$14 single for air-conditioned room and breakfast. At the smaller *Star Hotel,* $9.50 for air-conditioned room and breakfast. Comparable rates and comforts at the *Avenida* and *Kob Lodge*. A 10% service charge and 10% hotel tax are added to accounts; tips of 10% to 15% are also expected. The electricity in hotels is 220 volts, 50 cycles, A.C. There's a night club, *Mpamprom* (Beachcomber), in the Ambassador Hotel with Africa's only Polynesian restaurant featuring African dancers. Lunch costs about $2, dinner $3. Both continental and English-style cooking are available. There is an abundance of local fruit, and food specialties include ground-nut and palm-nut soup. Local beer, gin and spirits, and imported liquors are available but rather expensive. The water is generally safe to drink in major cities, but it's better to ask for boiled or bottled water.

Cooler than many other tropical countries, the weather is hot enough for swimming but not too hot for sightseeing in the towns and villages. Rainy months are May, June and October. Lightweight washable clothing is best, and dark-colored tropical suits are worn more than light ones.

To enter the country you will need a passport, visa, sufficient funds, and smallpox and yellow fever vaccination certificates. Airport tax is $1.40. The new Ghanaian currency has 100 pesewas to 1 cedi; 84 pesewas to U.S. $1. The official language is English.

SOURCES OF FURTHER INFORMATION ... State Tourist Corp., P.O. Box 2923, Accra. Pan American's office at Cocoa House, Kwame Nkrumah Ave., P.O. Box 1119, Accra (Tel. 64198). Ghana Information office at 565 Fifth Avenue, New York, N.Y. 10017.

GUINEA

Rich in natural resources, the completely independent Republic of Guinea lies on the west coast of Africa, its capital city of Conakry (population 112,000) less than 10 degrees north of the equator. The country has an area of 94,926 square miles, and a population slightly over 3,500,000. From New York, fly by Pan Am Jet Clipper, nonstop to Dakar in 7½ hours, then less than two hours to Conakry, or by Pan Am through flight in 15½ hours via Rabat. You need a passport, visa ($5) valid for 3 months, and onward transportation ticket; smallpox and yellow fever certificates; anti-malaria medication recommended. Reasonable amounts of cigarettes and liquor enter duty free. No Guinean francs may enter or leave the country. There are no restrictions on other currencies, but all money must be declared and a record of exchange transactions kept to be presented upon departure. Currency and travelers checks may be exchanged at the airport, your hotel and the Bank of the Republic of Guinea. The Guinea franc is valued at 247 to U.S. $1. French is the official language. Electric current is 220 volts, 50 cycles, A.C.

The average temperature in Conakry is 80° the year round. The wet season runs from May until late October; Conakry gets about 168 inches of rainfall a year. The dry season, and best time for a visit, is November to April. The most practical wardrobe is entirely of drip-dry cottons and synthetics (dark-colored business suits preferred).

The motel-type new *Gbessia Hotel* at the airport is air conditioned. Taxi fare from airport into Conakry (9½ miles) is 750 francs. Overlooking the sea in town are *Hotel Camayenne* and popular *Hotel de France*. Rates at all are from $10 single, $16 double, including 10% for service, but not the 5% tax. Small tips also expected; luggage porters get 50 francs per bag. The hotels are the best places to eat; lunch or dinner about $3.50-$5. Filtered water is served in the hotels; bottled water is also available and recommended. When it comes to stronger drinks, the hotels are again your best bet. There are interesting examples of Guinean sculptures and ethnographic displays at the Institute of Research and Documentation. See the university.

SOURCES OF FURTHER INFORMATION . . . Air Guinée is the general sales agent for Pan American in Conakry.

IVORY COAST

The attractive Republic of the Ivory Coast, with its tremendous forests, plantations and vast savannahs, combines the most exotically colorful aspects of tribal Africa with jet age conveniences. A land of 124,502 square miles and 3,665,000 population (including 20,000 Europeans), the Ivory Coast stretches northward from the Gulf of Guinea. The capital city of Abidjan (population 250,000) is only 5.16 degrees above the equator and has an average year round temperature of about 80°. Best time to visit is during the comparatively cooler period of August through November when the main rainy season is over. Pan Am-Air Afrique flights from New York to Abidjan take about 12¼ hours. You need a passport and visa, smallpox and yellow fever inoculation certificates, continuation or return ticket.

Business is booming in Abidjan, a new city of wide, tree-shaded avenues, splendid public buildings and beautiful residential sections. Newest hotel is the luxurious, completely air-conditioned *Ivoire Intercontinental* overlooking Ebrié Lagoon; single $13-$15, double $15-$17. In the same neighborhood is the modern *Hotel Relais de Cocody;* single $10-$11, double $12. In the city itself are the *Hotel du Parc,* the *Grand* and *L'Hotel de France.* Top hotels have swimming pools. Hotels and restaurants serve excellent meals which are rather expensive because so much of the food is flown in from France. Apart from hotel dining rooms, try the *Acapulco Restaurant,* the *Aquarium* and the *Palm Beach,* a few miles out of Abidjan. Dance in the evening to the typical Ivorian bands which beat samba-like rhythms in a Riviera atmosphere.

Local current is 220 volts, 50 cycles, A.C. City tap water is safe to drink. French is the language of the country, and the currency is 235 to 240 CFA francs to U.S. $1. Taxi fares from the airport into Abidjan (10½ miles) are rather high, but are cheap inside the city. Abidjan has both picturesque markets and fashionable shops. Be sure to visit the National Museum with its collection of African art, masks and sculpture. Impressive Banco National Park is only 5 miles from the capital, and there are excursions to the port of Grand Bassam and to the age-old town of Dabou.

SOURCES OF FURTHER INFORMATION ... Ivory Coast Visa Office, 521 Fifth Ave., New York, N.Y. 10017. In Abidjan, Pan Am-Air Afrique is at 2, Avenue General de Gaulle (Tel. 230-25).

KENYA

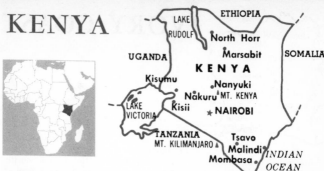

Set astride the equator in East Africa, Kenya is somewhat smaller than Texas (224,960 square miles) and has an estimated population of 9,104,000. The jet flight from Rome to Nairobi takes less than 8 hours and puts you down in a land where high adventure can be enjoyed in comfort. To enter the country, a U.S. citizen needs passport, visa, yellow fever and smallpox vaccination certificates. Duty-free allowances include ½ lb. tobacco or 200 cigarettes or 50 cigars, and 1 pint of spirits. Firearms and ammunition are admitted duty free, but a police permit must be obtained on arrival. The Kenya shilling is valued at U.S. 14¢, and is divided into 100 cents. Best times for seeing big game are June to October and December to March. Temperatures vary from the tropical beaches on the Indian Ocean to the snowy heights of Mt. Kenya (17,058 feet), but summer clothes are worn the year round. Evenings in the Highlands are cool.

Nairobi ... Clean-lined, ultramodern buildings and an ideal climate distinguish this capital of 267,000 people, which is 5,452 feet above sea level. Best hotels are the *New Stanley, Ambassadeur, New Avenue, Panafric* and *Norfolk*. Room with bath and breakfast is generally about $10 a day per person. Smart shops, sophisticated night clubs and sporting events give Nairobi a European atmosphere; but very near Embakasi international airport is the Nairobi National Park, where, in an area of 44 square miles, all kinds of big game roam freely. A 2-hour tour provides much the same thrill as a real safari.

You can travel independently by train, plane or hired car, but package tours are the most popular way to see Kenya, and travel agencies will handle all details. There are now very modern, comfortable hotels and lodges in the country's national parks and game reserves. A typical 7-day tour out of Nairobi goes through Tsavo Park to the slopes of Kilimanjaro, with countless opportunities to photograph wild animals in their natural surroundings. Advance reservations are necessary if you want to spend a night at *Treetops*, luxury hotel on stilts that overlooks a water hole where elephants, rhinos and huge wild buffalo drink under spotlights they think are the moon.

SOURCES OF FURTHER INFORMATION ... East Africa Tourist Travel Association, 750 Third Avenue, New York, N.Y.

LIBERIA

WEATHER IN ROBERTS FIELD (48 miles SE by road from Monrovia)
Lat. N6°45′

	JAN.	FEB.	MAR.	APR.	MAY	JUNE	JULY	AUG.	SEPT.	OCT.	NOV.	DEC.
Average Temp.	78°	80°	80°	81°	80°	78°	75°	75°	77°	79°	79°	79°
In. of Rain	1.9	3.1	4.4	6.1	13.	22.4	30.	18.7	28.8	17.1	6.8	2.7

This Negro Republic on the west coast of Africa, about 2 hours by Clipper from Dakar, was founded in 1822 by the American Colonization Society, organized to help U.S. Negroes return to Africa if they wished. This little country is a combination of modern Western efficiency and centuries-old African culture. Tourists find great friendliness and courtesy. The coastal area has beautiful beaches and good fishing. Best time to visit is November-March, which avoids the rainy months. Lightweight cotton and Dacron clothing is worn the year round. Passport and visa required. 1 lb. tobacco products, 1 bottle of liquor allowed duty free; smallpox and yellow fever certificates.

Monrovia, the capital city of 90,000, was named for U.S. President James Monroe, who once headed the Society. There's the air-conditioned *Roberts Field Hotel* at the airport, with bar and restaurant; from $9 single. It's 48 miles from Monrovia; fare into town is $5. In the city, the new *Ducor Intercontinental,* beautifully located on the top of Mamba Point, is air-conditioned and luxurious; it has a swimming pool, night club and restaurants; $13.50 single, $17.50-$21 double. The air-conditioned *City Hotel, French, Carlton* and *Ambassador* hotels are also comfortable. Rates in these, about $10 single, $15 double. Hotels add 10% service charge. Tip as you would at home; Liberian currency is on a par with the U.S. dollar. The electric current is the same as in the U.S. American and European foods are served, but it's interesting to try the delicious local dish, Country Chop, made from palm oil, rice, meat and fruits. *Heinz and Maria, Oscar's Chalet* and the *Tropical Hut* are popular restaurants.

Pan American is at 80 Broad Street, Monrovia (Tel. 21538).

LIBYA

"The shores of Tripoli" are a lushly productive coastal strip fringing the Mediterranean; 90% of Libya's 679,360 square miles is desert, but rich in oil. Foreigners live mostly in Tripoli (population 240,000) and Benghazi (136,641). Beida in Cyrenaica is the new capital. Flying time from New York is 8 hours to Rome by Pan American Jet Clipper; then 1¾ hours to Tripoli by jet. You need a passport, visa, smallpox vaccination certificate. Duty-free allowances of 200 cigarettes, 50 cigars, or 1 lb. tobacco; 1 bottle of liquor, 2 of wine. The Libyan pound, composed of 100 piastres, is valued at U.S. $2.80.

Tripoli, with a delightful climate, fairly glitters in dazzling sunshine. The best hotels, the *Uaddan, Libya Palace* and *National,* overlook the sea. Single rooms with bath, $8; double $12.50. Service charges of 20% cover most tips. Electric current is 125 volts, 50 cycles. Hotels and restaurants emphasize Italian cooking, but Arabic specialties are available. City tap water is safe to drink, and there is a wide choice of imported wines and liquors.

Tripoli's quaint narrow alleys are delightful; but there are also wide boulevards, modern buildings and a lovely seaside promenade. Note the Marble Arch of Marcus Aurelius, erected in A.D. 163. The sturdy old Castle now houses outstanding collections of Roman and other antiquities. Beautiful Gurgi and Caramanli mosques are open to visitors who obtain permits from the Tourist Department. Sandy beaches lie on both sides of the city, and facilities of the Shooting and Fishing Club are open to visitors. Wheelus Field Air Base is 6 miles from the city. Sabratha, on the coast 40 miles west of Tripoli, has a 2nd-century amphitheater still used for performances by visiting artists. Seventy-six miles east of Tripoli is Leptis Magna, probably the least visited, but best preserved of all ancient Roman cities.

Ghadames, oasis city in the desert of the Tuaregs, is fascinating.

Benghazi, founded in 466 B.C., is famous for rugs. *Berenice* and *Lux* hotels are recommended. The rich archaeological site of Cyrene is 140 miles northeast of Benghazi.

SOURCES OF FURTHER INFORMATION ... Tripolitania Tourist Dept., Tripoli. Pan Am office is c/o OTAL (Tel. 34658).

MOROCCO

WEATHER IN MOROCCO—Lat. 29°35′

Average Temp.	JAN.	FEB.	MAR.	APR.	MAY	JUNE	JULY	AUG.	SEPT.	OCT.	NOV.	DEC.
Tangier	54°	56°	57°	60°	65°	70°	73°	75°	72°	69°	59°	56°
Marrakech	53°	55°	61°	65°	70°	76°	84°	85°	77°	69°	59°	54°
Casablanca	53°	54′	57°	59°	66°	68°	72°	73°	71°	67°	60°	56°

LOCATION ... Morocco occupies the northwest corner of Africa.

CHARACTERISTICS ... Morocco is fascinating for the tourist. Except for the modern cities of Casablanca, Marrakech, Tangier and Rabat, much of the country has remained unchanged for centuries.

POPULATION ... Estimated 13,000,000. The population of Casablanca, the biggest city in Morocco, is about 1,200,000.

SIZE ... 174,471 square miles; 620-mile coastline.

CAPITAL ... Rabat, population 227,445.

GOVERNMENT ... The Kingdom of Morocco is a constitutional monarchy with a parliament of two houses.

HOW TO GET THERE ... By Pan Am Jet Clipper from New York direct to Rabat near Casablanca in 11 hours, 1¼ hours from Lisbon. Via Paris, 10¾ hours; via Lisbon, 12 hours. By ship, 5 days.

ACCOMMODATIONS ... In Casablanca, de luxe hotels in the business center are *El Mansour* and *Marhaba;* also good are the *Transatlantique* and *Noailles*. On Anfa Hill, easily reached by bus or taxi, is the famous *Anfa Hotel*. In Mohammedia, resort 15 miles north of Casablanca, is the glamorous *Miramar Hotel* with beautiful gardens and private beach. In Marrakech, *La Mamounia* and *Menara* are de luxe; *The Renaissance* is first class. In Rabat, the new *Hilton, La Tour Hassan* and the *Balima* are de luxe. In Fes, the *Palais Jamai*, and *El Zallagh* with swimming pool. In Tangier, *El Minzah* and the *Rif* are de luxe; *Velasquez Palace* and *Rembrandt* are good. De luxe rates from $8 single, $10 double; first class from $3 single, $4 double, plus service and about 20% tax; European Plan (without meals).

BALLET . . . During the winter, visiting troupes perform at the huge new Mohammed V Theater, Rabat; at municipal theaters in other principal cities.

BANKS . . . The Banque du Maroc and other banks are correspondents of many American banks.

CALENDAR OF HOLIDAYS . . . New Year's Day; Throne Day, March 3; Labor Day, May 1; Independence Day, November 18. Arab stores are closed during Moslem holidays; Jewish stores during Jewish holidays; other stores on Christian holidays.

CIGARETTES AND TOBACCO . . . American and English cigarettes cost about 65¢ a pack. French and Moroccan brands also available for about 25¢.

CLIMATE . . . Along the shore, from Tangier down to Agadir, the climate is similar to that of Southern California. It gets very hot in summer at Marrakech and in the south, up to 130°, but the air is dry and evenings are cool, especially in mountain resorts.

COMMON COURTESIES AND LOCAL CUSTOMS . . . Sweet mint tea is the Moroccan national beverage. Remove your shoes when entering a Moroccan home. Silverware is provided for visitors, but a Moroccan eats with his right hand, and would like you to, also.

COMMUNICATIONS . . . Fair long-distance telephone and normal cable service. Airmail to the U.S. costs 1 Dh. per 5 grams.

CURRENCY . . . The Moroccan dirham equals the French franc. The official rate is approximately 5 Dh. to U.S. $1.

CUSTOMS REGULATIONS AND DOCUMENTS REQUIRED FOR UNITED STATES CITIZENS . . . You may bring 1 carton of cigarettes, 50 cigars or 1 pound of tobacco duty free. 1 opened bottle of liquor. You need a passport, but no visa for up to 3 months. Importation and export of Moroccan dirhams is prohibited.

DRUGSTORES . . . French drugs and a few American and English drugs, as well as local brands, are available.

ELECTRIC CURRENT . . . U.S. electric appliances need only converter plugs. The current is 110-115 volts, A.C., 50 cycles.

FAUNA . . . Up in the Atlas Mountains, wild boar. In the south, gazelle, Moroccan fox, hyena.

FLORA . . . Towering palms, huge cacti, orange trees, cork forests, enormous roses. In the south, goats perch in squat, thorny argan trees.

FOOD . . . International food is served in hotels, but try some Moroccan specialties. Outstanding are *mechoui* (whole roast mutton), *pastilla* (immense flat pie with mutton, eggs, pigeon, chicken, vegetables, subtle spices), *couscous* (semolina steamed with mutton, chicken, vegetables, chick peas, raisins, with a hot sauce). Moroccan pastries are excellent; native bread is round and flat and is eaten warm. Ripe olives, served profusely, taste different, but good.

GAMBLING . . . There are the Casino of Mohammedia (15 miles from Casablanca), the Casino of Tangier and the Casino of Marrakech.

LANGUAGE . . . The official languages besides Arabic are French and Spanish. But English is understood almost everywhere.

LAUNDRY AND DRY CLEANING . . . Good 24-hour service in the principal cities and good hotels. Unreliable in the small towns.

LIQUOR . . . All kinds of imported liquors are available at reasonable prices. Morocco produces excellent wines and beer.

MEDICAL FACILITIES . . . Good hospitals in all cities.

MOTION PICTURES . . . Very modern theaters show newest American, European and Arabic movies with French sound tracks.

MUSIC . . . Symphony orchestras perform in principal cities, November through May. There's also Andalusian and Arabic music.

NIGHT CLUBS AND CABARETS . . . In Marrakech, dinner dancing at *Mamounia Hotel;* dancing and star entertainers at the *Casino*. In Casablanca, dinner dancing at the *Embassy, Don Quinchotte* and *Puerta del Sol;* all have floor shows. In Mohammedia, dinner dancing at the *Casino* and in the Miramar Hotel's *Kanguei*. Among many in Tangier, outstanding are the *Koutoubia Palace*, the *Casino*, *Hotel de France* and the *Tagada*. Moroccan night clubs are not expensive; cover charge, when imposed, is usually about $2.25.

PHOTOGRAPHY . . . All kinds of equipment and film available in large cities. Good 24-hour developing service.

RELIGION . . . Most Moroccans are Moslems. There are also Catholic and Protestant churches, and Jewish synagogues.

RESTAURANTS . . . Among the best in Casablanca for French food are *Le Doge, La Réserve, El Mansour, Le Panoramique* on top of the Marhaba Hotel and the roof restaurant on the Anfa Hotel; for seafood: *Le Petit Rocher, La Mer* and *Ma Bretagne;* Spanish food at the *Corrida*. In Marrakech, sumptuous décor and Moroccan food and folk dances at the *Gharnatta* restaurant; mainly French cuisine at hotels, the *Casino* and *Rex*. In Rabat, aside from the hotels, are *Casabella, Chez Pierre, La Pizzeria, Blue Notes* and the *Provençal*. Good Moroccan food at the *Koutoubia Restaurant* and *La Caravelle*. In Tangier, good Moroccan restaurants in the casbah section; European cuisine in restaurants along the seafront.

SHOPS AND STORES . . . Galeries Lafayette of Paris and other fine stores in principal cities. Tangier is best for imports. Fixed prices in stores; bargaining in *souks*.

SPECTATOR SPORTS . . . Try to see a *fantasia* for incredible horsemanship. Horse, bicycle and motorcycle races in winter. In autumn, Rallye Automobile du Maroc, followed by the International Automobile Race. Also soccer, rugby, hockey, boxing, basket and volley ball. Tennis tournaments, swimming meets in summer.

SPORTS . . . Good golf at Casablanca, Mohammedia and Marrakech. Fishing, hunting. A license is required for hunting. Scuba diving. Skiing at Oukaimeden, Ifrane and Azrou.

THEATERS . . . Performances in various languages at huge new Mohammed V Theater in Rabat, and other municipal theaters.

TIME... Noon in Casablanca is 7 A.M. in New York.

TRANSPORTATION... Plenty of taxis and buses. Good train service. Cars with or without chauffeurs can be hired at reasonable prices. Highways are well surfaced; special gas prices for tourists.

WATER... Usually safe to drink; bottled water available.

WHAT TO BUY... Native crafts, pottery, gold and silver jewelry, copper plates, hand-made rugs and carpets, fabulous leather goods.

WHAT TO WEAR... In summer, lightest weight materials. Swimming suits. In winter, warmer clothes; nights get really cold.

WHERE TO GO—SIGHTSEEING...

Casablanca... With its towering white buildings, modern Casablanca grew up around a small Arab village that is now the Old Medina, which is well worth a visit. Also to be seen are the King's Palace; the fine Aquarium; Anfa Hill residential section; the magnificent beaches, especially at Mohammedia, north of the city.

Rabat... The capital city is distinguished by its lovely gardens, the immense 12th-century Tower of Hassan, and impressive gateways cut through the ancient city walls.

Fes... Known for its 1100-year-old university, minareted mosques and interesting museums. See the city at sunset from the heights near the Tombs of the Merinides Princes. The nearby walled city of Meknes has a fine Moroccan Art Museum. In the cool Middle Atlas Mountains are Ifrane and Azrou summer resorts, which become ski centers in winter. See the eerie Ito region, pockmarked with extinct volcanoes.

Marrakech... A rose-pink oasis city looking to the snow-capped High Atlas Mountains, Marrakech is a sophisticated winter resort. Outstanding city sights are the Koutoubia Tower, Bahia Palace, Menara Pavilion, tombs of the Saadians and the activities in the Biblical-times Djemaâ El Fna Square. Marrakech has an elaborate Casino, superb golf course, is within easy reach of fishing and hunting in the mountains, which are alive with skiers in winter. Tours out of Marrakech are easily arranged. The huge old casbahs in the mountains have a timeless mystery. Principal centers are Ouarzazate, Zagora, Tiznit, the Valley of the Draa. At Goulimine are people with permanently blue skins, acquired from their blue robes. The little seafront towns of Agadir, Essaovira (formerly Mogador), El Jadida (formerly Mazagan) and Safi are charmingly picturesque.

Tangier... The "Crossroads of the World," Tangier's hills curve around a lovely bay and its beach resorts rival the Riviera's. Behind this glittering façade is a wonderfully conglomerate city populated with everything from robed Rifs to expatriate American artists who appreciate Tangier's ever-perfect climate and low prices. Fascinating medieval places in the nearby interior are Tetuan and Chechaouene.

SOURCES OF FURTHER INFORMATION... Royal Air Maroc is the General Agent for Pan American. Official tourist offices in major cities. The Moroccan National Tourist Office is at 341 Madison Avenue, New York, N.Y. 10017.

NIGERIA

WEATHER IN LAGOS—Lat. N6°27′ and **KANO**—Lat. N12°

	JAN.	FEB.	MAR.	APR.	MAY	JUNE	JULY	AUG.	SEPT.	OCT.	NOV.	DEC.
Aver. Temp. (Lagos)	91°	91°	91°	90°	88°	84°	82°	82°	84°	86°	89°	89°
Days of Rain	3	4	8	8	17	23	16	9	17	15	8	2
Aver. Temp. (Kano)	71°	75°	81°	87°	88°	84°	79°	78°	79°	81°	88°	72°
Days of Rain	0	0	0	1	6	9	13	17	11	2	0	0

This African Federation within the British Commonwealth (356,-669 square miles; 55,620,268 population) is divided by the Niger and Benue Rivers into 4 areas, each distinct in character, customs and language, with English as the common denominator. Vegetation ranges from tropical rain forests in the south through scrub plains to the sands of the Sahara Desert in the north. The capital is Lagos (population 675,352), 14½ hours by Jet Clipper from New York. In Lagos, principal hotels are the *Federal Palace* and the *Bristol,* each air-conditioned; $15 single, $25 double with breakfast. Slightly cheaper are the *Ikoyi, Mainland* and *Airport Hotel* in Ikeja. Meals at the *Regent* and *Cathay* restaurants and at night spots—*Domo* and *Bagatelle.* Drinking water should be boiled, except in Lagos area. Electricity is 220 volts, 50 cycles, A.C. In the handsome Moslem city of Kano, the *Central Hotel* is air-conditioned. The *Presidential* hotels in Port Harcourt and Enugu and the *Hamdala* in Kaduna are also highly recommended.

To enter Nigeria U.S. citizens need passport and visa, smallpox vaccination, yellow fever inoculation, onward transportation. Duty-free allowances: 200 cigarettes (also available locally), ½ bottle of liquor at Customs' discretion. Currency must be declared. No more than £50 Nigerian (on a par with sterling) may be taken out. Tipping ("dash") should be light, under 5%. Though expensive in the Lagos area, only metered taxis are suggested for transportation. Good buys are leather goods, camel-hair blankets, ebony and ivory carvings. Bargaining is essential; pay about ⅓ of price asked. Cool, drip-dry clothing is recommended and should be laundered personally.

SOURCES OF FURTHER INFORMATION ... The Pan Am office is on Broad Street, Lagos (Tel. 26191). There is a Nigerian information office in New York at 575 Lexington Avenue.

SENEGAL

WEATHER IN DAKAR—Lat. N14°40′—Alt. 100′

Temp.	JAN.	FEB.	MAR.	APR.	MAY	JUNE	JULY	AUG.	SEPT.	OCT.	NOV.	DEC.
Low	62°	61°	63°	64°	66°	76°	78°	77°	76°	74°	71°	65°
High	73°	76°	75°	77°	77°	86°	87°	87°	86°	84°	81°	77°
Average	68°	69°	69°	71°	72°	81°	83°	82°	81°	79°	76°	71°
Days of Rain	0	0	0	0	0	1	10	14	15	14	1	0

LOCATION . . . Senegal lies along the most westerly part of the coast of Africa. Its capital, Dakar, is the gateway to the group of new republics that are members of the French Community.

CHARACTERISTICS . . . This is a land of sunshine and bright colors, a land of contrasts between the old and the new. Dakar is a modern city with handsome buildings, spacious avenues. But only a few miles away, in country villages, the traditional African way of life continues with but little change.

POPULATION . . . 3,400,000—of which 40,000 are Europeans.

SIZE . . . 76,124 sq. miles; 250 miles long, 300 miles wide.

CAPITAL . . . Dakar, with a population of over 400,000 (of which about 30,000 are Europeans).

GOVERNMENT . . . Senegal is an independent Republic.

HOW TO GET THERE . . . By Pan American Jet Clipper from New York in about 7½ hours. By ship from New York, 10 days.

ACCOMMODATIONS . . . The *Grand Hotel de N'Gor,* situated on the beach 8 miles from Dakar, has frequent bus service into town. Rates single $11.50-$14; double $15-$17; continental breakfast, taxes and service included. In the city are the *Croix du Sud,* single $11.50-$15, double about $15 (excluding breakfast but including taxes and service); and the *Majestic,* from $6.50 single, $9 double, including only taxes and service. All three hotels are partially air-conditioned.

Rates apply year round. Reservations should be made well in advance. Electricity is 110 volts, 50 cycles, A.C. European-style plugs.

CLIMATE . . . In Dakar the rainy season, or *hivernage,* months of July to October are hot and humid, and not recommended for a visit. Ideal vacation weather the rest of the year, with warm, dry, sunny days and cool nights. Climate in the interior varies widely, but on the whole the winter months, December through May, are the best.

CURRENCY . . . Bank rate is about 240 Senegalese francs to U.S. $1; the rate given by hotels varies from 235 to 240.

CUSTOMS REGULATIONS AND DOCUMENTS REQUIRED FOR UNITED STATES CITIZENS . . . Passport, visa (obtainable from French Consulate of visitor's place of origin) and continuation or return ticket. Yellow fever and smallpox certificates. 1,000 cigarettes, or 1 lb. tobacco, or 250 cigars allowed duty free. No more than 75,000 francs in local currency may be imported or exported.

DRUGSTORES . . . Familiar products, but French brand names.

RESTAURANTS . . . There are a number of good restaurants in Dakar, serving first class French cuisine. Recommended are the *Croix du Sud, Hotel N'Gor* and *Folklore.* Lunch or dinner with wine runs about $7 to $10 per person. *Langouste* (crayfish) is a specialty. Filet steaks are good, but if you like them medium rare, ask for them well done or *a point.* For a lighter type of meal try the *Plaza Cafeteria,* or the Majestic Hotel snack bar. Another small restaurant that can be recommended is the *Lagon,* which is on the beach and specializes in seafood. Tap water in Dakar is safe to drink after it is filtered.

WHERE TO GO—SIGHTSEEING . . .

Dakar . . . See the native markets where the women in gaily colored costumes sell local produce, and where Moors from the northern deserts offer intricate silver work for sale. For a more comprehensive and compact sampling of African craftsmanship, visit the museum of the Institute Francais de l'Afrique Noir (IFAN); open daily except Mondays, Fridays and holidays.

Make sure to take a trip to Goree Island (about 20 minutes away by ferry), where slave traders imprisoned their victims before shipping them out of the country. There's an interesting museum here and a restaurant which serves good seafood.

If you have the time, a visit to the nature reserve of Niokolo-Koba is well worthwhile. There are a number of possible tours, according to how much time you have. The shortest takes 3 days and 3 nights. Accommodations are simple but satisfactory. The reserve is closed during the rainy season of June through mid-December. Further details can be obtained from the Pan Am office, listed below.

SOURCES OF FURTHER INFORMATION . . . The local Pan American office is in the Place de l'Independence (Tel. 265-86).

SOUTH AFRICA

WEATHER IN CAPE TOWN—Lat. S33°54′—Alt. 56′

Temp.	JAN.	FEB.	MAR.	APR.	MAY	JUNE	JULY	AUG.	SEPT.	OCT.	NOV.	DEC.
Low	60°	61°	59°	54°	51°	48°	47°	48°	50°	53°	55°	58°
High	80°	80°	78°	72°	67°	63°	62°	63°	66°	70°	74°	77°
Average	70°	70°	69°	63°	59°	56°	55°	56°	58°	62°	65°	68°
Days of Rain	4	4	4	7	10	12	11	11	9	7	6	5

LOCATION ... At the southern tip of Africa lies the Republic of South Africa, comprising the provinces of Cape of Good Hope (Cape Province), Natal, Orange Free State and Transvaal, where Johannesburg is located.

CHARACTERISTICS ... Here is a land of contrasts, of wonderful tropical beaches, lush foliage, bright sunshine and high cool mountains, rugged terrain and endless stretches of veld. Brilliant flowers bloom in profusion along the South African coast. Cape Town and Durban are cosmopolitan and gay. There are good hotels, excellent swimming and fishing and all the fun you want. Inland, Johannesburg is a busy, booming city with a marvelous cool climate. Kruger National Park, the sanctuary for wild animals, is an unforgettable spot. So, for that matter, is all of South Africa, with its color, strangeness and allure.

POPULATION ... Estimated 17,474,000. Cape Town has 787,000 inhabitants, Johannesburg 1,167,000, and Durban 659,934.

SIZE ... 472,359 square miles; 995 miles east-west, 805 miles north-south at its farthest points.

CAPITAL ... Pretoria is the administrative capital; Cape Town, the legislative capital; Bloemfontein, the judicial capital.

GOVERNMENT ... A completely independent republic.

HOW TO GET THERE ... By Pan Am Jet 22 hours from New

York to Johannesburg. By South African Airways, about 2 hours from Johannesburg to Cape Town and ¾ hour to Durban. Inquire about latest jet schedules. By ship about 17 days from New York.

ACCOMMODATIONS... Among the tops in Johannesburg are the *Langham,* Kerk Street; *Waldorf,* Bree Street; *Criterion,* Jeppe Street; *Dawson's,* President Street; *Whitehall,* Abel Road; *Ambassador,* Pretoria Street; *Astor,* King George Street; *Skyline,* Twist Street; and the *Park Royal,* Plein Street. Rates average from $10 single, $18 double, with bath and breakfast.

In Cape Town the most luxurious hotel is the *Mount Nelson,* slightly out of the city area and commanding a fine view of Table Mountain; from $14 single, $28 double with bath and all meals. Centrally located are the popular *Grand Hotel,* from $11.20 per person with bath, European Plan (without meals); the *Tulbagh,* from $9.80 per person with bath and breakfast; *Tudor House Hotel,* $3.85-$4.20 single, $8.40-$10 double with breakfast. At nearby Sea Point, *Arthur's Seat* is on the Atlantic coast near a beautiful public swimming pool. Farther out, on a famous beach, is the *Clifton Hotel;* $5.25-$9.80 single, $10.50-$22.40 double with bath and breakfast; good transportation facilities into the city. The *Alphen,* a skillfully restored Cape Dutch homestead, is 12 miles from Cape Town in Constantia Valley; $8.40-$15.40 per person with bath and breakfast. In lovely Stellenbosch Valley, 40 miles from Cape Town, is the excellent *Rawdon's Lanzerac* ranch-type hotel.

ARTS... In Johannesburg the Art Gallery in Joubert Park contains a fine collection of European paintings. The Africana Museum in the Public Library tells the chronological history of South Africa.

In Cape Town the Michaelis collection of Dutch and Flemish paintings is housed in the Old Town House, which was built in 1755 and is an excellent background for the paintings. Visit the South African Museum filled with items of archaeological and ethnological interest. The National Art Gallery, off Government Avenue, contains 14 galleries. Principal collections are the de Pass and Sir Abe Bailey exhibits. Koopmans-de Wet Museum contains a collection of Dutch antiques.

BALLET... Local ballet groups include the Festival Ballet, the Theater Ballet and the Cape Town University Ballet Company.

BANKS... Throughout the country there are branches of Barclay's Bank, Standard Bank, Netherlands Bank, Volkskas Bank and South African Reserve Bank. In Cape Town and Johannesburg, both First National City Bank and Chase Manhattan have banking offices.

CALENDAR OF HOLIDAYS... New Year's Day; April 6, Van Riebeeck Day; Good Friday; Easter Monday; Ascension Day; May 31, Republic Day; 2nd Monday in July, Family Day; First Monday in September, Settlers' Day; October 10, Kruger Day; December 16, Day of the Covenant; Christmas; and December 26, Boxing Day.

CIGARETTES, CIGARS AND TOBACCO... Local brands, very much like American cigarettes, cost U.S. 28¢ a pack. American brands are U.S. 46¢, or 33c a pack in local currency.

CLIMATE ... There are no extremes of climate, and a high average of daily sunshine. The seasons being reversed, September is spring here, winter extends from May to August. The Cape has its rains during winter and the rest of the country during the summer. Except on the east coast in summer, there is little humidity.

CLUBS ... Club life plays an important part in the social life of Johannesburg. There are many clubs which are glad to welcome visiting tourists to the city. Among the social clubs are the Rand, the New, the Union and the Automobile Club. For the ladies—the American Women's Club, Martha Washington Club, Rand Women's Club and the Vanguard. Visiting Rotarians are invited to phone the local secretary (834-8295). Sports clubs include the Rand Flying Club, Royal Johannesburg Golf Club, Inanda Polo Club, Jockey Club and Turf Club. The Transvaal Golf Union Club and Huddle Park Course are open to all. The Wanderers Club is one of the finest sports clubs, and honorary membership can be arranged through Pan Am.

In Cape Town the Rotary Club, Cape Town City Club, Royal Cape Yacht Club, Zeekoe Vlei Yacht Club, Cape Hunt and Polo Club, Mountain Club of South Africa, Royal Cape Golf Club, Mowbray Golf Club, King David Country Club.

COMMON COURTESIES AND LOCAL CUSTOMS ... The black people are pure-blooded aborigines of the Bantu races. Persons of mixed origin are referred to as "colored." The word "Bantu" refers to members of the black races only. South Africans are famous for their hospitality. City dwellers are great tea drinkers and country people great coffee drinkers.

Another South African institution is the "sundowner party," which means getting together at the end of the day for drinks. Another pleasant custom is the *braaivleis* (pronounced "bry-flace"—a combination of the Afrikaans words *braai*—to roast, and *vleis*—meat). It is similar to our barbecue.

COMMUNICATIONS ... A 3-minute phone call to the States costs R8.55 (U.S. $11.98); a cablegram is 17c a word. Airmail postage to the U.S. is 22½c per ½ ounce; airletter forms, 10c. Local phone calls cost 5c for 3 minutes.

CURRENCY ... There are 100 cents (c) in the South African rand (R), valued at U.S. $1.40.

CUSTOMS REGULATIONS AND DOCUMENTS REQUIRED FOR UNITED STATES CITIZENS ... All goods must be declared. Cameras, field glasses, typewriters, etc., are duty free but must be declared. Duty free allowances: 400 cigarettes, 1 opened bottle of liquor. Foreign currency can't be readily exchanged so take travelers checks. Passport and visa necessary. Proof of sufficient means and a return ticket, yellow fever and smallpox vaccination certificates.

DRUGSTORES ... As in England they are called chemist's shops and sell only pharmaceuticals, of which there is a big variety, including American brands. If you want a chocolate sundae, hamburger or hot dog, you'll get it at a milk bar, of which there are many.

ELECTRIC CURRENT ... The current is 220-250 volts A.C. The cycles are 50, as opposed to 60 cycles in use in the United States. If you have an electric razor, you should bear this in mind. The British type of plug is needed.

FAUNA ... South Africa carefully protects its wildlife and is a haven for antelopes from tiny blue duikers to huge elands, and for elephants, zebras, aardvarks, baboons. Unusual birds include the ostrich, bulbul, secretary bird, flamingo.

FLORA ... If you are a flower lover you will find endless joy in the many botanical gardens and wildflower reserves. South Africans are by nature garden-lovers and in the suburbs you'll see some magnificent gardens surrounding delightful homes.

Thousands of flowers are to be seen during the spring months (September through November). The national flower of the country is the protea. Wild arum lilies, chincherinchees with blooms that last for months, roses, dahlias, numerous types of erica—in fact, almost anything you can name is here. The silverleaf tree is indigenous and unique. In Natal you'll find some exotic tropical plants which do not flourish in harsher climes. Here you'll find guavas and avocados growing wild. Bougainvillaea grows in profusion, as do camellias, cannas, acacia, wild cosmos and hundreds of other flowers. Jacaranda trees and flamboyants are numerous. In Cape Town the Kirstenbosch Botanic Gardens on the shady slopes of Table Mountain specialize in the study of native South African flora.

FOOD ... You will enjoy South Africa's national dishes, her excellent wines and brandies and wide variety of fruits. There's no problem about purity of the drinking water and no need to fear any unhappy results from eating the food, which is much the same as ours. South African lobster tails are a great delicacy and are served in many ways, such as cooked in butter, simmered, then served on buttered noodles or browned rice. Young fresh *mealies* (corn on the cob) is a popular dish. South Africans are great meat eaters and their steaks are particularly good. The locally homemade sausage called *boerewors* ("farm sausage") is excellent. Fish is plentiful and good. The variety of fruit is enormous—tangerine, lemon, fig, pineapple, pawpaw, avocado, melons, orange, apple, pear and some of the finest peaches. Rock oysters and crawfish are excellent. National dishes lean towards stews and *braaivleis* (barbecues). Milk is plentiful and safe.

GAMBLING ... No casinos. Horse racing in Cape Town, Johannesburg and Durban with pari-mutuel betting. Every weekend and almost every holiday, meetings take place.

LANGUAGE ... The population is, in general, bilingual, speaking English and Afrikaans and various Bantu languages.

LAUNDRY AND DRY CLEANING ... Facilities are satisfactory and reasonably quick. Your hotel valet will attend to any requirements in this direction. Average price for dry cleaning a suit or dress is 85c (U.S. $1.19). There are many dry-cleaning establishments.

LIQUOR ... South Africa makes good brandy, and her wines rank with those of France and Germany. The most popular drinks are beer, brandy and whisky, which are lower priced than in the United States. *The* whisky is Scotch, but bourbon is obtainable. South Africa has a local liqueur called *Van der Hum,* which is brandy-based and delicious.

Although women are not allowed in some public bars, they are welcome in private lounges in hotels. Public bars are open from 10 A.M. to 11 P.M. daily except Sundays, when you can get a drink only at your hotel. Minimum legal age for drinkers is 18.

MEDICAL FACILITIES ... There are excellent doctors and dentists. The Johannesburg General Hospital is the largest of its type in the Southern Hemisphere. The hospitals in all cities and large towns are up to date and efficient.

MOTION PICTURES ... There are many modern movie houses throughout the country showing both British and American films and also some Continental ones. Of over 40 in Johannesburg the largest are the *Colosseum* and *Empire* in Commissioner Street, the *Metro* in Bree Street, the *20th Century* in President Street, and the *Monte Carlo* in Jeppe Street. These each seat about 3,000 people. In Cape Town the biggest are the *Colosseum* in St. George's Street, the *Alhambra* in Riebeeck Street, the *Metro* in St. George's Street, the *Van Riebeek* in Long Street. The *Broadway Theatre* and *Monte Carlo* on the Foreshore show Continental films. Durban's largest are the *Playhouse,* the *Metro,* the *20th Century* and the *Alhambra*—all in Smith Street. Shows are at set hours. Reserved seats are advisable and are a must on Friday and Saturday nights. Theaters are closed Sundays.

MUSIC ... Some of the big cities have a municipal orchestra. There are ballet and opera performances seasonally. Guest performers visit South Africa regularly from overseas. An *Eisteddfod,* or musical festival, is held annually in each province.

In Johannesburg interested visitors are invited to contact the Johannesburg Musical Society (838-4091).

NIGHT CLUBS AND CABARETS ... The clubs don't have floor shows, but in Johannesburg there is dancing nightly at the *Red Lantern,* the *Coconut Grove, Ciro's,* the *Moçambique, Diamond Horseshoe* and the *Colony,* among others. In Cape Town *Maxim's* is new and very chic: dancing nightly and a floor show on gala nights. Membership can be arranged but bring your own liquor.

PHOTOGRAPHY ... It's best to take with you all the film you'll need, although film is available. Also take cameras and other photo equipment. Film-developing facilities are comparable with those at home.

RELIGION ... All principal religions are represented. Main places of worship in Johannesburg are the Anglican Cathedral, 56 de Villiers Street; St. George's Presbyterian Church, Noord Street; Irene Dutch Reformed Church, Plein Street; Central Congregational Church, Bree Street; Baptist Church, de Villiers Street; Central Methodist Church, Pritchard Street; Swedish Church, Hancock Street; Roman Catholic Cathedral, End Street; Hebrew Synagogue, Wolmarans Street.

In Cape Town, among many others, there's an Anglican cathedral on Wale Street; a Dutch Reformed church on Adderley Street; St. Mary's Cathedral (Roman Catholic) on Roeland Street; Indian Mohammedan mosque, Long Street; a Methodist church in Greenmarket Square; a Lutheran church on Strand Street; a Presbyterian church on Somerset Road; a Christian Science church on Orange Street; a Jewish synagogue on Hatfield Street.

RESTAURANTS . . . The leading restaurants in Johannesburg include the *Criterion*, the *Waldorf, Dawson's, Café Royal,* the *Langham, Spaghi's, Caravelle, The Knight's Tavern, Tiffany's, Three Vikings* and *Rapallo Continental Restaurant*—all in the center of the city and ranging in price from $4.50 to $7 for lunch or dinner.

In Cape Town the most exciting restaurant is the *Sable Room* atop the Sanlam Skyscraper overlooking the city and Table Bay Harbour. Fully licensed and excellent food. The *Florentine Grill* in the Grand Hotel and *Café Royal* are both good and convenient. In Sea Point the *Ascot Grill* in Arthur's Seat is superior, and nearby *Fracarlo's Restaurant* is a must. In the suburbs the *Vineyard Grill* is charming; dancing nightly and music in the ladies' bar. Farther from town the *Plaza España* in Hout Bay is very smart; dancing, wonderful cuisine; reservations necessary.

SHOPS AND STORES . . . Stores are open Monday through Friday from 8:30 A.M. to 5:30 P.M.; Saturdays 8:30 A.M. to 1 P.M. The shopping streets in Johannesburg are Eloff, Joubert and Rissik Streets. On Eloff you'll find John Orr's; on Joubert Street there are Anstey's and Vanité (ladies), and on Rissik Street shop at Stuttafords. There are scores of other stores.

In Cape Town stores are open from 9 A.M. to 5 P.M.; Saturdays 9 A.M. to 1 P.M. Among the better stores in Cape Town are Stuttafords and Garlicks.

SPECTATOR SPORTS . . . Horse racing in Johannesburg at Turffontein and Newmarket; in Durban at Greyville and Clairwood; and in Cape Town at Kenilworth. At Greyville on the first Saturday each July they run the "Durban July," with one of the richest purses held anywhere. You'll find cricket played all over the country in summer. Rugby is the national game, and it is played in their winter. Soccer is popular and you'll find weekend matches in every city. Baseball is becoming popular, with weekend games in Cape Town, Johannesburg, Durban and Port Elizabeth.

SPORTS . . . Swimming is magnificent all along the coast. There are dozens of golf courses throughout the country. There are tennis courts and many tennis clubs, and countless bowling greens.

In and around Johannesburg there are about 18 golf clubs and 1 municipal course, innumerable swimming pools and tennis. There is excellent black bass and trout fishing.

Tuna fishing near Cape Town is popular. You may angle for sole, silver fish, geelbek (Cape salmon), mullet, mackerel and many other varieties. For superb deep-sea fishing there is Hermanus, False Bay, Saldanha Bay. You fish for carp and bass on the Cape Flats lake. There are wonderful trout, bass and perch to be found in the lakes and streams in the Western Cape Province, which are within easy range of Cape Town. Licenses are required for fresh-water fishing.

There are occasions when you can ski during the winter months about 80 miles from Cape Town. Information on mountain climbing is available at the Mountain Club of South Africa, Yorkshire House, 38 Strand Street, Cape Town.

THEATERS . . . Visiting companies appear in the season (middle of May through September and also in December). In Cape Town are the *Labia* and *Hofmeyer* theaters. Johannesburg theaters include *His Majesty's*, the *Reps, Brooke, Library* and the *Intimate*.

TIME . . . Seven hours later than Eastern Standard Time.

TIPPING . . . A 10% tip is tops. For small services tip 10c; 20c for larger ones. Hotels and sometimes restaurants add 10% service charges.

TRANSPORTATION . . . Taxis are plentiful and not expensive. Outside of the municipal area you must set your price with the driver. All main cities have bus services; cars are for hire at reasonable rates. This vast country is well served by rail and air services.

WATER . . . Safe to drink anywhere.

WHAT TO BUY . . . Native curios; spears; carvings; ostrich-skin bags; semi-precious South African stones; leather portraits; carved wooden animals; skins of African animals (antelope, snakes, leopards); carved ivory articles; *Karosses* (animal-skin blankets); stinkwood articles (brooches, trays, napkin rings, etc.); local pottery; tiles; wall plaques; beadwork; basketware; wooden earrings. Best sources in Johannesburg are the Gainsborough Galleries, Morris Davis and Ivy's; in Pretoria Ivy's; and in Cape Town Kottlers and Ivy's. In Durban the best place is in the native market.

WHAT TO WEAR . . . Remember that much of South Africa is plateau land, and that some parts lie at high altitudes. Johannesburg, for instance, has an altitude of nearly 6,000 feet, and during the winter months it can be cold in the early morning and after sunset. During the summer months women wear light dresses and men lightweight suits. For the cold months light overcoats and woolen sweaters are necessary. A raincoat is necessary. At dances or other formal evening functions women wear long evening dresses and the men black or white dinner jackets, according to the season. For casual wear at holiday resorts, or for traveling, men wear slacks or shorts and shirts and women wear skirts or slacks and blouses.

WHERE TO GO—SIGHTSEEING . . .

Johannesburg . . . Is quite naturally called the Golden City. You mustn't miss a trip down a gold mine—a thrilling experience. You can go down 6,000 feet below the streets and find yourself at sea level. Conducted tours of the mines take place Tuesday, Wednesday and Thursday mornings. Application must be made to the Public Relations Department, Transvaal Chamber of Mines (Tel. 838-8211).

Another interesting sight is the dances performed by the native mine workers on Sunday mornings at the mine compounds. They are a genuine example of African talent. Visitors should get in touch with the Johannesburg Publicity Association (Tel. 23-2324) to arrange for mine-dance visits.

Another tour of interest is through a diamond-cutting factory, permission for which is obtained from the Master Diamond Cutters Association (Tel. 23-2760). From the top of African Life Building, a 21-story building, round the corner from Pan American's office, you'll get a wonderful view of the city. Spend some time in the Herman Eckstein Park, where the Zoological gardens are situated. Don't miss a trip up to Northcliff where you get a sweeping view of the central Transvaal.

There are several tours of the city and suburbs which are worth taking and cost about $11.50 per 5-seater car. Don't miss a stroll through "The Wilds," a reserve devoted to native flora about 10 minutes from the center of the city. Johannesburg has a fine new planetarium.

Near Johannesburg are many pleasant resorts with good boating and fishing. Black bass and trout fishing at Florida Lake is known throughout South Africa. Hartebeestpoort Dam, a lovely spot, is near Pretoria, about 40 miles from Johannesburg.

Pretoria . . . 36 miles north of Johannesburg, Pretoria is known as the "Flower of the Transvaal." In the late spring during Jacaranda Week when the trees bloom there is a festival and a contest to choose the Jacaranda Queen. There are some interesting buildings: the house from which Winston Churchill escaped in the Boer War; President Kruger's house; the government buildings and gardens.

Good hotels include the *Assembly, Culemborg* and *Union.* About 25 miles from Pretoria is the famous Premier Diamond Mine, where the Cullinan diamond was found in 1905.

Victoria Falls . . . Among the great wonders of the world, Victoria Falls, on the Zambesi River between Zambia and Rhodesia, are about 820 miles from Johannesburg. Discovered by Dr. Livingstone in 1855, they have become the mecca of tourists. At their greatest height they are about twice as high as Niagara and are more than a mile wide. The main falls are 273 feet high; the Rainbow Falls about 325. The volume of water in April is so great that mist and spray obscure the view. During June to October (the best time to visit) it is warm in the daytime but very cool at night, so take warm clothing along. Motor launches will take you up the river to Kandahar Island, the campsite of Livingstone. This is a full-day excursion and really fascinating. You pass Lodando Island, where occasionally hippopotami are to be seen and where crocodiles abound.

The luxurious *Victoria Falls Hotel* here has an open-air swimming pool, dancing, excellent food and comfortable rooms. High season rates are $9.80 per person and up. There is a rest camp nearby.

Kimberley . . . This is a famous diamond-mining center on the Northern Cape about 300 miles from Johannesburg and 650 from Cape Town. You can get there by plane or rail. The Kimberley Diamond Mine is about a mile wide and is often referred to as "The Big Hole." This mine has been abandoned (shaft mining replaced open mining in the latter part of the 19th century), but special observation posts have been constructed so that visitors may see the amazing 3601-foot hole. It is a sidewalk-superintendent's paradise. There are, of course, active mines at Kimberley which may be visited. The dominating company, which arranges tours, is the de Beers Consolidated Mines, Ltd., founded by Cecil Rhodes and Barney Barnato. No uncut diamonds may be bought except from licensed dealers.

Kruger National Game Reserve ... In the northeastern Transvaal, along the border of Portuguese East Africa and just over 300 miles from Johannesburg, is the Kruger Game Reserve, some 200 miles long and from 30 to 60 miles wide. This is the world's most famous game sanctuary, where all the wild animals of the African jungles—elephants, lions, giraffes, crossword-puzzle animals like the kudu, impala, antelope, velvet monkey and many many others—are to be seen from your car. The reserve is subtropical and the open season is May 2 to October 15. The southern area, however, is open all the year. Travel agencies will arrange inclusive tours if you wish or you may hire a car and drive yourself. It's about 7 hours' drive from Johannesburg and you need about a week to see the reserve thoroughly. There are 14 rest camps in the area where tourists may stay. You are required to be in camp before sundown, so it is well to have a reservation. The largest and most luxurious camps are at Pretorius Kop and Skukuza, which accommodates 750 people. Less expensive camps are rustic and in keeping with a safari atmosphere.

From Johannesburg, the Pretorius Kop entrance (one of six) is the most convenient since the camp is only a few miles from the gate. From the Kop you will drive to Skukuza, passing the Hippo Pool en route. If you go north toward the Limpopo River (Kipling's "grey-green, greasy Limpopo"), you pass Letaba, a favorite spot for elephants, then to Shingwedzi, in the middle of the Mopani Forest. Plan if you can, to enter the reserve by one road and leave by another. Guides are not necessary as the roads are well marked. Undersized cars are not advisable. The whole place is fabulous, a sort of never-never land you will not forget. The camera has replaced the gun, and you have opportunities as nowhere else for photographing every type of animal from the safety of your car. Trans-Africa Safaris and Springbok Safaris both operate excellent inclusive tours to the Kruger Reserve.

Cape Town ... Cape Town is the parliamentary capital of the Republic of South Africa. It is a magnificent scenic city sometimes compared with Naples because of its location on Table Bay, with Table Mountain rising majestically behind the city. On either side of Table Mountain are the heights of Devil's Peak and Lion's Head. Beyond Lion's Head a series of peaks known as the Twelve Apostles stretches toward Cape Point. It is possible to reach the top of Table Mountain by cableway and have a wonderful view of both the Atlantic and the Indian Oceans. The foliage and flowers which abound in the valleys and glens are magnificent.

Cape Town is a blend of the old and the new; narrow streets recalling Dutch colonial days; tall office buildings modern as tomorrow. Visit the Michaelis Collection of Flemish and Dutch paintings, the South African Museum with its fascinating "Post Office Stones," the National Art Gallery, the Houses of Parliament, which may be visited during recess, the Flower Market opposite the Post Office, the Castle whose foundations were laid in 1666. Stop in at the Municipal Botanic Gardens, which are open daily until sunset. These gardens occupy the 17th-century site of the Dutch East India Company and contain magnificent specimens of trees and tropical plants. Take a 3-mile jaunt to the Aquarium, located at Sea Point, one of the dozens of delightful beach resorts within a 20-mile radius of Cape Town. Visit the Groote Schuur estate, the residence of the Prime Minister, which was left to the country by Cecil Rhodes. The residence is at Rondebosch, about 5 miles from town, and houses a fine collection of antiques. The Zoo is also at Rondebosch and so is the Rhodes Memorial.

Coastal suburbs stretch in each direction from Cape Town, some on the Atlantic Ocean and some on False Bay. The National Botanic Gardens at Kirstenbosch, on the eastern slopes of Table Mountain about 7 miles from the city, are famous. Admission to the Gardens is free. Groot Constantia, in Wynberg, about 12 miles out of the city, is one of the few remaining old Cape houses in Dutch colonial-period style and is now a state museum. Be sure to take beautiful Marine Drive, which runs for 100 miles around the Cape Peninsula and includes Muizenberg, one of the most famous resorts in the country. The Cape Town Publicity Association will give you details of some wonderful drives in the vicinity of Cape Town with prices ranging from $5.60 for an all-day bus tour to $36 for a chauffeured limousine.

The Garden Route tour from Cape Town to Durban (about 1300 miles, 6½ days) on the Indian Ocean is one of the most famous; all-inclusive price is $126. The trip takes in the fabulous Cango Caves and an ostrich farm at Oudtshoorn, proceeds over Montague Pass to George and on to the "Wilderness," a lovely seaside resort.

Durban . . . You may go to Durban from Cape Town or Johannesburg either by motor coach, rail or plane. A crack train, the *Orange Express,* runs between Cape Town and Durban. This delightful coastal city, about 400 miles from Johannesburg on the east coast, has fine hotels, swimming, fishing, and a colorful population. The Indian and native markets are fascinating. There is a Zulu reserve within 75 miles of the city to which motor trips are made. Durban itself has a Marine Parade and a residential section called the Berea, which is on a crest of hills.

The city is a riot of color. Its subtropical climate makes plant life luxurious. The wide streets are lined with flowering trees. This is a city of contrasts where proud Zulu ricksha boys, resplendent in skins and beads, carry Indian women dressed in exquisitely embroidered saris. Along the northern Natal coast are St. Lucia Bay and Richards Bay, where there is wonderful surf and lake fishing. The Durban Country Club has a championship golf course. There is excellent horse racing here, too. Hotels along the Marine Parade in Durban include the *Edward,* the *Marine, Claridge's, Edenroc,* the *Beach,* the *Killarney,* the *Park View* and the *Empress.* The new *Beverly Hills* overlooks the Indian Ocean from Umhlanga Rocks. In the city, try the *Mayfair,* the *Caister* or the *Butterworth.* By all means take in the *Café de Paris* at Claridge's and the *Causerie* at the Edward on the beach front. There are many night spots in and around the city.

Royal Natal National Park ... Is about half a day's run by car from Durban, a 20,000-acre reserve with magnificent scenery. Here are the Tugela River Falls, a game and flower sanctuary, and towering Mont Aux-Sources. There is an excellent hotel, the *Royal National Park Hostel,* with swimming, riding, fishing and lots of beauty.

The Drakensberg ... The mountain resorts of the Drakensberg Range bordering Natal and Orange Free State are popular tourist spots. There is some splendid and some very difficult mountain climbing here. The climate is fine—warm days and cool nights. The fishing is excellent; the hiking and riding magnificent. The hotels are modern, have swimming pools, cinemas, *braaivleis* (barbecues) and plenty of other entertainment. You may stay in a thatched *Rondavel,* or in the main hotel. Rates are about $4.50 a day and up.

About 190 miles from Durban in the heart of Zululand is Hluhluwe (pronounced "Shloo-shloo-wee"), where you see the rare white rhino, also plenty of black rhino, buffalo, impala, zebra, and other wild beasts. The views are wonderful, the foliage and flowers magnificent. There is an excellent rest camp with typical *Rondavel* huts. Bring your own food or purchase it en route. African servants will cook, if you like. Wear dark clothes; bright colors frighten the animals. Winter is the best time here. Two days are needed to make this tour.

Bloemfontein ... (438 miles west of Durban) is the capital of the Orange Free State Province and judicial capital of the Republic. Picturesquely situated 4,665 feet above sea level, it's a modern city of beautiful views, game reserves, flower-filled parks and fine public buildings and monuments. Among many hotels are the *Maitland* and the *Cecil.* Rates from $5 per person. North of Bloemfontein lie the fabulous Free State goldfields, important to South Africa's economic expansion. Uranium production is important here, too. Tours are arranged by the Transvaal and Orange Free State Chamber of Mines.

SOURCES OF FURTHER INFORMATION ... The Johannesburg Publicity Association, South Station Bldg., Eloff and De Villiers Streets (Tel. 23-2324) is an excellent organization which will go out of its way to help the tourist. Pan American's offices are at 517 Grand Parade Centre, Trafalgar Place (Tel. 22094) in Cape Town, and 29A Loveday Street (Tel. 834-6651) in Johannesburg.

The Cape Town Visitors' Bureau in Adderley Street and the Durban Visitors' Bureau in West Street have supplies of folders in English, city and country maps, information regarding local events, hotels, restaurants, tours, etc. In New York the South African Tourist Corporation at 610 Fifth Avenue has excellent travel information.

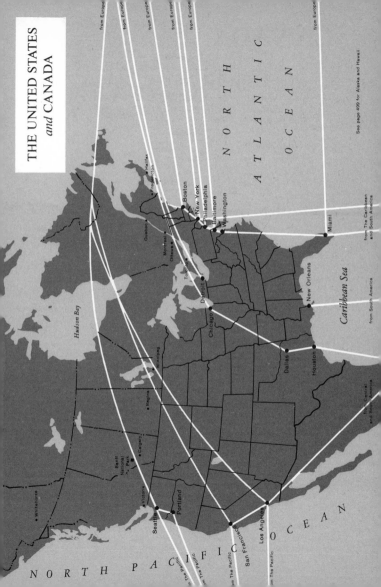

CANADA

WEATHER IN OTTAWA—Lat. N45°23′—Alt. 246′

Temp.	JAN.	FEB.	MAR.	APR.	MAY	JUNE	JULY	AUG.	SEPT.	OCT.	NOV.	DEC.
Low	3°	3°	17°	31°	43°	53°	58°	55°	48°	37°	26°	10°
High	21°	22°	34°	50°	65°	75°	80°	78°	69°	55°	40°	25°
Average	12°	13°	26°	41°	54°	64°	69°	67°	59°	46°	33°	18°

LOCATION ... Canada spans the top of the United States from the Atlantic to the Pacific.

CHARACTERISTICS ... City skylines seem to change daily as new buildings go up in an atmosphere of speed and sophistication. Yet there are hundreds of thousands of miles of empty wilderness to the north that still beckon with a promise of untapped riches. Canada is a land of Now and Tomorrow, but with charming remnants of the past.

POPULATION ... Nearly 20,000,000, 90% of whom live in the south within 200 miles of the U.S. border.

SIZE ... 3,851,809 square miles; only the Soviet Union is larger.

CAPITAL ... Ottawa, a city of 268,206 inhabitants.

GOVERNMENT ... An independent nation in the British Commonwealth. Queen Elizabeth is represented by a royally appointed Governor General; but Canadian affairs are decided by the elected Prime Minister, the Cabinet, and a Parliament composed of the Senate and House of Commons.

HOW TO GET THERE ... By car, train, plane, boat, bike or bus from the U.S.A. Pan Am Jets serve Canada from all parts of the world, through gateway cities of New York, Boston, Chicago, Detroit and Seattle via connecting carriers.

ACCOMMODATIONS... Hotels and motels in Canada are as modern and comfortable as those in the States, but rates are lower. The average single rate is $7 a night in motels, many of which are air-conditioned and have TV. City hotel rates, other than in Montreal, Toronto and Vancouver, are proportionately less than Stateside hotels. Canada is a paradise for campers. Along the 5,000-mile Trans-Canada Highway, extending from Victoria, B.C., to St. John's, Newfoundland, there are Day Parks every 50 miles for picnics and rest stops, and every 100-150 miles there are Overnight Parks equipped with all the conveniences campers need. At the other extreme is the sumptuous elegance of those much-photographed hotels, *Château Frontenac* in Quebec and *Château Lake Louise* near Banff, Alberta.

ARTS... The three principal art centers are Ottawa, Montreal and Toronto, but important galleries are also found in Vancouver, Calgary, Winnipeg, Quebec City and Fredericton in New Brunswick.

BALLET... Ballet groups are scattered all over the country, but the professional companies which have won international acclaim are the National Ballet of Canada, the Royal Winnipeg Ballet, and Montreal's Les Grandes Ballets Canadiens.

BANKS... Canada's commercial banks, which have branches all across the country, are the Royal Bank of Canada, Canadian Imperial Bank of Commerce, Bank of Montreal, Bank of Nova Scotia, Toronto-Dominion Bank, Banque Canadienne Nationale, Provincial Bank of Canada, Mercantile Bank of Canada.

CALENDAR OF HOLIDAYS... Nationally observed holidays are New Year's Day; Good Friday; Easter Monday (banks and government offices); Victoria Day, Monday preceding May 24; Dominion Day, July 1; Labor Day, first Monday in September; Thanksgiving, second Monday in October; Remembrance Day, November 11; Christmas Day. Many provinces also observe Boxing Day, December 26, and Civic Holiday, the first Monday in August.

CIGARETTES AND TOBACCO... Canadian, British and American tobacco products of all kinds.

CLIMATE... Extremely diverse, with abrupt temperature changes. An annual variation of 120 degrees is not unusual in many areas. Summers can be very warm as far north as the sub-Arctic region; winters are long and cold, but usually dry, crisp and invigorating, except on the Pacific Coast, which is mild and damp. Blazing autumnal colors are loveliest in the eastern provinces from mid-September through October. Spring is almost too brief to notice; suddenly it's summer.

COMMON COURTESIES AND LOCAL CUSTOMS... The same as in the States, except that Canadians of French descent are often rather determinedly French, and those of British descent never forget their respect for royalty. Canada is a very religious country, and Sunday is a quiet day.

COMMUNICATIONS... Same as in the States.

CLUBS... Visiting members are welcome at such international organizations as Lions, Rotary, Kiwanis, Knights of Columbus, among others.

CURRENCY ... Same denominations as in the States, and U.S. currency is everywhere acceptable. U.S. $1 is worth about $1.07 Canadian.

CUSTOMS REGULATIONS AND DOCUMENTS REQUIRED FOR UNITED STATES CITIZENS ... Native-born U.S. citizens need only some form of identification, such as a birth or voter's certificate. Naturalized citizens should carry naturalization certificates. Personal effects and sporting equipment enter free of duty, as well as up to 50 cigars, 200 cigarettes, 2 lbs. tobacco, 40 oz. alcoholic beverages per adult. Automobiles (proof of car insurance required in all provinces, with minimum limits of $35,000), motorcycles, bicycles and private boats receive free registration cards at point of entry that are good for 6 months. Temporary pilot permits are also free to visitors with private planes. To re-enter the States, have all sales receipts and invoices handy for inspection. U.S. citizens returning from Canada may take back, once every 31 days, goods for personal or household use to the retail value of $100, duty-free.

DRUGSTORES ... Same pharmaceuticals as in the States, but you may encounter some different brand names.

ELECTRIC CURRENT ... Same as in the States.

FAUNA ... Musk ox, caribou and moose still roam the northlands; deer of all kinds are wild farther south, even into the Great Lakes area. Grizzly and black bears are found in western provinces, brown bears in northeastern provinces, polar bears in the far north. Timber wolves inhabit all the great forests, where you'll also find such precious fur-bearers as silver fox, beaver, otter, marten and mink. Bighorn sheep pose dramatically on crags in the Rockies. Wild game birds abound, and coastal areas, lakes and rivers are teeming with fish.

FLORA ... The same flowers and trees as in our northern states. Canada's forests cover almost half the country's total land area.

FOOD ... As in the States, you'll eat most interestingly if you sample national and regional dishes ... the Canadian version of apple pie, Canadian bacon (called "back bacon"), cheese soup, *habitant* pea soup, buckwheat cakes, blueberry desserts of all kinds, Alberta's prime beef, wild game in season. And excellent fish: all kinds of freshwater fish inland (such as the Winnipeg Gold Eye trout); shellfish and salmon are great delicacies on the Pacific coast; along the Atlantic you'll feast on delicious lobsters; cod caught off Newfoundland has been known to European gourmets for centuries.

GAMBLING ... Pari-mutuel betting at racetracks.

LANGUAGE ... English and French are both official languages, but the whole country is not bilingual. French is spoken throughout Quebec Province, in many areas of the Maritime Provinces, northern Ontario and sections of Manitoba. With a few exceptions, English is understood in these areas, if not spoken. Americanese is a third language.

LAUNDRY AND DRY CLEANING ... Same as in the States.

LIQUOR ... Ever since 1920, Americans have been keenly aware of Canada's superb whiskies, beers and ales.

MEDICAL FACILITIES ... Excellent. Canada's medical schools rank with the world's best.

MOTION PICTURES ... Same as in the States. Canadian-made movies are, for the most part, documentary films.

MUSIC ... About 20 Canadian cities maintain symphony orchestras, and those of Montreal and Toronto are most outstanding. The National Youth Orchestra made its highly successful début during the 1960-'61 season. There are also numerous chamber music societies, string quartets and similar groups. Canada has produced many opera stars of international fame. Students of the Opera School of the Royal Conservatory in Toronto stage frequent productions, and the Canadian Opera Company appears regularly at Toronto's O'Keefe Center. The Montreal Opera Guild and the Vancouver Opera Associations also have professional performances. The most famous bands are those of the Royal Canadian Mounted Police and the Royal Canadian Air Force. During the summer, there are music festivals from one end of the country to the other.

NIGHT CLUBS AND CABARETS ... As in the States, night clubs with floor shows and visiting star entertainers are centered mostly in big cities. Montreal, like New York, is the acknowledged hub of night life in Canada.

PHOTOGRAPHY ... Same equipment and processing facilities as in the States.

RELIGION ... About 43% Roman Catholic; the largest Protestant denomination is the United Church, which combines Methodists, Congregationalists and some Presbyterians. Third major sect is Anglican (Episcopalian). There are, however, churches of all denominations and synagogues. You'll also find a Moslem mosque in Edmonton, a Shinto church in Toronto, and a Sikh temple in Vancouver.

RESTAURANTS ... These are regarded as among the most outstanding eating places in Canada: Nova Scotia—for lobster, seafood, blueberry pancakes and real home cooking—Mrs. Belle Baker's *Hotel Harbour View,* Marie Joseph; *Bluenose Inn,* Lunenburg; *Ragged Island Inn,* Allendale. New Brunswick—*Mrs. Sikorsky's Restaurant,* Magnetic Hill near Moncton; *Cy's Seafood Bar,* Moncton. Quebec City—for fine French food in elegant surroundings—the *Kerhulu, Le Vendôme* and *Château Frontenac; Manoir St. Castin,* about 8 miles out of the city. Montreal—best French cuisine—*Salle Bonaventure, Windsor Hotel, Café Martin, La Tour Eiffel;* for steaks, *Beaver Club;* for 101 kinds of French pancakes, *A La Crêpe Bretonne.* Ottawa—*La Touraine* (French), *The Rib Steak House, Château Laurier Hotel;* in Hull, across the river from Ottawa, *Madame Henry Burger's* and *La Savoie.* Toronto—*Ports of Call, Rathskeller, Julie's, La Scala, The Old Mill, Winston's Theatre Grill, The Victoria Room* at the Sheraton-King Edward; the *Imperial Room* at the Royal York Hotel. Winnipeg—*Charterhouse Rib Room, Hy's Steak Loft, Constellation Room* at the

Airport Hotel. Calgary—*The New Barney's,* Edmonton—*Sahara* (continental cuisine), *Seven Seas* (oriental). Vancouver—*Georgia Hotel Cavalier Room* (West Coast style seafood and steaks), *Hy's Encore* for steaks, *Geisha Gardens* and *Trader Vic's* (oriental). Victoria —*Princess Mary Restaurant* (seafood in a nautical atmosphere), *King Arthur's Round Table* (real Old English décor and food). Dinner prices average from $2.50 to $4.75.

SHOPS AND STORES ... Long-famous department stores (for woolens, furs, imported china and silver) which have branches across the country are Eaton's of Canada, Robert Simpson Co., Simpson Sears, Birks, Morgans and Hudson's Bay Company. "Duty-free" shops especially for American tourists are at Hill Island near the Thousand Island Bridge, in the Seagram Tower at Niagara Falls and in several other areas.

SPECTATOR SPORTS ... Rodeos begin in June in the west, the famous Calgary Stampede is in July. Highland Games are played by Scottish Canadians at many centers, such as Pugwash and Antigonish in Nova Scotia and Rothesay in New Brunswick. The St. John's Annual Regatta, held in Newfoundland in August, is the oldest organized sporting event in North America. Autumnal evenings and weekend afternoons are devoted to football, and Canada has two professional football leagues—the Eastern and Western Conferences—with championships decided at the Grey Cup Final, played alternately in Vancouver and Toronto. Canada's national game, hockey, is played at all levels, from such professional heights as the *Montreal Canadiens* and the *Toronto Maple Leafs* down to Little Leaguers. Basketball, invented by a Canadian, is tremendously popular as are curling and the Indian game of lacrosse. Harness racing is a big thing in the Maritime Provinces. The best-known thoroughbred tracks are those operated by the Ontario Jockey Club—Toronto's *Greenwood* and *Woodbine,* and *Fort Erie;* Montreal's *Blue Bonnet* and Vancouver's *Exhibition Park.* Soccer is gaining widespread popularity, and so are stock-car and sports-car events.

SPORTS ... For the active participant, there is no place like Canada. From mid-December to mid-March, the weather is ideal for skiing, skating, curling, tobogganing and every other winter sport. Many communities stage winter carnivals that go on for weeks and include packed programs of parades, dances and balls as well as sports. The most elaborate affairs are at Banff and Jasper in Alberta, and Montreal and Quebec, but there are others—smaller but just as lively— from the Yukon to Newfoundland. Golf, tennis, swimming, sailing are everywhere in summer. Real adventurers head north, where there are 2,500 miles of well-kept hiking trails through the immense National Parks, and there are horseback and canoe tours, too. Mountaineers come from all over the world to tackle the heights of the Canadian Rockies and Selkirks, and big game are still hunted in the wildernesses. Fishing is spectacularly good in every province. Information on hunting and fishing may be obtained from the Canadian Government Travel Bureau, Ottawa. As in the States, local laws must be observed.

THEATERS ... The Stratford Shakespearean Festival in Stratford, Ontario, about 85 miles west of Toronto, is the keystone of English drama in Canada. The Festival runs from mid-June to mid-September and embraces all the arts as well as top Shakespearean productions. The *Crest Theater* in Toronto is fully professional, and there are semi-professional performances at the *Manitoba Theatre Centre* in Winnipeg, and in the *Cambie Theatre* in Vancouver. French-language dramas thrive in Montreal and Quebec. The *O'Keefe Centre* and the *Royal Alexandra Theater* in Toronto and *Place d'Arts* in Montreal feature outstanding stage attractions.

TIME ... Same time-zoning pattern as in the States, except Newfoundland, which is ½ hour earlier than Eastern Standard Time.

TIPPING ... Luggage porters are tipped 25¢ a bag. Tip 10% of the bill in restaurants and taxis, at barber shops and beauty salons.

TOURIST TAXES ... Some provinces have sales taxes of from 3% to 6% which are added onto restaurant meals, hotel bills and store purchases.

TRANSPORTATION ... The Canadian Pacific and Canadian National transcontinental railways offer special reduced-fare rates to visitors from overseas; they give a 15% reduction on coach fares on all travel from port of entry cities to anywhere in the country, with freedom to depart from a different city than the one of entry. There are nearly 200 companies licensed to operate scheduled and nonscheduled airplane flights from city to city, or from city to fish-filled lakes deep in northern forests. Highways are excellent, and American motorists are delighted with the Imperial gallon, which is 1/5 larger than a U.S. gallon of gas. Your state driver's license is valid in Canada. For special information concerning the Alaska Highway, which runs from Dawson Creek, B.C., to Fairbanks, write the Canadian Government Travel Bureau in Ottawa. There is also an all-weather highway from Grimshaw, Alberta, to Yellowknife on the north shore of remote Great Slave Lake. One of the prettiest and most interesting trips in North America follows the St. Lawrence Seaway from Windsor (across the river from Detroit) to Quebec City. There is long-distance bus service across Canada, the same as in the States.

WATER ... Excellent everywhere.

WHAT TO BUY ... Canadian-produced specialties are cold-weather wear such as deerskin gloves, after-ski boots, Grenfell jackets and Viyella garments of all kinds; luxurious furs and parkas, Indian and Eskimo handicrafts are charming, and so are the wood carvings in the eastern provinces. Bargains in imported British woolens, china, crystal, and silver have been luring Americans across the border for years.

WHAT TO WEAR ... The same as you'd wear in any northern U.S. state at the same time of year. Despite its northern latitude, southern Canada gets hot in summer. Low humidity makes sub-zero winters crisply delightful.

WHERE TO GO—SIGHTSEEING ...

Ottawa ... The Parliament Buildings rise majestically above the

Ottawa River. There are daily conducted tours of the richly furnished chambers, and a colorful Changing of the Guard ceremony takes place every morning at 10 from June 30 to August 31. The National Gallery of Canada has perhaps the country's greatest collection of Canadian and European masterpieces. The National Museum of Canada has natural history exhibits and Indian and Eskimo artifacts. The Rideau Canal connecting Ottawa to Kingston is a delightful cruiseway for small boats, and there are 8 locks right in the center of the city. See the Flower Market, a block north of Rideau Street; the Bytown Museum, one of the oldest buildings in the city; Rideau Hall, residence of the Governor General; Laurier House; the official residence of the Prime Minister; Royal Canadian Mounted Police Barracks in Rockcliffe. Outstanding hotels are: *Château Laurier*, single $10-$20; double $14-$25; *Hotel Eastview*, single $6-$8, double $13-$15; *Lord Elgin Hotel*, single $7.75-$9.50, double $10.25-$12.50; *Bruce MacDonald Motor Hotel*, single $8.50-$11.50, double $10.50-$16.50; *Talisman Motor Inn*, single $10.75-$11, double $15.50-$16.50. North of Ottawa the lovely Gatineau Valley becomes a foremost skiing center in winter. Around Gracefield, only 60 miles north of the capital, lakes and rivers teem with trout and bass, and the autumn hunting season finds abundant moose, deer, bear and smaller animals.

Montreal ... Chosen as the site of the official World's Fair of 1967, bilingual (French-English) Montreal is tremendously attractive to visitors. A city of 1,191,062, Montreal, on an island in the St. Lawrence River, is Canada's national seaport. Rising 764 feet from the center of the city is beautiful Mount Royal, now a park where only horse-drawn vehicles are permitted on the upper slopes. In winter this is a lively sports center; in summer, weekly concerts and plays are held on the mountain. There is always something going on in Montreal. The most elaborate pageants and parades are on St. Jean Baptiste Day (June 24), St. Patrick's Day (March 17) and Labor Day. The wonderful Winter Carnival extends from the Laurentian Mountain resorts down into the city. The Festivals of the Arts and the International Film Festival take place in August. Both pro and college football in autumn at McGill University's Molson Stadium. Hockey, concerts, drama and art exhibits fill the winter months. The Montreal Museum of Fine Arts has, among other things, an unusual collection of antique glass; the Canadian Historic Wax Museum features replicas of historic figures from early Romans to early Canadians. Château de Ramezay, headquarters of the American Army briefly in 1775, is now a fascinating museum. Montreal has many beautiful churches. St. Joseph's Oratory, a point of pilgrimage for miraculous cures, is a semi-Renaissance basilica large enough for 10,000 worshipers. Notre-Dame-de-Montreal is the second-largest church in America and has exquisite stained-glass windows. St. Patrick's is famous for its pure Gothic architecture and magnificent interior décor. See, too, Manoir Lachine, a fur-trading post built in 1671, and handsome McGill University. St. Helen's Island features public swimming pools; the Montreal Military Museum in a former barracks; the Blockhouse (now a museum); the old powder magazine,

Changing of the Guard ceremonies are held before the Parliament Buildings in Ottawa every morning at 10 in July and August.

Château Frontenac towers behind Dufferin Terrace high above Quebec's Lower Town.

Motor vehicles are forbidden on Mt. Royal, Montreal's midtown mountain overlooking the city and the St. Lawrence River.

now the home of *La Poudriere* international theater; and the castle-like chalet restaurant, *Helene-de-Champlain*. La Fontaine Park, right in the city, has beautiful lagoons and gardens, a superb fountain, an open-air theater, and an enchanting fairytale "Garden of Wonders" (open daily from May 15–October 15). Montreal's leading hotels, all in the heart of the city are: *Berkeley Hotel,* single $8-$12, double $10-$16; *Laurentien,* single $7.50-$11.50, double $10.50-$14.50; *Ritz-Carlton,* single $11-$25, double $16-$30; *Sheraton-Mt. Royal,* single $8.50-$14.50, double $11-$18.50; *Queen Elizabeth Hotel,* single from $11, double $15-$22; *Windsor Hotel,* single $11-$21, double $15-$25; the new *Montreal Aeroport Hilton* near Dorval Airport, single $9.50-$13, double $14-$17.50.

The year-round vacation paradise of the Laurentian Mountains extends from 25 to 68 miles north of Montreal, and the hills are dotted with wonderful resort hotels. American Plan rates average $18 single, $28 double at smart inns featuring *haute cuisine* dining. Get complete details from The Laurentian Resorts Association, Queen's Hotel, Montreal, P.Q.

Quebec... Historic Quebec retains its medieval-looking walls, narrow twisting streets lined with cozy old stone buildings, and an air of quaintness duplicated nowhere else in North America. Its Winter Carnival is the most colorful in Canada, and the city (population 171,979) is delightful at any time of year. You can't miss the massive, yet graceful, *Château Frontenac,* and in front of it, Dufferin Terrace, a magnificent promenade overlooking the Lower Town and the vast sweep of the St. Lawrence River.

France lost Canada to England when Wolfe defeated Montcalm on the Plains of Abraham in 1759. Military reminders are the ancient Ramparts, Martello Towers, the battlefield itself (now a park), and the reconstructed Citadel. The Parliament Buildings are beautifully decorated, and guided tours are available. If you like museums, visit the Musée Historique, Inc. (Wax Museum), and the Provincial Museum. The Ursuline Convent, founded in 1639, is one of the oldest girls' schools on the continent, General Montcalm's skull is preserved in a glass case in the Chapel. The exquisite Basilica of Notre-Dame dates from 1647. Hotels: *Château Frontenac,* the most dramatically situated hotel in Canada, and one of the finest, single from $10, double from $13; *Victoria Hotel,* single $8.50-$10, double $12-$16; *Clarendon,* single from $9.50, double from $14. (All have lower rates in winter.)

Ten miles out of the city is Lac Beauport, one of Canada's finest resorts, where winter rates, including gourmet meals, are $80 and up weekly per person, at *Le Manoir St. Castin.* Go by car, bus or sightseeing cruise boat to the miraculous Shrine of St. Anne de Beaupré, 21 miles northeast of Quebec City; and to lovely Montmorency Falls, which foam down from a height of 274 feet. The falls are illuminated with colored lights from June to September.

The Gaspé Peninsula, a refuge for hay-fever sufferers, is one picturesque fishing village after another, and its panoramas of ocean, mountains and tidy little towns are painted by artists all summer. At the far end of the peninsula is Rocher Percé (Pierced Rock), rising nearly 300 feet out of the ocean. Resort hotels near this spectacular view are: *Au Pic de L'Aurore, La Côte Surprise* and *Hotel La Normandie.*

New Brunswick . . . The provincial capital of Fredericton is a little cultural center. A complete set of Audubon's bird paintings and other valuable paintings may be seen in the Legislative Buildings. Important manuscripts are displayed in the Bonar Law-Bennett Library on the University campus. The Beaverbrook Art Gallery and the York-Sunbury Museum are among the best in the country. *Lord Beaverbrook Hotel,* single $6-$8.50, double $10-$12. Go to Moncton to see "The Bore"—the thundering rush of the Petitcodiac River, which surges into Moncton at high tide. Waters are most dramatic in April and September. Try the eerie experience of coasting your car on what by optical iilusion appears to be up Magnetic Hill, 7 miles from Moncton. The famous "Reversing Falls Rapids" are at Saint John, where the Tourist Bureau has built a fine observation lounge overlooking the best view of the incoming tide's tumultuous clash with the St. John River. The first incorporated city in Canada, Saint John has the very good New Brunswick Museum of Indian, French and colonial British relics. *Admiral Beatty Hotel,* single $7-$15, double $9-$16.

Nova Scotia . . . No part of this hilly little province is more than 50 miles from the sea, and the whole region is a sportsman's heaven. You'll find golf courses, tennis courts, canoeing, yachting, horseback riding, surf bathing, deep-sea fishing, big-game hunting, bird shooting. There are 314 trout and salmon streams, 516 trout lakes! Delightful inns and motels provide modern, comfortable accommodations in scenic settings. The capital city of Halifax (population 90,000) has been a military and naval base since its founding in 1749. Its huge star-shaped Citadel today houses 3 museums. Halifax is a popular convention city. Centrally located hotels: *Nova Scotian, Lord Nelson* and *Carlton.* Rates from $8 single, from $12 double.

Toronto . . . Capital of the Province of Ontario and Canada's major industrial, commercial and financial center, metropolitan Toronto has a population of over 1,600,000. The huge Canadian National Exhibition is held here from mid-August to Labor Day; the Royal Agricultural Winter Fair is held in November; the Canadian National Sportsmen's Show is in March. A center of art and music, Toronto has some fine galleries and museums; the Royal Ontario Museum and the Art Gallery of Toronto are especially fine. See Casa Loma, the reconstructed château that was once a private home, and Old Fort York. Toronto is an exciting shopping center, with enormous department stores and duty-free bargains in furs, woolens, leather goods and diamonds. There is a sizable concentration of motels on Lake Ontario, west of the city center. Downtown hotels include the *King Edward-Sheraton,* single $6.50-$10.50, double $11.50-$14.50; *Lord Simcoe,* single $6.50-$10.50, double $10.50-$14.50; *Park Plaza,* single $10-$13, double $12-$17; *Four Season Motor Hotel,* single $9.50-$14.50, double

$16.50-$19.50; *Royal York,* single $10-$16, double $14-$20.50; *Westbury,* single $10.50-$14, double $14.50-$17.50. *Seaway Towers* (just out of downtown area on the lake front), single $9.75-$14. In the northeast section of the city are the *Inn-on-the-Park,* single $11-$15.50, double $10.50-$20.50; and the *Canadiana,* single $10-$12, double $13.50-$17. There are also numerous hotels near the city's airport.

Manitoba . . . With over 39,000 square miles of lakes, streams and rivers, the Province of Manitoba lures sportsmen with the promise of 30-lb. lake trout, pike, bass, grayling and char; and whirring overhead are Canadian geese, mallards, canvasbacks and similar game birds. Lakeside resorts offer swimming, sailing, water-skiing. Across the province is a summer-long program of regattas, exhibitions, concerts, summer theater presentations and festivals. Especially exciting is the Trout Festival (late June) at Flin Flon, featuring Indian dances, canoe derby and log-scaling contests. The capital city of Winnipeg (population 265,429) has handsome broad streets and an air of businesslike efficiency. See Lower Fort Garry, the only stone fur-trading fort still intact. Hotels: *Charterhouse,* single $9.50-$12.50, double $15-$18; *Fort Garry,* single $7.50-$13.50, double $13-$18.50; *Marlborough,* single $6-$13, double $8-$16; *Royal Alexandra,* single from $8, double from $12; *Gordon Downtowner Motor Hotel,* single $10-$12, double $12-$14. Twice every August the Canadian National Railway runs excursions from Winnipeg to Churchill on Hudson Bay, a back-of-beyond town with an unusual Eskimo museum.

Alberta . . . An immense vacationland, the Province of Alberta has some of the world's most spectacular scenery.

Banff National Park is more than twice as large as Rhode Island. The town of Banff is at an elevation of 4,538 feet, and within only 6 miles of it are 6 mountains over 9,000 feet high. Also in the Park are peaks up to 12,000 feet reflected in ice-blue lakes, and bridle paths lead through fragrant woods. Ski trails range from championship alpine runs to gentle slopes for amateurs. Of the many ski facilities, there is a 3,240-foot double chairlift that is one of the steepest in the world. Sunshine Village, 14 miles southwest of Banff, offers unexcelled skiing conditions from December through May. Other points of interest are the hot springs where you can swim summer or winter, Cascade Rock Gardens, and the Buffalo Paddocks. Throughout the park there are trailer camps, tent sites and motels. Scenic and luxurious are the *Banff Springs Hotel,* single $16-$19, double $21-24; and the lovely *Château Lake Louise,* single $16-$21, double $21-$27. Usually, both are open only in summer. The Banff School of Fine Arts is a lively cultural center in summer, and can accommodate over 600 guests. In July, Banff is the setting for a rousing Indian tribal celebration.

Jasper National Park is more than twice as large as Delaware, and is famous for its fish-filled Maligne Lake, its towering mountains, glittering ice fields, mineral hot springs, and summer-winter sports facilities. Accommodations range from tent sites to the elegant *Jasper Park Lodge* (open mid-June to mid-September), where rates, including

Cowboys and Indians help make the Calgary Stampede one of the most picturesque and exciting shows on earth. Bronco busters from the U.S. and Canada compete for prizes, and Indian chiefs in full tribal regalia proudly parade.

Even on a bright summer day, snow still covers the top of Victoria Glacier above Lake Louise in Banff National Park.

Legislative buildings in Victoria, B.C., suggest old-world charm and graciousness for which this very British city is famed.

all meals, are from $19.50 single, from $38 double.

Calgary is jammed for its Stampede (rodeo) every July. This city of over 275,000 people is a booming hub of oil, gas, ranching, farming, industry—and tourism, as it is conveniently near Banff National Park. The city's Zoological and Natural History Park is outstanding for its full-sized models of huge prehistoric animals. *Hotel Palliser,* single $8-$12, double $10-$14; the new *Calgary Inn,* single $10-$15, double $13-$19; *Hotel Wales,* single $6.50-$8.50, double $8.50-$11.

Vancouver... Today a city of 673,585, Vancouver was little more than a sawmill site until the Canadian Pacific Railway pushed through to the west coast in 1885. The beauty of its setting on mountain-fringed Burrard Inlet, its mild climate and its proximity to some of the world's best hunting, fishing and boating areas have made Vancouver a great vacation headquarters. Stanley Park, jutting out between English Bay and Burrard Inlet, is a 1,000-acre recreation area within a few minutes' drive of the business section. Here you'll find bowling on the green, cricket, a pitch and putt golf course, lagoon canoeing, the Public Aquarium, the Zoo, a collection of totem poles, and the *Theater Under the Stars.* The International Festival of Arts draws world-famous performers every June. Vancouver's City Museum displays a fine collection of Indian artifacts, and the Vancouver Art Gallery specializes in works by Canadians. The Grouse Mountain chairlift ride takes 30 minutes and culminates in a breathtaking view of the city and its great harbor. The Capilano Suspension Bridge in North Vancouver swings 230 feet above its rushing river in a preserve of huge Douglas firs and totem poles. Aside from bus sightseeing, in spring and summer there are delightful boat trips through sheltered waters. The ferry trip from Vancouver to the very British capital city of Victoria on Vancouver Island takes 1 hour 40 minutes. Some ferries have dance cruises on summer Saturday evenings. Victoria retains its Old England atmosphere, and the island is a notable sports paradise. Next to San Francisco, Vancouver has the largest "Chinatown" on the continent, and fine Chinese restaurants are abundant. Centrally located hotels in Vancouver are: *Abbotsford Hotel,* single from $6.50, double from $8.50; *Bayshore Inn* (with *Trader Vic's* restaurant), single $11-$16, double $15-$20; *Doric Howe Motor Hotel,* single $8.50-$10, double $13-$16; *Georgia Hotel,* single $10-$16.50, double $13.50-$20; *Grosvenor Motor Hotel,* single $7-$9, double $10-$13; *Hotel Vancouver,* single $11-$15, double $15-$20; *Castle,* single from $7, double from $9.

SOURCES OF FURTHER INFORMATION... Canadian Government Travel Bureau, Ottawa, Ontario. Branches in the States at Canada House, 680 Fifth Avenue, New York City; 102 West Monroe St., Chicago 1, Ill.; 1 Second Street, San Francisco, Cal. *Pan American Airways* at 91 Yonge St., Toronto; 1450 City Councillors St., Montreal; 1055 Alberni St., Vancouver; International Airport, Winnipeg.

UNITED STATES

Seattle, Wash.
Portland, Ore.
Sun Valley, Id.
Cody, Wy.
Minneapolis, Minn.
CANADA
Salt Lake City, Ut.
Lincoln, Neb.
Chicago, Ill.
Detroit, Mich.
Boston, Mass.
New York, N.Y.
San Francisco, Cal.
Aspen, Col.
Denver, Col.
Baltimore, Md.
Philadelphia, Pa.
WASHINGTON, D.C.
UNITED STATES OF AMERICA
Las Vegas, Nev.
Wichita, Kan.
St. Louis, Mo.
Louisville, Ky.
Los Angeles, Cal.
Santa Fe, N.M.
Nashville, Tenn.
Phoenix, Ariz.
Memphis, Tenn.
Atlanta, Ga.
Charleston, S.C.
Tucson, Ariz.
El Paso, Tex.
Birmingham, Ala.
ATLANTIC
OCEAN
PACIFIC
OCEAN
Dallas, Tex.
New Orleans, La.
Jacksonville, Fla.
MEXICO
Houston, Tex.
Sarasota, Fla.
GULF OF MEXICO
Miami, Fla.

WEATHER IN THE UNITED STATES
(See weather charts pages 18 and 19)

LOCATION ... Stretching between the Atlantic and Pacific Oceans, continental United States is bounded on the north by Canada and on the south by Mexico and the Gulf of Mexico. The 48 states in the temperate zone extend from approximately 24°30′ to 49° north latitude. Alaska (page 500), protruding into the Bering Sea from northwestern Canada, has almost exactly the same north-south latitudes as Norway, and is the largest state, with an area of 586,400 square miles. The tropical Hawaiian Islands (page 522), the 50th state, lie in the Pacific Ocean about 2400 miles west-southwest of San Francisco.

CHARACTERISTICS ... The United States is a land of great cities with soaring skyscrapers and traffic-jammed streets; deep, silent forests and lonely prairie farms; huge dams, roaring industrial plants and sleepy little towns; sky-high mountains and seemingly endless deserts; gleaming white beaches and enormous inland lakes. The average American is eager to talk to foreign visitors and to help them know and love America as he does.

POPULATION ... 195,129,000.

SIZE ... 3,614,210 square miles, including Alaska and Hawaii.

CAPITAL ... Washington, District of Columbia.

GOVERNMENT ... A republic of 50 semi-autonomous states,

each with its own governor, capital and legislative body. The federal government is headed by the President (elected for not more than two 4-year terms) and a Congress consisting of a Senate and a House of Representatives.

HOW TO GET THERE . . . By Pan American Airways, which has a wide choice of money-saving travel plans. The "Extra Cities" Bonus Plan takes you to any gateway city of your choice: Seattle, Portland, San Francisco or Los Angeles on the West Coast; Houston, Dallas, Atlanta, New Orleans or Miami in the South; Boston, New York, Philadelphia, Baltimore or Washington, D.C. in the East; Chicago or Detroit in the Midwest. You can then tour the country by domestic airlines and see any number of U.S. cities for just the price of a single round-trip ticket to the most distant destination. Group Fares, Family Fares and Excursion Fares also offer an appreciable savings on flights. Your travel agent can help you plan a trip which best fits your time, taste and budget.

ACCOMMODATIONS . . . As in all other countries, hotel rates in the States are noticeably lower in small towns than in large cities. In nonresort communities which are busy the year around, hotel rates are fairly stable all year although some hotels charge extra for the television set in your room. It is free in the better hotels. All the better hotels are air conditioned. There is no extra charge for steam heat, of which America seems to have an overabundance. While it is sometimes difficult to get a room with a private bath in many countries, the room-with-bath combination is standard in all modern American hotels and motels throughout the country. "American Plan," in which the room rate includes all meals, is seldom found nowadays except in an occasional resort. Only a few hotels include continental breakfasts in their room rates. In southern resorts such as Miami Beach, rates are drastically lower during the summer months. Northern resorts either close entirely or cut rates in winter, unless they are in snow-sports areas. American hotels are run efficiently but impersonally. To get service of any kind, use the telephone in your room. Motels, which began as rustic and very inexpensive accommodations for motorists, have grown into miniature resorts, with air conditioning, television in every room, and often with dining facilities and a swimming pool in the patio. Pan American offices around the world can supply information on, and make reservations at, most hotels and motels in the U.S. including *Holiday Inns,* a top-ranking chain which has nearly 550 motels in the U.S.A. and Canada.

ARTS . . . New York, Washington, Boston and Chicago may have the greatest concentration of art galleries and museums, but there are important collections in cities throughout the country, and excellent American and foreign art treasures are found—rather surprisingly—in small communities that have been endowed by wealthy residents. Outstanding examples include the Maryhill Museum of Fine Art, built in Washington State, miles from any city, by Samuel Hill; the Lauren Rogers Memorial Library and Museum, which displays European and American masterpieces in the little city of Laurel, Mississippi; the great Cunningham Art Gallery in Bakersfield, California; the controversial Chrysler Art Museum in Provincetown, Massachusetts; the lavish Vanderbilt mansion, turned museum, in Asheville, North Carolina; the Ringling Museum of Art with its paintings by Rembrandt and Rubens in Sarasota, Florida; the Amon Carter collection of Western American Art in Fort Worth, Texas; the Whitney Museum near Cody, Wyoming. There are also many, many galleries and museums sponsored by various cities and states. Admission is free to most of them, and exhibits may be photographed without charge, or by special permission.

BALLET... Major American ballet companies are the New York City Ballet Company, the American Ballet Theatre, National Ballet Company and Jerome Robbins Ballet, all of which are centered in Washington and New York, but there are a number of well-organized ballet groups in other cities, and many regional dance festivals are held in northern resorts in summer.

BANKS... Any town large enough to be incorporated has at least one bank, but except in gateway cities that are international sea or airports, American bankers are very reluctant to exchange foreign currency. Visitors from abroad should make money exchanges immediately upon arrival and carry their cash mostly in travelers checks. These are acceptable anywhere in the States, and leftover checks can be readily—and often profitably—exchanged back into your original currency when you get home.

CALENDAR OF HOLIDAYS... New Year's Day; Memorial Day (May 30); Independence Day (July 4); Labor Day (1st Monday in September); Veterans' Day (November 11); Thanksgiving (4th Thursday in November); Christmas, December 25. Stores, many restaurants, museums and various facilities are closed throughout the country on those days. In addition, there are local and state holidays when banks and schools may be closed, but stores usually stay open.

CIGARETTES, CIGARS, TOBACCO... Foreign-made tobacco products are available in large cities. The price of American cigarettes varies a little from state to state, depending upon local tax laws, but is generally around 40¢ a pack; cheaper by the carton.

CLIMATE... Despite its enormous range of latitude, continental U.S.A. is *everywhere*—at least briefly—cold in winter, hot in summer. The thermometer can reach 100°F. in Wisconsin in summer and 15°F. in Florida in winter, but neither unusual condition lasts very long. Spring and autumn are almost always reliably lovely in both the north and south. Air conditioning and central heating keep indoor temperatures practically impervious to outdoor conditions both in buildings and in public conveyances of all kinds.

CLUBS... International organizations, such as Rotary, Lions, Junior Chamber of Commerce and the Masonic and similar orders, have branches in nearly every city and town. Most golf clubs and yacht clubs are open only to members and their guests.

COMMON COURTESIES AND LOCAL CUSTOMS... Handshaking is not practiced nearly so much in the States as it is in other countries, but kissing is more prevalent between men and women, especially at parties, where it means nothing but "I'm glad to see you." Punctuality, both for business and social appointments, is a rule in northern states. Southerners drift in late for nearly everything. Americans laugh easily and often; they are casual and informal in their relationships, and feel that life's too short for stylized politeness, but they are almost never consciously rude.

COMMUNICATIONS... First-class surface mail (ordinary letter) costs 5¢ per ounce for the U.S., Canada and Mexico. Airmail is 8¢ per ounce for the U.S., Canada and Mexico; from 11¢ to 25¢ per ½ ounce to foreign countries, depending upon distance. Airletter forms can be sent anywhere in the world for 11¢. The charge for a 3-minute local call is 10¢ from public telephones, but if you call from your hotel room there is usually an additional service charge. To call someone in another city, dial the Long Distance Operator (the number is in the front of the directory). Rates are lower after 6 P.M. (lower still after 9 P.M.) on weekdays and all day Sunday. Dial the same number for calls to foreign countries and ask for the Overseas Operator. The charge for a 3-minute daytime call to most foreign countries is $12, plus 10% federal tax. Domestic telegrams are sent via Western Union and may be phoned in from your hotel room; the charges are added onto your bill. Overseas cablegrams are: (1) *full rate,* 5 words minimum, the fastest service; or (2) *cable letter* (LT); an overnight service with 22 words basic minimum. From New York City to most of Europe the full rate is 25¢ per word; cable letters of 22 words are $2.75, plus 12½¢ for each additional word.

CURRENCY... Coins are: 1¢ (penny), 5¢ (nickel), 10¢ (dime), 25¢ (quarter), 50¢ (half-dollar). Silver dollars are common in western states, but are comparatively scarce in the East. Paper money comes in denominations of $1, $2 (rare), $5, $10, $20, $50, $100 and up to $10,000 (even rarer).

CUSTOMS REGULATIONS AND DOCUMENTS REQUIRED FOR INTERNATIONAL VISITORS... To visit the United States, for business or pleasure, you need a passport, visa and international smallpox vaccination certificate. In most countries, it is no longer necessary to appear in person at a U.S. Consulate to obtain a visa. You can do this by mail merely by sending in your passport and one photograph. Pan American Airways sales offices can furnish application forms printed in your own language. Special permission is needed to bring into the U.S. any plants, flowers, vegetables, fruit, meat, birds or animals, but there are no restrictions on bringing in sports equipment, personal effects of all kinds, even a car or boat, as long as you take them with you when you leave. Duty-free items also include 300 cigarettes, or 50 cigars, or 3 lbs. tobacco, and 1 quart of wine or spirits.

DRUGSTORES... Are everywhere, but the drug-dispensing department is usually found deep at the back of the store, after you've run the gantlet of magazine racks, cigarette counter, cosmetic department, soda-and-lunch counter, housewares, toys, stationery, electrical and sporting goods. Every imaginable panacea is available, but prices are considered high by both foreigners and Americans.

ELECTRIC CURRENT ... 110 volts, A.C., 60 cycles. Appliances made to run on 220-volt current are inoperable.

FOOD ... American attempts to duplicate foreign cookery are often appreciated only by those who have never tasted the real thing, but genuine American regional dishes can be truly great. Pennsylvania Dutch cooking is especially outstanding. New England has its renowned lobsters, clam chowder, Boston baked beans. Virginia is famed for its hams. Around New Orleans, Creole cookery appeals to all visitors. The Midwest specializes in fruit pies, butter-dripping ears of corn, mammoth steaks and spareribs. California is one vast salad bowl with its superb fruits and vegetables, and its fish dishes are unbeatable. New York, San Francisco and New Orleans are recognized as the gourmet capitals of the States, but there is good food everywhere. One of the best places to find authentic regional cooking is at a small town "church supper." These money-raising affairs are most often held in the autumn and are hospitably open to strangers. Americans seldom drink wine or beer with their meals, but consume large amounts of ice water, coffee and, in summer, iced tea. Milk is pasteurized everywhere.

GAMBLING ... Pari-mutuel betting at race tracks in many states. Nevada is the only state with legalized gambling, and its cities of Reno and Las Vegas are famous for their roulette tables and slot machines. Only New Hampshire has a state lottery.

LANGUAGE ... Entirely English, although various foreign language groups can be found in many communities.

LAUNDRY AND DRY CLEANING ... Service is good, prices are reasonable. Coin-operated, automatic laundry and dry-cleaning facilities are found in all larger communities and many small ones.

LIQUOR ... Mississippi is still a "dry" state, but liquor is easily obtainable everywhere else, either in state-owned package stores or in independently owned liquor shops, depending upon local laws. Each community also makes its own laws for the hours that bars are open. Imported Scotch whisky is probably the most popular drink along the East coast, but the rest of the country is largely loyal to American rye (distilled from a mash of grain containing not less than 51% rye) and American bourbon (distilled from a mash of grain containing not less than 51% corn). Vodka and gin are used as bases for many cocktails, and Americans are masters at concocting these intricate formulae. American wines are produced mostly in California, Ohio and New York, and some compare very favorably with their European counterparts. American beers are somewhat lighter than the beers of other countries, but Americans like them that way.

MEDICAL FACILITIES ... Range from good to the very best in the world. They are costly for those who can afford to pay, but free for those who can't.

MOTION PICTURES ... "Art" theaters in larger cities show British, French, Italian and other imported films, but American-made movies predominate. Except in small towns, shows run continuously from mid-morning until late at night.

MUSIC ... Many cities maintain symphony orchestras with world-renowned conductors such as Jean Martinon in Chicago, George Szell in Cleveland, Erich Leinsdorf in Boston, Eugene Ormandy in Philadelphia and, of course, Leonard Bernstein of the New York Philharmonic. The concert season extends from autumn until late spring. In summer, music festivals sweep the country, featuring anything from Wagnerian operas and medieval chamber music to far-out jazz and atonal modern compositions. The songs of Broadway shows and Hollywood movies have become 20th-century classics, Dixieland jazz, blues songs and Negro spirituals are authentically American art forms; no other nation is as adept at composing danceable dance music.

NIGHT CLUBS ... Good places to dine, see a floor show and dance to an orchestra are generally found only in large cities, at smart resorts and in university towns. Other communities have bars and cocktail lounges, with possibly a juke box, or a pianist or an organist. All the better places are well advertised in newspapers and local city magazines. Most have a cover or minimum charge, and when there is entertainment there is an entertainment tax.

OPERA ... Opera, once rarely seen outside of New York, Chicago and San Francisco, has now been extended to cities all across the country through the touring Metropolitan Opera National Company.

PHOTOGRAPHY ... All kinds of American and imported photographic equipment are available, and processing services are speedy and good.

RELIGION ... Predominantly Protestant, Catholic and Jewish.

RESTAURANTS ... Breakfast is generally served from 7:30 to 10 A.M.; lunch from noon to 2 P.M.; dinner from 6 to 8:30 or later, with 7 o'clock being the most popular hour. That great American institution, the cocktail "hour," begins at 5 P.M. but seldom ends as early as 6. In large cities there is always a restaurant open somewhere, but in small towns the closing hour may be as early as 8 P.M. There are restaurants in all price ranges, depending a great deal upon atmosphere, decorations, service and the length of the menu. Drugstores are very popular for breakfast, and you can usually get a continental breakfast there, consisting of a roll and coffee, for about 25¢. A typical American breakfast of fruit juice, bacon and eggs, coffee and toast (plus hominy grits in the South) costs from 75¢ to $1.25. Quick lunch counters and cafeterias often provide hearty meals for less than a dollar. Hotel coffee shops, department-store dining rooms and medium-priced restaurants feature daily specials in which a satisfying meal, either lunch or dinner, can be had from 75¢ to $3. Even more unpretentious are those famous American favorites the tasty plump hot dog or juicy hamburger which you can buy for as low as 25¢ in many places. In more elegant establishments prices are considerably higher, and the food and service more elaborate.

SHOPS AND STORES ... The most famous stores in America include Macy's in New York; Rich's in Atlanta, Georgia; Neiman-

Marcus in Dallas, Texas; Marshall Field in Chicago, Illinois; and Gump's in San Francisco, with merchandise that could grace an art museum. But there are very good stores and specialty shops everywhere, and prices are much the same throughout the country in stores of similar category. A fairly recent innovation are the discount stores, huge emporiums where you can buy name-brand merchandise of all kinds at relatively low prices, but they are often crowded to the point of pandemonium, and there is not much personal service from sales people in most of them.

SPECTATOR SPORTS...The great national sport of professional baseball begins in late spring and culminates in the hotly contested World Series early in October, by which time collegiate and professional football are already under way. The college football season closes on New Year's Day with spectacular festivities and Bowl games in southern cities: the Rose Bowl in Pasadena, California; the Sugar Bowl in New Orleans; the Cotton Bowl in Dallas, Texas; and the Orange Bowl in Miami. Basketball and ice hockey (played indoors) are exhibition sports in winter; professional boxing and wrestling go on throughout the year. Horse racing's greatest events take place in May and early June with the Kentucky Derby in Louisville, Kentucky; the Belmont Stakes in New York City; and the Preakness Stakes at Pimlico in Baltimore, Maryland. Other great tracks are Hialeah in Miami; Santa Anita near Los Angeles; Arlington Park near Chicago; and the Fair Grounds in New Orleans. Harness racing is especially popular in New England. Large crowds attend track and field meets all over the country, and the National Open Golf Championship in June and the National Tennis Championships at Forest Hills, New York City, in September. The most famous auto racing event is held on Memorial Day (May 30) in Indianapolis, Indiana. Wild West rodeos may be seen occasionally in New York's Madison Square Garden, but are better in their natural element in Texas, Arizona, Wyoming, Montana and other Western states.

SPORTS...Public golf courses and tennis courts are found everywhere, all over the country. America's most famous ski centers are at Squaw Valley, California, Aspen, Colorado and Sun Valley, Idaho. On weekends, Easterners throng to the mountains of Vermont and New Hampshire, but in winter all the northern states almost always have enough snowy hills for skiing, tobogganing and bobsledding, with lakes and rivers for ice skating. The Rocky Mountains, which extend from Alaska (which has Mt. McKinley, 20,300 feet high—America's highest peak) down through western Canada and as far south as New Mexico, are a continual challenge to mountain climbers. The Grand Canyon in all its fantastic colors may be viewed from comfortable vantage points, or explored more venturesomely on surefooted mules. The lakes, rivers and seacoasts of America provide endless opportunities for water sports of all kinds, and most types of equipment can be rented. Every state in the nation has areas where the fishing and hunting are excellent. Probably the major indoor sport in the States is bowling, with billiards gaining rapidly.

THEATERS ... New York is the heart of America's theatrical world, but the stages of Broadway and Off Broadway are supplied with talent trained in theaters all over the country. Nearly every college and university has its drama group; more than 3,000 Little Theater clubs are scattered from coast to coast; and there are professional and semiprofessional stock companies in nearly a dozen cities. Actors who appear on Broadway and on television in winter often make star appearances in summer stock theaters throughout the New England states, other eastern states and near the large cities. The most famous of the many Shakespeare Festivals are those held in Stratford, Connecticut, and in New York's Central Park (admission free to the latter). A purely American theatrical enterprise, the Symphonic Drama, is a production weaving music, poetry, dance and pageantry around a dramatic historical event. The state of North Carolina is especially prolific in these entertainments.

TIME ... There are 4 standard time zones across continental U.S.A. When it is noon, Greenwich Mean Time, it is 7 A.M. in New York; 6 A.M. in Chicago; 5 A.M. in Denver; 4 A.M. in San Francisco; 2 A.M. in both Fairbanks, Alaska, and Honolulu, Hawaii. Daylight Saving Time is observed in summer by local option, but intercity trains, planes and buses run on standard time the year round.

TIPPING ... There is no tipping at all on airplanes, or to immigration or customs officials. Service charges are almost never included in restaurant or hotel bills. Chambermaids get no tip if you stay only a day or two; if you stay for a week and know that the same girl tidies your room every day, you might leave a dollar or two. The general rule is to give restaurant waiters 15% of the bill in most city restaurants; perhaps 20% in very expensive ones and in night clubs (deduct the amusement tax before you start figuring). The head waiter is not tipped unless he gives you some special service. Hatcheck girls get 10¢-25¢. Doormen get 15¢-25¢ for helping with luggage or getting a taxi on a rainy or busy day; otherwise nothing. Porters in hotels, at railway stations and at airports get at least 25¢ per bag. Tip taxi drivers about 15¢ for a short ride; 15% of the meter reading for a long one. Tip barbers 25¢-35¢ for a haircut; 25¢ for a shave; 10¢ for a shoeshine and 10¢ for having your clothes brushed. Tip washroom attendants 10¢-25¢. At better beauty parlors, tip the hairdresser about $1; 50¢ each to the shampoo girl and the manicurist.

TRANSPORTATION ... Traveling around America is now much easier for foreign visitors than it used to be. American and Canadian railroads have many reduced-fare plans especially for people from abroad, and a major one cuts 15% off the coach fares from any point of entry city to any other place in the interior of the U.S. or Canada; you see a lot, because you can go by one route and return by another, with any number of stopovers permissible within the 3-month limit of the ticket. Coach fares, without this reduction, average 2.8¢ a mile; reduced rates for children. The railroads also offer special family fares, group economy fares, party excursion rates, and so on. Many railroad lines feature all-expense escorted tours and organized prearranged individual tours which include transportation, hotels and sightseeing excursions. Some lines even own steamships which make rail-steamer trips possible in some areas.

American bus lines, too, have new, money-saving plans to enable foreign visitors to see more of the country. The most spectacular is the Greyhound Bus Lines' and Trailways' offer of 99 days of unlimited travel for $99. Go any place in the U.S.A. for just $1 a day! Buses are air-conditioned in summer, comfortably heated in winter; most have rest rooms and many carry snack bars. Other major bus lines also have special economy tours. Some include hotel accommodations, sightseeing and transportation—sometimes meals—all at remarkably low cost. A typical tour originating in New York City takes 13 days and includes exploration of New York City, Washington, D.C., Niagara Falls, and goes up into Canada, all for around $150—including transportation, hotels and sightseeing.

Domestic airlines in the U.S.A. have reduced family fare plans and special excursion rates. Many lines offer complete "package" tours including transportation, hotels, meals and sightseeing. And Pan American's "Extra Cities" Bonus Plan is a quick, economical way for overseas visitors to see a great deal of the country. For example, if you buy a round-trip ticket from London to Los Angeles, the "Extra Cities" plan enables you to stop off in as many as 20 cities along the way for no extra charge: New York, Philadelphia, Washington, Nashville, Memphis, Dallas, El Paso, Tucson, Phoenix, San Diego, Las Vegas, Amarillo, Wichita, Kansas City, St. Louis, Springfield, Chicago, Dayton, Columbus, Pittsburgh. The "Extra Cities" privilege may be used from any Pan Am gateway city, and the Pan American sales office nearest you can prepare a routing that will help you see the most and do the most for your least money.

If you want to see America by car, renting an automobile in the U.S. is much the same as in Europe. Costs are usually on a mileage basis, plus hourly, daily or weekly charges, and they include gasoline, oil, maintenance and insurance. All you need is a validated driver's license. The U.S. is currently validating licenses issued in some 65 countries. Any other national driver's license may be submitted for validation—without charge—at the American Automobile Association (International Division), 750 Third Avenue, New York, N.Y.; or at the Philadelphia, Boston, or Los Angeles offices of the American Automobile Touring Alliance.

There are car-rental agencies in cities all over the country, and it is often possible to pick up a car in one city and leave it in another without extra charge. Whenever return charges do apply, they are reasonable. It is not necessary to rent a large, unfamiliar American automobile. All kinds of European makes are available, too. The average daily cost of renting a car is $8-$10 a day, $50 a week—plus 10¢ a mile. The agency will usually make a reduction for long trips or longer rental periods. For real economy there is camping in beautiful state and national forests and in other sites where costs run from nothing at all to $2 a night to pitch a tent and use all the provided conveniences. Using a travel trailer is another economical and popular way to see the country, and there are trailer campsites in many state and national parks and forests.

The "fly-and-drive" combination trips are great time-savers. Suppose you enter the U.S. at Boston. You could pick up a car and wander all over New England and follow the Great Lakes down to Chicago; then turn your car in at the local branch of the rental agency and fly the long distance to, for instance, Houston, Texas (1,173 miles), where you could again rent a car and perhaps tour to the Grand Canyon and on to Los Angeles, San Francisco, Seattle or Portland, returning home from any one of these Pan Am gateway cities.

If you bring your own car to the States, remember that this country has reciprocal agreements with some 70 different countries whose citizens may use their own license plates and personal driver's licenses. It is advisable, though, that cars brought into this country have international Registration Markers and—to be entirely on the safe side—an International Driving Permit, although the latter is demanded only in the state of Massachusetts. The American Automobile Association (headquarters at 1712 G Street, N.W., Washington 6, D.C.) issues a booklet titled *Motoring in the United States,* which is especially written for motorists from abroad. Membership in the AAA, or Allstate Motor Club, both open to all drivers, includes excellent free tour books, maps, routings, emergency road service, personal accident insurance, bail bond protection and many other useful advantages. The major oil companies dispense free maps and information on accommodations and routes which are available at filling stations and from companies' central offices.

WATER . . . Safe to drink everywhere, but flavor differs from place to place.

WHAT TO BUY . . . Shoes, for men, women and children, are crafted to fit more perfectly than the shoes of any other country. Clothing which is partially or entirely of man-made fibers is comparatively inexpensive and almost unbelievably easy to care for. As with shoes, American clothing of all kinds is made in an enormous range of sizes in both the expensive and very inexpensive categories. Suits, dresses, hats, coats and underclothing of all kinds are made to fit *perfectly* even if mass-produced and low-priced. Dramatic costume jewelry is another American specialty. Labor-saving household products are also a specialty of the States, but visitors from abroad who want to take home refrigerators, washing machines or other electrical appliances should be careful to buy them only from dealers affiliated with manufacturers who make appliances especially for use on foreign electrical current, and who can handle the details of packing, shipping and necessary documentation. There are very few handicraft items in the States; nearly everything comes out of a factory or a laboratory.

WHAT TO WEAR . . . The same sort of sports or city clothes that you'd wear in any resort or city at home, but the excessive use of steam heat calls for cooler indoor clothing in winter than is worn in most countries. Evening clothes are seldom worn in the States.

WHERE TO GO—SIGHTSEEING . . .

WASHINGTON, D.C. . . . The impressive national capital, with its many beautiful, tree-lined streets, has grown from a small Southern town to a vital world influence. Here are the seat of the President, the Congress and the Supreme Court. Government offices are staffed with thousands of people from all over the nation, and almost every important country in the world has its ranking representative here.

POPULATION AND SIZE . . . Population 808,000; in the greater metropolitan district, 2,001,897. The District of Columbia, coextensive with Washington itself, covers about 61 square miles.

ACCOMMODATIONS . . . The huge new *Washington Hilton* is at Connecticut Avenue and Columbia Road, single from $12, double from $18. Other new luxury hotels in Washington: the handsome *Madison,* single from $16, double from $20; *International Inn* with year round outside swimming pool, single from $12, double from $16; and *Georgetown Inn,* where single rates start at $13, doubles from $17. Other principal hotels are: *Ambassador,* with indoor swimming pool, single from $8, double from $16. *Congressional,* single from $12, double from $15, on Union Station Plaza. *Dupont Plaza,* single from $13, double from $18; in the northwestern part of town, partly residential. *Fairfax,* single from $8, double from $10; conservative, pleasant. *Manger-Hay-Adams,* single from $17, double from $21; near White House, *Mayflower,* single from $10, double from $18; fashionable, scene of much political activity. *Roger Smith,* single from $9, double from $12; busy, popular. *Sheraton-Carlton,* single from $13, double from $19.50; excellent, sophisticated. *Sheraton-Park,* single from $10, double from $14; outside swimming pool near Rock Creek Park, partly residential. *Shoreham,* single from $12, double from $18; along Rock Creek Park, outdoor swimming pool, very fashionable. *Statler Hilton,* single from $16, double from $22; one of Washington's most modern hotels, in the heart of the city. *Willard,* single from $10, double from $16; well-known, traditionally important. The *Pick Lee Motor Hotel,* also serving as bus terminal for Friendship (Baltimore) and Dulles International airports, is from $11.50 single, from $14.50 double.

ARTS . . . *Corcoran Gallery of Art,* American paintings and sculptures; open Tuesday through Friday, 10-4:30, Saturday 9-4:30; free. *National Gallery of Art,* one of the outstanding museum buildings of the world, houses fine art collections; open weekdays 10-5, Sunday 2-10; free. *Phillips Collection,* mostly modern art; open weekdays 11-6, except Mondays when open until 10, Sundays 2-7; free. *Smithsonian Institution* (including Arts and Industries, Freer Museum of Natural History, Air and Space Building, Freer Gallery and the new History and Technology Building), U.S. Government establishments, almost overwhelming series of exhibits; open daily 9-4:30; free. *Dumbarton Oaks Museum,* library and art collection; open weekdays 10-4, Sunday 1-4; gardens open same hours.

The *National Symphony Orchestra* gives a regular series of concerts in winter. The U.S. *Army, Navy, Marine* and *Air Corps* orchestras and others, as well as celebrated singers, perform from a barge theater on the Potomac River and on the steps of the east front of the Capitol in summer. Performances are at the Watergate by the Lincoln Memorial; free admission. Throughout the year there are frequent performances by the *Washington Opera* and the *National Ballet.* The new *Kennedy Arts Center* is designed to house three sumptuous theaters for concerts, operas, ballet, plays and musicals.

CLIMATE . . . Summer in Washington is fairly hot, winter is fairly cold. Spring and fall, however, are usually pleasant.

FAIRS, EXHIBITIONS AND SPECIAL EVENTS . . . Among others, the Cherry Blossom Festival, usually in early April; President's Cup Regatta, mid-September; Lighting of the National Community Christmas Tree, around December 20.

LIBRARIES . . . Important national libraries are housed in the *Library of Congress* and the Smithsonian Institution. The Declaration of Independence, the Constitution and the Bill of Rights are displayed in the *National Archives* on Constitution Avenue; open weekdays 9 A.M. to 10 P.M., Sundays and holidays, 1-10. The *Folger Library* has a fine collection of Elizabethan relics and a complete reference collection for the study of Anglo-American civilizations. All government departments and offices maintain their own specialized libraries.

LIQUOR . . . The District of Columbia permits the sale of liquor weekdays from 8 A.M. to 2 A.M.; Saturdays from 8 A.M. to midnight; Sundays (beer and wine only) from 1 P.M. to midnight.

NIGHT CLUBS . . . In the summer, you can dine, dance and enjoy the floor shows on the *Terrace* of the Shoreham Hotel; in the winter the celebrated *Blue Room* opens. Dinner and dancing at the *Presidential Room* of the Mayflower Hotel. There are also numerous smaller restaurants with excellent entertainment. Check advertisements in the daily newspapers.

PARKS, ZOOS, AQUARIUMS AND GARDENS . . . *Rock Creek Park* with its Nature Center and adjoining *National Zoological Park.* The Cherry Blossom festivities are held in *East* and *West Potomac Park.* The *U.S. National Arboretum,* devoted to woody plants, has the country's most extensive collection of azaleas. *U.S. Botanic Gardens,* west side of Capitol.

POINTS OF INTEREST . . . Capitol district includes the *Capitol* itself, galleries open to the public when Congress is in session, 9 A.M.-4:30 P.M.; *Senate Office Buildings; Supreme Court Buildings; Library of Congress. Petersen House,* in which Lincoln died; open weekdays 9-5:30, Sundays and holidays 12:30-5:30, admission 10¢. Other Washington highlights include the *White House* (entrance on E. Executive Ave.), open Tuesday through Saturday, 10 to noon; *Washington Monument,* elevator ride to 500-foot-high observation room, open daily 9-5, 8 A.M. to 11 P.M. in summer; elevator 10¢, staircase climb free. The new *National Historical Wax Museum* features reproductions of famous persons and famous events in American history. Open daily

The Capitol of the United States. It has been greatly enlarged since President George Washington laid the first cornerstone on September 18, 1793.

The Washington Monument, over 555 feet high, dominates the skyline of the city and the Government buildings on Constitution Avenue.

9-9, admission 90¢ for adults, 50¢ for children under 12. See, too, the new *Navy Museum,* which displays historic American mementoes from earliest history to President Kennedy's ship-model collection. Along the Potomac River are such beauty spots as the *Lincoln Memorial,* lovely *Potomac Park, Jefferson Memorial.* In the delightful suburb of Georgetown, aside from the Dumbarton Oaks Park and Library, is *Dumbarton House* with its many colonial pieces. Visit *Arlington Cemetery, Christ Church* and *Washington Masonic Memorial.* A trip to *Mount Vernon,* George Washington's home, is a form of pilgrimage for Americans. A 4-hour tour to Mount Vernon is about $5. There are tours through the *Pentagon,* world's largest office building, which is open Monday through Friday, 7-6. There are numerous tours of Washington and vicinity, many of which include free pick-up at your hotel. A typical 3-hour tour is $6.

    RESTAURANTS... *The Jockey Club, Knife and Fork, Paul Young's, Trader Vic's, Golden Ox, Rive Gauche, Le Gourmet, La Salle du bois, Le Bistro, Sans Souci* and *Le Monicle* are all fairly expensive. The *Occidental,* steaks and chops; *O'Donnell's Sea Grill, Hogates,* sea food; *Blackie's House of Beef, Water Gate Inn* (Pennsylvania Dutch food), *Bassins, The Roma* (Italian), *Aldo's, Rhein* and *Old Europe*

(German), are moderately priced. *Charcoal Hearth* in Georgetown for beef. These are only a few of the many fine restaurants in Washington.

SPECTATOR SPORTS... *The Washington Senators* play professional baseball in the American League. The *Washington Redskins* are the local professional football team.

THEATERS... Broadway productions may be seen regularly at the *National Theater* and the *Arena Stage*. Summer theaters include the *Olney Theater, Shady Grove Music Fair* and the *Carter Brown Amphitheater*.

SOURCES OF FURTHER INFORMATION... International Visitors Information Service, 801 19th Street, N.W.; Washington Convention and Visitors' Bureau, 1616 K Street, N.W. (Tel. ST 3-3535). Pan American Airways, World Center Building, 16th and K Streets, N.W. (Tel. 757-8900), and at Friendship International and Dulles International Airports. The Tour Desks at hotels also have complete information on sightseeing, restaurants and theaters.

NEW YORK, NEW YORK... The largest city in the United States is in southeastern New York State at the mouth of the Hudson River. Manhattan Island, heart of the city, is the part most interesting to visitors. There are four other boroughs: Bronx (on the mainland north of Manhattan), Brooklyn and Queens (on Long Island, east of Manhatttan), and Richmond (Staten Island, south of Manhattan). Regardless of the season, New York men and women wear smartly conservative clothing, and most restaurants will not serve men in shirtsleeves or without ties. Women wear simple, well-cut dresses or suits —wool in winter, cotton in summer. Short cocktail styles for women and business suits for men are worn in the evening for nearly everything except great balls and gala theatrical affairs. New York is comparatively formal about daytime clothes and relatively informal about evening wear.

New Yorkers, rushing purposefully through their concrete canyons, appear to be totally engrossed in their own affairs, yet it is hard to find a friendlier city. Most New Yorkers were themselves once new to the place, and it makes them feel good to give directions and advice to strangers. And, while there is no limit to the amount of money you *can* spend, New York undoubtedly offers the most fun for the least money of any city in the world.

POPULATION AND SIZE... About 8,000,000; in the entire metropolitan region, 16,000,000. City area is 365 square miles, including 66 square miles of inland waters.

ACCOMMODATIONS... To be sure of getting a room in the hotel of your choice, always write or wire for a reservation and have it confirmed by the hotel, if at all possible. Checkout time is usually during the afternoon, and occasionally your room will not yet be available if you arrive early in the day. Budget-priced rooms (without private baths) start at $3.50 or $4 single, about $6 or $7 double. Reasonably priced rooms start at about $6 single, $10 double. Moderate prices are from about $10 single, $15 double. In the expensive category, a single room will start at about $18, and a double at $25. These are all minimum prices. Rooms with twin beds are more expensive than those with double beds. The following is merely a representative list:

Times Square District—West side of town from 42 St. to about 52 St. Hotels in this area are convenient to transportation, theaters, restaurants and night clubs. Somewhat noisy, busy at night, but near the center of activities. *Abbey*, 151 W. 51 St.; some rooms air-conditioned; many Spanish-speaking personnel; reasonable. The *Astor*, 1519 Broadway (at 44 St.); one of the meeting places of the city; features shops, banquet facilities, good food; moderate. *Bristol*, 129 W. 48 St.; popular with foreign tourists; reasonable. *Dixie*, 250 W. 43 St.: busy; Spanish-speaking staff; reasonable. *Edison*, 228 W. 47 St., 46 St. entrance: large commercial hotel; reasonable. *Manhattan*, 44 St. and Eighth Ave.: new; reasonable. *Paramount*, 235 W. 46 St.: large, popular; some rooms air-conditioned; reasonable. *Piccadilly*, 227 W. 45 St.: large commercial hotel; reasonable. *Taft*, 769 Seventh Ave.: extremely large, busy; some rooms air-conditioned; reasonable. *Woodstock*, 127 W. 43 St.: busy; many rooms air-conditioned; reasonable. Good budget-priced hotels in the area are the *Ashley*, 157 W. 47 St.; *Diplomat*, 108 W. 43 St.; *Iroquois*, 49 W. 44 St.; *Mansfield*, 12 W. 44 St.; *St. James*, 109 W. 45 St.; *Schuyler*, 57 W. 45 St. Free parking at: *Travelodge*, 515 W. 42nd St.; *Riviera Congress Motor Inn*, 40-41 St. & Tenth Ave.; *Skyline Motor Inn*, 49-50 St. & Tenth Ave.; *Sheraton Motor Inn*, 12th Ave. and 42 St.; *Howard Johnson Motor Inn*, 8th Ave. and 51 St.; *Loew's Midtown Motor Inn*, 8th Ave. and 48 St.; *City Squire Motor Inn*, 51 St. and Seventh Ave.; *Times Square Motor Hotel*, 43 St. west of Broadway; *Holiday Inn*, 440 W. 57 St.

Pennsylvania Station District—Conveniently located near the popular 34 St. shopping region, and close to the wholesale garment district. *Governor Clinton*, 31 St. & Seventh Ave.: Spanish-speaking personnel; very large, commercial; reasonable. *Sheraton-Atlantic*, Broadway & 34 St.: popular; pets allowed; moderate. *New Yorker*, 34 St. & Eighth Ave.: enormous commercial hotel; direct tunnel to Pennsylvania Station; moderate. *Statler-Hilton*, 33 St. & Seventh Ave.: very large, important commercially, a convention center; moderate. Budget-priced hotels in the area: *Breslin*, Broadway at 29 St.; *Wolcott*, 4 W. 31 St.

West Side—*Americana*, 53 St. at Seventh Ave.: luxurious new hotel near theater district; moderate-expensive. *Barbizon-Plaza*, 58 St. & Ave. of Americas (Sixth Ave.): very large; transient and residential; has a theater; well located; moderate. *Dorset*, 30 W. 54 St.: moderate-sized, residential and transient, on fairly quiet street; expensive. *Essex House*, 160 Central Park South: beautiful view of Central Park; luxurious; expensive. *Great Northern*, 118 W. 57 St.: some kitchenette apartments; French-speaking personnel; reasonable-moderate. *Henry Hudson*, 353 W. 57 St.: quiet; self-service laundry; indoor swimming pool and health club; reasonable. *New York Hilton*, Ave. of Americas at 53 St.: luxurious new hotel with convention and ban-quiet facilities; moderate-expensive. *Park Sheraton,* 55 St. at Seventh Ave.: large, commercial and transient; nightly entertainment in Mermaid Room; moderate. *Park Chambers,* 68 W. 58 St.: medium-sized, popular and busy; transient and residential; Spanish-speaking personnel; moderate. *St. Moritz,* 50 Central Park South; a favorite with foreign visitors; moderate-expensive. *Warwick,* 65 W. 54 St., fairly large, transient and residential; expensive.

East Side (all moderately priced)—*Beekman Tower,* 49 St. & First Ave.: near United Nations; transient and residential. *Belmont Plaza,* 49 St. & Lexington Ave.: large, residential and transient. *Beverly,* 125 E. 50 St.: moderate-sized, residential and transient. *Biltmore,* 43 St. & Madison Ave.: very large, partly commercial. *Commodore,* 109 E. 42 St.: adjacent to Grand Central Station; very large; specializes in banquets, conventions; kennel for pets. *Lexington,* Lexington Ave. & 48 St.: large, residential and transient; has the popular Hawaiian Room. *Manger-Vanderbilt,* Park Ave. & 34 St.: medium-sized; most rooms air-conditioned. *Roger Smith,* Lexington Ave. & 47 St.: small, quiet; features suites. *Roosevelt,* Madison Ave. & 45 St.: large, transient, with some commercial features. *Shelburne,* Lexington Ave. & 37 St.: residential and quiet at night. *Shelton Towers,* Lexington Ave. & 49 St.: busy commercial hotel. Budget-priced: the *Claredon,* 22 E. 31 St.

East Side (all quite expensive)—*Sheraton East,* formerly the *Ambassador,* Park Ave. & 51 St.: partly residential; quiet and dignified. *Barclay,* 111 E. 48 St.: moderate-sized, residential and transient. *Berkshire,* 52 St. & Madison Ave.: moderate-sized, luxurious; moderate-expensive. *Carlyle,* 76 St. & Madison Ave.: out of hotel area; quiet and luxurious; pets allowed. *Delmonico's,* Park Ave. & 59 St.: large, air-conditioned; all rooms with TV. *Drake,* Park Ave. & 54 St.: fairly large; centrally located and quite elegant. *Gotham,* 5 Ave. & 55th St.: quiet, dignified, convenient; residential and transient. *Pierre,* 5 Ave. & 61 St.: smart and exclusive; all rooms and suites have TV, most are air-conditioned. *Plaza,* Fifth Ave. & 59 St.: famous for its regal Edwardian atmosphere and unobstructed view of Central Park; pets allowed. *Regency,* Park Ave. at 61 St.: new and elegant. *St. Regis,* Fifth Ave. & 55 St.: large, residential and transient; convenient location. *Summit Hotel,* Lexington Ave. & 51 St.: international atmosphere; multilingual staff. *Tuscany,* 120 E. 38 St.: fairly small, residential and transient; quiet at night; color TV. *Waldorf-Astoria,* 50 St. & Park Ave.: world-famous, extremely large; all facilities for banquets and balls; shops; pets allowed, *Westbury,* 69th & Madison Ave.: residential and transient; quiet, dignified; pets allowed.

For Women Only—*Allerton House,* 130 E. 57 St.: transient and permanent; moderate. *Barbizon,* 140 E. 63 St.: transient and permanent, residential neighborhood; swimming pool; moderate. *Martha Washington,* 29 E. 29 St.: transient and permanent; in business district; busy during the day but quiet at night; reasonable.

Young Men's and Young Women's Christian Associations—Accommodations at very low rates are available for both men and women in various dormitories throughout the city, such as *Sloane House YMCA,* 34 St. & Ninth Ave., and *Spelman YWCA,* Eighth Ave. & 51 St. For information, write to YMCA, 422 Ninth Ave., New York 1, N.Y., or to YWCA, 610 Lexington Ave., New York 17, N.Y.

Queens—*Forest Hills Inn,* 1 Station Square, Forest Hills, Long Island: moderate-expensive; *International,* near entrance to New York's International Airport: moderate-expensive; *Holiday Inn,* at 175-15 Rockaway Blvd., provides free transportation to and from the airport.

Bronx—*Concourse Plaza*—161 St. & Grand Concourse; moderate-sized; near Yankee Stadium; reasonable.

Brooklyn—*St. George,* 51 Clark St.: extremely large; commercial; residential and transient; swimming pool; reasonable.

ARTS AND MUSIC: New York is fast becoming the art center of the world. In addition to the museums listed below there are always exhibits in privately owned art galleries that welcome visitors, and other events of special interest. These are publicized in the art and music sections of the newspapers, particularly the *N.Y. Times* and the *N.Y. Herald Tribune,* and in such magazines as *Cue* and *The New Yorker.*

Museums—*American Museum of Natural History,* 79 St. & Central Park West: enormous collection of plant and animal life, from their origins to the present; open weekdays 10 to 5; Sundays and holidays 1 to 5; free. In the *Hayden Planetarium,* part of the museum, afternoon lectures $1, evening $1.25 for adults, 50¢-75¢ for children. *American Numismatic Society,* Broadway & 156 St.: rare and unusual coins and medals; open Tuesday through Saturday 9-5; free. *Brooklyn Museum,* Washington Ave. & Eastern Parkway, Brooklyn: large general exhibit; open daily 10-5, Sundays and holidays 1-5; free. *Chase Manhattan Bank Money Museum,* 1254 Ave. of the Americas. *Cloisters,* Fort Tryon Park: priceless European medieval art in an exquisite setting; open daily except Monday 10-5, Sunday 1-6, May through September, other months 1-5; free. *Contemporary Crafts Museum,* 29 W. 53 St.: modern handicrafts in ceramics, fabrics, metals and woods; open weekdays noon to 6, Sundays 2-6; free. *Federal Hall National Memorial,* Wall and Nassau Sts. *Frick Collection,* Fifth Ave. & 70 St.: outstanding art treasures in a beautiful building; chamber music concerts in autumn; open Tuesday-Saturday 10-5, Sundays and holidays 1-5; free. *Gallery of Modern Art,* Columbus Circle; open 12-8 P.M. Tuesday through Friday, 12-6 Saturday and Sunday; adults $1, children 25¢. *Jewish Museum,* Fifth Ave. & 92 St.; open Monday-Wednesday 12-5, Friday 11-3, Sundays 11-6, closed holidays and month of August; adults 50¢, children 25¢. *Metropolitan Museum of Art,* Fifth Ave. & 82 St.: one of the great art museums of the world; open Monday through Saturday 10-5, Sundays and holidays 1-5; free. *J. P. Morgan Library,* 29 E. 36 St.: special exhibits. *Museum of the American Indian (Heye Foundation),* Broadway & 155 St.: Indian art of the Western Hemisphere; open Tuesday through Sunday 1-5; closed holidays and July and August; free. *Museum of the City of New*

York, Fifth Ave. & 104 St.; from Indian days to the present in displays and mementoes; open Tuesday through Saturday 10-5, Sundays and holidays 1-5; free. *Museum of Early American Folk Art,* 49 W. 53 St. *Museum of Modern Art,* 11 W. 53 St.: changing displays of modern art of all kinds; open daily Monday-Saturday 11-6, Thursdays to 10, Sundays 1-7; admission, adults $1, children 25¢, including free showings of old motion pictures. *New York Historical Society Museum,* Central Park W. & 77 St.: open Tuesday-Friday and Sunday 1-5, Saturday 10-5; closed during August; free. *Solomon R. Guggenheim Museum* (designed by Frank Lloyd Wright), Fifth Ave. & 89 St.: modern art, permanent and loan exhibitions; open Tuesday-Saturday 10-6, until 9 on Wednesdays, Sundays and some holidays noon to 6; admission 50¢. *Spanish Museum (Hispanic Society),* Broadway & 155 St.: Spanish art; open Tuesday-Saturday 10-4:30; Sunday 2-5; free. *Whitney Museum,* 22 W. 54 St.: contemporary American art; open daily except holidays, 1 to 5; free.

New York, the music center of the United States, offers at least two concerts daily even during the summer. For details consult the music pages of the *N.Y. Times,* the *N.Y. Herald Tribune,* and *The New Yorker* magazine. The New York Philharmonic is world-renowned, and now performs in the new *Philharmonic Hall* in Lincoln Center. The Metropolitan Opera presents a full program from September or October until spring. The principal concert halls are the *Brooklyn Academy of Music, Carnegie Hall, McMillin Theater* (Columbia University) and *Town Hall.* During the summer, there are outdoor band concerts in the *Central Park Mall,* and symphony concerts at *Lewisohn Stadium.* Leading ballet companies perform at different theaters during the winter season. The *New York State Theater* of Lincoln Center and the *New York City Center* present opera, ballet (top-quality companies) and other musical performances.

BANKS (FOREIGN): The following countries maintain banking facilities in New York City (see "Banks" in Manhattan *Yellow Pages* directory): Australia, Belgium, Brazil, Canada, China, Ecuador, France, Great Britain, India, Indonesia, Israel, Italy, Japan, Korea, Lebanon, Mexico, Netherlands, Nicaragua, Pakistan, Philippines, South Africa, Switzerland, Venezuela, Yugoslavia.

BUILDINGS: Many of the tallest buildings in the world are in New York—*Empire State* (102 floors), *Chrysler* (77), *60 Wall Street Tower* (66), *Bank of Manhattan* (71), *Radio Corporation of America* (70), *Chase Manhattan Bank* (60), *Woolworth* (60), *Pan Am Building* (59) with rooftop heliport. Other important structures: *City Hall,* City Hall Park, classic example of the architecture of its period (about 1811); *Grand Central Terminal,* 42 St. & Park Ave., huge railway station topped with the new Pan Am Building; *Port Authority Bus Terminal,* Eighth Ave. & 40 St., new general terminal with interesting shops. Park Avenue has become a dazzling boulevard of exciting new architecture with such outstanding buildings as the *Lever House* and the *Seagram Building. Rockefeller Center,* 48 to 52 St. on Fifth Ave. and Ave. of the Americas, consists of 17 buildings containing exhibits, offices, shops, theaters and television studios. Escorted tours start every 15 minutes daily, 9:30-5:30, from September 15-June 15, 9:30-9 during summer. *United Nations,* First Ave., 42 to 48 Sts.: when in session, the public may attend meetings; tickets available on a first come first served basis; guided tours; fascinating foreign shops. *Cathedral of St. John the Divine,* 112 St. & Amsterdam Ave.: Protestant Episcopal; largest church in the United States. *Grant's Tomb,* 122 St. & Riverside Drive: an impressive structure overlooking the Hudson River; mausoleum of General Ulysses S. Grant, Commander in Chief of the Union Army in the Civil War. *Riverside Church,* 122 St. & Riverside Drive; fine example of French Gothic-style architecture. *Trinity Church,* Broadway at Wall St., dates from the colonial era; Alexander Hamilton and Robert Fulton are buried in the quaint churchyard. *Fraunces Tavern,* 54 Pearl St. at Broad: built in 1719 and still serving meals in the first floor restaurant; setting for Washington's farewell to the officers of the Continental Army; museum on the 2nd, 3rd and 4th floors. The newest complex of buildings is Lincoln Center for the Performing Arts at 65th Street and Broadway.

CLIMATE: New York's variable weather is somewhat unpredictable. The coldest months, January through March, are often surprisingly mild. There is no set pattern for snowfalls; some years there is only a brief coating and other years the streets are alive with snowplows and shovelers. From June through September, it can be very warm and humid, but extreme heat usually lasts for only a few days at a time. Spring and fall—October, particularly—can be glorious. There are no definite rainy or dry seasons.

FAIRS, EXHIBITIONS AND SPECIAL EVENTS: In New York, probably not a day goes by that does not bring a dozen or more important and interesting events. The New York Convention and Visitors Bureau, 90 E. 42 St. & Park Avenue, issues a quarterly calendar of events as well as other folders, in various languages, which will be sent to you without charge. The following are typical of the various annual events: *January*—Chinese New Year Festival, Motor Boat show. *February*—track meets, Sportsmen's show, Kennel Club Dog Show. *March*—St. Patrick's Day Parade, track meets, basketball play-offs, Flower Show. *April*—opening of professional baseball season, Easter Sunday fashion parade, opening of horse racing season, Circus opening. *May*—outdoor art exhibition in Greenwich Village. *June to September*—"New York is a Summer Festival" season, with Lewisohn Stadium concerts, free performances of Shakespeare's plays in Central Park, fireworks, special concert, theatrical and sporting events. *October*—Philharmonic Symphony Orchestra season opens, and so does the Metropolitan Opera. *November*—various flower shows and exhibits, Thanksgiving Day Parade. *December*—lavish Christmas decorations and celebrations.

LIBRARIES ... The city's colleges and universities all have libraries; the *Columbia University Library* is one of the best. The *New York Public Library* system is extensive, its vast main building is at

42 St. and Fifth Ave., and there are many branches throughout the city. The main building of the *Brooklyn Public Library,* Grand Army Plaza, has a large collection and maintains foreign-language libraries at various of its branches. Other important libraries: *French Institute,* 22 E. 60 St.; *Frick Art Reference,* 10 E. 71 St.; *Goethe House,* 1014 Fifth Ave.

LIQUOR ... Bottled liquors may be purchased in liquor stores throughout the day and evening except Sunday. Liquor by the drink is served in restaurants, bars, cocktail lounges and night clubs, but not before 1 P.M. on Sundays.

NIGHT CLUBS ... Night-clubbing in New York can be fairly expensive, but it is rare to hear that anyone has been overcharged—unless you feel that the high prices are an overcharge to begin with. But there are also lots of unpretentious places where you can have a lot of fun for comparatively little money. Many of the important hotels have one or more rooms with music and dancing, although these are not night clubs in the strict meaning of the word.

Smart, expensive, not too large (some having dancing) *Bon Soir,* 40 W. Eighth St.; *Upstairs at the Downstairs* and *Downstairs at the Upstairs,* both at 37 W. 56 St.; *Little Club,* 70 E. 55 St.; *El Morocco,* 307 E. 54th St.

Music, modern style—*Hickory House,* 144 W. 52 St., good music played in an oval bar; *Eddie Condon's,* 330 E. 56 St., excellent musical improvisations; *Jimmy Ryan's,* 154 W. 54 St.; *Birdland,* Broadway at 52 St.; the *Round Table,* 151 E. 50 St.; *Village Vanguard,* 178 Seventh Ave.; *Village Gate,* 185 Thompson at Bleecker St.; *Bitter End* (coffeehouse), 147 Bleecker St.

Foreign atmosphere, moderately expensive—*Café Grinzing,* 323 E. 79 St., continental; *Café Tokay,* 1591 Second Ave.; *Chardas,* 309 E. 79 St., and *Viennese Lantern,* 242 E. 79th St., all Hungarian. *Chateau Madrid,* 42 W. 58 St., *El Chico,* 80 Grove St., both Latin American. *Two Guitars,* 244 E. 14 St., Russian; *La Chansonette,* 890 Second Ave., Parisian; *In Boboli,* Second Ave. at 82 St., and *Monsignore,* 61 E. 55 St., Italian.

Large and elaborate—*Latin Quarter,* 200 W. 48 St., long, elaborate floor show, continuous music, expensive; *Tavern-on-the-Green,* Central Park W. at 67 St., open-air dancing in good weather, fairly expensive; *Copacabana,* 14 E. 60 St., famous stars, showgirls; *International Theater Restaurant,* Broadway at 52 St., large with lavish floor show; *Basin Street East,* at 137 E. 48 St.

Much less expensive, but fun—*Roseland Ballroom,* 239 W. 52 St., highly respectable; *Peppermint Lounge,* 128 W. 45 St., birthplace of the Twist; *Open End,* 1471 First Ave. between 76 & 77 Sts., the Twist and everything since; *Gordian Knot,* York Ave. at 83 St., and *Red Onion* at Second Ave. and 82 St. are both very young and lively until 4 A.M.

For belly dancers and exotic Middle Eastern atmosphere—*Egyptian Gardens,* 301 W. 29 St.; *Port Said,* 257 W. 29 St.; *Britania,* 370 Eighth Ave.; *Arabian Nights,* 382 Eighth Ave.; *Afro-Caribbean re-*

vues at the *African Room*, 156 W. 44 St. For hearty German atmosphere, dancing and entertainment—*86th Street Brauhaus*, 249 E. 86 St.; *Platzl*, 225 E. 86 St.; *Student Prince*, 207 E. 86 St. Most of these places have no minimum charge on Tuesdays, Wednesday and Thursday evenings, and you can make one drink last a long time. Greenwich Village is full of coffeehouses where you'll find both genuine and phony Bohemian goings-on. Most of the popular Village night spots are clustered on Bleecker, MacDougal and Eighth streets.

PARKS, ZOOS AND GARDENS... *Battery Park*, lower Broadway at the Battery, Manhattan; *Botanical Gardens*, Bronx Park, Bronx; *Bronx Park and Zoo*, E. 180 St. and Boston Post Road, Bronx; *Brooklyn Botanical Gardens*, Flatbush Ave., Brooklyn; *Bryant Park*, 42 St. & Ave. of Americas, Manhattan; *Central Park and Central Park Children's Zoo*, 59 St. to 110 St. (zoo entrance at 64 St. and Fifth Ave.), Manhattan; *City Hall Park*, Broadway & Park Row, Manhattan; *Crotona Park*, Fulton Ave. & Claremont Pkwy., Bronx; *Fort Tryon Park*, 191 St. and Ft. Washington Ave., Manhattan; *Jacob Riis Park*, Rockaway, Queens; *Prospect Park*, Flatbush Ave. & Empire Blvd., Brooklyn; *Van Cortlandt Park*, Broadway & 242 St., Manhattan; *Washington Square Park*, Fifth Ave. & Fourth St., Manhattan.

POINTS OF INTEREST... *Airports* (La Guardia and John F. Kennedy Airport both have sightseeing decks); the *Bowery;* *Bronx Zoo* and *Botanical Gardens;* *Cathedral of St. John the Divine;* *Central Park* and its zoo; *City Hall* district and the *Foley Square* courthouse area; the *Cloisters* and *Fort Tryon Park;* *Chinatown;* *Columbia University;* *Coney Island;* the view from the top of the *Empire State Building;* *Grand Central Terminal;* *Grant's Tomb;* *Greenwich Village;* *Hayden Planetarium;* *Lincoln Center* (guided tours), *Little Italy* (Mulberry Street); *Port Authority Bus Terminal;* *Riverside Church;* *Rockefeller Center;* *St. Patrick's Cathedral;* *Shops and stores* from 34 St. and Seventh Ave. to Fifth Ave., and on up Fifth to 60 St. and avenues east of it; *Statue of Liberty* and *New York Harbor;* *Stuyvesant Town* and *Peter Cooper Village* (huge housing developments); *Times Square district;* *United Nations;* *Wall Street* district and the *Stock Exchange* (open to the public weekdays 10-3); *Washington Square* and *Washington Arch.* No trip to New York is complete without a visit to *Radio City Music Hall*, for which even resident New Yorkers queue up to see top-notch movies and magnificent stage shows featuring the world-famous precision dancing of the *Rockettes.*

Typical tours—There are daily boat rides around Manhattan Island for $2.75. During spring, summer and fall, the *Hudson River Day Line* has, for about $4, 1-day boat trips to Bear Mountain, West Point Military Academy, Poughkeepsie. A helicopter ride over New York with New York Airways costs about $5. For details, see the daily newspapers. A typical 2-hour bus tour of either lower or upper Manhattan costs $4-$4.50; a 4-hour combined tour is $5.50-$6.50. For only 5¢ you can take the interesting ferry ride from lower Manhattan to Staten Island.

In Brooklyn—Be sure to visit the *Brooklyn Botanical Gardens*,

Brooklyn Museum, Children's Museum, Prospect Park and Zoo.

In the Bronx—*City Island* and its yachting facilities, *Botanical Gardens, Bronx Zoo* (outstanding collection), *New York University* and the *Hall of Fame, Edgar Allan Poe Cottage.*

RESTAURANTS... New York is one of the great restaurant cities of the world. Dining out can be a very enjoyable occasion, whether expensive or economical. If you are going to one of the better-known (and expensive) places, a telephoned reservation made earlier in the day will facilitate your getting a table upon arrival. Should you be going to the theater, it is advisable to begin dinner no later than 6:30 or 7, and allow ample time to get from the restaurant to the theater, as traffic is heavy at the theater hour. In the following list, "reasonable" means $3 or less per person for dinner; "moderate" means from $3-$6; "expensive" means $6 or more. Very expensive restaurants average more than $8 per person. This list is only a sampling, to illustrate the wide choice available:

Seafood (moderate)—*Fisherman's Net,* 493 Third Ave.; *Grand Central Oyster Bar,* Grand Central Terminal; *Harvey's Seafood House,* 509 Third Ave., *King of the Sea,* 879 Third Ave., *Sea Fare,* 25 W. 56 St., also at 44 W. Eighth St., *Sweet's,* 2 Fulton St.

Steaks (expensive)—*Black Angus,* 148 E. 50 St.; *Cavanagh's,* 256 W. 23 St.; *Christ Cella,* 160 E. 46 St.; *Danny's Hide-A-Way,* 151 E. 45 St.; *Gallagher's,* 228 W. 52 St.; *Hickory House,* 144 W. 52 St.; *Keen's* 72 W. 36 St.; *McCarthy's Steak House,* 839 Second Ave.; *Old Homestead,* 56 Ninth Ave.; *Pen and Pencil,* 205 E. 45 St.; *Peter's Backyard,* 64 W. 10 St.; *Press Box,* 139 E. 45 St.; *Al Schacht's,* 102 E. 52 St.; *Steak Joint,* 58 Greenwich Ave.; *Toots Shor's,* 33 W. 52 St.

American Specialties (moderate)—*Hearthstone,* 102 E. 22 St.; *Patricia Murphy,* 260 Madison Ave., 12 E. 49 St.; *Stouffer's,* 100 E. 42 St.; *666 Fifth Ave.,* and under same management, atop the 666 building, "Top of the Sixes," with a fine view of the city; *Longchamps,* with 11 convenient locations in Manhattan; *Schrafft's,* with 29 locations.

Broadway and Theatrical Atmosphere (moderate to expensive)—*Lindy's,* 1655 Broadway; *Reuben's,* 6 E. 58 St.; *Sardi's,* 234 W. 44 St.; and *Sardi's East* at 123 E. 54 St.

Elaborate Decor and Menu (very expensive)—*Forum of the Twelve Caesars,* 57 W. 48 St.; *Four Seasons,* 375 Park Ave.; *La Fonda del Sol,* 123 W. 50 St.; *The Tower Suite,* 101 W. 50 St. (atop *Time-Life* Building with magnificent view).

Leading French Restaurants (very expensive)—*Baroque,* 14 E. 53 St.; *Brussels,* 115 E. 54 St.; *Chateaubriand,* 131 E. 54 St.; *Café Chauveron,* 139 E. 53 St.; *Colony,* 30 E. 61 St.; *L'Armorique,* Second Ave. at 54 St.; *Passy,* 28 E. 63 St.; *Pavillon,* 111 E. 57 St.; *Quo Vadis,* 26 E. 63 St.; *Twenty-One,* 21 W. 52 St.; *Voisin,* 30 E. 65 St.; *Charles V,* 34 W. 53 St.; *Les Pyrénées,* 251 W. 51 St.; *King Henri IV,* 142 E. 53 St.; *Maud Chez Elle,* 40 W. 53 St.

Other Foreign Restaurants (mostly reasonable to moderate)—
Armenian: *Golden Horn,* 122 W. 49 St.; *Balkan Armenian Res-*

taurant, 129 E. 27 St.; *Palace d'Orient,* 108 Lexington Ave.

Austrian: *Hapsburg House,* 313 E. 55 St.; *Viennese Lantern,* 242 E. 79 St.; *Wienerwald,* Park Ave. at 49 St.

Chinese: Some of the best-known are *Ho-Ho,* 789 Seventh Ave.; *House of Chan,* 52 & Seventh Ave.; *Ruby Foo's,* 240 W. 52 St.; *Sun Luck,* 143 W. 49 St., 157 W. 49 St., 935 Lexington Ave. and 75 E. 55 St.; *Lee's,* 36 Pell St.; *Peking,* 845 Second Ave.; *Gold Coin,* 994 Second Ave.; *Mandarin House,* 133 W. 13 St.

Czechoslovakian: *Bohemian National Hall,* 321 E. 73 St.

Danish: *Copenhagen,* 68 W. 58 St.

Dutch: *Holland House Taverne,* 10 Rockefeller Plaza.

French: *Le Bistro,* 827 Third Ave.; *Brittany,* 800 Ninth Ave.; *Le Moal,* 942 Third Ave.; *La Toque Blanche,* 359 E. 50 St.; *Veau d'Or,* 129 E. 60 St.; *Café du Soir,* 241 E. 86 St.; *Au Tunnel,* 306 W. 48 St.; *Du Midi,* 311 W. 48 St.

German: *Lüchow's,* 110 E. 14 St.; *Janssen's Hofbrau,* 430 Lexington Ave.; *Brauhaus,* 249 E. 86 St.; *Café Geiger,* 206 E. 86 St. There are many other good ones in the Yorkville area around and on 86 St.

Greek: *Pantheon,* 689 Eighth Ave.; *Britania,* 370 Eighth Ave.

Hungarian: *Chardas,* 309 E. 79 St.; *Tik Tak,* Second Ave. at 77 St.; *Emke,* 1494 Second Ave.

Indian-Pakistani: *Koh-i-noor,* 60 Second Ave.; *Pakistan India,* 183 Lexington Ave.; *Karachi,* 144 W. 46 St.; *Taj Mahal,* 216 E. 49 St.

Irish: *Shine's,* 426 Seventh Ave.

Italian: (expensive) *Angelo's,* 146 Mulberry St.; *Grotta Azzurra,* 387 Broome St.; *Mama Laura,* 230 E. 58 St.; *Romeo Salta,* 39 W. 56 St.; *Giovanni's,* 66 E. 55 St.; *Italian Pavilion,* 24 W. 55 St.; *San Marino,* 236 E. 53 St.; *Fontana de Trevi,* 151 W. 57 St.

Italian (moderate): *Gino,* 780 Lexington Ave.; *Leone's,* 239 W. 48 St.; *Red Devil,* 111 W. 48 St.; *Vesuvio,* 163 W. 48 St.; *Mimi's,* 161 E. 53 St.; *Luigino's Pizzeria Alla Napolitana,* 147 W. 48 St.; *Villa Doria,* 1460 Second Ave. and many others.

Japanese: *Miyako,* 20 W. 56 St.; *Saito,* 131 W. 52 St.; *Suehiro,* 35 E. 29 St.; *Tokyo Sukiyaki House,* 144 W. 55 St.

Jewish (Kosher): *Gluckstern's East Side Restaurant,* 135 Delancey St.; *Phil Gluckstern's,* 209 W. 48 St.; *Moskowitz and Lupowitz,* 40 Second Ave. Among good Jewish Dairy Restaurants are *Rapoports* at 93 Second Ave.; *Ratner's* at 111 Second Ave. and 138 Delancey St.; and *Steinberg's* at 2270 Broadway.

Korean: *Arirang House,* 30 W. 56 St.

Mexican: *Alamo,* 139 W. 47 St.; *El Charro,* 4 Charles St.; *Xochitl,* 146 W. 46 St.; *Kiko's,* 106 W. 43 St.; *El Paradore,* 561 2nd Ave.

Middle Eastern: *Baghdad,* 4 W. 28 St.; *Damascus Gardens,* 18 W. 31 St.; *Sheik,* 132 Lexington Ave.; *Mecca,* 6 E. 30 St.; *Cedars of Lebanon,* 39 E. 30 St.

Polynesian: *Tiki Village,* 59 E. 56 St.; *Luau,* 400 E. 57 St.

Russian: *Russian Bear,* 139 E. 56 St.; *Russian Tea Room,* 150 W. 57 St.; *Petroushka,* 23 E. 74 St.

Spanish: *Fornos* (also Mexican), 236 W. 52 St.; *Café Madrid,* 207

W. 14 St.; *Café Valencia,* 245 W. 14 St.; *Jai-Alai,* 82 Bank St.; *Sevilla,* 62 Charles St.; *Liborio's,* 150 W. 47 St.; *Fundador,* 117 W. 47 St.

Swedish: *Gripsholm,* 324 E. 57 St.; *Three Crowns,* 12 E. 54 St.; *Red Brick,* 212 E. 53 St.; *Stockholm,* 151 W. 51 St.

Swiss: *Swiss Pavilion,* 38 E. 50; *Chalet Suisse,* 45 W. 52 St.

See also the Manhattan classified directory *Yellow Pages* for a Restaurant Guide by nationalities, and *Visitors New York Restaurant Guide,* free from the New York Convention and Visitors Bureau, 90 E. 42 St.

For greatest economy and down-to-earth New York gastronomy, join the hundreds of thousands who dine quickly and cheaply in such famous chain restaurants as *Horn and Hardart Automats, Bickfords, Riker's, Chock Full O'Nuts, Nedick's, White Tower.*

SPECTATOR SPORTS . . . New York has two professional baseball teams—the *New York Yankees* of the American League (*Yankee Stadium,* River Ave. & 161 St.) and the *New York Mets* of the National League (new *Shea Stadium*). The baseball season is April through September; games start at 1:30 or 2 P.M., and there are also night games (8 P.M.) under artificial lights. Double-headers (two games for the price of one) are scheduled irregularly; details appear in local papers several days in advance. The *Columbia University Lions* play collegiate football at *Baker Field.* The nearest other important college games are played by Yale in New Haven, Conn., and by the University of Pennsylvania in Philadelphia, Pa. The *New York Giants* and *Jets* are the city's professional football teams. The *International Soccer League Tournament* includes the best clubs of 14 different nations competing in soccer games from mid-May to August at *Downing Stadium,* Randalls Island. During the winter, both college and professional basketball games may be seen, most often at *Madison Square Garden.* Ice-hockey matches feature the *New York Rangers.* Horse racing begins in March and ends in November at *Aqueduct* race track, fairly close to Manhattan. During August, however, most of the racing fraternity moves to Saratoga in upstate New York. Trotting races are held at *Roosevelt Raceway* and *Yonkers Raceway* during the summer, evenings only. Championship tennis matches are played at the *West Side Tennis Club* in Forest Hills, Queens. In the course of the year it is possible to attend many boxing and wrestling matches and, in fact, just about every conceivable type of sporting event. Details in the sports pages of the daily newspapers.

TELEVISION . . . Free tickets to shows can be obtained by writing to the broadcasting companies; write as far in advance as possible. Hotels often have tickets, too, which they give to guests. The local stations are: Channel 2—WCBS-TV (Columbia Broadcasting System); Channel 4—WNBC-TV (National Broadcasting Company), Channel 7—WABC-TV (American Broadcasting Company); Channel 11—WPIX (independently owned by *Daily News*); Channel 13 —WNTA-TV (educational).

THEATERS . . . In New York this means the legitimate theater as opposed to motion pictures. To get seats, of which there never seem to be enough for the hit shows, first try the box office of the theater (shows are listed in the newspapers, *The New Yorker* and *Cue*). If "sold out," try a theater ticket broker; he sells tickets at box-office price plus $1.65 service charge, plus tax for each ticket. If you know what shows you want to see before you come to New York, write in advance to the box office of the theater, offering at least 3 choices of dates (for details, get a New York newspaper or *The New Yorker* magazine in your home town); enclose your check or money order and a self-addressed, stamped envelope. The Off-Broadway theater movement has grown tremendously and offers easier-to-obtain seats at generally lower prices. These theaters often have Sunday performances, too.

SOURCES OF FURTHER INFORMATION ... New York Convention and Visitors Bureau, 90 E. 42 St.; open 9 A.M. to 6 P.M. every day of the year; answers questions and supplies maps and folders in various languages. Or call JU2-5555 (new Cultural Information Center) for word of artistic events. Other sources are: State Dept. of Commerce, 230 Park Ave.; Dept. of Public Events, 250 Broadway; Chamber of Commerce of the State of New York, 65 Liberty St.; Commerce and Industry Association of New York, 99 Church St.

Pan American World Airways offices in the new Pan Am Building, 200 Park Ave.; 120 Broadway; Fifth Avenue & 48 St.; 645 First Ave. (Airlines Terminal Building); 200 Livingston St. (Brooklyn); 512 Willis Ave. (Bronx). The telephone number is 973-7700 for all offices.

BOSTON, MASSACHUSETTS ... This state capital is in the eastern part of Massachusetts on the Mystic and Charles Rivers and the Atlantic Ocean. The older sections of the city have an old-world atmosphere with crooked, narrow streets (the mood sometimes broken by gasoline stations and parking lots), and many European visitors find Boston more appealing than any other U.S. city. Its cultural and historical backgrounds give Boston a major role in the American heritage.

POPULATION AND SIZE ... Population 700,000. In the greater metropolitan area, about 2,600,000 (including 83 separate towns and cities). City area is 43.18 square miles.

ACCOMMODATIONS ... The *Sheraton-Boston,* opened in April of 1965, was the city's first major hotel to be built in 38 years. Free parking in basement garage; indoor pool and health-club facilities; 3 ballrooms; 5 restaurants; 17 conference rooms; covered access to huge new War Memorial Auditorium; single rates from $12, double from $19, tower suites $36. Long-established Boston hotels include the *Ritz Carlton,* single from $12, double from $21; distinguished hotel with excellent accommodations. *Sheraton Plaza,* single from $11.75, double from $16.25; very good, at Copley Square in newer part of city. *Statler Hilton,* single from $14, double from $19.50; very large, busy, convention center. *Beaconsfield,* single from $9, double from $15; in a residential area. *Bradford,* single from $8.50, double from $12; busy, well located. *Kenmore,* single from $12, double from $17; very good, all rooms with TV. *Parker House,* single from $9, double from $14; centrally located, well known. *Somerset,* single from $10, double from $16; excellent, partly residential. The *Copley Square* and *Lenox,* both at Prudential Center, have rates from about $10 single, $14 double. *1200 Beacon Street Motel,* single from $10.50, double from $15. *Midtown Motor Inn,* single from $11, double from $16. *Charterhouse Motor Hotel* in Cambridge, single from $11.50, double from $17.50.

ARTS...*Museum of Fine Arts,* Roman, Greek, Oriental and Near East art objects; open daily except Monday, 10-5, Sunday, 1:30-5:30; free. *Institute of Contemporary Art,* open daily except Monday, 10-5, Sunday 2-6; admission 25¢. *Isabella Stewart Gardner Museum,* classic art, furniture in an Italian villa setting; open Tuesday, Thursday, Saturday 10-4, Sunday 2-5; closed August and holidays; free. *Children's Museum,* natural history exhibits; open daily except Monday, 9-5, Sunday 2-5; free. *Children's Art Center,* contemporary art, children's programs; open daily 9-5, Sunday 9-noon; closed July and August; free. *Museum of Science,* scientific exhibits; open Tuesday through Saturday 10-5, Sunday 1-5; admission 50¢ for museum, 50¢ for planetarium. The *Forbes House,* in suburban Milton, is an unusual museum of memorabilia from the great days of clipper trade with China; open Wednesday and Saturday 2-5; adults 50¢, children 25¢. The *Boston Festival of Arts* is held every summer from mid-June to mid-July; admission free.

The *Boston Symphony Orchestra,* one of the world's leading orchestral groups, performs during the winter, when there are also concerts by other groups, opera and ballet. The Boston "Pops" orchestra plays during May and June. There are Esplanade concerts outdoors at Hatch Memorial Shell during July and August; free.

CLIMATE...Rain is fairly evenly distributed throughout the year. Snowfall is quite heavy, averaging 42 inches, most of it falling from January to March. Winters are quite cold and damp. There are hot summer days, but temperatures drop at night. Spring and fall are the best seasons.

FAIRS, EXHIBITIONS AND SPECIAL EVENTS...*Poultry Show,* January; *Dog Show,* February; *Flower Show,* March; *Boston Arts Festival,* June-July; *Christmas Festival,* December.

LIBRARIES...Most important are the *Boston Public Library, Kirstein Business Library, Boston Medical Library, New England Historical and Genealogical Library, Social Law Library, Boston Athenaeum, State Library, Horticultural Hall, Zion Research Library, Bible Research Library* and *Creagh Research Library. Harvard University Library* in Cambridge is world-famous.

LIQUOR...Drinks are served in restaurants or hotels from 8 A.M. to 1 A.M. daily, except Saturday when the closing hour is midnight; Sunday from 1 P.M. to 1 A.M. Bottled liquor is sold in shops from 8 A.M. to 11 P.M. on weekdays. Taverns are open from 8 A.M. to midnight daily except Sunday; women may not be served.

NIGHT CLUBS...Dinner dancing at hotels *Sheraton-Boston, Bradford, Somerset* (in summer), and *Statler Hilton;* all fairly expensive.

PARKS, ZOOS, AQUARIUMS AND GARDENS...*Franklin Park* has rose gardens, golf course, woodland walk. *Boston Common,* laid out in 1634, is especially pleasant in summer. *Boston Public Garden,* next to the Common, has a pond with swanboats (great favorites with children) and good floral displays. *Arnold Arboretum* is known for its fine plants and trees. *Isabella Stewart Gardner Museum* has a Venetian garden with changing floral displays.

POINTS OF INTEREST...Most visitors enjoy wandering along the *Freedom Trail,* a marked walking tour of about 1¼ miles through historic Old Boston (starting point opposite the State House; allow about 2 hours) to see the Boston Common, Park St. Church and King's Chapel, Granary Burying Ground, City Hall, Old South Meeting House, Old State House, Faneuil Hall (often called the "Cradle of Liberty"), Paul Revere's House, Old North Church and Copp's Hill Burying Ground. Also of historical interest are the Bunker Hill Monument; "Old Ironsides"—the *U.S.S. Constitution*—on view daily in the Boston Navy Yard, 10-4; the impressive Christian Science Mother Church; and the *Mapparium,* a huge hollow replica of the world in the Christian Science Publishing House; the exciting new *City Hall* and complex of buildings in *Government Center.* In nearby Cambridge is *Harvard University,* founded in 1636, famed for its great libraries and the controversial new Le Corbusier art building. See, too, the *Fogg Art Museum,* the *Busch-Reisinger Museum,* and the *Harvard University Museum.* Also in Cambridge is the Henry Wadsworth Longfellow House, which is open to the public.

RESTAURANTS...*Durgin-Park,* hearty New England fare served family style, moderate; *Locke-Ober,* old and excellent, expensive; *Joseph's,* French cuisine, very good, expensive; *Jimmie's Harbor Side, Anthony's Pier Four* and *Yankee Fisherman,* seafood, expensive. More moderate-priced restaurants—*Jake Wirth's,* German dishes; *Red Coach Grill* and *Dinty Moore's,* steaks and lobsters. For such typical New England dishes as baked beans and brown bread, codfish balls, Indian pudding and New England boiled dinner, try *Patten's* and *Purcell's.* Fine seafood at *Pieroni's Sea Grill, Union Oyster House* (three locations), *Warmuth's* and the *Lobster House.* Fine Chinese restaurants around Hudson and Tyler streets; Italian ones in the North End; French in Back Bay and Cambridge.

SPECTATOR SPORTS...There is horse racing at *Suffolk Downs* from April to June, and dog racing at *Wonderland Dog Track* in Revere, May through early September. Professional baseball is played by the *Boston Red Sox* of the American League, basketball by the *Celtics,* football by the *Patriots,* and ice hockey by the *Boston Bruins.* There is also a wide choice of collegiate athletic events.

THEATERS...Broadway productions are presented at the *Shubert, Wilbur* and *Colonial* theaters; provocative Off Broadway dramas at *Charles Playhouse* and Harvard's *Loeb Drama Center.* Summer playhouses within easy reach of Boston are at Cohasset, Framingham, Beverly, Holyoke, Martha's Vineyard, Marblehead, Plymouth, Hyannis and Dennis.

SOURCES OF FURTHER INFORMATION ... Greater Boston Chamber of Commerce, 125 High Street, for maps, folders and tourist information. New England Council, Statler Office Building, Park Square, for information on the New England Area. Pan American Airways, 100 Federal Street (Tel. HU 2-6910).

MIAMI AND MIAMI BEACH, FLORIDA ... Miami is in southeastern Florida on Biscayne Bay. Miami Beach, 3½ miles to the east, is on the Atlantic Ocean and is the country's most fabulous winter resort, with over 8 miles of sandy, ocean beach-front lined with hotels. Stores and hotels have Spanish-speaking personnel for the convenience of the many Latin American visitors.

POPULATION AND SIZE ... The Miami area's permanent population is now estimated at over 1,000,000, including the communities and municipalities within a radius of 35 miles of the center of the city of Miami.

ACCOMMODATIONS ... There are over 500 hotels in metropolitan Miami. Rates are seasonal, particularly in Miami Beach, with the highest rates prevailing from December through April; February is the height of the season. After the winter months, rates drop gradually until they are at their lowest in July and August. It is not unusual for a $40-room to cost $10 off-season. Commercial hotels in Miami's business district, however, raise rates only about $3 to $6 during the December 15 to April 15 season. These include the *Du Pont Plaza, Biscayne Terrace, Columbus, Everglades* and *McAllister.* The *International Airport Hotel* is conveniently set right on top of Miami's air terminal. Key Biscayne, reached by the Rickenbacker Causeway, combines luxury and convenience with the feeling of being on a "remote" Atlantic island. The *Key Biscayne Hotel and Villas* is an outstanding resort on the island. There are also many "efficiency apartments" with small kitchens, convenient for extended visits. In view of the vast number of places to stay, it is impossible to list them here. The Miami Beach Chamber of Commerce will furnish information and rates on request.

ARTS ... The new *Bass Museum of Art* on Collins Avenue, Miami Beach; open Tuesday-Saturday 10-11:30 and 1-5; Sunday 1-5; free in the mornings, 50¢ afternoons. *Lowe Art Gallery,* on University of Miami campus; exhibits of sculptures and paintings. *Villa Vizcaya,* the old Deering estate, has art collections; tours through the buildings and gardens; open daily 10-5; adult admission $1.25, children 50¢.

CLIMATE ... Miami is subtropical. The winters are mild, although there are occasional cold days. Most days are clear, and fogs are rare. Rainfall may be expected during the summer and autumn. Humidity is high during early morning, but drops during the afternoon. The prevailing wind is from the southeast and ranges from

Within less than 50 years, Miami Beach has changed from a desolate mangrove swamp to one of the world's most glamorous resorts.

8 to 15 miles per hour.

FAIRS, EXHIBITIONS AND SPECIAL EVENTS...*Orange Bowl Festival,* parade and football game, January 1; *Flower Show,* March; *Pan American Week,* April; *Poinciana Festival,* early June; *Miss Universe Pageant,* mid-July; the famous Metropolitan Miami Fishing Tournament, open to everyone, runs from mid-December to mid-April. Numerous conventions throughout the year and, in winter, several major television programs are broadcast nationwide from Miami Beach.

LIQUOR...Dade County, in which Miami is located, permits the sale of liquor in package stores, which are open until 8 P.M. daily except Sunday. Bars and restaurants serve liquor until 1 A.M. or up to 5 A.M., depending upon individual licenses.

NIGHT CLUBS...All offer food, drinks, dancing and entertainment, but places of this kind are very impermanent, as ownership and popularity with clientele change frequently. Check advertisements in Miami newspapers. During the winter, well-known personalities make appearances. Many of the ocean-front hotels on Miami Beach have their own night clubs featuring world-famous entertainers.

PARKS, ZOOS, AQUARIUMS AND GARDENS...Outstanding gardens and plant displays may be seen at *Fairchild Tropical Garden* near Coral Gables, in *Everglades National Park* and at *Bayfront Park Sunken Gardens;* rare and exotic vegetation of all kinds. In the vicinity of Miami are the *Seaquarium, Parrot Jungle, Miami Serpentarium, Tropical Paradise* and *Monkey Jungle.* All have interesting exhibits; admission charges range from $1.50 to $2.20. *Crandon Park,* with its fine zoo, and *Bakers Haulover* are two of several county parks.

POINTS OF INTEREST . . . The hotels along the beach are really something to see. Walk through *Lincoln Mall* with its luxurious shops. Don't miss seeing the causeways connecting Miami Beach with the mainland. *Hialeah Park Race Track* with its pink flamingos; *Miami Marine Stadium;* the *Wax Museum; Vizcaya; University of Miami* campus; Miami's *Biscayne Boulevard; Venetian Pool; Tropical Park Race Track.* Wally's Motor Coach Lines and the Gray Line have regular conducted sightseeing tours of Miami and vicinity. A typical 4-hour tour costs $4.25. Boat trips around Miami offer a different view of the many beautiful homes. Blimp and helicopter trips are also available. If time permits, drive (or take a Greyhound Bus) on the *Overseas Highway* to Key West, a 3-hour trip, part of which is across the world's longest over-water road. Key West is delightfully quaint in atmosphere. Or go to the west coast of Florida on the *Tamiami Trail,* an extraordinarily straight road. A one-day trip to Hollywood Beach, Fort Lauderdale and Palm Beach is interesting, too.

RESTAURANTS . . . Among many in Miami: *El Centro* at the McAllister; *Top O' The Columbus* at the Columbus; *Red Coach Grill,* steaks and lobster, moderate to expensive. On Miami Beach: *Joe's Stone Crab,* good for seafood, expensive. For steaks, *Chandler's, The Embers;* excellent, expensive. *Lighthouse,* seafood; moderate to expensive. *Gatti's,* Italian; expensive. *Wolfie's* features delicatessen, sandwiches, cheesecake, Danish pastry; moderate to expensive. Good, reasonably priced meals may be had at *Curry's* and *Grandma's Kitchen.* Other reasonable places are *Gallagher's Steaks, Hurricane Harbor Lounge, New England Oyster House, Cupboard Steak House* and *St. Clair's Cafeterias.* In general, meals in the Miami Beach area are fairly expensive, especially during the winter months, and service is apt to be slow unless you eat early or after 8:30 P.M. when the rush has slacked off.

SPECTATOR SPORTS . . . Professional big-league baseball during the training season in March; boxing and wrestling events are scheduled throughout the year; golf exhibitions during winter months; football games are played by the University of Miami usually on Friday evenings in autumn; *Orange Bowl Game* on New Year's Day; jai-alai games are fast and furious; dog and horse racing are Miami's major attractions.

THEATERS . . . There are several theater groups at the University of Miami. During the winter, professional performances in Miami Beach and at the *Coconut Grove Playhouse.*

SOURCES OF FURTHER INFORMATION . . . Miami-Dade County Chamber of Commerce, 300 Biscayne Blvd.; Miami Beach Chamber of Commerce and Coral Gables Chamber of Commerce for questions about accommodations or tourism. Florida Development Commission, Tallahassee, Florida, for general information on industry and commerce. Pan American Airways, 2 Biscayne Boulevard, (Tel. NE 4-5444). *El Centro Club,* McAllister Hotel, has a Spanish-speaking information center.

NEW ORLEANS, LOUISIANA ... In southeastern Louisiana on the Mississippi River, New Orleans is about 60 miles north of the Gulf of Mexico. This romantic old city is famous for the graceful architecture in its *Vieux Carré* (Old French Quarter), its Creole cuisine and fine restaurants, its night clubs and Dixieland jazz.

POPULATION AND SIZE ... 665,300 people in the city itself; 1,000,482 in the metropolitan area, which extends over 199 square miles of land and 164 square miles of water.

ACCOMMODATIONS ... *Roosevelt,* single from $11, double from $13; a leading hotel, convention headquarters. *Sheraton-Charles,* single from $7.50, double from $11.50, comfortable, well-located. *Royal Orleans,* single from $8, double from $18; newest luxury hotel, located in the heart of the French Quarter. *Monteleone,* single from $9, double from $12; old, comfortable, French Quarter atmosphere. *Jung,* single from $8, double from $12; first class, slightly out of business district. *Pontchartrain,* single from $9, double from $14; residential and transient, 1½ miles from midtown. *Maison de Ville,* single from $15, double from $18.50; rates include continental breakfast; small and in French Quarter. *De Ville,* single from $8.50, double from $12.50; comfortable hotel-motel, about 2 miles from midtown. *Hilton Inn,* single from $12, double from $16; at Moisant Airport; swimming pool; kennels for pets. *Prince Conti,* single from $16, double from $20; small and in French Quarter; rates include continental breakfast. Also in French Quarter, *Provincial Motel,* single from $12, double $14; small; and *Chateau Motor Hotel,* same rates. Most hotels have French and Spanish-speaking personnel; all hotels are air-conditioned.

ARTS ... *Delgado Museum of Art,* especially fine Renaissance displays; open Tuesday through Saturday 12-5, Sunday 1-6; free. *Institute of Middle-American Research* at Tulane University, Mayan relics; open Monday-Friday 9-4; free. *New Orleans Jazz Museum,* open daily 10-5; admission 25¢. The New Orleans Philharmonic Symphony Orchestra performs at the *Municipal Auditorium,* October through April. *Musée Conti* is a particularly fine wax museum in the French Quarter where life-size figures dramatically portray events through 300 years of local history.

CLIMATE ... The best months are October, November, February, March and April. During the winter the weather varies from warm and mild to chilly, but it is seldom really cold. New Orleans has a heavy rainfall, heaviest from March through September. Summer months are hot and humid, followed by windy weather in the autumn.

FAIRS, EXHIBITIONS AND SPECIAL EVENTS ... *Sugar Bowl Football Game,* January 1; *Mardi Gras,* pre-Lenten celebration, the year's most important event; *Spring Fiesta,* April; *South Louisiana State Fair,* at Donaldsonville (40 miles from New Orleans), in the spring; *Cajun Pirogue Derby,* at LaFitte (26 miles from New Orleans), in May.

LIQUOR ... Can be bought at practically any hour, and is also sold in drugstores which have liquor licenses.

NIGHT CLUBS ... Dining, dancing and floor shows in most of the larger hotels. In the French Quarter the night clubs offer extremely informal entertainment, much of it rough-and-ready and not suited to all tastes; most places come to life about midnight. Best known are: *Old Absinthe Bar, Al Hirt, Famous Door, Jazz, Ltd., French Quarter Inn* (with Pete Fountain and his jazz clarinet), *Paddock*—all feature Dixieland jazz. Walk down Bourbon Street; it's famous for its honky-tonks, but you'll have to use your own judgment. Some are interesting, others are just joints. Don't miss *Dixieland Hall* and *Preservation Hall;* neither serves liquor but both feature jazz right out of this world.

PARKS, ZOOS, AQUARIUMS AND GARDENS ... *City Park* has a huge area with three public golf courses, many amusement and recreational facilities. *Audubon Park* has a zoo, aquarium, golf course, attractive grounds. There is a lively amusement center at *Pontchartrain Beach.*

POINTS OF INTEREST ... Undoubtedly the greatest attraction for tourists is the *Vieux Carré,* the Old French Quarter which still looks much as it did 170 years ago. Streets are narrow, buildings are laced with exquisite wrought-iron balconies and railings, and there are lovely patios and courtyards. Wandering through here on your own can be delightful. Royal Street, with its enticing antique shops, is the main street of the old quarter. Bourbon Street is at its best at night. See the *Cabildo,* erected in 1795, scene of the signing of the Louisiana Purchase and today housing the Louisiana State Museum; *St. Louis Basilica,* built in 1794; *Pontalba Apartments,* lovely Creole buildings reputed to be the first apartment housing in the U.S.; *Absinthe House,* former haunt of pirate-patriots, a bar-restaurant in business since 1806; new *Civic Center,* including City Hall, State Office Building, State Supreme Court and Civil Courts Buildings, and the Main Public Library, covering 14 acres in the central business district; the old *French Market.* Other interesting spots are the *International Trade Mart* (the "Buying Crossroads of the Hemisphere"); French cemeteries; *Ursuline Convent,* dating from 1734; *U.S. Customs House.* There are many conducted tours of New Orleans; a typical 2-hour tour costs $2.75; a 4½-hour night-life tour costs about $5.50. There are also horse-drawn carriages for hire, and boat trips on the Mississippi—a 2½ hour trip for about $3. Take the *Mark Twain* sternwheeler through historic bayous where Jean Lafitte and his buccaneers used to headquarter; daily tour leaves at 11 A.M., returns at 4 P.M.; adults $6, children $3.

RESTAURANTS ... Only New York and San Francisco can rival New Orleans for fine restaurants. Seafood, particularly shrimp, oysters and crabs, is renowned; local fish such as pompano, trout and redfish are superb. Famous New Orleans dishes include oysters Rockefeller (baked with a spinach-herb mixture), pecan pralines, gumbo soups thick with okra, and *café brûlot* (black coffee flavored with spices and ignited with brandy). French Quarter restaurants: *Antoine's,* most famous of all, exceptional food, expensive; *Arnaud's,* outstanding, many fine specialties, moderate-expensive; *Broussard,* good French and American food, outdoor patio, moderate; *Brennan's French Restaurant,* French, Creole and American food, famous for its great breakfasts, expensive; *Galatoire's,* wonderful crabmeat dishes, moderate-expensive; *Kolb's* (just out of French Quarter), German specialties, moderate; *Maylie's,* crab stews and boiled beef, moderate. In the Garden District; *Commander's Palace,* noted for steaks and crab imperial, patio, moderate; *Corinne Dunbar's,* luxurious home atmosphere, advance reservations essential (Tel. JA 5-2957), expensive. Near the lake, *Masson's Beach House,* very good French food, expensive. *Bali Hai,* at Pontchartrain beach park, specializes in Cantonese and Polynesian dishes, expensive. After a big night on the town, everyone in New Orleans goes to *Morning Call* in the French Quarter for probably the world's best coffee and doughnuts; open continuously.

SPECTATOR SPORTS... Horse racing at the *Fair Grounds* from Thanksgiving to March, daily except Sunday; night racing at *Jefferson Downs* from March to May, and again from September to November. College football, basketball and other sports.

SOURCES OF FURTHER INFORMATION... New Orleans Tourist Commission, 400 Royal St., booklets for tourists, business information. International House, 607 Gravier St., business information. Pan American Airways, 709 Common Street (Tel. 522-6391).

DALLAS, TEXAS... Dallas is in northeastern Texas on the Trinity River. It is a city known for its vigorous economic, civic and cultural interests, for its dynamic and pervasive personality and, not least, for its attractive, well-dressed citizens.

POPULATION AND SIZE... 1,083,601 in the metropolitan area. City area is 289 square miles; 808,400 population within the corporate limits.

ACCOMMODATIONS... *Sheraton-Dallas,* single from $11, double from $15.50; excellent hotel, drive-in garage. *Statler-Hilton,* single $10-$13, double $15.50-$18; dancing and floor shows in the Empire Room. *Adolphus,* single $7-$12, double $10-$16; popular, centrally located, pets allowed. *Baker,* single $5.50-$11, double $9.50-$13; drive-in motor lobby, centrally located. *Holiday Inn Central,* single, $8.50-$12.50, double $12.50-$16; *Cabana Motor Hotel,* single $12-$14; double $16-$18; *Marriott Motor Hotel,* single from $10, double from $13. The *Holiday Inn* (airport), *Executive Inn* and the *Ramada Inn* are all near Love Field Airport.

ARTS... *Dallas Museum of Fine Arts,* in Fair Park; large collection of paintings and sculptures, Southwestern and international; open 10-5 Tuesday through Saturday, 2-6 Sunday. *Hall of State* contains exhibits of Dallas and Texas folklore and historical collections; open 9-5 Monday through Saturday, 2-6 Sundays and holidays. The *Dallas Symphony* presents over 30 home concerts a year, often with outstanding guest artists.

CLIMATE... Winters are usually mild, with an annual snowfall of only 2.8 inches. Summer temperatures are high, with very low humidity.

FAIRS, EXHIBITIONS AND SPECIAL EVENTS... *Cotton Bowl Festival,* beginning with Thanksgiving Day parade and climaxing with the *Cotton Bowl Game,* January 1; *Vacation Show,* April; *Dallas Summer Musicals,* featuring top Broadway shows for 12 weeks; *Texas State Fair,* world's largest state fair, first 2 weeks in October; *Neiman-Marcus Fashion Fortnight,* October.

LIQUOR... Texas has "local option." In Dallas County, liquor may be purchased in package stores (open until 10 P.M.); setups available at night spots. Wines and beers may be bought at bars.

NIGHT CLUBS... *Century Room* at the Adolphus Hotel, big-name acts, outstanding, expensive. *Louanns,* the young folks' spot, is large, unpretentious, inexpensive. *Bon Vivant Club* in the Cabana Hotel features dining, dancing, star attractions; expensive.

PARKS, ZOOS, AQUARIUMS AND GARDENS... *Fair Park* is both the city park and the fair grounds site. Also on this 187 acres are the *Hall of State* and *Museum of Fine Arts, Museum of National History; Health and Science Museum; Aquarium* (watch fish-feeding at 3 P.M. Mondays and Thursdays); *Dallas Garden Center,* with permanent displays of tropical plants. During summer, there are musical productions at the *State Fair Music Hall.* The *Marsalis Park Zoo,* open daily from 8 to dark, is in Oak Cliff, easily accessible by R. L. Thornton Freeway. Major parks, such as *White Rock Lake,* all have good recreational facilities. The famous *Six Flags Over Texas* is 20 miles from Dallas on the Fort Worth road. The six sections of this park reproduce Texas as it was under the rule of Spain, France, Mexico, Republic of Texas, the Confederacy and the U.S. One admission price is good for all kinds of rides and attractions. Open daily in June, July, August; then Saturday and Sunday in April and May, and from early September through Thanksgiving. Adult admission $2.75, children $2.25.

POINTS OF INTEREST... *Dallas Theater Center,* only theater designed by Frank Lloyd Wright; *Observation Deck, Southland Center,* 41-story breathtaking view of city; the arena-type *Memorial Auditorium; John Neely Bryan's Cabin* preserved at County Courthouse; *Southern Methodist University* with its Georgian architecture; the fabulous *Neiman-Marcus* department store. *Industrial tours,* ranging from banks to factories; contact Dallas Chamber of Commerce.

RESTAURANTS... *Arthur's,* steaks and lobster, expensive; *Jardees,* Italian food, moderate; *Mexico City Café,* moderate; *Bounty,* excellent seafood and atmosphere; *Ports au Call,* Polynesian specialties, expensive; *Château Briand,* outstanding food and service, expensive; *Cattlemen's Steak House,* famous for steaks and barbecues, moderate; *Old Warsaw,* continental cuisine, expensive; *La Tunisia,* exotic Middle Eastern cookery, expensive; Neiman-Marcus's *Zodiac Room,* tops for lunch. *Dominique,* continental cuisine and wines, expensive; *Town & Country,* American and Chinese gourmet selec-

A horse ranch on the outskirts of Dallas.

Lunch time fashion show at the Neiman-Marcus Department Store.

tions, open for dinner only. The "Miracle Mile" near the Airport contains nearly two dozen good restaurants and clubs which feature every possible type of food. They range in price from 65¢ at *Fish 'n Chips* to moderately expensive, such as the French cuisine at *Mr. Pepe's*.

SPECTATOR SPORTS... Professional baseball is played by the Dallas Fort Worth *Spurs* in the Texas League at the new Turnpike Stadium. The Southern Methodist *Mustangs* play football in the Cotton Bowl on the Fair Grounds. The *Dallas Cowboys,* of the National Football League, also play in the Cotton Bowl. Top golfing events, Southwest Conference basketball, rodeos, sports car racing and yachting regattas on White Rock Lake are among the widely varied sports program.

THEATERS... The superb *Dallas Theater Center,* which houses a repertory group, offers top notch dramatic productions during the regular season. There are guided tours through the building. The *Pearl Chappell Playhouse* and *Theater Three,* two Little Theater groups, help round out a diversified choice of theatrical activities; State Fair musicals for 12 weeks in summer with Broadway stars and shows; the Broadway Theater League stages top New York shows in Dallas in the fall.

SOURCES OF FURTHER INFORMATION ... Dallas Chamber of Commerce, 1507 Pacific Ave., very helpful regarding local housing, business, tourist attractions. The *Texas Almanac,* published by the *Dallas Morning News,* is useful. Pan American Airways, 108 South Ervay St. (Tel. RIverside 8-9409).

CHICAGO, ILLINOIS ... Chicago, second-largest city in the country, is in northeastern Illinois on the southwestern shore of Lake Michigan. A gigantic industrial and economic center, Chicago is the focal point of the Midwest for conventions, cultural activities and shopping expeditions.

POPULATION AND SIZE ... Population 3,550,000 in the city itself; 7,000,000 in the metropolitan area. City area is 224 square miles, with 29 miles fronting on Lake Michigan.

ACCOMMODATIONS ... Downtown (close to shopping and business)—Newest is the very luxurious *Plaza* on North Michigan Avenue, single $15-$26, double $19-$34. *Essex Inn Motel,* single $13-$25, double $16-$30; overlooks Grant Park. *Bismarck,* single from $10.50, double from $13.50; good location. *Conrad Hilton,* single $14-$18.50, double $21.50-$24.50; world's largest hotel, many conventions. *Executive House,* single $20, double $16-$25; very modern. *La Salle,* single $8-$16, double $12.50-$21; financial district. *Palmer House,* single $10-$24, double $17-$30; Loop area, distinguished. *Pick-Congress,* single $10-$18, double $14-$24; overlooks Lake Michigan. *Sheraton-Blackstone,* single from $11.50, double from $15.50; a city landmark. *Sheraton-Chicago,* single from $10, double from $14; indoor swimming pool. *Sherman,* single $8-$16, double $15-$25; many conventions, Loop location.

North Side (near parks and beaches)—*Allerton,* single from $7, double from $12; quiet, convenient. *Ambassador East* and *Ambassador West,* single $14.50-$27.50, double $19-$30; luxurious twin hotels. *Drake,* single $10-$21.50, double $14.50-$24.50; a regal, long-time favorite. *Knickerbocker,* single $10-$16, double $14-$20; across from the Drake; caters to overseas visitors. *Water Tower Inn,* single $18-$20, double $22-$24; convenient to Michigan Avenue Shops. *Edgewater Beach,* single from $10, double from $15; outdoor swimming pool and cabanas. The new *Carriage House,* single from $14, double from $18; *Lake Tower Inn,* single $11-$18, double $15-$24.

South Side On U.S. 41 is the new, de luxe *50th On The Lake* motel on Southshore Drive at 50th Street; room service, cocktail lounge, dining room, pool, pets allowed; lake-front-view rooms from $16.50.

There are also numerous motels located near O'Hare International Airport, all built within the last few years. Among them are the *Holiday Inn, Flying Carpet, De Ville* and *Howard Johnson's Motor Inn.*

ARTS... *Adler Planetarium and Astronomical Museum; Art Institute of Chicago,* world-famous collection of paintings, prints and sculptures; *Chicago Historical Society,* especially noted for its Lincoln collection; *Chicago Natural History Museum,* extensive exhibits of anthropology, botany, geology and zoology; *Museum of Science and Industry,* very good exhibits pertaining to scientific, engineering, industrial and medical progress; *Oriental Institute,* distinguished museum of Near East antiquities; *Shedd Aquarium.*

The *Chicago Symphony Orchestra* performs on Thursday evenings, Friday afternoons and some Saturday evenings, in season. The famed *Lyric Opera* opens in the fall, and there are many other musical events throughout the year.

CLIMATE... Frankly hot in summer, cold in winter, but Lake Michigan tempers the weather in its immediate vicinity. Chicago, justifiably, is called "the Windy City" at any time of year.

FAIRS, EXHIBITIONS AND SPECIAL EVENTS... Major events are the *Automobile Show* in February; the *Flower Show* in March; *All-Star Football Game,* early August; *The Home Show* in January. Conventions of all kinds are constant throughout the year. For a complete list of attractions and activities during the time of your visit, write to the Chicago Association of Commerce and Industry, 30 W. Monroe St., Chicago 2, Illinois.

LIBRARIES... In addition to the extensive *Chicago Public Library* system, there are the *John Crerar Library* for technical and scientific literature; the *Newberry Library* for history, languages and fine arts; and the *Library of International Relations.*

LIQUOR... Drinks are served in restaurants, hotels and taverns weekdays from 8 A.M. to 2 A.M., Saturdays until 3 A.M., Sundays from noon to 2 A.M.

NIGHT CLUBS... *Polynesian Room,* at the Edgewater Beach Hotel, excellent Chinese food; *Boulevard Room* at the Conrad Hilton Hotel, features indoor ice-skating rink; *Empire Room* at the Palmer House, a paradise for generations of Midwesterners; *Camellia House* at the Drake Hotel, beautiful, name entertainers; *Mr. Kelly's,* 1028 Rush Street, famous entertainers; *London House,* 360 N. Michigan Ave., top musical entertainment; *Happy Medium,* 901 Rush St., musical-comedy revues. Rush Street, in fact, is one night club after another. Chicago has all kinds of after-dark entertainment.

PARKS, ZOOS AND CONSERVATORIES... Chicago is justly proud of its system of 168 public parks. Of special note are *Grant Park,* built along the downtown lake front on land reclaimed from Lake Michigan; *Jackson Park,* stretching along the lake shore on the South Side; and *Lincoln Park* on the lake to the north. The *Lincoln Park Zoo* has a varied collection and a special children's zoo. The famous *Brookfield Zoo,* where animals are exhibited in natural settings, is 14 miles west of the Loop. The *Lincoln Park* and *Garfield Park Conservatories*—the latter is the largest in the world under one roof—house permanent collections of tropical and exotic plants and feature special flower shows according to the seasons.

Looking north on Michigan Avenue on a quiet Sunday morning in Chicago.

POINTS OF INTEREST ... For a small admission charge you may see Chicago from the tops of its three tallest skyscrapers: *Board of Trade Building, Tribune Tower* and *Prudential Building.* Other famous landmarks are the *Buckingham Memorial Fountain, McCormick Place* exhibition center, the *Merchandise Mart, Chinatown, Hull House* social service center, the open-air market on *Maxwell Street.* Fabulous new buildings include the 60-story, circular, balconied towers of *Marina City;* the glass-façaded apartments designed by Mies van der Rohe on Lake Shore Drive; the immense new *Civic Center;* the new Chicago campus of the University of Illinois. There are conducted sightseeing tours by bus; also by motor launches which depart from the Michigan Avenue Bridge at Wacker Drive (April 15-Labor Day).

RESTAURANTS ...

American—Excellent dining rooms in all the leading hotels, ranging from moderate to expensive in price. Especially notable are *La Tour,* atop Outer Drive East; *Cape Cod Room* at the Drake; the *Pump Room* at Ambassador East and *Coach and Four* at Water Tower Inn, expensive. *Stockyards Inn* and *Ireland's* Oyster House, expensive; and the following moderately priced restaurants in the downtown area: *Younker's, Drake's, Forum, Epicurean, Harding's, Fred Harvey's, Stouffer's, George Diamond's Steak House.*

Foreign—*Scheherazade,* Arabian-Syrian, moderate; *Café Bohemia,* Bohemian, moderate; *Café de Paris, Chez Paul, Jacques, Maxim's,* all French, expensive; *Berghoff, Black Forest, Fritzel's, Math Igler's, Red Star Inn,* all German, moderate; *Athens Restaurant,* Greek, moderate; *111 Club,* Italian, moderate; *Armando's,* Italian, moderate; *Mme. A. Gilli's,* Italian, very reasonable; *Italian Village* and *Riccardo's,* both Italian and moderate; *House of Azuma,* Japanese, moderate; *El Jarocho, Su Casa* and *Joe's La Siesta,* Mexican and reasonable; *Bamboo*

Inn and *Jimmy Wong's,* Oriental and moderate; *Don the Beach-comber, Kon Tiki Ports* (in Sheraton-Chicago Hotel) and *Trader Vic's,* Cantonese, expensive; *Lenard's,* Polish, moderate; *Kungsholm,* Scandinavian, expensive. *Imperial House,* Continental, luxuriously elegant, expensive; *The Red Carpet,* exotic atmosphere, *Sasha's,* Russian.

SPECTATOR SPORTS ... Horse racing is in season from April through late fall. The *Chicago White Sox* play pro baseball in the American League; the *Chicago Cubs* are in the National League. The *Chicago Bears* play pro football, and the *Chicago Blackhawks* are the professional ice-hockey team. In addition, there is a good selection of college athletic events.

THEATERS ... Outstanding stage productions and first-run motion pictures are presented in Chicago. Theaters featuring dramatic and musical shows are in the central business district. There are motion picture theaters all over the city; the elaborate "movie palaces" are in the Loop. During the summer, stars of television, stage and cinema appear at "tenthouse" theaters in various suburban areas. *Drury Lane Theater,* on the southwest side, stages excellent entertainment the year round; *Aire Crown Theater,* in McCormick Place, offers everything from ballet to hootenannies.

SOURCES OF FURTHER INFORMATION: Visitors' Bureau, 30 W. Monroe St.; Pan American Airways, 30 S. Michigan Ave. (Tel. RA 6-6272), and at O'Hare International Airport.

DETROIT, MICHIGAN: Detroit is in southeastern Michigan on the Detroit River, which connects Lake Erie and Lake St. Clair and is a part of the International boundary between the United States and Canada. Rich, dynamic and progressive, Detroit is the world's largest automobile manufacturing city, and its river carries more tonnage than any other waterway in the world.

POPULATION AND SIZE: Population 1,670,144 in the city itself; 3,672,360 in the metropolitan areas. City area—139.6 square miles.

ACCOMMODATIONS: Newest and most luxuriously continental is *Hotel Pontchartrain,* single from $12.50, double from $17.50. *Sheraton-Cadillac,* single from $9, double from $15; extremely large, well-run hotel. *Statler Hilton,* single from $9, double from $14.50; very large, first-class rooms and food. *Pick-Fort Shelby,* single from $7, double from $10.50; very pleasant, nice rooms. *Tuller,* single from $6, double from $8; large, well-managed. Other important hotels are the *Henrose, Prince Edward* (Windsor), the *Whittier,* the *Park Shelton* and *Wolverine.* There are also numerous motels, such as: the *Algiers, Balmar* and the *Park Plaza.*

ARTS: *Detroit Institute of Arts,* a series of art galleries; during July and August, open Tuesday through Sunday 9-6, remainder of the year open Tuesday and Wednesday, noon to 9 P.M. Thursday through Sunday, 9 A.M. to 6 P.M., free. *Children's Museum,* art exhibits for young people; October through May, open Mondays through Fridays, 9 A.M.-5 P.M. Saturdays, 9 A.M.-4:30 P.M. Summer schedule: Monday through Friday, 1-4 P.M. Admission free. *Henry Ford Museum* and *Greenfield Village* are fascinating for their Americana exhibits, both scientific and historic; open weekdays 9-5, weekends and holidays 9-6; admission to each $1.25. *The Detroit Symphony Orchestra* gives a series of concerts in winter. Consult local papers for other musical events.

CLIMATE: The best months for a visit are May, June, September and October. July and August are often very hot. January and February are the coldest months with sub-freezing temperatures and considerable humidity. Annual rainfall is moderate and distributed fairly evenly throughout the year.

FAIRS, EXHIBITIONS AND SPECIAL EVENTS: *Auto Show,* annually; *Michigan State Fair,* September; *Home and Flower Show,* February; *International Freedom Festival,* latter part of June into early July; and the *Boat Races,* annually.

LIQUOR ... Michigan has "local option." Detroit permits purchases of packaged goods at state-operated stores from 10 A.M. to 6 P.M. and at licensed drugstores from 7 A.M. to 11 P.M. daily. On Sunday, beer and wine may be purchased from 12 noon until 2 A.M. the following day. Liquor is also served, of course, in hotels, restaurants and taverns.

NIGHT CLUBS ... Best-known are *London Chop House, The Rooster Tail, Baker's Keyboard Lounge, Wonder Bar, Showboat* and *The Caucus Club*—all have dining, dancing and some entertainment, expensive. *The Surrey Room* at Statler Hilton, music and good food; expensive. *Elmwood Casino,* across the river in Windsor, Ontario, star entertainment, expensive.

PARKS, ZOOS, AQUARIUMS AND GARDENS ... *Detroit Zoological Park;* large collection; free; open from May to November on weekdays 10-5, Sundays 9-6. *Belle Isle Park,* unique natureland on an island in the Detroit River; beautiful drives, symphony shell, golf course and athletic fields; all sorts of recreational facilities; a zoo and one of America's finest fresh water aquariums, both free, open during the summer 10-8; interesting Children's Zoo, admission 10¢. Other popular parks are *River Rouge* for golf, tennis and swimming; *Palmer Park,* with special exhibits, golf course, recreational facilities.

POINTS OF INTEREST ... Most people enjoy tours of the great automobile plants. *Plymouth* has the world's longest assembly line; also impressive assembly lines at *Cadillac, Chrysler, De Soto, Dodge, Ford, Lincoln-Mercury* and *Pontiac.* The *Ford River Rouge Plant* is 2 square miles of integrated industrial production; very interesting conducted tours; free. See, too, the animated displays in the *Ford Rotunda,* and the varied exhibits in the *Henry Ford Museum* and *Greenfield Village,* which includes the *Thomas A. Edison Buildings. Cobo Hall-Convention Arena,* a gigantic structure, is one of the world's finest convention, exposition and recreational buildings. Northwest of Detroit is *Cranbrook,* 6 famous cultural schools and institutions; worth seeing. Across the river from Detroit is *Windsor,* Canadian city with English china, woolens and other British goods at bargain prices. Typical conducted tours of Detroit take 4 hours, and cost $5.65.

RESTAURANTS ... *London Chop House, Berman's, Little Harry's* and *Gurney's,* all good for steaks, expensive; *Mario's,* Italian, moderate; *Muer's Oyster House,* seafood, moderate. *Stouffer's,* 3 restaurants in the Detroit area, moderate. Beautiful view of Windsor and Detroit from atop the Michigan Consolidated Gas Company's new restaurant, *Top of the Flame. Pontchartrain,* French, moderate; *Greenfield's* in 2 locations, excellent for cafeteria-style dining.

SPECTATOR SPORTS ... Tiger Stadium, with a capacity of 52,904, is the home of the *Tigers* (baseball) and the *Lions* (football). The Olympia, which seats up to 14,000, is the home of the *Detroit Red Wings* (hockey). The Convention Arena is the home of the *Pistons* (basketball). The *Thunderbirds* represent Detroit in bowling. Horse racing at *Detroit Race Course* and *Hazel Park* from May through early October. Harness racing at 3 parks from April through September. Important college football and other athletic events at Ann Arbor, 38 miles west, the home of the *University of Michigan.*

THEATERS ... The *Cass, Shubert,* and luxurious new *Fisher* theaters in midtown Detroit offer pre-Broadway premiers and top-ranking road company hits. The *Van Guard Theater* has a permanent repertory group with local and nationally known stars. Summer-stock productions at *Northland Playhouse* outside the city.

SOURCES OF FURTHER INFORMATION ... Greater Detroit Board of Commerce, 320 W. Lafayette Boulevard, business and industrial information. Convention and Tourist Bureau, 626 Book Building, best for general tourist information, maps and booklets about the city. Pan American Airways, 1231 Washington Boulevard (Tel. WO 3-0800).

LOS ANGELES, CALIFORNIA ... Los Angeles is in southwestern California, about 15 miles inland from the Pacific Ocean. Within the far-flung city limits, the elevation ranges from sea level up to 5,081 feet, and the inhabitants are just as diverse as the terrain. Hollywood, its most famous enclave, has made this the glamour city of the world.

POPULATION AND SIZE ... 2,660,000 in the city itself; 7,416,-450 in the metropolitan area. City area is 458.20 square miles, the largest land area of any city in the U.S. (as you will learn if you take a taxi).

ACCOMMODATIONS ... In the central business district—*Biltmore,* single from $9.50, double from $13.50; very large, a convention headquarters. *Clark,* single from $6, double from $8; conveniently located. *Mayfair,* single from $8, double from $9; pleasant, good hotel. *Mayflower,* single from $8, double from $11; well managed. *Statler Hilton,* single from $10, double from $13.50. Near the International Airport are the *Ramada Inn,* single from $10, double from $12; *Hayatt House,* single from $12.50, double from $16.50; *Sky-*

ways, single from $8, double from $10; and the *Airport Marina,* single from $13, double from $15; *International Hotel,* single from $14, double from $16; *Thunderbird Hotel,* single from $12, double from $16.

West of the business district—*Bel Air,* single and double from $18.50, very small, extremely luxurious. *Beverly Hills,* single from $16, double from $24; famous, luxurious, attractive setting. *Beverly Hilton,* single from $16, double from $21; very modern and de luxe. The ultra-new, ultra-smart *Century Plaza,* single from $16, double from $21. *Beverly Wilshire,* single from $16, double from $21, excellent, convenient to Beverly Hills district. In the Wilshire district—*Ambassador,* single from $13, double from $18; large, attractive, spacious grounds. *Gaylord,* single from $10, double from $12; good hotel on famous Wilshire Boulevard. *Sheraton West,* single from $14.50, double from $19.50; moderate-size, luxurious.

In Hollywood there are a number of very inexpensive hotels with considerable charm: the *Mark Twain,* single from $4, double from $5, all with bath; *Hollywood-Knickerbocker,* single from $9.50, double from $11.50; *Hollywood-Plaza,* single from $8, double from $10; *Hollywood-Roosevelt,* single from $8, double from $10, swimming pool. There are a great many motels in and around the city, such as the *Carolina-Hollywood,* single from $10, double from $12, swimming pool, and sightseeing buses from motel. On Sunset Strip: the *Continental Hotel,* single from $11, double from $15; *Hallmark House,* single from $9, double from $11; and *Thunderbird Inn,* single from $11, double from $14.

ARTS ... The new *Los Angeles County Museum of Art,* opened in April of 1965, consists of three pavilions holding up to $35 million worth of art treasures. Masterpieces on display include Rembrandt's *Titus* (acquired for $2,234,000) and the Ardabil Carpet, loomed in Tabriz in 1539. Outdoor décor of pools and fountains is embellished with remarkable sculptures and mobiles; open daily except Monday 10-5; free except for special showings. *Huntington Art Museum,* paintings, sculptures; open daily 1-4:30, except Monday; free; closed in October. *County Museum of History, Science and Art,* art and natural history exhibits; open daily except Monday 10-5; free. *Southwest Museum,* Indian handicrafts and relics; open daily except Monday 1-5; free; closed August 15-September 15. Principal musical groups are the *Los Angeles Symphony Orchestra, Light Opera Association* and *Hollywood Bowl Association,* which sponsors the famous *Symphony Under the Stars* in July and August. *The Pavilion,* first building completed in Los Angeles' new *Music Center for the Performing Arts,* has been hailed by both musicians and architects as one of the world's most "perfect" buildings for concerts and musical productions.

CLIMATE ... The region is famous for its good weather, although Los Angeles is equally famous for its "unusual" weather that comes along occasionally. Winters are very mild. Some summer days are hot, but the average temperature is pleasant. Rainfall is negligible from

May through October, but some heavy showers may be anticipated from December through March. High humidity is present in the early morning, but it usually disappears by early afternoon. The principal problem is "smog"—atmospheric pollutants that cause some eye and respiratory irritation; steps are being taken to resolve this difficulty.

FAIRS, EXHIBITIONS AND SPECIAL EVENTS ... Among many, many others: *Tournament of Roses* and *Rose Bowl Football Game,* January 1; *Easter Sunrise Service* in Hollywood Bowl; *Los Angeles County Fair* at Pomona, September; *Christmas Week Celebration,* Hollywood.

LIBRARIES ... The *Huntington Library,* San Marino, has many rare books in its outstanding collections. The *Los Angeles Public Library* has 60 branches.

LIQUOR ... Liquor may be bought in package stores and served in bars, restaurants and hotels from 6 A.M. to 2 A.M. daily.

NIGHT CLUBS ... Many of the hotels have rooms with the customary night-club attractions; the best-known of these is the *Coconut Grove* in the Ambassador Hotel. Whether you're on a champagne or a beer budget, there is an enormous choice of places to go for fun in Hollywood, Los Angeles, the suburbs.

PARKS, ZOOS, AQUARIUMS AND GARDENS ... *Marineland* at Palos Verdes, ocean fish and whales in a modern, open aquarium; admission charge. *Griffith Park Zoo,* good collection; open in summer 10 A.M.-5:30 P.M. *Fern Dell,* adjoining Griffith Park, has beautiful rare ferns. *Rose Garden,* in Exposition Park, is also interesting; also the *Pacific Ocean Park* (open daily in summer, week-ends the rest of the year).

POINTS OF INTEREST ... To see the old Spanish landmarks, visit *Olvera Street* with its shops, restaurants, curiosities; most interesting in the evening. *Old Mission Church; Avila Adobe,* a reconstructed Spanish ranch house, open Wednesday and Sunday 2-5; free. In central Los Angeles, visit *Chinatown* and eat in a typical restaurant. See *Little Tokyo,* recently restored as an authentic Japanese community of shops, gardens, restaurants and night clubs. A few blocks north of this region is *El Pueblo de Los Angeles State Historical Monument* covering 11 blocks and depicting California life as it was in the days of the Indians, Mexicans and pioneer Americans. See *Rodia's Towers,* the unique craftsmanship of one man. The *La Brea Tar Pits, Civic Center* (beautifully illuminated at night), *Forest Lawn Memorial Park.* The art galleries on La Cienega Boulevard are especially interesting on open-house Monday nights when Angelenos promenade to view the latest paintings and sculptures. Hollywood radio and television studios are all interesting. There are new tourist tours of *Universal City* where both movie and TV shows are produced; cost is $2.50 and you get a close-up look at sets and stars. The *Farmers Market* is best visited in the middle of the day; enjoy an outdoor lunch there. If time permits, see the Los Angeles-Long Beach Harbor, San Pedro harbor and Terminal Island Navy Base. Drive through Los Angeles' suburban residential areas. Apart from the homes of celebrities, the houses of ordinary citizens, too, are unique for their landscaped lawns and gardens. World-famous *Disneyland,* in nearby Anaheim, delights both adults and children; amusements, rides, many attractions (closed Monday and Tuesday, September through May). There are interesting boat rides and flights to Catalina Island, 25 miles off shore; round trip can be made in a day. Visiting the motion picture studios is difficult without a letter of introduction, but several of the conducted sightseeing tours include a trip through a studio or two. There are numerous tours of the city to choose from; a typical 3-hour tour costs $3.75.

RESTAURANTS . . . In the midtown section—*La Golondrina,* Mexican food and music, moderate; *Cook's Steak House,* moderate; *New Ginza,* Japanese, floor shows, moderate. In the western section on Restaurant Row on La Cienega Boulevard—*Lawry's Prime Rib, The Islander, Tail of the Cock, Stears For Steaks, Oyster House, Beefeater's, Mediterrania;* all expensive but worth it. In the Beverly Hills area—*Trader Vic's, The Luau;* expensive. *Paul's Steak House, Frascati;* moderate. In the Hollywood section—*Brown Derby, Au Petit Jean, Four Trees, Beachcomber;* expensive. *Musso and Franks, Fogcutter;* moderate. The restaurants mentioned here are only a very small sampling of what Los Angeles has to offer in all price ranges.

SPECTATOR SPORTS: Horse racing at *Santa Anita* and *Hollywood Park;* at Del Mar track, just north of San Diego; on Saturday and Sunday at Agua Caliente. Many football games in the area are scheduled by USC and UCLA, plus a varied program of other college sports. Los Angeles has two major professional baseball teams, the *Los Angeles Angels* and the *Los Angeles Dodgers.* The *Rams* play pro football. The *Blades* play pro hockey. The *Los Angeles Coliseum* and the *Sports Arena* book a wide choice of sporting events.

THEATERS . . . Many Broadway presentations can be seen at the *Shrine Auditorium.* Nearby is the famous *Pasadena Playhouse.* The *Padua Hills Theater* in Claremont specializes in plays with a Spanish flavor. Outstanding among many little theater groups are *The Player's Ring* and *Player's Gallery.*

SOURCES OF FURTHER INFORMATION . . . Los Angeles Chamber of Commerce, 404 S. Bixel St.; All Year Club of California, 628 W. Sixth St., 2nd floor; tourist information on the city and general area; write for their maps and literature. Pan American Airways, Sixth and Grand Streets (Tel. MA 9-3292).

SAN FRANCISCO, CALIFORNIA . . . Beautifully situated on the central coast of California, San Francisco is on a hilly peninsula bounded by the Pacific Ocean on the west, Golden Gate on the north and San Francisco Bay on the east. A sophisticated and cosmopolitan city, San Francisco can boast of having some of the best-dressed citizens in the country, and of being one of America's gourmet capitals. The city has painfully steep streets and frequent fogs, but no San Franciscan would change a bit of it, and visitors succumb at once to the city's unique spell.

POPULATION AND SIZE ... Population 745,000 in the city itself; 3,933,700 in the entire metropolitan area. The city covers 93.1 square miles, of which 48.28 are water.

ACCOMMODATIONS ... San Francisco ordinarily has no shortage of hotel space unless a convention is on. Leading hotels include: the new *San Francisco Hilton,* "wrapped around" its own parking garage downtown, single from $12, double from $16; *St. Francis,* from $13 single, from $16 double, excellent location on Union Square opposite Pan Am office; *Fairmont* and *Mark Hopkins,* both atop Nob Hill, single from $17, double from $22; the *Huntington,* also on Nob Hill, from $14 single, $18 double; *Clift,* single from $15, double from $19; *Sheraton-Palace,* single from $12, double from $16; *Sir Francis Drake,* single from $12, double from $15. Other popular hotels—*Stewart,* single from $8, double from $10; *Californian,* single from $8, double from $10; *Drake Wilshire,* single from $9, double from $11.50; *Plaza,* single from $9, double from $11.50; *Manx,* single from $7.50, double from $10; *Bellevue,* single from $9, double from $12. There are also many new motels.

ARTS ... *M. H. de Young Memorial Museum,* open daily, 10-5; *San Francisco Museum of Art,* open daily 10-5—both have varied art exhibitions. The *Palace of the Legion of Honour,* permanent collections of painting and sculpture, open daily 10-5. The *San Francisco Symphony Orchestra* gives concerts on Wednesday and Friday evenings and Wednesday afternoons, December-April. The *San Francisco Ballet* appears in the spring. The *San Francisco Opera* is outstanding; performances September-November and May-June.

CLIMATE ... It gets neither very hot or very cold. Most of the time it's what women call "good suit weather," and suits are the favorite uniform of smartly dressed San Francisco ladies. Unlike other American cities, San Francisco's warmest months are September and October. Summer rainfall is slight, but rain is fairly heavy during the winter. There are heavy (but picturesque) sea fogs that roll over the city in the early evening and are burned away by the morning sun.

FAIRS, EXHIBITIONS AND SPECIAL EVENTS ... *Shrine East-West Football Game,* January 1; *Chinese New Year* celebration, late January or early February; *Imported Car Show, Boat Show,* February; *St. Patrick's Day* parade, March; *Maiden Lane Festival,* late March; *Easter Sunrise Service; Fashion Show* in Union Square, mid-July; *Grand National Livestock Show,* October; *Autumn Film Festival; California-Stanford Football Game,* November.

LIBRARIES ... In addition to the city's public library system, there are the *John Hammond Mining Library, California Academy of Sciences, Lane Library* and *Mechanics Mercantile Library.*

LIQUOR ... Sold in bars and restaurants from 6 A.M. to 2 A.M.

NIGHT CLUBS ... Dining and dancing at these hotels—*Fairmont, Mark Hopkins, Hilton* and *Sheraton-Palace;* all fairly expensive. *Bimbo's, Chinese Sky Room, Goman's Gay Nineties, Forbidden City, Alexis Discotheque, Whisky A-Go-Go, Tiger A-Go-Go, Jazz Workshop* and *Sinaloa;* all with dancing. For that very special San Francisco humor, the *hungry i* and the *Purple Onion* are tops, and you'll also like *El Matador*. San Francisco's famous coffeehouses are mostly centered in the North Beach area on, or near, Grant Avenue. In nostalgic contrast and offering almost continuous floor shows are the *Roaring Twenties, Gold Street* and many others along busy Broadway.

PARKS, ZOOS, AQUARIUMS AND GARDENS ... *Golden Gate Park* is a beautiful man-made area with a playground, conservatory, Dutch windmills, the Steinhard Aquarium, planetarium and Japanese tea garden. *Lincoln Park* has fine views of the harbor. Also interesting are *Aquatic Park* and *San Francisco Zoological Gardens*, open daily from 10 to sundown; free.

POINTS OF INTEREST ... Just wandering around San Francisco is a fascinating experience. Every visitor wants to ride the famous cable cars which scale the city's most precipitous streets. Try several different destinations—they're all fun. *Chinatown*, probably the largest Chinese community outside Asia; *Civic Center; Cliff House* and *Seal Rocks; Embarcadero*, the waterfront district; *Farmer's Market*; the *Gas Buggy Memories History Museum; Golden Gate Bridge; Livestock Pavilion*, better known as the "Cow Palace"; *United States Mint; Mission Dolores;* the very beautiful *Opera House;* the *Presidio*, a U.S. military reservation since 1776; the *San Francisco-Oakland Bay Bridge; Stern Memorial Grove; Wells Fargo Historical Collection*. San Francisco's first pedestrian promenade is charming *Maiden Lane* on Union Square, 2 blocks long, and closed to cars from 11:30 A.M. to 2:30 P.M. There are many conducted tours of the city. A typical 3-hour Gray Line bus tour costs $4.00; an afternoon excursion to see the giant and beautiful *Muir Woods* across Golden Gate Bridge in Marin County is $4.30; it's only 45¢ for the Greyhound trip across the Bridge to picturesque Sausalito. If time permits, try one of the several boat trips on San Francisco Bay for a memorable view of the city. Many sightseeing boats leave from *Fisherman's Wharf;* a 1-hour trip costs $1.75.

RESTAURANTS ... San Francisco's seafood specialties and French bread are worth crossing the continent for. Try the local shrimp, giant crabs, red sole, abalone, sand dabs and clams; *cioppino*, a great favorite, is a cross between a soup and a stew, made with several kinds of seafood. There are hundreds of really fine restaurants in the city. Some of the better-known ones are: *Amelio's*, Italian, attractive, expensive; *Alfred's*, good for crab, steaks, expensive; *Cliff House*, superb view of the ocean and Seal Rocks, fairly expensive; Fisherman's Wharf has many good restaurants, so take your pick. A well-known spot is *Fisherman's Grotto*, moderately expensive; *Grison's Chicken and Steak Houses* are both good, both fairly expensive; *Julius' Castle*, French-Italian dishes, quite expensive; *Skipper Kent* and *Trader Vic's*, Chinese-Polynesian food, unusual surroundings, very expensive; *Vanessi's*, Italian, fairly expensive; *Ernie's, Jacks* and the *Blue Fox* are excellent, all expensive. For other foreign cuisines, try some of these—*Alexis* (truly elegant) and *Omar Khayyam*, Armenian; *Fleur-de-Lys, Charlie's*, French; *Señor Pico*, Mexican and early Californian dishes; *Canlis,* steaks; *Tao Tao* and *Cathay House,* Chinese; *Taj of India,* East Indian; *Yamato Sukiyaki House,* Japanese. Full of atmosphere but very inexpensive restaurants in China- town include the *Far East Cafe, Songhay, Universal Cafe, Sun Hung Heung* and *Sam Wo's. The Buena Vista,* just south of Fisherman's Wharf, serves excellent, moderately priced meals in a picture-win- dowed room overlooking Golden Gate Bridge. The *Hippo* is the place to go for wildly imaginative hamburgers. You can also find German, Mexican, Russian, Spanish, Swedish, and Swiss restaurants in San Francisco, which, like the others, come in all price ranges.

SPECTATOR SPORTS . . . Professional baseball is played by the *San Francisco Giants* at Candlestick Park. The *San Francisco 49ers* play pro football at Kezar Stadium. Boxing and wrestling matches at *Oakland Auditorium;* pro basketball and ice hockey in the huge *Cow Palace.* College athletic events are scheduled by the University of California in Berkeley and at Stanford University at Palo Alto. There is horse racing at *Golden Gate Fields* in Albany, at *Tanforan* in San Bruno, and at *Bay Meadows* in San Mateo.

THEATERS . . . San Francisco is an active theatrical city, with regular professional productions at the *Curran* and *Geary* theaters, as well as at the *Opera House.* Little theaters: *Playhouse, Contemporary Dancers Center;* also *Encore, Interplayers, Lamplighters, Little Fox, Opera Ring, Actors' Workshop, Off Broadway* and *Sheraton-Palace Dinner-Theater.* The University of California also presents stage pro- ductions at *Wheeler Auditorium.*

SOURCES OF FURTHER INFORMATION . . . San Francisco Chamber of Commerce, 333 Pine St.; Convention and Visitors Bu- reau, Civic Auditorium; Californians, Inc., 703 Market St.; Visitors Information Center, 476 Post St. All are helpful with information on hotels, restaurants, amusements. Pan American Airways, 222 Stock- ton St. (Tel. EX 7-5200) and also at the International Airport.

Nearly every house has a good view in hilly San Francisco. In the dis- tance, the Coit Memorial Tower on Telegraph Hill overlooking the Bay.

INDEX AND KEY TO PRONUNCIATION

OTHER USEFUL TRAVEL GUIDES

Carry abroad any of these Pan Am books. They won't be weighed as baggage:

Complete Reference Guides ... to *Britain* ... to *France* ... to *Italy* ... to *Germany* ... to *Scandinavia* ... to *Spain and Portugal* ... to *Austria and Switzerland* ... to the *Low Countries.* (In addition to many useful travel facts these handy books include currency converter, menu translator, major events and details on low cost travel throughout each country); *New Horizons Living Abroad,* a fascinating encyclopedia of living conditions in 90 countries; *Passports and Profits,* useful guide to doing business in 105 countries. *New Horizons in Education,* covering universities and boarding schools abroad; *Ski New Horizons,* about ski facilities in 30 countries. Other Pan Am books include *New Horizons U.S.A.,* covering 100 U.S. cities and resorts; *Round the World Cookbook,* with 600 recipes from 81 countries.